THE CAMBRIDGE HANDBOOK OF ISLAM AND ENVIRONMENTAL LAW

Environmental challenges require diverse legal approaches. In this expansive handbook, global scholars examine the nexus of Islam and environmental law as a significant yet understudied framework for contemporary governance. Spanning fourteen centuries of legal development, Islamic environmental jurisprudence offers sophisticated approaches to stewardship, resource management, and climate policy. Chapters include detailed case studies of Pakistan's constitutional courts and Malaysia's environmental legislation, Gulf economic transitions, and water-governance innovations, all demonstrating how Islamic legal principles inform real-world environmental solutions. Each contribution provides a nuanced analysis of how traditional concepts adapt to contemporary contexts across diverse Muslim-majority nations. Timely and innovative, this handbook is an ideal resource for environmental law scholars, comparative legal researchers, policy analysts, and development practitioners working in pluralistic contexts.

Nadia B. Ahmad is a professor of law at Barry University, where she serves as Coordinator of the Environmental and Earth Law certificate program. She teaches property, energy law, and environmental regulation with her work situated at the convergence of legal scholarship, data science, human rights, and environmental governance.

Saba Kareemi is a Pakistani Canadian legal scholar and lawyer specializing in Islamic law, corporate law, and constitutional law. She has taught at the Asian Institute of Management in the Philippines, Pakistan College of Law, and Westminster International University in Tashkent. She holds an LLM from the University of Toronto and LLB from the International Islamic University, Islamabad.

Erum K. Sattar is a lecturer at Tufts University with degrees from Harvard Law School and the University of London and is a member of the Bar of England and Wales and the Honourable Society of Lincoln's Inn. Her interdisciplinary research examines the impact of water governance and transboundary water sharing on food production, livelihoods, and migration requiring legal and institutional adaptation structures globally. Her scholarly articles and book chapters have appeared in leading academic publications.

Oluwakemi A. Ayanleye is a law lecturer at Olabisi Onabanjo University, Nigeria, specializing in Islamic finance and sharia legal systems. She has published extensively on Islamic finance regulation, presented at Harvard Law School, and received TETFund research grants. Her interdisciplinary expertise spans Islamic law, intellectual property, and international trade law.

The Cambridge Handbook of Islam and Environmental Law

Edited by

NADIA B. AHMAD
Barry University

SABA KAREEMI

ERUM K. SATTAR
Tufts University

OLUWAKEMI A. AYANLEYE
Olabisi Onabanjo University

CAMBRIDGE
UNIVERSITY PRESS

CAMBRIDGE
UNIVERSITY PRESS

Shaftesbury Road, Cambridge CB2 8EA, United Kingdom

One Liberty Plaza, 20th Floor, New York, NY 10006, USA

477 Williamstown Road, Port Melbourne, VIC 3207, Australia

314–321, 3rd Floor, Plot 3, Splendor Forum, Jasola District Centre, New Delhi – 110025, India

Cambridge University Press is part of Cambridge University Press & Assessment, a department of the University of Cambridge.

We share the University's mission to contribute to society through the pursuit of education, learning and research at the highest international levels of excellence.

www.cambridge.org
Information on this title: www.cambridge.org/9781009332088

DOI: 10.1017/9781009332118

When citing this work, please include a reference to the DOI 10.1017/9781009332118

First published 2026

Cover image: Part of Garden Majorelle in Marrakesh. Image: Alan_Tow / iStock Unreleased / Getty Images

A catalogue record for this publication is available from the British Library

Library of Congress Cataloging-in-Publication Data
NAMES: Ahmad, Nadia Batool editor | Karemi, Saba editor | Sattar, Erum K. editor | Ayanleye, Oluwakemi A. editor
TITLE: The Cambridge handbook of Islam and environmental law / edited by Nadia B Ahmad, Barry University School of Law; Saba Karemi; Erum K. Sattar, Tufts University, Massachusetts; Oluwakemi A. Ayanleye, Olabisi Onabanjo University, Nigeria.
DESCRIPTION: Cambridge, United Kingdom ; New York, NY : Cambridge University Press, 2026. | Series: Cambridge law handbooks | Includes index.
IDENTIFIERS: LCCN 2025042848 (print) | LCCN 2025042849 (ebook) | ISBN 9781009332088 hardback | ISBN 9781009332118 epub
SUBJECTS: LCSH: Environmental law (Islamic law) | Environmental law–Religious aspects
CLASSIFICATION: LCC KBP3127 .C36 2026 (print) | LCC KBP3127 (ebook)
LC record available at https://lccn.loc.gov/2025042848
LC ebook record available at https://lccn.loc.gov/2025042849

ISBN 978-1-009-33208-8 Hardback

To Akmal, Senan, Safiya, and Sarah, and my parents, Ejaz and Aneesa

—Nadia

To my parents, Aunty Alia, Uncle Saleem, Aunty Syeda, and Waqar Sahib

—Saba

To my grandfather, my dada, *Abdus Sattar Moosa Didi*

—Erum

To my granddaughters Sakeenah and Sameeha

—Kemi

Contents

Figures

Contributors

Dalal Aassouli is an assistant professor of Islamic and sustainable finance at Hamad Bin Khalifa University, Qatar. She is a distinguished academic and development finance leader with extensive international experience across Europe, Southeast Asia, the Middle East, and North Africa. She specializes in leveraging emerging technologies such as blockchain and artificial intelligence to drive innovation in Islamic and sustainable finance.

Nadia B. Ahmad is a professor of law at Barry University, where she serves as Coordinator of the Environmental and Earth Law certificate program. She teaches property, energy law, and environmental regulation with her work situated at the convergence of legal scholarship, data science, human rights, and environmental governance.

Saleem H. Ali is the chair of the Department of Geography and Spatial Sciences and Blue and Gold Distinguished Professor of Energy and the Environment at the University of Delaware (USA). He is also a member of the United Nations International Resource Panel.

Hooshmand Alizadeh is an associate professor of urban design at the University of Kurdistan, Iran. His areas of expertise include urban resilience, socio–spatial dynamics of public space, and participatory urban governance. His research also explores the intersections of sociopolitical polarization, intersectional and gendered urban experiences, and migrant integration practices, often using participatory and collaborative methods.

Wardah Alkatiri obtained her PhD from the University of Canterbury, New Zealand. She is a human ecologist and sociologist of Islam whose interdisciplinary work focuses on the transition to a postcarbon world. She is a senior lecturer in environmental health, community development, philosophy, and development studies at Universitas Nahdlatul Ulama Surabaya, Indonesia.

Mohamed A. ʿArafa is a professor of law at Alexandria University Faculty of Law, Egypt, and an adjunct professor and the Clarke Initiative Visiting Scholar at Cornell Law School. In 2025, he taught comparative law as a visiting professor at the Brazilian Institute of Education (IDP) in Brasília, Brazil. His recent visiting positions include Chandigarh University Institute of Legal Studies (India), Monash University Faculty of Law (Australia), and Prince Sultan University College of Law (Saudi Arabia).

Oluwakemi A. Ayanleye is a law lecturer at Olabisi Onabanjo University, Nigeria, specializing in Islamic finance and sharia legal systems. She has published extensively on Islamic finance regulation, presented at Harvard Law School, and received TETFund research grants. Her interdisciplinary expertise spans Islamic law, intellectual property, and international trade law.

Nematollah Azizi is a visiting professor at the School of Education at the University of Glasgow. His ongoing research project, funded by Leverhulme Trust, reconceptualizes the role of universities in creating and developing learning and creative cities in light of Islamic academic tradition.

Anke Iman Bouzenita obtained her PhD in Islamic sciences, corporate governance and state structure as well as sovereign debt from Ruhr-Universität Bochum, Germany, in 2001. Her main research interests are in Islamic bioethics, history of Islamic law, Ibadi studies, and international relations. She is currently working as a professor at Sultan Qaboos University, College of Education, in the Islamic Education Department.

Saffet Abid Catovic is an environmental leader, having co-chaired the Parliament of the World's Religions Climate Action Task Force. He serves as GreenFaith's Senior Muslim Advisor and one of the drafters of "Al-Mizan" Covenant for the Earth and the FCNA fossil fuel divestment fatwa. He also advises the Yale Forum on Religion and Ecology and serves as Drew University's Muslim Chaplain.

Erin Daly is Professor Emerita of Law and the director of the Dignity Rights Institute. Since 2021, she has directed the Dignity Rights Clinic. Previously, she served as Interim Dean and Vice Dean of Widener University Delaware Law School. She is a Fulbright Specialist with an appointment in Brazil in 2025 and has lectured on dignity and environmental rights in more than two dozen countries including Pakistan where she co-chaired the UN Environmental Judicial Institute.

Lutfallah Gari is an environmental historian based in Saudi Arabia specializing in traditional conservation systems. His expertise includes the history of Arabic medicine, environmental protection, and the *ḥimā* conservation system.

Jawad Hassan is a judge of the Lahore High Court in Pakistan. He is an expert on public and private international law. He has been actively involved in legislative and judicial reforms on child labor, domestic workers, and environmental rights.

Golshan Hemati completed a doctoral degree at the University of Kurdistan, Iran, specializing in urban planning and design. Her research focuses on water rights and sustainable urban development in Islamic contexts.

Mehran Kamrava is Professor of Government at Georgetown University, Qatar. He also directs the Iranian Studies Unit at the Arab Center for Research and Policy Studies. An expert on Iran, the Persian Gulf, and the politics of the Middle East, Kamrava is the author of a number of journal articles and books.

Saba Kareemi is a Pakistani Canadian legal scholar and lawyer specializing in Islamic law, corporate law, and constitutional law. She has taught at the Asian Institute of Management in the Philippines, Pakistan College of Law, and Westminster International University in Tashkent. She holds an LLM from the University of Toronto and LLB from the International Islamic University, Islamabad.

Ridoan Karim is a senior lecturer and deputy director of the Centre for Commercial Law and Regulatory Studies (CLARS) at the Malaysia Hub, School of Business, Monash University Malaysia. His teaching and research span the dynamic intersection of law, science, and technology with a particular focus on areas such as energy and natural resources law and cyber law.

Hassan Khalilieh is a senior lecturer in the departments of maritime civilizations and interdisciplinary studies at the University of Haifa. He is a specialist in medieval Islamic admiralty and maritime law, and international law of the sea. He is the author of *Islamic Maritime Law: An Introduction* and *Admiralty and Maritime Laws in the Mediterranean (ca. 800–1050): The Kitāb Akriyat al-Sufun vis-à-vis the Nomos Rhodion Nautikos.*

James R. May is Richard S. Righter Distinguished Professor of Law at Washburn University, where he teaches environmental and constitutional law and human rights, and codirects the program in environmental, energy, and resources law. May is a human rights lawyer who co-founded the Dignity Law Institute and established the Dignity Rights Practicum. He has published extensively on rights to dignity and a healthy environment, visited at the Pakistan College of Law, and co-chaired the UN Environmental Judicial Institute in Pakistan.

Damilola S. Olawuyi is a professor and UNESCO Chairholder on Environmental Law and Sustainable Development at the College of Law, Hamad Bin Khalifa University. He is also Chancellor's Fellow and Director of the Institute for Oil, Gas, Energy, Environment and Sustainable Development (OGEES Institute), Afe Babalola University, Nigeria. Olawuyi has published close to 100 articles, book chapters, and books on petroleum law, energy, and international environmental law.

İbrahim Özdemir is the vice president of academic affairs at the American Islamic College. Formerly, he was a professor of philosophy at Uskudar University, Istanbul, and the dean of the Faculty of Humanities and Social Sciences. He is a pioneering Islamic environmental philosopher and ethics scholar, serving as a core team member for *Al-Mizan: A Covenant for the Earth* and former member of the *Islamic Declaration on Global Climate Change* drafting team.

Shazny Ramlan is a legal scholar, trained at the National University of Singapore, specializing in religious law and environmental governance. His research examines the implementation of Islamic environmental law through constitutional frameworks and religious rulings in Southeast Asia.

Erum K. Sattar is a lecturer at Tufts University with degrees from Harvard Law School and the University of London and is a member of the Bar of England and Wales and the Honourable Society of Lincoln's Inn. Her interdisciplinary research examines the impact of water governance and transboundary water sharing on food production, livelihoods, and migration requiring legal and institutional adaptation structures globally. Her scholarly articles and book chapters have appeared in leading academic publications.

Sarra Tlili is an associate professor of Arabic language, literature, and culture at the University of Florida. She graduated from the University of Pennsylvania, Department of Near Eastern Languages and Civilization. Her primary research interests are stylistics of the Quran, animals in Islam, and Arabic literature.

Foreword

Dan Danielsen

More than a decade ago, when I served as faculty reviewer for the Institute for Global Law and Policy writing workshop session in Doha in 2013, I had the privilege of witnessing the first encounter between Nadia Ahmad and Oluwakemi A. Ayanleye. Neither participant, nor I as their faculty reviewer, could have anticipated the remarkable intellectual trajectory that would follow. Their subsequent collaboration with Saba Kareemi and Erum Sattar beginning in 2018 exemplifies how ambitious intellectual projects emerge from unexpected encounters, a reminder that the most transformative scholarship can begin in the margins of established academic discourse. That Harvard Law School's Institute for Global Law and Policy international convening provided the venue for these initial connections speaks to its broader mission of disrupting conventional boundaries in international legal scholarship.

The Cambridge Handbook of Islam and Environmental Law arrives at a moment when the machinery of global environmental governance has revealed its limitations. As someone who has long examined how corporate power intersects with legal institutions and global governance, I find this volume's timing especially significant. The familiar repertoire of international environmental law in the form of treaties, protocols, market mechanisms, and technocratic expertise has proven inadequate to the scale and urgency of our ecological crisis. This handbook does not simply add Islamic perspectives to existing frameworks. Rather, it exposes how those frameworks themselves rest on unexamined assumptions about the relationship between law, corporate power, and environmental governance.

The environmental crisis that confronts us is fundamentally a crisis of expert rule and institutional capture. The same technocratic vocabulary that promised rational management of global environmental challenges has become detached from its distributional consequences and increasingly serves corporate rather than public interests. Climate negotiations produce elaborate procedural architectures while carbon emissions continue their upward trajectory. Environmental impact assessments proliferate while ecosystems collapse. The gap between expert knowledge and environmental outcomes suggests something more fundamental than implementation failure. It reveals how corporate influence has compromised expertise itself as a mode of global governance.

Islamic environmental law, as presented in this volume, offers more than alternative doctrinal approaches. It provides a different vocabulary for thinking about environmental governance, one that refuses both the separation between technical and ethical questions and the subordination of environmental protection to corporate profit maximization that characterizes so much contemporary environmental expertise. The concept of *khilāfa* (stewardship), for instance, is not simply an Islamic equivalent of Western environmental ethics. It embeds environmental responsibility within a framework of accountability that extends beyond shareholder value to encompass relationships of trust and responsibility that technocratic expertise typically cannot capture. The editors and contributors demonstrate how Islamic legal thought has been continuously adapting to environmental challenges, not through wholesale adoption of Western corporate-dominated frameworks, but through creative interpretation that maintains normative coherence while addressing novel problems. This process of adaptive expertise offers insights into how professional knowledge operates across different legal cultures, revealing both the possibilities and constraints of legal translation in contexts where corporate power is less entrenched.

Consider the transformation of the *ḥimā* system that Lutfallah Gari traces in Chapter 10. What began as a pre-Islamic practice of elite resource control was reimagined within Islamic legal frameworks as a community-centered conservation mechanism. This institutional innovation anticipated modern commons governance by centuries, yet it operated according to logics quite different from contemporary environmental management dominated by market mechanisms and corporate actors. The *ḥimā* system embedded resource conservation within social relationships and religious obligations in ways that made environmental protection inseparable from community welfare, a stark contrast to systems where environmental protection is treated as a constraint on corporate profitability.

Such examples reveal how Islamic environmental law challenges the assumption that environmental problems require primarily technical solutions mediated by corporate actors. The handbook's treatment of corporate environmental responsibility illustrates this point with particular clarity. In Chapter 2, Saba Kareemi's examination of how Pakistani courts deploy concepts like *maṣlaḥa* (public interest) and *amāna* (trust) to constrain corporate environmental harm suggests pathways beyond the familiar regulatory frameworks that treat environmental protection as a constraint on economic activity rather than as constitutive of legitimate economic relations. This resonates with my own work on how law can serve to constrain rather than enable corporate power in environmental contexts.

The volume's engagement with Gulf states provides another lens through which to examine the relationship between expertise, corporate interests, and environmental governance. In Chapter 6, Mehran Kamrava's analysis reveals how oil wealth has entrenched institutional arrangements that frustrate environmental reform, despite clear Islamic ethical imperatives supporting ecological protection. This scholarship illustrates how corporate economic structures can render expert knowledge politically irrelevant, regardless of its technical sophistication or ethical grounding.

The handbook's treatment of constitutional environmental litigation in Pakistan offers yet another perspective on how expertise operates when confronted with entrenched corporate interests. Chapter 5 by James R. May and Erin Daly, and the judicial opinion by Justice Jawad Hassan in Chapter 16, demonstrate how Islamic legal principles can be mobilized to challenge environmental harm through the courts. Yet they also reveal the limitations of legal expertise when confronted with the structural forces driving environmental degradation, including the political power of corporations whose business models depend on environmental exploitation.

Most significantly, this volume demonstrates how Islamic environmental law integrates questions typically separated within Western environmental discourse. Environmental protection cannot be disaggregated from questions of social justice, economic distribution, and political authority, including the authority of corporations to externalize environmental costs. In Chapter 7, Nadia Ahmad's analysis of militarism and climate emissions exemplifies this holistic approach, showing how environmental harm intersects with other forms of violence in ways that technical environmental expertise typically cannot address, particularly when such expertise is compromised by corporate funding and influence.

The handbook's contributors write from diverse positions within the landscape of Islamic legal scholarship, some as practitioners navigating between traditional principles and contemporary challenges, others as scholars examining how Islamic legal thought adapts to novel circumstances. This diversity of perspective reveals how expertise itself operates differently across institutional contexts and professional cultures, offering alternatives to the corporate-captured expertise that dominates much contemporary environmental discourse.

What emerges from this collection is a different understanding of how law relates to environmental governance. Islamic environmental law, as presented here, embeds environmental protection within frameworks of social relationship and religious obligation that resist both the compartmentalization characteristic of technocratic expertise and the subordination of environmental values to corporate profit maximization. The handbook succeeds in demonstrating that Islamic environmental law offers such a vocabulary. Whether this vocabulary can be translated into effective environmental governance capable of constraining corporate environmental harm remains an open question, one that will be answered not by scholars but by practitioners navigating the complex terrain where religious principles, legal institutions, corporate power, and environmental realities intersect. This project is rigorous comparative legal scholarship that avoids both romanticization and dismissal of Islamic legal traditions. The contributors present Islamic environmental law as a complex intellectual tradition that offers different ways of understanding the relationship between law, society, corporate power, and natural systems.

Preface

This *Cambridge Handbook of Islam and Environmental Law* emerged from a shared conviction among its editors, Nadia Ahmad, Saba Kareemi, Erum Sattar, and Oluwakemi Ayanleye, that the intellectual, ethical, and legal traditions of the Islamic world hold untapped potential for responding to the environmental crises of our time. We were inspired to create this volume because we felt that our voices, histories, and epistemologies have been silenced or sidelined in the global environmental discourse. The frameworks that dominate environmental law and policy frequently overlook the moral imagination and legal sophistication embedded in Islamic jurisprudence. In this process, entire civilizations' contributions to understanding stewardship, justice, and sustainability have been neglected. This handbook seeks to fill that gap. It brings together scholars from across disciplines to explore how Islamic law, ethics, and philosophy engage with environmental governance, sustainability, and justice. The chapters collectively reimagine environmental law through the lens of Islamic thought, connecting the spiritual with the ecological, the legal with the moral, and the global with the local.

At its core, this project reclaims the classical constructs of *mīzān* (balance), *khilāfa* (stewardship), and *amāna* (trust) as living principles of environmental order. These values emphasize equilibrium among all forms of creation, accountability to the Creator, and a moral responsibility to sustain the natural world. While the field of environmental law has developed largely in secular and technocratic terms, Islamic jurisprudence offers a deeply relational understanding of justice that integrates ecological, social, and spiritual well-being.

The handbook is structured to move from foundations to frontiers. It begins with the theological and jurisprudential roots of environmental ethics in Islam, then turns to governance, institutions, and public policy. Subsequent chapters address land and water law, biodiversity conservation, energy transitions, and climate adaptation, alongside regional and comparative perspectives. The contributors employ diverse methodologies of textual analysis, case studies, comparative frameworks, and policy critique to highlight how Islamic legal traditions can inform contemporary environmental governance.

Our intended audience includes legal scholars, Islamic studies researchers, policymakers, practitioners, and students who seek to understand how Islamic perspectives can enrich global environmental debates. We assume no prior specialization in either Islamic or environmental law; rather, we invite readers to an interdisciplinary dialogue that situates Islamic jurisprudence as a critical voice in global sustainability efforts. The intersection of Islam and environmental law has never been more urgent. As societies confront accelerating climate crises, resource conflicts, and ecological degradation, the ethical and legal wisdom embedded in Islamic thought provides tools for renewal, offering pathways toward justice that are rooted in faith, humility, and community. This collaboration grew out of many years of teaching, research, and advocacy across multiple regions. Each of us brings distinct scholarly and cultural experiences, yet we share a commitment to recovering and advancing an Islamic environmental consciousness that is both ancient and forward-looking. In bringing this volume to fruition, we hope to contribute to a global conversation about how law and faith together can sustain the earth and its people.

Acknowledgments

This handbook represents a collaborative effort that would not have been possible without the dedication and expertise of numerous scholars and practitioners who shared their knowledge at the intersection of Islamic law and environmental stewardship. Above all, I give thanks to Allah (*sub-ḥānahu wa-ta'ālā*) for granting me the strength, patience, and clarity of purpose to complete this work, and for allowing me to walk, even imperfectly, in the moral example of the Prophet Muhammad (peace and blessings be upon him), who embodied mercy to all creation (*raḥma li-l-'ālamīn*). His life continues to remind me that faith and action, knowledge and humility, are inseparable paths toward justice and stewardship. This volume is an intellectual journey as much as a spiritual one. In bringing it to life, I have drawn deeply on traditions that teach that seeking knowledge is an act of worship and that justice is the highest form of service to humanity and the earth.

I am profoundly grateful to my co-editors, Saba Kareemi, Erum Sattar, and Oluwakemi "Kemi" Ayanleye, whose scholarly expertise, editorial insight, and commitment made this project possible. Their deep understanding of both Islamic jurisprudence and environmental law was instrumental in shaping this work and sustaining our shared vision throughout its development.

We are deeply grateful to the exceptional team at Cambridge University Press who brought this handbook to fruition: Matt Gallaway, Laura Blake, Jadyn Fauconier-Herry, Deepthi Anaparthi, Nabila Rojob, and Hariharan Jayamoorthy. Their professionalism and dedication made this ambitious project possible. Special thanks are owed to Matt. Our collaboration began at the 2016 American Association of Law Schools meeting, when I was in my first year on the tenure track and Matt had just joined the Press. Nearly a decade later, his patience, guidance, and editorial wisdom have proven invaluable. From the earliest conversations about this project through the rewarding challenge of coordinating contributors across multiple continents, Matt and Laura provided steady support, skillful triage, and thoughtful troubleshooting at every turn. This handbook is immeasurably better for their involvement. Gratitude to Nabila for her language and editorial support as we tracked down archival manuscripts and navigated the complexities of translation and transliteration.

I extend heartfelt thanks to the mentors, colleagues, and friends whose scholarship, mentorship, and example have guided and inspired me: Berta Esperanza-Truyol Hernandez, Don Smith, Taja-Nia Henderson, Seema Mohapatra, Nancy Cantalupo, Catheren Page, Jamila Jefferson, Khaled Beydoun, Cliff Villa, Rebecca Bratspies, Carmen Gonzalez, Leila Nadya Sadat, Cyra Choudhury, Tayyab Mahmud, Wil Burns, Kevin Leske, Rachel Deming, Usha Natarajan, Julia Dehm, Chaumtoli Huq, Sahar Aziz, Nicholas Robinson, Jason Czarnezki, Hari

Osofsky, Danielle Conway, Asifa Quraishi-Landes, Richard Albert, Ozan Varol, Marcy Winograd, Imam Tom Facchine, Yasir Qadhi, Haidar Hamoudi, Faisal Kutty, Hatem Bazian, and Hamza Yusuf. Their ideas and engagements have sharpened my thinking and deepened my commitment to pluralism, justice, and the difficult work of dialogue even in disagreement. Each of them, in distinct ways, has influenced how I imagine the relationship between law, faith, and environmental stewardship.

I am immensely grateful to all the contributors who trusted us with their work.

I also owe special thanks to David Kennedy at Harvard's Institute for Global Law and Policy (IGLP), who facilitated the connections that made this collaboration possible. The IGLP offered an invaluable forum for interdisciplinary dialogue between Islamic legal scholars and environmental law experts, helping to nurture the intellectual space in which this project could take shape. My profound thanks to Dan Danielsen, who facilitated our first workshop in Doha in 2013 and provided the feedback that made the seeds of this work possible.

I am deeply grateful to our research assistants, Brooke Lynn Smith, Crescenzo Benkiran, Stanley Ciesielski, Shazmina Khan, Mercedes Da Silva, Mostafa Blassy, and Melissa Bryan, as well as librarians Whitney Curtis, Diana Botluck, and Jason Murray, for their diligence, insight, and attention to detail. Their work in research, review, and organization was indispensable in bringing this volume to completion.

At Barry University, I also want to thank Judy Koons, Sr. Patricia Siemens, Leticia M. Diaz, Margaret Stewart, John Murray, Pablo Ortiz, Michael Allen, Smilka Melgoza, J. J. Meyers, Whitney Mutch, Jason Murray, Louis Rosen, Lucinda Machado, and Renita Culpepper. for their encouragement and institutional support. Their belief in the scholarly and societal significance of this work created the conditions that allowed it to flourish.

At Yale University, I extend my gratitude to Indy Burke, Heather Gerken, Ian Ayers, Dan Esty, Gerald Torres, Sarah Insley, Jordan Colbert, Kristina Lynch, Michelle Bell, Peter Raymond, Jessica Quagliaroli, Ryan Wempler, Julie Vance, Jonas Elbousty, Omer Bajwa, Anthony Kronman, and Bradley Hayes.

I am especially grateful to my husband, Akmal, and our children, Senan, Hanan, and Jihan, for their patience, humor, mischief, and resilience throughout this long journey. They have been both my grounding and my inspiration. I thank my parents, Ejaz and Aneesa Ahmad, for instilling in me a deep sense of Islam, nurturing my curiosity, and tolerating my many indulgences. Their recoveries from cancer reaffirmed for me the profound connection between human health and environmental well-being, and the sacred duty to protect both. I thank my siblings, Shazia, Osman, and Rubina, for their love and laughter. I am grateful to my in-laws, Iqbal Ahmed and Ashrafun Nisa.

I also want to thank the teachers, tutors, coaches, students, and staff who tolerated my tardiness, disarray, and disorganization, and the various grocery stores and restaurants who delivered the meals that kept our household running through many late nights and early mornings of writing and editing.

The insights and perspectives shared by all contributors reflect a collective commitment to bridging Islamic jurisprudence with urgent contemporary environmental concerns. Any errors or omissions remain my own responsibility.

Finally, I thank my extended family, mentors, and community for their encouragement and understanding throughout this process. This volume is dedicated to all who seek environmental justice through faith, scholarship, and collective care for creation, and the world to develop the political will and courage to make change possible.

—Nadia Ahmad

I want to extend my heartfelt thanks to my co-editors, Nadia Ahmad, Oluwakemi Ayanleye, and Erum Sattar. Their exceptional collaboration and shared vision for this book, which transcends Islamic law to explore its impact on other disciplines, such as urban planning, has been truly inspiring. I have learned invaluable lessons in humility, empathy, and leadership from my team, particularly from Nadia, who has been instrumental in uniting us all.

I am also grateful to the Institute for Global Law and Policy (IGLP) for bringing us all together.

Susan Barker, Bogdan Smarandache, Mohammad Fadel, and Sarah al-Ghamidi made this project possible for me with their constant support and feedback. I owe my passion for Islamic law and ethics to Imran Ahsan Khan Nyazee and Sheikh Nuh Ha Mim Keller. Sheikh Nuh's daily live sessions proved instrumental in understanding the Quranic ethos.

Finally, I would like to thank my parents and my late grandfather, Dr. Abdul Khaliq Kareemi, for instilling in me a love and respect for the natural environment. I am writing these words in Lahore, which has one of the worst air quality indices in the world. My elders have told me of a time when wild peacocks and finches populated the city, until corporate interests led to urban development that drove them away. I hope the book changes policy toward a more sustainable future.

—Saba Kareemi

This volume would not have been possible without the insight, vision, and leadership of my co-editor, Nadia Ahmad. Many years ago, she approached me during a panel I was moderating at a conference at Harvard's Institute for Global Law and Policy (IGLP), sparking the idea of co-editing a volume such as this. From that initial conversation, an inspiring team of women came together, our fellow editors Saba Kareemi and Oluwakemi Ayanleye. It has truly been an honor to be part of this collective effort. Working also with contributors from around the world – especially during the challenges of the COVID-19 pandemic – has been both demanding and deeply rewarding.

As I reflect on this journey, I am moved to honor the deep wisdom, kindness, and generosity of my paternal grandfather – my *dada* – the late Abdus Sattar Moosa Didi, originally from the Maldives. His integrity always shone through, and the fact that he taught his grandchildren games and played with us continues to uplift me! When I was a child, he gifted me a beautiful fountain pen and a typewriter, quite concretely expressing his confidence that I could – and that he expected me to – express myself in writing. In this era of growing climate vulnerability, the fate of small island nations, such as the one from which my *dada* hailed, can serve as a beacon that lights the way toward more just and compassionate action among us humans and on the earth that sustains us.

To all those who work in the daily toil of life in obscurity and to scholars throughout history who have advanced human understanding, I sincerely hope our collective efforts contribute to living in harmony with nature, healing past missteps, and forging a wiser, more humane future. I hope this volume helps to advance and live up to that vision.

—Erum Sattar

All praises and adoration are due to Almighty Allah, the Lord of All the Worlds, for giving me the grace to be part of this project. I send peace (*salām*) on the Prophet Muhammad (peace and blessings be upon him), whose teachings and guidance continue to guide and illuminate my path.

I express my deepest gratitude to Nadia Ahmad for inviting us to share in the vision for this project. I am grateful to my other co-editors, Saba Kareemi and Erum Sattar, we became sisters in the course of this project. Their tireless efforts, intellectual rigor, collaborative spirit, and contributions were invaluable. I am indeed honored to have worked alongside them.

I also extend my sincere appreciation to all the authors who contributed to this project for their scholarly expertise, excellent research, dedication, and patience. We are grateful for the opportunity to showcase their work.

I thanks Harvard's Institute for Global Law and Policy (IGLP) for creating an avenue for collaboration with scholars which brought me in contact with Nadia in 2013.

I am grateful to Professors Olusesan Oliyide, Olanrewaju Adeojo, Idowu Adegbite, and Gbade Akinrinmade for their mentorship. I am also indebted to other members of the Faculty of Law at Olabisi Onabanjo University, Ago-Iwoye. Their camaraderie and shared passion for academic excellence have been inspiring and stimulating. I thank my friends and sisters, Drs. Adeejat Kubra Kolawole and Adekunbi Johnson-Odusanya, for their peer mentoring, support, words of encouragement, and constructive feedback.

Finally, I would like to thank my husband, Abiola Ayanleye, my children, Tobi, Tomi, Toba, Tola, and Yinka, and my mother, Mrs. Muslimat Sanni, for their steadfast support, patience, and understanding. Their love, encouragement, and sacrifices have enabled me to pursue my academic passions.

—Oluwakemi Ayanleye

Introduction

Traditional Foundations and Contemporary Directions in Islamic Environmental Law

Nadia B. Ahmad, Saba Kareemi, Erum K. Sattar, and Oluwakemi A. Ayanleye

In an era of unprecedented environmental transformation, the intersection of religious principles, legal frameworks, and ecological sustainability has never been more critical. This handbook emerges as an exploration of Islam and environmental law, presenting a nuanced and multifaceted examination of how Islamic legal traditions address the most pressing environmental challenges of our time. Far from being a static historical artifact, Islamic environmental law reveals itself as a dynamic, evolving system of thought and practice that offers profound insights into environmental conservation, governance, and ethical responsibility. At the heart of Islamic environmental law lies a fundamental theological and ethical concept: humans as stewards (*khalīfa*) of God's creation. This principle transcends mere resource management, embedding a profound spiritual and moral responsibility for environmental protection. The Quranic concept of *mīzān* (balance) provides a framework that recognizes human needs and the intrinsic value of the natural world. Unlike perspectives that view nature as a resource to be exploited, Islamic environmental ethics establishes a delicate covenant of care, respect, and sustainable interaction. The philosophical underpinnings of this approach are revolutionary in their implications. Where many contemporary environmental frameworks view human beings as external to ecological systems, Islamic thought positions humanity as an integral, responsible participant in the complex web of creation. This perspective demands a proactive engagement with environmental protection that goes beyond passive preservation.

Contrary to simplistic narratives that portray traditional legal systems as inherently static, the contributions in this volume reveal the sophistication of classical Islamic environmental institutions. Islamic jurisprudence has developed intricate environmental protection frameworks that anticipated modern ecological concerns by centuries. The *ḥimā* (private pasture) system exemplifies this institutional innovation. Originally a pre-Islamic practice of exclusive land use by powerful chieftains, Islam transformed the concept into a community-centered conservation mechanism. This institutional evolution represents more than a legal adaptation; it reflects a profound philosophical shift towards collective environmental responsibility and shared ecological stewardship.

The handbook examines the landscape of contemporary environmental governance in Muslim-majority contexts. Analyses of institutional dynamics in Gulf states reveal the challenges of translating traditional principles into modern environmental policy. The tension between resource abundance, institutional inertia, and environmental imperatives creates a nuanced narrative of adaptation and resistance. Research on Pakistani constitutional jurisprudence offers a particularly illuminating perspective by demonstrating how Islamic legal principles can be interpreted to support environmental rights through the lens of human dignity. This approach transcends legal interpretation, presenting environmental protection as a fundamental human right deeply rooted in religious and ethical principles.

Groundbreaking work on Islamic ethics and climate change mitigation represents a bridge between historical principles and contemporary global challenges. By exploring how Islamic environmental heritage can inform decarbonization strategies, the research moves beyond theoretical discourse into practical, implementable solutions. The chapters collectively argue that Islamic environmental law is a living, evolving system with genuine potential to address complex global ecological challenges. The framework offers unique perspectives on environmental governance that complement and, in many instances, challenge dominant Western environmental paradigms. Several interconnected themes emerge as central to understanding Islamic environmental law. These include a holistic approach of principled stewardship that views environmental protection as a spiritual and moral obligation; institutional flexibility that adapts traditional principles to contemporary governance challenges; a human-centric approach to environmental protection that links ecological rights directly to human dignity; strategies for sustainable development that balance economic progress with ecological preservation; and approaches for integrating emerging technologies and environmental challenges with established legal and ethical principles.

The handbook presents a robust intellectual framework for understanding environmental governance through an Islamic lens. The research demonstrates that Islamic environmental law represents a sophisticated, adaptable system of thought capable of addressing global ecological challenges. This perspective is particularly critical in an era of increasing environmental uncertainty. Climate change, resource depletion, and ecological disruption demand innovative, culturally responsive approaches to environmental governance. Islamic environmental law offers a rich, nuanced framework that goes beyond regulatory compliance to address fundamental questions of human–nature relationships. As global communities seek innovative approaches to environmental governance, the insights presented in this handbook provide a rich, nuanced framework for understanding and addressing our most pressing ecological challenges. Islamic environmental law emerges not as a peripheral perspective but as a central, transformative approach to reimagining our relationship with the natural world. The journey continues, and the dialogue is just beginning.

In Chapters 1 and 4, Professor Mohamed ʿArafa delves into Quranic themes such as *fasād* (corruption), *iṣlāḥ* (reform), and *tazkiya* (purification), emphasizing the legal and spiritual imperative of environmental stewardship. He articulates how Islamic law operationalizes ecological ethics through mandates for cleanliness, prohibition of waste (*isrāf*), and preservation of natural resources. These chapters form the theological backbone of the handbook, emphasizing continuity between Islamic ethics and environmental duty.

In Chapter 2, Professor Saba Kareemi analyzes how Pakistani courts interpret corporate environmental obligations through the lens of Islamic principles such as *maṣlaḥa* (public interest) and *amāna* (trust). The chapter evaluates the tension between federal and provincial authority in environmental regulation and the role of Islamic law in balancing corporate power with public welfare. It highlights jurisprudential creativity in adapting classical norms to modern governance challenges.

In Chapter 3, Professor Saleem Ali explores the tensions between fossil fuel dependency and Islamic environmental ethics in Gulf economies. He advocates for ethical decarbonization grounded in *maqāṣid al-sharīʿa* (objectives of Islamic law), emphasizing ecological integrity, intergenerational justice, and public interest (*maṣlaḥa*). This chapter positions Islamic ethical thought as a guidepost for climate mitigation policy in oil-dependent states.

In Chapter 5, Professors James May and Erin Daly examine human dignity and environmental outcomes in Pakistan. Focusing on Pakistan's judiciary, the authors illustrate how constitutional courts have interpreted environmental degradation as a violation of the Islamic value of human dignity. They show how judges mobilize religious and legal arguments to link clean environments with human rights. Their work demonstrates the adaptability of Islamic principles in modern public interest litigation.

In Chapter 6, Professor Mehran Kamrava's political economy analysis examines how oil wealth has entrenched institutional inertia and hindered environmental governance in the Gulf. He argues that despite Islamic ethical imperatives, rentier structures obstruct ecological reform, creating a gulf between theory and practice. The chapter underscores the need for structural transformation to align policy with Islamic environmental ideals.

In Chapter 7, Professor Nadia Ahmad examines how military emissions contribute to climate change while being largely exempt from international climate protocols with Muslim-majority countries bearing disproportionate environmental burdens. The chapter draws on Islamic principles like *khilāfa* (trusteeship), *mīzān* (balance), and *ʿadl* (justice) to argue for demilitarization and ecological justice, using case studies from Iraq, Gaza, and Afghanistan. It advocates for reconceptualizing national security and climate action through Islamic environmental ethics that emphasize spiritual responsibility, ecological stewardship, and transnational solidarity.

In Chapter 8, Professor Hassan Khalilieh reconstructs premodern Islamic maritime law, revealing early environmental regulations that protected marine ecosystems and ensured sustainable use of coastal resources. Drawing from legal manuals, maritime codes, and *fiqh* (jurisprudence), the chapter offers a historical precedent for marine conservation rooted in Islamic tradition. His analysis demonstrates how Islamic law anticipated many of today's pressing marine legal frameworks.

In Chapter 9, Professor Erum Sattar addresses the legal and environmental marginalization of landless agricultural workers in South Asia, examining Islamic doctrines on land tenure and distributive justice. She emphasizes the role of *waqf* (Islamic endowment) and equitable land allocation in fostering sustainability and social cohesion. The chapter advocates for legal reforms inspired by Islamic land ethics to address climate vulnerability among rural populations.

In Chapter 10, Professor Lutfallah Gari revisits the *ḥimā*, an Islamic conservation institution for communal resource management, and traces its transformation from pre-Islamic to Islamic contexts. He highlights how the *ḥimā* was reimagined as a collective good serving ecological and social justice, rather than elite privilege. This chapter bridges historical practice with contemporary efforts to revive indigenous conservation mechanisms.

In Chapter 11, Professors Hooshmand Alizadeh and Golshan Hemati examine how Islamic law conceptualizes water as a communal resource and human right. Focusing on Iran, the authors show how Islamic ethics have influenced water distribution policies and environmental planning. They argue for reviving Islamic water ethics to ensure equitable access and sustainable water governance in arid regions.

In Chapter 12, Professor Oluwakemi Ayanleye explores the intersection of intellectual property rights and environmental protection through an Islamic lens. She critiques the monopolization of green technologies and promotes knowledge-sharing rooted in Islamic values of collective benefit (*maṣlaḥa*) and trust (*amāna*). The chapter proposes alternative intellectual property (IP) models aligned with environmental sustainability and Islamic ethics.

In Chapter 13, legal scholar Shazny Ramlan investigates how Malaysia incorporates Islamic legal principles into environmental legislation. The chapter analyzes how Islamic institutions, such as muftis and sharia councils, contribute to legal interpretations that uphold environmental protection. Malaysia's experience provides a model for harmonizing religious law with state-based environmental governance.

In Chapter 14, Professor Wardah Alkatiri critiques consumerism and reimagines the Islamic concept of *ḥayāt ṭayyiba* (good life) through ecological values. She argues that spiritual well-being must include environmental harmony, challenging development paradigms driven by materialism. The chapter calls for a return to prophetic simplicity as a model for sustainability.

In Chapter 15, Professor Anke Iman Bouzenita analyzes the permissibility of genetically modified food (GMF) under Islamic law, considering both ethical and scientific dimensions. The chapter assesses halal certification, risk-benefit calculations, and the precautionary principle from a juristic standpoint. It offers a balanced framework for assessing emerging biotechnologies within Islamic legal ethics.

In Chapter 16, Justice Jawad Hassan of Pakistan presents *Sheikh Asim Farooq v. Federation of Pakistan*, a landmark case study on how Pakistan's judiciary interpreted environmental protection as a constitutional and Islamic obligation. The case catalyzed a broader legal movement linking environmental harm with the violation of public trust and human dignity. Justice Hassan provides a practical example of strategic litigation within Islamic legal frameworks.

In Chapter 17, Professor İbrahim Özdemir presents Al-Mizan as an Islamic declaration for environmental justice developed through multi-faith and international collaboration. The chapter emphasizes the theological underpinnings of ecological harmony and interspecies ethics. Al-Mizan exemplifies how Islamic principles can be mobilized for global environmental diplomacy.

In Chapter 18, Professor Nematollah Azizi explores how Islamic theology and philosophy contribute to epistemologies of sustainability. He calls for rethinking environmental education and ethics through the integration of revelation, reason, and experience. The chapter offers a visionary blueprint for developing sustainable worldviews grounded in Islamic knowledge systems.

In Chapter 19, Professor Lutfallah Gari surveys historical Arabic medical and scientific texts that addressed environmental degradation and public health. These writings show a long-standing awareness of pollution and environmental impacts in Islamic thought. The chapter uncovers early environmental science embedded within Islamic intellectual traditions.

In Chapter 20, Professor Ridoan Karim argues for establishing Islamic environmental law as a formal subdiscipline within Islamic legal studies. He outlines its theoretical basis, sources, and methodologies, advocating for curriculum development and scholarly investment. The chapter highlights the need to institutionalize environmental law within *fiqh* scholarship.

In Chapter 21, Sarra Tlili examines animal welfare within Islamic jurisprudence, challenging anthropocentric interpretations of Islamic law. She foregrounds hadiths and legal rulings that advocate compassion, prohibition of cruelty, and animal dignity. This chapter contributes to broader environmental ethics by emphasizing the intrinsic value of nonhuman beings.

In Chapter 22, Professors Dalal Aassouli and Damilola Olawuyi evaluate the potential of Islamic finance as a tool for environmental protection. Drawing on the shared ethical underpinnings of Islamic finance and green finance, the chapter explores how instruments like green *ṣukūk* can support climate change mitigation. It also highlights legal and institutional gaps hindering broader adoption in Muslim-majority countries.

In Chapter 23, Imam Saffet Catovic offers a deeply theological argument for fossil fuel divestment and renewable energy adoption. Grounded in the principles of *tawhid* (oneness of

God) and *khilāfa* (stewardship), he positions ecological protection as a spiritual duty. The chapter advocates for sustainability as a core component of sharia compliance and moral living.

In Chapter 24, Professor Mohamed ʿArafa presents a framework for sustainable development in Islamic jurisprudence. He examines the protection of water, air, land, and animals through legal mechanisms rooted in *amāna* (trust) and *maṣlaḥa* (public interest). The chapter highlights Islamic law's emphasis on ecological balance, waste prevention, and intergenerational justice.

In Chapter 25, Professor Nadia Ahmad broadens the lens by examining how diverse faith traditions, including Islam, Christianity, Judaism, and Eastern religions, can offer moral guidance for environmental law. She argues that faith-based ethics can complement legal norms to restore ecological harmony. The chapter draws from historical and scriptural sources to propose new paradigms for environmental protection, as discussed in Chapter 26.

The volume explores several interwoven themes:

1. The translation of classical Islamic legal institutions into contemporary governance models, such as the transformation of *ḥimā* and the expansion of Islamic jurisprudence to regulate marine and corporate behavior.
2. The fusion of ethical and legal principles, particularly how courts and scholars interpret *khilāfa*, *mīzān*, and human dignity in ecological terms.
3. The challenge of institutional and political reform, where rentierism and modernization pressures often dilute or block implementation of Islamic environmental principles.

This handbook showcases a living legal system, replete with moral resources, juridical tools, and institutional innovations, capable of responding to the planetary crisis. Whether through the courtroom, the mosque, or the policymaking arena, Islamic principles offer pathways to ecological justice rooted in ethical responsibility and collective stewardship. The future of Islamic environmental law lies in creative engagement between scholars and practitioners, between tradition and innovation, and between local knowledge and global frameworks. As this volume shows, environmental protection in Islam is not a marginal concern but a core component of justice, faith, and law.

1

Islamic Policy of Environmental Conservation

1,500 Years Old – Yet Thoroughly Modern

Mohamed A. 'Arafa[*]

If anyone travels on a road in search of knowledge, Allah will cause him to travel on one of the roads of Paradise.[1]

—The Prophet Muhammad

Knowledge is a treasure, but practice is the key to it.[2]

—Ibn Khaldūn, *al-Muqaddima*

1.1 INTRODUCTION AND OVERVIEW

As is generally known,

> man has the fundamental right to freedom, equality, and adequate conditions of life, in an environment of a quality that permits a life of dignity and well-being, and he bears a solemn responsibility to protect and improve the environment for present and future generations. In this respect, policies promoting or perpetuating apartheid, racial segregation, discrimination, colonial and other forms of oppression and foreign domination stand condemned and must be eliminated.[3]

Environmental security is a focal issue of the new epoch, because the degradation of the environment by human actions is continuously increasing and becoming one of the primary struggles of the present time.[4] Domestic and international legal mechanisms are becoming increasingly effective in protecting against environmental destruction.[5]

* The author wishes to thank and express sincere appreciation to Avv. Professor Ignazio Castellucci for inviting him to present an earlier version of this chapter at the 'Crossroads East and West: Visions of the Economy in the Islamic and Western Legal Traditions' International Workshop at the International University Turin College of Law, Turin, Italy, in 2013. Further, the author thanks Michael Blackwell for his insightful comments and invaluable feedback on this chapter. An earlier version of this chapter appeared in the *European Journal of Law Reform*.

1 M. al-Bukhārī, *Ṣaḥīḥ al-Bukhārī*, Book 3: Knowledge, hadith nos 311, 356, vol. 1, trans. University of Southern California Center for Muslim–Jewish Engagement, available at https://crcc.usc.edu/cmje/.

2 Ibn Khaldūn, *al-Muqaddima*, vol. 21 (Cairo: Dār al-Shāb, 1959). See also Ibn Khaldūn, *The Muqaddimah: An Introduction to History*, trans. F. Rosenthal, ed. N. J. Dawood (Princeton, NJ: Princeton University Press, 1958).

3 See M. R. al-Ḥalw, *Qānūn ḥimāyat al-bī'a fī ḍaw' al-sharī'a* (Beirut: Dār al-Maṭbū'āt al-Jāmi'iyya, 1999), 34–47.

4 Ibid.

5 Ibid., 42–44.

For many Muslim nations, Islamic sharia is considered the main, or one of the main, sources of legislation. Meanwhile, these countries represent a hazardous source of environmental pollution to the world.[6] Accordingly, Muslims must examine the Islamic rules for environmental protection in order to effectively regulate the performance of those countries that do not admit to being bound only by Islamic rules and confirm that Islamic law is both a legal system and a form of public social order at all times and in all places.[7]

Since the 1970s, the jurisdictional reach of environmental law has extended from a national to a transnational level to cover detrimental undertakings and offer greater environmental fortification.[8] Thus, the failure to entirely attain this purpose supports the idea of finding another source of commitment, such as Islamic rules, which would bind Islamic nations that have become a significant source of ecological pollution.[9] Environmental threats are pressing all throughout the world. Consequently, the earth needs to be protected through the adoption of universally applicable legal rules, and the right to a healthy environment needs to be elaborated on in international measures.[10] It is very important to understand Islam's overall view of the universe to comprehend the gap between Islamic theories and practice in Muslim countries.[11] The universe is full of diverse creatures that aim to fulfil man's needs and prove God's greatness.[12] In this domain, the Quran – which is the primary source of Islamic environmental law – states: 'Have you not seen that God is glorified by all in the heavens and on earth, such as birds with wings outspread? Each knows its worship and glorification, and God is aware of what they do.'[13] In the same vein, Allah (God) has created everything in this universe in due proportion and measure, both qualitatively and quantitatively.[14]

In Islamic environmental law, all creatures in the universe perform two specific roles: a *religious* role that evidences God's perfection and presence, and a *social* role that serves man and other creatures.[15] The outcome is the solidarity of the universe and the realisation of its common good (*maṣlaḥa*). According to sharia law, the preservation of the environment is a religious duty demanded by God, as He said, 'Do good, even as God has done you good, and do not pursue corruption in the earth'; 'Verily, God does not love corrupters'; 'Eat and drink, but waste not by

6 Ibid. It should be borne in mind that a comparative analysis of different legal systems' approaches to environmental law contributes to the extensive literature on this area of law in numerous areas of the world such as the United States, Europe, and the Middle East. However, that literature appears to have had little coverage of the treatment of environmental law in Islamic law, one of the three main global legal systems together with common and civil law.

7 A. A. Bagader, A. T. El-Sabbagh, M. Al-Glayand, and M. Y. Samarrai, 'Environmental Protection in Islam', *IUCN Environmental Policy & Law Paper*, no. 20 (1994): 2.

8 J. McCormick, 'The Role of Environmental NGOs in International Regimes', in N. J. Vig and R. S. Axelrod (eds), *The Global Environment* (Washington, DC: CQ Press, 1999), 52. See also A. Bouvier, 'Protection of the Natural Environment in Time of Armed Conflict', *International Review of the Red Cross* 285 (1991): 567–71.

9 al-Ḥalw, *Qānūn*; J. Donnelly, 'Ethics and International Human Rights', in J.-M. Coicaud and D. Warner (eds), *Ethics and International Affairs: Extent and Limits* (Tokyo: United Nations University Press, 2001), 128, 134.

10 Bagader et al., 'Environmental Protection in Islam', 2.

11 M. A. H. Haneef, 'Islam, the Islamic Worldview, and Islamic Economics', *IIUM Journal of Economics and Management* 5, no. 1 (1997): 39–65; R. Al-Sayyid, 'Contemporary Muslim Thought and Human Rights', in *Proceedings of the Seminar on Islamic Perspectives on the Universal Declaration of Human Rights*, UN Doc. HR/IP/SEM/1999/1 (Part II, Section 2), 1999, 253, 260.

12 Q 2:164. All Quranic translations are taken from ʿA. Y. ʿAlī, *The Meaning of the Holy Qurʾān*, 11th ed. (Beltsville, MD: Amana Publications, 2006); al-Ḥalw, *Qānūn*, 26.

13 Q 24:41.

14 Q 44:38–39, 54:49, 13:8, 55:7.

15 R. al-Ḥamd and M. S. Ṣabārīnī, *al-Bīʾa wa-mushkilātuhā* (Kuwait: ʿĀlam al-Maʿrifa, 1979), 150. ('The introduction by man into any part of the environment of waste matter or surplus energy, which so changes the environment as directly or indirectly adversely to affect the opportunity of man to use or enjoy it.') See J. McLoughlin, *The Law and Practice Relating to Pollution Control in the United Kingdom* (London: Graham & Trotman, 1976), xxiii.

excess; verily, He loves not the excessive'; 'Do not cause corruption in the earth, when it has been set in order.'[16] These previous Quranic verses are dominant in international environmental law; they recurrently denounce any environmental damage.

It was not only the Quran that addressed the main principles of Islamic protection of the environment. The Prophet Muhammad's Sunna emphasised the same Islamic norms that guarantee the maintenance of the environment and natural resources.[17] Sunna – the second primary source of sharia – underlines the environmentally friendly nature of various sections in the Quran. The Prophet Muhammad ordered Muslims to protect their environment when he said in a prophetic speech, 'If any Muslim plants a tree or sows a field, and a human, bird, or animal eats from it, it shall be reckoned as charity from him.'[18] Therefore, harming the environment and not bearing any liability in contributing to its fortification is considered to be a violation and a great *ithm* (sin) of God's orders and that of His messenger, which will beget an eternal punishment.[19]

In Islamic law, man does not possess the earth, but has been granted a stewardship to manage it in accordance with the objectives envisioned by the Creator (God) and to utilise it for the benefit of himself and for the benefit of other creatures.[20] As a result, the environment should be kept healthy and safe by contemporary generations for inheritance by future generations, since environmental ruin interrupts public interests, particularly when it causes water, air, and soil pollution.[21]

Islamic law premises man's position in the universe on two Islamic juristic principles: (a) *khilāfa* (stewardship) of man, which means that man is not only a creature but also God's *khalīfa* (steward) on earth, as God is the only proprietor of earth and man is a mere beneficiary, and man can exploit nature for his and other creatures' benefit without depleting it; and (b) the principle of *amāna* (trust), namely that all natural resources created by God are placed as a trust in man's hands and the needs of coming generations must be taken into consideration by man.[22] Islamic environmental law uses a 'duty paradigm' in the sphere of the right to a healthy environment, as human beings cannot destroy, deplete, or misuse natural resources, but rather have an

16 Q 28:77, 7:31, 56. See also D. D. Caron, 'Protection of the Stratospheric Ozone Layer and the Structure of International Environmental Lawmaking', *Hastings International and Comparative Law Review* 14 (1991): 755, 760–61. See also 'Antarctic Ozone Hole Larger Than Ever', CNN, 6 October 1998, https://edition.cnn.com/TECH/science/9810/06/ozone.destruction/.

17 M. Ahmad, 'Safeguarding Environment through Religion: A Study of Prophet Muhammad (PBUH) Sunnah', *Central Asian Journal of Social Sciences and History* 2, no. 4 (2021): 94–101.

18 See the hadith reported by Aḥmad b. Ḥanbal in his *Musnad* and by al-Ṭabarānī in *al-Muʿjam al-kabīr*, on the authority of Abū al-Dardāʾ, with a reliable chain of transmission. See also the hadith related by Anas b. Mālik in the *Musnad* of Aḥmad, and by ʿAbdullāh b. ʿUmar and Abū Hurayra in al-Bukhārī's *al-Adab al-mufrad*, Abū Dāwūd's *Sunan*, and Muslim's *Ṣaḥīḥ*, all available in English translation at https://crcc.usc.edu/cmje/.

19 The Prophet Muhammad warned that a 'person who starves an animal to death is punished by God in the fire of hell' and stated that 'a person's sins are pardoned by God for the act of giving water to a dog in desperate thirst'. M. b. I. al-Bukhari, *The Translation of the Meanings of Sahih Al-Bukhari: Arabic–English*, trans. M. M. Khan, 9 vols. (Riyadh: Darussalam Publishers, 1997), vol. 4, hadith 3482, vol. 8, hadith 6009.

20 Bagader et al., *Environmental Protection in Islam*, 27; Q 20:53–54. See also *Ṣaḥīḥ Muslim*, hadith on the authority of Abū Saʿīd al-Khudrī.

21 S. Khan, 'An Islamic Approach to Environment', Envirocivil, 1 November 2012, http://envirocivil.com/environment/an-islamic-approach-to-environment. See also M. Hassan, 'Teaching Environmental Law from an Islamic Point of View', paper presented in Arabic at the Conference on Environmental Legislation in the Arab Region, 30 September–2 October 2000, 34.

22 Khan, 'An Islamic Approach to Environment'. See also Hassan, 'Teaching Environmental Law from an Islamic Point of View', 34.

obligation to develop and enhance them.[23] Any disturbance to God's equilibrium in the universe is a transgression, a great sin, against the divine system.[24]

In Islam, the creation of environmental damage may be considered to go beyond the mistreating of God's property, where environmental damage could be interpreted as a violation of private interests as well.[25] The difference between these two views, God's property as public property and private property, reflects the nature of the penalty that results from the destruction of both.[26] Every action that represents a breach of public interest is considered a crime against society and entails the punishment of *ta'zīr*, which used to be a preventive sentence, and for which reconciliation was not accepted.[27] The imam (leader) applies such sanctions even if there is no plaintiff, where the qadi (judge) fulfils this role.[28] On the other hand, if the environmental contravention is interpreted as an abuse of private interest, the punishment of *ḥudūd* or *qiṣāṣ* will be implemented; however, compromise or reconciliation can always be made in such kinds of criminal acts.[29]

Based on the fundamental Islamic environmental norms, Section 1.2 discusses the right to a clean environment as it exists within the 'duty' paradigm and solidarity rights. Chapter 4 presents the Islamic protection of basic natural resources and man (environmental challenges) in the Middle Eastern region, followed by an analysis of Islamic law norms on sustainable development and the environment, highlighting the case of clean water laws within the Islamic perspective. Chapter 24 addresses the Islamic strategy for environmental security and the Islamic institutions responsible for the preservation and protection of nature. It concludes by saying that Islamic environmental safety is based upon the principle of 'use' without 'abuse'. Environmental protection in the Islamic legal scheme does not differ from any modern environmental legal system (environmental international law) and calls attention to the significance of having a clear agenda towards the current debate. This plan may be intended primarily by principles of Islamic law that establish the protection of the environment.

1.2 A RIGHT TO A CLEAN AND HEALTHY ENVIRONMENT WITHIN ISLAMIC THEORY: DUTY PATTERN AND SOLIDARITY RIGHTS

Under Islamic environmental standards, humanity is viewed as having *khilāfa* (vice-regency) over, or being a trustee of, the environment.[30] A human being is a distinctive and unique part of this universe and has a special position among its other parts, the components of which are

23 Khan, 'An Islamic Approach to Environment'. See also Hassan, 'Teaching Environmental Law from an Islamic Point of View', 34.

24 Khan, 'An Islamic Approach to Environment'; al-Ḥalw, *Qānūn*.

25 Hassan, 'Teaching Environmental Law from an Islamic Point of View', 34. For instance, the damage of an agricultural field maintained by a private person by the waste of nearby plants is considered a violation of both God's property and individual property.

26 A.-H. B. A. Masri, 'Islam and Ecology', in F. Khalid and J. O'Brien (eds), *Islam and Ecology* (New York: Cassell, 1992), 1, 3; N. Al-Duaij and E. Al-Anzi, 'The Environmental Laws and Regulations in Islamic Waqf: Application to the Situation in Kuwait' (2009), 3–4.

27 A. Mohamed, 'Corruption and Bribery in Islamic Law: Are Islamic Ideals Being Met in Practice?', *Annual Survey of International & Comparative Law* 18 (2012): 188–95.

28 Ibid. See also Hassan, 'Teaching Environmental Law from an Islamic Point of View', 34.

29 Al-Duaij and Al-Anzi, 'The Environmental Laws and Regulations in Islamic Waqf', 3.

30 D. Fisher-Ogden and S. Ross Saxer, 'World Religions and Clean Water Laws', *Duke Environmental Law & Policy Forum* 17, no. 63 (2006): 11. ('One of the basic beliefs in Islam is the concept of human stewardship. Building on the idea that God created the earth, the Qur'an reveals that God provides for humanity by putting everything in service to humans.') See also F. Denny, 'Islam and Ecology: A Bestowed Trust Inviting Balanced Stewardship', *Earth Ethics* 10 (1998): 10.

complementary to one another in a cohesive whole.[31] In this regard, the Quran makes the following assertion:

> Allah is he who created the heavens and the earth and caused water to come down from the clouds, and brought forth therewith fruits for your [human] sustenance. He has constrained to your service the winds that vessel may sail through the sea by [His] command, and the rivers also he has constrained to your service. He has also constrained to your service the sun and the moon, both carrying out their functions incessantly; and He has subjected to you the night as well as the day. He has given you all that you asked to Him; and if you try to count the favours of Allah, you will not be able to number them.[32]

The notion of stewardship is strengthened even more by the philosophies of order and equilibrium that are found elsewhere in the Quran.[33] Humankind is to follow God in sustaining order, as He said, 'Create not disorder in the earth after it has been set in order.'[34]

Egypt, for instance, has followed the Muslim teachings in its legislation and jurisprudence.[35] The Egyptian courts have given the constitutional provision in Article 2 of both the 1971 Constitutional Charter and the 2014 Constitution a narrow interpretation, and hence allowed room for some modern legal thought, such as Egyptian environmental laws.[36] In this sense, the Egyptian government supports the Islamic model of human stewardship, as there is no precise mention of it in the main Egyptian Law No. 4 of 1994: Promulgating the Environment Law.[37] Instead, these are embodied in the Islamic Declaration on Sustainable Principles, and refer to humans as having a 'lieutenancy mission on Earth'.[38] It remains to be seen how effective the environmental statutes and regulations will be.

However, it could be claimed that Islamic traditions are sympathetic to the general values of environmental protection, yet achieving environmental safety through human rights in a Muslim state may obscure application.[39] Islamic nations and secular countries may have central

31 Bagader et al., 'Environmental Protection in Islam', 2.

32 Q 14:33–35. See also K. Stilt, 'Islamic Law and the Making and Remaking of the Iraqi Legal System', *George Washington International Law Review* 36 (2004): 695, 725. See, generally, B. Taylor, *Encyclopedia of Religion and Nature* (New York: Continuum, 2005), 597–98. ('Environmental ethics can be defined, in very general terms, as efforts to articulate, systematize, and defend systems of value guiding human treatment of and behaviour in the natural world. Philosophical and religious environmental ethics, however, did not emerge until the last three decades of the twentieth century. The roots of modern environmental philosophy predate the emergence of "environmental ethics" as an academic field.')

33 Q 7:57.

34 M. Rafiq and M. Ajmal, 'Islam and the Present Ecological Crisis', in O. P. Dwivedi (ed.), *World Religions and the Environment* (New Delhi: Gitanjali Publishing, 1989), 119.

35 Stilt, 'Islamic Law and the Iraqi Legal System', 720.

36 Ibid., 723 (quoting the 1971 Egyptian Constitution). See Constitution of the Arab Republic of Egypt, 18 January 2014, Art. 2. Cf. Abrogated Constitution of the Arab Republic of Egypt, 11 September 1971 (amended 22 May 1980, 25 May 2005, 26 March 2007; replaced 20 March 2011), Art. 2. See also Law No. 4 of 1994 on the Protection of the Environment, amended by Law No. 9/2009, *al-Jarīda al-Rasmiyya* (Egypt), Arts 2–5, 8–83 (formerly available at www .eeaa.gov.eg; URL inactive as of 2025). [Executive regulation amendments: Prime Minister's Decree No. 1741 of 2005.]

37 Stilt, 'Islamic Law and the Iraqi Legal System', 724.

38 'Islamic Declaration on Sustainable Development', United Nations World Summit on Sustainable Development, Johannesburg, 26 August–4 September 2002, 7, https://tinyurl.com/4snhrfaf/. ('1. Generalizing assessment of environmental and health impacts of development projects. 2. Legal and Institutional Aspects of Environment: (a) conducting a comparative study on Islamic countries' environmental laws and conferring an Islamic character on their contents, (b) making Islamic countries' environmental laws consistent with their commitments under related international conventions.')

39 al-Ḥalw, *Qānūn*. See also Hassan, 'Teaching Environmental Law from an Islamic Point of View'.

differences in their attitude towards environmental defence within their legal systems.[40] The standard that there is a 'universal consensus on the ethical basis of nature conservation, and secondly, that human rights standards are or at least should be universally applicable throughout the world'[41] is based on the evidence that there are no differences between rights-based perceptions of environmental protection in secular and Islamic countries, and that all key world religions comprise common ethical doctrines and social values promoting conservation of the living environment and imposing an obligation to protect this environment.[42]

Although there are various Quranic verses (roughly 500) that refer to the correlation between man and the environment, the Quran does not have a rights-based attitude towards protection of the environment, instead underlining the duty of the individual Muslim to care for the natural environment and not to deplete it.[43] This paradigm duty is deeply rooted in the divine orders (beliefs) that the earth in its entirety is a creation of God, and that both man and the state are charged with taking responsibility for God's creation as part of their religious commitments.[44]

One should bear in mind that there is global coherence on there being a human right to a clean environment under international law, which occasionally takes the form of using religious texts to support general statements on there being human rights to a clean environment in Islamic law.[45] In this regard, Article 17(a) of the 1990 Cairo Declaration on Human Rights in Islam states: 'Everyone shall have the right to live in a clean environment, away from vice and moral corruption, an environment that would foster his self-development and it is incumbent upon the State and society in general to afford that right.'[46]

The concept of environment is used extensively in sharia law, including its application in discussions of the natural environment, the social environment, and the economic environment.[47] This notion of environmental security demonstrates itself in many particular areas. First, in the area of pollution, the Prophet Muhammad indicated: 'No one shall urinate on stagnant water, [and] avoid thou the abhorrent act of emptying your bowels near water sources, in the middle of the road, and in the shade.'[48]

40 K. Ahmad, 'Introduction', in S. A. A. Maududi, *The Islamic Law and the Constitution*, ed. and trans. K. Ahmad (Lahore: Islamic Publications, 1960), v–vii. See also A. A. An-Na'im, 'Civil Rights in the Islamic Constitutional Tradition: Shared Ideals and Divergent Regimes', *John Marshall Law Review* 25 (1992): 267–68.

41 M. Lau, 'Islam and Judicial Activism: Public Interest Litigation and Environment Protection in the Islamic Republic of Pakistan', in A. Boyle and M. R. Anderson (eds), *Human Rights Approaches to Environmental Protection* (Oxford: Clarendon Press, 1996), 286. See also M. Palmer, 'The Encounter of Religion and Conservation', in J. R. Engel and J. G. Engel (eds), *Ethics of Environment and Development* (London: Belhaven Press, 1990), 50; J. W. Nickel, 'The Human Right to a Safe Environment: Philosophical Perspectives on Its Scope and Justification', *Yale Journal of International Law* 18 (1993): 281.

42 Lau, 'Islam and Judicial Activism', 285–302.

43 Masri, 'Islam and Ecology'. For a fuller discussion, see M. Y. Izzi Deen (Samarrai), 'Islamic Environmental Ethics, Law, and Society', in J. R. Engel and J. G. Engel (eds), *Ethics of Environment and Development* (London: Belhaven Press, 1990), 189.

44 Izzi Deen, 'Islamic Environmental Ethics'. The emphasis on religious duties rather than rights is common in the discourse of human rights in Islam. See An-Na'im, 'Civil Rights in the Islamic Constitutional Tradition'.

45 See *Final Report of the Special Rapporteur on Human Rights and the Environment*, UN Doc. E/CN.4/Sub.2/1999/9. The report opens with a quotation attributed to the first caliph, Abū Bakr al-Ṣiddīq, illustrating Islamic moral obligations towards environmental protection. It further suggests that the right to a clean environment may be grounded in either a rights-based or duties-based framework.

46 Ibid.

47 A. M. Nasir, 'Islam and the Protection of the Environment', *Islam Today* 13 (1995): 67–68, 84–96.

48 See *Ṣaḥīḥ Muslim* and *Ṣaḥīḥ al-Bukhārī*, supra note 18. A. Nanji, 'The Right to Development: Social and Cultural Rights and Duties to the Community', in *Proceedings of the Seminar on Islamic Perspectives on the Universal Declaration of Human Rights*, UN Doc. HR/IP/SEM/1999/1 (Part II, Section 2), 1999, 355.

In the light of this provision, Professor Al-Khayyat notes that

> what is striking in these commands is the use of the word *'la'n'* (curse) which involves expulsion, repudiation, and exile from the community unless *twabaa*(*h*) (repentance) is proved.[49] Consequently, she who intentionally pollutes or damages the environment to harm the public interest becomes accountable and banishable.[50]

Environmentalism 'stands on the basis of faith ... [and] any kind of corruption whatsoever – whether in the natural or social environment – is considered a violation of God's law.'[51] The role of individuals as vicegerents deeply impacts the misuse of natural resources when such misuse occurs. In terms of capitalism, which is based on self-interested individuals, 'exploitation' carries the negative implication of using the environment for personal interest.[52] On the contrary, under the Islamic ideal based on stewardship, exploitation carries the positive meaning of a trusteeship with God, meant to benefit the group.[53]

Professor Nasir relates that, in sharia law, 'ownership is a social [r]esponsibility, a fact which confirms the relationship between [community] and land, and the extent of Islam's interest in regulating it.'[54] Accordingly, through both the policy of trust and stewardship placed in creatures by God, environmental abuse or mistreatment becomes a divinely motivated responsibility of group improvement, not a self-motivated form of obliteration.[55] However, in spite of the numerous Islamic divine commandments (laws) against environmental exhaustion, unfortunately, the existing Muslim world, in general, is not incedibly concerned about environmental conservation. Islamic environmentalists illustrated that even though vice-regency makes man the main authority on earth, he should not be wasteful, but rather should apply his power sensibly and only in ways that serve God's will.[56] By the same token, because Islamic values hold that

[49] M. H. Al-Khayyat, 'On the Preservation of the Environment: An Islamic Perspective', *The Hassanian Lectures* (Morocco: Ministry of Waqfs and Islamic Affairs, 1998), 152–65.

[50] Ibid., 166. In this context, the importance of personal cleanliness in Islam is worth noting. The Prophet said, 'Cleanliness is half of faith.' See Nasir, 'Islam and the Protection of the Environment', 100. Nasir emphasises: 'Islam links faith and Iman (belief) to purity and cleanliness. Some of the pillars of Islam, such as Salat (prayers) and Hajj (pilgrimage), can only be accomplished in a state of purity using clean water. This rule teaches the community how to protect sources of water from contamination.' Ibid., 99–100.

[51] Nanji notes that 'the role of stewardship entrusted to human beings also necessitates an ethical stance towards the development of natural resources and the public space inhabited by human beings. This stewardship, thus defined, is both a right and a duty to perpetuate these gifts of Allah.' See Nanji, 'The Right to Development'. See also Nasir, 'Islam and the Protection of the Environment', 73–82.

[52] al-Ḥalw, *Qānūn*, 50–59.

[53] J. Morgan-Foster, 'Third Generation Rights: What Islamic Law Can Teach the International Human Rights Movement', *Yale Human Rights & Development Law Journal* 8 (2005): 67. ('The right to a healthy environment is a new development in international human rights law, first discussed in the 1970s and codified in international human rights instruments in the past twenty years. Against these recent developments on the international level, a right and duty towards environmental protection have existed in Islam since the time of the Prophet Mohammad, present in both of the foundational Islamic textual sources (the *Qur'an* and the *Sunnah*).')

[54] Ibid., 82. See also J. Abraham, 'An Ecological Reading of the Qur'anic Understanding of Creation', *Bangalore Theological Forum* 33, no. 1 (2001), https://tinyurl.com/mwbmxecp/. Citing Abd-al-Hamid, 'Exploring the Islamic Environmental Ethics', in A. R. Agwan (ed.), *Islam and the Environment* (New Delhi: Institute of Objective Studies, 1997), 47–48.

[55] Morgan-Foster, 'Third Generation Rights', 13. Environmental deprivation generally becomes a matter of concern only when pollution poses a threat to economic development.

[56] M. R. Hassanien, 'Greening the Middle East: The Regulatory Model of Environmental Protection in the United States–Oman Free Trade Agreement, a Legal Analysis of Chapter 17', *Georgetown International Environmental Law Review* 23 (2011): 465.

each of God's creation serves His will in its own way, man should avoid destroying nature to the point where it can no longer accomplish the purpose that God envisioned.[57]

Furthermore, Arab environmental scholars consider the principle of non-corruption the cornerstone of Islamic theory on environmental defence.[58] The Quran reads thus: 'mischief has appeared on land and sea because of (the meed) that the hands of men have earned that (God) may give them a taste of some of their deeds, in order that they may turn back from Evil.'[59] Also, God says, 'And when he goes away, he strives throughout the land to cause corruption therein and destroy crops and animals. And Allah does not like corruption.'[60] In this respect, Professor ʿAbd al-ʿAzīz Fahmī distinguished between the principle of non-corruption under sharia law and the rule of the fruit of the poisonous tree (which is known in European Roman law as *fraus omina corrumpit*), and he realised that the Islamic norm is more inclusive than the Roman standard one as corruption includes more than deception and fraud.[61] Islamic international environmental law comprises great norms and attitudes on environmental care. Environmental experts should pay more attention to these green principles advocated by Islam.[62] To summarise, this chapter has discussed how the notions of creation, natural purity, stewardship, and non-corruption enrich and conceptualise the Islamic attitude on transnational protection of the environment. Islam, which represents the religion of more than 20 per cent of the world population, will be a driving force in strengthening international environmental law. Chapter 4 discusses Islamic protection of the basic natural resources and man (environmental encounters), followed by an analysis in Chapter 24 of jurisprudential *fiqh* (Islamic juristic rules) on sustainable development and the environment, addressing the responsible Islamic institutions for the preservation and protection of nature.

57 Ibid.; G. E. Roughton, 'The Ancient and the Modern: Environmental Law and Governance in Islam', *Columbia Journal of Environmental Law* 32 (2007): 99, 102. In this sense, the Quran states: 'He it is Who created for you all that is in the Earth; then He turned towards the heavens, and He perfected them as seven heavens; and He knows all things.' And again: 'Say, "Shall I seek a lord other than Allah, while He is the Lord of all things?" ... Then to your [Lord] will be your return, and He will inform you of that wherein you used to differ.' See Q 2:30, 6:165.

58 N. Mohamed, 'Revitalizing an Eco-Justice Ethic of Islam by Way of Environmental Education: Implications for Islamic Education', (PhD diss., Stellenbosch University, 2012), https://core.ac.uk/download/pdf/37348584.pdf.

59 'It is Allah Who has created you, and then He has provided for you; then He will cause you to die, and then He will bring you to life. Is there any of your "partners" who can do any of these things? Glorified be He and exalted above that which they associate with Him.' See Q 30:41.

60 In the same vein, 'And remember Allah during the appointed number of days; but whoso hastens to leave in two days, it shall be no sin for him; and whoso stays behind, it shall be no sin for him. This is for him who fears God. And fear Allah and know that you shall be brought together before Him ... And of men there is he whose talk on this life would please thee, and he would call Allah to witness as to that which is in his heart, and yet he is the most contentious of quarrellers.' See Q 2:204–5.

61 See, generally, 'A. 'A. Fahmī, *al-Qawāʿid al-Rūmāniyya wa-l-fiqhiyya* (Houston, TX: Islamic University of North America (Mishkāh), 2013), https://www.muslim-library.com/dl/books/English_Legal_Maxims_of_Islamic_Jurisprudence.pdf. See also Hassanien, 'Greening the Middle East', 12.

62 Islamic scholars should undertake further research and examination into the Islamic position on nature and the environment to improve its condition and its compatibility with all features of modern life.

2

Acknowledging Environmental Externalities in Islamic Legal Critiques of Corporate Personhood

Saba Kareemi

Blighted corruption has appeared on land and sea, because of what humans' own hands have earned; That He may let them taste something of what they have worked, that haply they may turn back.

—Q 30:41

2.1 INTRODUCTION

This chapter analyzes contemporary Islamic legal scholarship on the validity of corporate persons through the backdrop of a Federal Shariat Court of Pakistan judgment regarding the sharia review of the Companies Ordinance 1984. Section 2.2 discusses the court's rationale, political factors, and individual stakeholders that influenced the judgment in favor of corporate persons. Section 2.3 discusses dissenting scholarship on the corporate form, which stresses the impact of fictitious persons on Islamic law's structure in its entirety, but suffers from similar faults as the majority reasoning, because of its compromise with the postcolonial economic and political realities of Muslim-majority jurisdictions. Sections 2.4 and 2.5 demonstrate how these scholars have theorized the corporation based on frameworks existing in common law jurisprudence, while ignoring social and environmental justice paradigms based on Islamic law. The chapter also highlights criticisms on how Islamic law's nonrecognition of corporations held back Muslim-majority countries economically. This chapter demonstrates how Islamic and Roman commercial laws operated on similar legal principles, and later divergences resulted from private contracting in European enterprises and Islamic jurists' noncomprehension of modern commercial contracts. While Islamic law promotes private enterprise, its primary aim is to develop socioeconomic justice and environmental equilibrium. Lastly, historical Islamic regulatory institutions provide guidelines to deal with market failures, including environmental degradation.

2.1.1 *The Companies Ordinance 1984 and* Federal Government v. Provincial Governments

In October 2008, Pakistan's Federal Shariat Court delivered a judgment in the *Federal Government v. Provincial Governments* case,[1] which decided whether the provisions of the Companies

[1] *Federal Government v. Provincial Governments*, [2009] PLD FSC 1.

Ordinance 1984 complied with the sharia. The court's action was in line with the general trend following the Zia era to ensure that legislation enacted in Pakistan was not repugnant to Islam.[2] The case, initiated under the court's suo moto jurisdiction in 1987, had been pending for almost twenty-two years. The same year, the court had directed the Federal[3] and Provincial governments, the Securities and Exchange Commission of Pakistan (SECP), and the Ministry of Finance to explain why the ordinance's provisions were not repugnant to the injunctions of Islam. The court also invited scholars of Islamic law from all over Pakistan to express their opinions on the subject.

Among the issues under debate was the validity of corporate personhood in Islam, which is the focus of this chapter. In defending the concept, the respondents provided the following responses. The Punjab government, as well as SECP, for example, argued that anything not prohibited in the Quran and Sunna is permitted, citing the legal maxim: *al-aṣl fī al-ashyāʾ al-ibāḥa* (the original rule for all things is permissibility).[4] The Quran and Sunna do not mention corporate personhood. Therefore, the concept was compliant with Islamic law. The North-West Frontier Province (NWFP, now Khyber Pakhtunkhwa) government argued that profits accrued from companies did not fall under the interpretation of *ribā* (usury),[5] and were not part of any exploitative practice in production, trade, and commerce.[6] In addition, the current economic environment necessitates promoting industrial capitalism to allow families to sustain themselves. Therefore, Islamic law should permit corporate personhood, a vital ingredient of the legal frameworks that preserve capitalist economies, based on public interest. The NWFP government then quoted Mufti Taqi Usmani's article on companies limited by shares, published in his magazine, *al-Balāgh*. In the article, Usmani states that permissibility was the original rule for *muʿāmalāt* (civil matters). This rule extended to companies limited by shares. The judgment lacks reference to arguments made by other provinces.

2.2 THE FEDERAL SHARIAT COURT'S RATIONALE

The judgment states that the company limited by shares is like the slave permitted by his master (*al-ʿabd al-maʾdhūn*) under Islamic law to conduct the latter's business. In this case, the master would provide the slave with the initial capital required for a commercial transaction, which the slave could execute freely. The slave's earnings belonged to his master; however, if the slave incurred any debts, the assets the slave had in his possession would be used to set them off. If doing this failed to match the amount owed, the creditor had a right to sell the slave and settle their claims from his bid price. If any unpaid debt remained, the creditors would be unable to satisfy their claims from the master's assets.[7] As per the judgment, while the phrase "juridical person" might have been unknown to classical Islamic jurists, the idea was not. The court cited the *waqf* (charitable trust), the mosque

2 Which legislation the Federal Shariat Court takes up for review is often a matter of politics. See Shoaib A. Ghias, "Defining Shari'a: The Politics of Islamic Judicial Review" (PhD diss., UC Berkeley, 2015).

3 The judgment lacks an explanation of why the Federal Government was the petitioner in this case.

4 *Federal Government v. Provincial Governments*, at para. 10.

5 Imran Ahsan Khan Nyazee demonstrates that the relationship between shareholders and the corporation is, in fact, usurious, since the corporation is not the shareholder's agent; shareholder capital passes into the corporation's ownership as a debt and the corporation has to distribute its entire net profit to shareholders while retaining only the expenses it incurs for its operations, while the shareholder has no liability for the corporation's debts. Imran Ahsan Khan Nyazee, *Islamic Law of Business Organization: Corporations* (Islamabad: The Islamic Research Institute Press, 1998), p. 133.

6 *Federal Government v. Provincial Governments*, at para. 13.

7 The idea that the corporation is like a slave permitted by its master also exists in Western jurisprudence. See Katharina Pistor, *The Code of Capital: How the Law Creates Wealth and Inequality* (Princeton, NJ: Princeton University Press, 2019), p. 54.

(again a type of charitable trust), and the *bayt al-māl* (public treasury) as examples of juridical persons recognized by Islamic law.[8] The judges seemed to be basing their argument on the legal maxim *al-ʿibra li-l-maʿānī laysat li-l-alfāẓ wa-l-mabānī* (meanings, rather than words and constructions, are given weight), even though the judgment does not mention it.[9]

The Federal Shariat Court had also hired jurisconsults to issue independent opinions on the validity of corporate personhood and its legal manifestations. Maulana Taseen, who had passed away before the court delivered the judgment, submitted that shares in a company, being mere paper, fell short of the definition of *māl* (property or a thing of value) under Islamic law and therefore transacting with them was impermissible.[10] He added that the market value of shares always experiences highs and lows, creating an unstable economy, which is against the economic system Islam envisages.[11] He likened trading in shares to gambling.[12]

In response, instead of addressing Taseen's point, the judges argued that all prominent Arab scholars of Islamic law had declared companies and legal personality permissible.[13] These scholars consider the joint stock company, the forebearer of the company limited by shares, akin to the *sharika* (partnership) in Islamic law. The judgment also cited the Organization of Islamic Cooperation's (OIC) Islamic Fiqh Academy, which stated in its resolution number 7/1/65[14] that companies limited by shares were permissible according to Islamic law if formed for lawful objectives.

From the opinions presented before the court, the judges agreed with the arguments referencing Usmani's position. They held that the *waqf* and the *bayt al-māl* were juridical persons recognized by Islamic law, citing in addition to Usmani, ʿAbd al-Qādir ʿAwda,[15] Muṣṭafā al-Zarqā,[16] and ʿAlī al-Khafīf.[17] Proponents of fictitious personality argue that a *waqf* is a legal person because when a donor declares a property to be a *waqf*, they no longer own it. The beneficiaries of a *waqf* benefit from its corpus, or proceeds, yet they are not its owners. A property purchased with the *waqf*'s income, however, does not automatically become a part of the *waqf*. The law treats this property as being owned by the *waqf*. They further argue that the money donated to a mosque is not part of the *waqf*. Instead, it becomes the mosque's property, which is a *waqf*. The *waqf* can buy or sell property; it may become a creditor or debtor and can sue and be sued. A *waqf*, therefore, like a natural person, may own property. They therefore concluded that corporate entities could also have legal personalities.

8 A similar argument exists in Western jurisprudence, with scholars citing the *societas publicanorum* as an example of a body corporate with tradable shares, called *partes*, that existed in Roman law. In fact, it exemplified a partnership with individual and unlimited liability, where adding a partner without consent created a sub-partnership, thus limiting its scale. The structure lacked the market systems needed for public share trading. See: Geoffrey Poitras and Frederick Willeboordse, 'The Societas Publicanorum and Corporate Personality in Roman Private Law.' (2021) 63(7). Business History 1055–1078.

9 Aḥmad ʿAlī ʿAbdullāh has quoted this maxim as an argument in favor of corporate personhood. Aḥmad ʿAlī ʿAbdullāh, *al-Shakhṣiyya al-iʿtibāriyya fī al-fiqh al-Islāmī* (Khartoum, n.d.), p. 109.

10 *Federal Government v. Provincial Governments*, at para. 21.

11 Daromir Rudnyckyj while discussing his book *Beyond Debt* on the New Books Network states that his instructor at International Centre for Education in Islamic Finance (INCEIF) Malaysia made a similar argument about the prevalent global economic system: Daromir Rudnyckyj, *Beyond Debt: Islamic Experiments in Global Finance* (Chicago: University of Chicago Press, 2019). Podcast at https://newbooksnetwork.com/daromir-rudnyckyj-beyond-debt-islamic-experiments-in-global-finance-u-chicago-press-2018/.

12 Richard Ney has made similar arguments. See Richard Ney, *The Wall Street Gang* (New York: Praeger, 1974).

13 *Federal Government v. Provincial Governments*, at para. 15.

14 The judgment misnumbers Resolution No. 63 (1/7). Online at https://iifa-aifi.org/en/32438.html.

15 ʿAbd al-Qādir ʿAwda, *al-Tashrīʿ al-jināʾī al-Islāmī muqāranan bi-l-qānūn al-waḍʿī* (Beirut: Muʾassasat al-Risāla, 1963), vol. 1, p. 393.

16 Muṣṭafā Aḥmad al-Zarqā, *al-Madkhal al-fiqhī al-ʿāmm* (Damascus: Dār al-Qalam, 2004), vol. 3, pp. 253, 258. Originally published in 1968.

17 ʿAlī al-Khafīf, *al-Sharikāt fī al-fiqh al-Islāmī* (Cairo: Arab League, 1962), p. 25.

Aslam Khaki, the name-bearer of a previous famous judgment on *ribā*,[18] argued that the concept of limited liability was against Islamic law. Under Islamic law, the liability to pay off a debt extends to the debtor's entire personal property. When limited liability companies are liquidated, the exchequer or the public directly bears the loss if the company's loans remain unpaid. The Quran states, "Nobody shall bear the burden of another."[19] By transferring the company's debts onto others, its shareholders and directors violate Quranic injunctions. Khaki pointed out that this loss-shifting would lead to harm and would contravene the principle of *lā ḍarar wa-lā ḍirār* (neither getting harmed nor harming others is permissible).

In response, the court stated that this hadith is of a general nature and is not restricted to business transactions.[20] The court provided no further explanation as to why the hadith was inapplicable in this case. The court agreed that, as per the Quran, no one should bear the burden of another. While the liabilities of a company's shareholders were indeed unlimited, the company was a separate legal entity, and its assets and liabilities were distinct from those of the shareholders. If a company owed debts to its creditors, its liability to them as an independent entity would also be unlimited.

The unanimous judgment reads as a detailed argument favouring corporate personhood, rather than an engagement with various dissenting voices in contemporary Islamic legal scholarship. The judgment misquotes some authors, leading to intellectual dishonesty. For example, the judgment quotes Imran Ahsan Khan Nyazee as follows:

> We find that there are many things in this modern world, at least for which an explicit hukm (ruling) cannot be found in the light of the Quran and Sunnah and it is difficult to derive a hukm for it on the basis of analogy.[21]

While Nyazee did state this in *Theories of Islamic Law*, he had written a separate book on corporations in which he was largely critical of Taqi Usmani's thesis. The judgment also quoted the Hanafi jurist al-Sarakhsī's *al-Mabsūṭ* to show that *waqfs* had independent legal personalities. However, al-Sarakhsī, in his book *al-Uṣūl*, explicitly stated that human beings are the only bearers of legal capacity and, therefore, the only subjects of Islamic law.[22]

In short, with some highly creative legal engineering, the judgment declared corporate personhood valid but failed to engage with significant policy issues, such as the role of corporations in shaping our economies, societies, and the environment.

2.3 THE CASE'S BACKGROUND

To understand the case's trajectory and the court's decision, this chapter investigates why the court decided to issue a judgment in 2008 when it had initiated the case in 1987. Furthermore, why did it cite promoting industrial capitalism as the only value judgment Islamic law recognizes? Why did the court not take the opportunity to reflect on corporate actions, their colonial history, and their impact on human rights and the environment?

[18] *Aslam Khaki v. Syed Muhammad Hashim*, [2000] PLD SC 225.

[19] Q 53:38.

[20] *Federal Government v. Provincial Governments*, at para. 24.

[21] Imran Ahsan Khan Nyazee, *Theories of Islamic Law: The Methodology of Ijtihad* (Islamabad: Islamic Research Institute and International Institute of Islamic Thought, 1994), p. 47.

[22] Muḥammad b. Aḥmad b. Abī Sahl Abū Bakr al-Sarakhsī, *Uṣūl al-Sarakhsī*, 2 vols. (Beirut: Dār al-Kutub ʿIlmiyya, 1993), vol. 2, p. 340.

The answer lies with the person of Mufti Taqi Usmani. Usmani is a renowned Pakistani scholar of Islamic law. He was a judge at the Supreme Court of Pakistan's Shariat Appellate Bench from 1982 to 2002, until the military dictator Pervez Musharraf removed him.[23] He was also vice-chairman of OIC's Islamic Fiqh Academy when it passed Resolution No. 63 (1/7) on the permissibility of corporate personhood in Islam, which the Federal Shariat Court referenced in its judgment.[24] Due to his long tenure at the Shariat Appellate Bench, and his global renown, he exercised unparalleled influence in shaping Islamic law's application in Pakistan.

Before Usmani, several scholars of Islamic law had written about the validity of corporate personhood in the twentieth century. As mentioned above, they included Abdur Rahim,[25] Muṣṭafā al-Zarqā, ʿAlī al-Khafīf, and ʿAbd al-Qādir ʿAwda. Most of this scholarship, however, was apologetic – written either to show that Islamic law was not antiquated or to refute Joseph Schacht's statement that it did not recognize juristic persons.[26]

Usmani, however, integrated the issue of corporate personhood within the Islamic finance framework he was promoting. In 1998, he authored *An Introduction to Islamic Finance*,[27] which focused on the diverse types of contracts that Islamic banks could sell as products to the Muslim faithful. The entire last chapter deals with the issue of corporate personhood.[28]

The book drew considerable criticism from other Deobandi[29] scholars.[30] They argued, among other things, that corporate personhood was against Islamic law, because the latter does not recognize limited liability, since it is unjust to creditors. Usmani, however, had enough endorsement within the Deobandi fraternity to issue his opinions as fatwas.[31] He then used his influence at the Federal Shariat Court to promote his ideas further. Since Pervez Musharraf had removed him as a judge of the Shariat Appellate Bench, based on Usmani's judgment on *ribā*, Usmani decided to focus on the question of corporate personhood. While the *Federal Government* judgment briefly considered alternative viewpoints, judges did not consult Usmani's critics from within the Deobandi school. Other quoted scholars, including Nyazee, refused to participate, because they felt the judges had determined the outcome before the proceedings began.[32]

In the book, Usmani used textual and policy arguments to promote the concept of legal personality. The textual arguments cited the same examples as the *Federal Government* case, including the example of the *waqf*. However, Usmani also considered recognizing the limited

[23] Musharraf was unhappy with his judgment in *Dr. Aslam Khaki v. Syed Muhammad Hashim*, PLD 2000 SC 225.

[24] Mufti Taqi Usmani has remained Pakistan's permanent representative to the academy since 1983. He served as its deputy chairman from 1991 to 2000. The academy passed the above resolution in May 1992. See https://hikmahinstitute.org.pk/mufti-muhammad-taqi-usmani-db/. See also www.albalagh.net/qa/ifa.shtml.

[25] Abdur Rahim, *The Principles of Muhammadan Jurisprudence according to the Hanafi, Maliki, Shafi'i and Hanbali Schools* (London: Luzac, 1911).

[26] Joseph Schacht, *An Introduction to Islamic Law* (Oxford: Clarendon Press, 1966), p. 125.

[27] Mufti Muhammad Taqi Usmani, *An Introduction to Islamic Finance* (Karachi: Idaratul Ma'arif, 1998). The book has an Urdu version too: Muḥammad Tāqī ʿUsmānī, *Islām awr jadīd maʿīshat wa-tijārat* (Karachi: Quranic Studies Publishers, 2009).

[28] Usmani supplemented his scholarship through service as an advisor to the sharia advisory boards of various Islamic banks. Today, he runs a sharia-compliant advisory service, Usmani & Co., with his son, Imran Usmani, who also served as a jurisconsult on the *Federal Government* case. The service also gives recommendations regarding buying shares in publicly listed companies that Usmani considers to be sharia compliant.

[29] Deobandi is a Sunni Hanafi revivalist movement that started in Deoband, India, in the late nineteenth century. The movement runs several madrasas in Pakistan.

[30] In 2008, Deobandi critics of Usmani held conferences against his concept of Islamic finance. They collectively wrote a book called *Murawwaja Islami Bankari* (Prevalent Islamic Banking) the same year.

[31] Ghias, "Defining Shari'a," p. 215.

[32] I asked Nyazee about his involvement in the case via WhatsApp on June 21, 2020.

liability of corporations in view of the Muslim community's greater interest.[33] He argued that the concept had proven vital in mobilizing large amounts of capital from a wide range of investors.[34] Other scholars have made similar policy-based arguments in favor of the corporate form. For example, Anowar Zahid, a Malaysian scholar, argues that in the absence of any clear text from the Quran and Sunna, corporate personality may be accepted from a *maṣlaḥa* (public interest) viewpoint, because corporations might bring economic prosperity and felicity to society.[35]

Despite supporting the corporate form, Usmani recognizes the pitfalls of limited liability. He argues that the concept should be restricted to publicly listed companies, because the shareholders are so numerous that holding each of them liable for the company's daily affairs and debts exceeding its assets would be unfeasible.[36] Conversely, private companies and partnerships should have unlimited liability because shareholders and partners can easily ascertain their business's daily management activities. Therefore, they should be held personally accountable for any losses their businesses incur.[37]

Usmani's argument against limited liability for private companies has some precedence in American jurisprudence. In a 1992 article, Larry Ribstein advocated limited liability for both public and private companies because it reduces externalities for owners and wards off litigation from employees and others affected by the company's actions.[38] In response, Robert W. Hillman argued that limited liability makes sense for large publicly held companies, because there is a separation between ownership and control.[39] In private companies, however, the company's owners participate actively in management. Limited liability, therefore, should not be allowed in such cases. Hillman also argued that shielding owners from liability must be balanced with the interests of creditors and employees.[40] Hillman was barely the first to critique the private limited company. In *Broderip v. Salomon*,[41] the case preceding *Salomon v. Salomon*,[42] L. J. Lindley made the same argument in the Court of Appeal vis-à-vis private companies enabling sole traders to defeat the claims of those who traded with them.[43] For similar reasons, Usmani argues that governments should regulate private companies and partnerships more closely than public limited companies.

His argument runs counter to the global trend following the 2008 financial crisis. Governments are regulating public companies more closely, because the externalities they produce, including environmental disasters like the 2010 British Petroleum oil spill in the Gulf of Mexico, affect society en masse. Private companies provide different social challenges, given that they have become the preferred business form for international military and security companies.[44]

33 Usmani, *An Introduction to Islamic Finance*.
34 Ibid.
35 Anowar Zahid, "Corporate Personality from an Islamic Perspective," *Arab Law* 27, no. 2 (2013): 125–50.
36 Usmani, *An Introduction to Islamic Finance*, p. 231.
37 Ibid.
38 Larry E. Ribstein, "The Deregulation of Limited Liability and the Death of Partnership," *Washington University Law Quarterly* 70 (1992): 417–75.
39 Robert W. Hillman, "Limited Liability and Externalization of Risk: A Comment on the Death of Partnership," *Washington University Law Quarterly* 70 (1992): 477–87.
40 Ibid., p. 484.
41 *Broderip v. Salomon* [1895] 2 Ch. 323.
42 *Salomon v. A Salomon & Co. Ltd* [1897] AC 22.
43 Paddy Ireland, "The Rise of the Limited Liability Company," *International Journal of the Sociology of Law* 12, no. 3 (1984): 239–60, at 253.
44 Christopher Kinsey, *Corporate Soldiers and International Security: The Rise of Private Military Companies* (Oxford: Routledge, 2006).

2.4 ADDITIONAL ARGUMENTS FOR AND AGAINST THE CORPORATE FORM

In response to Usmani, Nyazee argues that corporate personhood should be analyzed within the framework Islamic law's general principles create rather than *ad hoc* examples such as the *waqf* and the *bayt al-māl*. The *waqf* is suspended property (*ḥabs al-ʿayn*). Its revenue is a beneficiary's right and not a part of the *waqf*. The beneficiary pays for its maintenance expenses because of the principle of *al-kharāj bi-l-ḍamān* (entitlement to profit has a corresponding liability for bearing loss). He quotes Ibn ʿĀbidīn, explicitly stating that the *waqf* has no *dhimma* (here translatable as "personality"). Further, in law, legal personality is not dependent on the ownership of wealth. The *waqf*, however, can only exist with suspended property. The *waqf* ceases to exist if the property is destroyed.

The *bayt al-māl* is merely a *māl mushtarak* (joint wealth) of the *umma* (Muslim community), which the ruler administers as their *wakīl* (agent). Since the *bayt al-māl* is considered the collective property of the Muslims, if someone steals from it, the *ḥadd* (fixed) punishment for theft is waived because the thief is considered part owner of the *bayt al-māl*.

According to Nyazee, human beings are the only subjects of divine command and, therefore, the only beings with legal capacity according to Islamic law.[45] However, Nyazee recognizes corporate personality as an effective organizational tool. He proposes that if Islamic law is to accept them, corporate persons should not be expected to perform religious duties because they are not subjects of divine command.[46] He stipulates that some form of *ʿaql* (intellect) be associated with the fictitious entity. This intellect may be that of an individual or a group of individuals, which is similar to a board of directors in a corporation.

Lastly, dual title of ownership should be associated with the fictitious person. Any property the fictitious person holds in its name will be assumed to be held on behalf of the members constituting the fictitious person through *khalṭ*, or mingling of capitals.[47] Nyazee imagines this type of business organization as a *wakāla* (agency contract) rather than a *sharika* (partnership).[48] In associating a dual title of ownership to the corporation and requiring the mingling of capitals, Nyazee advocates a hybrid between a corporation and a partnership. The entity Nyazee devises has legal personality but with unlimited liability. The corporation is the agent of its members, acting on their behalf. Unlimited liability companies are no mystery to corporate lawyers. Multiple jurisdictions recognize them in various forms. Some of these companies are successful large-scale enterprises. This type of business organization is usually subject to less regulation and benefits from tax advantages, making it attractive to investors,[49] and demonstrates how corporate structurization results from conscious government policy-making. The core issue, though, is Nyazee's conceptualization of legal personality, due to its impact on assigning liability.

When discussing legal personality for nonhumans in Islamic law, he draws from al-Sarakhsī and al-Ghazālī to argue that the intellect, *ʿaql*, is a condition for legal capacity existing in Islam and that animals lack this.[50] However, Nyazee grants legal personality to the corporation, based on a passage by the fourteenth-century Central Asian Hanafi jurist al-Taftāzānī. He states that al-

45 Imran Ahsan Khan Nyazee, *Islamic Law of Business Organization: Partnerships* (Islamabad: International Institute of Islamic Thought, 2002), p. 91.

46 Ibid., p. 94.

47 Ibid., p. 181.

48 Ibid., p. 177. I will explain the concept of *wakāla* later in this chapter.

49 Land Rover, for example, was an unlimited liability company registered in the United Kingdom till 2013.

50 Nyazee, *Islamic Law of Business Organization: Corporations*, p. 93.

Taftāzānī seems to recognize that animals can have some category of intellect and are therefore capable of possessing limited, unsound legal capacity.[51] He then extends this rule to corporations, stating that as long as human intelligence directs them, fictitious persons may be assigned a limited *dhimma* provided they have no liability for failing to perform religious duties.[52] The passage he translates from al-Taftāzānī is as follows:

> The intellect is merely to understand the *khitab* (communication from God), while the obligation is based upon an attribute that is called the *dhimmah*, so much so that if the existence of *'aql* is assumed without this attribute, like the mounting of intellect on to an animal other than a human, no obligation for or against it can be established.

Al-Taftāzānī made the above statement while arguing that only human beings have complete legal capacity in Islamic law. He wrote this in response to the Mu'tazilī claim that the intellect is a source of law. For him, the intellect was merely a condition to understand God's communication.[53] However, the cause (*sabab*) for acquiring legal capacity was *dhimma*, which he deemed the covenant (*'ahd*) man had made with God based on the following Quranic verse:

> And (remember) when thy Lord brought forth from the Children of Adam, from their reins, their seed, and made them testify of themselves, (saying): Am I not your Lord? They said: Yea, verily. We testify.[54]

Based on this covenant between God and the Children of Adam that implied a duty to worship Him, al-Taftāzānī concluded from the preceding verse that God had chosen human beings among all animals to bear rights and obligations, making human beings the only bearers of legal capacity.[55] Therefore, even if God gave intellect to any other animal, only human beings would be considered to have legal capacity as per Islamic law.

Nyazee's stipulation to attach some form of intellect to the corporation demonstrates a shift in Islamic jurists' understanding of *'aql*. Sarakhsī defines *'aql* as a light in the chest with which the heart sees when observing clear proofs related to God.[56] In contrast, when Nyazee refers to the intellect in the context of corporate identity, he views it as a function of the brain, resembling the common law conception. While classical jurists believed that intellect facilitates a person's experience of the Divine, and their ability to distinguish right from wrong, modern jurists focus on whether a legal entity is capable of rational thought.[57]

Nyazee does not explain why he prefers analogizing the corporation to an animal rather than an authorized slave.[58] The owners of both animals and authorized slaves have limited liability when both commit unauthorized acts. However, it seems that Nyazee is circumventing the issue created when the slave rather than the master is entitled to profits earned from excess credit

51 Ibid.

52 Ibid., p. 94.

53 Sa'd al-Dīn Mas'ūd b. 'Umar al-Taftāzānī, *Sharḥ al-talwīḥ 'alā al-tawḍīḥ*, 2 vols. (Cairo: Maktabat Ṣubayḥ, 1957), vol. 2, p. 322.

54 Q 7:172.

55 Ibid.

56 al-Sarakhsī, *Uṣūl al-Sarakhsī*, vol. 1, pp. 336–47.

57 All Sunni legal theories agree that the heart is the intellect's locus, based on various Quranic verses, including 7:179 "... they have hearts they do not understand with ..." Hanafis also recognize the prefrontal cortex's (*nāṣīa*) executive function as a regulator of emotions, based on verse 96:16, "A hideous, lying, willfully evil brow [*nāṣīa*]." The intellect is light that flows into the brain from the heart: Shihāb al-dīn Maḥmūd al-Ālūsī, *Rūḥ al-ma'ānī fī tafsīr al-Qur'ān al-'azīm wa-l-sab' al-mathānī*, (Beirut: Dār al-Fikr, 1997) vol. 1.

58 See Nyazee, *Islamic Law of Business Organization: Corporations*, p. 171, for a detailed discussion of why according to him the corporation is dissimilar to an authorized slave.

purchases due to the former's separate, yet defective, legal capacity as a human. While Islamic law recognizes animals as capable of exercising choice, they still lack intellectual capacity and *dhimma*.[59] This lack of capacity ensures the owner's automatic entitlement to any profits the animal earns. However, this is mere speculation about Nyazee's reasoning.

Nyazee's preference for using the analogy of an animal corresponds with his proposal that the corporation become the shareholders' agent. However, Islamic law stipulates that both the agent and the principal must have independent wills with complete legal capacity. Minors and slaves cannot become agents for this very reason.[60] Their owners or guardians must ratify any financial transactions they undertake.[61] A fictitious person lacks an independent will. Therefore, it lacks the capacity to become an agent. It is important to note that cases such as the authorized slave are exceptions to the general rule.[62] Islamic law prohibits using analogy to extend exceptions, because they erode the law's foundation and defeat its spirit. Nyazee's approach to anthropomorphizing (in this case, zoomorphizing) the corporation has precedent in Western jurisprudence. In American legal jurisprudence, Paul Vinogradoff analogized the corporate form to a human body in the following manner:

> How is the law to deal with such superindividual undertakings? The usual expedient is to assimilate them to live persons. We assign to them a will, i.e., the faculty of taking resolves in the midst of conflicting motives; a governing brain and nerves, in the shape of institutions and agents; a capacity for the promotion and the defence of interests by holding property, performing acts in law, and exercising rights of action in courts.[63]

Vinogradoff inspired Lord Denning to make the following statement in *H. L. Bolton (Engineering) Co. Ltd v. T. J. Graham & Sons Ltd*:

> A company in many ways may be likened to a human body. It has a brain and a nerve centre which controls what it does. It also has hands which hold the tools and act in accordance with directions from the centre. Some of the people in the company are mere servants and agents who are nothing more than hands to do the work and cannot be said to represent the mind or will. Others are directors and managers who represent the directing mind and will of the company and control what it does. The state of mind of these managers is the state of mind of the company and is treated by the law as such.[64]

Similarly, the United States Supreme Court used the real entity theory to extend to the corporation the right to equal protection of the law given to individuals under the fourteenth amendment.[65]

The United States Supreme Court has used other metaphors, such as that of the aggregate entity, to grant corporate rights under other constitutional amendments.[66]

[59] Peter Adamson, "Abū Bakr al-Rāzī on Animals," *Archiv für Geschichte der Philosophie* 94, no. 3 (2012): 249–73, at 256.

[60] Burhān al-Dīn Abū al-Ḥasan ʿAlī b. Abī Bakr al-Marghīnānī, *al-Hidāya fī sharḥ bidāyat al-mubtadī*, 4 vols. (Beirut: Dār Iḥyāʾ al-Turāth al-ʿArabī, n.d.), vol. 3, p. 6.

[61] Ibid. See also the Ottoman Islamic Civil Code of 1876, drafted by a team of ulema: *Majallat al-aḥkām al-ʿadaliyya* (Karachi: Nūr Muḥammad, Karkhāna Tijārat-e Kutb, n.d.), pp. 255–56, para. 1333.

[62] Gaius, *Institutes*, trans. Edward Poste (Oxford: Clarendon Press, 1904), Book IV, sec. 71–73.

[63] Paul Vinogradoff, "Juridical Persons," *Columbia Law Review* 24, no. 6 (1924): 594–604, at 595.

[64] *H. L. Bolton (Engineering) Co. Ltd v. T. J. Graham and Sons Ltd* [1956] 3 All ER 624.

[65] Gregory A. Mark, "The Personification of the Business Corporation in American Law," *University of Chicago Law Review* 54 (1987): 1441–83, at 1460. See also Jess M. Krannich, "The Corporate Person: A New Analytical Approach to a Flawed Method of Constitutional Interpretation," *Loyola University Chicago Law Journal* 37 (2005): 61–109, at 61.

[66] Krannich, "The Corporate Person," p. 97.

2.5 THE LIMITATIONS OF ANTHROPOMORPHIZING THE CORPORATION

Krannich criticizes using metaphors to extend individual rights to corporations.[67] He argues that reliance on metaphors focuses on a results-based approach to corporate legal theory and ignores fundamental principles of statutory interpretation. In turn, this approach leads to instability in corporate theory jurisprudence.[68]

Criticizing the use of metaphors has precedent in jurisprudence for perpetuating uncertainty and distracting from the real issues in a case.[69] In *Yukong Line Ltd v. Rendsburg Investment Corporation*, Justice Toulson stated that metaphors are a substitute for analysis and may, therefore, obscure reasoning.[70] An example is analogizing inventors to farmers who toil to create fruits and, therefore, must be allowed to reap what they have sown. Intellectual property laws deem attempts to copy their work theft or robbery when, in reality, entire industries use these analogies to protect themselves regardless of the social costs.[71] To illustrate, if one farmer is toiling to produce a particular fruit, should they now be able to restrict others from producing it? After all, one of the earliest critiques of monopolies was that such businesses would render other craftsmen idle.

The real issues, for example, in landmark US judgments such as *Santa Clara*,[72] *Dartmouth*,[73] and the *Railroad Tax*[74] cases, which all conferred individual rights to corporations, were related to property rights.[75] *Salomon* was an insolvency law case. However, the effect of granting individual rights to institutions, such as corporations, is that they aggregate more power than natural persons and even governments.[76] For this reason, rethinking the real entity metaphor is crucial. A natural person can reason but will also express emotions such as laughter or anger. When jurists call a corporation a person, one immediately focuses on the element of reason, because this characteristic is closer in manner to how we conceptualize individuals. However, this approach ignores that corporations are aggregates, and their decisions are also the effects of collective resolve.[77]

Under Hanafi jurisprudence, which both Nyazee and Usmani follow, the corporate person metaphor would be considered *qiyās al-shabah*, which is reasoning based on resemblances between properties,[78] or which Judge Aldisert would call enumeration of relevant resemblances.[79] Anita Schnee states that this enumeration of instances, which she calls "induced

67 Ibid., pp. 62, 63.

68 Ibid.

69 Justice Kim Lewison, "Metaphors and Legal Reasoning," *Judicial Review: Selected Conference Papers: Journal of the Judicial Commission of New South Wales* 12, no. 4 (2016): 375–92, citing Lord Hoffmann in *Serco Ltd v. Lawson* [2006] UKHL 3.

70 Ibid.

71 Isabelle Richard, "Metaphors in English for Law: Let Us Keep Them!," *Lexis: Journal in English Lexicology* 8 (2014): 1–20, at 10.

72 *Santa Clara County v. Southern Pacific R. Co.*, (1886) 118 U.S. 394.

73 *Trustees of Dartmouth Coll. v. Woodward*, (1875) 17 U.S. 518.

74 *State Railroad Tax Cases*, (1875) 92 U.S. 575.

75 Mark, "Personification of the Business Corporation," p. 1464.

76 Krannich, "The Corporate Person," pp. 96, 100.

77 Richard, "Metaphors in English for Law," p. 11. Single shareholder companies are an exception.

78 Shahid Rahman, Muhammad Iqbal, and Youcef Soufi, *Inferences by Parallel Reasoning in Islamic Jurisprudence: Al-Shīrāzī's Insights into the Dialectical Constitution of Meaning and Knowledge* (Cham, Switzerland: Springer Nature, 2020), p. ix.

79 Ruggero J. Aldisert, *Logic for Lawyers: A Guide to Clear Legal Thinking*. 3rd ed. (National Institute for Trial Advocacy, 1997), p. 80. See also Imran Ahsan Khan Nyazee, *The Methodology of Ijtihad: Old and New (Comparative Jurisprudence)* (Islamabad: Federal Law House, 2021), p. 96.

generalisation," depends on the quantity of resemblances. She contrasts this to analogies, called *qiyās al-ʿilla* in Islamic law, which depend on the quality of the resemblances.[80]

To illustrate, when Vinogradoff or Lord Denning argue that a corporation is a person, they enumerate the qualities or characteristics resembling human beings figuratively,[81] such as a will, brain, nerves, or hands. They argue that a corporation is a person based on these numerous, resembling qualities. When employing this methodology, they ignore each resemblance's value in mapping personhood onto a corporation. Similarly, none of these qualities may be the essential factor that grants personhood to any being. For example, in Islamic law personhood is tied to legal capacity, and capacity is tied explicitly to the single attribute called *dhimma*, which is distinct from *ʿaql* as per al-Taftāzānī's argument above. In Western jurisprudence, determining the single correlational factor in the corporate person metaphor is difficult. In most cases, jurists seem to argue that this correlational factor is the capacity to think and to have a will.[82]

Hanafi jurists reject the use of *qiyās al-shabah*, because this form of legal reasoning amounts to a personal opinion, which lacks reference to the underlying proof that gives the original case its legal ruling.[83] For them, the only valid method of analogy is *qiyās al-ʿilla*, because it requires an investigation into the real underlying determinant for a legal ruling that later becomes the single correlational factor in extending that rule to a new target domain.

By creating a fictitious person, the human actors behind its actions redirect liability, creating uncertainty in associating *dhimma*. While limited liability encourages adventurism with other people's money, fictitious personhood enables immunity from tortious and criminal culpability.

2.6 SEEING THE FOREST FOR THE TREES: THE VALUE OF A *MAQĀṢID* FRAMEWORK

From a *maqāṣid* (objectives) framework, despite their differences, both Nyazee and Usmani advocate preserving and protecting the Muslim community's wealth in response to corporations as a colonial enterprise funneling wealth into colonizing nations. Both scholars are concerned that prohibiting this form of business organization would be destructive to the Muslim community.

Various stakeholders echoed this concern in the 2022 judgment regarding prohibiting usury before the Federal Shariat Court in Pakistan.[84] For example, as a party to the case, the State Bank of Pakistan argued that a completely Islamic financial system is impossible in the current economic framework.[85]

Historically, Islamic law has permitted types of business organization that would otherwise be prohibited based on recognizing the benefit they bring in generating and acquiring wealth.[86] An example is the *ʿinān* partnership in Hanafi fiqh, based on the concept of agency and trust.

80 Anita Schnee, "Logical Reasoning 'Obviously,'" *The Journal of the Legal Writing Institute* 3 (1997): 105–26, at 107; Rahman, *Inferences by Parallel Reasoning in Islamic Jurisprudence*, p. viii; Nyazee, *The Methodology of Ijtihad*, p. 97.

81 In Islamic jurisprudence, a metaphor that is based on resemblance in meaning rather than form is called *istiʿāra*.

82 This idea originated with Thomas Hobbes. See Sean Fleming, "The Two Faces of Personhood: Hobbes, Corporate Agency and the Personality of the State," *European Journal of Political Theory* 20, no. 1 (2021): 5–26, at 13.

83 Abū Zayd al-Dabbūsī, *Taqwīm al-adilla* (Beirut: Dār al-Kutub al-ʿIlmiyya, 2001), p. 304. See also Nyazee, *The Methodology of Ijtihad*, p. 91. The other schools of Islamic jurisprudence are more accepting of *qiyās al-shabah*.

84 Shariat Petition No.30-L of 1991.

85 "No Alternative to Interest-Based Economy, SBP Tells FSC," *The News*, October 30, 2015, www.thenews.com.pk/print/15439-no-alternative-to-interest-based-economy-sbp-tells-fsc.

86 Nyazee, *Partnerships*, pp. 103–4, quoting al-Kāsānī.

'Inān is a contract based primarily on *wakāla* that permits both sides to participate with wealth, work, or credit-worthiness and profit sharing in an agreed-upon ratio.[87] Equal contribution, or even equal entitlement to profits, is not necessary to form the partnership, which is in contrast to the *mufāwaḍa*,[88] because one party may be contributing more to the partnership physically and financially and thus demanding a larger share of the profits.[89] The Hanafis permit this type of partnership because it promotes wealth acquisition.[90] The Shafiʿis and Malikis do not permit partnerships based on credit-worthiness.[91]

Even though Islamic law recognizes wealth acquisition as a legitimate benefit, contemporary scholarship fails to consider corporations' effect on human rights and the environment.

Aḥmad ʿAlī ʿAbdullāh, a Sudani scholar, is the exception among contemporary scholars.[92] While generally accepting of fictitious personality, he argues that corporate personhood allowed the accumulation of capital to an unprecedented extent. The concept opened the doors to colonization and supplied cheap raw materials and labor to the West, leading to exploitation and endangering human rights and the planet.[93] The sharia allows for increasing one's wealth, but not at the expense of avoiding liability for one's harmful actions. Human advancement and land cultivation are among Islam's purposes. For this reason, God created the earth, made it subservient to humans, and deposited all means of life into it. However, taking advantage of the earth's resources is subject to the limits the sharia has prescribed – this means abstaining from injustice, unpaid labor, and exploitation.[94]

Based on ʿAbdullāh's argument, if corporate personhood is permitted within the *maqāṣid* framework to increase the Muslim community's wealth, protecting the earth lies in the realm of a higher purpose of Islamic law – the preservation and protection of life. The Quran states in Sura al-Baqara:

> And spend in the cause of Allah and do not throw yourselves into destruction and do good. Surely, Allah loves the righteous.[95]

Based on the prohibition in the above verse, destroying the environment is akin to destroying oneself, as there will be no life if there is no earth. Therefore, permitting actions that allow destroying the earth is against Islamic law.

The Quran states further that the property we possess is not ours. Instead, God has given it to humanity as a trust:

> . . . and spend of that whereof He has made you trustees . . .[96]

Therefore, the privileges we enjoy are, in fact, a responsibility. While the Muslim community has the right to increase its wealth, the higher purpose of religion is to reach unity with God, to

87 Ibid., p. 102.

88 The *mufāwaḍa* partnership requires both equal investment and profit sharing from all partners. *Majallat*, p. 255, para. 1331.

89 al-Marghīnānī, *al-Hidāya*, vol. 3, p. 9. While Islamic law allows profit sharing to be asymmetrical between partners, they must bear losses equally. Ibid.

90 Nyazee, *Partnerships*, p. 104.

91 Ibid., p. 40.

92 ʿAbdullāh, *al-Shakhṣiyya al-iʿtibāriyya*, p. 236.

93 Ibid., p. 235.

94 Ibid.

95 Q 2:195.

96 Q 57:7.

worship Him as though we see Him.[97] A Muslim, and indeed any human being, can only attain this by nourishing and sustaining that which God has entrusted to them.

In this context, the Arabic word for personality, *dhimma*, makes more sense. *Dhimma* also means something owed to God. If we take Nyazee's argument that a fictitious person can be created if there are no religious responsibilities attached to it, how do we make this Islamized corporation liable[98] for violations of resources placed on earth for humans to hold in trust?

However tempting a regulatory compliance-based approach for corporate liability may be, it risks standing on shaky jurisprudential foundations that use metaphors to formulate liability. Furthermore, even compliance policy is increasingly steering towards individual liability for unethical corporate commercial activities because human actors lack the incentive to act responsibly when personal liability is absent.[99]

The question arises: If not the corporate form, then what? After all, Timur Kuran argued that the corporate form's absence in Islamic law bridled economic development in Muslim-majority countries[100] – his larger argument being that excessive regulation stifles innovation and market growth.

Kuran's criticism is based on two assumptions. The first singles out Islamic law as being intrinsically unprogressive and arrested. The second sees unbridled economic development as the ideal aim of all legal design. Historically, Western, and Islamic commercial jurisprudence operated on the same fundamental principle: profit and loss sharing. According to Roman law, the person who receives the profit should also bear the loss (*cujus est commodum ejus debet incommodum*).[101]

Islamic law had an advantage over Western legal systems because it recognized limited liability for certain partnerships. Nyazee states that the Hanafi school had a developed concept of agency where the principal could not be sued for performance, a remedy Roman law lacked.[102] According to the school, the right of performance belongs to the agent in a *wakāla* contract. The principal cannot be sued for performance. In a partnership based on *wakāla*, if a partner buys something for the business as an agent, the other partners are deemed his principals

97 See the hadith of Jibrīl in Muslim b. al-Hajjāj, *Ṣaḥīḥ al-Muslim*, book 1.1.

98 In *Bank Islam Malaysia Berhad v. Adnan Omar* [1994] 3 CLJ 735; [1994] 3 AMR 44; [1994] 4 BLJ 372: BBA the court ruled that corporations, like Bank Islam Malaysia Berhad, cannot have a religion, thus falling outside the sharia court's jurisdiction. In contrast, the US Supreme Court in *Burwell v. Hobby Lobby Stores, Inc.* recognized that corporations can possess religious beliefs. See: 573 U.S. 682 (more) 134 S. Ct. at 2768.

99 See, for example, the discussion on directors' duties post *re Caremark International*: Jennifer Arlen, "How Directors' Oversight Duties and Liability under Caremark Are Evolving," *The CLS Blue Sky Blog*, October 13, 2022, https://clsbluesky.law.columbia.edu/2022/10/13/how-directors-oversight-duties-and-liability-under-caremark-are-evolving/.

100 Timur Kuran, "The Absence of the Corporation in Islamic Law: Origins and Persistence," *The American Journal of Comparative Law* 53, no. 4 (2005): 785–834.

101 Giuseppe Dari-Mattiacci, Oscar Gelderblom, Joost Jonker, and Enrico C. Perotti, "The Emergence of the Corporate Form," *The Journal of Law, Economics, & Organization* 33, no. 2 (2013): 193–236, http://dx.doi.org/10.2139/ssrn.2223905. Spanish courts recently applied the maxim to impose liability on polluters for damage caused by toxic gases, waste, water, and mines. See: Pemmaraju Sreenivasa Rao, *Third Report on the Legal Regime for the Allocation of Loss in Case of Transboundary Harm Arising out of Hazardous Activities*, 2006, Doc. A/CN.4/566. Newly independent states have employed it as the principle of non-inheritance of obligations to avoid their colonizers' financial liabilities – see the case of Eritrea and Italy: Alona E. Evan, "Federation of Ethiopia and Eritrea Case Note," *The American Journal of International Law* 62, no. 1, (1968): 202–204.

102 The *wakāla* contract in Hanafi jurisprudence, for example. Nyazee, *Partnerships*, p. 66. Watson states that the concept of agency only developed fully in common law in the nineteenth century. Susan Watson and Lynn Buckley, "Directors' Positive Duty to Act in the Interests of the Entity: Shareholders' Interests Bounded by Corporate Purpose," *Journal of Corporate Law Studies* 24, no. 1 (2024): 233–65, at 256.

to the extent of their shares. Parties that deal with the partnership can only demand payment from the partner who made the transaction. The other partners are not liable for the debts a copartner incurs for the business without their approval. European jurisprudence did not recognize limited liability in partnerships and agency contracts.[103] Nyazee argues that the corporate form was created to resolve this issue.[104]

The corporation's development in Europe was a result of private contracting backed by judicial sanction in addition to government recognition of its utility in colonizing missions. The world's first multinational corporation, the Dutch East India Company (VOC), was initially organized as a limited partnership, based on the *commenda*,[105] a tenth-century Italian contract, which in turn was modeled after the Arabian *muḍāraba*.[106] However the *commenda* is different from the Islamic concepts of *ʿinān* and *muḍāraba*, because in the latter two the managing partner has no personal liability, provided they acted in good faith and can recover any amount creditors demand from the investing partners.[107]

Under the VOC's 1602 Charter, the company's directors were considered active partners and had unlimited liability. Investors were considered sleeping partners and had limited liability due to limited control over business activities. This changed in 1623 after the directors too declared themselves limitedly liable through a unilateral resolution which the Dutch court later upheld. Directors' limited liability, therefore, was a contractual rather than legislative innovation.[108]

Historically, sea trade partnerships would end once the ship returned, and the profits would be distributed at the port. To ensure long-term investment, company directors introduced capital lock-in, ensuring the company would remain active even after the end of a trade voyage. This gave investors less control over their property but ensured that the VOC was able to achieve dominance in trade with Asian countries as well as eventually controlling various ports. The VOC's military expenditure eventually made it take on extensive debt. This debt allowed the VOC to continue operations despite running at a loss – a problem endemic to the corporate form. Based precisely on this ability to raise large amounts of debt while investors continue to claim limited liability, critics argue that incorporation allows businesses to keep functioning even when unprofitable.[109]

Returning to Kuran's critique, Islamic jurists – rather than Islamic law – were the reason for the lack of economic development.[110] Crafting business organizations like the limited liability

[103] In medieval Europe, unlimited liability was considered an effective insurance in risky business enterprises. Traders equated unlimited liability with honor, discretion, and fairness. The *commenda*, an Italian innovation to bear the high risks of sea trade, was the exception to the general rule. The Napoleonic code of 1807 systemized this form of business organization across Europe. See Marie-Laure Djelic, "When Limited Liability Was (Still) an Issue: Mobilization and Politics of Signification in 19th-Century England," *Organization Studies* 34, nos. 5–6 (2013): 595–621, at 602.

[104] Nyazee, *Partnerships*, p. 67. The reality, at least in the United Kingdom, was more complex. Shortly after 1851, when Robert Slaney, a British member of Parliament, advocated that limited liability be introduced in the law of partnerships, Christian socialists began campaigning for working class cooperatives to have cheap and easy access to both corporate identity and limited liability. See: Djelic, "When Limited Liability Was (Still) An Issue," pp. 605, 607, and 610.

[105] Dari-Mattiacci, "The Emergence of the Corporate Form," p. 207.

[106] Hassan S. Khalilieh, "The Lex Mercatoria Maritima: An Abridgement of the Jurisprudential Principles of the Early Islamic Maritime Qirad," *Comparative Studies of South Asia, Africa and the Middle East* 40, no. 2 (2020): 266–76, https://doi.org/10.1215/1089201X-8524193.

[107] Nyazee, *Partnerships*, p. 89.

[108] Dari-Mattiacci, "The Emergence of the Corporate Form," p. 213.

[109] Ibid., p. 212.

[110] Harris argues there were geographical, political, and legal reasons for why the corporation might not have been needed in Islamic and South Asian countries at the outset. See Ron Harris, *Going the Distance:*

company requires some creativity. Lawyers in Western countries were the leading force behind creating, in Katharina Pistor's words, codes of capital, including the corporate form, which helped create and preserve large amounts of wealth.[111]

The last few centuries, however, saw a steady decline in the general quality of Islamic legal scholarship. The reason behind this was a lack of engagement with, and understanding of, complex issues related to property, contracts, insolvency, and trusts, which is where Western lawyers were the most creative in their coding.[112]

For instance, citing the *waqf*, a charitable trust, as an example of a corporate person, shows unawareness of how trusts operate in the present world, particularly in the context of the history of antitrust laws. Just as Usmani's critics state, the trust is suspended property. Unlike the corporation, which the state creates, the trust results from private contracting, allowing modern-day trusts to hold large amounts of wealth while property owners can escape liability from taxes and regulation. If the corporation is a device to collect and mobilize large amounts of capital, the trust is a device to preserve it.[113]

Contemporary Islamic legal scholarship's unfamiliarity with antitrust issues became apparent when I began teaching competition law in Tashkent. While developing my course outline, I searched for Islamic law publications on the subject out of curiosity. I found only two articles, one of which started by citing references to the permissibility of horse racing in Islam. In a time when competition authorities routinely scrutinize giant tech corporations such as Apple, Google, and Facebook, I found this comically tragic. At least we can credit the author for addressing a topic few others have delved into.

This neglect of competition law research is unfortunate given that the office of *ʿāmil al-sūq* or *ḥisba*, which the Prophet established himself, was a cornerstone in regulating competition and business-related environmental damage and ensuring compliance[114] – demonstrating thereby that the Islamic economic system prioritizes ethics and sustainability rather than just pure economic gain. Western competition authorities now also include environmental regulation in their mandates, because competition law and environmental law share the common objectives of maximizing social well-being and correcting market failures.[115] Competition authorities are in the ideal position to regulate upstream supply chain issues, including environmental degradation and exploitation, while also monitoring downstream margin squeezing. International organizations such as the OECD have recognized these common objectives and are creating policies whereby competition authorities calculate

Eurasian Trade and the Rise of the Business Corporation, 1400–1700 (Princeton, NJ: Princeton University Press, 2020), p. 331.

111 Pistor, *The Code of Capital*. When the Royal Commission on Mercantile Laws 1854 sent out its questionnaire, lawyers favored introducing limited liability in the UK in contrast to bankers and merchants. Djelic, "When Limited Liability Was (Still) an Issue," p. 610.

112 For a detailed discussion of precolonial Islamic jurists creating effective contractual devices for trading, see Fahad Ahmad Bishara, *A Sea of Debt: Law and Economic Life in The Western Indian Ocean, 1780–1950* (Cambridge: Cambridge University Press, 2017).

113 For a discussion on the trust acting as a substitute for the corporation after the Bubble Act 1720 because it is a private contract rather than a creature of the state, see Susan Mary Watson, "The Corporate Legal Entity as a Fund," *Journal of Business Law* 6 (2017): 467–84, at 475.

114 Luṭf Allāh Qārī, *Iḍāʾa zawāyā jadīda li-l-taqniyya al-ʿArabiyya al-Islāmiyya* (Riyadh: Maṭbūʿāt Maktabat al-Malik Fahd al-Waṭaniyya, 1996), p. 95.

115 Romana Coêlho de Araujo and Jorge Madeira Nogueira, "Environmental Law & Competition Law: Conflicts & Complementarities from an Environmental Economics Perspective," *Direito e Desenvolvimento* 11, no. 1 (2020): 92–105, at 95.

environmental efficiencies,[116] moving into the more holistic direction Islamic law already envisions for market regulation.

Contrary to Usmani's opinion, political factors such as democratization, rather than just corporate personification, influence the economic stability required to create large businesses. Dari-Mattiacci argues that traders are more likely to invest large sums of capital when the risk of public expropriation is low.[117] This explains why developing countries trail behind in their economic systems despite introducing the corporate form, as weak property rights lead to unstable economies.

History illustrates that the corporate form was a product of various political and social forces. Djelic argues that tracing its history shows us that the legal structures we take for granted are frail and that decrystallizing them is possible. Retracing the socioeconomic dynamics that created the limited liability corporation will allow us to construct alternatives.[118]

As Blanco and Grear argue, constructing legal persons is a political act that continues predatory legal structures of privilege.[119] This practice will continue when Western states eventually grant personhood to new technologies such as artificial intelligence, deploying jurisprudential techniques comparative to those they used for corporations. Muslim scholars should be wary of perpetuating systems of injustice.

2.7 CONCLUSION

This chapter demonstrates that contemporary scholars disregard basic tenets of Islamic jurisprudence in applying the law concerning corporations. Accepting the corporate form modifies the concept of legal capacity and shifts liability to creditors and other stakeholders, including vulnerable, colonized communities, leading to unprecedented environmental exploitation in the name of trade.[120] While this impacts Islamic law's fundamental structure, accepting the corporate form in its entirety also defeats the social and environmental justice values that Islamic law espouses.

The *Federal Government* case could have been a trailblazer in postcolonial environmental and human rights activism. It could have provided a framework to bolster corporate accountability in Muslim countries. Instead, the judges chose to follow the global status quo without meaningful engagement with the corporate form's impact on the foundations and aims of Islamic law. The case gained little publicity in Pakistan, and the parties to the litigation viewed it as a mere intellectual exercise. Even Aslam Khaki, one of the jurisconsults the Federal Shariat Court engaged, failed to recall the case when I contacted him to inquire about its proceedings.

Islamic jurists should advocate strong property rights and condemn exploitative business practices. They should follow al-Sarakhsī's lead in speaking truth to power, steering the Muslim community to create alternative environmentally sustainable solutions that promote

116 OECD, "Environmental Considerations in Competition Enforcement: Background Paper by the Secretariat," (2021), DAF/COMP(2021)4, https://one.oecd.org/document/DAF/COMP(2021)4/en/pdf.

117 Dari-Mattiacci, "The Emergence of the Corporate Form," p. 214.

118 Djelic, "When Limited Liability Was (Still) an Issue," pp. 616–17.

119 Elena Blanco and Anna Grear, "Personhood, Jurisdiction and Injustice: Law, Colonialities and the Global Order," *Journal of Human Rights and the Environment* 10, no. 1 (2019): 86–117, at 98.

120 Wim Huisman and Daniel Sidoli, "Corporations, Human Rights and the Environmental Degradation–Corruption Nexus," *Asia Pacific Journal of Environmental Law* 22, no. 1 (2019): 66–92. See also Emmanuel Sarpong Owusu, "Environmental Degradation and Human Rights Violation: A Cursory Overview of the Potential of the Existing Frameworks to Hold Multinational Corporations Accountable," *Groningen Journal of International Law* 9, no. 1 (2021): 143–73.

fair business practices but allow collecting and mobilizing large amounts of capital for public purposes.

Islamic law is concerned with the well-being of creation and the careful stewardship of resources. *Dhimma*, as it would apply to corporate entities, gives us tremendous insight into the spirit of Islamic law. Additionally, the *maqāṣid* framework can help evaluate corporate personhood more holistically. Islamic jurists should move their focus from the preservation and protection of the *umma*'s wealth to higher *maqāṣid*. The first is preserving and protecting life, for which promoting environmental conservation is essential. The second is protecting the religion, which requires holding accountable those whom Islamic law deems responsible.

3

Islamic Ethics, Decarbonization, and Climate Change in the Middle East

Saleem H. Ali

In August 2015, a remarkable gathering of Islamic leaders from twenty countries met in Istanbul, Türkiye, to launch an "Islamic Declaration on Climate Change." The stated goal of the symposium was to reach broad unity and ownership from the Islamic community around the declaration.[1] The initiative came about through a coalition of nonprofit organizations working on environmental education in Muslim societies. However, in addition to civil society groups, the declaration also had three significant institutional partners that suggest the mainstream credentials of this initiative: the Islamic Educational, Scientific and Cultural Organization (ISESCO), which models itself on UNESCO for Muslim countries and is based in Morocco; the Organization of the Islamic Conference, which is the largest intergovernmental organization of Muslim states; and the International Islamic Fiqh Academy based in Saudi Arabia.

What was also notable about the declaration was its willingness to challenge the fossil fuel economy of the Middle East, a region that remains the heartland of Islam's origin and holy sites despite the dominant demographic dispersal of the Muslim diaspora in South and Southeast Asia. Although statements made by the attendees were not reflective of official national policies of governments like Saudi Arabia, the fact that scholars were comfortable making them indicates that space for such discussions can open even in the fossil fuel economies. One could also argue that the fossil fuel economies did not object to these statements because they see the initiative as inconsequential to political decisions on high. However, this would be a cynical reading of the changing reality of environmental consciousness in the Middle East. The transformation of Dubai from an oil economy to a service economy has shown that using capital accumulated through the age of oil and gas to diversify is possible and prudent. There has also been a concern among Saudi investors such as Prince Al-Waleed bin Talal regarding the challenge of "stranded assets" that could result from investments in fossil fuels.[2] Furthermore, the Saudi government has been following an ambitious renewable energy research and development program since 2010, when a royal decree established the King Abdullah City for Atomic and Renewable

[1] For details on the full declaration and the event participants, see https://unfccc.int/news/islamic-declaration-on-climate-change.

[2] Ed King, "Saudi Prince Says Oil Markets Are 'in Decline,'" *Climate Home News*, July 29, 2013, https://climatechangenews.com/2013/07/29/saudi-prince-says-oil-markets-are-in-decline/.

Energy (KCARE), and has shown its willingness to engage with climate change discourse due to its own vulnerabilities to global warming.[3]

This was not the first time that Islamic scholars had convened to focus on climate change. In 2008, twenty-two participants from Islamic NGOs, academia, government, and Muslim environmental activist groups from fourteen countries convened a forum under the auspices of the United Nations Development Programme (UNDP). They drew up a "Seven Year Plan for Islamic Action on the Environment." This workshop was the first step of a project initiated by the Earth-Mates Dialogue Centre (EMDC) and the Alliance of Religions and Conservation (ARC) "to harness the teachings, values and ethical law of the Islamic faith in the service of humanity, in order to meet one of the most serious challenges in the contemporary world."[4] Although there has not been a detailed review publicized of the seven-year mandate of this group, 2015 was also opportune to reinvigorate this effort, marking the seventh anniversary of the plan's launch.

The Istanbul Declaration of August 2015 amply referenced Quranic verses and hadith (sayings and traditions of the Prophet Muhammad) and quite specifically set targets for Muslim countries. There was even a call for businesses in Muslim countries to divest from fossil fuels in clause 3.4.[5] Such bold statements being supported by a fairly robust and influential group of organizations will undoubtedly lead to some pressure on countries in the Middle East to respond to this global challenge. Given the advent of the United Nations major climate change conference (the 21st Conference of the Parties on the United Nations Framework Convention on Climate Change in Paris), the timing was opportune. The subsequent "Paris Agreement" has become the touchstone for international consensus on decarbonization. There is perhaps some interfaith competition to show relevance and tenacity on this issue following Pope Francis's landmark encyclical on the environment. However, it may be worth considering how we reached this point and the likelihood of this bold declaration gaining real traction in the Middle East.

3.1 ENVIRONMENTAL ETHOS IN ISLAMIC SOCIETIES

The advent of Islam as an organized religion occurred in the desert environment of Arabia, and hence there was considerable attention paid to ecological concerns within Islamic ethics. While Islamic theology is not pantheistic, and shares many of the anthropocentric attributes of other Abrahamic faiths, there is a reverence of nature that stems from essential pragmatism within the faith. Due to resource constraints, early Muslims realized that long-term development was only possible within ecological constraints that were shared by all of humanity. Furthermore, Islam considers environmental deterioration as symptomatic of social injustice, and hence, development and the environment are inextricably linked. As the foundational scripture of Islam, all doctrines must be legitimized through Quranic injunctions and curricular efforts must first acknowledge that there is indeed a scriptural basis for this linkage between the environment and development.

3 Michal Nachmany, Sam Fankhauser, Jana Davidová, et al., *Climate Change Legislation in Saudi Arabia* (London: Grantham Institute on Climate Change and the Environment of the London School of Economics and Political Science, 2015), www.GranthamInstitute/wp-content/uploads/2015/05/SAUDI_ARABIA.pdf.

4 Alliance of Religions and Conservation (ARC), "The Muslim Seven Year Action Plan to Deal with Global Climate Change," 2008, https://loe.org/images/content/090731/M7YAP_draft.pdf.

5 Arthur Lyon Dahl, "Islamic Declaration on Global Climate Change: A Review," August 29, 2015, https://yabaha.net/dahl/env/2015IslamicDeclCC.html.

The first linkage is made through the concept of *mīzān* (Q 42:17, 55:7–9, 57:25) or balancing the material and immaterial worlds (*dunyā* and *dīn*). The concept of *mīzān* was also invoked in the Istanbul Declaration. Unlike the ascetic traditions in Hinduism or Buddhism, seeking wealth is considered a worthy goal in Islam (Q 62:10). Thus the Quran recognizes that economic development is essential but that it must not be undertaken in excess or by compromising earthly limits (Q 47:12). There is thus a clear distinction made between consumption for improving the human condition and wanton consumerism. A most salient aspect in the Islamic scriptural tradition is the constant reference to the natural world. Repeatedly Muslims are reminded to reflect upon the natural systems and their obligations of stewardship through the concept of *khilāfa* (Q 2:30). The Islamic Declaration on Climate Change referenced this context and noted that we are now living in the Anthropocene (the epoch of humans) and hence the duties of *khilāfa* have particular applicability.

Several organizations have been taking root in the Muslim world to further manifest these environmental norms. Of course, given the vast geographic expanse of Islamic countries from Indonesia to Morocco, there is a wide spectrum of ideas and perspectives, and therefore it is important to highlight that Muslims, like others engaged in the environmental movement, may have many different ideas influencing their decision to join this global effort. This responsibility is built upon a connection between primary textual sources from the Quran and hadith, which highlights the interconnectedness of the Islamic ethos, in theory *and* practice, for Muslims. It is upon this interconnectedness that individuals, communities, and governmental organizations are establishing a solid foundation, which has reinvigorated Muslims' commitment to sound environmental practices.

Environmental activism in Muslim societies has often been galvanized by charismatic political or religious leaders or by a pressing ecological challenge. For example, the rapid urbanization of the United Arab Emirates (UAE) led to a concomitant rise in environmental leadership. In particular, a sheikh of the Emirate of Ajman, Abdul Aziz Al-Nuaimi, labels himself "the Green Sheikh," and has initiated a growing movement in the region to focus on ecological conservation in sync with Islamic culture. Contemporary organizations are also trying to link Islamic architecture in desert regions with energy conservation principles. The development of the low-carbon Masdar City in Abu Dhabi is an example of a centrally planned effort to instill environmental education and design within an urban development initiative. However, this project remains an enclave within a more conventional swath of infrastructure development in the region. The challenge will be to upscale the lessons from Masdar City and replicate features of the environmental impact mitigation therein across the region.

At the grassroots level, the Islamic Foundation for Ecology and Environmental Sciences in Birmingham, UK, established by Sri Lankan Muslim Fazlun Khalid in 1996, was among the first organizations to focus on environmental education at the community level within an Islamic context. Numerous other organizations have also developed in North America with a similar mandate. There is also a growing genre of scholarship around Islam and the environment from the elementary school level all the way to tertiary education. For example, the Pesantren Lingkungan Giri Ilmu (an Islamic religious school in Central Java, Indonesia) has a structured experiential education curriculum for students who learn to grow crops through organic methods as an example of their service to Islam.[6] There are also increasing numbers of courses in Islam and the environment in universities, and centers of higher learning are now

[6] Anna Gade, "Tradition and Sentiment in Indonesian Environmental Islam," *Worldviews: Global Ecology, Culture and Religion* 16, no. 3 (2012): 263–85.

keeping pace with environmental movements in other religious traditions. The Zaytuna College in Berkeley, California, hosted a meeting in 2013 to bring Muslim schoolteachers across America together to train them in experiential environmental education within an Islamic context.[7]

3.2 THE TRUE GREENING OF THE MIDDLE EAST?

In order for a more coherent "greening" process to be realized in the Middle East itself, there needs to be a clear analysis of the direct linkage between political, economic, and environmental factors. There are specific areas where such connections have much potential for positive impact. For instance, environmental scarcity could fuel greater conflict and humanitarian crises in the region. There is already research showing that the Syrian conflict could be linked *partly* to climate change conditions impacting water availability, agricultural productivity, and social distress.[8] No doubt overexploitation of water resources due to population growth and affluent high-impact lifestyles are a primary cause of water insecurity. Climate change is further increasing vulnerabilities and conflicts in what is already a precarious situation.

Climatic changes are also being exacerbated by wars that can cause extensive pollution and resource stress, as noted in a report by the United Nations on the Gaza conflict that suggested the region would soon be uninhabitable.[9] EcoPeace Middle East, a unique organization with joint offices in Israel, Jordan, and Palestine, has noted the urgency of addressing these challenges in much of its recent work as well as realizing the potential for using environmental issues as a peacebuilding strategy.[10] Environmental peacebuilding around the common threat of climate change also has potential in Iraq as a means of bringing Shia and Sunni communities closer towards a superordinate goal on which there is no theological disagreement.[11]

At the same time there is also a need to mainstream the greening of the Middle East beyond boutique projects. For example, the Masdar City initiative, though laudable, is designed to accommodate only about 40,000 people and it is not clear how the broader economy of the UAE might be impacted by this effort.[12] If the initiative is considered as a prototype to transform the fossil fuel economy of the Gulf states, then that is indeed a transformative approach. However, if the city is merely a tourist attraction, with a university as its centerpiece, then the impact may be more limited. An important positive step taken by the UAE has been to provide support for the establishment of the International Renewable Energy Agency (IRENA) and to host its headquarters in Abu Dhabi, eventually within Masdar City itself. Countries in the Middle East should lead the way towards empowering IRENA to play a more transformative role in the current energy economy in sync with traditional norms within their dominant Islamic traditions.[13]

[7] Elaine Pasquini, "Zaytuna College Hosts Historic Workshop on Environmental Education in Islamic Schools," *Washington Report on Middle East Affairs*, April 2013, 48–49.

[8] Peter H. Gleick, "Water, Drought, Climate Change, and Conflict in Syria," *Weather, Climate, and Society* 6, no. 3 (2014): 331–40.

[9] United Nations Conference on Trade and Development (UNCTAD), *Report on UNCTAD Assistance to the Palestinian People: Developments in the Economy of the Occupied Palestinian Territory* (Geneva, 2015).

[10] See www.ecopeaceme.org.

[11] Saleem H. Ali, ed., *Peace Parks: Conservation and Conflict Resolution* (Cambridge, MA: MIT Press, 2007).

[12] Danyel Reiche, "Renewable Energy Policies in the Gulf Countries: A Case Study of the Carbonneutral 'Masdar City' in Abu Dhabi," *Energy Policy* 38, no. 1 (2010): 378–82.

[13] Tallal Alie Turfe, *Energy in Islam: A Scientific Approach to Preserving Our Health and the Environment* (Elmhurst, NY: Tahrike Tarsile Qur'an, 2011).

Although such major changes to truly "green the Middle East" may take time, the positive momentum being built in the region around addressing climate change is a sign that substantive change is being considered. Veteran environmentalist writer Bill McKibben summed up his reaction to the Islamic Declaration on Climate Change as "an ongoing shift in the zeitgeist."[14] There is little doubt that Islam has been more inertial than other Abrahamic faith traditions because of its more dominant literalist interpretation of scripture. This in turn has also led to greater inertia on many social policy changes in the Middle East. However, environmental issues are emerging as an area where liberal politics are now finding some congruence with dominant scriptural interpretations. There is thus potential for both policy unity in the Middle East around environmental issues as well as for harnessing peace dividends of environmental engagement for the region.

3.3 THE UAE AND COP28

The decision of the UAE to appoint the head of the Abu Dhabi National Oil Company (ADNOC), Sultan al-Jaber, as the chair of the COP28 climate change meeting in 2023 has caused major controversy in environmental advocacy circles. The UAE is considered a relatively progressive Muslim country with a vibrant multinational community and as the host country for IRENA. The country also sees itself as an ecumenical locus of conversations, particularly since it officially recognized Israel and opened diplomatic relations with the country in 2020.

Sultan al-Jaber has been using the country's credentials in this regard, and in October 2023 hosted the Global Faith Leaders' Summit, which brought together twenty-eight faith leaders to sign the "Confluence of Conscience: Uniting for Planetary Resurgence," known as the "Abu Dhabi Interfaith Statement for COP28." A Changemakers Majlis, titled "Faith and Science: Actioning an Ethic of Care for the Environment," was also held during the summit and united faith leaders, scientists, and decision-makers to foster knowledge-sharing and trust-building for a more secure and sustainable world.[15]

Hosting such an event, and high-level meetings with faith leaders such as Pope Francis, has been a differentiating feature of COP28's "big tent" approach to climate change problem-solving. The UAE has also responded to criticism of its willingness to embrace and engage with fossil fuel companies as part of the COP28 reform agenda by noting the need for balance and pragmatism. This approach is often justified on the basis of the Islamic concept of *mīzān*, or balance. The UAE has also directly linked Islamic law and fatwas to the COP28 agenda. The "UAE Council for Fatwa" held a separate meeting in November 2023 with scholars, as well as politicians, to highlight the role of Islam in promoting a more climate-friendly ethos. However, Dr. Rashid bin Mohammed Al Hajeri, chairman of the Sunni Endowments Council, Bahrain, suggested that it was important for the Islamic community to come to a collective conclusion on what was needed in terms of sharia regarding climate change and sustainability.[16]

3.4 CONCLUSION

The period from 2015 to 2023 has seen a growth in Islamic engagement with climate change concerns despite the historic reluctance for many of the powerful Gulf economies in

[14] Bill McKibben, "Climate Change: A Warning from Islam," *New York Review of Books Daily*, August 24, 2015, www.nybooks.com/blogs/nyrblog/2015/aug/24/climate-change-warning-islam/.

[15] Refer to "Global Faith Summit – Interfaith Statement Released in Pre-COP28 Event," International Partnership on Religion and Sustainable Development, November 13, 2023, https://tinyurl.com/2bv592b4.

[16] Nasreen Abdulla, "UAE Expert Calls for Fatwas on Preserving Environment," *Khaleej Times*, November 8, 2023, www.khaleejtimes.com/uae/sustainability-is-central-part-of-islam-uae-expert.

confronting the obsolescence of fossil fuels. Although there is still considerable disagreement among Muslim states about prioritization of environmental issues within the portfolio of global problems, the leadership being shown by some countries, such as the UAE, in furthering the renewable energy agenda and decarbonization more broadly is a promising sign. Islamic theology is being invoked for promoting environmental norms and many of the anthropocentric voices of earlier days of environmental education in Muslim countries are less strident. Instead, a pragmatic approach aligned with ecological modernization is taking root in much of the Muslim world. Technologies such as carbon capture and storage or conversion of carbon emissions to useful products are being promoted as "win-win" options in many of the fossil fuel economies, which continues to create anxiety among environmental advocates. The "moral hazard" of technological optimism in many of the wealthier Muslim countries could lead to complacence about reducing consumption of natural resources. Islamic stigmatization of *isrāf* (wastage) and *tabdhīr* (extravagance) deserves to be further invoked to mitigate the moral hazard concerns of "techno-optimism." With such a confluence of collective action towards environmental norms that consider green technologies and reduction in aggregate consumption, Islamic countries in the Middle East can move more swiftly towards a more sustainable economic and social profile.

BIBLIOGRAPHY

Abdulla, Nasreen. "UAE Expert Calls for Fatwas on Preserving Environment." *Khaleej Times*, November 8, 2023. www.khaleejtimes.com/uae/sustainability-is-central-part-of-islam-uae-expert.

Ali, Saleem H., ed. *Peace Parks: Conservation and Conflict Resolution*. Cambridge, MA: MIT Press, 2007.

Alliance of Religions and Conservation (ARC). "The Muslim Seven Year Action Plan to Deal with Global Climate Change." 2008. http://www.arcworld.org/downloads/ARC-Windsor-press-release-website-M7YP1.pdf.

Dahl, Arthur Lyon. "Islamic Declaration on Global Climate Change: A Review." August 29, 2015, https://yabaha.net/dahl/env/2015IslamicDeclCC.html.

Gade, Anna. "Tradition and Sentiment in Indonesian Environmental Islam." *Worldviews: Global Ecology, Culture and Religion* 16, no. 3 (2012): 263–85.

Gleick, Peter H. "Water, Drought, Climate Change, and Conflict in Syria." *Weather, Climate, and Society* 6, no. 3 (2014): 331–40.

King, Ed. "Saudi Prince Says Oil Markets Are 'in Decline.'" *Climate Home News*, July 29, 2013. www.climatechangenews.com/2013/07/29/saudi-prince-says-oil-markets-are-in-decline/.

McKibben, Bill. "Climate Change: A Warning from Islam." *New York Review of Books Daily*, August 24, 2015. www.nybooks.com/blogs/nyrblog/2015/aug/24/climate-change-warning-islam/.

Nachmany, Michal, Sam Fankhauser, Jana Davidová, et al. *Climate Change Legislation in Saudi Arabia*. London: Grantham Institute on Climate Change and the Environment of the London School of Economics and Political Science, 2015. www.GranthamInstitute/wp-content/uploads/2015/05/SAUDI_ARABIA.pdf.

Pasquini, Elaine. "Zaytuna College Hosts Historic Workshop on Environmental Education in Islamic Schools." *Washington Report on Middle East Affairs*, April 2013, 48–49.

Reiche, Danyel. "Renewable Energy Policies in the Gulf Countries: A Case Study of the Carbonneutral 'Masdar City' in Abu Dhabi." *Energy Policy* 38, no. 1 (2010): 378–82.

Turfe, Tallal Alie. *Energy in Islam: A Scientific Approach to Preserving Our Health and the Environment*. Elmhurst, NY: Tahrike Tarsile Qur'an, 2011.

United Nations Conference on Trade and Development (UNCTAD). Report on UNCTAD Assistance to the Palestinian People: Developments in the Economy of the Occupied Palestinian Territory. Geneva, 2015.

4

Environmental Stewardship in Islamic Law

Principles, Institutions, and Ecological Governance in the Muslim World

Mohamed A. 'Arafa[*]

Islamic law adopts a duty paradigm to realise the right to a healthy environment. According to Karel Vašák, third-generation solidarity rights 'can be realised only through the concerted efforts of all the actors on the social scene'.[1] Vašák discovered his well-known notion on third-generation human rights. Also, a cluster of distinguished Muslim scholars defined the concept in almost equal terms in their scholarly writings to explain Islamic philosophies of human rights at the Vatican colloquium on economic, social, and cultural rights in Islam.[2]

However, although third-generation solidarity rights are feeble and self-improving in the international legal discourse, Muslim jurists mention them as a basic principle in the Islamic view of the human rights movements.[3] Owing to the equivalents between the Islamic standards and the basics of solidarity rights, the right to a healthy and clean environment is one of the most commonly proposed solidarity rights in the Islamic legal tradition.

4.1 LEGAL FRAMEWORK: THE FUNDAMENTAL PRINCIPLES OF ISLAMIC LAW'S ENVIRONMENTAL PUBLIC POLICY

The responsibility for doing the right deed lies solely with the individual, who will be judged on the Day of Resurrection by God for what he did in his life, irrespective of the procedures that were taken in favour of or against him by the public authorities, administrative and municipal agencies, and the courts.[4] Therefore, every Muslim should be committed to the protection of the environment and the salvation of its natural resources within the notion of a mandatory duty to protect himself and the community, on the basis of his faith in accountability before God.[5]

[*] The author wishes to thank and express sincere appreciation to Avv. Professor Ignazio Castellucci for inviting him to present an earlier version of this chapter at the 'Crossroads East and West: Visions of the Economy in the Islamic and Western Legal Traditions' International Workshop at the International University Turin College of Law, Turin, Italy, in 2013. Further, the author thanks Michael Blackwell for his insightful comments and invaluable feedback on this chapter. An earlier version of this chapter appeared in the *European Journal of Law Reform*.

[1] J. Morgan-Foster, 'Third Generation Rights: What Islamic Law Can Teach the International Human Rights Movement', *Yale Human Rights & Development Law Journal* 8 (2005): 67–91, at 85.

[2] Ibid.

[3] Ibid. See, generally, J. P. Martin and T. Stahnke (eds), *Religion and Human Rights: Basic Documents* (New York: Columbia University, 1998).

[4] M. R. al-Ḥalw, *Qānūn ḥimāyat al-bīʾa fī ḍawʾ al-sharīʿa* (Beirut: Dār al-Maṭbūʿāt al-Jāmiʿiyya, 1999), 44–47.

[5] Ibid., 45.

Under Islamic ethics, rules, and social values in dealing with the environment, it should be taken into account by every Muslim that there should be (a) no wastage or overconsumption of natural resources; (b) no improper obstruction or demolition of any element of natural resources; (c) no harm, injury, or exploitation of the natural environment in any way; and (d) sustainable development of the earth's resources and elements. The protection and enrichment of the earth and its resources is a religious obligation in Islamic doctrine.[6]

As explained by various Quranic provisions, and verified thoroughly by the Sunna's teachings, God is the owner of the universe, and man has only a usufruct right. Use of this right is subject to the juristic norm inferred from the Prophetic tradition: 'there shall be neither damage nor an infliction of damage.'[7] The right shall be exercised only within its scope and for the achievement of its goal, and Muslims are prohibited from exploiting that right in causing any sort of harm or injury, whether intentionally or unintentionally, to a particular individual or the whole community.[8] In other words, the exercise of the usufruct is counterbalanced by accountability.[9] All individuals are entitled to reasonably benefit from common sources, and each person is entitled to use the common resource according to their necessities and needs, without causing any infringements or violations of the equal rights of other community members.[10]

Islamic law authorises the intervention of public authorities to secure the common welfare and eliminate injustice or unfairness as an original and primary responsibility. The abilities of each social class must be taken into consideration by the public authorities. Should a common source be insufficient, prioritisation of usufructs is made according to (a) the degree of need, accurately assessed both quantitatively and qualitatively; (b) the impact on the resource; and (c) the priority of claim in time for use of the resource.[11] In light of that, Prophet Muhammad stated, 'The benefit of a thing is in return for the liability attaching to it,' and, 'Liability for a thing is an obligation accompanying the benefit thereof.'[12]

There is no doubt that a leader's undertakings become illicit or illegitimate if they are based on autocracy without any care for the community's public interest.[13] The Islamic public policy

[6] H. Cissé, 'Islamic Law and the Environment', in United Nations Environment Programme and United Nations Educational, Scientific and Cultural Organization (UNEP–UNESCO), *Draft Papers on Religion and Sustainable Development* (Nairobi: UNEP, 2008).

[7] Ibid.

[8] G. Smith, 'Islam and the Environment: World and the Spirit', *Earth Island Journal*, March 2008, http://islamawareness.net/Nature/environment.html. ('Despite the apocalyptic premise of Samuel Huntington's book, *The Clash of Civilizations* (which prophesies an inevitable war between the armies of the God and the armies of Allah), Islam and Christianity have much in common. In their view of the natural world, both the Bible and the Qur'an share many of the same stories, heroes, and ethical concepts. But there are some differences. The Qur'an might even be said to be the "greener" of the two holy books.')

[9] Ibid.; I. Abdul-Matin, *Green Deen: What Islam Teaches about Protecting the Planet* (San Francisco: Berrett-Koehler Publishers, 2010). He argued: 'The Prophet Muhammad, peace be upon him, said that the Earth is a mosque. Since everything on the planet is sacred, nothing can be debased.'

[10] al-Ḥalw, *Qānūn*. See O. A. Bakhashab, 'Islamic Law and the Environment: Some Basic Principles', *Arab Law Quarterly* 3 (1988): 287–98, at 293, 298. See also, generally, A. M. Ḥashīsh, *al-Mafhūm al-qānūnī li-l-bī'a fī ḍaw' mabda' aslama al-qānūn al-mu'āṣir* (Alexandria: Dār al-Fikr al-Jāmi'ī, 2001); M. A. El-Gamal, *A Basic Guide to Contemporary Islamic Banking and Finance* (Houston: Rice University, 2000), www.ruf.rice.edu/~elgamal/files/primer.pdf.

[11] F. Rahman, *Islam and Modernity: Transformation of an Intellectual Tradition* (Chicago: University of Chicago Press, 1982), 32 (quoting Professor Santillana).

[12] *Ṣaḥīḥ Muslim* and *Saḥīḥ al-Bukhārī* (English translation available at www.usc.edu/org/cmje/).

[13] See M. Izzi Dien, 'Islam and the Environment, Theory and Practice', *Journal of Beliefs and Values* 18, no. 1 (1997): 47–57, at 47, providing a paradigm solution for many forms of environmental degradation, including that of water distribution, underlining Islam's role as an important potential ground for settling disputes from which environmental international law may proceed. ('Despite the fact that Islam's attitude in the theoretical environmental debate is both straightforward and well respected, many parts of the Muslim world are currently witnessing a cultural environmental

governing the actions of the imam/hakim (ruler) stipulates that the management of a subject's affairs by the rules shall be according to their welfare, as this represents the final goal of the Islamic environmental legislation within the agenda of balancing these conflicting interests.[14]

In Islamic law, all actions are assessed in terms of their outcomes as social *maṣāliḥ* (benefits) or social *mafāsid* (evils). Muslim rulers are required to promote the public welfare of society's members. The failure to do so is assessed and potentially mitigated by different factors, such as the significance and urgency of numerous goods involved; inevitability or possibility of injury or benefit; ordering by raising the welfare of the greatest number; and the capability of those affected to secure their interests without assistance.[15]

Public policy and decision-makers must always seek the maximisation of public welfare through their policies. If an action simultaneously realises welfare yet leads to harm, the juristic principle of 'the averting of harm takes priority over the realisation of benefit' applies.[16] In his landmark statement, the well-known Muslim scholar Ibn Taymiyya declared that

> what is required to safeguard is to safeguard all benefits and bring them to perfection, and to eliminate all determinates and minimise them. And if they prove irreconcilable, it is to safeguard the greater good by the exclusion of the lesser, and to remove the greater harm by acceptance of the lesser. This is the mandate of the law.[17]

From this doctrine, it is clear that under Islamic law the interests of the Muslim community (public interest) take precedence over the individual (private) benefits based on the principle that 'priority is given to preserving the universal interest over particular interest'.[18] This, in other words, means achieving and protecting the mutual interest of the general public based on sharia law that 'the lesser of two evils shall be chosen', 'severe damage shall be removed by means of lighter damage', and 'if one of two opposing determinates is unavoidable, the more injurious is averted by the commission of the less injurious'.[19] Muslim intellectuals advocate that priority should be given to the actual and well-known benefit over the probable one.[20]

rupture which can be ascribed to two causes. The sudden, almost shocking, introduction of the industrial age to these countries was not supported by a value system compatible with the prevalent Islamic values. The outcome has been a sad alteration of "satisfaction" with the little that can be acquired from the environment, to a "dissatisfaction" which can only be appeased by ever increasing consumption. Both Islamic values and industrial values need to be re-examined to extract from them a new value system that fits modern human beings, without rejecting the bedrock of Islam and the environmental elements that it supports.')

14 A. A. Bagader, A. T. El-Chirazi El-Sabbagh, M. A. Al-Glayand, M. Samarrai, and O. A. Barbour, *Environmental Protection in Islam*, 2nd ed. (Gland, Switzerland: International Union for Conservation of Nature and Natural Resources, 1994), 18.

15 Ibid., 19. See Smith, 'Islam and the Environment'.

16 Taqī al-Dīn Aḥmad Ibn Taymiyya, *al-Siyāsa al-shar'iyya fī iṣlāḥ al-rā'ī wa-l-ra'iyya* (Arabic Book Review, 2008).

17 Ibid.

18 Ibid. And from this rule, the juristic principle 'a private injury is accepted to avert a general injury to the public' has emerged. Muslim scholars use this tool to answer new questions. Imam al-Ghazālī, a very well-respected Islamic scholar, created this doctrine in his mission for clarifications to new economic, environmental, social, and political concerns that arose with the expansion of Islamic community. This source refers to all new notions and ideas that have neither been allowed nor forbidden by one or more agreed-upon sources of Islamic law. In arbitrating whether an idea or solution is appropriate according to *maṣlaḥa mursala* (consideration of public interest), scholars look to whether it endorses social welfare. Further, the rule derived from this secondary source of this law source must be logical and must not oppose or contradict the principles of the Quran, Sunna, and the overall spirit of the sharia. M. Hashim Kamali, *Principles of Islamic Jurisprudence*, 3rd ed. (Cambridge: Islamic Texts Society, 2003), 238.

19 Ibid. See also Ḥashīsh, al-Mafhūm al-qānūnī; W. Montgomery Watt, *The Faith and Practice of Al-Ghazali* (London: George Allen & Unwin, 1951).

20 See also Kamali, *Principles of Islamic Jurisprudence*; Ḥashīsh, *al-Mafhūm al-qānūnī*.

Social interests and public benefits are addressed according to their significance, actuality, and certainty in this regard. Islamic law classifies interests into (a) *ḍarūriyyāt* (necessities), or those things indispensable to the preservation of the *al-ḍarūriyyāt al-khams* (five sharia objectives of life, religion, lineage, property, and prosperity); (b) *ḥājiyyāt* (needs), meaning those things whose absence leads to actual hardship and suffering; and (c) *taḥsīniyyāt* (supplementary benefits), which are things that refine life and enhance ethical values.[21]

Furthermore, the public authorities' (state) intervention in the dealings of society for environmental security necessarily requires that the aversion of harm to the poor take priority over the aversion of harm to the wealthy, that the welfare of the poor take precedence over the benefit to the rich, and that averting harm generally overrides the acquisition of benefits.[22]

In the same vein, and within the duty of public authorities, two key features are included with regard to the remedy for environmental damage and its prevention. These establishments are obliged to take all necessary measures to *avoid* any environmental damage or minimise it before its occurrence. For instance, the state would have the right to suspend any perpetual or temporary activity if it were to cause environmental misuse, limit the scope of action (time, place, quality, kind, etc.), apply scientific technical standards or particular methods to avert the occurrence of damage or restrict its impact, and educate and socially advise the general public about real environmental hazards.[23] Further, public authorities may plan the exploitation and development of natural resources.[24]

Moreover, the state's institutions are obliged to take all necessary measures to *eliminate* existing damage. For example, individuals along with institutions may be held liable for any environmental damage, whether intended or not. The Islamic juristic principle states: 'The author of an act is responsible, even if the act is not intentional,' and, 'Dire necessity renders prohibited things permissible'; social activities violating the environment must be stopped, and violators of the environment and animal rights must be punished in cases of clear negligence (recklessness) or disobedience of the general directions set out by the government for the promotion of ecological safety.[25] In addition, the government has the right to require

[21] Ibid. According to Islamic fiqh rules, Muslim scholars emphasised that urgency and precedence should be given to basic desires and needs. In the case of conflict between the lesser needs and supplementary benefits, lesser needs should have priority over the supplemental needs. As Islamic jurisprudence is unique in assuring the right of personal security and social order, Imam al-Ghazālī recognised what are known today as the 'five essentials' and these became the neutral criteria for scholars to identify whether an idea or solution stimulates the public interest. Accordingly, Islam assures five essential things (*maqāṣid al-sharī'a al-Islāmiyya/al-ḍarūriyyāt al-khams*) to all individuals and prohibits unjustified violation of them by the state. These essentials are (a) protecting religion; (b) protecting lives; (c) protecting mind; (d) protecting posterity and intellect; and (e) protecting property. On the other hand, Islamic law presents the structural framework for the community by maintaining the legal relationships among persons and protecting the interest of one person from being attacked by another. See J. Naify, 'Al-Ghazali', in R. H. Popkin (ed.), *The Pimlico History of Western Philosophy* (London: Pimlico, 1999).

[22] Ibid. See also Kamali, *Principles of Islamic Jurisprudence*; Ḥashīsh, *al-Mafhūm al-qānūnī*. ('Regardless of law enforcement mechanisms, preservation of nature is every individual's religious duty.'); Q 3:104.

[23] Specialists, consultants, and experts in all the various areas (e.g., biology, biochemistry, overhunting, overgrazing, etc.) should be encouraged, trusted, and delegated the power to determine the proper criteria and suitable standards. Authorities have the right to design the guidelines in planning sustainable development in this time of greater human impact on the natural world. All development projects have to be evaluated according to their possible benefits and harm, either in the short or long run, before receipt of approval. Such development should be accomplished within the legislative principles and Islamic institutions highlighted under the Islamic environmental legal system underlined.

[24] al-Ḥalw, *Qānūn*, 255.

[25] See also Ḥashīsh, *al-Mafhūm al-qānūnī*. The state's foundation has a right to intervene to protect animals (local and wild) rights, whether in private possession, scientific institutes, zoos, etc. for any illicit purposes (killing, using methods to harm them). Under Islamic law, if the animal's owner mistreats, fails to provide, or is unable to afford care and

compensation and indemnity (insurances, securities, and collaterals) for irreparable environmental harms effected by establishments, enterprises, corporations, and the like.[26] All of this shall be supported by the Islamic legal framework and attained by the institutional framework under Islamic environmental law.

4.2 INSTITUTIONAL FRAMEWORK: ISLAMIC INSTITUTIONS FOR THE MAINTENANCE OF NATURE

One of the most important requirements for the active and effective preservation of the natural environment is the inclusion of official institutional measures, through which the operators may be made responsible for appropriate conservation programming for patterns, enticements, and incentives aimed at the positive enrichment and conservation of the environment.

4.2.1 Iḥyāʾ al-Arḍ al-Mawāt *(Land Revitalisation or Reclamation)*

According to the duty model in Islamic law, all individuals are required to share in the duty of bringing life to unpossessed land through its retrieval, cultivation, or beneficial use as private property.[27] In other words, the reclamation of arid, unowned land is a means to the acquisition of proprietorship (ownership) rights. In Islamic law, *iḥyāʾ* provides persons with an influential motivation to invest and participate in the appropriate use of the land and to offer the land for the prosperity and welfare of the community.[28] Public authorities have the right and duty to prevent the development of vacant land if such improvement would result in any form of environmental abuse. This includes power over all sorts of lands that are set aside for public benefit, such as inviolable zones, reserves, and all land that has resources crucial to the public interest.[29]

In this respect, the state has the right to make *iqṭāʿāt* (grants) of the unowned land for public beneficial purposes such as farming, building, and agriculture. In addition, these grants can be used to provide a means of reimbursement to individuals whose land is intended for public use or limited to the public utility.[30] Should the beneficiary fail to reclaim the unowned land successfully within a reasonable period, the recipient is obliged to return the land to the state for development by other parties in various ways.[31] Lastly, the state may grant *ijārāt* (long-term leases) or grant the right to *ijāra manfaʿa/istighlāl al-arḍ* (usufruct/exploitation) to channel investments via effective control, actual supervision, and active management over its consumption.

suitable maintenance (food, water, shelter, and the like), authorities are to force him to afford appropriate conditions, and if he refuses or is unable to do so, he will be compelled to sell it or slaughter it for food.

26 Ibid. It should be noted that individuals and organisations should not be held accountable for damages that may result from exceeding their legal commitments and practising their proper obligations in the terms of their contracts, licences, permits, and conditions under the notion that 'legal permission cancels liability'.

27 al-Ḥalw, *Qānūn*, 301.

28 Ibid., 297–300. For further details on the environmental damages of the Second Gulf War, see Kuwait Foundation for the Advancement of Sciences, *An Environmental Assessment of Kuwait: Seven Years after the Gulf War* (Geneva: Green Cross International, 1998).

29 al-Ḥalw, *Qānūn*, 302. In other words, reclamation cannot be executed in natural reserves or inviolable lands.

30 Ibid. These grants are regulated according to the principles of *iḥyāʾ*, and they may not include resources based on public goods. These grants do not guarantee a property right in itself unless the beneficiary (recipient) resuscitates it effectively and efficiently, when it practically becomes their own property.

31 Ibid.

4.2.2 Al-Ḥimā *(Reserves)*

The state may establish reserves for the procurement of the public good, such as management of forests, wildlife, watersheds, and other development. Prophet Muhammad established the first public natural reserve in Islam to attain mutual benefit and for the public good after eliminating the private reserves that were for the elite use of powerful classes. Government organisations are required to launch these reserves in appropriate spots and strategic sites for the purpose of rapid natural improvement and ecological enhancements.[32]

4.2.3 Al-Ḥarīm *(Inviolable/Protective Zone)*

The state may institute *al-ḥarīm* (an uninfringeable zone) where use and development is proscribed or circumscribed to avert damage to utilities and the mutilation of natural resources.[33] In sharia law, towns and settlements should be surrounded by inviolable zones so as to secure people's basic necessities and needs.[34] Each settlement has a right to construct such zones managed by the persons and where use is rigorously limited.[35]

4.2.4 Al-Waqf *(Charitable Endowments)*

Waqf etymologically means *ḥabs* (tying up). *Waqf* is a religiously motivated donation of a property that generates revenues, and is managed and regulated by Islamic law. The Hanafi school defines *waqf* as 'the extinction of the proprietor's ownership in the thing dedicated and its detention in the implied ownership of God in such a manner that the profits may revert to and be applied for the benefit of mankind'.[36] There is no explicit Quranic verse defined or

[32] Woodcutting, cropping, and hunting may be forbidden or constrained within the particular objectives of each reserve to protect the environment from any potential damage.

[33] M. Hassan, 'Teaching Environmental Law from an Islamic Point of View', paper presented in Arabic at the Conference on Environmental Legislation in the Arab Region, 30 September–2 October 2000; A. B. M. Ben Saad Al-Konain, 'The Efforts of Saudi Judiciary in Developing Environmental Protection', Arabic paper presented at the Conference on the Role of the Judiciary in the Development of Environmental Law in the Arab Region, 26–28 October 2002.

[34] Watercourses, roads, canals, lakes, squares, and the like are surrounded by inviolable zones to facilitate their use in order to achieve public welfare. These sources should have these zone-approaching easements to preclude any harm and maintain their mutual proper usage. S. H. Nasr, *Man and Nature: The Spiritual Crisis in Modern Man* (London: Unwin Hyman, 1990). It should be noted that the sacred territorial areas in both Makka and Madina are known as *al-ḥaramayn* (inviolable sanctuaries), where plants (trees) cannot be cut down and wildlife (animals) are protected from any environmental harm or damage within their borders. They serve as examples of best practice. All construction, development, and the like should be carried out with care and sensitivity. In this domain, the Prophet said: 'It is sacred by virtue of the sanctity conferred on it by God till the Day of Resurrection. Its thorn tress shall not be cut down, and its game shall not be disturbed, and the objects lost in it, shall be picked up only by one who will announce them, and its fresh herbage shall not be cut.' See also Abū Dāwūd's *Sunan* and Muslim's *Ṣaḥīḥ*, both available in English translation at www.usc.edu/org/cmje/.

[35] Nasr, *Man and Nature*. Furthermore, it is acceptable to create these zones adjacent to sources of water and other utilities. L. J. Kotzé and A. Paterson (eds), *The Role of the Judiciary in Environmental Governance: Comparative Perspectives* (Alphen aan den Rijn, the Netherlands: Wolters Kluwer, 2009). This volume explains constitutional rights to a healthy environment; reconciliation of environmental and aboriginal rights; recognition of public environmental rights within property law; clarification of the mandates of environmental authorities; and the creation of specialist environmental courts.

[36] M. Z. Abbasi, 'The Classical Islamic Law of Waqf: A Concise Introduction', *Arab Law Quarterly* 26, no. 2 (2012): 121–53. While Imam Abu Hanifa originally held that the founder retained ownership with restricted use, the position of his disciples Abu Yusuf and Muhammad al-Shaybani that ownership transfers irrevocably to Allah became the

mentioned directly or indirectly about the *waqf*, though it promotes charity, including *waqf*.[37] Further, Prophet Muhammad motivated Muslims to make charities, saying, 'When Adam's son dies, he will be disconnected except from three: continuous charity, useful knowledge, or well-raised offspring who pray for him.'[38] In this sense, some modern, non-Islamic legal systems were inspired by the Islamic system of *waqf*.[39] According to the *wāqif*'s (the donor of *waqf*) will, *waqf* may be dedicated to serving relatives and society. It can be dedicated to helping financially incapable persons to marry, feed infants and children, assist the sick, disabled, orphans, and elderly, and to cover the expenses of the needy.[40]

Waqf is subject to the supervision and control of governmental institutions, where ministries and public offices were established in Muslim nations to regulate and govern the *waqf* properties.[41] The status of its ownership (assets) as *waqf* is debated by Muslim scholars.[42] According to Islamic rules, once the *waqf* is created, the corpus will be devoted to God. Jurists acknowledge that although the dedication of the property does not result in the loss of the proprietorship itself, the usufruct is thereafter devoted to charitable commitments.[43]

In this regard, Muslim ulema (jurists) classified *waqf* as follows: *waqf dā'im* (permanent *waqf*, which lasts as long as the possessions last and is productive) and *waqf muwaqqat* (temporary *waqf*, which occurs for a limited period).[44] Accordingly, *waqf* can be (a) self *waqf* (for the *wāqif*'s benefit); (b) *waqf ahlī* (for the relatives' or family's welfare); (c) *waqf khayrī* (for the benefit of the community's public interest); and (d) *waqf mukhtalaṭ* (mixed grant) (for the benefit of the self, the public, and/or relatives).[45] In charitable *waqf*, the earnings and usufruct

authoritative Hanafi doctrine. The main notion of *waqf* under sharia is the fact that definite assets should be protected in peacetime and in wartime (times of armed conflict and aggression) from all sorts of destruction.

37 God says, 'They ask thee what they should spend (in charity). Say: Whatever ye spend that is good, is for parents and kindred and orphans and those in want and for wayfarers. And whatever ye do that is good, Allah knoweth it well' (Q 2:215); and, 'If ye loan to Allah, a beautiful loan, He will double it to your (credit), and He will grant you Forgiveness: for Allah is most Ready to appreciate (service), Most Forbearing' (Q 2:245).

38 *Ṣaḥīḥ Muslim* and *Ṣaḥīḥ al-Bukhārī*. Also, Prophet Muhammad told his companion ʿUmar b. al-Khaṭṭāb to 'tie up the property and devote the usufruct to human beings'. W. F. Fretcher, 'Islamic Wakf', *Missouri Law Review* 36, no. 2 (1971): 153–55, http://scholarship.law.missouri.edu/mlr/vol36/iss2/1.

39 Ibid. It is worth mentioning that the English trust legal system is based on the notion of *waqf*. The trust legal system in England was used to give part of the income to individuals who are not able to share these assets and belongings. M. M. Gaudiosi, 'The Influence of the Islamic Law of Waqf on the Development of the Trust in England: The Case of Merton College', *University of Pennsylvania Law Review* 136 (1988): 1231–61, at 1231.

40 A. V. W. Thomas, 'Note on the Origin of Uses and Trusts – Waqfs', *Southwest Law Journal* 3 (1949): 162–64.

41 R. A. al-Shurunbāṣī, *Aḥkām al-waṣiyya wa-l-waqf fī al-sharīʿa al-Islāmiyya* (n.p., 2005). ('A *waqf* known as *waqf al-awlād* is an absolute religious endowment in Islamic law, typically denoting a building or part of land for Muslim religious or charitable objectives. The donated assets are held by a charitable trust. The grant is known as *masrūʿat al-khidma*, while a person making such devotion or dedication is known as a *wāqif*. Ibn ʿUmar (God be pleased with him) reported: ʿUmar b. al-Khaṭṭāb got land in Khaybar, so he came to Prophet Muhammad (peace be upon him) and asked him to advise him about it. The Prophet said (peace be upon him), "If you like, make the property inalienable, and give the profit from it to charity."')

42 Ibid. In other words, *waqf* means the permanent dedication by a Muslim of any property for any purpose recognised by the Muslim law as religious, pious, or charitable. It allows private contribution to public good as it is not subject to transactions, and the endowment's yield is devoted to the needy people. T. Mahmood, 'Islamic Family Waqfs in Twentieth Century Legislation', *Islamic and Comparative Law Quarterly* 8 (1988): 1–20, at 1.

43 al-Shurunbāṣī, *Aḥkām al-waṣiyya*, p. 144. ('Most of the Islamic *waqfs* are subject to similar principles and norms and Muslim scholars argued about its details that may reflect on its roles (functions).')

44 Ibid., 145.

45 Ibid., 146–49. In the meantime, some specific *waqfs* can be *ahlī* (family based) and temporary at the same time, or *khayrī* (charitable) and permanent during the same period.

are donated to generous purposes that may be defined by the *waqf* statement, in which the qadi (judge) has the right to designate these goals according to society's needs.[46]

On the basis of the background of the advisors, the benefactor may decide to offer his *waqf* for general welfare, to improve upon goals such as educational needs, construction of worship places, or for service to the elderly.[47] Moreover, if the consultant has experience with environmental issues and is able to persuade and encourage the *wāqif* that environmental safety is vital and necessary for a clean and healthy environment, the donor may well be inspired to attain that purpose.[48] The benevolent *waqf* can result in three conservational circumstances:

1. Charitable *Waqf* (Grant) with a General Environmental Objective: In this scenario, an environmental *waqf* is devoted generally to environmental security and the greening of the environment without identifying which area needs to be sponsored.[49] Under the qadi's control and authorisation, the supervisor has the authority to determine which environmental needs should take precedence and be treated as a priority before advancing the next one.[50] But in the case of an environmental disaster, such as the occurrence of an earthquake or a flood, the manager can, by the judge's permission, move the grant's resources, either wholly or partially, to address new and crucial environmental harms. Such emergency manoeuvres may reallocate resources to other parts of the environment as long as the new objective falls within the overall environmental purpose indicated by the donor.[51]
2. Charitable *Waqf* (Endowment) with Explicit Environmental Goal: Here the environmental *waqf* is dedicated to the fulfilment of a precise, express ecological goal, such as the cleaning up of the marine environment or sponsorship of certain environmental research.[52] When this detailed and specific objective is accomplished, the administrator – under the full control, managerial supervision, and approval of the judge – has to satisfy other new requests (necessities) such as those provided in the *wāqif*'s statement.[53]
3. Charitable *Waqf* (Donation) without Any Environmental Purpose: Generally speaking, benevolent grants may be intended for purposes distinct and apart from any environmental goals, such as assistance for the needy. In such a case, the administrator has no discretionary power and should be restricted within these parameters.[54] Nevertheless, in cases of unexpected environmental crises, the officer, with the qadi's consent, may

[46] Ibid. See also F. M. Goadby, 'Waqf in Egypt', *Journal of Comparative Legislation & International Law* 10 (1928): 319–20.

[47] See, e.g., Egypt, *Law No. 48 of 1946*, Art. 7, concerning the rules of *waqf*, amended by *Law No. 180 of 1952* (abolishing non-charitable *waqf*), issued by Decree of 14 September 1952, published in *al-Jarīda al-Rasmiyya*, 14 September 1952, Art. 3 (Egypt). See also A. M. Tawfiq, 'The Awqaf in Modern Egypt', *The Islamic Quarterly* 4 (1998): 257–65.

[48] Tawfiq, 'The Awqaf in Modern Egypt'. For further information about the historical development of *waqf* in the Islamic world, especially Egypt, see F. J. Ziadeh, 'Land Law and Economic Development in Arab Countries', *American Journal of Comparative Law* 33, no. 1 (1985): 93–106, www.jstor.org/stable/840119.

[49] al-Shurunbāṣī, *Aḥkām al-waṣiyya*, 153.

[50] Ibid., 154. Accordingly, if the grant was committed to the clean-up of the nautical area, the public official's efforts should emphasise this environmental part.

[51] Ibid., 157.

[52] Ibid., 158–59. ('Officers should assure that the adjacent environment beyond the *waqf* property is safe and the protection of their *waqf* is guaranteed too.')

[53] Ibid. In the previous cases, the administrator should find another contaminated maritime or naval area to clean, and another educational and research institution to maintain.

[54] Ibid.

direct the whole or part of the *waqf*'s proceeds towards environmental conservation initiatives.[55]

It should be borne in mind that the protection and enrichment of the natural environment should be understood and interpreted in charitable terms as serving the public interests and sustaining God's properties, over which human beings have only vice-regency.[56] Therefore, it is highly recommended that *waqf* be established permanently as a means to improve environmental safety in specific environmental sectors as a fixed time period makes no sense and wastes time, effort, and financial resources.[57] In contrast, temporal environmental *waqf* can be valuable in situations of environmental difficulties, as in cases of natural or human disasters that affect the normal ecological and economic systems (as this sort of donation directly supports recovery efforts in such catastrophic conditions).[58]

Meanwhile, where nature is under day-to-day threats, under the sharia principles it is suggested that *wāqifs* (contributors) direct wholly or partially their *waqf*'s payments to serve environmental protection.[59] Consequently, numerous efforts should be undertaken to persuade *wāqifs* (future donors) about the significance of environmental rehabilitation, and spending should occur to assist in environmental protection so as to serve descendants and future generations.[60] Islamic organisations should play a predominant role in raising public awareness of the vitality of the environmental *waqf* by establishing a strategy for inspiring the launch of dedicated *waqfī* funds.[61]

Both the administrator and the qadi of the environmental *waqf* should maintain a minimum level of attentiveness to environmental issues, and should consult and collaborate with experts and attorneys in the environmental field.[62] Accordingly, the environmental administrator is bound by the *wāqif*'s statement to manage the *waqf* in such a way that it promotes, prioritises, and protects the natural environment. For example, if the donor includes the natural protection in the statement, the manager is obliged to follow such a requisite and devote the incomes to that purpose.[63]

55 Ibid.

56 Thus, *wāqifs* (donors) must give environmental protection the same high precedence as the maintenance of mosques.

57 For instance, funding agrarian efforts in a desert zone may eradicate the several efforts completed throughout the previous period of supply if the fund is terminated, where plants will die and sandstorms will cover the region.

58 In this sense it is highly recommended that the *waqf*'s revenues be directed into cleaning up polluted areas from lethal waste and harmful substances that were dumped perilously from nuclear settings up into lands and watercourses. At all times, it is possible that some extraordinary circumstances that could not have been predicted by the *wāqif* may ascend in course of time and require the alteration of the original terms of the *waqf* tool. These conditions cannot be a reasonable ground for abolishing the original situation created by the *wāqif* unless they were eligible as necessary and under them the receivers will not be able to use their dividends. H. Cattan, 'The Law of Waqf', in M. Khadduri and H. J. Liebesny (eds), *Law in the Middle East*, vol. 1 (Washington, DC: Middle East Institute, 1955), 210.

59 Ibid.

60 Ibid. See also Goadby, 'Waqf in Egypt'.

61 Each account is focused on a definite area to invite and convince persons to donate their possessions (assets) as *waqf* in monies and then use the returns to attain its objectives.

62 In investigative cases, the judge may refer to consultants and professionals in each field, including the environmental field, and their appointment will be based on professional skills and experience in the required fields (trade, environment, business management, etc.) to select the most capable one to care and keep the *waqf*.

63 al-Shurunbāṣī, *Aḥkām al-waṣiyya*, 153. For instance, in order to protect a machining factory from any ecological hazards, environmentalists should plant trees rather than construct a barrier (fence) around it. It is worth mentioning that Muslim scholars recognised *waqf* as perpetual, irrevocable, and inalienable. The eternity of the *waqf* means that it lasts as long as the corpus itself, where the corpus's proprietorship does not belong to the *wāqif* anymore, but to God. Irrevocability means that once a *waqf* is established there is no right for its cancellation as inevitability guarantees the stability of the Muslim *umma* (community), where recipients cannot live vulnerably by being prevented any time from the *waqf*'s income. Finally, inalienability averts the *waqf* from being subject to any legal disposition, such as mortgage, sale, pledge, lease, gift, inheritance, or any sort of alienation. See Cattan, 'The Law of Waqf', 203–8.

Under Islamic environmental law, it is highly recommended that environmental courts be launched to inspect and examine environmental issues and to oversee the management of the environmental administrator.[64] If the commissioner decides that the corpus is not productive anymore and does not cover the beneficiaries' needs, they can replace or exchange it from the same value with another one under the judge's observation.[65] So Muslim overseers, as believers in God, should keep, care, protect, and serve *waqf* to be creative and dynamic in advancing environmental safety to match God's highness.

4.3 CONCLUSION AND POLICY RECOMMENDATIONS: THE FUTURE OF ISLAMIC ENVIRONMENTAL LAW AND THE MIDDLE EAST'S UPRISINGS – A POSSIBLE THOUGHT?

Under Islamic law norms, environmental preservation and nature's care are imperative commands of God that must be obeyed by all beings. Environmental maintenance by man leads to the improvement of his welfare, is a benefit to the whole universe, and the satisfaction of the Lord's will. Although ecological resiliency is problematic and has existed and been recorded throughout history, it has been extremely exaggerated in modern times, as man's aptitude to affect it has extended with incredible speed, while in terms of his accountability as a *khalīfa* (vice-regent) on earth, he remains unfair, reckless, and unwise.

Even though it may be conceivable to integrate the rules of Islamic environmental law within the statutory programmes of Muslim nations, serious environmental problems will persist unless proper and effective institutional measures are taken to replace the old and now virtually redundant ones. It is also interesting that secular efforts to meet environmental challenges in Muslim countries fail to follow and adopt the Islamic model in the sharia code (Quran and Sunna). It is highly recommended that the role of the Muslim environmental scholars be redefined owing to the fact that the nature of the Islamic state has changed and needs to be brought into conformity with modern standards and the sharia requirements of updating and maintaining flexibility through the principles of *qiyās/ijtihād* (individual reasoning, analogical deduction, public interest considerations, and the use of secondary sources of Islamic law). Islamic law supports all means necessary to lead to the advancement of public utilities, mutual values, and common welfare of the community.

In light of this, the maintenance of the natural environment is an important ethical and moral principle under sharia law. Moral consciousness along with religious awareness at the individual, institutional, and social levels can inspire individuals to think positively about sacrifices committed for the common good rather than simply focusing on personal (self) interests. These ethical values should be incorporated within the environmental legislation and regulation, and effective implementation of necessary sanctions should be attained. The state (governmental institutions) is in charge of bringing environmental justice and equity through the fair allocation and distribution of natural resources. Technical knowledge, advanced scientific research, and the monitoring of natural resources are required under Islamic law. Ecological public consciousness and the social cognisance of ecological concerns in basic education are highly

64 In environmental *waqf*, the environmental judge has the right to supervise the administrator after being designated, guarantee that he is satisfying his task of better environmental care, and see that his authorisation is not abused, and to take indispensable actions, including the right to replace him, in case of proven negligence or recklessness (unqualified) and hold him liable.

65 al-Shurunbāṣī, *Aḥkām al-waṣiyya*.

encouraged among schools and universities, enabling the general public to contribute to the advancement of environmental security measures.

Before any developmental action with potential environmental impact is undertaken, it is highly recommended that the Arab governments give due consideration to the minimisation (calculation) of any potential environmental damage, exploration of all environmental impacts, and due attention to all environmental aspects (health, science, and natural beauty). Any domestic progress should not be accomplished at the injury or expense of others, or by the utilisation of any tool that may bring harm to any individual.

In Islamic countries, government administration is generally uncommitted to continuous implementation and review of environmental standards. The above understanding of the law regarding the upholding and greening of the environment requires efforts of a contemporary and continuous nature to be undertaken by Muslim governments to reinforce and strengthen their environmental statutes and enforcement procedures. There is no reasonable justification for incomplete interpretation and implementation of Islamic environmental law in these societies unless regimes are wholly rejecting Islamic environmental law. In such a case, these nations are not sufficiently entitled to embrace these philosophies and norms. As it were, though, these principles of environmental law establish a legal prerequisite; they are mandatory for Muslim nations.

In sum, Islamic law regards man as a creature of elevated status. In Islamic environmental law, humans are not owners of nature but are *mere* beneficiaries. Islamic environmental safety is based upon the principle of 'use' without 'abuse'. Environmental protection in the Islamic legal scheme does not differ from any modern environmental legal system, as Islamic teachings support all undertakings and deeds whether local, national, or international in their scope of applicability and call for mutual collaboration and joint assistance in all areas to save the environment from any degradation.

These proposals cannot be executed without dedicated laws that comprehensively provide for the protection of the environment and nature in the Arab Middle East. Contemporary events dictate that now is the time for applying such drastic procedures. The Arab Spring uprisings of 2010–12 gave rise to much political and legal chaos. This turmoil could be moderately alleviated by remodelling laws and regulations in various sectors to bolster a sense of community in Arab countries, and environmental law is a topic ripe for such reform. The challenges and the tests facing us are extraordinary in their status and size. The accomplishment of the environmental mission requires massive utilisation of resources, sound strategies, operational plans, and definite actions so that we may, God willing, conserve and propagate a good life and achieve prosperity for the present and future generations of all beings in the universe.

5

Dignity Law and the Environment in Pakistan

James R. May and Erin Daly

A judge today must be conscious and alive to the beauty and magnificence of nature, the interconnectedness of life systems on this planet and the interdependence of ecosystems.

—Syed Mansoor Ali Shah, CJ
Asghar Leghari v. Federation of Pakistan, 2018

5.1 INTRODUCTION

In Pakistan, as elsewhere in the world, the right to human dignity is the central axis around which other rights revolve. In seeking to fulfill the constitutionally protected right to dignity, Pakistani courts have recognized that a healthy environment and a stable climate are essential. Thus, although Pakistan is one of about sixty countries that do not recognize an express right to a healthy environment in some way,[1] courts in Pakistan have issued pioneering environmental jurisprudence under Article 14, which provides that "the dignity of man . . . shall be inviolable."[2] Relying on this provision, both the Lahore High Court[3] and the Supreme Court of Pakistan[4]

[1] James R. May, The Case for Environmental Human Rights: Recognition, Implementation and Outcomes, 42 *Cardozo Law Review* 983 (2021); Environmental Rights Map, https://envirorightsmap.org; James R. May, Making Sense of Environmental Human Rights and Global Environmental Constitutionalism, in *The Routledge Handbook of International Environmental Law* (Sumudu Atapattu, Carmen G. Gonzalez, and Sara Seck, eds., 2021). See also James R. May, Constituting Fundamental Environmental Rights Worldwide, 23 *Pace Environmental Law Review* 113 (2006); James R. May and Erin Daly, *Global Environmental Constitutionalism* (2015); James R. May and Erin Daly, Learning from Constitutional Environmental Rights, in *The Human Right to a Healthy Environment* (John H. Knox and Ramin Pejan, eds., 2018); Erin Daly and James R. May, Comparative Environmental Constitutionalism, 6 *Jindal Global Law Review* 9, 10–11, 30 (2015); James R. May and Erin Daly, Global Constitutional Environmental Rights, in *Routledge Handbook of International Environmental Law* (Shawkat Alam, Md Jahid Hossain Bhuiyan, Tareq M. R. Chowdhury, and Erika J. Techera, eds., 2012), 603–4.

[2] The Constitution of the Islamic Republic of Pakistan 1973, Art. 14(1): "The dignity of man and, subject to the law, the privacy of home shall be inviolable."

[3] See, e.g., Asghar Leghari v Federation of Pakistan, PLD 2018 Lahore 364. ("Fundamental rights, like the right to life (Article 9) which includes the right to a healthy and clean environment and right to human dignity (Article 14) read with constitutional principles of democracy, equality, social, economic and political justice include within their ambit and commitment, the international environmental principles of sustainable development, precautionary principle, environmental impact assessment, inter and intra-generational equity and public trust doctrine.")

[4] See, e.g., D.G. Khan Cement Co. v. Government of Punjab, C.P.1290-L/2019. ("The legislative policy of organized and planned growth, under the Ordinance, also synchronizes well with our constitutional values, set out in the preamble of the Constitution, as well as the Fundamental Rights and the Principles of Policy, in particular, the right to

have issued landmark decisions seeking to improve environmental outcomes relating to water, sanitation, and a stable climate.

We posit that Pakistani courts have aligned environmental protection with human dignity for good reason. To many, it might seem obvious that one cannot realize human dignity in an unhealthy environment; ask people who live near toxic dumps and experience higher than normal rates of cancer, or anyone who has lost a home, a limb, or a loved one in record-setting freezes, droughts, fires, and storms, or people, like those in all four provinces of Pakistan who experienced cataclysmic flooding in recent years.[5] Simply, environmental degradation diminishes human dignity and erodes community.

In a tacit conversation among courts on every continent, Pakistan is serving as a model for recognizing the relationship between human dignity and environmental outcomes. To examine this development, this chapter proceeds in three steps. First, we describe how courts in Pakistan have recognized human dignity as a pre-eminent constitutional value in line with the global commitment to dignity rights and with conceptions of dignity in Islam. We then highlight the intricate relationship between human dignity and environmental conditions, as has been recognized globally at the international and constitutional levels. We conclude that courts in Pakistan are serving as a global model in using dignity rights to advance environmental outcomes, thereby enhancing the ability of people to live with dignity in a healthy environment, and we show why a dignity lens is valuable. These decisions are implicitly and explicitly grounded in Pakistan's identity as an Islamic Republic.

5.2 DIGNITY UNDER LAW IN PAKISTAN AND IN ISLAM

With deep roots in philosophic and religious traditions, dignity is also a legal right that is enforceable in courts around the world.[6] The first and most important recognition of human dignity in a global legal instrument after the Charter of the United Nations (UN) is in the 1948 Universal Declaration of Human Rights (UDHR), the preamble of which begins with an emphatic acknowledgment of every person's dignity and a commitment to its centrality to human rights: "Whereas recognition of the inherent dignity and of the equal and inalienable rights of all members of the human family is the foundation of freedom, justice and peace in the world."[7]

The UDHR's first substantive article sets the stage: "All human beings are born free and equal in dignity and rights. They are endowed with reason and conscience and should act towards one another in a spirit of brotherhood."[8] This indicates dignity's dual nature that is evident in Islamic tenets as well: dignity describes both the immanent and equal worth of every human being, and

life and dignity, promotion of social and economic wellbeing of the people and safeguarding the legitimate interest of backward and depressed classes.")

5 According to UNICEF, six months after the floods "more than 10 million people living in flood-affected areas remain deprived of safe drinking water, leaving families with no alternative but to drink and use potentially disease-ridden water." UNICEF, Devastating Floods in Pakistan, www.unicef.org/emergencies/devastating-floods-pakistan-2022 (July 17, 2023).

6 See, e.g., Erin Daly and James May, *Dignity Law: Global Recognition, Cases and Perspectives* (2021); Erin Daly and James May, *Dignity under Law: A Global Handbook for Jurists* (2021); Erin Daly and James May, A Dignity Rights Primer, 3 *Juriste Internationale* 21 (2018); James May and Erin Daly, Why Dignity Rights Matter, 2 *European Human Rights Law Review* 15 (2019); Erin Daly, *Dignity Rights: Courts, Constitutions, and the Worth of the Human Person* (2nd ed., 2020).

7 UN General Assembly, Universal Declaration of Human Rights [UDHR], December 10, 1948, UN Doc. A/Res/217 (III), Preamble.

8 UDHR, Art. 1.

it reads that inherent worth as imposing responsibilities on people to treat each other in a way that respects each person's human dignity.

From there, dignity became a binding value, as it was incorporated in the common language of both UN International Covenants, which begin by recognizing that the rights enumerated therein "derive from the inherent dignity of the human person."[9] And at the same time, constitutions around the world began to incorporate dignity as an enforceable right and a foundational value.[10]

The qualities and role of dignity in Islam are consistent with the judicial treatment of dignity in courts around the world. Throughout, we see dignity's dual nature as both an existential fact and as a source of legal obligation. In Islam, as elsewhere, dignity is inherent: "Human beings possess a special value intrinsic to their humanity and as such are worthy of respect. A person is inherently and by nature venerable and honourable."[11] And, again consistent with the global understanding of dignity, it is, in Islam, universal and equal; simply put, "this dignity is equal for every human being irrespective of their caste, creed and gender."[12] And, as elsewhere, dignity in Islam is inviolable: "The concept of human dignity (*Karamatu al-Insani*) is rooted in Islamic thought which denotes inviolable value of all mankind which cannot be destroyed."[13]

But dignity in Islam, as elsewhere, does not only describe a fact of human existence, but also imposes social obligations as a function of that fact. As Mohammad Ali Shomali explains:

> We are all dignified from birth. Allah has given us some level of honour as our capital:
>
> وَلَقَدْ كَرَّمْنَا بَنِي آدَمَ
>
> "Certainly We have Honoured the Children of Adam" (17:70).
>
> Our responsibility is to utilise our capital and add to it.[14]

Islamic teachings further explain how we add to human capital in ways that align with international human rights norms and constitutional rights throughout the world. First, there are certain actions that are precluded by the recognition of dignity: "Everything that diminishes human dignity, such as torture, insult and humiliation, contradicts the principle of honour and respect."[15] Second, as Mohammad Hashim Kamali explains, "It is a basic right of all human being[s] to live a life of dignity, complemented by peace and comfort and the freedom to pursue what brings them happiness and perfection through all lawful means."[16]

[9] International Covenant on Civil and Political Rights [ICCPR], December 16, 1966, 999 UNTS 171, Preamble; International Covenant on Economic, Social and Cultural Rights [ICESCR], December 16, 1966, 993 UNTS 3, Preamble. "Dignity" appears twice in the preambles in both covenants and one additional time in each. In the ICCPR, it appears in connection with liberty: "All persons deprived of their liberty shall be treated with humanity and with respect for the inherent dignity of the human person" (Art. 10 (1)). In the ICESCR, it appears in connection with education: "The States Parties to the present Covenant recognise the right of everyone to education. They agree that education shall be directed to the full development of the human personality and the sense of its dignity, and shall strengthen the respect for human rights and fundamental freedoms" (Art. 13).

[10] On dignity rights generally, see Daly and May, *Dignity Law*; Daly and May, *Dignity under Law*; Daly, *Dignity Rights*.

[11] Umer Riyaz, Understanding Right to Dignity in Islam, *Kashmiri Reader* (December 14, 2022), https://kashmirreader.com/2022/12/14/understanding-right-to-dignity-in-islam/.

[12] Id., citing, inter alia, Q 49:13.

[13] Vaffi Foday Sheriff, Concept of Human Dignity in Islamic Thought, 3 *International Journal of Research and Innovation in Social Science* 148 (2019), https://tinyurl.com/38sz4543.

[14] Mohammad Ali Shomali, Honour and Dignity in Islam, 18 *Message Of Thaqalayn* (2017), https://tinyurl.com/5n83k4hz.

[15] Riyaz, Understanding Right to Dignity.

[16] Mohammad Hashim Kamali, *The Dignity of Man: An Islamic Perspective* (2002), 8.

Dignity is thus both an inherent quality of being human and a legal entitlement. It signifies, in the simple but profound words of Hannah Arendt, "the right to have rights."[17] It is thus recognized as both a right in and of itself and the progenitor and justification for all other rights, whether social or political, individual or collective, or environmental.[18] These various ways of thinking about dignity rights are reflected in current global constitutionalism: nearly 160 of the world's constitutions have incorporated dignity in some fashion, and hardly a new constitution is adopted without reference to the right to dignity. Many of these constitutions address dignity in multiple ways – as a foundational value, as a general personality right, and/or as a right associated with some specific interest (work, detention, etc.) or with a particularly vulnerable segment of the population (persons with disabilities, elderly, children, etc.). Some constitutions, either by text or by judicial implication, make it clear that the obligation to respect the dignity of every human being is imposed on all the organs of the state.[19] Thus, dignity, the common ancestor to all modern human rights law, is also its future – informing and implicating most other human rights at international and national levels.[20]

Because of these provisions and the global movement to appreciate the fundamental role that the recognition of dignity plays in the application of human rights, litigants around the world are framing claims in terms of human dignity, and courts are listening. In the last two decades alone, dignity rights have been invoked, interpreted, and applied by courts in thousands of cases and in a wide variety of factual settings.[21] Notable examples include: Argentina, where dignity is the foundation for freedom of speech and the right of association;[22] South Africa, where civic dignity protects voting rights and other rights associated with the political process;[23] Israel, where it is a "mother right";[24] Colombia, where dignity is a measure of the state's obligation to provide health care;[25] Germany, where the level of pension benefits must allow a person to live in dignity;[26] and India, where dignity guarantees the right to travel.[27] These broad affirmations of the role of human dignity in all state action also reveal the indivisibility of human rights – a characteristic that is all the more poignant in the context of sustainable environmental health and environmental justice.

[17] Hannah Arendt, *The Origins of Totalitarianism* (1958), 296.

[18] Daly, *Dignity Rights*, 133–35.

[19] These provisions are discussed at length in Daly, *Dignity Rights*, 11–25. See, e.g., Basic Law of Germany, Article 1: "Human dignity shall be inviolable. To respect and protect it shall be the duty of all state authority." See also, for judicial implication, the following excerpt from a judgment of the Constitutional Court of Colombia: "This means that the principle of human dignity must be understood: (i) as a founding principle of the legal system; (ii) as a constitutional principle, and (iii) as an autonomous fundamental right. Additionally, the Court has established that the 1991 [Medellin] Charter is essentially humanistic, insofar as the entire normative system has been constructed to protect dignity and personal autonomy, not in the abstract, but from a material and concrete dimension: that is why the respect for human dignity should inspire all actions of the State." Center for Social Justice Studies et al. v. Presidency of the Republic et al., Judgment T-622/16, Constitutional Court of Colombia (November 10, 2016).

[20] Iain Currien and Johan De Waal, *Bill of Rights Handbook* (2005). See also Halton Cheadle, Dennis Davis, and Nicholas Haysom, *South African Constitutional Law: The Bill of Rights* (2014), at 5.1, 5.2.2.

[21] See generally Daly, *Dignity Rights*.

[22] Asociación Lucha por la Identidad Travesti-Transexual v. Inspección General de Justicia, Argentina Supreme Court of Justice (November 21, 2006).

[23] August and Another v. Electoral Commission and Others (CCT8/99) [1999] ZACC 3; 1999 (3) SA 1; 1999 (4) BCLR 363 (April 1, 1999).

[24] Golan v. Prison Services (1996) IsrSC 50 (4) 136; Gal-On v. Attorney General, HCJ 466/07 (2012).

[25] Sentencia T-292/09 (Constitutional Court of Colombia).

[26] BVerfG, Judgment of the First Senate of 09 February 2010 – 1 BvL 1/09, paras. 1–220.

[27] Maneka Ghandi v. Union of India (1978) 2 SCR 621.

Dignity is also a constitutional cornerstone in Pakistan. Indeed, the Constitution of the Islamic Republic of Pakistan expressly recognizes a right to dignity, declaring that it "shall be inviolable."[28]

Dignity rights are consequential in law and life in Pakistan, where courts have widely applied this mandate to circumstances including capital punishment;[29] treatment of those arrested, detained, and incarcerated;[30] proclamation;[31] privacy;[32] child custody;[33] sexual harassment;[34] and more. The High Court of Lahore and the Supreme Court of Pakistan have been particularly vigilant in adumbrating the importance of dignity to legal rights and obligations in a range of legal and factual contexts. A few recent examples will suffice to illustrate the place of dignity in law in Pakistan.

First, the Supreme Court has on numerous occasions explained what the concept of dignity means. In a case about the treatment of rape survivors, the court said that: "Dignity means *human worth*: simply put, every person matters. No life is dispensable, disposable or demeanable."[35] Moreover, the court has recognized dignity's equality imperative: "Human dignity encapsulates the notion that every person has inherent equal worth; no one's life and liberty is more important than any other person's."[36]

The fact that dignity is inherent and invariably equal means that it is "not granted by law or cannot be taken away by law." Thus, it is "an absolute constitutional standard, which is not subject to law."[37] This is a profound jurisprudential development in keeping with the growing role that courts in Pakistan have played in achieving therapeutic jurisprudence[38] and social justice.[39] The place of dignity in Pakistani constitutional law is further explained in the rape case:

> Human dignity hovers over our laws like a guardian angel; it underlies every norm of a just legal system and provides an ultimate justification for every legal rule. Therefore, right to dignity is the crown of fundamental rights under our Constitution and stands at the top, drawing its strength from all the fundamental rights under our Constitution and yet standing alone and tall, making

[28] Constitution of the Islamic Republic of Pakistan, Art. 14(1). Art. 11 also provides that "no compulsory service shall be of a cruel nature or incompatible with human dignity."

[29] See, e.g., Shagufta Omar, Abolition of Death Penalty with Special Reference to Pakistan Part 2, 35 *Hamdard Islamicus* 15 (2012).

[30] Ibn Abdur Rehman, The Dignity of Person, *The Dawn* (September 20, 2018), www.dawn.com/news/1434057: "In short, patriarchy, feudal practices, refusal to accept the rights of the poor and the marginalised, and the *ulema*'s reluctance to properly interpret religious injunctions create a cultural blend that not only allows the people to commit excesses against one another's dignity but also provides justification for the state's doing so."

[31] See, e.g., Munir Ahmad Mughal, Law of Proclamation, *SSRN* (November 23, 2011), https://ssrn.com/abstract=1963765.

[32] See, e.g., Faisal Daudpota, Fundamental Scope of the Right to Privacy in Pakistan – Need for a New Data Protection Law, *SSRN* (November 8, 2016), https://ssrn.com/abstract=2866416.

[33] Fahad Siddiqi, Application of the Principles of Fair Play, Natural Justice and Due Process, in Guardianship / Child Custody Legal Proceedings in Pakistan, *SSRN* (January 22, 2018) https://ssrn.com/abstract=3107198.

[34] See, e.g., Shamreeza Riaz, Sexual Harassment: A Threat to Gradual Women Emancipation, 6 *Pakistan Journal of Gender Studies* 233 (2012).

[35] Zareef v. The State (in both cases), Criminal Appeal No.251/2020 & Criminal Petition No.667/2020, para. 11.

[36] Id.

[37] Id.

[38] See, e.g., Muhammad Amir Munir, Mainstreaming Therapeutic Jurisprudence in Pakistan: A Historical Discourse, *SSRN* (August 18, 2017), https://ssrn.com/abstract=3021643.

[39] See, e.g., Munir Ahmad Mughal, Legal and Judicial Education Reforms in Pakistan: Role of Legislature, Judiciary and Executive, *SSRN* (December 3, 2013), https://ssrn.com/abstract=2362973.

> *human worth* and *humanness* of a person a far more fundamental a right than the others, a right that is absolutely non-negotiable.[40]

The reason for dignity's primacy is that dignity goes directly to a person's identity and therefore can never be degraded. As the court put it in the rape case:

> Similarly Article 14 of our Constitution mandates that dignity shall be inviolable, therefore, reporting sexual history of a rape survivor amounts to discrediting her independence, identity, autonomy and free choice thereby degrading her human worth and offending her right to dignity ... *Every person has the right to live, and the right to live means right to live with dignity. A person should live as "person" and no less.*[41]

Tying together the textual guarantee of dignity in the constitution, the notion of dignity as protecting the equal and inherent worth of every person, and the absolute right to have one's dignity respected and protected, the court indicates that dignity gives each person a claim to live "as a person."

The High Court of Lahore in Pakistan has been the source of some of the most thoughtful and expansive articulations of constitutionalized dignity in the world. For example, in Hafiz Junaid Mahmood v. Government of Punjab, the court noted that "right to life and right to dignity are the epicentres of our constitutional architecture."[42]

The same court has also written about the relationship between the dignity that is protected in the Constitution of Pakistan and Islam. For example, in Dr. Kumail Abbas Rizvi v. Punjab University, a case concerning a teacher who was terminated after his voluntary resignation was not accepted, the court noted the "fundamental right of the Petitioner to be treated by the Respondent with dignity."[43]

In Ameen Masih v. Federation of Pakistan, the same court held that Christians in Pakistan have the same divorce rights as Christians in Christian-dominated countries because "human dignity dictates that the state must create a system of laws that recognises the right of every person to create a familial relationship as he desires ... The dignity of a human being is his free will: the freedom to shape his life and fulfill himself. It is a person's freedom to write his life story."[44]

Then, in the context of protecting the dignity under law of persons with disabilities in the Hafiz Junaid case, the Lahore High Court held that "the right to life and dignity of a person with disabilities can only be realised if the State and its institutions take steps to provide reasonable accommodation that will facilitate and ensure that the person with disabilities can enjoy life with honour and dignity like others in the society."[45] In Barrister Asfandyar Khan v. Government of the Punjab, the same court forbade the government from using the term "disabled," "physically handicapped," and "mentally retarded" because "dignity has its roots in the simple idea that justice consists of the refusal to turn away from suffering ... [It] unites the other human rights into a whole."[46]

In Arshad Mehmood v. the Commissioner of Elections in Pakistan, a case about the dignity implications of the malapportionment of political districts, the Lahore High Court observed that the right to dignity "carries perhaps the most vital of fundamental rights."[47]

40 Zareef v. The State (in both cases), para. 11.
41 Id.
42 PLD 2017 Lahore 1 (the "Hafiz Junaid" case), at 18–19, para. 19.
43 PLC (CS) 2017 Lahore 569 (the "Kumail Abbas" case), at 575, para. 8.
44 PLD 2017 Lahore 610 at 636, para. 41.
45 Hafiz Junaid Mahmood v. Government of Punjab, PLD 2017 Lahore 1, at 19, para. 19.
46 PLD 2018 Lahore 300, at 313, para. 13, quoting Aharon Barak, *The Judge in a Democracy* (2008), 85–86.
47 PLD 2014 Lahore 221, at 253, para. 28.

This right includes the right to live in a healthy environment and in a stable climate. For instance, in D. G. Khan Cement Co. v. Government of Punjab, the Supreme Court upheld the denial of a permit to expand a cement factory into an ecologically fragile area finding an alignment with the government's environmental and dignity-based social obligations:

> In the facts of the case, the Provincial Government was obliged to take a precautionary approach and act in-line with the principle of *in dubio pro natura*, till, inter alia, a detailed hydrogeological study assessing the potential of groundwater resources for industrial purposes of the project area is carried out. This approach is also constitutionally compliant as the courts are to protect the fundamental rights of the public and in this case right to life, sustainability and dignity of the community surrounding the project remains paramount till such time that the Government is of the view that the project has no adverse environmental effects.[48]

We further examine the relationship between human dignity and environmental quality in Section 5.3.

5.3 DIGNITY AND THE ENVIRONMENT

The link between human dignity and environmental outcomes has been subject to increasing attention in recent years.[49] Simply, when there is a violation of an environmental right, the effect is experienced as a deprivation of human dignity.[50]

International law has taken some small but significant steps to acknowledge that the right to human dignity embeds a right to live in a quality environment. The Stockholm Declaration in 1972 first noted that people should enjoy the "fundamental right to freedom, equality, and adequate conditions of life, in an environment of quality that permits a life of dignity and well-being."[51] In 1989, the Hague Declaration expressly acknowledged "the right to live in dignity in a viable global environment."[52] Then, the first Special Rapporteur on a Right to a Healthy Environment concluded in 1994:

> Environmental damage has direct effects on the enjoyment of a series of human rights, such as the right to life, to health, to a satisfactory standard of living, to sufficient food, to housing, to education, to work, to culture, to non-discrimination, to dignity and the harmonious development of one's personality, to security of person and family, to development, to peace, etc.[53]

In recent years, the UN's 2015 Sustainable Development Goals (SDGs) come closest to recognizing the link between human dignity and the environment.[54] The sustainability framework features seventeen goals to be achieved by 2030, including protecting biodiversity,

[48] C.P.1290-L/2019, at para. 16.

[49] Erin Daly and James May, Exploring Environmental Justice through the Lens of Human Dignity, 25 *Widener Law Review* 167 (2019).

[50] Erin Daly and James May, Bridging Constitutional Dignity and Environmental Rights Jurisprudence, 7 *Journal of Human Rights and the Environment* 218 (2016).

[51] UN Environment Programme (UNEP), Declaration of the United Nations Conference on the Human Environment (1972) ("the Stockholm Declaration").

[52] Hague Declaration on the Environment, 28 *International Legal Materials* 1308 (1989), reprinted in Selected International Legal Materials for Global Warming, 5 *American University Journal of International Law and Polity* 513, 567 (1990).

[53] Fatima Zohra Ksentini (Special Rapporteur) through UN Commission on Human Rights, *Human Rights and the Environment: Final Report*, 248 (U.N. Doc. E/CN.4/Sub.2/1994/9, 1994).

[54] See UN Sustainable Development Goals, adopted by all UN member states in 2015, https://sustainabledevelopment.un.org/?menu=1300.

ensuring clean water, air, land, and food, ending poverty, hunger, and discrimination, and providing access to justice and opportunity for the future.[55] Dignity is the thread that stitches these SDGs together, reflected in the SDGs' core provisions, which carry the word dignity several times in connection with the ideas of sustainability and environmental protection.[56]

In addition, the UN Special Rapporteur on Human Rights and the Environment determined:

> Human rights are grounded in respect for fundamental human attributes such as dignity, equality and liberty. The realisation of these attributes depends on an environment that allows them to flourish ... Human rights and environmental protection are inherently interdependent.[57]

These developments suggest that inexorably, if belatedly, international law recognizes the relationship between human dignity and environmental rights,[58] including in 2021 by the UN Human Rights Committee,[59] and in 2022 by the UN General Assembly.[60]

Yet, at the domestic level, linking dignity and environmental outcomes has been more sporadic. Only Belgium's constitution expressly entwines environmental and dignity rights textually: "Everyone has the right to lead a life worthy of human dignity ... [including] the right to enjoy the protection of a healthy environment."[61] Still, a few courts have recognized the relationship between human dignity and environmental conditions. For instance, in a case involving illegal mining in a Colombian river, the Colombian Constitutional Tribunal stressed that "this situation has multiple harmful effects since, for example, it threatens the food security of the ethnic communities ... and violates the fundamental rights to a healthy environment, to life, human dignity, health, water, territory and culture."[62]

It is in the constitutional domain that the most important and effective work can be done, as illustrated in Section 5.4. In particular, constitutions are more effective than international instruments at articulating local values and integrating a wide range of interests – including all types of rights – into a single holistic and integrated document. Moreover, constitutional courts can enforce these rights and bring them to life in a way that eludes international instruments. This is because courts are open to the population in order to vindicate their rights and interests, and people, usually through media, are able to observe the development of the

55 Id.

56 Id.

57 Human Rights Council, *Report of the Independent Expert on the Issue of Human Rights Obligations Relating to the Enjoyment of a Safe, Clean, Healthy and Sustainable Environment*, December 24, 2012, U.N. Doc. A/HR/22/43. See also Daniel J. Whelan, *Indivisible Human Rights: A History* (2010); Erin Daly, *Environmental Human Rights: Paradigm of Indivisibility*, unpublished paper (2011), https://works.bepress.com/erin_daly/24/: "The constitutional right to a healthy environment is perhaps the paradigmatic example of the indivisibility claim. Environmental rights are inseparable from many other rights, including (depending on the factual nature of the claim) the right to life, to health, to dignity, to subsistence, to employment, to property and so on."

58 Daly and May, Bridging Constitutional Dignity; D. Lupin Townsend, The Place of Human Dignity in Environmental Adjudication, 3 *Oslo Law Review* 27 (2016); Erin Daly and James May, Environmental Dignity Rights, in *Encyclopedia of Human Rights and the Environment: Legality, Indivisibility, Dignity, and Geography* (James May and Erin Daly, eds., 2019); Daly and May, Exploring Environmental Justice; Tiwajopelo O. Dayo, Environmental Dignity Rights in Nigeria, 25 *Widener Law Review* 183 (2019); Erin Daly and James May, Environmental Dignity Rights, in *The Effectiveness of Environmental Law* (Sandrine Maljean-Dubois, ed., 2017).

59 A/HRC/RES/48/13 (October 8, 2021).

60 The Human Right to a Clean, Healthy and Sustainable Environment, United Nations General Assembly, A/RES/76/300 (August 1, 2022).

61 The Constitution of the Kingdom of Belgium, Title II, Art. 23(4).

62 Judgment T-622/16 (The Atrato River Case), Constitutional Court of Colombia 2016 (translation by Erin Daly, James R. May, and Thomas Swan, in consultation with Hugo Echeverria), https://tinyurl.com/439u3v5r.

domestic law. Additionally, constitutions have more impact than any law or set of regulations because they have this character as both law and instantiation of national values; people are therefore more likely to know about and be mindful of what constitutions say, either explicitly or through their expositors.

It is here that courts in Pakistan have taken the lead. As mentioned, Pakistan's constitution does not say a word about the environment, or a right to a healthy environment, clean water, or a stable climate. Yet, it is cases out of Pakistan that put the country's constitutional right to human dignity[63] into service for the environment.

5.4 DIGNITY AND THE ENVIRONMENT AND PAKISTAN

While Pakistan lacks any textually explicit constitutional environmental rights, including the right to climate protection, water, or a healthy environment, it has been in the vanguard of juridical use of a right to dignity as a basis for hearing claims and requiring action to improve environmental conditions. This reflects an emerging global trend of the judicial recognition of the impact that environmental degradation has on human dignity.

In the landmark case of Ms. Shehla Zia et al. v. WAPDA,[64] the Supreme Court of Pakistan expanded the fundamental rights to life and dignity by interpreting these rights to incorporate a right to a healthy environment. Residents petitioned the Supreme Court to challenge the Water and Power Development Authority's (WAPDA) plan to build a powerplant, concerned that the electromagnetic hazards associated with the construction of an electrical grid station would pose a health risk. The court held that risks violated the fundamental right to life and and to dignity which include a right to a healthy environment. Even though the court determined the scientific evidence inconclusive, it applied the precautionary principle, whereby the lack of full scientific certainty should not be used as a reason to prevent environmental degradation.[65]

The court issued a novel remedy. Instead of enjoining the project, the court in Zia ordered a review and report of the grid project by the National Engineering Services of Pakistan (NESPAK) to suggest alterations and location alternatives and directed the government of Pakistan to establish a commission of internationally known and recognized scientists to review and rule on future grid station projects. "In the problem at hand the likelihood of any hazard to life by magnetic field effect cannot be ignored. At the same time the need for constructing grid stations which are necessary for industrial and economic development cannot be lost sight of," the court explained.[66] Because the government had proceeded without any attention to the hazards the grid might cause to human health, the court appointed "NESPAK as Commissioner to examine and study the scheme, planning, device and technique employed by [the government] and report whether there is any likelihood of any hazard or adverse effect on health of the

[63] Constitution of Pakistan, Art. 14(1): "The dignity of man and, subject to law, the privacy of home, shall be inviolable"; Art. 11: "no compulsory service shall be of a cruel nature or incompatible with human dignity."

[64] PLD 1994 Supreme Court 693.

[65] See also Muhammad Ayaz v. Government of Punjab through Its Chief Secretary & Others (High Court of Lahore, 2017), in which the court upheld the Punjab Environmental Protection Agency's (EPA) decision to seal a steelworks factory that was noncompliant with an environmental protection order and was causing air and noise pollution. The court noted that the EPA's legislative authority to take this action was based on the precautionary principle. Cognizant of the growth of jurisprudence on the establishment of environmental justice in Pakistan, the court considered it necessary to ensure that enforcement mechanisms responded swiftly, especially where public safety, public health, and the environment must be protected from irreparable harm.

[66] Id.

residents of the locality."[67] The court also ordered the government to submit all the relevant information to NESPAK and to issue public notices and invite objections (orally or in writing) prior to installing or constructing any grid station or transmission line. In addition, the court ordered WAPDA to allow public consultation and objection procedures for all projects concerning grid stations and power lines.

The Supreme Court of Pakistan has also held that environmental rights are embedded in the constitutional right to life. In re Human Rights Case (Environmental Pollution in Balochistan), for example, the court took judicial notice of a newspaper report that "business tycoons are making attempts to purchase coastal area of Balochistan and convert it into dumping ground" for nuclear and highly hazardous waste. Finding this violates the right to life, the court ordered the agency charged with implementing environmental laws in the area to monitor land allocations in the affected area and forbid such use because "to dump waste materials including nuclear waste from the developed countries would not only be [a] hazard to the health of the people but also to the environment and the marine life in the region."[68] The court also suggested that the responsible authorities "should insert a condition in the allotment letter/license/lease that the allottee/tenant shall not use the land for dumping, treating, burying or destroying by any device waste of any nature including industrial or nuclear waste in any form."[69]

Likewise, in West Pakistan Salt Miners v. Industries and Mineral Development, Punjab, Lahore, the court upheld a claim that the right to life included a right to water free from contamination from mining activities: "the right to have unpolluted water is the right of every person wherever he lives."[70]

Under the leadership of former Justice Syed Mansoor Ali Shah, lower courts in Pakistan have gone even further in rooting environmental protection and environmental justice in the weft of the constitutional fabric. In a case involving the legality of the Lahore Development Authority's review process of an environmental impact assessment, the court explained that "protection of the environment is, therefore, an inalienable right and perhaps more fundamental than the other rights. It emerges from the right to life, liberty and dignity under Articles 9 & 14 of the Constitution."[71] Explaining that it was "moving on" from its initial analysis in the Shehla Zia case, the court elaborated:

> To us, environmental justice is an amalgam of the constitutional principles of democracy, equality, social, economic and political justice guaranteed under our Objectives Resolution, the fundamental right to life, liberty and human dignity (article 14) which include the international environmental principles of sustainable development, precautionary principle, environmental impact assessment, inter and intra-generational equity and public trust doctrine. Environment and its protection has come to take center stage in the scheme of constitutional rights. Right to environment that is not harmful to the health or well-being of the people and an environment that protects the present and future generations is an essential part of political and social justice and even more integral to the right to life and dignity under our Constitution.[72]

67 Id.

68 In re Human Rights Case (Environmental Pollution in Balochistan) PLD 1994 Supreme Court 102.

69 Id.

70 West Pakistan Salt Miners v. Industries and Mineral Development, Punjab, Lahore 1994 SCMR 2061.

71 Tiwana v. Government of Punjab, Lahore W.P. No.7955/2015, at 36. See also Muhammad Tariq Abbasi and Others v. Defence Housing Authority and Others, 2007 CLC 1358, expanding the public trust doctrine to include rights of public access, discussed in Muhammad Wajid Munir, Putting Public Trust Doctrine to Work: A Study of Judicial Intervention in Environmental Justice, *SSRN* (July 17, 2018), https://papers.ssrn.com/sol3/papers.cfm?abstract_id=3203467.

72 Id., at 37.

The court ultimately set aside the EIA approval as being "violative of the right to life, dignity of the citizenry besides offensive to environmental justice and due process protected under Articles 4 and 10A of the Constitution."[73] It is precisely because environmental and social justice are so deeply embedded in the human rights provisions of the Pakistan constitution that public interest litigation may be so broadly accepted by the judiciary, particularly in environmental cases.[74]

The climate crisis provides a vivid example of the relationship between environmental conditions and human dignity. Climate change "directly and indirectly implicates" important human rights and responsibilities because it "connects the many dangerous climate impacts to the human rights commitments states have already undertaken."[75] Hence, a right to human dignity can be especially important in ascertaining whether, and to what extent, climate change diminishes the human right to a quality environment. Catastrophic climate events implicate "rights to life, dignity, and personal security – core civil and political rights."[76] Drought and desertification, for example, endanger food security, the lack of which diminishes dignity.[77] People living on small island nations are particularly vulnerable to climate change impacts[78] and climate change may well turn entire populations into refugees, raising human rights issues to a new level.[79] Under some circumstances, such impacts can be litigated as constitutional rights cases involving the right to dignity.

Some courts are beginning to appreciate the linkages between human dignity and environmental outcomes, especially regarding access to potable water and the climate crisis, with courts in Pakistan leading the way. In the pioneering ruling, Ashgar Leghari v. Federation of Pakistan, a farmer argued that the government's climate policies violated his rights to life and dignity protected by the Constitution of Pakistan. The Lahore High Court invoked continuing mandamus jurisdiction following a 2015 decision to require the government to implement climate change mitigation and adaptation plans to fulfill a constitutional right to life and dignity. The court reviewed at some length the threats of climate change in Pakistan, considering its effects on water resources as well as forestry and agriculture, among other things, but found that the commission had been the driving force in sensitizing the governments and other stakeholders regarding the gravity and importance of climate change, and had accomplished 66 percent of the goals assigned to it. The Climate Change Commission (CCC) was established by the Lahore High Court in the Ashgar Leghari case to monitor and oversee the implementation of Pakistan's climate change policies and framework. The court then dissolved the CCC and established a Standing Committee to act, on an ongoing basis, as a link between the court and the executive and to render assistance to the government to further implementation. Here, the

[73] Id., at 56.

[74] Atta Ullah Khan Malik v. Federation of Government of Pakistan, I.C.A No.105/2010 etc. ("Any citizen or person (part of the public) has 'sufficient Interest' and is, therefore, an aggrieved person under article 199 of the Constitution, if public property is being acquired, held, used, or disposed of by public functionaries in violation of the law. Public functionaries, as trustees of the people, cannot have any personal interest in any public property, therefore if there is any abuse of trust or violation of law, it qualifies any member of the general public as an 'aggrieved person' with the right to invoke the constitutional jurisdiction of this court, subject to fulfilling other requirements of article 199.")

[75] Maxine Burkett, A Justice Paradox: On Climate Change, Small Island Developing States, and the Quest for Effective Legal Remedy, 35 *Hawai'i Law Review* 633, 646–47 (2013).

[76] Id.

[77] Graham Frederick Dumas, A Greener Revolution: Using the Right to Food as a Political Weapon against Climate Change, 43 *New York University Journal of International Law and Politics* 107 (2010).

[78] Burkett, A Justice Paradox, 645.

[79] See, e.g., Ioane Teitiota v. New Zealand, CCPR/C/127/D/2728/2016, UN Human Rights Committee (HRC), January 7, 2020.

court recognized the indivisibility of environmental and human rights and the centrality of environmental human rights in the constitutional landscape:

> Fundamental rights, like the right to life (article 9) which includes the right to a healthy and clean environment and right to human dignity (article 14) read with constitutional principles of democracy, equality, social, economic and political justice include within their ambit and commitment, the international environmental principles of sustainable development, precautionary principle, environmental impact assessment, inter and intra-generational equity and public trust doctrine. Environment and its protection has taken a center stage in the scheme of our constitutional rights.[80]

The court also recognized the urgent threats that the global climate situation poses to human beings:

> It appears that we have to move on. The existing environmental jurisprudence has to be fashioned to meet the needs of something more urgent and overpowering i.e., Climate Change. From Environmental Justice, which was largely localized and limited to our own ecosystems and biodiversity, we need to move to Climate Change Justice. Fundamental rights lay at the foundation of these two overlapping justice systems. Right to life, right to human dignity, right to property and right to information under articles 9, 14, 23 and 19A of the Constitution read with the constitutional values of political, economic and social justice provide the necessary judicial toolkit to address and monitor the Government's response to climate change.[81]

The corresponding Pakistani Climate Change Act of 2017 established the Pakistani Climate Change Council, headed by the prime minister, and consisting of the ministers in charge of climate change, finance, agriculture, food security and research, planning, development and reform, petroleum and natural resources, science and technology, water and power, and foreign affairs; the chief ministers of the provinces; ministers in charge of the department of environment in the provinces; thirty other appointed members; chairman of the National Disaster Management Authority; chairman of the Pakistani Climate Change Authority; and the secretary of the division of climate change, who served as the secretary of the council.[82] The 2017 Act gave the Council the authority to

> (a) coordinate and supervise enforcement of the provisions of this Act; (b) monitor implementation of international agreements relating to climate change specified in the Schedule; (c) coordinate, supervise and guide mainstreaming of climate change concerns into decision-making by Federal and Provincial Government's ministries, divisions, departments and agencies so as to create enabling conditions for integrated climate-compatible and climate-resilient development processes in various sectors of the economy; (d) approve and monitor implementation of comprehensive adaptation and mitigation policies, strategies, plans, programmes, projects and other measures formulated by the Authority to meet Pakistan's obligations under international conventions and agreements relating to climate change including in particular the Sustainable Development Goals; (e) monitor implementation of the National Adaptation Plan and its constituent provincial and local adaptation action plans, the National Appropriate Mitigation Action Framework and National Communication submitted to the concerned Secretariat of the United Nations Framework Convention on Climate Change; approve guidelines for the protection and conservation of renewable and non-renewable resources, species,

80 Ashgar Leghari v. Federation of Pakistan.
81 Id.
82 Pakistan Climate Change Act of 2017, https://tinyurl.com/2bkpts5n.

> habitats, and biodiversity in general adversely affected or threatened by climate change; and (f) consider the National Climate Change Report and give appropriate directions thereon: The Act also establishes the Pakistan Climate Change Authority.[83]

These developments have induced various responses from the government to promote climate mitigation and adaptation. In 2019, the Pakistan Ministry of Climate Change and Environmental Coordination (MOCC) issued the "Ten Billion Trees Tsunami Project," which set out to plant ten billion trees by 2023.[84] In 2020 the government launched the "Protected Areas Initiative," which aimed to increase protected areas such as national parks, wetlands, and wildlife reserves to 15 percent of the country's total area by 2023.[85] The National Climate Change Policy (NCCP) is Pakistan's primary policy framework for addressing climate change. In 2021, Pakistan updated the NCCP to steer Pakistan toward more climate-appropriate development, including integrating climate change policy with other interrelated national policies, building climate-resilient infrastructure, and implementing the SDGs.[86]

Developments in Pakistan have both been inspired by and have inspired global juridical recognition of the linkage between human dignity and environmental outcomes. For example, Kenya's Environmental and Land Court recently acknowledged that environmental rights are part and parcel to a right to human dignity:[87]

> The Preamble to the Constitution ... proclaims that the people of Kenya, when making the Constitution were committed to nurturing and protecting the well-being of the individual, the family, communities and the nation. Likewise, the national values and principles that bind this Court ... include human dignity, equity, social justice, human rights, non-discrimination, protection of the marginalised and sustainable development.[88]

Decisions like this are hardly outliers.[89]

Similarly, in Gbemre v. Shell Petroleum Development Company Nigeria Limited and Others,[90] a Nigerian court held that gas flaring violated the petitioners' constitutional "right to respect for their lives and dignity of their persons and to enjoy the best attainable state of physical and mental health as well as [the] right to a general satisfactory environment

83 Id., https://mocc.gov.pk/.

84 See Ten Billion Trees Tsunami Programme, Pakistan Ministry of Climate Change and Environmental Coordination, https://tinyurl.com/5n942z6e.

85 See "Pakistan's Protected Areas Initiative," *IUCN* (July 13, 2020), www.iucn.org/news/pakistan/202007/pakistans-protected-areas-initiative.

86 Updated National Climate Change Policy (NCCP) 2021, LEAP, https://tinyurl.com/8bmvk5ex. Further developments from MOCC are available at www.mocc.gov.pk/Policies.

87 The Constitution of Kenya, 2010, Art. 10(2)(b) and (2)(d)

88 Friends of Lake Turkana Trust v. Attorney General & 2 Others [2014] eKLR, in the Environment and Land Court at Nairobi ELC Suit No. 825 of 2012 (finding insufficient evidence of actual violations of the right to dignity, life, livelihood and cultural and environmental heritage by the Gibe III hydroelectric project at the planning and implementation stages, but finding that the risks "that the harnessing of such electricity in Ethiopia is likely to affect its right to life and a livelihood and its cultural and environmental heritage ... imposes a positive duty upon the Respondents and Interested Party to provide the Petitioner with the all relevant information in relation to importation and/or purchase and transmission of electric power from Ethiopia").

89 See, e.g., Abu Masad v. Water Commissioner, Israel Supreme Court, 2011 (finding that right to dignity requires government to provide some water to Bedouin community).

90 Gbemre v. Shell Petroleum Dev Corp & the Nigerian National Petroleum Corporation [2005] 6 AHRLR 152 (Nigeria).

favourable to their development" and that the gas flaring activities formed "a violation of their said fundamental rights to life and dignity of human person and to a healthy life in a healthy environment."[91]

The Nepalese Supreme Court has articulated a similar commitment to environmental dignity:

> Article 12(1) of the Interim Constitution has also incorporated the right to live with dignity under the right to life. It . . . should be understood that all rights necessary for living a dignified life as a human being are included in it. Not only that, it cannot be imagined to live with dignity in a polluted environment[;] rather it may create an adverse situation even exposing human life to dangers.[92]

Yet, it should not take the impending threat of climate change or the threat of severe flooding or drought to prove the interrelatedness of dignity and environmental rights. As the cases from Pakistan and elsewhere show, the concept of human dignity can help us understand how environmental conditions affect the full range of the human experience – from access to water and food, to educational and employment opportunities, to culture and solidarity with others. Weaving all of these human needs together is the idea of human dignity that expresses how we live as individuals and in stable communities with others. Dignity – and the legal rights associated with human dignity – are therefore useful tools in environmental litigation for several reasons.

First, dignity provides a vocabulary for foregrounding the damage *to people* of environmental and climate harms; to see climate change as a dignity harm is to see how it impacts the lives of human beings. Second, it draws attention to how environmental harms affect all of the essential aspects of a person's life; where food security, access to clean water, and breathable air are threatened, a person's ability to design their own life plan is weakened and their ability to live in material comfort is impossible. Thus, it draws attention to *how* people live in their environments and seeks to ameliorate the impacts that adverse environmental conditions have on people's ability to live *as people of worth*. Third, and relatedly, inherent in the concept of human dignity is that the right must be enjoyed at all times by every person on an equal basis, a principle that has particular salience in the context of environmental injustice, which places the burden of environmental destruction disproportionately on vulnerable communities.[93]

Dignity can be useful not only at the stage of identifying violations, but also at the stage of crafting remedies. Environmental cases are among constitutional law's most complicated to remedy because the injuries can be multifaceted, layered, and interdependent; defendants can be recalcitrant and are often among the country's most politically powerful and economically resourceful; and the damage to both humans and their environment can be literally irremediable. In addition, it can be daunting to quantify the damage not only to present but also to future generations. Most courts are keenly aware of the limitations of their own power and of the fact that courts have no particular resources other than their own legitimacy to ensure respect for or compliance with judicial orders.[94]

Just as recourse to the right to dignity can help identify violations, it can also help define remedies: increasingly, courts are pegging remedies to the standards necessary to ensure that people can live with dignity. Dignity-based remedies can be both substantive and procedural.

[91] See James May and T. Dayo, Dignity and Environmental Justice in Nigeria: The Case of Gbemre v. Shell, 25 *Widener Law Review* 183–97 (2019).

[92] Pro Public v. Godavari Marble Industries Pvt. Ltd. and Others (Supreme Court of Nepal, 2015).

[93] Daly & May, Exploring Environmental Justice.

[94] Id., 149.

When the Supreme Court of India ordered the closure of tanneries that had been polluting the River Ganga, it required that the new operation protect the jobs and rights of the displaced workers, including requiring that they be paid during the period of closure and that they be given a substantial "shifting bonus" to help them settle at the new location.[95] Similarly, when landfills were being closed in Colombia, the court took special care to assure the dignity of those individuals whose only means of support had been collecting recyclables from the landfill. The court's extensive remedial order required each affected municipality to, within a few months, adopt necessary measures to protect the recyclers' rights to health, education, dignified living, and food, ensuring in each particular case that the means were connected to specific social programs.[96] And without risking charges of judicial activism, courts could even go further: they could ensure that governmental decisions that impact the environment would be made only on the basis of human dignity, in its various manifestations. After all, the protection of human dignity in present and future generations is arguably how we know how much clean water is needed, what constitutes appropriate environmental safeguards for the extraction of natural resources, or how to advance climate justice.

5.5 CONCLUSION

Human dignity has become the standard by which justice is measured. It is a universal value, equally at home in Islamic republics as in other nations. And, increasingly, courts have recognized the dignity implications of environmental and climate conditions.

We conclude that this is a positive development. As a conceptual matter, attention to human dignity foregrounds the impacts on human beings of environmental decisions, including decisions that contribute to climate change, and requires courts to address the ways in which those decisions diminish the ability of people to manage their own lives, often in ways that disproportionately affect those who are already the most vulnerable and marginalized. Thus, in the context of judicial implementation, attention to dignity can also help shape the contours of environmental human rights by providing a measure of when a violation of an environmental right has occurred. Dignity can also serve as a benchmark for remedies, showing courts the way to ensure that environmental harms are remedied to the extent that they remediate the harms done to the dignity interests of those who are most affected. In recent years, courts, led by those in Pakistan, have increasingly recognized the links between environmental protection and the enjoyment of human rights, including the human right to dignity. One can only hope that these judicial trends continue in Pakistan and are studied carefully elsewhere.

[95] MC Mehta (Calcutta Tanneries' Matter) v. Union of India and Others, Writ Petition (C) No. 3727 of 1985 (1996).
[96] Sentencia T-291/09 (Colombia Constitutional Court, 2009), 9.2.5.

6

Oil and Institutional Stasis in the Persian Gulf

Mehran Kamrava

The debate on whether resource abundance in general, and resource dependence in particular, is a curse or a blessing is an old one. Paradoxically, despite a proliferation of studies on rentierism in the last two decades or so, the specific notion of a "resource curse" has seldom been studied systematically in relation to the Persian Gulf. In this chapter, I introduce some of the broader aspects of the resource curse phenomenon in relation to the evolution of states in the Persian Gulf region. More specifically, I argue that one of the most pronounced consequences of resource abundance and dependence in the region has been a freezing of state institutions – especially those institutions through which political power is exercised – at the moment in which oil revenues began flowing into the coffers of the state.

Across the Arabian Peninsula, oil wealth began accruing to the state at a particular juncture in the state-building process, when traditional, largely informal, patterns of sheikhly rule were relatively well established, but the formal institutional apparatuses of the state were not yet fully formed. Oil wealth had a direct impact on subsequent developments in these two complementary areas. On the one hand, the control and distribution of petrodollars enabled political elites to solidify existing patterns of rule, through deepening clientelist practices, and also by establishing new, dependent clients. On the other hand, rent revenues gave state leaders the opportunity to establish and shape state institutions in ways that solidified their political control. Tribally rooted patron–client practices were superimposed upon and reinforced through an ostensibly modern bureaucratic apparatus. Rent-seeking, clientelism, and patronage dictated the logic of institutional change and evolution.

A combination of rent-seeking and patron–client relations froze some institutions in place, slowed or skewed the change that other institutions might otherwise have experienced, and enabled state leaders to shape the direction and pace at which institutional change occurred. The consequence was neopatrimonialism, which informed, and continues to inform, the institutional makeup and functions of the state and its larger approach towards society. If one adopts the terminology commonly used to refer to the consequences of resource dependence, whatever "curse" has befallen the states of the Arabian Peninsula has been more institutional than economic or developmental.

Before elaborating on these points, a few preliminary remarks about the overall causes and consequences of the resource curse are in order. The chapter then focuses on the specific relationship between resource abundance and the development of state institutions in the Persian Gulf region. In addition to providing a summary of the analysis here, Section 6.4 will offer some thoughts on future directions for research on the topic.

6.1 WHITHER THE RESOURCE CURSE?

An important early observation is that the resource curse is not inevitable and is, in fact, conditional on bad governance.[1] Political institutions in general and fiscal institutions in particular can help turn a resource curse into a blessing.[2] By itself, wealth does not generate lack of financial discipline or pathologies such as corruption or inefficiency. For example, one of the negative side effects of reliance on resources is living off capital rather than income, and relying on revenues from a nonrenewable source. One remedy would be to turn these earnings into financial assets, investing them into a diversified portfolio, and treating the interests accrued as income.[3] As Elbadawi and Soto have argued, "while macroeconomic mismanagement and oil abundance are important determinants of performance, these factors are shaped primarily by the prevailing political institutions, which predate resource discovery."[4] In fact, whether derived from natural resources or through other means, wealth can facilitate the implementation of development strategies, many of which have been ambitiously pursued by the states of the Arabian Peninsula.[5]

There are, of course, a number of economic drawbacks to overreliance on a single commodity – in the case of the Persian Gulf states, oil and gas. The oil monarchies, for example, perform far below their potential.[6] Despite good-faith efforts in literally all regional countries to escape oil dependence, its symptoms can be found in three areas: the state and the macroeconomy still remain vulnerable to oil price volatility; there is massive overemployment and inefficiency in the public sector; and there is low growth in labor productivity.[7] Other pathologies include boom-and-bust cycles, dependence on foreign labor, and "a culture of complacency among many of the Gulf nationals, many of whom could easily find 'work' in government."[8]

Nor have most Gulf Cooperation Council (GCC) countries increased non-oil revenues in any meaningful ways.[9] Oil dependence continues to be the norm across the board, with the possible exception of the Emirate of Dubai, although the degree to which the "Dubai model" can survive without the cushion of oil revenues was put to serious test during the 2008 financial meltdown.[10] The Qatari government, for example, had stated that it hoped to finance the country's budget fully from non-hydrocarbon revenues starting from 2020, a goal that seemed highly unlikely.[11] Invariably, regional states also remain vulnerable to fluctuations in the oil

[1] Elbadawi and Soto, "Resource Rents, Political Institutions and Economic Growth," *Understanding and Avoiding the Oil Curse in Resource-Rich Arab Economies*, ed. Elbadawi and Selim (2016), p. 188.

[2] Schmidt-Hebbel, "Fiscal Institutions in Resource-Rich Economics: Lessons from Chile and Norway," *Understanding and Avoiding the Oil Curse in Resource-Rich Arab Economies*, ed. Elbadawi and Selim (2016), p. 228.

[3] Humphreys, Sachs, and Stiglitz, "Introduction: What Is the Problem with Natural Resource Wealth?," *Escaping the Resource Curse*, ed. Humphreys, Sachs, and Stiglitz (2007), pp. 8–9.

[4] Elbadawi and Selim, "Overview of Context, Issues and Summary," *Understanding and Avoiding the Oil Curse in Resource-Rich Arab Economies*, ed. Elbadawi and Selim (2016), p. 8.

[5] As Jeffrey Sachs points out, a successful development strategy needs to have at least three components: public investments suited to national circumstances; a policy framework that supports private sector economic activity; and a political framework to ensure rule of law and macroeconomic stability. Sachs, "How to Handle the Macroeconomics of Wealth," *Escaping the Resource Curse*, ed. Humphreys, Sachs, and Stiglitz (2007), p. 178.

[6] Ibid., p. 174.

[7] Soto and Haouas, "Has the UAE Escaped the Oil Curse?," *Understanding and Avoiding the Oil Curse in Resource-Rich Arab Economies*, ed. Elbadawi and Selim (2016), p. 373.

[8] Foley, *The Arab Gulf States: Beyond Oil and Islam* (2010), p. 144.

[9] Sommer, et al., *Learning to Live with Cheaper Oil: Policy Adjustments in Oil-Exporting Countries of the Middle East and Central Asia* (2016), p. 18.

[10] Davidson, "The Dubai Model: Diversification and Slowdown," *The Political Economy of the Persian Gulf*, ed. Kamrava (2012), pp. 195–220.

[11] "Qatar: Managing the Limits of Economic Growth," Gulf States Newsletter 37.956 (2013), p. 11.

market. Severe declines in oil prices, especially since 2014, have necessitated deep structural reforms and much needed diversification, as well as fiscal consolidation and adjustments.[12] The effects of lower oil prices are also being compounded by a number of simultaneous developments, including intra- and inter-state conflicts in Iraq, Syria, Yemen, and elsewhere; serious discord among the members states of the Gulf Cooperation Council; the further strengthening of the dollar; slowing growth in China and its spillover effects; and recession in Russia.[13]

Given the rapid economic and infrastructural development of the oil monarchies through their deployment of their massive financial resources, and the concurrent improvements they have fostered in the lives of their citizens, it is difficult to point to oil as a catalyst for an economic resource curse in the region. The primary consequences of oil dependence, in fact, have mostly been institutional and political rather than economic. The Persian Gulf's oil states, for example, have benefited from a certain amount of built-in adaptability and enhanced capacity, which has in turn accorded them greater political resilience over time. The petrostates may be suffering from the institutional consequences of resource dependence, but whatever "development" their institutions may have had so far has been sufficient to allow them to ride out, or fend off altogether, crises of the kind that engulfed many of the other Arab states in 2011. The contrast with other oil states in crisis, for instance Libya, is striking. In 2005, the Libyan government attempted to implement subsidy reforms for foodstuffs and energy that had been in place since the 1970s. Food subsidies varied from 39 percent to 96 percent of the market price, with flour, rice, sugar, and vegetable oil accounting for the bulk of the state's subsidies. Although the elimination of food and energy subsidies could have saved the Libyan state budget the equivalent of about 2 percent, it would have cut household expenditure by about 10 percent and doubled the poverty level.[14] Just before the eruption of the 2011 unrests, the state started to roll back on subsidy reforms, but the measures proved insufficient to stem the tide of the revolution. In the end, despite its best efforts, the state could do little to overcome the cumulative effects of its self-inflicted wounds and to reverse its disintegration.

In the Persian Gulf region, oil may have skewed or impeded changes to political institutions, but it has bestowed on them a certain amount of resilience to withstand or to blunt possibilities for societal pressures for change altogether. It is to an examination of these resource-influenced institutional dynamics that the chapter turns next.

6.2 OIL AND INSTITUTIONAL CHANGE

With the exception of Saudi Arabia, formal independence did not come to the Persian Gulf area until 1961 when Kuwait became independent, and even later, in 1971, to the rest of the region. Ruling families, already firmly entrenched in power, now gained unprecedented access to economic resources that enabled them to forge new forms of clientelism and patronage and to deepen existing ones. Meanwhile, the emerging fiscal structures of the petrostates institutionalized a permanent tendency toward rent-seeking, and perpetuated "traditional concepts of authority as the personal patrimony of the ruler."[15] Rentierism became a potent source of

[12] Sommer et al., *Learning to Live with Cheaper Oil*, p. 7.

[13] Ibid., p. 11.

[14] Araar, Choueiri, and Verme, "The Quest for Subsidy Reform in Libya," The World Bank Policy Group: Research Working Paper 7225 (2015), pp. 3–4.

[15] Karl, *The Paradox of Plenty: Oil Booms and Petro-States* (1997), pp. 62–3. Contrary to what Karl maintains, there is no evidence to suggest that, at least in the Arabian Peninsula, oil abundance "delayed the development of a modern consciousness of 'the state'" (ibid., p. 62). In fact, oil appears to have further facilitated such a consciousness by helping political leaders deepen the state's practical and symbolic presence in people's daily lives.

legitimacy. In other words, oil shaped subsequent patterns of institutional development, but only in the direction of reinforcing preexisting processes and practices.[16] It also allowed the state to develop new agencies, enhanced its extractive capacities and activities, and shaped the behavior and preferences of policymakers.

When the flow of oil rents and the early stages of the state-building process coincide, rents tend to go directly to the state and are not mediated through domestic private actors. At the same time, economic power, and ultimately the political authority of these states, resides in their ability to extract rents externally from the global environment and then to distribute the revenues internally.[17] There are, therefore, multilevel and multidimensional causal relationships between oil and institutional development. In the countries of the Arabian Peninsula, as elsewhere, oil revenues made possible the growth and strength of some institutions and the underdevelopment or total absence of others. For example, state leaders were enabled by the flow of oil revenues to excel at taxing foreign oil corporations instead of making unpopular domestic fiscal decisions. They also became good at monitoring, regulating, and promoting the oil industry, both domestically and internationally, at the expense of the state's ability to develop a coherent, penetrating bureaucracy.[18]

However, successful promotion of the domestic oil industry is far from being the only accomplishment of the Arabian Peninsula's petrostates. In the postindependence era, in particular, oil has also brought them a number of other broad advantages, both institutional and otherwise. To begin with, oil can, at the broadest level, offer three huge benefits to oil-producing states: it can boost real living standards by increasing levels of public and private consumption; it can finance higher levels of investment; and, by developing the public sector, it can facilitate state efforts at fostering development.[19] Natural resources can also enhance the state's ability to deliver public goods. In fact, oil-rich states tend to outperform their non-oil neighbors in terms of private consumption and higher levels of well-being, as seen in decreased child mortality and increased life expectancy, paved roads, and per capita electricity. The large income generated by oil enables the state to develop capacities that states without oil do not have – for example, alleviating poverty, becoming bureaucratically expansive, and hiding the extent of their income.[20] Moreover, although rent revenues may foster institutional underdevelopment in certain instances, they are also likely to stimulate state capacity, market capitalism, and industrialization.

We will explore how, in the context of the Arab petrostates, as in the larger Middle East, rent revenues have undermined rather than enhanced prospects for democracy. But it is hard to deny that rent has also been instrumental in stimulating state capacity, economic growth, and, broadly defined, development. In other words, whether and to what extent rent revenues become a "blessing" or a "curse," depends both on context and on different institutional arenas. There are undoubtedly numerous deleterious economic, political, and institutional consequences of natural resources abundance and the overwhelming reliance on rent revenues accrued from them. But in the strict sense of the term, oil in itself has not been an economic curse.[21] Oil and minerals actually have a positive effect on development. It is not a *resource* curse that causes

[16] For an accessible history of oil in the Persian Gulf region, see Askari, *Collaborative Colonialism: The Political Economy of Oil in the Persian Gulf* (2013).
[17] Karl, *The Paradox of Plenty*, p. 49.
[18] Ibid., p. 61.
[19] Sachs, "How to Handle the Macroeconomics of Wealth," *Escaping the Resource Curse*, ed. Humphreys, Sachs, and Stiglitz (2007), pp. 174–75.
[20] Ross, *The Oil Curse: How Petroleum Wealth Shapes the Development of Nations* (2012), p. 225.
[21] Ibid., p. 196.

underdevelopment but an *institutions* curse. States are cursed not by their resources but by their institutions. The economic dependence on natural resources, and the pathologies attributed to it, are caused by weak state capacity, low-quality institutions, and policies pursued by state leaders.[22]

States with weak or inadequate institutions have a hard time imposing and collecting taxes, attracting foreign investments, and otherwise raising revenues. Thus their dependence on revenues from natural resources is all the more pronounced.[23] Moreover, since states with low-quality institutions cannot create vibrant and diversified economies, natural resources enable them to enjoy the benefits of substantial revenues.[24] In the Arabian Peninsula, albeit under British protection, patterns of rule with tribally rooted systems of patronage and clientelism were already robustly in place before the advent of the oil era. Once rent revenues started flowing into the state, they strengthened rather than altered these patterns, and in the process they also enhanced the autonomy of state leaders.

The key variable is the timing of institutional development in relation to the flow of rent revenues. State leaders can employ rent revenues to strengthen those preexisting institutions on which they rely, and from which they derive their legitimacy. In the Arabian Peninsula, these are the same institutions that perpetuated patronage and clientelism. In Norway and Canada, where democratic institutions were already in place when oil production began, oil enhanced the state's economic performance and helped deepen the state's democratic legitimacy.[25] In Chile, where strong financial institutions predated the flow of rents into the economy, what could have been a resource curse was turned into a resource blessing.[26] Some scholars have argued that the political institutions found in the Arab world before the discovery of oil were weak, and that the effects of this weak institutional setup from the pre-oil era have lingered on.[27] Weakness is relative; in the Arabian Peninsula, those institutions from which states emerged – the family, tribal practices and confederations, patronage, and the like – were actually quite strong in relation to the communities over which they began to rule, and subsequently their strength was only enhanced as a result of oil revenues.

Reliance on natural resources wealth does, of course, lead to various negative economic side effects. In the case of oil, there is often unequal expertise between the state and the international oil companies (IOCs), and the latter frequently have leverage over state leaders in terms of information, resources, and access to global markets. There have also been numerous examples of corporations cheating states out of the terms of their contracts, both large and small,[28] and there is also market volatility and unsteadiness of income. Three specific developments can lead to the volatility of income: variations over time in the rates of oil exportation; fluctuations in the value of natural resources; and variability in the timing of payments by the corporations to the

22 Menaldo, *The Institutions Curse: Natural Resources, Politics, and Development* (2016), p. 11. Menaldo is adamant that "there is no resource curse and oil is not the devil's excrement." Indeed, there is ample evidence that "natural resources wealth improves infrastructure, investments, living standards, helps improve the quality of political and economic institutions, strengthening the state, democracy, and the rule of law" (ibid., p. 3). While there is much to be said about the blessings of resource abundance, linking it to democracy and the rule of law may be somewhat of an analytical stretch.

23 Ibid., p. 18.

24 Ibid., p. 11.

25 Ross, *The Oil Curse*, p. 234.

26 Schmidt-Hebbel, "Fiscal Institutions in Resource-Rich Economies," p. 225.

27 Elbadawi and Selim, "Overview of Context, Issues and Summary," p. 3.

28 Stiglitz, "What Is the Role of the State?," *Escaping the Resource Curse*, ed. Humphreys, Sachs, and Stiglitz (2007), p. 25.

states.[29] Resource-dependent states can also be turned into "honey pots" that can be raided by all sorts of domestic and foreign actors,[30] while most states that rely on natural resources income tend to suffer from higher rates of corruption and underinvestment in education.[31] And, as other countries learned the hard way when their natural resources ran out, oil income can easily be used for short-term consumption instead of for longer-term growth and focused investment.[32]

Dependence on single commodity exports shapes classes, regime types, state institutions, decision-making bodies, and policy.[33] It is also likely to spark off what is known as Dutch Disease: this refers to the condition in which favorable changes in one sector of the economy, such as in the oil sector, cause distortions in other sectors, like agriculture. Income from the export of a natural resource often makes exports from nonnatural commodities more difficult and more expensive, especially in the manufacturing and agriculture sectors. When revenues accrued from natural resources are used for consumption, as they are in the states that make up the GCC, Dutch Disease is a likely outcome.[34] In cases where Dutch Disease has set in, when the market for natural resources slows down, other sectors may find it hard to recover.[35]

In the Arab petrostates, Dutch Disease has manifested itself in declining shares of tradable services, bloated bureaucracies, and a falling off in agriculture and manufacturing. In the Arab economies, in addition to a general neglect of the agricultural sector, rents from natural resources have led to a diminishing share of services, agriculture, and manufacturing in relation to GDP.[36] In resource-rich Arab countries, it is mostly the domestic production of non-tradable services, such as hotels, restaurants, and real estate, that has grown.[37] This is representative of the rest of the Arab world, where the bulk of the services sector is comprised of travel and transport industries (some 78 percent in 2008).[38]

6.3 POLITICAL ECONOMY OF INSTITUTIONAL STASIS

In addition to its economic consequences, rent-seeking behavior tends to be self-reinforcing and deepens path dependence, thereby impeding institutional change. This occurs especially during periods of economic boom, when rent revenues are at their height. In oil economies, such boom effects exacerbate petrolization, reinforcing public and private oil-based interests. Political stasis, as will shortly be seen, is also a likely outcome. In rentier states, rulers often maintain support by distributing rent revenues to allies, friends, relatives, and supporters. As one observer has noted,

[29] Humphreys, Sachs, and Stiglitz, "Introduction," pp. 5–6.

[30] Karl, "Ensuring Fairness: The Case for a Transparent Social Contract," *Escaping the Resource Curse*, ed. Humphreys, Sachs, and Stiglitz (2007), p. 257.

[31] Humphreys, Sachs, and Stiglitz, "Introduction," p. 10.

[32] Sachs, "How to Handle the Macroeconomics of Wealth," p. 173. Perhaps the most extreme example of a resource-dependent country in which overconsumption led to depletion of the resource on which the economy depended is that of Nauru, where the once prosperous Pacific island nation was on the brink of becoming a failed state following the collapse of the country's phosphate industry. See Connell, "Nauru: The First Failed Pacific State?," The Round Table 95.383 (2006), pp. 47–63.

[33] Karl, *The Paradox of Plenty*, p. 7.

[34] Sachs, "How to Handle the Macroeconomics of Wealth," p. 185.

[35] Dutch Disease can be overcome, or at least lessened, by properly investing oil proceeds as part of a national development strategy. Oil income should be turned into public investment rather than private consumption. Sachs, "How to Handle the Macroeconomics of Wealth," pp. 176–77, 184.

[36] Diop and de Melo, "Dutch Disease in the Services Sector: Evidence from Oil Exporters in the Arab Region," *Understanding and Avoiding the Oil Curse in Resource-Rich Arab Economies*, ed. Elbadawi and Selim (2016), p. 100; Elbadawi and Selim, "Overview of Context, Issues and Summary," p. 6.

[37] Diop and de Melo, "Dutch Disease in the Services Sector," p. 100.

[38] In South Asia, by contrast, it is the ICT and finance industries that predominate in the sector. Ibid., p. 85.

during the first oil boom in the 1970s, oil wealth created an "irrational and symbolic universe" that fostered "societal autism" and helped keep authoritarian systems in place in Algeria, Libya, Iran, and the Arabian Peninsula.[39] Poorer states in particular are more likely to engage in oil exploration and to market it aggressively, as much for political reasons as out of economic necessity.[40]

Reliance on natural resources tends to have negative consequences for institutional and political dynamism. Dependence on oil is particularly harmful to the emergence of accountable, politically representative government. Michael Ross sees oil as a curse, because "the revenues it bestows on governments are unusually large, do not come from taxation, fluctuate unpredictably, and can be easily hidden."[41] It is little wonder that petrostates are burdened with a host of difficulties in governance. They often suffer from an information deficit, in the form of lack of feedback mechanisms from citizens to policymakers. In addition, they repeatedly have multiple incentives to develop or employ regulations, and therefore possess the inherent potential for overcentralization of power. Finally, they frequently feature few, or ineffective, institutional means of connection between citizens and state leaders.[42]

Oil states also tend to spend far more than comparable non-oil states on their military, and are more likely to be involved in conflicts.[43] For instance, in most GCC states, military spending constitutes a higher percentage of GDP than the world average.[44] Since the early 1990s, oil-producing countries have also been about 50 percent more likely to have civil wars.[45]

Additionally, oil states are more likely to be ruled by autocrats, and very seldom do such states report their revenues from oil – for them, political secrecy tends to be the norm rather than the exception. All too frequently, this enables state leaders to divert oil revenues for their own, often corrupt, purposes, lining their own pockets and engaging in cronyism.[46]

Oil abundance can be particularly detrimental to the prospects of democratization. The relationship between oil and democracy is context-specific; if nondemocratic institutions are already in place by the time oil production begins, then changing and democratizing them becomes more difficult. But, as the examples of Canada, the US, and Norway demonstrate, oil on its own does not undermine democratic institutions and practices *if* they are already in place prior to oil's introduction into the economy.

Oil abundance can undermine prospects for democratization through two, interrelated ways. First, oil can impede the emergence of social forces that are likely to press for political participation and accountability. Natural resource extraction can take place without the participation of large segments of the labor force, is often independent of other developments in the economy, and encourages rent-seeking behavior.[47] What has undermined democracy, especially in the Middle East, is not so much the revenues derived from oil, but rather the ways in which oil was discovered and oil pipelines were built, the way oil was transported, and the manner in

39 Martinez, *The Violence of Petro-Dollar Regimes: Algeria, Iraq and Libya*, trans. Schoch (2012), p. 41.

40 Menaldo, *The Institutions Curse*, p. 12.

41 Ross, *The Oil Curse*, p. 6.

42 Karl, "Ensuring Fairness," pp. 264–65.

43 Humphreys, Sachs, and Stiglitz, "Introduction," p. 13.

44 Jarzabek, "G.C.C. Military Spending in Era of Low Oil Prices," *MEI Policy Focus 2016–19* (2016), p. 4. In 2016, Saudi Arabia's total defense budget was estimated at $82 billion and was set to rise to $87 billion in 2020, and the UAE's was set at $15.1 billion in 2016 and estimated to reach $17 billion in 2020. Carvalho, "Gulf States to Maintain Defense Spending Despite Oil Price Slump," *Reuters*, February 18, 2017.

45 Ross, *The Oil Curse*, p. 145.

46 Ibid., p. 59.

47 Humphreys, Sachs, and Stiglitz, "Introduction," p. 4.

which its exports and sales were financed.[48] The developments that followed from the production of oil in the Middle East weakened rather than strengthened various forms of political participation. International oil companies collaborated amongst themselves to delay the emergence of an indigenous oil industry in the Middle East, while state leaders saw the control of oil facilitated by overseas interests as an effective means of weakening democratic forces at home.[49]

Once in place, petrostates tend to have oil-based social forces that have a strong vested interest in perpetuating oil-led development. Therefore, any decision by the authorities to build an alternative fiscal base through taxation is very much resisted by the middle classes and the private sector.[50] Timothy Mitchell observes that, whereas the age of coal facilitated the birth of democracy by making political mobilization possible, the birth of oil, and the ways in which the global oil industry has grown, has limited possibilities for the emergence of democracy.[51]

Another reason for the inverse relationship between oil abundance and lowered prospects for democratization lies in the enhanced autonomy of state actors. Natural resources are likely to undermine democracy through lessening the government's need for accountability to the citizenry. As unearned income, rent revenues make it more difficult for citizens to mobilize and press the state for accountability. Low taxation as a percentage of total state revenues tends to reduce the incentive for public scrutiny of the government.[52] Rulers, and especially autocrats, remain in power when citizens believe that governments are delivering benefits relative to their revenues. Since oil revenues are easier to hide, autocrats can boost their popularity by concealing portions of their oil revenues from the public.[53] At the same time, oil revenues also enable states to invest in and enhance their coercive capacities.[54]

Of course, oil wealth does not necessarily stop democratization; it just makes it more difficult. The example of Kuwait, no matter how imperfect its parliamentary system may be, shows that rents do not necessarily make it impossible to constrain the state through representative institutions.[55] However, as Michael Ross observes, "the more oil that an authoritarian government produces, the less likely it will make the journey to democracy."[56]

Even in its most extreme forms, rentierism does not altogether eliminate the possibilities of discontent. Those who are recipients of direct rent transfers often assume they could do better, and the assumption that people can always be bought off politically for the right price has not proved to be universally true.[57] Nevertheless, rent revenues do strengthen state institutions and, more importantly, freeze their development at the stage in which the revenues begin flowing into the coffers of the state. At the very least, such revenues cause the pace at which state institutions change and develop to slow down considerably. In other words, in the case of the Persian Gulf monarchies oil has fostered institutional stasis.

48 Mitchell, *Carbon Democracy: Political Power in the Age of Oil* (2011), p. 253.
49 Ibid., p. 8.
50 Karl, *The Paradox of Plenty*, p. 54.
51 Mitchell, *Carbon Democracy*, p. 254.
52 Schmidt-Hebbel, "Fiscal Institutions in Resource-rich Economies," p. 227.
53 Ross, *The Oil Curse*, p. 71.
54 Humphreys, Sachs, and Stiglitz, "Introduction," pp. 12–13. Luis Martinez makes a related argument, maintaining that control over oil revenues enabled former colonies – beset by "a deep sentiment of revenge against the former colonial powers" – to vent their bitterness on their neighboring states, such as Kuwait and Iran in Iraq's case, Morocco in Algeria's case, and Chad in Libya's case. Martinez, *The Violence of Petro-Dollar Regimes*, p. 42. Warfare, and more broadly the "rally around the flag" effect, make demands for democratization more difficult.
55 Herb, *Wages of Oil: Parliaments and Economic Development in Kuwait and the UAE* (2014), p. 192.
56 Ross, *The Oil Curse*, pp. 65–66.
57 Kamrava, *Inside the Arab State* (2018), pp. 166–70.

6.4 CONCLUSION

On their own, natural resource endowments are a blessing and not a curse. What turns this blessing into a curse is the ways in which it is managed or, more accurately, mismanaged. For some time, policymakers have known the nature of the remedies for dealing with the resource curse: minimizing the risks of Dutch Disease; instituting policies that enhance growth in short to medium terms; promoting good governance and reducing corruption; preparing for the depletion of oil resource income; and regularly assessing the appropriate policy mix.[58] Long-term savings plans, in the form of investments by sovereign wealth funds, can also help alleviate some of the pitfalls of dependence on and depletion of natural recourses.[59] Of these policy options, the GCC states have already made good use of their sovereign wealth funds and, with varying degrees of conviction and success, they have slowly begun to diversify their economies. But on most other scores, including economic diversification, the political will and the capacity to make difficult decisions seem to be conspicuously absent.

Wealth on its own does not buy state capacity. The capacity that the petrostates have so far enjoyed is rooted in other complementary phenomena, such as state evolutionary patterns and state–society linkages. But whether these on their own, without the additional element of oil-driven patronage, are sufficient to enable the Gulf states to operate as they have been in the past, without substantial changes to their actual institutional setup, is an open question. Within the region, state leaders and opinion makers frequently talk of the need to be prepared for the inevitable arrival of the post-oil era. With the notable exception of Dubai, little of this talk has so far been translated into reality. How readily the rest of the region can adapt and adopt the Dubai model, and whether by doing so this will impede or expedite the need for other political changes, is a question that only time can answer.

There are, to state the obvious, differences among Gulf states in terms of patterns of state-building, social cohesion, rent-driven policies, the relationship between ruling families and tribes, and bureaucracies. These differences have been stimulated by implicit understandings between ruling families and other stakeholders, such as the merchants, both before and since the discovery of oil. Clientelism and marital bonds between ruling families and these stakeholders have contributed to the resilience and adaptability of the social contracts between ruling families and stakeholders, and the establishment of enduring ruling bargains.

Further research is needed to explore a number of persisting questions concerning the relationship between resource abundance and institutional evolution in the states of the Persian Gulf. Regional states have invariably responded to economic downturns by promoting nationalization of their labor force, which has decreased the efficiency of state institutions. Some states, however, have taken additional measures to clamp down on any signs of economic or political discontent – most notably, Saudi Arabia, Bahrain, and the UAE – whereas Qatar, Kuwait, and Oman have remained as comparatively benign dictatorships. These variances raise the question of the conditions that shape the responses of these states to oil-induced changes in economic and political conditions. In this particular regard, the entrepreneurial classes deserve special attention. In countries where the state establishes strong clientelistic relationships with the merchant class through offering contracts, the merchant class becomes more dependent on the state, especially during times of downturn. How do these entrepreneurial classes and the

[58] Sachs, "How to Handle the Macroeconomics of Wealth," p. 191.

[59] Collier, "Savings and Investment Decisions from Natural Resource Revenues: Implications for Arab Development," *Understanding and Avoiding the Oil Curse in Resource-Rich Arab Economies*, ed. Elbadawi and Selim (2016), p. 286.

state react to different cycles of oil bust and boom? And what does this tell us about institutional evolution in the interim period between the boom-and-bust cycles?

BIBLIOGRAPHY

Araar, Abdelkarim, Nada Choueiri, and Paolo Verme, "The Quest for Subsidy Reform in Libya," The World Bank Group: Policy Research Working Paper 7225 (2015), https://tinyurl.com/k7xw454r.

Askari, Hossein, *Collaborative Colonialism: The Political Economy of Oil in the Persian Gulf* (New York: Palgrave Macmillan, 2013).

Collier, Paul, "Savings and Investment Decisions from Natural Resource Revenues: Implications for Arab Development," *Understanding and Avoiding the Oil Curse in Resource-Rich Arab Economies*, edited by Ibrahim Elbadawi and Hoda Selim (Cambridge: Cambridge University Press, 2016), pp. 284–300.

Connell, John, "Nauru: The First Failed Pacific State?," *The Round Table* 95.383 (2006), pp. 47–63.

Davidson, Christopher, "The Dubai Model: Diversification and Slowdown," *The Political Economy of the Persian Gulf*, edited by Mehran Kamrava (New York: Columbia University Press, 2012), pp. 195–220.

Diop, Ndiame, and Jaime de Melo, "Dutch Disease in the Services Sector: Evidence from Oil Exporters in the Arab Region," *Understanding and Avoiding the Oil Curse in Resource-Rich Arab Economies*, edited by Ibrahim Elbadawi and Hoda Selim (Cambridge: Cambridge University Press, 2016), pp. 82–102.

Elbadawi, Ibrahim, and Hoda Selim, "Overview of Context, Issues and Summary," *Understanding and Avoiding the Oil Curse in Resource-Rich Arab Economies*, edited by Ibrahim Elbadawi and Hoda Selim (Cambridge: Cambridge University Press, 2016), pp. 1–15.

Elbadawi, Ibrahim, and Raimundo Soto, "Resource Rents, Political Institutions and Economic Growth," *Understanding and Avoiding the Oil Curse in Resource-Rich Arab Economies*, edited by Ibrahim Elbadawi and Hoda Selim (Cambridge: Cambridge University Press, 2016), pp. 187–224.

Foley, Sean, *The Arab Gulf States: Beyond Oil and Islam* (Boulder, CO: Lynne Rienner Publishers, 2010).

Herb, Michael, *Wages of Oil: Parliaments and Economic Development in Kuwait and the UAE* (Ithaca, NY: Cornell University Press, 2014).

Humphreys, Macartan, Jeffrey D. Sachs, and Joseph E. Stiglitz, "Introduction: What Is the Problem with Natural Resource Wealth?," *Escaping the Resource Curse*, edited by Macartan Humphreys, Jeffrey D. Sachs, and Joseph E. Stiglitz (New York: Columbia University Press, 2007), pp. 1–20.

Jarzabek, Jaroslaw, "G.C.C. Military Spending in Era of Low Oil Prices," *MEI Policy Focus 2016–19* (2016), www.mei.edu/sites/default/files/publications/PF19_Jarzabek_GCCmilitary_web.pdf.

Kamrava, Mehran, *Inside the Arab State* (New York: Oxford University Press, 2018).

Karl, Terry Lynn, *The Paradox of Plenty: Oil Booms and Petro-States* (Berkeley: University of California Press, 1997).

Karl, Terry Lynn, "Ensuring Fairness: The Case for a Transparent Social Contract," *Escaping the Resource Curse*, edited by Macartan Humphreys, Jeffrey D. Sachs, and Joseph E. Stiglitz (New York: Columbia University Press, 2007), pp. 256–85.

Martinez, Luis, *The Violence of Petro-Dollar Regimes: Algeria, Iraq and Libya*, translated by Cynthia Schoch (London: Hurst, 2012).

Menaldo, Victor, *The Institutions Curse: Natural Resources, Politics, and Development* (Cambridge: Cambridge University Press, 2016).

Mitchell, Timothy, *Carbon Democracy: Political Power in the Age of Oil* (London: Verso, 2011).

"Qatar: Managing the Limits of Economic Growth," Gulf States Newsletter 37.956 (2013), www.gsn-online.com/downloadable/2036.

Ross, Michael L., *The Oil Curse: How Petroleum Wealth Shapes the Development of Nations* (Princeton, NJ: Princeton University Press, 2012).

Sachs, Jeffrey D., "How to Handle the Macroeconomics of Wealth," *Escaping the Resource Curse*, edited by Macartan Humphreys, Jeffrey D. Sachs, and Joseph E. Stiglitz (New York: Columbia University Press, 2007), pp. 173–93.

Schmidt-Hebbel, Klaus, "Fiscal Institutions in Resource-Rich Economies: Lessons from Chile and Norway," *Understanding and Avoiding the Oil Curse in Resource-Rich Arab Economies*, edited by Ibrahim Elbadawi and Hoda Selim (Cambridge: Cambridge University Press, 2016), pp. 225–83.

Sommer, Martin, et al., *Learning to Live with Cheaper Oil: Policy Adjustments in Oil-Exporting Countries of the Middle East and Central Asia* (Washington, DC: The International Monetary Fund, 2016), www.imf.org/external/pubs/ft/dp/2016/mcd1603.pdf.

Soto, Raimundo, and Ilham Haouas, "Has the UAE Escaped the Oil Curse?," *Understanding and Avoiding the Oil Curse in Resource-Rich Arab Economies*, edited by Ibrahim Elbadawi and Hoda Selim (Cambridge: Cambridge University Press, 2016), pp. 373–420.

Stiglitz, Joseph, "What Is the Role of the State?," *Escaping the Resource Curse*, edited by Macartan Humphreys, Jeffrey D. Sachs, and Joseph E. Stiglitz (New York: Columbia University Press, 2007), pp. 23–52.

7

Militarism, Climate Emissions, and Islamic Environmental Ethics

A Transnational Perspective on Demilitarization and Ecological Justice

Nadia B. Ahmad

The contemporary global landscape presents a critical intersection of militarism, climate change, and environmental ethics that demands rigorous interdisciplinary scholarly examination. This chapter explores the relationship between military activities, greenhouse gas emissions, and Islamic environmental ethics, offering analysis of how Islamic philosophical and theological principles can inform a transformative approach to demilitarization and climate action. Through an Islamic lens, we examine the spiritual, ethical, and material implications of unchecked militarism on the ecological health of the planet and vulnerable communities worldwide. The global military-industrial complex represents an overlooked yet significant contributor to climate change. Military operations, extensive infrastructure networks, and complex supply chains generate vast quantities of greenhouse gas emissions that remain largely invisible in international climate negotiations. This invisibility stems from deliberate policy decisions that specifically exempt military emissions from reporting requirements under major international climate agreements. These exclusions hinder global accountability mechanisms and allow the environmental consequences of military action to persist without adequate scrutiny. The climate consequences of war zones, military bases, weapons testing sites, and strategic fuel transportation corridors require urgent and sustained investigation.

Beyond emissions, military operations lead to ecosystem disruption on a massive scale. The establishment of bases, live-fire training, deforestation for military installations, and post-conflict toxic contamination contribute to irreversible environmental damage. These impacts are not incidental but inherent to the structure and strategy of modern warfare, where control over land, water, and resources forms a central axis of power. The collateral damage inflicted on flora and fauna, topsoil erosion, and biodiversity loss extends far beyond combat zones. The environmental impact of military activities falls disproportionately on Muslim-majority countries, where decades of conflicts, fueled by external military powers, have resulted in devastating ecological and social consequences. Countries such as Iraq, Afghanistan, Syria, Yemen, Somalia, Libya, and Palestine have faced relentless air strikes, bombings, infrastructure collapse, and humanitarian crises that further weaken already fragile ecosystems. These regions have experienced a dual burden of environmental degradation: the immediate consequences of bombings, drone strikes, and heavy troop presence, and the longer-term effects of resource exploitation, war economy dynamics, and infrastructural collapse.

Environmental devastation in Muslim-majority countries coincides with broader geopolitical objectives. Oil-rich and resource-abundant regions become sites of prolonged militarization, where ecosystems are sacrificed at the altar of strategic interests. In southern Iraq, decades of conflict and oil spills have transformed fertile marshlands into arid wastelands. In Gaza, the destruction of water systems and agricultural land by repeated bombings compounds environmental vulnerability. The militarized extraction and control of natural resources, particularly fossil fuels, operate as mechanisms of neocolonial economic control. These dynamics reinforce cycles of poverty, dislocation, and environmental vulnerability.

Critical scholarship has illuminated the mechanisms of ecological violence perpetrated through military interventions. This violence extends beyond immediate physical destruction, creating long-lasting systemic vulnerabilities that fundamentally reshape environmental and social landscapes. Military interventions operate as mechanisms of environmental transformation, disrupting local ecological systems, traditional resource management practices, and community resilience. They degrade agricultural productivity, destroy watersheds, and generate toxic waste that lingers in soil and water for generations. The physical, psychological, and cultural dislocation that accompanies such transformations often leads to forced migration, compounding the problem through climate displacement.

A critical theoretical lens such as transmodern coloniality reveals how contemporary military operations serve as conduits of transnational corporate interests and ecological extraction. The environmental damage wrought by military engagements is not accidental; it is integral to the functioning of a globalized system that prioritizes economic dominance, often in the guise of security or liberation. Military campaigns thus double as extractive projects, displacing populations while paving the way for multinational control over reconstruction and redevelopment contracts. Corporate–military alliances further entrench environmental inequities, especially in the Global South.

Through the framework of transmodern coloniality, militarism is exposed as a modern manifestation of colonial power structures. Environmental degradation becomes a form of structural violence against marginalized communities, extending beyond immediate physical destruction to create long-lasting ecological and social disruptions. This perspective challenges traditional narratives of military intervention, revealing the profound environmental and social costs borne disproportionately by vulnerable populations. Climate justice, from this vantage point, becomes inseparable from anti-imperialist resistance.

Technological infrastructure is another dimension of military-induced ecological harm. Military research and development continuously prioritize innovations that enhance destructive capabilities, hypersonic missiles, autonomous drones, satellite-guided weaponry, while largely ignoring ecological implications. These systems are not neutral or contained; they impose a logic of domination upon ecosystems and amplify the reach of environmental harm. The carbon-intensive supply chains that enable the global flow of weaponry, armor, and surveillance tools perpetuate a cycle of destruction that spans continents. Weapons development involves extensive extraction of rare earth elements, toxic byproducts, and energy-intensive manufacturing. Moreover, the maintenance and disposal of military hardware, especially nuclear weapons and submarines, create long-term radioactive contamination threats. The result is an accumulation of technological debris that functions as a slow-acting environmental poison, with consequences that span centuries. The Pacific islands, Central Asian test sites, and Middle Eastern conflict zones have become unwitting laboratories of environmental experimentation with lasting damage.

The ecological footprints of military operations extend into peacetime. The ongoing maintenance of military bases, the fuel demands of routine exercises, and the carbon-heavy logistics of global troop deployment all contribute to military emissions that are rarely included in national climate inventories. These peacetime emissions reinforce a permanent state of ecological destabilization, even in the absence of active conflict. US military bases in Okinawa, Qatar, and Djibouti, for instance, continue to exert local environmental pressures through noise pollution, habitat fragmentation, and water stress.

Islamic environmental ethics provides a robust philosophical framework for challenging militaristic environmental destruction. The Quranic conception of humans as *khalīfa* (trustees) of the earth establishes a sacred responsibility for environmental protection. This spiritual designation reframes environmental stewardship as a divine mandate, positioning ecological well-being as a moral and theological imperative. Trust in this context is not passive – it entails active guardianship over the balance and integrity of the earth. This foundation offers a profound alternative to extractive and destructive approaches to environmental management. Unlike dominant Western environmental paradigms that often conceptualize nature as a resource to be managed or exploited, Islamic environmental ethics emphasizes an intrinsic connection between ecological systems and spiritual well-being. The earth is not a possession but a trust, a creation imbued with signs of the Divine, worthy of reverence and protection. This ethical orientation encourages restraint, compassion, and sustainability as religious virtues.

Islamic environmental ethics is grounded in three fundamental theological principles. The first, *mīzān* (balance), underscores the harmony and equilibrium within natural systems. Disrupting this balance – whether through excessive consumption or military aggression – violates the natural order. The second, *ʿadl* (justice), requires fairness not only among humans but between humanity and the rest of creation. Environmental degradation that disproportionately affects the poor, the marginalized, and future generations is inherently unjust. The third, *isrāf* (wastefulness), forbids excessive use of resources and condemns actions that result in ecological harm. Together, these principles provide a framework for nonviolence, stewardship, and systemic justice.

The Quranic verse "Do not commit abuse on the earth, spreading corruption (*fasād*)" (Q 2:60) encapsulates these ethical imperatives. Corruption, in this context, is more than moral depravity – it includes the degradation of ecosystems, the poisoning of water, the destruction of habitats, and the exploitation of earth's bounty for unjust ends. This verse transcends a simple environmental directive, representing an ethical framework that challenges the fundamental logic of militaristic environmental destruction. It calls for a holistic approach to environmental stewardship that prioritizes ecological balance and social justice. These values are echoed in Prophetic traditions that emphasize mercy to all creatures and equitable resource distribution.

Historical Islamic governance offers remarkable examples of environmental conservation that challenge contemporary militaristic approaches to resource management. The *ḥimā* system, for instance, designated areas of land for protected use, prohibiting certain forms of exploitation to ensure ecological sustainability. These were not arbitrary designations but the result of community consensus and ecological observation. *Ḥimā* regions included pastures, forests, and water sources protected from overuse.

Ottoman environmental policies, including extensive forest conservation and *waqf* (charitable endowments) for environmental protection, reflect a sophisticated understanding of ecosystem management. These institutions illustrate the integration of environmental ethics into governance, law, and community practice, offering instructive models for contemporary ecological justice movements. In Morocco, Tunisia, and Egypt, traditional Islamic jurisprudence (*fiqh*) has informed customary environmental laws that emphasize sustainable irrigation, water rights, and land use.

Addressing military climate emissions requires international cooperation and transformative policy strategies. These must begin with the development of robust methodologies for measuring and reporting military-related emissions. Without accurate data, accountability remains elusive. Transparent mechanisms for tracking environmental impacts of military installations, deployments, and supply chains are essential. Satellite imagery, environmental audits, and open-source intelligence can complement these efforts. Policy reform should also include integrating military emissions into national climate targets and international agreements. This would mean closing existing loopholes in frameworks like the Paris Agreement and establishing clear benchmarks for military decarbonization. Nations must be compelled to treat military emissions with the same seriousness as civilian sectors, dismantling the notion that security justifies ecological destruction. Civil society and international institutions have a critical role to play in demanding this shift.

Demilitarization offers significant opportunities for economic and ecological transformation. Redirecting military budgets toward environmental protection, disaster preparedness, and climate adaptation could generate profound societal benefits. Investments in renewable energy, sustainable infrastructure, and ecological restoration would not only reduce emissions but build long-term resilience. This redirection also supports job creation in green industries and peacebuilding programs. Such a transformation would require reimagining the very concept of security. Current paradigms define security in terms of military might and territorial defense. But true security is rooted in ecological stability, food and water access, social cohesion, and resilience to climate shocks. An Islamic perspective reinforces this broader definition, emphasizing that peace and justice are inseparable from environmental balance. Security through stewardship, rather than dominance, emerges as a moral and practical imperative.

Despite growing awareness, significant obstacles remain. The military-industrial complex represents a powerful institutional barrier to meaningful climate action. Defense contractors, geopolitical rivalry, and entrenched economic interests perpetuate a system where militarism is normalized and protected. Environmental regulations often exempt military operations, perpetuating a dangerous exceptionality. To overcome this, targeted advocacy, faith-based campaigns, and academic pressure must converge. Overcoming these challenges requires building broad coalitions among environmentalists, faith-based organizations, academics, and civil society actors. Islamic ethical teachings can serve as a unifying force within such coalitions, offering a moral vocabulary to articulate shared goals. The sacredness of life, the duty of care for the earth, and the imperative of justice offer powerful tools for mobilization. Interfaith alliances, community organizing, and international solidarity can challenge the dominance of militarized policy.

The path forward demands a fundamental transformation of our understanding of security, moving from a militaristic paradigm to one grounded in ecological justice and human well-being. Islamic environmental ethics provides a compelling philosophical foundation for this transformation, offering a holistic approach that integrates spiritual, ethical, and practical considerations.

Demilitarization is an environmental strategy for human and planetary security. By challenging the military-industrial complex and centering principles of ecological balance and justice, we can develop more sustainable and peaceful global systems. This process involves dismantling the ideology of militarism itself, replacing it with frameworks that value life, cooperation, and stewardship. The intersection of militarism, climate change, and Islamic environmental ethics calls for a transformative approach to global challenges. It demands that we move beyond narrow conceptualizations of security and environmental management, embracing a more holistic, just, and ecologically sustainable worldview. This perspective calls upon policymakers, religious leaders, scholars, and citizens to recognize the moral urgency of environmental action and to act with courage and clarity.

The principles of Islamic environmental ethics offer a powerful framework for this transformation, providing both a philosophical foundation and practical guidance for creating a more just and sustainable global future. This approach recognizes the fundamental interconnectedness of ecological systems, social justice, and human flourishing, offering a path toward genuine planetary well-being. As we stand at the precipice of environmental collapse, these principles call us to reclaim our role as stewards, not conquerors, of the earth.

Islamic teachings thus invite a paradigm shift in how we conceptualize power, responsibility, and the environment. They ask us to resist the seductions of militaristic strength and instead build a world rooted in mercy, balance, and justice. This is the ethical revolution we need, one that embraces the sacredness of creation and commits to the difficult, necessary work of healing the earth. The devastation wrought by militarism on the environment can be seen clearly through specific case studies in Muslim-majority regions. In Iraq, successive wars have not only decimated human life and infrastructure but have severely impaired ecological systems. The draining of the Mesopotamian Marshes, once the largest wetland ecosystem in the Middle East, is a glaring example. A rich biodiversity hotspot, the marshes were intentionally dried by Saddam Hussein's regime in retaliation against Marsh Arab resistance. Post-2003 US military presence exacerbated this loss through fuel pollution, disrupted hydrological cycles, and the collapse of local agricultural practices.

In Gaza, repeated Israeli military campaigns have led to widespread ecological devastation. Wastewater treatment facilities have been bombed, leaving raw sewage to flood urban areas. Bombings have destroyed solar energy infrastructure and farmland, resulting in long-term degradation of arable land and access to clean water. The 2021 airstrikes alone caused damage to 500 agricultural structures. Combined with the Israeli blockade, this creates an artificial ecological disaster zone, where civilians experience daily environmental precarity.

In Afghanistan, decades of foreign intervention and civil war have devastated irrigation systems, forest coverage, and local wildlife. Military hardware abandoned in conflict zones leaks hazardous substances into the soil and groundwater. Deforestation for firewood due to fuel shortages, often exacerbated by wartime logistics, has stripped once-forested valleys of their ecological cover, increasing the risks of landslides and flooding.

7.1 ISLAMIC LEGAL INSTRUMENTS AND ECO-FATWAS

Islamic jurisprudence (*fiqh*) has historically governed the use and management of land, water, and natural resources. These legal instruments are now being revived to inform modern environmental governance. Contemporary eco-fatwas (legal opinions) have emerged to guide Muslims in practicing environmental responsibility. For example, the Indonesian Council of Ulama issued a fatwa in 2014 declaring illegal wildlife trafficking and deforestation as *ḥarām* (forbidden), grounded in Quranic ethics and the Prophetic tradition. Similarly, scholars such as Sheikh Ali Gomaa of Egypt and Mustafa Ceric of Bosnia have articulated legal opinions that support sustainable water use, antipollution regulations, and the protection of endangered species, all rooted in Islamic theology. These eco-fatwas serve as moral and legal tools to counter both state inaction and militarized exploitation of ecosystems.

7.2 ISLAMIC ENVIRONMENTAL MOVEMENTS AND INSTITUTIONS

There is a growing transnational Islamic environmental movement that emphasizes climate justice, biodiversity preservation, and the critique of militarism. Organizations like the Islamic

Foundation for Ecology and Environmental Sciences (IFEES) in the UK, Green Muslims in the United States, and the Global Muslim Climate Network work at the grassroots level to educate, mobilize, and implement sustainable practices rooted in Islamic principles. In Muslim-majority countries, faith-based initiatives have supported large-scale environmental campaigns. In Türkiye, mosque-based outreach has been used to plant trees and educate congregations about water conservation. In Malaysia, Islamic environmental ethics are taught in madrasas, linking Quranic verses to climate science. These programs demonstrate the potential for integrating religious identity and ecological action to counterbalance the militarized worldview.

7.3 MILITARIZED BORDERS AND CLIMATE MIGRATION

Another key dimension of militarism's ecological cost is its role in exacerbating climate migration. As climate shocks intensify and ecosystems collapse, large populations are forced to flee. Militarized borders, surveillance technologies, and detention regimes turn these migrations into humanitarian crises. Muslim refugees from Syria, Bangladesh, Sudan, and Yemen are disproportionately affected. Islamic environmental ethics offers an alternative framework grounded in hospitality (*karam*), refuge (*amān*), and justice (*'adl*). These principles can guide both Muslim-majority and global societies in moving from punitive border policies to compassionate climate response systems. Instead of building walls and drones, societies can build green infrastructure, renewable energy cooperatives, and safe corridors of human mobility.

Redirecting military expenditure into climate adaptation could transform vulnerable communities. For example, funds currently allocated to fighter jets and naval fleets could be redirected toward mangrove reforestation in coastal Bangladesh, solar infrastructure in Sudan, or climate-resilient housing in flood-prone Pakistan. Islamic finance tools, such as *sukuk* (Islamic bonds) and *waqf* (charitable endowments), can be mobilized to finance such transitions.

Scholars have proposed a zakat for the earth – a system where Muslims donate a portion of their wealth specifically to environmental restoration. This could fund reforestation projects, clean water initiatives, and conservation education, creating a religiously sanctioned mechanism for ecological justice. Such tools can complement national and international mechanisms in the shift from militarism to sustainability.

While some Muslim-majority states remain dependent on military expenditure and fossil fuel exports, others are beginning to lead in climate diplomacy. Morocco hosted the 2016 UN Climate Conference (COP22) and committed to sourcing over 50 percent of its energy from renewables by 2030. The UAE launched the Masdar initiative, a clean energy city, though critics note contradictions in its continued arms sales and fossil fuel production. There is an urgent need for Muslim-majority nations to lead calls for the inclusion of military emissions in climate negotiations. As stewards of vast natural resources and as moral voices in the Global South, these nations can pressure global institutions to address militarism's environmental toll. The Organisation of Islamic Cooperation (OIC) could become a platform for collective action on climate justice and demilitarization.

7.4 CONCLUSION: A COVENANT OF ECOLOGICAL JUSTICE

Islamic environmental ethics equips us with the spiritual courage and moral clarity to confront militarism's role in ecological degradation. It offers not just a critique but a blueprint – a model for living in balance with the earth, for redistributing power, and for protecting the most vulnerable. In a world dominated by military logics, it dares to propose mercy over might, stewardship over extraction, and justice over domination. The profound theological concept of *khilāfa* (trusteeship) represents more than a passive environmental management strategy – it is a radical reimagining of human–planetary relationships. This principle challenges the dominant paradigms of militaristic extraction and environmental violence, proposing instead a holistic approach to ecological justice that centers on reciprocity, compassion, and profound interconnectedness.

At its core, Islamic environmental ethics demands a fundamental reconfiguration of power dynamics. The principle of *ʿadl* (justice) extends far beyond human-to-human interactions, encompassing a vision of justice that includes nonhuman entities, ecological systems, and future generations. This expansive understanding directly confronts the military-industrial complex's logic of destruction and domination, offering an alternative framework of mutual care and sustainable coexistence.

The transformation this chapter envisions requires more than policy change; it demands a paradigm shift of unprecedented magnitude. From educational institutions to religious spaces, from legal frameworks to international climate negotiations, we must amplify the voices calling for ecological peace. The Quranic injunction to walk gently on the earth is not a metaphor, it is a profound mandate that challenges the very foundations of militaristic and extractive global systems.

This approach calls for concrete actions that dismantle the structures of ecological violence. This includes:

1. Redirecting military budgets toward ecological restoration
2. Developing robust international mechanisms for environmental accountability
3. Centering the voices and experiences of communities most impacted by ecological destruction
4. Creating educational frameworks that teach ecological stewardship as a spiritual and ethical imperative

The spiritual dimension of this transformation cannot be overstated. Islamic environmental ethics offers a powerful alternative to the dominant secular paradigms of environmental management. It reconnects ecological action with spiritual purpose, transforming environmental protection from a technical challenge to a sacred responsibility. We stand at a critical juncture in human history. The ecological crisis is not a future threat but a present reality, disproportionately impacting marginalized communities and ecosystems. The military-industrial complex has been a primary driver of this destruction, perpetuating cycles of violence that extend far beyond human communities to encompass entire ecological systems. Yet, there is profound hope in this moment of crisis. Islamic environmental ethics provides a transformative vision that is at once ancient and urgently contemporary. It reminds us that our relationship with the earth is fundamentally sacred, a covenant of care, respect, and mutual flourishing. This is not a passive stance but an active commitment to ecological justice that requires continuous effort, imagination, and spiritual courage.

The path forward demands collective action rooted in spiritual principles. We must build transnational networks of ecological solidarity that transcend geopolitical boundaries. This means creating spaces of dialogue, developing collaborative ecological restoration projects, and challenging the dominant narratives of militarism and environmental destruction. Let us respond, not with silence or complicity but with action rooted in faith, solidarity, and hope. Our covenant as *khalīfa* is both a profound privilege and an immense responsibility. We are called to be active agents of ecological healing, to challenge systems of destruction, and to cultivate a vision of planetary well-being that honors the intricate web of life. Only then can we truly honor our sacred role as trustees of this fragile, magnificent planet. The journey is challenging, but the spiritual and ecological imperative is clear. We must walk gently, act courageously, and live with profound reverence for the intricate, interconnected miracle of existence.

BIBLIOGRAPHY

Belcher, Oliver, Patrick Bigger, Ben Neimark, and Cara Kennelly. "Hidden Carbon Costs of the 'Everywhere War': Logistics, Geopolitical Ecology, and the Carbon Boot-Print of the US Military." *Transactions of the Institute of British Geographers*, vol. 45, no. 1 (2020), pp. 65–80.

Crawford, Neta C. *Pentagon Fuel Use, Climate Change, and the Costs of War*. Providence, RI: Brown University, Watson Institute for International and Public Affairs, 2019.

Edwards, Paul N. *The Closed World: Computers and the Politics of Discourse in Cold War America*. Cambridge, MA: MIT Press, 1996.

Escobar, Arturo. *Encountering Development: The Making and Unmaking of the Third World*. Princeton, NJ: Princeton University Press, 1995.

Foltz, Richard C. *Islam and Ecology: A Bestowed Trust*. Cambridge, MA: Harvard University Press, 2003.

Foran, John. "Climate Change, Conflict, and Militarism: Interconnected Challenges for Global Sustainability." *Global Environmental Politics*, vol. 15, no. 3 (2015), pp. 45–68.

Garcia, Denise. "Redirect Military Budgets to Climate Change Mitigation." *Nature*, vol. 584 (2020), pp. 521–22.

Grosfoguel, Ramón. "Transmodernity, Border Thinking, and Global Coloniality." Eurozine (2008).

Ibrahim, Malik. "Environmental Ethics in Islam: Principles and Perspectives." *Journal of Islamic Studies*, vol. 25, no. 2 (2014), pp. 187–210.

Khalid, Fazlun M. *Signs on the Earth: Islam, Modernity and the Climate Crisis*. Leicester: Kube Publishing, 2019.

Levy, Barry S., and Jonathan A. Patz. "Climate Change and Collective Violence." *Annual Review of Public Health*, vol. 36 (2015), pp. 569–88.

Light, Sarah E. "The Military-Environmental Complex." *Boston College Law Review*, vol. 55, no. 4 (2014), pp. 879–910.

Nasr, Seyyed Hossein. *Religion and the Ordeal of Modern Man*. London: Traditional Studies Press, 2009.

Nazaryan, Alexander. "The US Department of Defense Is One of the World's Biggest Polluters." *Newsweek* (2014).

Nevitt, Mark P. "Climate Change and the Law of National Security Adaptation." *Northwestern Law Review Online*, vol. 118 (2023), pp. 126–58.

Parkinson, Stuart. "Cutting Military Spending for Climate Action." *Responsible Science*, vol. 2, no. 2 (2020), pp. 18–23.

Parkinson, Stuart. "Military Emissions and Climate Change: A Critical Analysis." *Sustainability*, vol. 12, no. 8 (2020), pp. 3245–62.

Pulido, Laura. "Geographies of Race and Ethnicity II: Environmental Racism, Racial Capitalism, and State-Sanctioned Violence." *Progress in Human Geography*, vol. 42, no. 4 (2018), pp. 590–602.

Sachedina, Abdulaziz. "Islam and the Environment." *Journal of Islamic Studies*, vol. 13, no. 1 (2002), pp. 1–20.

Sassen, Saskia. *Expulsions: Brutality and Complexity in the Global Economy*. Cambridge, MA: Harvard University Press, 2014.

Tucker, Mary Evelyn, and John Grim (eds.). *Religions of the World and Ecology*. Cambridge, MA: Harvard University Press, 1998.

Zarook, Ruqaiyah. "Why the Pentagon Is the World's Biggest Single Greenhouse Gas Emitter." *Mother Jones* (2022).

8

A Concise Overview of the Classical Islamic Coastal and Marine Environmental Law

Hassan S. Khalilieh

Islam places great significance on the environment and ecology. The Quran and Prophetic tradition (Sunna) keenly recognize the necessity of a suitable environmental and ecological equilibrium and acknowledge the human's right to life, health, and security. By the same token, classical Muslim scholars have showcased a profound commitment to environmental and ecological matters whether through their dedication to religious teachings, establishment of behavioral norms, or active engagement in practical scientific applications. Their dedication is clearly manifested through the authorship and dissemination of literature that addresses a broad spectrum of topics specifically related to ecology and the environment. They have authored treatises covering a diverse array of subjects, such as hydrology and water sciences, atmospheric phenomena, soil and marine sciences, flora and botany, fauna and zoology, ornithology, and beyond.[1] The goal of the forthcoming discussion is not to offer a comprehensive overview of Islamic environmental and ecological ethics but rather to focus on the relatively underexplored coastal and marine dimensions, which have received limited attention in contemporary scholarship.

8.1 COASTAL JURISDICTION AND SPATIAL PLANNING

With Caesarea (19/640) and Alexandria (20/641) falling into Muslim hands, the Syrian and Egyptian littorals were exposed to constant threats of the Byzantine navy. Moreover, the population's composition in the newly captured territories constituted a serious challenge to Muslim authorities. Primarily consisting of Byzantine Greeks and Arab Christians, they

[1] Muḥammad b. Aḥmad al-Tamīmī al-Maqdisī, *Māddat al-baqā ʾ fī iṣlāḥ fasād al-hawā ʾ wa-l-taḥarruz min darar al-awbā ʾ* (Cairo: Maʿhad al-Makhṭūṭāt al-ʿArabiyya, 1999); Abū Yūsuf Yaʿqūb b. Isḥāq al-Kindī, *Risāla fī al-ʿilla al-fāʿila li-l-madd wa-l-jazr*, www.hindawi.org/books/51419736/2.1/; Abū ʿAbd Allāh Muḥammad b. Abī Ṭālib al-Qazwīnī, *Nukhbat al-dahr fī ʿajāʾib al-barr wa-l-baḥr* (Saint Petersburg: Imperial Academy, 1865); Lutfallah Gari, "Arabic Treatises on Environmental Pollution up to the End of the Thirteenth Century," *Environment and History* 8.4 (2002), 475–88; Omar A. Bakhashab, "Islamic Law and the Environment: Some Basic Principles," *Arab Law Quarterly* 3.3 (1988), 287–98; Muḥammad Abṭawī, "Matn al-muʾallafāt al-ʿArabiyya fī al-awbiʾa: Qāʾima awwaliyya maʿ taʿālīq mukhtaṣara," https://arsco.org/article-detail-1647-8-0; Philippe Provençal, "Marine Biological Report in the *Nukhbat al-Dahr fī ʿAjāʾib al-Barr wa-al-Baḥr*," *Arabic Sciences and Philosophy* 24 (2014), 169–80; Asep S. Jahat et al., "The Use of *Maqāṣid al-Sharīʿa* in Maritime and National Resilience Context," *Al-Risalah* 21.1 (2021), 97–110; Samira Idllalène, *Rediscovery and Revival in Islamic Environmental Law* (Cambridge: Cambridge University Press, 2021).

frequently rebelled with the Byzantine navy's assistance.[2] In response to the coastal frontiers' weak security situation, ʿUmar b. al-Khaṭṭāb (r. 13–23/634–44) and his successor, ʿUthmān b. ʿAffān (r. 23–35/644–56), brought new populations to these regions. The establishment of military towns and installations assisted this policy of transferring populations to the coastal frontiers, along with other supportive measures, including the construction of mosques, allocation of landholdings (*qaṭāʾiʿ*) and houses for new settlers, the development of sources of livelihood, and stationing of volunteer defenders in the maritime *ribāṭ*s (garrisoned outposts).[3] ʿUmar b. al-Khaṭṭāb's caliphate also set up *dīwān*s for paying of stipends and distributing of tracts of land to enlisted soldiers and volunteers among the *muhājirūn* (immigrants).[4] These measures led to gradual stabilization of the security situation along the Syrian coast.[5] It was also during that time when the post of the "governorship of the coasts" was founded. Administratively, the coastal frontiers of the *ajnād* (sing. *jund*, military district) were detached from their hinterlands and transferred to the territorial jurisdiction of the governor of the coasts. The governor, who was normally an army commander, was appointed directly by the caliph and drew his authority from the central government.[6] The first military commander to hold the post was ʿAbd Allāh b. Qays al-Jāsī al-Fazārī.[7] With the establishment of this distinct coastal administrative entity, the caliph laid the official and legislative foundations for the post of admiralty.[8]

The significant change in the Islamic naval strategy and administration in the eastern Mediterranean was tangible during the Sufyanid period (41–64/661–84). The seventh- and eighth-century papyri furnish us with a great deal of historical data on the formation, organization, and financing of the early military fleet.[9] Notwithstanding, these documents together with

[2] Aziz Abu Ahmad, "The *Ribāṭs* of Palestine as a Forerunner of the Coastal Defense System in Islamic Mediterranean" (PhD diss., University of Haifa, 2017), 28–30.

[3] Rana Mikati, "The Creation of Early Islamic Beirut: The Sea, Scholars, Jihad and the Sacred" (PhD diss., University of Chicago, 2013), 23; Yumna Masarwa, "From a Word of God to Archaeological Monuments: A Historical-Archaeological Study of the Umayyad Ribāṭs of Palestine" (PhD diss., Princeton University, 2006), 178–79; Mehdi K. Kader, "On the Origins and Strategic Dynamics of Pre-Legal Jihad 610–680" (PhD diss., King's College London, 2016), 201–4; Ḥusayn Muḥāfaẓa, "al-Taḥṣīn al-ʿaskarī li-l-thughūr al-Shāmiyya al-barriyya wa-l-baḥriyya fī al-ʿahd al-rāshidī," *Majallat al-Mishkā li-l-ʿUlūm al-Insāniyya wa-l-Ijtimāʿiyya* 3.2 (2016), 354–58.

[4] Patricia Crone, "The First-Century Concept of *Hijra*," *Arabica* 41.3 (1994), 364–66.

[5] Abū al-ʿAbbās Aḥmad b. Yaḥyā al-Balādhurī, *Futūh al-buldān* (Beirut: Muʾassasat al-Maʿārif, 1987), 175.

[6] Anwar M. al-ʿAwwa, "Tārīkh al-sāḥil al-Shāmī mundhu maṭlaʿ al-ʿaṣr al-rāshidī ḥattā nihāyat al-ḥukm al-Sufyānī: Futūḥātuhu, taʾsīs al-arbiṭa, inshāʾ al-quwā al-baḥriyya" (PhD diss., Damascus University, 2012), 133; Mikati, "Creation of Early Islamic Beirut," 42.

[7] Abū Jaʿfar Muḥammad b. Jarīr al-Ṭabarī, *Tārīkh al-rusul wa-l-mulūk* (Cairo: Dār al-Maʿārif, 1969), 4:64, 67: "*istaʿmala ʿAbd Allāh b. Qays ʿalā al-sawāḥil min kull kūra*" (ʿAbd Allāh b. Qays governed the shorelines of every coastal district); Abū al-Qāsim ʿAlī b. al-Ḥasan b. ʿAsākir, *Tārīkh madīnat Dimashq* (Beirut: Dār al-Fikr, 1996), 32:118–21: "*wallahu Muʿāwiya ghazw al-baḥr*" (he, i.e., al-Fazārī, was appointed by Muʿāwiya to undertake naval campaigns); ʿAbd Allāh al-ʿUmarī and Maḥmūd Jubrān, "Ishkāliyyat al-baḥriyya al-Islāmiyya fī ʿahd al-khalīfa ʿUmar b. al-Khaṭṭāb: Qirāʾa fī al-riwāyāt," *al-Majalla al-ʿArabiyya li-l-Ādāb* 3.1 (2006), 126; Christophe Picard, *Sea of the Caliphs: The Mediterranean in the Medieval Islamic World* (Cambridge, MA: Harvard University Press, 2018), 58, 192; Mikati, "Creation of Early Islamic Beirut," 44–45.

[8] al-Ṭabarī, *Tārīkh al-rusul wa-l-mulūk*, 4:260; Mikati, "Creation of Early Islamic Beirut," 45; Avraham Elmakias, *The Naval Commanders of Early Islam: A Prosopographical Approach* (Piscataway, NJ: Gorgias Press, 2018), 57; Antoine Borrut, "L'espace maritime syrien au cours des premiers siècle de l'Islam (VIIe-Xe siècle): le cas de la region entre Acre et Tripoli," *Annales d'histoire et d'archéologie* 10.11 (1999–2000), 14–15.

[9] Aly Mohamed Fahmy, *Muslim Naval Organization in the Eastern Mediterranean from the Seventh to the Tenth Century A.D.* (Cairo: National Publication and Printing House, 1966), 87–114; Jelle Bruning, "Imperial Policies and the Organization of the War Fleet in Early Islamic Egypt," in *Christians and Muslims in Early Islamic Egypt*, ed. Lajos Berkes (Michigan: Michigan University Press, 2022), 35–39; Jaser Abu Safieh, *Bardiyyāt Qurra Ibn Sharīk al-ʿAbsī* (Riyadh: Markaz al-Malik Fayṣal li-l-Buḥūth wa-l-Dirāsāt al-Islāmiyya, 2004), 100–107; Ghaydāʾ ʿĀdil, *al-Usṭūl al-umawī fī al-maṣādir wa-l-wathāʾiq al-bardiyya* (Amman: Dār al-Fāris li-l-Nashr wa-l-Tawzīʿ, 2018), 39–78; Mikati, "Creation of Early Islamic Beirut," 43–57, draws our attention to the fact that classical Arabic sources use different

early historical accounts do not enable us to draw a clear thematic view of the admiral's (*amīr al-baḥr*) naval administration, coastal and offshore jurisdiction, and military and civil responsibilities in times of war and peace. By contrast, the executive power vested in the admiral is tacitly defined by the renowned Abbasid scholar and administrator Qudāma b. Jaʿfar's (261–337/873–948) treatise *The Book of Land Tax and the Art of Writing*. In regard to the admiral's territorial jurisdiction, the author writes:

> [The admiral] is commanded to oversee [the frontiers'] observation places and watchtowers, maintain close supervision on the garrisoned troops there, provide them with the *arzāq* (wheat allowances), and avoid holding back anything from [their allowances]. ... He is commanded to be vigilant of the enemy's deception to lay hands on any weapon or other arms, or any treachery against Islamic territory. He must prohibit merchants from carrying any [weapons] to the enemy, or clearing the way [to the enemy's] land. Whoever is caught committing such violations, [the admiral] must inflict severe punishment on him and make an example of him, as a warning for all to see. ... He is commanded to dock all ships at their berths and to appoint trustworthy and valiant [port superintendents] to take care of them so that no ship can depart from the ports without his knowledge, or come into them without his permission. ... He is commanded to be on high alert against the enemy's spies and secret agents and to assign on his behalf a supervisor in every city who is acquainted with it. The city's gatekeepers and guards shall not enable easy entry to every person except after obtaining information about his identity and the purposes, intentions, and desires of his visit.[10]

It is evident from the writ of appointment that the admiral enjoyed supreme administrative, judicial, and military authority over the coastal frontiers. He was charged with maintaining good order and securing maritime frontiers and guarding them in order to defend the coastal frontiers against external naval attacks, facilitating the flow of commerce, sheltering wayfarers and caravans, and protecting merchants and postal systems against piratical raids and highway robbers. The admiral was responsible for the construction of caravanserais, *ribāṭ* fortresses, and watchtowers (or lookouts), official and private.[11] The *ribāṭ* fortresses and watchtowers, which characterized the rural coastal landscape of the Islamic Mediterranean, were generally built outside the urban centers. Their locations and distances between them were primarily dictated by military and topographical considerations. Therefore, they were not uniformly spaced, but rather were situated at high gravel ridges, artificial mounds, and flatlands, provided that signals and alerts could clearly be transmitted and observed from one *ribāṭ* to the next.[12]

The *ribāṭs*' architectural plan and features were unique to the religio-military landscapes of the Islamic Mediterranean. As prototypes of the Umayyad desert castles, the *ribāṭ* fortresses

names and titles to denote "admiral": *ṣāḥib al-thughūr al-baḥriyya*/commander of the maritime frontiers (42n65), *ʿalā al-baḥr*/governorship of the sea (45n73), *ṣāḥib al-baḥr*/commander of the sea/fleet (47n79), *wilāyat ghāziyat al-baḥr*/governor of maritime expeditions (49n85), *wilāyat thaghr al-baḥr*/governor of the maritime frontier (57n108), *amīr al-sāḥil*/governor of the coast (57n107), *ṣāḥib ghazw al-baḥr*/commander of maritime expeditions (167n22).

[10] Qudāma b. Jaʿfar b. Ziyād al-Baghdādī, *Kitāb al-kharāj wa-ṣināʿat al-kitāba* (Baghdad: Dār al-Rashīd li-l-Nashr, 1981), 47–51.

[11] Abū Bakr ʿAbd Allāh b. Muḥammad al-Mālikī, *Riyāḍ al-nufūs fī ṭabaqāt ʿulamāʾ al-Qayrawān wa-zuhhādihim wa-nussākihim wa-siyar min akhbārihim wa-awṣāfihim* (Beirut: Dār al-Gharb al-Islāmī, 1983), 1:420, 422. In fact, endowed or state-owned *ribāṭs* could not be placed randomly at any point on the coast without the admiral's official approval. Positioning the proper location was the admiral's prerogative, who had to take into account the topographical, military, economic, social, and religious factors in order to avoid any negative impacts on the environmental surroundings, neighboring strongholds, and local residents, as in the case of the third-century AH construction of Qaṣr b. al-Jiʿd and Qaṣr Ziyād.

[12] Hassan S. Khalilieh, "The *Ribāṭ* of Arsūf and Coastal Defence System in Early Islamic Palestine," *Journal of Islamic Studies* 19.2 (2008), 167–69.

shared a similar architectural structure and plan but varied in size. A typical *ribāṭ* was a squared-built enclosure strengthened by square buttresses along its external walls with four round towers at the corners. Two semicircular towers protected the main gate leading into a courtyard surrounded by arms and food warehouses, stables for cattle and horses, larger and smaller rooms, reservoirs, a small mosque, and prayer niches. In the middle of the courtyard were cisterns and drill areas for warriors. At the highest point were the command headquarters. Most *ribāṭ*s were several stories high and typically housed over a hundred cavalrymen.[13] Between one *ribāṭ* and the next were square *miḥrās*es (small watchtowers), each one ranging between 50 and 60 square meters.[14]

The establishment of the *ribāṭ* institution along the Islamic Mediterranean littoral not only changed the demographic balance but also introduced new settlement patterns and landscapes to the coastal rural areas. The practice of defensive jihad created a new lifestyle in the frontier landscape where heterogeneous warrior-saints, garrisoned soldiers, and volunteers from all over the empire moved to perform their *ribāṭ* religious duty in the maritime borderlines.[15] In spite of the *ribāṭ* practitioners' diverse ethnic, social, economic, cultural, and sectarian backgrounds, they were unified in their devotional mission and way of life.[16] As an administratively autonomous and self-sustaining entity, every *ribāṭ* was managed by an *amīn* (trustee) or imam (leader/commander), who gained his authority from the district commander.[17]

The selection of the *ribāṭ* sites stemmed from military, administrative, ideological, religious, social, economic, and ecological perceptions.[18] Ecologically, its location was highly dependent on the existence of natural resources for the garrisoned stationers' livelihood, mostly from cultivating the lands, farming, herding, and fishing.[19] Moreover, due to its strategic and presumable religious importance as a frontline against the enemy's naval raids, central and regional authorities endowed vast estates, including *ḥimā*s (reserved pastures), and granted

[13] Hassan Khalilieh, "May the Umayyad Coastal *Ribāṭ* Fortress of Kafr Lāb Have Been Built in Memory of Mujāhid ibn Jabr?," *Al-Masāq: Journal of the Medieval Mediterranean* 34.3 (2022), 310–311; Hassan Khalilieh, "The *Ribāṭ* of Arsūf," 165–66; Sarah K. Raphael, *Azdud (Ashdod-Yam): An Early Islamic Fortress on the Mediterranean Coast* (Oxford: Archaeopress, 2014), 22–24; Hervé Barbé and Itamar Taxel, "Habonim-Kafr Lām: A *Ribāṭ* of the Levantine Coastal Defensive System in the First Centuries of Islam," in *The Art of Siege Warfare and Military Architecture from the Classical World to the Middle Ages*, ed. Michael Eisenberg and Rabei Khamisy (Oxford: Oxbow Books, 2020), 153–63; Harvé Barbé et al., "Ha-Bonim," *Hadashot Arkheologiyot: Excavations and Surveys in Israel* 114 (2002), 31–32; Abu Ahmad, "*Ribāṭ*s of Palestine," 105; Masarwa, "From a Word of God," 18–29, 44–50; Yumna Masarwa, "The Mediterranean as Frontier: The Umayyad Ribāṭs of Palestine," in *Western Monasticism Ante Litteram: The Spaces of Monastic Observance in Late Antiquity and the Early Middle Ages*, ed. Hendrik Dey and Elizabeth Fentress (Turnhout: Brepols, 2011), 194; Keppel A. C. Creswell, *A Short Account of Early Muslim Architecture* (Cairo: American University Press, 1989), 287–89; Richard Ettinghausen and Oleg Grabar, *The Art and Architecture of Islam 650–1250* (Middlesex: Penguin Books, 1987), 101; Lucien Golvin, "Note sur le mot *ribat* (terme d'architecture) et son interprétation en occident musulman," *Revue de l'occident musulman et de la méditerranée* 6 (1969), 95–101; Alexandre Lezine, "Deux ribāṭ du sahel Tunisien," *Les cahiers de Tunisie* 4 (1956), 279–88; Néji Djelloul, *al-Ribāṭāt al-baḥriyya bi-Ifrīqiya fī al-ʿaṣr al-wasīṭ* (Tunis: Markaz al-Dirāsāt wa-l-Buḥūth al-Iqtiṣādiyya wa-l-Ijtimāʿiyya, 1999), is one of the best comprehensive studies written on the origins, diffusion, and evolution of the maritime *ribāṭ*s of the early Islamic Ifrīqiya.

[14] Khalilieh, "The *Ribāṭ* of Arsūf," 166.

[15] Ibid., 169–73; Djelloul, *al-Ribāṭāt al-baḥriyya*, 185–88, 191, 204–6; Gideon Avni, *The Byzantine–Islamic Transition in Palestine: An Archaeological Approach* (Oxford: Oxford University Press, 2014), 202, 230–31.

[16] Djelloul, *al-Ribāṭāt al-baḥriyya*, 194; Asa Eger, "The Spaces between the Teeth: Environment, Settlement, and Interaction on the Islamic–Byzantine Frontier" (PhD diss., University of Chicago, 2008), 26.

[17] Muḥammad Ballan, "Fraxinetum: An Islamic Frontier State in the Tenth-Century Provence," *Comitatus: A Journal of Medieval and Renaissance Studies* 41 (2010), 73; Djelloul, *al-Ribāṭāt al-baḥriyya*, 191; Eger, "Spaces between the Teeth," 26.

[18] Eger, "Spaces between the Teeth," 411.

[19] Djelloul, *al-Ribāṭāt al-baḥriyya*, 201; Eger, "Spaces between the Teeth," 56.

offshore fishing rights over limited marine space for the communal benefit of the *ribāṭ*'s occupants.[20]

Whether or not the seas should have *ḥarīm* zones was also dealt with in the early jurisprudential compendia. The Maliki jurist Ashhab b. ʿAbd al-ʿAzīz al-Qaysī (140–204/757–820) made a clear distinction between property rights on land as distinct to those pertaining to maritime spaces, arguing that – contrary to the sea – land can be occupied. The inquiry reads as follows:

> Ashhab was asked about a group of voluntary guards who arrived in some town, set up boundary lines, and settled therein for the performance of garrison duty (*ribāṭ*); a woodland area separated their settlement from the sea. Along the coast there were deserted towns occupied by *ribāṭ* practitioners, too. Since these were exposed to immediate threat and frequent raids by the Byzantines (Rūm), governors refused the practitioners' appeal to extend their boundaries. Their living conditions have improved in due course and, as a result, they have expanded their woodland zone so that their territorial rights extended to the seacoast. Are they entitled to do so? Do you think that the sea should have a *ḥarīm* zone on the pretext of repulsing Byzantine [maritime] threat? Or can their zone be expanded under the pretense of feeding their animals?
>
> He answered: They shall not be forbidden from developing their woodlands as much as they wish, provided that their territorial extension should not get close to populated areas and cause harm to local residents. If that were to happen, they shall be forbidden from doing so. I do not think that the sea should have its own inviolable zone.[21]

In line with the Prophetic tradition that maintains that every land has its *ḥarīm*, by extension, the coast must also have its *ḥarīm* to include part of the maritime space along the shoreline. However, Ashhab offers a different interpretation. As land, the coast can have a *ḥarīm* extending over a limited and clearly visible seaward distance. However, the sea itself does not have a *ḥarīm*.[22] Thus, the sea bordering the coast can be an appurtenant to the coastland, but not vice versa.[23] This legal opinion does not suggest that nonlocal residents may exploit marine natural resources off coastal settlements, *ribāṭ*s, or installations other than their own according to their free will. Contrary to the open sea, which is common and openly accessible to all, maritime zones contiguous to populated coastal frontiers enjoy a different legal status, although they still may not be subject to private ownership. Dwellers in coastal settlements, garrisoned warriors, and volunteers at *ribāṭ*s could claim exclusive fishing rights, restrict access, or exclude outsiders from exploiting marine resources. Even so, they still could not prevent nonthreatening vessels from freely navigating these waters.[24]

Coastal urban and rural residents, including *ribāṭ* occupants, made a living from farming, local, regional, and overseas trading, manufacturing, gathering hay, collecting wood, producing salt, and catching fish.[25] Abū al-Ḥasan Muḥammad b. Khalaf al-Qābisī (324–403/935–1012)

[20] Djelloul, *al-Ribāṭāt al-baḥriyya*, 201–2.

[21] Abū ʿAbd Allāh b. ʿAbd al-Raḥmān b. Abī Zayd al-Qayrawānī, *al-Nawādir wa-l-ziyādāt ʿalā mā fī al-mudawwana min ghayrihā min al-ummahāt* (Beirut: Dār al-Gharb al-Islāmī, 1999), 10:521: "*wa-lā arā li-l-baḥr ḥarīman.*"

[22] Anke I. Bouzenita, "The Division of the Seas in International and Islamic Law and the Concept of *Ḥarīm al-Baḥr*: A Comparative *Fiqh* Study," *Ilahiyat Studies* 12.2 (2021), 165–72. Sunni jurists unanimously contend that the sea does not have *ḥarīm* zones. By contrast, the Omani Ibadi jurists argue that the *ḥarīm* of the sea extends over 500 cubits from the coastline, whereas others equate it to rivers and opine 40 cubits from the coastline.

[23] Muḥammad Ḥamīdullāh, *The Muslim Conduct of State* (Lahore: Sh. Muhammad Ashraf, 1968), 93–94.

[24] Hassan S. Khalilieh, *Islamic Law of the Sea: Freedom of Navigation and Passage Rights in Islamic Thought* (Cambridge: Cambridge University Press, 2019), 120–21.

[25] Djelloul, *al-Ribāṭāt al-baḥriyya*, 88, 111, 114–15, 118, 119–20, 137, 139, 150, 168, 177, 194, 202–3; Roxani Margariti, "The Rasūlids and the Bountiful Sea: Marine Resources, State Control, and Maritime Culture in the Southern Red Sea and the Gulf of Aden (626/1229–854/1454)," *Der Islam* 98.1 (2021), 71.

was asked about fish vendors purchasing fish from garrisons at the Ribāṭ of Monastir (Tunisia) and selling them in different towns. He responded with concern that this activity could negatively affect the economy of the *ribāṭ*:

> In my view, fishing in [the Sea of Monastir] is like collecting hay and wood from its woodland areas; outsiders cannot exploit them, except if harm is not caused to them, or its occupants do not yield benefits from leaving them [i.e., marine species] unfished. It is not something attainable, like collecting hay and wood in land, which are always within reach. This means that any resident of Monastir who catches fish in this sea has to sell them in its market; whoever wishes may buy [fish] provided that he neither pays a very low price to the seller nor fixes the rate of sale. They must, however, be sold in conformity with what God has assigned to him at that time, regardless of whether they fetch a greater or lesser price. Whatever is left over from the purchase for the consumption of the residents of Monastir, the catcher/fisherman (*al-ṣā'id*) can dispose of and sell [them] as he wishes and at his own free will.
>
> If the catcher intends to fish in this sea with the intention of selling them in the local market, then no one is eligible to buy the fish at the gateway to the sea, or when heading for the market; they must, however, be sold at the marketplace. Merchants who take up residence in these strongholds are associates of other occupants. Nevertheless, if they inflict harm on occupants, their affiliation will be terminated and their residence revoked because they are disqualified from meeting the *ribāṭ*'s religious duties and conditions. Their way of earning a livelihood is equivalent to that of shopkeepers (*ahl al-aswāq*); therefore, they must be forbidden from residing due to the harm they may inflict. Those who inflict harm in one way or another on practitioners of the strongholds must be expelled. Any merchant who arrives in this place for fishing therein with the purpose of trading them in various places other than Monastir must not be permitted to do so because he inflicts harm on those who fish in Monastir. However, if the residents of Monastir have taken what is sufficient to supply their want, there is no harm, if God wills, in transporting what they caught from this sea on the condition that such an action neither inflicts harm nor straitens their conditions; this is because sea fishing is dissimilar to land hunting, where the land prey [is easier to attain]. If someone inclines to leave them unexploited in that place, I do not see any reason why local people should be prevented from reaping the benefits of fishing! This is what seems to me [is happening] in the case of the Sea of Monastir. May God grant us success![26]

A number of legal inferences can be gleaned from the above responsum. First, and consistent with the Prophetic tradition, being part of the land, every coast has its own *ḥarīm*. Second, local residents of coastal settlements enjoyed exclusive rights to exploit marine resources available within a specified distance from the coast. Therefore, access to any offshore *ḥarīm* was either conditional or denied outright to outsiders. Third, although exact boundaries for the maritime *ḥarīms* were not fixed, it is reasonable to assume that they ranged up to the seaward distance at which a vessel could be sighted from the coast. Fourth, exploitation of natural resources in the "protected maritime zones" – if such a term is appropriate – required prior approval from local, and at times peripheral, governing authorities. Fifth, in order to conserve the marine ecosystem and not to affect the economies and livelihoods of the local residents, both native and foreign fishermen alike were obliged not to overfish and deplete the resources, since the needs of the community held precedence over those of the individual;[27] local coastal residents had the rights

[26] Abū al-ʿAbbās Aḥmad b. Yaḥyā al-Wansharīsī, *al-Mi'yār al-mu'rib wa-l-jāmi' al-mughrib 'an fatāwā ahl Ifrīqiya wa-l-Andalus wa-l-Maghrib* (Beirut: Dār al-Gharb al-Islāmī, 1981), 2:5–6.

[27] For a deeper insight into the impact of poaching and overfishing on the environment in view of Islamic law and jurisprudence, see Abū al-Khayr N. Atta, "Athar al-ṣayd al-jā'ir 'alā al-bī'a: Dirāsa fī ḍaw' al-fiqh al-Islāmī," *Majallat al-Zahrā'* 31 (2021), 301–424.

to exclude nonlocals from fishing in their own coastal waters. Sixth, even though the sea is considered to be the property of no particular person but instead common to all, and although fishermen could freely set sail for any destination, they were not licensed to fish unrestrained within sighting distance of populated coastal areas other than those of their own hometowns. In other words, the maritime spaces bordering coastal settlements may be considered to have had the status of *res communes*, whereby local residents held exclusive rights over – but could not deny nonlocal vessels from passing through – these natural resources.[28]

8.2 FISHERIES

With the exception of amphibians, all kinds of seafood – animals and plants, either alive or dead – are lawful to eat pursuant to the Quranic verses and the Prophetic tradition.[29] Seafood constituted an integral part of the typical diet of coastal residents, seamen, and sea travelers due to its accessibility and affordability.[30] In times of drought and famine, fish was the main staple

[28] Offshore waters, rivers, and springs must be freely accessible and shared by all people. Individuals are not authorized to erect private constructions that may hinder or prevent access to aquatic resources. Abū ʿAbd Allāh ʿAbd al-Raḥmān b. al-Qāsim b. Khālid b. Junāda al-ʿUtqī al-Miṣrī, known as Ibn al-Qāsim (133–91/751–806), an Egyptian-born jurist and one of Mālik's disciples, was asked about a person who prevents others by different means from reaching and exploiting natural resources. Ibn al-Qāsim rules: "No one has the right to block a sea bay [inlet] or a valley with a barrier thus excluding people from fishing in it; he and other people alike enjoy similar fishing rights. Muḥammad b. Rushd decrees: This is quite true because the river is common to all Muslims. No one has fishing rights over others even if his estate is adjacent to either edge of the riverbanks. He neither has right to block it with a barrier, nor allocate an exclusive fishing area for himself. If he does so, he is more deserving to fish in it in for his own need only. Then, let the people share fishery with him in it. This opinion has been endorsed by Muṭrif [b. ʿAbd Allāh al-Hilālī, d. 220/835] and Ibn al-Mājishūn [d. 212/827] in the *Wāḍiḥa*. In my opinion, he is entitled to fish for his own need only. May God bless us with success." See Abū al-Walīd Muḥammad b. Aḥmad b. Rushd al-Qurṭubī, *al-Bayān wa-l-taḥṣīl wa-l-sharḥ wa-l-tawjīh wa-l-taʿlīl fī masāʾil al-mustakhraja* (Beirut: Dār al-Gharb al-Islāmī, 1984), 3:314–15.

[29] "Lawful to you is the pursuit of water-game and its use for food – for the benefit of yourselves and those who travel" (Q 5:96); "Nor are the two bodies of flowing water alike – the one palatable, sweet, and pleasant to drink, and the other, salty and bitter. Yet from each [kind of water] do ye eat flesh fresh and tender, and ye extract ornaments to wear; and thou seest. The ships therein that plough the waves that ye may seek [thus] of the Bounty of God that ye may be grateful" (Q 35:12); all Quranic translations are taken from ʿAbdullāh Y. ʿAlī, *The Meaning of the Holy Qurʾān* (Brentwood: Amana Corporation, 1991). In regard to the lawfulness of seafood, the Prophet Muhammad decrees: "Two types of dead animals and two types of blood have been made lawful for us: the two types of dead animals are locusts and fish [seafood], while the two types of blood are the liver and the spleen"; and "It is whose water is pure and its dead [animals] are lawful [to eat]." Ibn Rushd, *al-Bayān wa-l-taḥṣīl*, 3:275–76, 299–301; Rāshid M. al-Ḥarbī, "al-Aḥādīth al-nabawiyya al-wārida fī al-baḥr jamʿan wa-dirāsatan wa-takhrījan" (master's thesis, Jordan University, 2004), 42–51; Aḥmad ʿA. Ismāʿīl, "Min aḥkām al-asmāk fī al-fiqh al-Islāmī," *Majallat al-Jāmiʿa al-ʿIrāqiyya* 53.1 (2021), 195–212.

[30] Margariti, "The Rasūlids," 69–99; Elizabeth A. Lambourn, *Abraham's Luggage: A Social Life of Things in the Medieval Indian Ocean World* (Cambridge: Cambridge University Press, 2018), 65, 107, 110–11, 181–82, 184, 215–17, 254–67; Nalini Sadhale and Y. L. Nene, "On Fish in Manasollasa (c. 1131 AD)," *Asian Agri-History* 9.3 (2005), 177–99; Alan G. Walmsley, "The Cities and Districts of Palestine and East Jordan during the Early Islamic, ʿAbbāsid, and Early Fāṭimid Periods" (PhD diss., University of Sydney, 1987), 76, 94, 99, 176, 191; Djelloul, *al-Ribāṭāt al-baḥriyya*, 202–3; Tahar Kaddouri, "al-Samak wa-l-taghdhiya bi-l-gharb al-Islāmī fī al-ʿaṣr al-wasīṭ," *ʿUṣur al-Jadīda* 10 (2013), 46–48; Ali Ashi, "al-Ṣayd al-baḥrī fī al-Maghrib al-awsaṭ bayn al-mumārasa al-ḥirafiyya wa-l-ḥayāt al-maʿīshiyya," *Journal of Social and Human Science Studies (Oran)* 10.2 (2021), 366–68; Mohamed Benamira, "al-Tharwa al-samakiyya fī al-sawāḥil al-mutawassiṭiyya min bilād al-Maghrib fī al-ʿaṣr al-wasīṭ," *Dirāsāt fī Āthār al-Waṭan al-ʿArabī* 12.12 (2009) 503–18; Mohamed Benamira, "Hijrat samak al-tun (tūna) wa-iṣṭiyādihi bi-bilād al-Maghrib fī al-ʿaṣr al-wasīṭ," *Dirāsāt fī Āthār al-Waṭan al-ʿArabī* 15.15 (2012), 1796–803; Nawal Belmadani, "al-Tharwa al-samakiyya bi-l-Maghrib al-Islāmī khilāl al-ʿaṣr al-wasīṭ," *Majallat al-Mawāqif li-l-Buḥūth wa-l-Dirāsāt fī al-mujtamaʿ wa-l-tārīkh* 10 (2015), 180–84; John Cooper, "The Medieval Nile: Route, Navigation, and Landscape in Islamic Egypt" (PhD diss., University of Southampton, 2008), 158–59; ʿAbd Allāh ʿAbd al-Majīd, "al-Asmāk wa-l-ḥaywānāt al-nīliyya wa-l-baḥriyya wa-atharuhā ʿalā al-ḥayāt al-ʿāmma bi-Miṣr fī al-ʿaṣr al-Mamlūkī fī ḍawʾ kitābāt al-raḥḥāla wa-l-jughrāfiyyīn (648–923/1250–1517)," *Majallat Kulliyyat al-Ādāb* 14.1 (2022), 2255–88; Ibrāhīm ʿAbd al-Majīd,

food for starving and impoverished people; for example, during the 535/1140 famine in the Maghrib.[31] Since marine resources – fisheries in particular – had long been acknowledged by provincial and central governments, the Abbasid senior courtier and fiscal administrator of Syria and Egypt Abū al-Ḥasan Aḥmad b. Muḥammad b. al-Mudabbir (ca. 868–71 CE) founded the bureau of Kharāj Maḍārib al-Awtār wa-Maghāris al-Shibāk (Tax on Fish Trap Strings and Aquaculture Nets),[32] which is considered apparently the oldest bureau of fisheries and aquaculture in the Islamic Mediterranean.[33] Together with professional scribes, witnesses, and tax collectors, the chancellor's primary purposes were to issue fishing licenses (*maṣāyid*), collect taxes on fisheries, and regulate fish farming in the Gulf of Alexandria, Lake of Alexandria, Lake of Burullus, Nastarū, Damietta frontier, Aswan, and natural inlets and artificial farms and marine plantations along the Nile and the coastal frontiers.[34] In order to promote the growth of sustainable fish farming, provincial and central administrations dug canals and built fish farms, erected dams on rivers, streams, and estuaries, dredged canals and waterways, assigned watchmen to protect and preserve aquaculture against man-made and natural pollution, regulated fisheries within the state's inland waters, particularly to avoid excessive and unjust consumption of fishery resources, established fish markets in specific places, and monitored the fish market prices and environmental cleanliness.[35]

In a similar vein, rulers of the Maghrib established regulations governing the extraction of corals. Located near the port-city of Bône (in Algiers today), Marsā al-Kharaz (La Calle) held a reputation as a major source of coral reefs, particularly the highly sought-after red corals.[36] In a

"Tanmiyat al-tharwa al-samakiyya bi-Miṣr khilāl al-ʿaṣrayn al-Ayyūbī wa-l-Mamlūkī (567–923/1171–1517): Dirāsa muqārana," *Majallat Kulliyyat al-Lugha al-ʿArabiyya bi-Ītāy al-Bārūd* 33.3 (2020), 3511–23; Ulfat J. Muḥammad, "al-Tharwa al-samakiyya fī Miṣr khilāl al-ʿaṣr al-Fāṭimī (358–567/969–1171)," *Majallat Buḥūth Killiyyat al-Ādāb* 121 (2020), 1837–39, 1844–48, 1850–54, 1862; Michelle Alexander et al., "Diet, Societ, and Economy in Late Medieval Spain: Stable Isotope Evidence from Muslims and Christians from Gandía, Valencia," *American Journal of Physical Anthropology* 156 (2015), 265–68; Nawal Nasrallah, *Best Delectable Foods and Dishes from al-Andalus and al-Maghrib: A Cookbook by Thirteenth-Century Andalusi Scholar Ibn Razīn al-Tujībī (1227–1293)* (Leiden: Brill, 2021), 361–82, describes the varieties of dishes with various types of fish in Andalusia.

31 Ibn al-Zayyāt Abū Yaʿqūb Yūsuf b. Yaḥyā al-Tādilī, *al-Tashawwuf ilā rijāl al-taṣawwuf wa-akhbār Abī al-ʿAbbās al-Sibtī* (Rabat: Manshūrāt Kulliyat al-Ādāb wa-l-ʿUlūm al-Insāniyya, 1984), 183; Bahījah al-Shādhilī and Amīn al-Buddādī, "Tafāʿul al-mutaṣawwufa maʿ al-majāl al-baḥrī bi-l-Maghrib al-wasīṭ: Mulāḥaẓāt wa-maẓāhir wa-asbāb," *Revue Lixus* 38 (2021), 34.

32 Taqī al-Dīn Aḥmad b. ʿAlī al-Maqrīzī, *al-Mawāʿiẓ wa-l-iʿtibār bi-dhikr al-khiṭaṭ wa-l-āthār* (Beirut: Dār al-Kutub al-ʿIlmiyya, 1998), 1:202; Muḥammad, "al-Tharwa al-samakiyya," 1858; Yomna M. Osman, "Fisheries and Fishing Boat Building Traditions in Egypt during the Islamic Period," in *Maritime Archaeology Graduate Symposium 2021: Short Report Series* (London: Honor Frost Foundation, 2023), 2.

33 A similar administrative office with the same functions called *ʿāmil al-maḍārib* (inspector of fisheries) existed in the Maghrib. Among the inspector's administrative duties, who gained his authority from the port superintendent, were the regulations of fisheries, collection of fishery tax, and distribution of fish to the needy and poor people. Shihāb al-Dīn Aḥmad b. Muḥammad al-Maqqarī al-Tilmisānī, *Azhār al-riyāḍ fī akhbār ʿiyāḍ* (Cairo: Maṭbaʿat Lajnat al-Taʾlīf wa-l-Tarjama wa-l-Nashr, 1939), 1:42–43.

34 al-Maqrīzī, *al-Mawāʿiẓ*, 1:202; ʿAbd al-Majīd, "al-Asmāk," 2257, 2264, 2266; Aḥmad b. ʿAbd Allāh al-Qalqashandī, *Ṣubḥ al-aʿshā fī ṣināʿat al-inshā* (Cairo: al-Maṭbaʿa al-Amīriyya, 1919), 3:307–8, refers to the four major Egyptian lakes; Abū al-Ḥasan ʿAlī b. ʿUthmān al-Makhzūmī, *Kitāb al-minhāj fī ʿilm kharāj Miṣr*, ed. Claude Cahen and Yūsuf Rāghib (Cairo: Institut Français d'Archéologie Orientale, 1986), 16–17, 27–28, 58, refers to taxes on fishing boats; Hassanein M. Rabie, "The Financial System of Egypt 564–741 A.H./1169–1341 A.D." (PhD diss., University of London, 1968), 170–72.

35 ʿIṣām M. ʿAbd al-Mawlā, "al-Taktīkāt al-ʿArabiyya fī tanmiyat al-tharwa al-samakiyya fī bilād al-Maghrib al-Islāmī khilāl al-qarnayn al-thānī wa-l-thālith li-l-hijra," *Majallat Madārāt Tārīkhiyya* 3.1 (2021), 96–106; Muḥammad, "al-Tharwa al-samakiyya," 1854–61; ʿAbd al-Majīd, "Tanmiyat al-tharwa," 3523–36; Belmadani, "al-Tharwa al-samakiyya," 191; ʿAbd al-Majīd, "al-Asmāk," 2266–67.

36 Abū ʿAbd Allāh Muḥammad b. Aḥmad al-Muqaddasī, *Aḥsan al-taqāsīm fī maʿrifat al-aqālīm* (Leiden: Brill, 1906), 226; Abū ʿUbayd Allāh ʿAbd Allāh b. ʿAbd al-ʿAzīz al-Bakrī, *al-Mughrib fī dhikr bilād Ifrīqiya wa-l-Maghrib* (Baghdad:

bid to curb the overexploitation of these precious resources, Ibn Ḥawqal (331–68/943–78), who praises the exceptional quality of these coral reefs, emphasizes their unparalleled uniqueness when compared to reefs from other seas. According to him, these rulers appointed trustees, overseers, and laborers to closely monitor the extracted quantity, quality, and sale process of these minerals. He further adds: "Given the region's abundant coral reserves, about fifty boats were designated for coral extraction, each roughly carrying twenty men at any given time."[37]

The Quran views the sea and its natural resources as among God's bounties therefore they must be accessible to all mankind.[38] This principle is broadly applicable to the high sea but less implementable on territorial waters. Documentary, historical, and legal evidence from the Islamic Mediterranean and Indian Ocean assert that local coastal communities enjoyed privileged access to their offshore marine natural resources. An extraordinary example is documented in a royal decree issued by the Fatimid caliph al-Ḥāfiẓ (r. 525–44/1131–49) on Rajab 21, 528/May 17, 1134. Based on this caliphal decree, access to the Lake of Burullus, laying to the west of Rosetta on the Mediterranean, was exclusively restricted to local residents and the *ḍāmin* (tax-farmer), who normally paid a sum determined in advance to the treasury in return for keeping tax revenues for himself from a defined district or area, including a limited offshore zone. Save for local residents and the *ḍāmin*(s), outsiders were denied access to fishing in the Lake of Burullus and its adjacent Mediterranean waters.[39] Nonlocals and aliens were required to abide by the rules and regulations of fisheries in every province and coastal zone, as discussed earlier with reference to the *ribāṭ* practitioners.

Islam emphasizes the significance of maintaining cleanliness on spiritual, physical, and communal levels. A tradition attributed to the Prophet Muhammad, on the authority of Saʿīd b. al-Musayyib (13–94/642–712), states: "God is good and He loves what is good; He is clean and He loves cleanliness; He is kind and He loves kindness; and He is generous and He loves generosity. So clean" – I think he said – "your courtyards."[40] In compliance with the sharia, *ḥisba* (marketplace) manuals instruct Muslims to refrain from causing environmental harm.[41] Fishermen, fish vendors, and cooks were required to keep the marketplace clean and avoid causing harm and inconvenience to market-goers, shoppers, and merchants. Ensuring the tidiness and impeccable state of the spaces in front of seafood stores and restaurants was of utmost importance. Fishery wastes had to be dumped away from streets, fresh water-tanks, and waterways for the sake of preventing leachate and emission of stinks.[42]

Maktabat al-Muthannā, 1968), 55; Sydney J. Hickson, *An Introduction to the Study of Recent Corals* (Manchester: University of Manchester, 1924), 240.

37 Abū al-Qāsim Muḥammad b. Ḥawqal, *Ṣūrat al-arḍ* (Beirut: Dār Maktabat al-Ḥayāt, 1992), 76.

38 Khalilieh, *Islamic Law of the Sea*, 31–41.

39 Geoffrey Khan, "A Copy of a Decree from the Archives of the Fāṭimīd Chancery in Egypt," *Bulletin of the School of Oriental and African Studies* 49.3 (1986), 441–43. The decree reads as follows: "Fishermen from outside of this province living in the province of al-Gharbiyya are fishing along the shores of the Lake (of Burullus) in the said province and all this is causing damage to the *ḍāmins* and to the finances of the *dīwān* (custom house). . . . (It enjoins) the prevention of whomsoever of those who are not their tenants encroaches upon the shores of their province. . . . Let the Chosen *Amīr*, the diligent representative of its *dīwān* – may God save him (and all the *amīrs*, governors, and employees) – ensure that all the commands and prohibitions contained in this decree are carried out; let him stand within the bounds of his office in loyalty and absolute obedience."

40 Abū ʿĪsā Muḥammad b. ʿĪsā al-Tirmidhī, *al-Jāmiʿ al-kabīr* (Beirut: Dār al-Gharb al-Islāmī, 1996), 4:495, hadith no. 2799; Tāj al-Dīn Abū Naṣr al-Kāfī, *Ṭabaqāt al-Shāfiʿiyya al-kubrā* (Cairo: Dār Iḥyāʾ al-Kutub al-ʿArabiyya, 1979), 6:289; Nomanul Haq, "Islam and Ecology: Toward Retrieval and Reconstruction," *Daedalus* 130.4 (2001), 164–67.

41 Ḥajj Aḥmad ʿAbd Allāh, "Dawr al-muḥtasib fī ḥimāyat al-bīʾa," *Majallat al-Wāḥāt li-l-Buḥūth wa-l-Dirāsāt* 12.2 (2019), 189–208.

42 Évariste Lévi Provençal (ed.), *Thalāth tasāʾil fī al-ḥisba* (Cairo: L'Institut Français d'archéologie orientale, 1955), 45, 97–98; Belmadani, "al-Tharwa al-samakiyya," 193.

Ḥisba manuals provide guidance to both fish vendors and buyers on proper conduct and behavior in the marketplace. Fish vendors had to routinely clean their saddlebags, scales, and all their gear, including the bags used by carriers. Before leaving, they had to sprinkle a layer of salt on these items to prevent any lingering odors. However, whoever violated this rule and his saddlebag was left unclean with the carrier was subjected to discipline and rebuke. Whoever purchased fish for personal consumption had to carry it in a container to prevent spreading offensive odors to others' clothes in the marketplace. Had anyone been found holding fish in his hand would have it placed on his lap, thereby setting a disciplinary example for others to observe.[43]

8.3 MARINE POLLUTION

The principles guiding the preservation and protection of the earth's natural environment – terrestrial, oceanic, and aerial dimensions – are evidenced in the two fundamental sources of Islamic law, the Quran and the Prophetic tradition. The need to conserve the environment and protect natural resources from pollution is framed in various ecological terms in the Quran, the Sunna, and exegetical literature.

These sources apply several expressions of preservation of nature from pollution, namely *fasād*[44] (corruption), *ḍurr*[45] (harm), and *nahī*[46] (prohibition). They clearly indicate the prohibition of applying changes in the various components of nature, both marine and terrestrial; a prohibition against the violation of the environmental equilibrium (*mīzān*)[47] in nature and causing irreversible damage in all that God has created on land and sea, changes in the patterns of human environmental conceptions, determination of the fact that man bears responsibility for the pollution of the environment, with emphasis on those activities that endanger the continued

[43] Muḥammad b. Aḥmad b. Bassām al-Muḥtasib, *Nihāyat al-rutba fī ṭalab al-ḥisba* (Baghdad: Maṭba'at al-Ma'ārif, 1968), 53.

[44] The triliteral Arabic root *f-s-d* and its derivatives are widely mentioned (approximately 150 times) across 22 chapters of the Quran, applying to different aspects of the worldly life of mankind. It broadly denotes activities and actions that cause physical or spiritual harm to any individual and society, or tangible change in the earth's ecological equilibrium. For further details, see Fethi B. Jomaa Ahmed, "Corruption according to the Main Sources of Islam," *Intellectual Discourse* 26.1 (2018), 91–110; Mohammed A. al-Jubouri, "Mafhūm al-fasād wa-l-ifsād fī al-Qur'ān al-karīm," *Majallat Kulliyyat al-Tarbiya al-Asāsiyya* 7 (2012), 36–51; Tareq T. Abdallah, "al-Fasād wa-madlūlātihi fī ḍaw' al-Qur'ān al-karīm wa-l-sunna al-nabawiyya," *Prosiding Konferensi Nasional Bahasa Arab VII* (2021), 234–48; Omamah Hamasha, "Bayān mafhūm al-fasād fī siyāq al-āyāt al-Qur'āniyya wa-l-aḥādīth al-nabawiyya wa-anwā'ihi," *IUG Journal of Islamic Studies* 30.2 (2022), 762–99; Khalilieh, *Islamic Law of the Sea*, 170–79, refers to piracy and brigandage.

[45] The term *ḍurr* and its derivatives occur in the Quran sixty-six times.

[46] *Nahī* and its derivatives are found in the Qur'ān in twenty-five verses.

[47] In conformity with the concept of *mīzān*, God has created the whole world in a harmonious condition, subjugated it to mankind's stewardship for the benefit of all His creatures on the planet, provided that they conserve its equilibrium and not cause harm to it. Muhammad R. Akhtar, "Towards an Islamic Approach for Environmental Balance," *Islamic Economic Studies* 3.2 (1996), 57–76; Dina M. Abdelzaher et al., "Eco-Islam: Beyond the Principles of *Why* and What, and into the Principles of *How*," *Journal of Business Ethics* 155.3 (2019), 631–33; Djamel Ghernaout, "Environmental Principles in the Holy Koran and the Sayings of the Prophet Muhammad," *American Journal of Environmental Protection* 6.3 (2017), 76–77; Rania Kamla et al., "Islam, Nature and Accounting: Islamic Principles and the Notion of Accounting for the Environment," *Accounting Forum* 30.3 (2006), 249–55; Labeeb Bsoul et al., "Islam's Perspective on Environmental Sustainability: A Conceptual Analysis," *Social Sciences* 11 (2022), 4–5, 8; Riham R. Rizk, "Islamic Environmental Ethics," *Journal of Islamic Accounting and Business Research* 5.2 (2014), 196; Willis Jenkins, "Islamic Law and Environmental Ethics: How Jurisprudence (*Usul al-Fiqh*) Mobilizes Practical Reform," *Worldviews* 9.3 (2005), 342–44; Yūsuf al-Qaraḍāwī, *Ri'āyat al-bī'a fī sharī'at al-Islām* (Cairo: Dār al-Shurūq, 2001), 214–15.

existence of the various living creatures and plants as mentioned in different Quranic verses.[48] Both sources refer to human influence and natural factors as the main contributors to environmental pollution.[49] All this is said alongside guidance given to humans and instructing them on how to protect the marine environment from the various causes of pollution in view of the negative effects of pollution on mankind, plants, and animals.[50] Marine pollution may cause damage to aquatic plants, ore deposits, gems, and minerals found in the depths, offshores, and littorals and change the ecological balance.[51]

Q 30:41 lays the responsibility for spoiling the terrestrial and marine environment upon the bad and careless behavior of human beings.[52] As a result of the widespread pollution on both masses, there is a decrease in the benefits that could be derived from them, and prices are increased. Many irreversible damages and plagues that are caused by pollution may afflict people, plants, and living creatures causing blindness, death, pestilences, dearth of natural resources, and harm to their quantity and quality,[53] as noted by Muḥammad b. Aḥmad al-Qurṭubī (611–71/1214–73):

> Corruption (*fasād*) in the sea results from the sins of the Children of Adam causing a cessation of fishing. ʿAṭiyya[54] said: "If the rain is lessened, there is also less diving into the depths of the sea, fishermen fail in their catching, and marine animals could lose much of their eyesight." Ibn ʿAbbās said: "If rains fall in abundance, oystershells in the sea would open and every rain drop from the sky falls into them is a pearl." It is said that *fasād* denotes price stagnation and lack of livelihood. It is also said that *fasād* signifies commitment of evil acts, highway robbery, and oppression, that is, this action has become an obstacle to planting, building, and trading. … The lack of rain and high prices become discernible. Evil deeds have appeared on land and sea, therefore God has withheld rain and the prices have risen (*ẓahara qillat al-ghayth wa-ghalāʾ al-siʿr*).[55]

48 "There is the type of man whose speech about this world's life may dazzle thee and he calls God to witness about what is in his heart; yet is he the most contentious of enemies. When he turns his back his aim everywhere is to spread mischief through the earth and destroy crops and cattle. But God loveth not mischief" (Q 2:204–5); see also Q 5:32, 7:74, 30:41.

49 Nature plays a role in the pollution of the sea and the marine and aquatic environment through physical forces and natural phenomena such as earthquakes, volcanoes, hurricanes, tornadoes, storms, and floods. See Q 7:133, 10:22, 13:17, 34:16, 46:24, 99:1–2. Some commentators contend that these verses refer to famine, diseases, drought, and the sinking of ships. Others, however, argue that the reference here is to false opinions or the corruption of morals in general.

50 Tirmidhī, *al-Jāmiʿ al-kabīr*, 4:495, hadith no. 2799; al-Kāfī, Ṭabaqāt al-Shāfiʿiyya, 6:289: "the religion is built on hygiene"; Haq, "Islam and Ecology."

51 ʿAbd al-Raḥmān b. ʿAbd Allāh al-Suhaylī, *al-Durr al-manthūr fī al-tafsīr bi-l-maʾthūr* (Cairo: Markaz Hajar li-l-Dirāsāt al-ʿArabiyya wa-l-Islāmiyya, 2003), 21:48; Muḥammad Murtaḍā al-Ḥusaynī al-Zabīdī, *Tāj al-ʿarūs min jawāhir al-qāmūs* (Kuwait: Maṭbaʿat Ḥukūmat al-Kuwait, 1965), 1:114.

52 ʿAbd Allāh Shaḥāta, *Tafsīr al-Qurʾān al-karīm* (Cairo: Dār Gharīb, 2000), 11:4157; Muḥammad J. al-Qāsimī, *Tafsīr al-Qāsimī al-musammā Maḥāsin al-taʾwīl* (Cairo: Dār Iḥyāʾ al-Kutub al-ʿArabiyya, 1957), 13:4787; Shazia Chaudhry, "Environmental Stewardship: Perspectives from the Islamic Teachings," *African Journal of Sociological and Psychological Studies* 1.1 (2022), 127–28.

53 Abū al-Fidā ʿImād al-Dīn Ismāʿīl b. ʿUmar b. Kathīr, *Tafsīr al-Qurʾān al-ʿaẓīm* (Riyadh: Dār Ṭība li-l-Nashr wa-l-Tawzīʿ, 1999), 6:319; Ṭanṭāwī Jawharī, *al-Jawāhir fī tafsīr al-Qurʾān al-karīm al-mushtamil ʿalā ʿajāʾib badāʾiʿ al-mukawwanāt wa-gharāʾib al-āyāt al-bāhirāt* (Cairo: al-Bābī al-Ḥalabī, 1922), 15:96–100; Shaḥāta, *Tafsīr*, 11:4157; Fahad al-Refaei, "The Protection of the Marine Environment from Oil Pollution by Ships in the Arabian Gulf and the Role of Saudi Arabia: A Study in International Law with Special Reference to Islamic Law" (PhD diss., University of Portsmouth, 2009), 12.

54 Abū Muḥammad ʿAbd al-Ḥaqq b. Abī Bakr Ghālib b. ʿAṭiyya (481–541/1088–1146) is a renowned Andalusian jurist, hadith transmitter, exegete, and the author of *al-Muḥarrar al-wajīz fī tafsīr al-Kitāb al-ʿazīz* (*The Compendious Record in the Interpretation of the Mighty Book*), which is considered one of the leading Sunni commentaries of the Quran in the Maghrib.

55 Abū ʿAbd Allāh Muḥammad b. Aḥmad al-Anṣārī al-Qurṭubī, *al-Jāmiʿ li-aḥkām al-Qurʾān* (Cairo: Dār ʿĀlam al-Kutub, 2003), 14: 40–41.

In line with Quranic verses,[56] exegetes contend that damage caused to the marine environment – high seas, shorelines, residential coastal zones, settlements bordering estuaries and riverbanks, and islands – is essentially the result of improper, sinful, unethical, and immoral behavior of humans, who violate the scheme of the Creator.[57] The deviant and imprudent behavior of people is the main factor bearing responsibility for the pollution of the environment. Pollution is also perceived by exegetes as activities that contradict and oppose the precepts of religion, justice, and truth.[58] It is argued that prior to the existence and evolution of the human race there was no environmental pollution at all.[59] The cause of environmental pollution is people; however, everything that has not been touched by humans remains free of environmental pollution.[60] This explains why the Quran assigns great importance to the preservation of the natural environment and strongly urges humans to protect and maintain it.[61]

Protecting and sustaining the environment is considered an act of worship that generates reward in this life and the hereafter.[62] The reward promised by God might be tangible and reflected by the wealth of resources from which the maximum can be derived.[63] Exegetes contend that the very offering of reward has many consequences. They argue that the threat of punishment is meant to serve as a warning against those who do not safeguard and protect the marine environment against pollution as expected and demanded, with the assumption that the kind of deterrence and penalties mentioned in the Quran will prevent mankind from activities that cause environmental damage.[64] Besides the reference to the punishments awaiting those who bear the main responsibility for pollution and damage to the sea, the commentators also stress the need for the supervision and guardianship over the sea and marine environment, including the rights, benefits, and even the protection that can be derived from the sea by those

[56] "that the hands of men have earned" (Q 30:41); "When he turns his back his aim everywhere is to spread mischief through the earth" (Q 2:205).

[57] Q 2:205, 30:41; al-Qurṭubī, *al-Jāmiʿ*, 14:14; ʿAbd al-Razzāq b. Hammām al-Ṣanʿānī, *Tafsīr ʿAbd al-Razzāq* (Beirut: Dār al-Kutub al-ʿIlmiyya, 1999), 3:20; al-Ḍaḥḥāk b. Muzāḥim al-Hilālī, *Tafsīr al-Ḍaḥḥāk* (Cairo: Dār al-Salām, 1999), 2:664; Shaḥāta, *Tafsīr*, 11:4157.

[58] Abū al-Barakāt ʿAbd Allāh al-Nasafī, *Tafsīr al-Nasafī* (Beirut: Dār al-Nafāʾis, 2005), 3:396; Shaḥāta, *Tafsīr*, 11:4157; Muḥammad M. Shaʿrāwī, *Tafsīr al-Shaʿrāwī* (Cairo: Dār Akhbār al-Yawm, 1999), 18:11474–78; Rāshid al-ʿAjmī, "Itlāf al-bīʾa al-barriyya min manẓūr al-sunna al-nabawiyya," *Majallat Kulliyyat Dār al-ʿUlūm* 37 (2020), 22–25.

[59] Muḥammad M. Shaʿrāwī, "al-Kawn, al-ḥaḍāra, al-talawwuth," *Majallat al-Tanmiya wa-l-Bīʾa* 9 (1987), 6–7.

[60] Shaʿrāwī, *Tafsīr*, 18:11471; Qaraḍāwī, *Riʿāyat al-bīʾa*, 221–22.

[61] Q 2:30, 2:60, 16:65, 21:32, 28:77, 30:41.

[62] Shaʿrāwī, *Tafsīr*, 18:11471.

[63] Abū Jaʿfar b. Jarīr al-Ṭabarī, *Jāmiʿ al-bayān ʿan taʾwīl al-Qurʾān* (Cairo: Dār Hājar, 2001), 18:513; Ibn Kathīr, *Tafsīr*, 6:320; Refaei, "Protection of the Marine Environment," 28–30.

[64] "taste of some of their deeds" (Q 30:41); "but God loveth not mischief" (Q 2:205); "and heaped therein mischief (on mischief). Therefore did thy Lord pour on them a scourge of diverse chastisements. For thy Lord (as a Guardian) on a watchtower" (Q 89:12–14); "and refrain from evil and mischief on the earth" (Q 7:74); "Say: Travel through the earth and see what was the end of those before (you): most of them worshipped others besides God. But set thou thy face to the right Religion before there comes from God the Day which there is no chance of averting: on that Day shall men be divided (in two). Those who reject Faith will suffer from that rejection: and those who work righteousness will spread their couch (of repose) for themselves (in heaven). That He may reward those who believe and work righteous deeds, out of His Bounty. For He loves not those who reject Faith" (Q 30:42–45). Quranic verses emphasize the punishments expected for all those who violate the commandment of God, as well as the reward expected for the community of believers who observe His precepts. With regard to the reward for believers, these will be granted a reward that is ten times and even up to 700 times more than what they have done, all in accordance with the will and considered judgment of God, while the reward and payment for heretics is perdition and doom (*halāk*). Many religious regulations can be found that deal with the issue of punishment for all those who contaminate the sea and its environment. See Jalāl al-Dīn al-Suyūṭī, *Sunan al-Nasāʾī* (Beirut: Dār al-Bashāʾir al-Islāmiyya, 1994), 8:75–77; Ali M. al-Damkhi, "Environmental Ethics in Islam: Principles, Violations, and Future Perspectives," *International Journal of Environmental Studies* 65.1 (2008), 18; Refaei, "Protection of the Marine Environment," 30–31.

who act to protect and care for it and its environment.[65] They note that divine scriptures contain references to messengers who were sent by God especially to transmit His tidings and instructions regarding the struggle against corruption and pollution in order to save mankind from such damage.[66]

The exegetes' and jurists' attitude toward the complex issues relating to the protection of the sea and aquatic environment focus on three dimensions: conceptual, theoretical, and practical. They promulgated regulations and responsa that were meant to protect the aquatic environment from corruption and contamination. These regulations were based on the perception of total responsibility that applies to every Muslim wherever he/she may be, and obliges him/her to protect the oceans, seas, rivers, and other aquatic environments and refrain from dumping wastes into them. This implies positive behavior, mainly in protecting the quality of water, which is paramount to the observance of the commandments that atone for sins,[67] as presented in the following responsum:

> Imam Mālik [97–179/715–95] was asked: Consider the Gulf of Alexandria. If the Nile flows into it, ships sail in it and its water is clear and pure. However, when the Nile recedes, its water's color changes and it has a pleasant smell, yet ships continue to sail in it, and it becomes abundant with water. People pour their toilet waste into it, and its water is used for washing clothes and performing ablutions for prayer. He responded: If toilet waste is poured into it causing discoloration, I do not like this. [ʿAbd Allāh] b. ʿUmar [10–73/610–92], who was well-known among people for his piety, used to say: "I like to leave between me and unlawful [things] a veil of lawful things." Mālik commented: "You should stick to what you have no doubt about and let people think what they want, as they may have different opinions."[68]
>
> Muḥammad b. Rushd [450–520/1058–1126] rules: It is indeed true, as he has asserted, because even if the water [in the Gulf] is abundant and clear enabling ships to sail in it, it is inappropriate to perform ablution with when it becomes stagnant and changes its color, due to the possibility that toilet waste is poured into it. It is likely that its discoloration may have resulted from the pouring of such toilet waste into it, but not due to its stagnation and stillness at its spot. If it is discovered that its discoloration has not resulted from the pouring of said toilet waste into

65 Shaʿrāwī, *Tafsīr*, 18:11472; Akrum Helfaya et al., "Qur'ānic Ethics for Environmental Responsibility: Implications for Business Practice," *Journal of Business Ethics* 150 (2018), 1105–28; Asmawati Muhamad et al., "Quranic Messages on Environmental Sustainability: An Expository Study of Its Relevance," *Al-Bayān: Journal of Qur'ānic and Ḥadīth Studies* 17 (2019), 38–59.

66 Q 28:77; Ibn Kathīr, *Tafsīr*, 6:320; Shihāb al-Dīn Abū al-Faḍl b. Ḥajar al-ʿAsqalānī, *Fatḥ al-Bārī sharḥ Ṣaḥīḥ al-Bukhārī* (Riyadh: Dār al-Salām, 2000), 11:443; Wahba al-Zuḥaylī, *Tafsīr al-munīr fī al-ʿaqīda wa-l-sharīʿa wa-l-manhaj* (Beirut: Dār al-Fikr al-Muʿāṣir, 1997), 21:101: "Abū Hurayra recounts, on the authority of the [Messenger of God], may peace be upon him: 'God has commanded the believers as He has commanded His messengers.' The spread of corruption and deviation phenomenon throughout the globe is labeled as the greatest evil after polytheism. They are the cause for damage and significant decline, drought, famine, the lack of sufficient plant growth, disappearance of blessing, disobedience, highway robbery, injustice, and other iniquities and sins. When one speaks about the world, the reference is both to land and sea, which are recognized in language among people. It is corruption that brings destruction and desolation to this life and the hereafter. The reference is to despicable and wicked actions that men commit around the globe both on land and across the seas; they cause lack of rainfall, rise of prices, outbreak of wars, quarrels, disputes and continual disquiet, and other negative phenomena that could be prevented if only the people return to faith in God and follow the path of righteousness, clinging to His commandments and refraining from committing wicked acts. All mankind should study the required lessons and deduce the necessary conclusions, and learn from past experience since history has proved beyond all doubt that entire peoples and nations who denied God, did not believe in Him, and committed sins have all met their punishment, were destroyed, and disappeared from the stage of history."

67 Ibn Kathīr, *Tafsīr*, 6:320.

68 The responsum was first addressed to Ashhab b. ʿAbd al-ʿAzīz al-Qaysī (145–204/762–819), cited in the *ʿUtbiyya*, and quoted by al-Qayrawānī, *al-Nawādir*, 1:81.

> it, then it is permissible to use its water for ablution. Moreover, if it is discovered that the discoloration is due to the pouring of [toilet waste], it is unlawful to use it for ablution; it is consensually regarded impure. However, if one does not know the factor behind the change in its color, it is more prudent to consider it impure. By contrast, if the discoloration factor is known but it has not arisen from tangible filthiness that contains analogous color characteristics, it is more appropriate to be considered pure. May God grant [us] success.[69]

Scholars unanimously agree that when impurities enter large bodies of water like the sea and great rivers – the Nile, Euphrates, and the Tigris – and the water maintains its original color, taste, and smell, it remains pure, allowing individuals to use it for purification purposes. This does not imply that people can dispose of their waste and garbage into these water bodies. On the contrary, Islam places the highest importance on preserving and safeguarding the pristine condition and natural state of these waters.

The Prophet placed great importance on conserving, safeguarding, and rehabilitating the natural environment by designating spaces as inviolable in order to protect natural resources. A tradition attributed to the Prophet rules that "every land has its inviolable (*ḥarīm*) appurtenance [to other than the proprietor]" (*li-kull arḍ ḥarīman*).[70] Following this principle, to which the Prophet and his successors abided, spaces adjacent to water sources have been declared as *ḥarīm*. The *ḥarīm* boundaries of public and private wells were fixed at a forty-cubit (*dhirā'*)[71] radius (21.86 yards/20 meters);[72] for natural springs, the *ḥarīm* area extended to a radius of 500 cubits (273.25 yards/250 meters).[73] With respect to rivers, Abū Ḥanīfa stated that "there is no reserved public space for rivers" because all people are partners in the water of great rivers. However, other jurists maintained that lands along the riverbanks should be reserved for the maintenance of water and for other activities and so no one may claim these spaces as private property.[74] All jurists agreed that the great rivers are akin to public highways and must be traversable, clear, and unobstructed on all sides. Governing authorities had to ensure the removal of any construction, private and public, which may have caused damage or affected the safe passage of vessels. Any person who built a structure that caused damage to river crafts, their contents, or their human element was held liable for any losses.[75]

69 Ibn Rushd, *al-Bayān wa-l-taḥṣīl*, 1:134–35.

70 Ḥamīdullāh, *Muslim Conduct of State*, 95.

71 *Dhirā'*, a measurement of the arm from the elbow to the tip of the middle finger, that is, a cubit, and also the name given to the instrument for measuring it. *Al-dhirā' al-shar'iyya* equals 0.5465 yards/0.49875 meters.

72 Aharon Ben Shemesh, *Taxation in Islam: Abū Yūsuf's Kitāb al-Kharāj* (Leiden: Brill, 1969), 1:72–74; 2:63–64; Abū al-Ḥasan 'Alī b. Muḥammad b. Ḥabīb al-Māwardī, *The Ordinances of Government (al-Aḥkām al-Sulṭāniyya wa-l-Wilāyāt al-Dīniyya)*, trans. Asadullah Yate (London: Ta-Ha Publishers, 1996), 260–61. Jurists argued that the reserved area of a well differs from one well to another. A new well maintains a reserved space of 25 cubits (13.66 yards/12.5 meters) on all sides, whereas an ancient well is fixed at 50 cubits (27.32 yards/25 meters). As for an agricultural well, it assumes an inviolable zone of 300 cubits (163.93 yards/150 meters) on all sides.

73 Ben Shemesh, *Taxation in Islam*, 1:73–74, 2:63, 123–24; al-Māwardī, *Ordinances of Government*, 261–62.

74 Ben Shemesh, *Taxation in Islam*, 2:60, 64, 3:127; Abū 'Abd Allāh Muḥammad b. Abū Bakr b. Qayyim al-Jawziyya, *Zād al-ma'ād fī hadī khayr al-'ibād* (Beirut: Mu'assasat al-Risāla, 1998), 5: 709: "the great rivers are common to all people" (*al-anhār al-kabīra al-mushtaraka bayna al-nās*); Aḥmad A. Ḥasan, *Qānūn al-biḥār wa-l-anhār al-duwaliyya fī al-Islām* (Cairo: Ma'had al-Buḥūth wa-l-Dirāsāt al-'Arabiyya, 1988), 22–24.

75 Ben Shemesh, *Taxation in Islam*, 3:128; 'Alī b. Aḥmad b. Sa'īd b. Ḥazm, *al-Muḥallā* 880.969 (2003): "There is no difference between a sea coast and riverbank in religion; there is no preference for one coast over another" (*lā farq bayn sāḥil baḥr wa-sāḥil nahr fī al-dīn, wa-lā faḍl li-shay' min dhālik*). Legally, inland and internal waters were recognized as being under state sovereignty and proprietorship. The government in charge of regulating navigation on rivers and in harbors was held responsible for embanking the rivers and prohibiting private construction within a specific distance from the riverbanks. A space of 200–500 ells/yards (100–250 meters) from the banks of a river was to be kept clear of all buildings. Ibn 'Abdūn reports that the local governor of a port-city "has to be very vigilant against any enterprise that might have a harmful effect on the port, and that the superintendent of the port is under obligation

A tradition attributed to the Prophet Muḥammad states: "Muslims are partners in three things: green pastures, water, and fire."[76] In keeping with this tradition, scholars unanimously concurred that great rivers such as the Nile, Tigris, Euphrates, and comparable rivers should indiscriminately be open and accessible for public use, serving the purpose of drinking, irrigation, purification, and other personal and domestic needs. People are entitled to dig small canals, construct irrigation systems for transporting water to their lands, and employ various methods to utilize the water for drinking and other household needs. However, it is forbidden for any individual to claim exclusive ownership over others; for example, by diverting or withholding the water from them, thus resulting in harm. Additionally, jurists mandate that such rivers must be kept clean, free from pollution, and uncontaminated.[77]

Water, as the primary element essential for life, not only sustains the survival of humankind but also underpins the existence of all terrestrial creatures, the diverse array of plant life, and the hidden treasures found both on land and in the depths of the seas and oceans.[78] Preserving the natural purity of water and shielding it from potential pollution is a fundamental principle. Water is crucially needed for innumerable human necessities, such as drinking, personal hygiene, food preparation, the irrigation of arid lands, and the cultivation of plants for both aesthetic and practical purposes. It also holds great significance in the fulfillment of religious obligations, especially in the context of ablution. Therefore, conserving the purity of rivers, seawater, and ocean water is vital for preventing the spread of diseases, ensuring the perpetuation of humanity and all living beings on earth, protecting plants from pests and diseases, utilizing it for ablution, and facilitating safe navigation in inland waters, bays, ports, and offshore areas.[79]

Islam views mankind as the planet's designated custodian. Of all the creatures that God created, He has bestowed him the title *khalīfa* (God's vicegerent on earth), who must guard and take care of the environment and defend it from all possible harm. Since this implies a divine trust (*amāna*) that is given to humanity's care, the duty of guarding this trust is considered a divine commandment that obliges one to treat nature in the right way, to observe and defend it, and avoid causing any damage to it, even if there are good intentions to use its resources for the benefit of humankind. In such cases, all activities of this kind are considered illegal and even transgressions from a religious point of view.[80]

not to permit selling plots of lands in the port." Muḥammad b. Aḥmad b. ʿAbdūn al-Tujībī, *Séville Musulmane au début du XIIe Siècle, le Traité d'Ibn ʿAbdūn*, ed. Évariste Levi-Provençal (Paris: G.P. Maisonneuve, 1947), 60, 64–65; Évariste Levi-Provençal, *Thalāth rasāʾil Andalusiyya fī ādāb al-ḥisba wa-l-muḥtasib* (Cairo: L'Institut Français d'archéologie orientale, 1955), 29–30; ʿAbd al-Raḥmān b. Abī Bakr b. Muḥammad al-Suyūṭī, *al-Ḥāwī li-l-fatāwī* (Cairo: al-Ṭibāʿa al-Munīriyya, 1933), 1:133–43; Khamīs b. Saʿīd al-Shiqṣī, *Manhaj al-ṭālibīn wa-balāgh al-rāshidīn* (Muscat: Wizārat al-Awqāf wa-l-Shuʾūn al-Dīniyya, 1983), 13:6–7; Bouzenita, "Division of the Seas," 165–67.

76 Abū ʿAbd Allāh Muḥammad b. Yazīd Ibn Mājah, *Sunan Ibn Mājah* (Cairo: Dār Iḥyāʾ al-Kutub al-ʿArabiyya, 1952), 2:826, hadith no. 2473; al-Jawziyya, *Zād al-maʿād*, 5:707; Muḥammad Nāṣir al-Dīn al-Albānī, *Irwāʾ al-ghalīl fī takhrīj aḥādīth manār al-sabīl* (Beirut: al-Maktab al-Islāmī, 1985), 6:6–7.

77 Lutfallah Gari, "A History of the Ḥimā Conservation System," *Environment and History* 12.2 (2006), 226; Muhammad Akthar, "Towards an Islamic Approach for Environmental Balance," *Islamic Economic Studies* 3.2 (1996), 64–66; Chaudhry, "Environmental Stewardship," 129–32; Bakhashab, "Islamic Law," 292–94.

78 Q 35:27–28.

79 Khalilieh, *Islamic Law of the Sea*, 118–19.

80 Ahmad Akhtaruddin, *Islam and the Environmental Crisis* (London: Ta-Ha Publishers, 1997), 230; Giuseppe Poderati, "An Islamic Perspective of Environmental Law and Policy," *Rivista Giuridica Ambiente Diritto* 21.1 (2021), 7–11; Bambang Irawan et al., "Applying Ibn ʿArabī's Concept of *Tajallī*: A Sufi Approach to Environmental Ethics," *Teosofia: Indonesian Journal of Islamic Mysticism* 10.1 (2021), 26–27, 31–33; Norita M. Nasir et al., "Environmental Sustainability and Contemporary Islamic Society: A Shariah Perspective," *Asian Academy of Management Journal* 27.2 (2022), 4; Abdelzaher et al., "Eco-Islam," 627–28; Bsoul et al., "Environmental Sustainability," 2–3; Damkhi, "Environmental Ethics," 16–17; Ghernaout, "Environmental Principles," 77; Chaudhry, "Environmental

8.4 MARINE SALVAGE

Marine salvage had four major objectives: saving goods and items from impairment and destruction, rescuing endangered vessels, recovering wrecks of sunken vessels for reuse and shipbuilding, and averting environmental damage and pollution. In principle, property found onshore had to be delivered to the rightful owner providing the latter rewarded the salvor in return.[81] In saying so, classical Muslim jurists evidently regulated the rule of "the polluter pays principle," meaning that the party which produced damage to the coastal and aquatic environment was held liable for paying compensation in accordance with the harm inflicted.[82]

Jurists authorized salvage divers to take possession of derelict maritime properties provided that the actual owners relinquished their claims to them or could not be identified. However, if the owner of the maritime property did not relinquish his possessions, he had to grant the salvor an equitable indemnity consisting of a wage comparable to his exertions, and other expenses incurred during the salvage operation.[83] Documentary evidence confirm that professional divers offered their services in major port-cities. Shipowners, shippers, and merchants negotiated and contacted these divers to recover shipwrecked properties and bring them safely to shore. Salvors were ordinarily compensated on the basis of successful services taking into account the peril involved in reaching the property and its monetary value.[84]

After discovering maritime property on the coast, floating in sight of land, or at the bottom of the sea, the salvor was bound to observe proper juridical procedures to avoid criminal prosecution. The distinguished Cordovan jurist and notary Ibn al-ʿAṭṭār (330–99/941–1008) rules that the salvor could either preserve salvaged items or deliver them to the qadi or local governor if the name of their rightful possessor was obliterated or unmarked. If he decided to retain the property, he had to write a deed, which served as formal notice of his possession of it, depicting the quality and quantity of salvaged items, as well as the location and date (day, month, year) of discovery, and make known the public places, such as city gates, mosques, marketplaces, and baths, where the find was advertised. Salvaged valuables habitually remained in the salvor's custody for one lunar year from the moment they were brought to the public's attention.[85] Committing the deed to writing ensured that if the salvor died unexpectedly during that interval of his retention of the goods, his heirs would have to transmit the salvaged items to the actual owner if he showed up during the allotted time. Only if the period elapsed and the real owner did not appear, or the actual proprietor decided to relinquish the damaged portion, the salvor would be at liberty either to keep the goods or donate them to pious foundations after recording

Stewardship," 125–28; Rizk, "Islamic Environmental Ethics," 197–98; Jenkins, "Islamic Law," 352; Qaraḍāwī, *Riʿāyat al-bīʾa*, 208–13.

[81] Abū al-Qāsim b. Aḥmad al-Burzulī, *Fatāwā al-Burzulī: Jāmiʿ masāʾil al-aḥkām li-mā nazala min al-qaḍāyā bi-l-muftīn wa-l-ḥukkām* (Beirut: Dār al-Gharb al-Islāmī, 2002), 5:310; Khalilieh, *Islamic Maritime Law*, 111.

[82] Aḥmad Ibn Taymiyya, *Majmūʿ al-fatāwā* (Al-Mansoura: Dār al-Wafāʾ li-l-Ṭibāʿa wa-l-Nashr wa-l-Tawzīʿ, 2005), 30:224–25; Ḥasan, *Qānūn al-biḥār*, 97–101.

[83] al-Burzulī, *Fatāwā*, 5:312; Khalilieh, *Islamic Maritime Law*, 110.

[84] Shelomo D. Goitein and Mordechai A. Friedman, *India Traders of the Middle Ages: Documents from the Cairo Geniza* (Leiden: Brill, 2008), 527 (doc. TS 13 J 8, f. 17), 534 (doc. PER H 161); Shelomo D. Goitein, *Letters of Medieval Jewish Traders* (Princeton, NJ: Princeton University Press, 1973), 189 (38), TS 24.64; Moshe Gil, *In the Kingdom of Ishmael: Texts from the Cairo Geniza* [in Hebrew] (Tel Aviv: Tel Aviv University Press, 1997), 3:614 (485), TS 12.545, l.20: "the divers salvaged nine bales and brought them to the al-Askariyya" (*kharrajū lakum al-ghaṭṭāsīn 9 [aʿdāl] ilā al-Askariyya*); Khalilieh, *Islamic Maritime Law*, 110; Ranabir Chakravarti, "Ship-Owning Merchants in the West Coast of India (c. AD 100–1500)," *Journal of the Economic and Social History of the Orient* 43.1 (2000), 46.

[85] Salvors could keep an object worth twenty dinars or more after one lunar year, that is, 355 days, and lower-priced articles after a few days. Muḥammad b. Aḥmad Ibn al-ʿAṭṭār, *al-Wathāʾiq wa-l-sijillāt* (Madrid: Academia Matritense del Notariado Instituto Hispano-Árabe de Cultura, 1983),128; Ibn Rushd, *al-Bayān wa-l-taḥṣīl*, 15:375.

the date of release on the deed.[86] Otherwise, if he violated legal procedures, either by selling or retaining the salvaged property before the scheduled period had elapsed, he would pay a penalty corresponding to the value of the salvaged object.[87]

A salvor might also petition the local court to obtain free and clear title of the salvaged goods. The qadi would call upon him to testify before the court about the date of discovery and the circumstances of the salvage. If the qadi could verify the testimony, based upon the testimony of two credible witnesses, he would issue a written declaration designating the salvor's identity, the date and location of the salvage, the type and quantity of salvaged items, public places where notice of the salvage had been advertised, and the duration of the waiting period. The judicial authorities never issued such a certificate of discharge or enabled salvors to seize salvaged property, unless the stated interval had elapsed and the actual owner had not appeared to claim it. Finally, when the qadi substantiated the salvor's testimony, he would conclude the judicial process by issuing the deed.[88] In instances when the salvor transferred the property to the court during the period of retention, the qadi would entrust it to a reliable guardian for safekeeping, and he would advertise the discovery in public places. If the interval elapsed, but the owner had not appeared before the court, the qadi would call upon "persons of knowledge" (*ahl al-maʿrifa*, i.e., experts), the guardian, and the salvor to endorse three copies of the certificate of discharge: one copy went to the court archive, another to the guardian, and the third to the salvor. Such a certificate normally described the quality and quantity of the cargo, the public centers where the salvage had been advertised, the duration of the intervening period, and the dates of issuing the judgment and releasing the salvaged cargo.[89]

Islamic–Christian international, commercial, and diplomatic treaties that survived from the eleventh century onward reflect the actual life and legal status of alien merchants, shipowners, and seamen in Islamic territories. The authorities on both sides acknowledged that whatever was rescued from danger, be it human lives, a ship and its gear, cargo, or their wrecked remains, should be released to the rightful owner(s). Maritime property found in Islamic territorial waters or on coasts was not considered derelict unless the real owner(s) voluntarily relinquished it, or did not show up during the period designated by international treaties, local custom, or sacred law. Most importantly, many such treaties included conditions requiring both parties to assist imperiled ships and goods in coastal and/or inland waters. Muslim judicial and civil authorities frequently delivered items salvaged from jetsam or flotsam within Islamic territorial waters to the rightful owner(s) in person. Alternatively, the authorities would transfer the salvaged maritime property, if it was established with certainty that it belonged to an alien merchant, to a consul who returned it to its owner.[90] Despite the lack of written evidence from earlier times, it is not

[86] Ibn al-ʿAṭṭār, *al-Wathāʾiq*, 127–32; ʿAbd al-Wāḥid b. ʿAlī al-Tamīmī al-Marrākishī, *Wathāʾiq al-murābiṭīn wa-l-muwaḥḥidīn* (Cairo: Maktabat al-Thaqāfa al-Dīniyya, 1997), 614–16.

[87] Ibn Rushd, *al-Bayān wa-l-taḥṣīl*, 15:375.

[88] A Geniza letter dated from January 1143 deals with a foreign Jewish merchant who drowned off the coast of Alexandria. His salvaged cargo was first handed over to the qadi. When he verified that it belonged to a Jew, the qadi called for two Jewish witnesses to endorse the transfer of the salvaged shipment to Samuel ha-Nagīd, head of the rabbinical court in Alexandria. Doc. TS 13 J 3, f. 4; Shelomo D. Goitein, *A Mediterranean Society: The Jewish Communities of the Arab World as Portrayed in the Documents of the Cairo Geniza* (Berkeley: University of California Press, 1967), 1:62; Khalilieh, *Islamic Maritime Law*, 112–13.

[89] Ibn al-ʿAṭṭār, *al-Wathāʾiq*, 130–31; al-Marrākishī, *Wathāʾiq al-murābiṭīn*, 616–17.

[90] Michele Amari, *I Diplomi Arabi del R. Archivio Florentino* (Firenze: Dalla Tipografia di Felice le Monnier, 1863), 7–13, 17–22, 29–35, 45–47, 70–71, 86–111, 123–64, 169–80, 184–209, 214–17, 221–36; John Wansbrough, "The Treaties of the Early Mamluk Sultans with the Frankish States," *Bulletin of the School of Oriental and African Studies* 43.1 (1980), 67–76; John Wansbrough, "The Safe-Conduct in Muslim Chancery Practice," *Bulletin of the School of Oriental and African Studies* 34.1 (1971), 20–35; John Wansbrough, "Venice and Florence in the Mamluk

unreasonable to postulate the existence of prior customary arrangements between the Christian and Muslim worlds for such transfers.

8.5 MARITIME BURIAL

The death of a sailor or sea traveler during the maritime journey was not a rare or unusual event. Letters of merchants and travel accounts show that throwing the corpse of a deceased seaman, merchant, and passenger into the sea was a prevalent practice especially when sailing across the open sea for days and even longer durations. Burying a corpse at sea aimed to cover up personal disgrace and avoid its decomposition and the spread of stench, viruses, and possible damage to cargo.

The treatment of dead bodies on board ships and on Islamic shores is thoroughly elaborated by jurists. They offered three methods for disposing of a corpse at sea. After washing the deceased person and the performance of the ceremonial funeral prayer, the body should be bound to a heavy object of metal or stone allowing it to sink into the sea. Such a procedure was applicable if the ship was sailing across the high sea and at a distance of a few days' journey from the nearest coast. The second method, in the case of coastwise trade, was to place the dead body in a coffin and throw it into the water, provided the ship was sailing off Islamic coastal territories. The waves would carry the coffin to the shore, and it was hoped that local Muslims would bury it after conducting the appropriate funeral rituals. The last method required the crew and passengers to keep the corpse in a tightly closed compartment in order to delay the process of decomposition before they reached their destination inasmuch as there is no fear of decomposition. A corpse that is found on Islamic shores had to be buried by the local residents. It had to be washed and shrouded if it was found naked followed by the Islamic ceremonial funeral prayer if the deceased's identity was unknown.[91]

8.6 CONCLUSION

Early historical and administrative records reveal that the development of rural and urban coastal frontiers of the Islamic Mediterranean was the result of careful strategic planning and coordination by the central government, with the admiral acting as its supreme representative authority. Irrespective of whether the defensive posts were constructed by the state or benefactors, the admiral had to approve their locations, taking into account military importance, topographical settings, and living conditions. Interestingly, the architectural design and characteristics of the *ribāṭs* were distinctive within the religio-military environments of the Islamic Mediterranean. Serving as prototypes for the Umayyad desert castles, these *ribāṭ* fortresses exhibited comparable architectural structures and layouts, though they differed in terms of size. Each *ribāṭ* possessed a designated *ḥimā*, agricultural acreage, reserved pasture, as well as offshore areas for fishing and marine agriculture.

Seafood has always been the traditional diet of coastal residents, mariners, and travelers due to its readily accessible nature and cost-efficiency. In order to regulate fisheries and aquaculture, central and provincial governments instituted specialized bureaus with the aim of revenue

Commercial Privileges," *Bulletin of the School of Oriental and African Studies* 28.3 (1965), 483–523; John Wansbrough, "A Moroccan Amīr's Commercial Treaty with Venice of the Year 913/1508," *Bulletin of the School of Oriental and African Studies* 25.1 (1962), 449–71; John Wansbrough, "A Mamluk Letter of 877/1473," *Bulletin of the School of Oriental and African Studies* 24.2 (1961), 200–213; Khalilieh, *Islamic Law of the Sea*, 132–33, 164.

91 Khalilieh, *Islamic Maritime Law*, 168–71.

collection and the supervision of fishing activities in both inland waters and coastal regions. These bureaus had also the duty of issuing fishing licenses, conserving marine ecosystems, and averting overfishing and the depletion of fish stocks within these waters. To prevent environmental harm, fish vendors were ordained to follow strict cleanliness regulations in the marketplace. This entailed routine cleaning of their saddlebags, scales, and all their gear, along with a commitment to avoid disposing their fishery waste in the streets.

Marine pollution covers a wide array of contamination that affects not only all bodies of water on earth – oceans, seas, rivers, lakes, and other inland waters – but also their surrounding marine ecosystem. Although the Quran regards mankind as God's vicegerent on earth, entrusted with its care, jurists and exegetes have pinpointed that marine pollution and environmental deterioration stem from human misconduct, described as *fasād* (corruption). As a result, the act of safeguarding and preserving the environment is seen as a form of worship that yields rewards in this life and the hereafter. Hence, safeguarding the purity of water is of utmost significance in fulfilling the commandments that atone for sins.

The primary purpose of marine salvage was to rescue and preserve the property of shipwrecked vessels, thereby reducing the losses incurred by unfortunate merchants and shippers. In line with the "polluter pays principle," jurists mandated that the party responsible for environmental harm to the coastal and aquatic ecosystem was obligated to pay compensation corresponding to extent of harm caused. Finally, in cases of deaths occurring on board a vessel, maritime burial was the most appropriate course of action. This practice aimed to prevent the spread of diseases, protect the cargo from damage, and ensure that the deceased was treated with the respect and dignity they deserved. Submerging the deceased by attaching a weighty stone to the corpse and allowing it to sink into the sea was never considered to result in environmental harm.

9

Property Rights for Landless Agricultural Workers and the Flexibility of Hanafi Land Law Jurisprudence

A Solution for Rural Displacement?

Erum K. Sattar

9.1 LANDLESS AGRICULTURAL WORKERS ON THE OKARA MILITARY FARMS

In the year 2000, the Pakistani military along with other powerful interest groups that run the complex of the Okara Military Farms in southern Punjab province, decided to change its relationship with the landless agricultural workers who work on the farms from a system established by the British in the first decade of the twentieth century. The military unilaterally changed the terms of the landless agricultural workers' working relations by replacing a system of sharecropping to one of "cash rent." As a leader of landless workers explained, "In Kulyana Estate alone, the farm authorities introduced the (cash rent) system at a very minimal rate of Rs. 300 per acre per annum. The rate has reached up to Rs. 30,000 per acre per annum now and, resultantly, 50 percent of the original tenants have been deprived of these lands because they could not pay the rent on time."[1] Under the new system, the tenants would become "contractors" who would have to vacate the land within a period of six months upon receiving a notice. As a response to the changes introduced by the military, and the violent evictions that they had to face from both paramilitary forces and private contractors – one of whom caused the death of three landless agricultural workers in April of 2009 – amongst others, the landless agricultural workers, estimated to number over one million, have slowly begun to organize themselves into a political and resistance movement, the Anjuman-e-Mazareen Punjab (AMP) – in English, the Tenants Association of Punjab. The slogan "*Malki ya Maut*" (ownership or death) adopted by the landless agricultural workers captures their sense of desperation as well as their new aspirations, going beyond the previous sharecropping arrangement. As the General Secretary of the AMP explained in an interview when asked if the slogan was an extreme one,

[1] Aoun Sahi, "Pakistan: The Tenants' Struggle on Okara Military Farms – Analysis and an Interview with the Leader of Anjuman Mazarain Punjab," April 19, 2009, www.sacw.net/article847.html. The landless agricultural workers' struggle in Okara has to date only generated limited press coverage and limited academic and research work, perhaps because of the difficulty of conducting fieldwork. In light of this, and for the purposes of this chapter, I rely almost exclusively on reports by independent journalists. In addition, the largest newspaper group in Pakistan, *The News*, produced a special report in April 2009 on the plight of the landless agricultural workers: http://jang.com.pk/thenews/apr2009-weekly/nos-19-04-2009/spr.htm#5. Human Rights Watch has also carried out a study based on over one hundred interviews: "Soiled Hands: The Pakistan Army's Repression of the Punjab Farmers' Movement," *Human Rights Watch*, July 20, 2004, https://tinyurl.com/w4fb32vs.

"For outsiders it can be a crude slogan but for us who have faced the wrath of the security agencies there is no other option. Our stance means that we are willing to pay any price for our rights. We will die of hunger if thrown out of this land. It would be the end of the world for us. We have no other source of income and nowhere to go." When the interviewer asked, "So what's the solution?" he replied, "Very simple: give land ownership rights to the tenants."[2]

In light of this critical situation of the landless agricultural workers on the Okara Farms, as well as the plight of millions of landless agricultural workers working on feudal farm holdings across Pakistan, it is crucial to explore ways to make the state more socially and economically inclusive. In Pakistan's federal constitutional structure, the control of government land is a provincial subject. Therefore, the changes that need to be implemented will need to take place at the provincial level. Nevertheless, it is the premise of this chapter that if there is normative legal consensus at the national level, the provinces will be more likely to align their administrative frameworks with this national consensus. I suggest that one possible solution to the plight of the agricultural poor may be found from a study of the history of classical Islamic land law for its potential for making agricultural relations more just in present-day Pakistan. This chapter explores this possibility and recommends potential research and policy proposals for study, leading perhaps to change on the ground in the form of the adoption of new legal norms inspired by and grounded in classical Islamic land law. Of necessity at this stage of the inquiry, this is a conceptual, theoretical, legal study that is beginning to ask the question of where change could come from.

9.2 JOHANSEN'S STUDY OF THE CHANGE IN THE HANAFI SYSTEM OF LAND TAX AND RENT

This chapter applies lessons from Baber Johansen's challenge to scholarly orthodoxy. His research on Hanafite[3] law in the Mamluk and Ottoman periods shows that, contrary to the long-held view that the main body of Islamic law was fully developed by the end of the "classical period," what is referred to as the so-called "closing of the gates of ijtihad," Islamic law did in fact change significantly in the realm of public law between the eighth and tenth centuries. In addition, Johansen goes further and shows by his comparison of the legal opinions of preclassical and classical jurists with those of Mamluk and Ottoman jurists between the tenth and sixteenth centuries, how these changes were in fact structural and normative. He posits that these changes clearly show the central role of the muftis and their responsiveness to changing social conditions. This means that, in essence, while the social and cultural practices of the states themselves were the vital background in which the muftis were developing the legal doctrines, the muftis themselves were of crucial importance to the development of the law. Although Johansen leaves out a discussion of the historical development of the norms, he is nevertheless cognizant of the need to develop such an historical understanding of the internal changing of the norms. Such a study will provide us with a framework to understand the complex interplay of the role of the muftis in their response to changing social needs, while at the same time being the shapers of a cohesive set of legal doctrines aimed at making society

[2] Interview of Mehar Abdul Sattar, the thirty-seven-year-old general secretary of AMP at the time in *The News* Special Report on Okara Military Farms, April 2009, http://jang.com.pk/thenews/apr2009-weekly/nos-19-04-2009/spr.htm#5.

[3] Throughout this chapter I use the terms "Hanafi" and "Hanafite" interchangeably; in South Asia the prevalent form is "Hanafi."

more inclusive. Developing such a dynamic model of legal and social change will help us situate and develop a program of legal change.

As per Johansen's original research we know that the older classical doctrines of Hanafi law were aimed at greater economic and social integration. As Johansen makes clear, the idea behind the older doctrines was the creation of a common interest between tillers of the land and the lessors of the land. This motivation was slowly eroded in the later interpretations of the Hanafi doctrine during the Mamluk and Ottoman periods during a period of five centuries from the fifth to the tenth centuries. Johansen argues that the change in the interrelationship between property, rent, and taxation of arable lands redefined the essential concept of landed property during the Mamluk and Ottoman periods, to the benefit of the lessors and to the detriment of the landless agricultural workers. His research leads to two crucial insights; one normative, in which the content of the law itself changed, and the other structural, in which he shows the very significant fact of the elusive goal of legal change taking place. It is therefore necessary to separate the very fact of the change of Islamic law from its change for the benefit of lessors at the cost of landless agricultural workers. The fact that the law itself changed can be of significant help in a program of law reform designed to benefit Pakistani landless agricultural workers. Meanwhile, because of how the law historically changed for the benefit of the well-off, it must be situated in its context and studied for possible lessons on how to utilize it in a program of legal change, designed this time around to benefit landless agricultural workers.

In the historical change of concepts, what is interesting to note is the important role played by the muftis who created a holistic system of norms in the service of society's practical needs. The changes they wrought in the system of law during the Mamluk and Ottoman periods gave more power to lessors over tenants. While Johansen's findings that the legal doctrines did in fact change is a very heartening boost to the cause of Islamic law reform, nevertheless, this particular instance of the change in norms shows that in fact the legal changes were affected to serve the privileged at the expense of the landless agricultural workers. In the present case, I aim to utilize the key insights that Johansen's research provides in the service of landless agricultural workers, so as to reverse the trend of juristic opinion as developed during Mamluk and Ottoman rule. Therefore, I aim to learn from the wealth of Johansen's crucial insight to use it as the basis of modern law reform to be undertaken in the realm of a nation state, so that we might utilize how Islamic law itself has changed while rejecting, reversing, or mitigating the direction in which that change took place.

9.3 THE INTERRELATED CONCEPTS OF TAX AND RENT UNDER HANAFI LAW

In the Hanafi tradition, the very idea of legal personality is based upon "the idea of the property-owning legal person."[4] It is important to understand the complex relationship between tax and rent, as the two were inextricably linked together as parts of one integrated system. Particularly, the rate of taxation largely determines the rent that a lessor can charge. For this reason, the base of the economic order is built on the right of the state to charge tax on arable land, upon which the remaining economic order is structured. In addition, as in the Middle East where cereals have historically been planted on arable land, in southern Punjab, in the first decade of the twentieth century, the British not only established agricultural farms but also set up livestock farms. Johansen focuses on the Hanafi concepts of the two types of land tax (*kharāj al-waẓīfa* and

[4] Baber Johansen, "IV. Property as an Institution of Social Integration," in *Contingency in a Sacred Law: Legal and Ethical Norms in the Muslim Fiqh* (Leiden: Brill, 1999), 189–218.

kharāj al-muqāsama), the related contracts of particular relevance to a cereal planting economy, the contracts of tenancy (*ijāra*) and sharecropping (*muzāra'a*), and the change in their meanings wrought by the jurists over time. He shows how during the preclassical and classical periods of the development of Hanafite law these legal concepts were similar across the class of landed property holders and landless agricultural workers' landholdings. However, in their development during both Mamluk and Ottoman times, differentiated concepts of tax and rent were developed for landed holdings and landless agricultural workers' holdings. During the emergence of these new concepts, "the law of the 'old jurists' was dismissed in favour of 'the choice of the modern jurists,'"[5] which was to the detriment of the landless agricultural workers.

9.4 THE INTERPRETIVE ROLE OF THE MUFTIS IN THE DEVELOPMENT OF THE LAW

As Johansen explains, over a period of five centuries, from the tenth to the fifteenth, the muftis revised the interrelated concepts of property, tax, and rent to give greater rights to lessors at the cost of historical protections and opportunities offered to landless agricultural workers. The historical protections in the preclassical and classical periods of Hanafi law flowed from a complex set of interconnected assumptions about the needs of different social classes and the particular need to integrate the least powerful into society by giving them a stake in its functioning and future outcomes.

As a normative starting point, the Prophet is reported as saying: "Till it or grant it free of charge to your brother."[6] Johansen traces the development of the law that flows from this hadith and shows that in relation to the preclassical and classical periods of Hanafite law, the eleventh century jurist Sarakhsi explained that religious scholars understood it to mean that there was no justification in Islam for validating the concept of tenancy (*ijāra*). In addition, Sarakhsi also explained that Imam Abu Hanifa did not accept the principle of sharecropping (*muzāra'a*). Despite the possibly prohibitive effects of these opinions based on the hadith, the inhibiting effects of these more religious conceptions as one way of understanding the role of religion in defining economic and social arrangements were relaxed by successive generations of muftis. In light of the preclassical and classical objections to these types of legal relations, it is almost ironic that Johansen chooses both of these contracts as paradigmatic examples of Hanafi contracts in relation to land and property.

It is important to realize that even though the muftis did not develop a formal system for the protection of landless agricultural workers' rights, by their development of the law the muftis constructed a system of legal doctrines that gave protections to landless agricultural workers. This systematic coherence resulted from a particular perspective of the law such that it could be made to serve social ends of constructing a more integrated society.

9.5 THE IMPLICATIONS OF THE *KHARĀJ* OR LAND TAX

Despite the Western debates about the effects of paying the *kharāj*, it seems clear that *kharāj* has historically proven ownership in Hanafi law going back a thousand years. Johansen clearly shows

[5] Baber Johansen, "Preliminary Remarks," in *The Islamic Law on Land Tax and Rent: The Landless Agricultural Workers' Loss of Property Rights as Interpreted in the Hanafite Legal Literature of the Mamluk and Ottoman Periods* (Abingdon: Routledge, 1988), 4.

[6] Baber Johansen, "The Contract of Tenancy (*Ijāra*): The 'Commodification' of the Productive Use of Land," in *The Islamic Law on Land Tax and Rent: The Landless Agricultural Workers' Loss of Property Rights as Interpreted in the Hanafite Legal Literature of the Mamluk and Ottoman Periods* (Abingdon: Routledge, 1988), 25.

this from the extensive quotations of Hanafi jurists he offers as part of his review of the legal conceptions and implications of paying *kharāj*, culminating in the Ottoman Land Code of 1858.[7] As I shall explore in Section 9.6, the true implications of the Hanafi conception of *kharāj*, in terms of standing as proof of ownership of land, are critical to both the historical and present conceptualization of landless agricultural workers on the Okara Military Farms and, more generally, to landless workers in Pakistan from the time of British rule to the present. Johansen quotes Morony to show that it is quite likely that after Muslim conquests, "peasant cultivators became proprietors of some of these lands."[8] Johansen goes on to say:

> The Muslim conquest must in fact have led to a partial emancipation of the landless agricultural workers. Hanafite law supports this emancipation. By transforming land into a commodity and the land tax into a proof of property, the Hanafite legal position on *kharaj* stands in the way of an attempt to consider the landless agricultural workers as a serf bound to the soil.[9]

This insight is crucial for understanding a comparative image of the landless agricultural workers in Pakistan. It is also proof of the great power of the law to shape the legal, social, and economic conceptualization of particular groups and to be able to change the way these groups are viewed by society.

9.6 THE CONCEPT OF THE LANDLESS AGRICULTURAL WORKERS IN PAKISTAN

The crucial insight that Johansen's research brings to light is that it is imperative to understand the starting points in terms of the values that a legal system holds at its core. In our application of this crucial insight to Pakistan, we find that it is precisely at this conceptual starting point that the paths of the Pakistani and the classical Hanafi doctrines diverge. This is because in the Hanafi system the goal is to create a more cohesive and socially integrated society. Yet, in present-day Pakistan, the goal appears to be keeping people tied to the land, to the extent that it may be possible to do so. And even if not necessarily to keep them tied to the land, the goal could even be to displace if that proves more beneficial. To make such a claim is not to state that this is a policy of any government in particular, or of society more broadly. However, it does mean that there is an entrenchment of a decision-making feudal elite that takes its rule over land and landless agricultural workers tied to it as a birth right, and hampers any reconceptualization of the landless agricultural workers as well as the structures of the agricultural economy.

Legally, under the Punjab Tenancy Act 1887 (the "1887 Act") that governs the Okara Farms, landless agricultural workers can either be simple tenants or occupancy tenants.[10] Simple tenants are on the land because of a contract with their landlord and can be removed by a simple notice, while occupancy tenants have an interest in the land itself and can only be evicted on a decree passed by a court of law. This is the extent of the legal and technical conceptualization of the landless agricultural workers that makes them co-sharers in the produce and only acknowledges their rights in rem to a limited extent. More importantly than the letter of the law, for our purposes we must look to the prevalence of the feudal mindset in Pakistan to

7 See, in general, Baber Johansen, "The Birth of the *Kharāj* Payer," in *The Islamic Law on Land Tax and Rent: The Landless Agricultural Workers' Loss of Property Rights as Interpreted in the Hanafite Legal Literature of the Mamluk and Ottoman Periods* (Abingdon: Routledge, 1988), 7–24.

8 Ibid., 11.

9 Ibid., 11–12.

10 The Punjab Tenancy Act, 1887 (Act No. XVI of 1887), http://punjablaws.gov.pk/laws/11.html.

gain a fuller understanding of the normative conceptualization of landless agricultural workers. Upon such an examination, we find that the feudal view of a landless agricultural worker is the exact opposite of the normative conceptualization of landless agricultural workers as understood and constructed by Hanafi jurists, such that in the feudal mindset the landless agricultural worker is viewed as a serf who is tied to the soil through successive generations. This generational tie to the land is maintained and exploited by a constant and never-ending indebtedness. I argue that this sociological conceptualization of the landless agricultural worker in the feudal mindset is more important than the description and place of landless agricultural workers in the legal structures of the state, at least to the extent that it comes before the legal conceptualization as subsequently embodied in the relevant laws.

To complete the picture, it is important to distinguish the conceptualization of landless agricultural workers by the military in Pakistan from the traditional view of landless agricultural workers, as described above, held by Pakistan's feudal class as well is its more traditional large farmers, which to a large extent is also its ruling political class. Although, of course, there are significant overlaps that affect the overall status of the peasantry.[11] For the purposes of the military farms, the military does not take the place of the feudal landlord on the farms under its control. Therefore, landless agricultural workers are not in a state of perpetual indebtedness to the military. Outside the circle of the traditional debt trap, the ability of the military to circumscribe the possible claims of the landless agricultural workers to the land itself is limited. Therefore, it is necessary to put in place a system that, from the outset, denies any potential claims of the landless agricultural workers to the land. This is not to claim that there is some kind of well-thought-out plan of finding an alternate way of a priori denying landless agricultural workers' claims to land. But barring how it does transpire that small-scale landless agricultural workers become entrapped in debt, another legal way to limit such claims has evolved that nevertheless leads to their indebtedness in a roundabout way. This explains the new normative imagination that frames the landless agricultural workers in terms of the market economy and characterizes them as mere "contractors" who, instead of being able to pay in kind, will now be forced to pay cash rent. It is important to realize that while framing the landless agricultural workers in this new way, the military has gone outside the structure of the 1887 Act. Further, the legal image of the contractor is that of someone who is on the land purely at the discretion and pleasure of the lessor – in this case the Pakistani military that leases the land from the provincial government of the Punjab.[12]

9.7 BACKGROUND CONDITIONS IN PAKISTAN

Although there have been several rounds of attempted land reforms in Pakistan going back to Partition, then significantly in 1959 and throughout the 1970s, to date no government has been able to end feudalism in the country, and the tillers of the land remain tied to it as serfs under the

[11] These have to do with military officers getting agricultural land as part of their retirement packages from the government and means that post-retirement, at least, their interests as landholders are aligned with the dominant conceptualization of landless agricultural workers as held by the existing larger landholders. It is also the case that it is hard to disentangle the actions of officers while they are in military service from their post-retirement benefits because, certainly, while they are serving military officers they can easily be assumed to have knowledge of their expected post-retirement benefits. This is a continuation and extention of British land policy as Imran Ali detailed masterfully in *The Punjab Under Imperialism: 1885–1947*.

[12] Even though the military is technically the lessor from the provincial government, in Pakistan's well-understood power structure, it is the more powerful institution against which the provincial government, even if it wanted to assert more rights, is definitely the weaker party.

control of all-powerful landlords.[13] In addition, the process of land reform is further hampered by, and flows from, the entrenchment of vested interests by the perpetuation of colonial era legislation as the basis of the agricultural structure of the state.

As Johansen makes clear, it is imperative that we develop a clear understanding of the motivating background economic and social conditions to which the relevant actors react and respond. While such a full contextual understanding of Pakistan's agricultural economy is beyond the scope of this chapter, some attempts to understand the motives of the military in the year 2000 will benefit the inquiry found here and enable more practical policy recommendations to be made, especially when further research is undertaken to broaden the scope of this inquiry. From the interviews available to us, it is clear that the military's change of the landless agricultural workers' status from sharecroppers to contractors who have to pay a cash rent to the military means it has become easier for the landless agricultural workers to fall into debt. As a result of this change a very large number, perhaps up to half the landless agricultural workers, have been unable to pay the cash rent and have been ordered to vacate the land. The reason the military had to go outside the 1887 Act to impose its new system of cash rent is that under it only *occupancy* tenants may be made to pay cash rent, but they have the added protection of the necessity of a court order to evict them from the land. An official memorandum summarized the Ministry of Defence's position as follows:

> The Military Farm Authorities explained that the decision of switching over from previous "*Bittai* System" [rent paid in kind, so a portion of the crop being cut] to "Cash Rent System" was taken by the GHQ [General Head Quarters] at [*sic*] the best interest of both the parties. It would not only generate more funds for the Govt., but also save the management and tenants from many corrupt practices. Rather, it would be more beneficial for the present tenants, as they would be able to get more yield by using more inputs and labor.[14]

While this is a very rich statement and needs to be unpacked fully, for now we must focus on the difference between how the circular is trying to characterize interests and conditions and put into the mix some other possible self-stated explanations. In contrast to these reasons offered by the military, the landless agricultural workers suspect that this policy was adopted as it was the easiest way to empty the land of its occupants and clear the way for the military to allot the land to retired military officers, supposedly under the pretext of setting up stud farms. This practice goes back to British colonial rule of India, under which it tied an influential local group to empire. It is thus a practice that the Pakistani military inherited from past foreign rulers, but as clearly as the laws and norms continue to serve its interests into the present, it explains their continued existence. It is important to note that while agricultural and residential plots of land are given to retiring officers as compensation for their services and in lieu of lower salaries throughout the course of their military careers, in recent years the buying and selling of allotted military land has become a lucrative business. Officers are given several plots, out of which their residential requirements are easily met by one plot alone. While such a policy for the removal of landless agricultural workers remains officially unconfirmed by the military, it is certainly a plausible explanation for the unilateral change in a long-standing legal, social, and economic set of relations. In this regard, further research will be beneficial to develop a fuller understanding of the motivations behind the change, to see how they have evolved in the intervening period, and

[13] See, generally, Syed Nawab Haider Naqvi, Mahmood Hasan Khan, and M. Ghaffar Chaudhry (eds.), *Land Reforms in Pakistan: A Historical Perspective* (Islamabad: Pakistan Institute of Development Economics, 1987).

[14] Executive District Office, Okara to the Board of Revenue, Punjab (Letter No. 45/DOR/TSC, September 22, 2001), excerpted by Rafay Alam, "On the Military Farms, Okara," *Chowk*, July 3, 2003, http://www.chowk.com/articles/6314.

to help inform any suggested program of law reform that aims to integrate landless agricultural workers into an agricultural economy more equitably. Surely, this is a worthy goal.

9.8 THE HANAFI DOCTRINE ON LAND TAX AND RENT AS THE "IDEAL"

For the purposes of this chapter, it is relevant to compare the key components of the Hanafi doctrine on land tax with the present system of land management and revenue in Pakistan. If we take for the present the classical Hanafi system as the ideal, the implementation of which will increase social inclusiveness, the contrasts between the ideal and the actual serve as pointers for law reform in Pakistan. My starting assumption regarding the conceptualization of the classical Hanafi doctrine of land tax does not mean that I do not admit that there may be details of the system that are partially or completely unsuited to modern conditions. These details, both in terms of Pakistan's present agricultural needs as well as any future goals for the agricultural sector as a whole the country may have, will certainly affect the direction of legal change. I admit that there are likely to be components of the Hanafi doctrine that may require adjustment and reinterpretation to suit Pakistani conditions. However, for the present, I can do no more within the scope of this chapter than to highlight the possibility of such unsuitability and the need for relevant reform. With this caveat, I believe that an evaluation of the present state of the legal and administrative organization of Pakistan's agricultural sector against the backdrop of the Hanafi system as the "ideal" will serve us well.

9.9 THE FOUR CORE COMPONENTS OF THE HANAFI SYSTEM AND ITS IMPLICATIONS FOR PAKISTAN

Johansen lists the essential components of the Hanafi doctrine on land tax that lend themselves to the protection of the landless agricultural workers. In this framework, the first principle is that land is considered a commodity. In my research, I cannot find a similar conceptualization of land as a commodity in present-day Pakistan. This will become clear from the discussion of the second interconnected core principle that Johansen highlights as it flows from the image of land as a commodity. In contrast to other urban commodities that may not have been subject to taxation, productive land under the Hanafi system was always subject to taxation. In Pakistan, by contrast, while the government suffers from its inability to collect direct taxes and therefore has to resort to the imposition of higher indirect taxes, no government to date has yet been able to impose a tax on agriculture despite many demands from the International Monetary Fund to impose such a tax. The idea of taxation is important, as it links to the idea of ownership as the third core element of the Hanafi system of land tax. Hanafi law applied the assumption that it was the lessor who had the obligation to pay the tax and this brought with it the accompanying claim of ownership of the land, therefore vesting the lessor with requisite rights in the land. Johansen suggests that this device enabled the jurists to recognize the existing property rights of the landless agricultural workers as it helped them distinguish between tax and rent. In addition, this meant that a distinction did not need to be made between small and large landholdings, therefore enabling the recognition of property rights of landless agricultural workers.

The most important element of Hanafi land law that Johansen identifies is the fourth one, which has two interlinked components as the normative source of landless agricultural workers' rights. The first of these is that the landless agricultural workers are seen to regain their primordial rights upon their confirmation by the Imam (religious leader) and payment by the landless agricultural workers of the *kharāj*, or the land tax. In the case of Pakistan, the

Government of Pakistan was the successor entity to the British Government at the time of Partition in 1947. This legal substitution took place under the authority drawn from the Government of India Act 1935, which vested all rights and responsibilities in the successor government itself, and passed when the British were devolving some powers to provincial or state governments. For the purposes of this chapter, we may be able to draw a plausible parallel between confirmation of the rights of landless agricultural workers by the Imam and the Government of Pakistan, the successor government to the departing British rulers. However, it is in the second element of the fourth component that Johansen identifies, as mentioned above, which is the weak link in the context of Pakistan. At the time of confirming property rights, the Imam also imposed the *kharāj*, which, as indicated above, is the missing element from the Pakistani context; it is through the responsibility of paying the land tax that the payee's ownership is perfected.

9.10 WEAKNESSES OF THE HANAFI SYSTEM: NO PROTECTION FROM THE DEBT TRAP

Johansen highlights the fact that while the Hanafi system works to give property rights to landless agricultural workers and mitigates the harm that would result from conceiving of them as serfs tied to the land, it does not clearly put in place a robust system to protect them from falling into indebtedness. The fact that the Hanafi jurists did not construct an accompanying doctrine to protect the landless agricultural workers from falling into the debt trap means that the landless agricultural workers are left at the mercy of exploitative forces. This leads to a weakening of their position and aids in the de facto perpetuation of their serf status. He explains that to the extent the Hanafi system does not serve as a buffer against debt, it enables larger landholders to take over the smaller landholdings of landless agricultural workers. In Pakistan, it is this very indebtedness of the landless agricultural workers that is the worst element of their situation, and this makes it nearly impossible for them to break free of the traps of their social conditions. However, it is necessary to realize that in Pakistan the position of the landless agricultural workers is also weak in the accompanying sense, as the all-important Hanafi element of their normative conceptualization, as owners of land, is missing.

In addition, although the situation and context are not exactly the same, and we must be careful in drawing parallels, we see that Hanafi jurists allowed for a *kharāj* of up to 50 percent of the produce of the land. As is clear, this burden would be compounded if, in addition to it, the landless agricultural workers would also need to pay rent. The combination of these two types of claims on the meagre resources of a landless agricultural worker would lead to a long-term debt cycle that would attach to their lands, leading to a situation in which the landlords would have a claim on the only valuable tangible asset of the peasant, namely the plot of land. In the context of the Okara landless agricultural workers, until the year 2000, the tenants gave between 50 and 60 percent of their crops to the military, while the 1887 Act set a limit of 43 percent as the portion a landlord may receive.

9.11 GOING FORWARD WITH RESEARCH

It is clear that there is need for further research on the system of land tenure in Pakistan. I envisage this future research to be both intra-provincial as well as inter-provincial. It will also be important to evaluate whether the provinces can learn from one another. Currently, the system of land tenure is affected by the particularities of the feudal, military, and other power structures of each province.

As part of the further research I envisage undertaking, it will be crucial to study the social and economic developments that shaped the development of the Hanafi legal doctrines in order to draw parallels with present-day Pakistan. If commonalities are found to the extent of similar social and economic pressures between the four periods, the preclassical and classical, the Mamluk and Ottoman, under British rule when the present legislation in effect was enacted, and present-day Pakistan, this will help to develop a modern program of law reform in the service of landless agricultural workers. Pressures that could harm their interests will have been studied and relevant lessons learnt from the history.

In addition, I envisage that additional work will include the juristic development of legal concepts to meet people's aspirations and social development goals, as well as those that will take account of emergent environmental challenges and goals. In the current structure of the state, this burden will fall on modern-day judges who are under-equipped to take the lead on such a reform effort; their day-to-day work is focused on applying the law, not reconceptualizing it with the aid of these legal historical tools, for which they are untrained in the ways of scholars of Islamic jurisprudence, in particular. Further, I would submit that it is likely that the Hanafi conception of landless agricultural workers and the goal to build a more inclusive society are not their top priorities, given the framework of the current law. Further, within the realm of the current law, judges are bound to apply the law of the statute books. Therefore, parliament is better placed and more suited to legislate a wholesale program of law reform. However, it is quite unlikely for parliament to have the capacity to study and effect such a wholesale reform effort. In this regard, Johansen's scholarship will be extremely useful as the starting point of a holistic and wide-ranging program of legal, economic, social, and political research covering the span of preclassical to modern times. Another institutional element in the law-making structure of Pakistan that may be relevant in this effort is the Council of Islamic Ideology, which is tasked by the constitution to suggest ways for the government to bring all laws in line with the injunctions of Islam. Although, we must acknowledge that it has never attempted to undertake anything even remotely so expansive, and it may be found to be singularly unsuited to the task, even if there were political will for such a reform effort. Our main goal is legal reconceptualization, by enabling us to search for the most likely places from which such change could occur.

In practical terms, there is always a trade-off between having the best information possible and taking the necessary action to meet pressing social needs. Therefore, parliament will need to make a political commitment to change. I am, of course, assuming that such political will exists in parliament. This is a big assumption in the present circumstances, as those elected to parliament are the largest landholders in the country, who benefit personally from the exploitative colonial era land revenue laws that have been perpetuated in the country to the benefit of the feudal ruling class. In light of the prevailing ground realities, it may be the case that a broad-based social movement will need to be built around the plight of the Okara landless agricultural workers, in which the media and other civil society groups can come together to give a voice to the demands of the landless agricultural workers who have only recently begun to organize themselves politically. Such a cause will be strengthened significantly by Johansen's research into the particular areas of Islamic law discussed here.

10

A History of the *Ḥimā* Conservation System

Lutfallah Gari

10.1 CONSERVATION IN ANCIENT CIVILIZATIONS

Early in their development, humans realized that it is an essential task to master the art of prudent manipulation of renewable and nonrenewable resources. Religion, mythology, and social pressures – along with a genuine desire to conserve – all influenced the development of conservation practices in early times.

The actual motives varied widely. To some nations, such as the ancient Egyptians, Indians, and Incas, some animals had special religious significance. Some other species were left aside because they were considered unclean or inauspicious. On other occasions, the interest of rulers in hunting was the reason behind habitat enhancement as a means of stimulating game production. Construction of royal pleasure or hunting parks and zoological gardens was widely practiced in ancient Mesopotamia, Egypt, China, Inca and Aztec lands, and Roman Italy. The regulations varied in those parks. Some banned tree cutting, while others prohibited netting on certain fish species. Some periods of hunting prevention were specified, and some species were protected by royal edicts. Incans and Assyrians banned killing females of "useful" species, namely the animals that could be used for food, transportation, hunting, agriculture, and so on.[1]

10.2 DEFINITION OF *ḤIMĀ*

Those ancient steps towards the conservation of nature were not long-term trends. Measures were adopted sporadically, and no specific evolutionary development can be traced. The case of the *ḥimā* system is different, as we review it here. The word *ḥimā* (*ḥemā* in some references) literally means "protected or forbidden place." The term was used in the pre-Islamic Arabian Peninsula for an expanse of ground with some vegetation, access to and use of which were declared forbidden by the man or men who had arrogated possession of it to themselves.[2] Later, its meaning became: a reserve, sometimes a seasonal pasture set aside to allow its regeneration.[3]

[1] R. M. Alison, "Conservation by the Ancients," in 1983 *Yearbook of Science and the Future* (Chicago: Encyclopaedia Britannica, 1983), 112–25.

[2] J. Chehod, "Ḥimā," in *Encyclopaedia of Islam* (Leiden: Brill, 1971), 3:393.

[3] J. W. Bruce, *Legal Bases for the Management of Forest Resources as Common Property* (Rome: Food and Agriculture Organization of the United Nations, 1999), 48.

The area under the *ḥimā* protection was not to be built upon or used as a trade commodity, nor was it to be cultivated for financial gain. It can imply closing certain areas to grazing for a specified period; this period starts with the first showers, in the rainy season or winter, and continues into the dry season to allow sufficient time for grasses, forbs, shrubs, and trees to grow and set seed for subsequent regeneration. The system sets aside an area as a grazing reserve for restricted use by a village community, clan, or tribe as part of a grazing management strategy.[4]

10.3 TYPES OF *ḤIMĀ*

The studies about *ḥimā* show that the following types existed since pre-Islamic times in Arabia:

1. Grazing is prohibited, yet cutting is permitted during specific periods. This timing occurs when plants reach a certain height of growth, after they flower and bear fruit. The cut branches are taken outside the *ḥimā* to feed the livestock. The tribe council specifies the number of people from each family allowed to do the cutting. Certain trails are specified for the workers, to prevent destruction of soil fertility. Certain days are allocated for men, others for women.[5]
2. Grazing and cutting is allowed only after flowers and fruits are produced. This allows natural seeding of the soil for the next year or season.
3. Grazing is allowed all year, and the number and type of animals are specified. No restriction on grass cutting.
4. Reserve for beekeeping. Grazing is allowed only after the flowering season. These reserves are closed for five months of the year, including the spring months.
5. Reserve for forest trees, such as *Juniperus procera*, *Acacia*, and *Haloxylon persicum*. Cutting is only allowed for great emergencies or acute needs.[6]
6. Reserving a woodland to stop desertification of an area or sand dune encroachment.[7]

10.4 THE *ḤIMĀ* IN PRE-ISLAMIC ARABIA

This institution, which dates back to pre-Islamic Arabia, seems to have a secular origin. To protect their flocks from the ill effects of drought, the powerful nomadic lords used to reserve for themselves the grazing and watering rights in certain rich pasturages.[8] As stated by Llewellyn, "A good ruler or tribal chieftain would presumably have used the *ḥimā* for purposes pertaining to the welfare of his people; however, according to al-Shāfiʿi (died 820 A.D.), the pre-Islamic institution of the *ḥimā* was widely regarded by the common people as an instrument of oppression."[9] This was also mentioned by medieval Muslim historians when discussing the Islamic regulations of the *ḥimā*, to compare its status before and after the Islamic state.[10]

[4] A. A. Alabsi, *Country Pasture/Forage Resource Profiles: Yemen* (Rome: Food and Agriculture Organization of the United Nations, 2002).
[5] O. Draz, "The Ḥimā in the Arabian Peninsula" [in Arabic], al-ʿArabī 211 (Kuwait, 1976), 52–59.
[6] S. Nomanul-Haq, "Islam and Ecology: Toward Retrieval and Reconstruction," in *Islam and Ecology*, ed. R. C. Foltz et al. (Cambridge, MA: Harvard University Press, 2003), 121–54.
[7] Draz, "The *Ḥimā*," 55.
[8] Chehod, "Ḥimā," 393.
[9] O. A. Llewellyn, "The Basis for a Discipline of Islamic Environmental Law," in *Islam and Ecology*, ed. R. C. Foltz et al. (Cambridge, MA: Harvard University Press, 2003), 185–247, at 212.
[10] A. al-Samhūdī, *Wafāʾ al-wafā bi-akhbār dār al-Muṣṭafā* (Cairo: Saʿāda Press, 1954), 3:1087.

A famous incident took place when the chief Kulayb, having appropriated certain meadows, fixed as the limits of his *ḥimā* the points within earshot of his dog's bark. A strange she-camel strayed into the middle of his herd, and he shot an arrow which wounded it mortally. In reprisal, his brother-in-law killed him, and this was the originating event of the forty-year Basus war.[11]

Although it is likely to be of secular origin, the *ḥimā* was sometimes placed under the protection of the tribal deity. It was then assimilated with an inviolable zone (*ḥaram* or *ḥarīm*)[12] in whose privileges it participated. Its fauna and flora were protected, and it enjoyed the right of asylum. Some idols' *ḥimā*s were inviolable, as reported in literature. The animals consecrated to them grazed there safely, and no one dared to kill or steal them. The straying animals that crossed over the boundary were lost to their owner, for they then came under that god's tutelage.[13]

10.5 IN EARLY ISLAM

Islam promoted this institution, but in doing so abrogated the earlier practices and transformed the *ḥimā*'s functions. It was still characterized by great flexibility. To be valid in Islamic law it had to meet four conditions, which were derived from the practices of the Prophet and the early caliphs:

1. It must be constituted by the legitimate Islamic governing authority.
2. It must be established in the way of God, that is, for purposes pertaining to the public welfare.
3. The area to be declared as *ḥimā* should not be so large as to cause undue hardship to the local people, and it should not deprive them of indispensable resources.
4. It must realize greater actual benefits to society than detriments. The overriding aim of the *ḥimā* was the economic and environmental benefit of the people.[14]

The caliph 'Umar b. al-Khaṭṭāb (r. 634–44 AD) instructed the manager of Rabadha *ḥimā* by saying:

> Lift your wing from the people! Heed the complaint of the oppressed for it will be heard by God. Let enter those who are dependent on their camels and sheep; and turn away the livestock of Ibn 'Awf and Ibn 'Affān (two rich Companions[15]) for they can fall back to their palms and fields if their livestock should perish. Whereas the needy ones, if their livestock perish, will come to me crying (i.e. asking for financial help). It is easier for me to provide them with pasture than to

[11] Chehod, "Ḥimā," 393.

[12] In pre-Islamic Arabia, the term *ḥaram* was used to define inviolable zones. In Islam the same term became specific to define Mecca and Medina as inviolable sanctuaries within which the injury of wild animals and plants is forbidden. The term *ḥarīm* stands for inviolable zones within which developments are prohibited or restricted to prevent the impairment of utilities and natural resources. In Islamic jurisprudence, every town and village should be surrounded by an inviolable zone within which the right to acquire vacant land for its development is restricted. These municipal common lands are to be managed by the people of the settlement to provide for their needs, such as forage and firewood, and to facilitate their use and development of it in the manner most conducive to their long-term welfare. Sources of water, such as seas, lakes, rivers, springs, wells, and watercourses, and utilities such as roads and squares should have inviolable zones resembling easements to prevent their impairment, to facilitate their use and maintenance, and to preclude nuisances and hazards. The governing authorities have the right and obligation to prevent the violation of these zones. A. A. Bagader et al., *Environmental Protection in Islam*, 2nd ed. (Gland, Switzerland: IUCN – The World Conservation Union, 1994).

[13] Chehod, "Ḥimā," 393.

[14] Nomanul-Haq, "Islam and Ecology," 144; Llewellyn, "The Basis for a Discipline," 213.

[15] The term "Companion" is used for the followers and contemporaries of the Prophet Muhammad who met him.

> spend on them gold or silver. Indeed it is their land, for which they fought in the time of ignorance (i.e. before Islam) and upon which they embraced Islam.

He also said: "All property belongs to God and all creatures are but servants of God. By God, if it did not bear upon the cause of God, I would not have reserved a hand's span of the land."[16]

The Prophet established the *ḥimā* of al-Naqīʿ near Medina for the cavalry and made Mecca and Medina two inviolable sanctuaries (*ḥarams*). Hunting was forbidden within a radius of four miles around Medina, and destruction of plants within twelve. The caliphs who succeeded him established additional *ḥimās* for the cavalry, the camels allocated for charity, and the livestock of the poor.[17]

Strong rules were set forth by the Prophet and the early caliphs regarding *ḥimā*. The Prophet said: "Nobody has the right to declare a place as *ḥimā* except God and His Messenger."[18] In this way, *ḥimā* became a symbol of redress and restoration of justice, and acquired a status similar to an inviolable zone (*ḥaram* or *ḥarīm*), in that it denoted a sanctuary, with its flora and fauna receiving special protection.[19]

During the reign of ʿUmar b. al-Khaṭṭāb, the Companion and commander Saʿd b. Abī Waqqāṣ found a slave man cutting the trees of the *ḥimā*. He beat him and took his axe away. A female relative of the man went to the caliph complaining to him about what Saʿd had done to her relative. ʿUmar said to Saʿd: "Return the axe and clothes, may God's mercy be upon you." Saʿd refused, saying: "I do not give away that which the Prophet has granted to me. But, if you like, I can reimburse you for its cost." Then Saʿd told the attendees that he heard the Prophet saying: "Everyone who finds anybody cutting in the *ḥimā* he should beat the cutter and confiscate his things." Saʿd used the axe on his farm until he passed away (in 675 AD).[20] Similarly, if anyone was caught trespassing and violating the *ḥimā* regulation, he was severely beaten by the caliph ʿUmar b. ʿAbd al-ʿAzīz (718–20 AD).[21]

In Medina, when the Companion Abū Saʿīd al-Khudrī (d. 693) found a bird in the hands of a youth, he took it from him and let it go free. This happened on two other occasions; once with the Companion Zayd b. Thābit (d. 665) and another with ʿUbāda b. al-Ṣāmit (d. 654). When Abū Ayyūb al-Anṣārī (d. 672) saw some boys besieging a fox, he ousted them while saying: "Is this in the *ḥaram* of God's Messenger?" Abū Hurayra (d. 679) used to say: "If I see gazelles in Medina, I wouldn't bother them."[22]

10.6 DURING THE MIDDLE AGES

The system enjoyed a long life throughout the Middle Ages. As we see in this chapter, some traditional *ḥimās* were the best managed rangelands in the Arabian Peninsula; they have been grazed correctly since early Islamic times and are among the most long-standing examples of rangeland conservation known. As mentioned by Llewellyn, "few established systems of protected areas are known that have a history comparable in length with traditional *ḥimās*."[23]

[16] Llewellyn, "The Basis for a Discipline," 213.
[17] Ibid., 212; M. S. al-Alūsī, *Bulūgh al-arab fī aḥwāl al-ʿArab* (Cairo, 1925), 3:31–36.
[18] *Ṣaḥīḥ al-Bukhārī*.
[19] Nomanul-Haq, "Islam and Ecology," 144.
[20] Bruce, *Legal Bases*, 49; M. Ibn al-Athīr, *Jāmiʿ al-uṣūl fī aḥādīth al-Rasūl* (Damascus: Halawānī Bookshop, 1970), 9:309–12.
[21] Abū ʿUbayd al-Bakrī, *Muʿjam mā istaʿjama min asmāʾ al-buldān wa-l-mawāḍiʿ*, ed. Muṣṭafā al-Saqqā (Cairo: Committee for Composition, Translation and Publishing, 1945), 3:1035.
[22] Ibn al-Athīr, *Jāmiʿ al-uṣūl*, 9:311–12.
[23] Llewellyn, "The Basis for a Discipline," 213.

According to information that we find in jurisprudence and geography and history literature, the *ḥimās* continued to exist both around the cities and in rural and nomadic areas throughout that period. They varied in size from a few hectares to hundreds of square kilometres. Jurisprudents like al-Khaṭṭābī (d. 998), al-Māwardī[24] (d. 1058), Abū Ya'lā (d. 1066),[25] and al-Suyūṭī[26] (d. 1505) discussed the legal aspects of *ḥimās* in their writings. History books tell us that the Rabadha *ḥimā* deteriorated in 931 AD as a result of a long civil war between the Rabadha and Dhariyya people. The Dhariyya people sought the help of the strong Carmathian state. Hence, the Rabadha people left their homes and *ḥimā* to escape. Before that date, the Rabadha area was the most beautiful on the pilgrimage road between Baghdad and Mecca. The Dhariyya *ḥimā* was known during the time of al-Samhūdī (d. 1506).[27]

Recently, in 2005, a doctoral thesis was completed about the site of Dhariyya in the Department of Archaeology in Riyadh. After describing the modern town there and presenting a detailed history of the *ḥimā* and the water sources in the area, the author describes the archaeological findings. These include the following:

1. Foundations of buildings in the ancient town.
2. The water supply structures: wells, underground conduits and shafts of springs, above-ground channels and ponds, and the dam there.
3. Surface finds: fragments of pottery and glass, and pieces of soapstone.
4. Inscriptions on mountain versants.

Excavations revealed two periods of dwelling in the area. The earlier period (seventh to early eighth centuries) was characterized by simple artifacts. The finds of the latter period (late eighth to early tenth centuries) were sophisticated pieces. These included glossy chinaware adorned with tin and lead, and delicate glassware.[28] The archaeological fieldwork informs us that the town was a place of inhabitancy until the early tenth century only, while al-Samhūdī mentions its existence in the sixteenth century. This means that it was known later to the nomads as a pasture, not a pilgrimage transit town as it was before.

Around cities, the *ḥimās* followed the system of charitable endowments (*waqf*).[29] They were endowed properties. During the reign of Nūr al-Dīn b. Zangī (Nureddin in English literature, r. 1146–49), an area close to the old town of Damascus, called al-Marj al-Akhḍar (the green lush meadow), was reserved for the aged, retired horses. It remained as such until around 1930, when Damascus started expanding beyond the old town. It occupied a large area that extends now from the Umayyad Square to al-Marja Square, including the old Damascus International Fair

[24] al-Alūsī, *Bulūgh al-arab*, 3:33–34.
[25] Abū Ya'lā, *al-Aḥkām al-sulṭāniyya*, 3rd ed. (Cairo: al-Bābī al-Ḥalabī Publisher, 1987), 231–33.
[26] Llewellyn, "The Basis for a Discipline," 213.
[27] al-Samhūdī, *Wafā' al-wafā*, 1091–93.
[28] Sa'īd D. al-'Utaybī, "Mawqi' Dhariyya" (PhD diss., King Saud University, 2005), 178–81.
[29] As stated by Bagader et al.: "Islam encourages individual Muslims to participate in the conservation and wise development of the environment through various gifts, bequests, and loans. The most important institution of Islamic law in this regard is the charitable endowment (*waqf*), which constitutes the major avenue for private contribution to the public good. The *waqf* may take the form of a land trust dedicated in perpetuity to charitable purposes such as agricultural and range research, wildlife propagation and habitat development, a village woodlot, or a public cistern, well, or garden; or it may take the form of a fund or endowment for the financing of such projects. The governing authorities may set provisions and standards for such *waqf* lands and funds, and for the qualifications of their managers, so that the benevolent objectives of such projects may be effectively fulfilled." Bagader et al., *Environmental Protection*; D. Behrens-Abouseif et al., "Waqf," in *The Encyclopedia of Islam* (Leiden: Brill, 2002), 11:63–74.

(DIF).[30] In 2004, the Syrian government decided to use the DIF land for building an amusement park for keeping the area lush, as per the endowment.[31]

Because the rural and nomadic areas were not under the firm control of central governments, the local authorities were the custodians. For centuries, local inhabitants of the rural and nomadic lands have successfully established environmental planning and management strategies which balanced the settlements' growth and use of the natural resources according to Islamic laws and the tribal self-government.[32] Tribes were given the authority by the Prophet to be the custodians of their *ḥimās* and to control them on behalf of the central government. Chieftains and tribe delegates used to visit him and obtain his approval for a *ḥimā* around their villages or camps.[33]

10.7 DURING THE TWENTIETH CENTURY

As shown by most of the researchers who have studied this subject, tribal self-government continued to control the *ḥimās* and to take care of pastures through the first half of the twentieth century. This was the case in Jordan, Syria, Yemen, and Saudi Arabia, where studies were conducted.

Environmental management was fundamental to both the cultural and spiritual survival of the tribal society. The control of land use and urban form in tribal society was through consensus rather than prescribed legislative or institutional control. Such consensus brought political control and influence, which were vital in the effort to bring ecological sensibility to the management of natural resources in tribal lands.

The traditional political system in tribal society settlements was administered by a *shaykh* (chieftain, or sheikh in English literature) of the settlement, or the *nā'ib* (representative) of the tribe. The chieftain or the *nā'ib* had the full power to implement agreed-upon environmental rules, and to punish persons found guilty of an infraction. He was assisted by a planning commission in the form of a permanent committee, equally representing the kin groups living in the settlements, two to eight persons from the council, and other administrative groups appointed by the settlement council. One group was involved in the management of rainwater runoff, guaranteeing its fair distribution. Another group, in charge of the natural landscape, especially quarries, forests, or grazing lands, reported environmental misconduct to the settlement council. The council would decide the type of punishment and the value of a fine. The group members were also responsible for proposing improvements to the vernacular landscape and preventing any expected hazards. A third group was in charge of the tithe, one-tenth of the total agricultural harvest, to be allocated to the settlement treasury. A fourth group was in charge of business transactions, the weekly market, and the settlement's affairs. Any expenditure needed for improvement of landscape and local issues was approved by the planning commission and the chieftain, who verbally authorized the release of settlement moneys.[34]

30 Draz, "The *Ḥimā*," 55.

31 Syrian News Agency (SANA), "Damascus International Fair: A Story of Success Resonating Across the Region," July 28, 2018, https://archive.sana.sy/en/?p=143586.

32 M. A. Eben-Saleh, "Environmental Planning and Management for the Assarawāt Highland Region of South-Western Saudi Arabia: The Traditional versus the Professional Approach," *The Environmentalist* 20, no. 2 (2000): 123–39.

33 S. al-ʿAlī, "The *Ḥimā* in the First Hijra Century (7th Century AD)" [in Arabic], al-ʿArab (1969), 7:577–95.

34 M. A. Eben-Saleh, "Land Use and Planning of Vernacular Landscape in Highlands of the Southwest of Saudi Arabia," *Journal of Sustainable Forestry* 7, nos. 3–4 (1998): 53–76.

Several key elements of the *ḥimā* system allowed it to survive for many centuries:

1. A high degree of militarization of society, which allowed violent retribution against rule breakers.
2. The slow pace of movement to a given pasture (on foot).
3. Herding was carried out directly by the owners of the animals.
4. Actual herd sizes were smaller, implying less competition for pastures.[35]

Violations of the *ḥimā* were traditionally punished by the slaughtering of one or more of the trespassing animals, but in more recent times sanctions have generally been fines and – in case of repeated offence – imprisonment.[36]

These conditions have all been transformed within the first half of the twentieth century. The nomads have come under control of central governments of relatively small countries (compared to the Ottoman empire and the preceding dynasties), and tribal lands have been nationalized. The herders acquired trucks to transport animals, herding is largely done by hired shepherds, and herd sizes are now very large. A growing population has demanded more land for housing, farms, and pasture, and the needs of village farmers have changed.

In Jordan, these new changes in society have led to a situation where grazing is virtually uncontrolled on various rangelands.[37] In Saudi Arabia, the government wanted the tribes to be unified under one umbrella. Hence, it took the responsibility of management and security of the rural lands through governmental agencies. In 1954, a decree was issued designating the Ministry of Agriculture and Water as the custodian of the rural lands. This created a new statute for the *ḥimās* that became public lands. There was no immediate alternative conservation system. The first national park in the country (i.e. Asir National Park) was established in 1980. The National Commission for Wildlife Conservation and Development (NCWCD) was established in 1986. The period between the banning of the *ḥimā* system and the constructing of national parks and protected areas was characterized by severe destruction of plant cover through overgrazing and the felling of trees as well as overhunting of wild animals. This period expanded the tasks of the governmental agencies, not only to conserve the continuity of the plant cover which was depleted, but also to restore part of it.[38] Overgrazing was aggravated by a number of factors, including a rapid increase in the number of animals to meet the demand for red meat of a growing population.[39] An estimated three thousand *ḥimās* existed in Saudi Arabia in the 1950s.[40] The studies that were conducted until 1990 mentioned that some *ḥimās* still exist.[41] Yet, a report issued by the NCWCD in 2003 mentions only four that are called "old *ḥimās*," which are managed by the Ministry of Agriculture, and a few dozen *ḥimās* that are still managed by local communities in "isolated" rural areas. The NCWCD report says: "Many of the traditional *ḥimās* as well as many terraces have been either abandoned or disappeared under fields that are suitable for mechanical cultivation. In some cases, this has replaced sustainable systems of land use with ones that require increasing inputs of water and

35 R. Blench, *Rangeland Degradation and Socio-economic Changes among the Bedu of Jordan: Results of the 1995 IFAD Survey* (Rome: Food and Agriculture Organization of the United Nations, 1999), 17.
36 Bruce, *Legal Bases*, 48.
37 Blench, *Rangeland Degradation*, 4, 17.
38 Eben-Saleh, "Environmental Planning," 130.
39 Saud L. al-Rowaily, "Rangeland of Saudi Arabia: Tragedy of Commons," *Rangelands* 21, no. 3 (1999): 27–29.
40 Draz, "The *Ḥimā*," 54.
41 Eben-Saleh, "Land Use and Planning," 64–65.

management to maintain their productivity, but it has also markedly reduced the diversity of habitats."[42]

In Syria, the role of local authorities in resource management underwent a dramatic change in the years after independence in 1946. During their mandate (1925–46), the French had recognized tribal authorities and territories and regulated these through special acts. Tribes were legally recognized and their territories mapped. Even before independence, land use on the steppe had begun to change in important ways. In the years after 1940, mechanization for wheat cultivation spread rapidly in these rangelands. The government of independent Syria considered nomadism a backward way of life, and nomads were pressured to settle. New villages were created and landholdings allocated. Boreholes and earth dam construction increased water availability for livestock. Act No. 166 of September 28, 1958, abolished the tribal administration and effectively brought an end to the *ḥimā* system of tribal land use regulation. The provision of new water sources in the absence of social control of land use gave rise to widespread degradation of land resources.[43]

During the period 1961–65, Omar Draz, a Syrian FAO (Food and Agriculture Organization of the United Nations) adviser, worked in Saudi Arabia and observed the *ḥimā* system. He was struck by its potential and the religious sanction behind the system. On his return to Syria, he began to promote the restoration of the tribal control of grazing. A new regulation (Act No. 140 in 1967) prohibited the expansion of cultivation and ordered that in the future all state steppe grazing land was to be managed under range improvement and sheep husbandry cooperatives. The cooperatives created under the decree were identified according to geographical distribution instead of by tribal name. Homogeneity of members was maintained. Cooperative boundaries were mapped. The cooperatives' *ḥimās* were demarcated on the ground by piles of stones and by ploughed strips along the perimeters. The borders of the cooperative *ḥimās* were announced in a ministerial decree. Cooperative boards were mainly elected from among the chieftains and *'urafā'* (dispute settlers) of the tribes. Individual licenses bearing the member's photo were distributed as grazing permits. Natural resources, such as trees on the range, were put under the supervision of the cooperative, marked, and inventoried.[44]

While a promising start was made, the program lost its impetus through political changes. In 1974, the cooperatives became part of the Peasant Union, a syndicalist group that reoriented the program towards water provision and other projects, rather than effective range management. There was widespread failure to enforce the prohibition of trespass on cooperatives' land, on the grounds that revival of the system could revive tribal antagonisms. The *ḥimā* system still continues to be applied effectively on private rangelands, and some cooperatives maintain the winter–summer rotation, though their *ḥimā* areas are not guarded in their absence. The condition of the range has deteriorated.[45]

The following are some of the variations of the Syrian cooperative system from the traditional *ḥimā* system:

1. Ranges were under the control of tribal councils; each tribe had its own council and chieftain. Loyalty of individuals was voluntary and not due to pressure. The cooperative

[42] A. H. Abu Zinada et al., *First Saudi Arabian National Report on the Convention on Biological Diversity* (Riyadh: The National Commission for Wildlife Conservation and Development, 2003), 35.

[43] Bruce, *Legal Bases*, 113.

[44] Ibid.

[45] Ibid.

members and other Bedouin groups using the range lacked a common interest that was established by tribal affiliation.

2. Only a small percentage of range users during the winter season seem to be cooperative members. Nonmembers of the cooperatives claim seasonal rights and use of areas of "cooperative lands" that traditionally belonged to their tribes. On the other hand, the cooperative members who are mobile herders end up paying fees for stubble grazing. Having said this, there is a concurrent insistence in the project literature that (a) there was once a *ḥimā* system that has now disappeared; (b) no clear land tenure arrangement exists; and (c) there is now an organizational gap that must be filled. The mechanisms of resource use that are in use today are not a focus of attention and therefore become invisible or are perceived as "unclear."
3. Large animals, such as camels and horses, eat the leaves of grown trees, while other animals, such as goats, act like locusts: they destroy the pasture by overgrazing if not controlled. The *ḥimā* system established over the 1970s was seized as an opportunity for some tribes to reestablish social distinctions with others. Once sheep-raising became widespread at the expense of camel-raising, the distinction between the "noble-patron" tribes (traditionally the camel-raisers) and the "common-client" tribes (the sheep-raisers) became blurred and could no longer be upheld on this basis. To reestablish this distinction, members of the "patron" tribes did not join the cooperatives, hence the government-sponsored *ḥimā* cooperatives were composed mainly of "client" tribal groups.[46]

In Yemen, it was reported that the system was effective and widespread until the first part of the second half of the twentieth century, when it began to decline in some areas due to socioeconomic factors. The cited sources did not specify those factors, but most probably they are similar to changes in society that were mentioned earlier reagrding the case of Jordan.[47]

The following four traditional grazing management systems are practiced in the Central Highlands of Yemen and are also found elsewhere:

1. Temporary *maḥjūr* [*ḥimā*]: a sort of short-term reserve consisting of a slope or grazing area adjacent to cultivated land, which is declared protected. The protected area is closed to grazing from sowing time until harvest each year.
2. Temporary village *maḥjūr*: part of a village's communal grazing land [that] can be declared as protected for a specific period for the purpose of reserving forage to be used in the dry season.
3. Permanent *maḥjūr*: the area of a hill or mountain slope of variable size opened for common grazing use during dry season and the period needed. It is privately owned, usually by more than one family. Trees in *maḥjūr* areas are always privately owned and are utilized by owners only.
4. Semi-rotational system: found in the desert plain and practiced by Bedouins. In this case, their grazing land comprises many sites that are used at different times each year. Their use depends on vegetation regrowth and rainfall.[48]

A study was conducted in Kuḥlān ʿAffār, in the northern mountains of Yemen, where rangelands are the principal feed resource for livestock. They provide a major source of income to

[46] L. Triulzi, "Empty and Populated Landscapes: The Bedouin of the Syrian Arab Republic between Development and State," in *Land Reform 2001/2* (Rome: Food and Agriculture Organization of the United Nations, 2002), 30–47.
[47] Alabsi, *Country Pasture*.
[48] Ibid.

farmers as well as wood for fuel, charcoal production, and construction. Covering about 30 percent of the area, they include woodland, bare rocky ground, steep slopes unsuitable for cultivation, and collapsed terraces. The investigation assessed plant cover, biomass, and species composition under various systems of grazing in the mid-slopes and highlands in the spring and summer of 1996. The results showed that the various systems of grazing led to varying degrees of degradation: communally owned range showed all signs of overgrazing, while restricted, privately owned range had a high density of palatable plants. The impact of different systems of grazing was clear on the mid-slopes. There, the richest vegetation was in a site where grazing was restricted by the range owners during the growing season. Grasses are first harvested by the owners before the range is opened for grazing.[49]

At a mid-altitude site, the community generally allowed open access, but periodically chose to restrict grazing to permit regeneration. Unpalatable species covered 60 percent of this land, and palatable plants only 6 percent. This pattern was repeated in the highlands. An open range was exposed to erosion, with just 30 percent total plant cover (66 percent of which was unpalatable species). In comparison, a restricted rangeland, where the community decides which slopes shall be grazed each year, had twice the plant cover, 60 percent of which were palatable grasses.[50]

10.8 MODERN POLICIES AND *ḤIMĀ*

As we saw in Syria's experience, they tried to utilize the concept of *ḥimā* to manage their pastures, but their experience needs some revision. Do we really benefit from this traditional system? And, if so, in which fields? What modifications or improvements are needed to use it?

The first question is answered by Llewellyn as follows:

> The value of *ḥimās* for the rehabilitation of rangeland, the stabilization and control of nomadic grazing, as indicators of range potential and better animal husbandry practices, and for the proper management of water catchment areas has been identified by a succession of researchers. Many *ḥimās* are also located in areas of high species diversity or support woodlands and other key biological habitats and are thus important in preserving biological diversity. Their great potential for ecological and socio-economic research and development has received less attention. The importance to ecological research of areas that have been protected under a more or less defined management regime for a substantial period of time cannot be stressed too strongly. Reclamation of the grazing resources and their level of use during and after rehabilitation will be difficult to plan in the absence of base-line information on which to judge recovery and the capacity of the range to support wild or domestic herbivores at different stages during recovery. Such information is difficult to obtain in the absence of trial range sites protected from overgrazing. Well-protected *ḥimās* provide a measure of potential plant species diversity and standing plant biomass under particular climatic conditions and management treatments.[51]

Most countries in the region have established their own environmental government agencies in the last three decades of the twentieth century. But, as Hamed says,

> unless communities are well-informed and consulted during the development planning process, new projects and programs will not benefit from local knowledge and may never gain the support of the community. Movement toward environmentally sustainable development by any

[49] M. Bounejmate, B. Norton, and A. Gruggeman, "Changes Suffered by the Mediterranean Rangelands in the Recent Past: ICARDA's Experience," Medias Newsletter, June 13, 2002, 21–30.

[50] Bounejmate et al., "Changes Suffered," 27.

[51] Llewellyn, "The Basis for a Discipline," 215.

society involves more than establishing an environmental protection agency, raising environmental awareness, or providing technical training. It requires comprehensive efforts on all fronts to strengthen the sustainable development institution as a whole and to shift the priorities of the society at large. No significant progress in history was ever accomplished without an ethical emphasis, sincere loyalty, genuine affection, and authentic convictions.[52]

Certain conditions need to be met in order for any society to build the capacity to attain sustainable development while managing its environmental resources. The key conditions are organizations and institutions, human resources, information base, and public involvement. These four conditions are highly interactive, mutually dependent, and self-reinforcing. Significant synergy exists among them. Improvements in one condition can often improve the effectiveness of the other conditions, while deterioration in one condition may erode the effectiveness of the others.[53]

Based on these reasons, the researchers and planners in the region call for adopting the *ḥimā* system in future plans. The NCWCD report states that some of the measures that are needed to achieve this include investigating "different methods of rangeland management, including systems based on nomadic pastoral as well as traditional *ḥimā* systems."[54]

In another part of the report, it says:

The National Commission for Wildlife Conservation and Development (NCWCD) adopted a rational approach for the selection and prioritisation of potential protected areas from the outset. This aims to provide the most effective conservation of the biodiversity and to optimize the socio-economic benefits that are derived from the protected areas.

The criteria are summarized below . . .:

Socio-economic:

• Traditional and local conservation initiatives, such as *ḥimās*, wildlife conservation initiatives, agricultural terraces and other rainwater harvesting systems.[55]

Also in the same report we read:

With over six thousand years of bio-cultural diversity in the region it is only to be expected that there is a wealth of indigenous knowledge on how to use natural resources sustainably. Local traditions for use of resources provide a basis that can be elaborated into programmes for linking the conservation of renewable natural resources with sustainable national development. Functioning local *ḥimās*, agricultural terraces, rainwater harvesting methods and wildlife populations that are protected by local people all provide initiatives of tremendous value for achieving the objectives of the conservation of biodiversity.[56]

Some traditional *ḥimās* serve as new tourism sites after restoration. The NCWCD conservation body has been responsible for surveying, recommending, and administering a number of protected areas. It identified fifty-six terrestrial sites and forty-seven marine and coastal sites as suitable for proclamation as protected areas. It started with a few of them to increase the number gradually. The newest one is Ajā Mountain range and the north of Ḥā'il city, where a traditional

[52] S. A. Hamed, "Capacity Building for Sustainable Development: The Dilemma of Islamization of Environmental Institutions," in *Islam and Ecology*, ed. R. C. Foltz et al. (Cambridge, MA: Harvard University Press, 2003), 403–21, at 409.

[53] Ibid., 416.

[54] Abu Zinada et al., *First Saudi Report*, 53.

[55] Ibid., 59–60.

[56] Ibid., 62.

ḥimā existed in the near past.[57] It is of importance to wildlife, as the site lies at the center of the spring flyway for the threatened African wintering population of *Gus virgo*. In addition, there is an impressive spring migration of swifts, larks, and wheatears, together with a wide range of raptors. Other characteristic avifauna are the houbara bustard (*Chlamydotis undulata*), Lichensteins sandgrouse (*Pterocles lichtensteinii*), and chestnut-bellied sandgrouse (*Pterocles exustus*).[58] Recently, in 2005, the site was declared a protected reserve with facilities to be developed for desert tourism.[59]

The research in this field needs to continue until we establish suitable guidelines for using the traditional systems and make every environmental agency in the area aware of the importance of them. Adopting traditional systems cannot be possible without modifications and improvements in today's world, which is completely different from the nineteenth-century Middle East. These are some of the factors that need to be considered:

1. The new generations of the tribespeople in the area work in modern jobs. The residential areas are no longer composed of one tribe. The demography has changed from homogeneous tribes to heterogeneous communities. This necessitates new forms of authorities to replace chieftains and tribe councils. Loyalty is now for the community and the employing company.
2. Transportation, felling of trees, and agriculture are being carried out with machines. This new powerful machinery requires strong rules and modern methods of control (e.g. aircraft). The state alone can handle this task. For these reasons, the NCWCD report is mentioning the traditional *ḥimā* system as *one of* the measures or criteria to be considered. The modern ways of administering natural reserves can replace the traditional system in urbanized and large-scale areas.
3. Politicians need to give more authority to researchers and the scientific approach. As we saw before in the case of Syria, Omar Draz's approach of reviving the traditional system was altered. This experience is telling us that many countries in the region are unfortunately lacking some of the essential factors that contribute to achieving sustainable development. Whether we revitalize the cultural heritage or do not, decision-makers and politicians need to listen to expert advice. Hence, the first factor to reach this situation is not environmental but political. Unless we see changes in the political thought and decision-making, we cannot expect improvements on ecological destruction and resource depletion.[60] In the case of Saudi Arabia, where a decree was issued in 1954 to declare the *ḥimā*s as public lands, and in the case of Syrian state intervention to alter the system that was designed by experts, Taylorism and democracy were on vacation.

[57] National Commission for Wildlife Conservation and Development (NCWCD), *Wildlife Newsletter* 6 (May 2005), and personal communications with an NCWCD researcher.
[58] R. Llewellyn-Smith, *Red Sea Nubo-Sindian Tropical Desert and Semi-Desert* (Washington, DC: World Wildlife Fund, 2001).
[59] NCWCD, *Wildlife Newsletter*, 6.
[60] Hamed, "Capacity Building," 417.

11

The Right to Water in Islamic Thought and Its Manifestation in the Islamic-Iranian Cities

Hooshmand Alizadeh and Golshan Hemati

11.1 INTRODUCTION

Water, a colorless and chemical-free substance, is a fundamental component of life on earth. It covers 70 percent of the global surface and comprises a significant portion of the human body, making it essential for the survival of all organisms. Throughout history, water has been a vital requirement for the existence of humanity, with settlements and communities often forming around water sources such as streams, rivers, and lakes. Ancient philosophers recognized water as one of the four primary components of the universe, alongside earth, air, and fire, and considered it a symbol of life. Ethically, it is crucial to acknowledge that water is not just a commodity but a vital resource and a right for every human and nonhuman being. Its use should not be solely guided by market forces and economic considerations. Instead, people should care for the natural environment as a whole, including ecology, water, land, air, and society, irrespective of economic fluctuations. Ensuring an adequate quantity of safe and affordable water at all times is the present and future challenge.

Considering the significance of water, it is unsurprising that Islam places great emphasis on its conservation. In Islamic thought, water is seen as a divine gift, symbolizing profound wisdom and quenching the thirst of the soul. Islam encourages its followers to consider equity, justice, and sustainability when utilizing natural resources. Scholars argue that water is mentioned over sixty-three times in the Quran, with specific terms related to water, such as river and drinking water, cited fifty-four and thirty-nine times, respectively. Various forms of precipitation, including rainfall, dew, and snow, are mentioned over 100 times. The Quran states, "And we created from water every living thing" (21:30). This verse highlights the significance of water as the source of life. Islamic teachings, as found in the Quran and the hadith, emphasize principles of social justice, equity, and the preservation of natural resources. Islam views water as a communal resource and a right for all humankind. The Prophet Muhammad emphasized this by stating that Muslims have a common share in three things: grass (pasture), water, and fire (fuel). Wise use and conservation of water are not only encouraged but also considered a moral obligation to perpetuate life on earth.

Water supplies have played a significant role throughout history, contributing to the rise, disintegration, and even disappearance of civilizations. Understanding the history of water and sanitation services is crucial in addressing current water management and policy issues and anticipating future implications. Muslim cities, shaped by hot climates and the sun, often exhibit distinctive "solar architecture." However, it is equally important to recognize the sophisticated "water architecture" developed in these cities due to the scarcity of water and the care devoted to it. Traditional Muslim cities were influenced by water, shaping their morphology and emphasizing the importance of this vital resource.

The long-standing expertise of Muslim jurists in allocating water rights in arid lands showcases a remarkable example of sustainable resource utilization. Muslim societies across diverse regions, from Russia and China to Spain, Southern Europe, the Middle East, North Africa, and Somalia, have contributed to the world heritage in various areas, including water supply, sanitation, and hygiene practices. This societal and geographic diversity has resulted in a wide range of experiences, considerations, and practices in the field.

In this chapter, we will explore the right to water in Islamic thought and its manifestation in Islamic-Iranian cities. By delving into Islamic principles, historical perspectives, and the rich heritage of Muslim societies, we aim to highlight the significance of water and its preservation as a fundamental aspect of Islamic teachings and the urban development of Iranian cities.

11.2 ISLAMIC ENVIRONMENTAL THEORY

Islamic principles dictate that the natural environment is divinely ordained by Allah (God) and entrusted to humankind as a sacred responsibility (Amery, 2001). The Islamic environmental philosophy asserts that all creatures, human and nonhuman, exist independently of their utility to human beings. The universe, with all its components, is a creation of God, deserving of love and admiration. This love stems from the recognition that all elements of the world are divinely crafted (Gada, 2014). Islamic environmental philosophy transcends mere romanticizing of wilderness or equating other organisms with humans; rather, it views environmental protection as a sacred duty based on the environment's exalted position as a higher authority responsible for the treatment of all creatures (Gada, 2014).

According to Islamic views, environmental crises arise when humans overexploit the ecosystem bestowed upon them by God (Gada, 2014). The Quran enjoins people to preserve the natural environment (Özdemir, 2003). An Iranian Islamic scholar, Seyyed Hossain Nasr, beautifully articulates that nature is a theater wherein the signs of God are manifested (Özdemir, 2003). Thus, the relationship between God and nature is that of a creator and creature (Gada, 2014). The root of environmental crises, according to Islamic scholars, lies in the separation of worldly living from religious teachings (MacAlister & Subramanyam, 2018). To halt the destruction of nature, some propose redesigning environmental policies and regulations according to religious-oriented principles (Shomali, 2008).

In contrast to Western environmental ethics, which include anthropocentrism, biocentrism, liberation/rights theory, and ecocentrism, the Islamic view is theocentric, centered on God (Abedi-Sarvestani & Shahvali, 2008). The Quran repeatedly emphasizes that nature is the creation of one Almighty God. For example, it states, "There is no God but He, the Creator of all things," including nature (Gada, 2014). Islamic civilization's perspective on water and the environment is deeply rooted in its theocentric understanding, recognizing divine presence and purpose in all elements of the natural world.

11.3 ISLAMIC FRAMEWORK ON INTEGRATED WATER RESOURCES MANAGEMENT

Water holds a central position in all sacred texts, highlighting its significance for life, agriculture, livestock breeding, climate, and the environment. The Quran eloquently describes water as the life-giving force, bringing rain to irrigate lands and revive barren farms, thus fostering human civilization (Gada, 2014). It is considered the greatest bounty from God, and its scarcity is seen as a potential curse that could devastate life.

Islamic water management is governed by Islamic sharia law, with two fundamental concepts related to water rights: *shafa*, the right of thirst, entitling humans and their animals to quench their thirst, and *shirb*, the right to irrigate lands (Hussein & Al-Jayyousi, 2001). These concepts prioritize human and domestic use, followed by animal, agricultural, industrial, and recreational uses (Brooking, 2021). However, interpretations of these concepts may differ among Islamic states due to geographical, social, ethical, and cultural variations (Amery, 2001).

Islamic ethics of water use intertwine faith, behavior, and responsibility. All Muslim activities, including those related to water supply, sanitation, and hygiene, are expected to conform to Islamic guidance and rules, as outlined in Quranic verses and Prophetic teachings (Dien, 1997). Muslim jurists have thoroughly studied the development of water law in Islam, with overlapping themes or domains of *fiqh* (religious law) dealing with water and land rights, among others (UN-HABITAT, 2005). Water in Islam is classified as either public or private, with the former shared equally and the latter subjected to regular forms of usufruct and transactions (Ben-Hamouche, 2008). Islam emphasizes the importance of balance, conservation, and harmony in water use. Priority is given to drinking water, and wastewater, greywater, and saline water are recognized for their various uses, such as food sources, jewelry, and transportation. Good management and water conservation are essential obligations under Islamic law, prohibiting wasteful practices, even in religious rituals like washing before prayer. Water pollution is deemed unacceptable, as it hinders water's social, religious, and ecological functions. Islam recognizes water as a resource for all time, necessitating its protection for future generations (Brooking, 2021).

11.4 CONCEPTUAL FRAMEWORK: ISLAMIC WATER ETHICS AND THE MANIFESTATION OF THE RIGHT TO WATER IN ISLAMIC-IRANIAN CITIES

As a result of the above review, the following aspects can be highlighted for this chapter to explore the right to water in Islamic thought and its manifestation in Islamic-Iranian cities (Figure 11.1). It revolves around two main pillars: Islamic Environmental Theory and an Islamic Framework on Integrated Water Resources Management. These pillars serve as the foundation for understanding the ethical and practical aspects of water management within the context of Islamic teachings and traditions.

11.4.1 *Islamic Environmental Theory*

The first pillar, Islamic Environmental Theory, is based on the theocentric worldview present in Islamic thought. It posits that the natural environment is divinely ordained by Allah and deserves reverence and protection. In this perspective, all creatures, human and nonhuman, have inherent value and exist independently of their utility to humans. Humans are entrusted with the responsibility of caring for the environment as a sacred duty.

- Divine-Centric Relationship: The conceptual framework emphasizes the relationship between God and nature as one of a creator and creature. The environment is seen as a manifestation of God's wisdom and is, therefore, deserving of care and preservation.
- Environmental Crises and Spiritual Separation: The framework highlights that environmental crises arise when humans overexploit the ecosystem without considering the

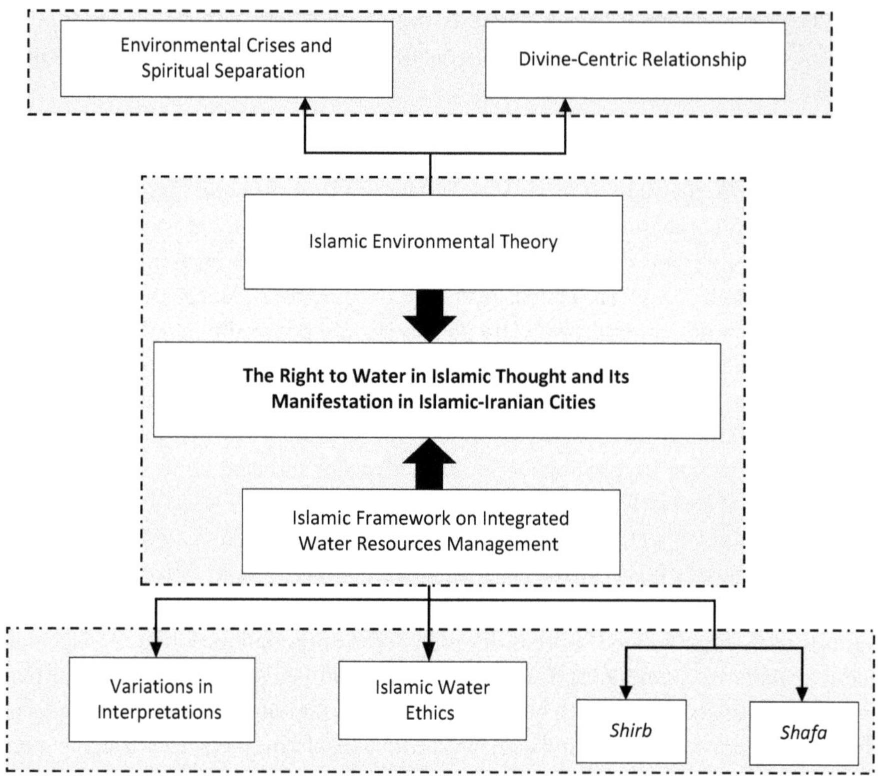

FIGURE 11.1 Conceptual framework: Islamic water ethics and the manifestation of the right to water in Islamic-Iranian cities

sacredness of nature. The separation of worldly living from religious teachings is identified as a root cause of environmental degradation.

11.4.2 *Islamic Framework on Integrated Water Resources Management*

The second pillar, an Islamic Framework on Integrated Water Resources Management, focuses on the principles and guidelines found in Islamic teachings for managing water resources sustainably and justly. Islamic water management is governed by Islamic sharia law, with the fundamental concepts of *shafa* and *shirb* guiding water rights.

- *Shafa* and *Shirb*: The framework acknowledges the concepts of *shafa* (the right of thirst) and *shirb* (the right to irrigate lands) as fundamental principles in Islamic water rights. The framework highlights the priority of human and domestic water needs over other uses.
- Islamic Water Ethics: The framework delves into the ethical considerations of water use in Islam. It emphasizes the importance of balance, conservation, and harmony in water use, with a focus on drinking water as a primary need. The ethical guidelines discourage wasteful practices, promote water conservation, and condemn water pollution.
- Variations in Interpretations: The framework recognizes that interpretations of Islamic water management may vary among different Islamic states due to geographical, social, ethical, and cultural differences.

Overall, this conceptual framework provides a basis for understanding the Islamic perspective on water as a divine gift and the responsibility of Muslims to protect and manage water resources sustainably. It also acknowledges the historical significance of water in shaping the development of Islamic-Iranian cities, where water scarcity has influenced sophisticated "water architecture." By examining the ethical principles and practical applications of water management in Islamic thought, the framework aims to shed light on the importance of water preservation and the manifestation of the right to water in Islamic-Iranian cities.

11.5 WATER IN ISLAMIC CITIES

The Arabian Peninsula's arid landscape heavily influenced the significance of water in Islam. Pre-Islamic Arab tribes, in their quest for water resources, established territories, shaping their understanding of water's hidden value. Islam, with its doctrine focusing on the rights of use, transformed the concept of water, elevating it to an act of charity in regions plagued by arid conditions and scarce water networks.

Islamic empires drew inspiration and technologies from Egyptian and Persian civilizations, utilizing innovative water-lifting devices such as the Persian wheel, shadoof, saqiya, and qanat (underground aqueducts) to harness and conserve water across the Islamic world.

Islamic cities, often centered around mosques, ensured the availability of running water and basins for ablution and provided public drinking fountains and troughs for animals. These water installations were adorned with Quranic inscriptions underscoring the centrality and sanctity of water in Islam. Islamic architecture incorporated water not only for its functional and aesthetic values but also as a reflection of the tolerant teachings of Islam, emphasizing water conservation.

11.5.1 *Water Management in Islamic History: Engineering Innovations and Sustainable Practices*

Sabīls (Public Water Fountains): In Islamic history, the provision of drinking water for the public was considered an act of charity. These public water fountains, known as *sabīls*, were established to serve the people's needs (Al-Sawy, 1995). The construction of *sabīls* at the al-Aqsa Mosque dates back to the Ayyubid and Mamluk eras, and many of them were renewed or restored in the Ottoman era under the order of Sultan Suleiman the Magnificent (926–74 AH/1520–66 AD), who emphasized their construction (Haddad, 2012).

Aflaj: The term "Aflaj" refers to an ingenious water management system found in Oman. It comprises a network of canals, including subsurface water channels, that has a remarkable historical legacy. Although the precise date of its origin is uncertain, it is believed to have evolved through numerous construction campaigns dating back to around 500 AD or possibly even earlier (Haddad, 2012). The Aflaj system involves the harnessing of valuable water resources, including groundwater, springs, and surface water. These resources are efficiently transported through gravity-driven channels that span long distances, ultimately reaching cities and villages. Once delivered, the water serves crucial domestic and agricultural purposes, supporting the needs of the local communities. This remarkable system demonstrates the ingenuity and sustainable water management practices developed by ancient civilizations in Oman.

Dams and Water Support Structures: Islamic civilizations built significant dams during the Abbasid and Fatimid periods, as well as in regions like the Levant and Andalusia. Notable examples include the Nahrawan Dam in the Levant and various dams in Syria. Islamic engineers introduced innovative dam-building techniques, such as water level control gates and channels for draining silt or mud from the dam's bottom. Similar advancements in dam construction were observed in Spain, with structures like the Cordoba Dam, the Segura River Dam, and the Turia River Dam showcasing the Muslims' engineering prowess (Haddad, 2024).

Waterwheels (Noria): In some Islamic countries, waterwheels, known as norias, were used to irrigate farms and fields. These waterwheels, powered by animals or the force of water, raised water from rivers for irrigation purposes. Initially, wooden compartments were used along the wheel's rim, but later ceramic compartments replaced them in 870 AD (De Miranda, 2007). An example of these norias can be seen on the Orontes River in Hama, Syria.

Water Devising: Muslims have been adept at devising groundwater sources, a practice known as "hidden waters" in their ancient traditions. Devising involved the use of field experiences, sense, imagination, and wisdom to locate groundwater sources, determining their depth and proximity to the surface. Various indicators, such as soil smell, the smell of plants in the area, and the movement of specific animals, helped Muslim scientists and experts in identifying groundwater sources (Hassan, 2020).

Qanats: Qanats, a method of dry-land irrigation dating back to the pre-Islamic era, were crucial for providing water in arid regions. This system, originating from the Achaemenid period, involved a series of wells linked at a considerable distance to accumulate underground water (Morgan, 2008). Qanats relied solely on gravity for water flow, minimizing evaporation and pollution, and ensured a balanced and reliable supply of water for hundreds of years (Haddad, 2024). Diggers created gently sloping tunnels connected to the surface with vertical shafts, forming a "chain of wells" (Amery, 2015). Qanats spread through the Islamic era, becoming a prominent method of water supply in the Mediterranean and central European countries (Khaled, n.d.).

11.6 WATER AND ARCHITECTURE: SYMBOLISM AND SIGNIFICANCE IN IRANIAN CITIES

Water holds great significance in Iranian culture, both from ancient times and throughout the emergence of Islam. Iranian cities, like many ancient cities, were strategically located near water sources due to Iran's relatively dry climate and scarcity of permanent rivers and springs. The Iranian people have long recognized the value of water as a life-giving and precious substance. Water's scarcity and the natural need for it have elevated its importance and made it a revered element among Iranians.

In Iranian cities, there are three main types of water systems: those based on underground water, running water, and surface water. Additionally, some cities have combined systems that utilize multiple water sources. Examples include cities like Meibod, Ardestan, and Yazd, which rely on underground water sources; cities like Bukhara, Isfahan, and Semnan, which utilize running water systems; and cities like Lar, which rely on surface water. These water systems play a crucial role in meeting the water needs of Iranian cities (Karamati, 2005).

With the advent of Islam, Iranian Muslims integrated their existing customs and beliefs about water with Islamic teachings, enriching their culture in the context of the relationship between humans and nature, specifically water. The location of Iranian cities, both before and after Islam, continued to be determined by the presence of water. Cities that developed along rivers, expanded around springs, or were constructed with the help of aqueducts maintained their reliance on water. Water served as a guiding force for the growth and development of these cities. For instance, the city of Kashan's location has been influenced by surface water movements for centuries (Karamati, 2005). Architects in Islamic-Iranian cities recognized the spiritual aspects of water and incorporated them into their designs, symbolizing various meanings. Water was represented in three states: flowing, eruptions, and stagnant. Each state carried its own symbolism and significance.

Flowing State: In Iranian gardens of the Islamic period, water was not only used for irrigation but also brought freshness, vitality, and movement to the gardens. The flow of water in gardens symbolized the transient nature of the world. Examples of flowing water can be seen in gardens such as the Fin Garden in Kashan, where water flows through the garden, and the Shahzadeh Mahan Garden, where water cascades like a stair-like flow. This type of water representation symbolizes the concept of streams in paradise and the journey from nothing to everything, as streams return to their source (Johnson, 1929). The traditional Iranian garden construction gradually sank into oblivion. Modern public parks were created, overwhelmingly in the rich neighborhoods, where ever-flowing rivers and high precipitation create favorable conditions (Alizadeh & Habibi, 2022).

Eruptions State: In traditional houses and palaces, water fountains represented light, cleanliness, and purity. The interaction between sunlight and turbulent water symbolized the eternal battle between light and darkness. These fountains were often strategically placed in the south of porches or in front of palaces, signifying the clash between light and darkness during prayer times (Khoshnevis, 2001).

Stagnant State: The stagnant state of water was utilized for reflection, silence, and peace. Architects aimed not only to reflect the physical architecture of buildings in water but also to evoke spirituality and firm beliefs. For example, the front pond of Chehel Soton (Forty Pillars) in Esfahan was designed to reflect the twenty pillars in the water, symbolically representing forty pillars, a sacred number in Islamic belief. In mosques, water symbolized silence and peace. For instance, in the Imam Mosque in Esfahan, the pond reflects the sky, symbolizing the connection between the material and spiritual worlds. It creates an atmosphere where worshippers feel as if they are entering heaven and the celestial realm. Water, representing the holiness of the Supreme Being, is positioned in the middle of the mosque's courtyard, symbolizing purity, brightness, and light. Symbols play a crucial role in Islamic-Iranian architecture, particularly in mosques. The large pools in mosque courtyards have deep roots in people's beliefs. Water positioned in the center of the mosque represents spiritual cleansing and the purification of Muslims' inner selves. The water pool in the mosque courtyard serves multiple purposes, including air conditioning, hand washing, and, symbolically, the presence of water and its reflection of the sky (Siavoshi, 2013).

11.6.1 Water in Tehran Metropolis

Tehran, the capital of Iran, has a rich history of water abundance and innovative water technologies. Originally a large village with twelve neighborhoods, Tehran expanded and developed into a prosperous city of Shahneshin. In its early stages, Tehran was blessed with ample water resources, with rivers and streams such as Shamiranat, Jajrud, and Karaj ensuring the prosperity of agriculture and horticulture. During the Qajar dynasty, as the population of Tehran grew rapidly, the issue of water scarcity started to demand attention. The ruler Fath Ali Shah Qajar showed interest in addressing this issue, but it was during the reign of Mohammad Shah Qajar that significant progress was made. The construction of numerous qanats, underground water channels, became the primary solution to supply water to the expanding city. Mirza Agassi, the chancellor at that time, oversaw the peak period of qanat construction in

Tehran. However, as the population continued to increase and living standards improved, the qanats could no longer meet the growing demand for water. Efforts were made to bring water to Tehran from the Karaj and Jajrud rivers, but it was still insufficient. The open soil streams used for water flow resulted in significant evaporation, subsidence, and contamination, leading to various water-related diseases. To address these challenges, plans and projects for water piping in Tehran were proposed, starting from the early twentieth century. These initiatives aimed to provide a more reliable and efficient water supply system for the city's growing needs.

In the past, Tehran employed various water technologies to ensure access to clean water. Two significant examples are *saqqakhane* (drinking fountains) and cisterns. *Saqqakhane* were small structures built along public roads, allowing residents and businesses to provide water to thirsty passers-by. These drinking fountains held a special place in Islamic cities, often regarded as socioreligious phenomena. *Saqqakhane* contained stone containers filled with drinking water and were equipped with chained cups for people to use. They also became sacred places over time, with candles lit to guide passers-by and fulfill vows.

Cisterns, on the other hand, were crucial water storage structures in Tehran. These cylindrical tanks were often placed below ground level, and their construction became common due to the dryness and heat of the region. Cisterns were situated near mosques, schools, markets, and government palaces, serving as centralized water sources. They played a vital role in providing water to many houses in old Tehran, primarily filled with river water from sources like the Karaj River. Some prominent cisterns included Seyed Ismail Cistern and Baba Nowruz Ali Cistern.

Lastly, public baths held significant importance in Tehran's water technology. These underground facilities, often luxurious and magnificent, offered spaces for cleaning and washing the head and body. Iranian baths, built below ground level, provided natural temperature regulation, keeping them cool in summer and warm in winter. They were not just places for personal hygiene but also served as social gathering spots for discussions and sharing news.

The water technologies in Tehran's metropolis reflected the ingenuity and adaptation of Islamic-Iranian cities. *Saqqakhane*, cisterns, and baths were integral parts of the city's water infrastructure, ensuring access to clean water and promoting communal well-being. The preservation and recognition of these historical water technologies are essential for understanding Tehran's past and its continued manifestation in Islamic thought.

11.7 CONCLUSION

The right to water holds a significant place in Islamic thought, and its importance is further highlighted in the context of Islamic cities in Iran. Islamic teachings emphasize the fundamental right of all individuals to access clean and safe water for their basic needs. This right is not only recognized but also promoted in the Quran, hadith, and the practices of the Prophet Muhammad and his Companions. Islamic teachings emphasize the ethical responsibility to preserve and protect the natural environment, including water, as a divine gift and a communal right. The rich heritage of Muslim societies in water management and conservation practices showcases remarkable examples of sustainable resource utilization. From ingenious water-lifting devices to innovative water management systems, Islamic civilizations have demonstrated their engineering prowess and commitment to balancing water needs with environmental preservation. Iranian cities, with their diverse water systems and architectural integration of water symbolism, exemplify the close relationship between water, culture, and spirituality. By studying the right to water in Islamic thought and exploring its manifestation in Islamic-Iranian cities, we can gain valuable insights into the importance of water conservation and sustainable urban development from an Islamic perspective. It is our collective responsibility to ensure the availability of safe and affordable water for present and future generations, guided by the principles of justice, equity, and ecological balance.

In conclusion, recognizing the right to water in Islamic thought and applying it to the context of Islamic cities in Iran represents a harmonious integration of faith, culture, and practicality. By upholding this right and implementing effective water management strategies, we can ensure that Islamic cities continue to thrive as models of sustainable urban living, where access to clean water remains a cornerstone of human dignity, social justice, and environmental stewardship.

REFERENCES

Abedisarvestani, A., and M. Shahvali (2008). "Environmental Ethics: Toward an Islamic Perspective." *American-Eurasian Journal of Agricultural & Environmental Sciences*, vol. 3, no. 4, pp. 609–17.

Alizadeh, H., and K. Habibi (2022). "Urban Park Traditions in Iran and Tehran." In R. Murray (ed.), *Why Cities Need Large Parks*. London: Routledge, pp. 65–77.

Amery, H. A. (2001). "Islamic Water Management." *Water International*, vol. 26, no. 4, pp. 481–89.

(2015). *Arab Water Security: Threats and Opportunities in the Gulf States*. Cambridge: Cambridge University Press.

Ben-Hamouche, M. (2008). "Islamic Law for Water and Land Management and Its Impact on Urban Morphology." *Cities*, vol. 69, no. 2, pp. 208–24.

Brooking, E. T. (2021). "Before the Taliban Took Afghanistan, It Took the Internet." *Atlantic Council*, August 26.

De Miranda, A. (2007). *Water Architecture in the Lands of Syria: The Water-Wheels*. Rome: L'Erma di Bretschneider.

Dien, M. I. (1997). "Islam and the Environment: Theory and Practice." *Journal of Beliefs and Values*, vol. 18, no. 1, pp. 47–57.

Gada, M. Y. (2014). "Environmental Ethics in Islam: Principles and Perspectives." *World Journal of Islamic History and Civilization*, vol. 4, no. 4, pp. 130–38.

Haddad, M. (2012). "An Islamic Perspective of Food Security Management." *Water Policy*, vol. 14, pp. 121–35.

(2024). "Flowing Through History: Water Management in Muslim Civilization." *Muslim Heritage*, 12 March. https://muslimheritage.com/water-management/.

Hassan, A. B. (2020). "Arab Contributions to Hydronymy: The Detecting of Underground Water that Led to the Construction of Water Wells." *WIT Transactions on the Built Environment* vol. 197, pp. 13–25.

Hussein, I., and O. Al-Jayyousi (2001). "Management of Shared Waters: A Comparison of International and Islamic Law." In N. I. Faruqui, A. K. Biswas, and M. J. Bino (eds.), *Water Management in Islam*. New York: United Nations University Press.

Johnson, J. (1929). *The Persian Garden*. San Francisco, CA: Windsor Press.

Karamati, G. (2005). "Jaigah-e Aab Dar Shahr-e Iraniye Diroz Va Emroz." In *Congress on the History of Iranian Architecture and Urbanism*. Bam, Iran.

Khaled, A. (n.d.). "Al-Karaji and the Secrets of Hydrology." *1001 Inventions*. www.1001inventions.com/feature/devices/.

Khoshnevis, A. (2001). "Symbol Perspective of an Iranian Garden." *Manzar Magazine*, no. 15.

MacAlister, C., and N. Subramanyam (2018). "Climate Change and Adaptive Water Management: Innovative Solutions from the Global South." *Water International*, vol. 43, no. 2, pp. 133–44.

Morgan, M. H. (2008). *Lost History: The Enduring Legacy of Muslim Scientists, Thinkers, and Artists*. Washington, DC: National Geographic Books.

Özdemir, I. (2003). "Toward an Understanding of Environmental Ethics from a Qur'anic Perspective." In R. C. Foltz, F. M. Denny, and A. Baharuddin (eds.), *Islam and Ecology: A Bestowed Trust*. Cambridge, MA: Harvard University Press, pp. 3–37.

Sarvestani, A. A., and M. R. Shahraki (2023). "Climate Change Adaptation Methods at the Community Level: Evidence from the Oghan Watershed, North of Iran." *Environmental Science & Policy*, vol. 142, pp. 42–49.
Al-Sawy, A. (1995). "Al-Asbela (Free Water Fountains), the Water of Civilization." *Horus*, April–June.
Shomali, M. (2008). "Aspects of Environmental Ethics: An Islamic Perspective." *Thinking Faith*, no. 11.
Siavoshi, M. (2013). "Water in Islamic Architecture and Mosques." *Architectural Thinking Magazine*.
UN-HABITAT (2005). *Islamic Land Tenures and Reform*. Nairobi: UN-HABITAT. https://bit.ly/43CtpHd.

12

Intellectual Property and the Protection of the Environment in Nigeria

Lessons from Sharia

Oluwakemi A. Ayanleye

Like winds and sunsets, wild things were taken for granted until progress began to do away with them. Now we face the question whether a still higher 'standard of living' is worth its cost in things natural, wild, and free. For us of the minority, the opportunity to see geese is more important than television, and the chance to find a pasque-flower is a right as inalienable as free speech.[1]

12.1 INTRODUCTION

Technology has been the bedrock of human existence from time immemorial as every aspect of human life is dependent on one form of technology or the other. From the era of fruit gathering, to the Stone Age and the present-day information age, technology has consistently played a part in human development. Technology is thus pivotal to human existence as all basic human needs are dependent on one form of technology or the other for their satisfaction.[2] Technology and intellectual property (IP) systems have been described as some of the most important factors in nation building, wealth creation and economic development.[3] 'Innovation and creativity provide the alchemy that drives human development and welfare, that empowers individual and national economic growth – perhaps even contributes to democratic self-governance and longer healthier lives.'[4] This millennium is the age of the knowledge economy (KE), where research and innovation are central to development and economic growth.[5] Just as raw materials and

[1] Aldo Leopold, A *Sand County Almanac: And Sketches Here and There* (Oxford: Oxford University Press, 1949); Michael A. Gollin, 'Using Intellectual Property to Improve Environmental Protection', *Harvard Journal of Law & Technology* 4 (1991): 193–235, at 193.

[2] Meeting basic human needs like food, clothing and shelter are dependent on technology. Even human biological needs are met by the use of technology, whether crude or advanced.

[3] Ita Okon Bassey Ewa, 'Enhancing Technology and Intellectual Property Rights as Tools for Economic Development in Nigeria', speech delivered by the minister of science and technology on the occasion of the commemoration of African Day for Technology and Intellectual Property on 13 September 2012 in Abuja.

[4] Fernando de Santos, 'Foreword', in Shirin Elahi and Jeremy de Beer (eds), with Dick Kawooya, Chidi Oguamanam and Nagla Rizk, *Knowledge and Innovation in Africa: Scenarios for the Future* (Cape Town: Open A.I.R. Network, 2013), 1.

[5] Bámidélé Adémólá-Olátéjú, 'Beyond Selfies: Zuckerberg's Visit and the Knowledge Economy', *Premium Times Opinion*, 6 September 2016, http://opinion.premiumtimesng.com/2016/09/06/bamidele-ademola-olateju.

labour were key resources in the first industrial revolution, intellectual property is a central asset in an information- or knowledge-based economy.[6]

All economic and social progress ultimately depends on new ideas that challenge the inertia of the status quo with possibilities for change and improvement.[7] Innovation is an integral part of human existence and development. Indeed, 'the history of the human race is a history of the application of imagination, or innovation and creativity, to an existing base of knowledge in order to solve problems. Imagination feeds progress in the arts as well as science.'[8] Knowledge and innovation are propelling today's global economy as human development, including economic growth and the capability for longer, healthier and more fulfilling lives, depends on innovation and creativity.[9] However, with technology and innovation comes the attendant environmental pollution and degradation. There is an increased recognition that much of the technology employed in manufacturing, agriculture and transportation damage the environment.

The environment is the life supporting system for human existence and survival and provides much of the physical milieu and raw materials required for socio-economic progress. Humanity has no choice but to interact with it. Unfortunately, human interaction, natural disasters and climate change are putting unprecedented pressure and impact on the quality of environmental conditions.[10]

Innovation policies, together with environmental laws, thus play an important role in addressing many global environmental issues. Intellectual property rights (IPRs), as temporary privileges over the products of intellectual activity, determine who controls information and technology.[11] Intellectual property rules fundamentally affect the quality and availability of innovative ideas and products, and are therefore extremely important in achieving sustainable development, ensuring human health and protecting the environment.[12] The level and scope of IP protection influences the flow of technologies between industrialised and developing countries. These standards also impact the control communities have over their traditional knowledge, their access to medicines and education, as well as other such issues fundamental to sustainable development.[13]

From time immemorial, all societies in the world have evolved various means of drawing boundaries around certain kinds of knowledge resources. Knowledge systems evolve within a socio-cultural and institutional context, and analysis of the interactions between private, community and public domain knowledge helps the understanding of the evolution of knowledge, innovation and practice. The green future is dependent on the world's ability to create sustainable alternatives to the existing pollutive way of life. Globally, innovative technology remains a key driving force in the quest to transit to a green future. Technological innovation and IP are intertwined and cannot be discussed in isolation. Intellectual property rights are the

6 Audrey R. Chapman, 'Approaching Intellectual Property as a Human Right: Obligations Related to Article 15 (1) (c)', *Copyright Bulletin* 35, no. 3 (2001): 4–47.

7 Shirin Elahi and Jeremy de Beer, with Dick Kawooya, Chidi Oguamanam and Nagla Rizk, *Knowledge and Innovation in Africa: Scenarios for the Future* (Cape Town: Open A.I.R. Network, 2013), 17.

8 Kamal Idris, *Intellectual Property: A Power Tool for Economic Growth* (Geneva: World Intellectual Property Organization, 2003), 10–11.

9 Jeremy de Beer, Chidi Oguamanam and Tobias Schonwetter, 'Innovation, Intellectual Property and Development Narratives in Africa', in Jeremy de Beer, Chidi Oguamanam and Tobias Schonwetter (eds), *Innovation and Intellectual Property: Collaborative Dynamics in Africa* (Cape Town: UCT Press, 2014), 1.

10 National Environmental Standards and Regulations Enforcement Agency (NESREA), 'Nigeria: National Policy on the Environment (Revised 2016)', https://nesrea.gov.ng/wp-content/uploads/2025/05/nig176320.pdf.

11 Center for International Environmental Law, 'Intellectual Property', www.ciel.org/issue/intellectual-property/.

12 Ibid.

13 Ibid.

heart and soul of innovation. In the unending conversation on the effect of climate change, technology has been at the forefront of providing succour, with IP playing a key role.[14] Innovation is fundamental to the realisation of a green future as IPRs are fundamental to making innovation work. Hence, the progress and well-being of humanity are now dependent on IPRs.

This chapter considers the issue of IP and the environment from two perspectives. The first is encouragement of green innovation and the second is non-patentability of inventions contrary to public order and morality. The chapter is divided into five sections. Section 12.1 is the introduction. Section 12.2 deals with the concept of property generally and IP from different perspectives. Section 12.3 discusses the notion of the environment and its protection from the traditional African perspective and that of Islamic law. Section 12.4 appraises the legal framework for protection of IP especially as it affects the environment. In this regard, it discusses the issue of green technology and using the instrumentality of the law to exclude the patenting of innovations and registration of marks contrary to public order and morality. Section 12.5 is the conclusion and includes recommendations.

12.2 THE CONCEPT OF INTELLECTUAL PROPERTY

In understanding the concept of intellectual property, it is imperative to understand the concept of property itself as private ownership property is the foundation of IP. Control over property rules is foundational to the sovereignty of a state and its people and it is perhaps the most fundamental instrument that a state can use to plan its own development.[15] By the changing definitions of property, the creation of new rights of property and limitations on rights of property the state can decide who owns resources, who can exploit resources, who benefits and who loses from resource allocation and consumption.[16] The concept of property, especially private property, has continually generated much debate amongst scholars. Property connotes different things to different people with a variety of meanings depending on the context in which it is used. According to Roman law, property is the 'right to use and abuse one's own within the limits of the law – *jus utendi et abutendi re suâ, guatenus juris ratio patitur*'.[17] Abuse in this sense does not signify senseless and immoral abuse, but absolute domain or control.[18] Property consists of a package of legally recognised rights held by one person in relationship to others with respect to an object or resource.[19] This bundle of rights consists of the right to exclude, the right to transfer and the right to possess and use.[20] Concepts of property are used to describe the legal and ethical entitlements that particular people or groups have or use to manage particular resources.[21] Islam

[14] Nta Ekpiken and Emmanuel Nkamare, 'Innovate for a Green Future', *Mondaq*, 5 May 2020, www.mondaq.com/nigeria/trademark/928076/innovate-for-a-green-future.

[15] Peter Drahos, 'Thinking Strategically about Intellectual Property Rights', *Telecommunications Policy* 21, no. 3 (1997): 201–11, at 201.

[16] Ibid.

[17] Pierre-Joseph Proudhon, 'What Is Property? An Inquiry into the Principle of Right and of Government', 1840, www.marxists.org/reference/subject/economics/proudhon/property/ch02.htm; Oluwakemi Amudat Ayanleye, 'Protection of Intellectual Property and Promotion of Indigenous Technology in Nigeria through University Industry Collaboration' (PhD diss., Babcock University, 2022), 27.

[18] Proudhon, 'What Is Property?'.

[19] John G. Sprankling, *Understanding Property Law* (Newark, NJ: Matthew Bender & Company, 1999), 2.

[20] Ibid.

[21] Hugh Breakey, 'Property', *Internet Encyclopeadia of Philosophy*, www.iep.utm.edu/prop-con.

recognises private ownership of property. It grants individuals a high degree of freedom in dealing with property and its use in a proper manner.[22]

The concept of IP is one aspect of property, albeit incorporeal. It belongs to the class of property referred to as choses in action in that it is intangible. Intellectual property can be broadly defined as 'creations of the mind, inventions, literary and artistic works, and symbols, names, images, and designs used in commerce'.[23] Intellectual property is a broad concept that covers several types of legally recognised rights arising from some type of intellectual creativity, or that are otherwise related to ideas.

12.2.1 *Justifications for IP*

There are a number of traditional justifications for IPRs which tend to provide support for, or to influence, the jurisprudence and general objective of intellectual property. Despite subtle or nuanced distinctions between competing justifications, some of the reasons adduced for IP tend to overlap.[24] Intellectual property has reportedly been grounded and validated over time by natural, social, moral and economic narratives.[25] The philosophical, legal and economic rhetoric for protecting the creations and innovations of authors, inventors and producers has, dating back to Roman times, employed terms as 'incentive', 'reward', 'natural rights', 'public interest', 'utilitarian', 'welfare' and, more recently, 'stakeholder'.[26] Consequently, theories have been constructed around these terminologies as jurisprudential foundations of modern IPRs. The Kantian or the Hegelian natural, ethical or human rights justification for the protection of authorial personality and the Lockean concept of property have formed the cornerstones of modern IP rights systems.[27]

Justifications for the creation of IP fall within four fundamentally different lines of argument, each of which starts from a different point but arrives at the same conclusion.[28] The first type of argument is that a person has a natural property right to their own ideas. The appropriation of such ideas by others must be condemned as stealing and society is morally obligated to recognise and protect this property right. Enforcement of the exclusive property right by the use of a patented invention is the only appropriate way for society to recognise this right.[29] The second type of argument posits that justice requires that a person receives, and that society secures to them, reward for their services in proportion to the usefulness of these services to society. Inventors render useful services, and the most appropriate way to secure rewards commensurate with their services is by means of exclusive patent rights to their inventions. The third type of argument posits that industrial progress is desirable to society and inventions and their exploitation are necessary to secure industrial progress. Neither invention nor exploitation of invention

[22] Hayatullah Laluddin, Mohd Nasran Mohamad, Zaini Nasohah and Shofian Ahmad, 'Property and Ownership Right from an Islamic Perspective', *Advances in Natural and Applied Sciences* 6, no. 7 (2012): 1125–29, at 1126.

[23] World Intellectual Property Organization, 'What Is Intellectual Property?', www.wipo.int/edocs/pubdocs/en/wipo_pub_450_2020.pdf, 2.

[24] Chidi Oguamanam, 'Beyond Theories: Intellectual Property Dynamics in the Global Knowledge Economy', *Wake Forest Intellectual Property Law Journal* 9, no. 2 (2009): 104–54, at 105.

[25] Adebambo Adewopo, *According to Intellectual Property: A Pro-Development Vision of the Law and the Nigerian Intellectual Property Law and Policy Reform in the Knowledge Era* (Lagos: NIALS, 2012), 5.

[26] Ibid.

[27] Ibid., 6–7. See also Graham Dutfield and Uma Suthersanen, *Global Intellectual Property Law* (Cheltenham, UK: Edward Elgar Publishing, 2008), 47–48.

[28] Fritz Machlup and Edith Penrose, 'The Patent Controversy in the Nineteenth Century', *The Journal of Economic History* 10, no. 1 (1950): 1–29, at 10.

[29] Ibid.

will be obtained to any adequate extent unless inventors and capitalists have hopes that successful ventures will yield profits, which make it worth their while to put in their efforts and risk their money. The simplest, cheapest and most effective way for society to hold out these incentives is to grant exclusive patent rights in inventions.[30] The fourth type of argument holds that industrial progress is desirable to society, and to secure it at a sustained rate it is necessary that new inventions become generally known as parts of the technology of society. In the absence of protection against immediate imitation of novel technological ideas, an inventor will keep his invention secret. The secret will die with him, and society will thereby lose the new art. Hence it is in the interest of society to induce the inventor to disclose his secret for the use of future generations. This can best be done by granting exclusive patent rights to the inventor in return for public disclosure of his invention.[31]

Justifications for protection of IP centre on two basic sets of principles, the utilitarian and non-utilitarian. The utilitarian principles are basically the economic justifications for IPRs while the non-utilitarian principles are the philosophical justifications for the granting of property rights to IP. They all, however, meet at the convergence of incentive, that is, the need to grant some concession to the inventor in order to encourage more inventions for the benefit and betterment of society.[32]

12.2.2 *Islamic Perspective of IP*

While there are diverse views on Islam and IP, the general opinion of scholars is that Islam supports IP protection.[33] In pre-Islamic societies, works of the mind were highly valued and may have qualified as a form of IP. Though this recognition was rudimentary, society gave authors moral rights to their works. For example, poetry was deeply respected in the pre-Islamic era, and authors enjoyed an enhanced social standing and esteem. As recognition of the value of their work, poets were compensated for the publication and distribution of their work.[34] The process of recitation and mentioning the name of the author constituted a basic form of a moral type of IPR of the author. Unauthorised use could have shown disrespect to the poet and, for this reason, might have led to public outcry. The process of public recitation in that era is akin to present-day IPRs. The Prophet Muhammad stated: 'A Muslim who achieves something before another Muslim who has not achieved is entitled to that.'[35]

However, with regard to *ʿilm* (knowledge), it has been reported that the Prophet warned Muslims against the concealment of knowledge as it is common property and the shared heritage of all humankind, the owner of which is God.[36] Beneficial knowledge (*al-ʿilm al-nāfiʿa*) is highly valued in Islam. Muslims are encouraged to supplicate by praying: 'O Allah, indeed I ask You for beneficial knowledge (*al-ʿilm al-nāfiʿa*).' From an Islamic perspective, beneficial and useful creativity and innovation in all kinds of knowledge is rewarding and merit making both in this world and the hereafter (*ākhira*), and for as long as people benefit from such

30 Ibid.
31 Ibid.
32 Ayanleye, 'Protection of Intellectual Property', 98–99.
33 Ezieddin Elmahjub, 'An Islamic Perspective on the Theories of Intellectual Property', *Law Explorer*, 11 October 2015, https://lawexplores.com/an-islamic-perspective-on-the-theories-of-intellectual-property.
34 Bashar H. Malkawi, 'The Alliance between Islamic Law and Intellectual Property: Structure and Practice', *University of St. Thomas Law Journal* 10, no. 3 (2013): 618–649, at 618.
35 Rehana Anjum, 'An Introduction of Intellectual Property Rights in Islamic Law', *SSRN*, 18 April 2019, https://papers.ssrn.com/sol3/papers.cfm?abstract_id=3397868.
36 Elmahjub, 'Theories of Intellectual Property'.

knowledge, the reward will go to the person who created it. In a hadith the Prophet states, 'When a man dies, his deeds come to an end except for three things: *ṣadaqa jāriya* (ceaseless charity), a knowledge which is beneficial, or a virtuous child who prays for him.'[37]

Although sharia is based more on social order and cohesion rather than private interests, sharia does clearly recognise IPRs as the Quran emphasises the notion of profitable trade as well as one's right to enjoy the fruits of one's work.[38]

12.2.3 *Traditional Protection of IP in Nigeria*

Property rights are not novel to African traditional communities or their knowledge systems. African history disproves the notion that there were no property rights.[39] The protection of IP is not entirely new in Nigeria as evidence showed the appreciation of IP even before colonialism. There is evidence to show that the technology of a tribe in Africa, such as techniques of hunting and gathering of wild products to elaborate systems of agriculture, differs with location, and the mechanisms are owned by the parties concerned.[40] There is evidence that copyright has been and is an intrinsic part of the customs and traditions of the people of Nigeria.[41] A case in point refers to the practice of dancers and singers paying homage to their ancestors and predecessors in the trade before commencement of performance. The intent of the acknowledgment is the traditional belief that if the current performers desire success, they must appreciate their ancestors and predecessors in trade to attract the requisite blessings.[42] The practice of giving money, gifts, refreshment and other forms of remuneration to the performers is another evidence of recognition of literary and creative works. These practices go to the root of modern copyright concepts of moral and economic rights.[43]

Earlier proprietary rights in intangibles vested exclusively in groups, such as families, clans, age or sex group, cults, professional guilds, or individuals, such as particular elders, chiefs or kings. The enforcements of these rights were based on magical or religious beliefs, taboos or punishments administered by the group.[44] Proprietary rights in intangibles were often exercised in form of monopolies maintained by guilds.[45] Traditional doctors protected their trade by a system of trade secrets and magical beliefs and practices. The trade secrets were maintained as often only members of their family were trained, thereby reinforcing the belief that only a particular lineage had magical powers to heal.[46] In some cases certain clans were known as the

[37] Cited in Mohammad Manzoor Malik, 'Ethical Medical Innovations and Their Applications: An Islamic Perspective', *Al Ameen Journal of Medical Sciences* 12, no. 3 (2019): 115–20, at 116.

[38] Lolwa Alfadhel, 'Shariah Law and Trademark Protection in the GCC Member States', in David Price and Alhanoof AlDebasi (eds), *Intellectual Property Rights: Development and Enforcement in the Arab States of the Gulf* (Berlin: Gerlach Press) 109–32.

[39] Ayoyemi Arowolo, *Intellectual Property Rights, Traditional Knowledge Systems and Jurisprudence in Africa* (Ibadan, Nigeria: Ababa Press, 2012), 159.

[40] Ibid., 165.

[41] Kunle Ola, 'Evolution and Future Trends of Copyright in Nigeria', in Brian Fitzgerald and John Gilchrist (eds), *Copyright Perspectives* (Cham, Switzerland: Springer, 2015), 97–124.

[42] Ibid.

[43] Ibid.

[44] Adebambo Adewopo, 'Developments in Intellectual Property in Africa', *ATRIP*, June 2016, http://atrip.org/wp-content/uploads/2016/06/Adewopo-Dev.-of-IP-in-Africa.doc.

[45] Bankole Sodipo, *Piracy and Counterfeiting: GATT, TRIPS and Developing Countries* (London: Kluwer Law International, 1997), 44.

[46] Ibid.

medicine people and were licensed as such by the king.[47] As a result of their expertise, they were under the special protection of the king and often went unpunished for crimes. In a manner akin to the development of the patent system in medieval Europe, kings also invited medicine men from other tribes to their towns and bestowed favours on them to keep them in such towns.[48]

12.2.4 *Statutory Protection of IP in Nigeria*

Basically, IP is divided into two categories, copyright and industrial property. Industrial property includes patent, industrial designs and trademarks. In Nigeria, several laws have a bearing on the protection of the different rights that make up IP. Hitherto, there are three main statutes governing the protection of IP in Nigeria, the Copyright Act (CA) 2022, the Patents and Designs Act (PDA)[49] and the Trademarks Act (TMA).[50] The enactment of the Plant Variety Protection Act (PVPA) of 2021 brought a new paradigm to IP protection in Nigeria.

The CA provides for the protection of copyright and neighbouring rights, prescribes appropriate exceptions and improves the effective administration, regulation and enforcement of copyright in the digital environment in Nigeria. The objective of the CA, as contained in section 1, are to inter alia protect the rights of authors to ensure just rewards and recognition for their intellectual efforts and provide appropriate limitations and exceptions to guarantee access to creative works.

The PDA makes comprehensive provisions for the registration and proprietorship of patents and designs in Nigeria and other ancillary matters. The objective of the patent system is to protect an inventor's right to control the exploitation of their invention in the marketplace by giving them exclusive rights over its use for twenty years. To enjoy patent protection, an invention must be new, result from inventive activity and must be capable of industrial application.[51] Patent protection helps companies to recoup the research and development costs of bringing new products or services to market.

Plant Variety Protection Act 2021 (PVPA) is designed to protect plant breeders. It is a form of IP protection law that helps encourage plant breeders and enthusiasts by granting them an IPR over their planting materials.[52]

12.3 LEGAL FRAMEWORK FOR PROTECTION OF THE ENVIRONMENT

12.3.1 *Nigeria's Indigenous Customary Laws on Environmental Protection*

The Indigenous legal tradition in communities now known as Nigeria was woven around the land and the belief that the soil feeds man from infancy to adulthood, and at death provides

47 Samuel Johnson, *The History of the Yoruba from the Earliest Times to the Beginning of the British Protectorate*, ed. Obadiah Johnson (Lagos: C.S.S. Bookshops, 1973), 121.

48 Ibid., 122. Johnson relates the story of a particular family of Efon (a town in present-day Ekiti State, Nigeria) descent living at one time at Oyo and said to have belonged to the Ondasa tribe. Their ancestors were said to have been invited to Oyo by one of the early kings for medical advice when all the king's wives were barren. His prescriptions were successful and he was retained at Oyo and rewarded with a high position in the palace amongst the household officers.

49 Patents and Designs Act Cap P2 Laws of the Federation of Nigeria (LFN) 2004.

50 Trademarks Act Cap T13 LFN 2004.

51 PDA, s. 1.

52 Nigeria Economic Summit Group, 'Plant Variety Protection Act 2021: Fact Sheet', www.pvp.gov.ng/assets/pdf/fact.pdf.

housing for his corpse. The Indigenous peoples have laws governing land use and the interrelations between all living beings. Traditional laws, cultures and knowledge systems recognise the relational connection of man to land. The law is encoded right into the language, as stories and cultural practices manifest in discussions made in Indigenous languages.

Before the advent of colonialism, Islam and Christianity in Africa, the African lived in harmony with nature. Environmental conservation is not a novel phenomenon to the African communities. Past generations knew about environmental degradation and the need for its preservation. This found expression in the traditional religious practices because of the belief that everything belongs to the ecosystem and the environment has a strong spiritual meaning for humans. Their attitude to nature is deeply rooted in the belief that all things were created by the Supreme Being for a harmonious continuity, and as such there must be a relationship of mutual obligations between all created things. The awareness of the fact that the well-being, survival and the physical, spiritual and material development of man depend largely on the state of the environment has since time immemorial fuelled the drive to protect, preserve and conserve natural resources among Africans in general and Nigerians in particular.

The need to protect the environment is seen as a communal, spiritual and sacred duty. For instance, land is in some parts referred to as mother earth, since it brings forth the food that feeds the world's population, and its protection is therefore viewed and considered a sacred and religious responsibility.[53] The practice of environmental conservation was prevalent and well accepted throughout Africa and traditional and peculiar strategies which were indigenous to Africa were employed as protective and conservative means of preserving the environment.[54] These include taboos, folktales, totemism and a conception of natural resources as common property, among others.[55] Diawuo and Issifu also agreed that Africans were using norms, myths, taboos, totems and a closed season in the preservation, conservation and management of natural resources.[56]

Kwashirai observed that superstition was actually employed for the purpose of preserving game and forests.[57] The customary law of the Iroko people in the Western part of Nigeria frowns at the burning of bushes for the purpose of hunting game, and it is thus a taboo to engage in this act which can incur the wrath of the gods.[58] Among the Ajah people of Lagos State, the killing of pregnant animals during hunting is a taboo. The killing of pregnant animals, for example, was forbidden by customary law even during hunting festivals.[59]

Also, in the area of habitat and species protection and preservation, some trees in Africa were given special recognition, protection and preference.[60] Apart from their value in food production, medicine and timber, the trees were accorded spiritual status and worshipped. People also

[53] Shallon Asiimire, 'The Unwritten Law: Traditional Ways of Conserving Environment', *New Vision*, 8 December 2014, https://tinyurl.com/j72bdp65. See also Adekunbi O. Johnson-Odusanya, 'The Environment and Right to Life: An Appraisal of the Legal Framework for Air Pollution in Nigeria' (PhD diss., Babcock University, 2020).

[54] Johnson-Odusanya, 'The Environment and Right to Life'.

[55] Muyaradzi Mawere, 'Traditional Environmental Conservation Strategies in Pre-Colonial Africa: Lessons for Zimbabwe to Forget or to Carry Forward into the Future', *Afro Asian Journal of Social Sciences* 4, no. 4 (2013): 1–23, at 6.

[56] Johnson-Odusanya, 'The Environment and Right to Life'.

[57] Vimbai C. Kwashirai, 'Environmental History of Africa', *Encyclopedia of Life Support Systems*, www.eolss.net/Sample-Chapters/C09/E6-156-35.pdf.

[58] Adamu Kyuka Usman, *Environmental Protection Law and Practice* (Ibadan, Nigeria: Ababa Press, 2012), 1.

[59] Ibid.

[60] Vimbai C. Kwashirai, 'Environmental Change, Control and Management in Africa', *Global Environment* 6, no. 12 (2013): 166–96.

avoid the indiscriminate felling of such trees.[61] Certain areas within communities are designated as sacred groves or forests. These actually serve to protect biodiversity, as they could otherwise have been endangered or become extinct.[62] Africans hold the genuine belief that spiritual entities reside in trees, land and rivers, and that man must be cautious in his interaction with them or face the wrath of the gods.[63]

Customary practices and responses to environmental protection in Nigeria include the use of taboos, the dedication of some animals as sacred beings, the protection and preservation of certain plants species as sacred trees, shifting of cultivation, the designation of hills and mountains as sacred, and dietary restrictions.[64] These are enforced by the elders, chiefs and community leaders.[65]

12.3.2 *Statutory Protection*

Protection of the environment is guaranteed under the Nigerian constitution, section 20 of which provides that the 'State shall protect and improve the environment and safeguard the water, air and land, forest and wild life of Nigeria.'[66] The main objective of section 20 is to ensure a healthy environment for Nigerian citizens.[67] The protection of the environment is essential for the realisation of the right to life. This formed the foundation upon which various bodies of legislation on the protection of the environment and the preservation of the right to a healthy environment were enacted. In addition, Nigeria is party to several international treaties and conventions governing environmental issues. There are several statutes enacted for the protection of the environment,[68] however, the National Environmental Standards and Regulations Enforcement Agency (NESREA) Act 2007, as amended in 2018, is the major enactment on environmental protection. The Act established an agency charged with the responsibility of the enforcement of environmental standards regulations, rules, laws, policies and guidelines. The agency established under the Act is also charged with the responsibility of the protection and development of the environment biodiversity conservation, and development of Nigeria's natural resources. The functions and powers of the agency are set out under sections 7 and 8 of the Act which inter alia include the enforcement of laws, guidelines, policies and standards on environmental matters including pollution of the environment.[69]

[61] Ibid.

[62] A. Rim Rukeh, G. Irerhievwie and I. E. Agbozu, 'Traditional Beliefs and Conservation of Natural Resources: Evidences from Selected Communities in Delta State, Nigeria', *International Journal of Biodiversity and Conservation* 5, no. 7, (2013): 426–32.

[63] Ibid.

[64] Raphael Oladele Adeoluwa, 'An Examination of Customary Practices Related to Environmental Protection in Nigeria', *International Journal of Education and Human Developments* 3, no. 2 (2017): 38–51.

[65] Ibid.

[66] The Constitution of the Federal Republic of Nigeria 1999, s. 20.

[67] Abdulkadir Bolaji Abdulkadir, 'The Right to a Healthful Environment in Nigeria: A Review of Alternative Pathways to Environmental Justice in Nigeria', *Afe Babalola University: Journal of Sustainable Development Law and Policy* 3, no. 1 (2014): 118–31, at 122.

[68] Examples of such laws are the Federal Environmental Protection Act; Associated Gas Re-Injection (Continued Flaring of Gas) Act; National Environmental Protection (Effluent Limitation) Regulations and Environmental Impact Assessment Decree; Factories Act Cap F1 LFN 2010; State Environmental Protection Agencies Laws; Associated Gas Re-Injection Act (Cap A24) LFN 2004; Environmental Impact Assessment Act of 1992; and National Environmental (Protection Pollution Abatement in Industries and Facilities Generating Waste) Regulation 1991, among others.

[69] Ebiemere Osaro, 'Legal Framework on Protection of Environmental and Foreign Direct Investment Rights in Nigeria: A Reflection on the Oil and Gas Industry', *African Journal of International Energy & Environmental Law* 4, no. 1 (2023): 41–56.

Another important statute is the Environmental Impact Assessment Act 1992. This Act requires an assessment of public or private projects that are likely to have a significant impact on the environment. The Act establishes cases where an Environmental Impact Assessment is required and creates liability for non-compliance. Accordingly, an assessment of the potential negative impact of a proposed gas project on the natural environment in Nigeria is mandatory.

12.4 IP AND PROTECTION OF THE ENVIRONMENT

Innovation, environmental sustainability and IP are closely intertwined and enjoy a synergetic, interdependent relationship. Intellectual property rules fundamentally affect the quality and availability of innovative ideas and products, and are therefore extremely important in achieving sustainable development, ensuring human health, and protecting the environment. Innovation policies, together with environmental laws, play a key role in addressing many global environmental issues. Intellectual property rights, as temporary privileges over the products of intellectual activity, determine who controls information and technology.[70]

Protection of the environment through the instrumentality of IP comes in two ways. The first is the encouragement of green technology. When innovation is of the green variety, the value added is the yielding of environmental benefits such as energy savings, pollution prevention and mitigation, deployment of clean technology and so on.[71] Copyright impacts environmental protection in many ways. In the environmental field, they can range from eco-friendly architectural plans and buildings, literature (e.g. scientific articles, newspaper or magazine articles, instruction manuals detailing processes that accomplish environmental benefits), charts, diagrams, maps, photographs, and even films about the weather, climate, the size of glaciers and so on. Also, software and databases used for forecast or analysis of weather, climate, temperature patterns, changes in fauna and flora, drought control and so on. In short, literary and artistic works of various kinds as well as audiovisual works and films.[72]

12.4.1 *Non-Patentable Inventions*

An invention may be novel, result from inventive activity, be capable of industrial application and still not be patentable if it falls within the category of inventions excluded from patentability under the PDA. Under the Act patents cannot validly be granted or obtained in respect of the following:

a. plant or animal varieties, or essentially biological processes for the production of plants or animals (other than microbiological processes and their products);[73] or
b. inventions the publication of or exploitation of which would be contrary to public order or morality (it being understood for the purposes of this paragraph that the exploitation of an

[70] Center for International Environmental Law (CIEL), 'Intellectual Property', www.ciel.org/issue/intellectual-property.
[71] Adejoke Oyewunmi, 'Green Innovation and Intellectual Property (Trademarks): Prospects and Challenges'. Presented at 'An Executive Look at the Role of Trademark Law in Advancing a Green Future in Nigeria', a workshop organised by World Intellectual Property Organisation (WIPO) Nigeria office and International Trademark Association on 27 April 2020.
[72] Estelle Derclaye, 'The Role of Copyright in the Protection of the Environment and the Fight against Climate Change: Is the Current Copyright System Adequate?', in Joshua D. Sarnoff (ed.), *Research Handbook on Intellectual Property and Climate Change* (Cheltenham, UK: Edward Elgar Publishing, 2012).
[73] PDA, s. 1 (4) (a). See also Simisola Oluwatoyin Akintola, 'Intellectual Property Rights and Biomedical Research: Problems and Challenges under the Nigerian Law', *NIALS Journal of Intellectual Property* 2 (2012): 78–100, at 98.

invention is not contrary to public order or morality merely because its exploitation is prohibited by law).[74]

12.4.1.1 Plant and Animal Varieties and Biological Processes

There is no doubt that biotechnology is revolutionising production in both industry and agriculture in certain areas. It has the potential to provide the answers to some of the world's most intractable problems concerning agriculture, health, nutrition and the environment.[75] The PDA prohibits the granting of patents for plant or animal varieties, or essentially biological processes for the production of plants or animals. Article 27(3) of the Trade-Related Aspects of International Property Rights (TRIPS) agreement permits World Trade Organization (WTO) members to exclude from patentability 'plants and animals other than micro-organisms, and essentially biological processes for the production of plants or animals other than non-biological and microbiological processes'.[76] This prohibition has far-reaching implications for the patentability of biotechnological inventions and genetically engineered plant varieties in Nigeria. Varieties of living organisms obtained through new processes in horticulture, animal husbandry and others are excluded from patentability, and this extends to cross-breeding and cross-planting if biological in nature.[77] However, the Act is silent on what it means by 'essentially biological', nor does it define 'microbiological process'.[78] Thus it may be difficult to distinguish between what is biological and what is a microbiological process, or determine the scope of each concept and how they are so materially different that a microbiological process merits the grant of patents and a biological process does not. Kur opines that under the concept of 'essentially biological processes', classical plant breeding methods would be excluded from patentability while genetic engineering processes and technique would be patentable.[79] To him, the difference between the two concepts lies only in the degree of technical intervention, scientific growth and industrial capacity or intervention in natural traits of plants and animals.[80] In the US case of *Diamond v. Chakrabarty*[81] the court concluded that Congress intended statutory subject matter to 'include anything under the sun that is made by man'. Other cases confirmed the patenting of live organisms.[82] The issue of patenting live organisms is not only complex but also contentious. It involves highly intricate political questions, such as domestic food supply, as well as ethical considerations, and may have negative implications. The government and certain amici curiae argued in *Diamond v. Chakrabarty*[83] that patenting living organisms would present substantial risks to society and the environment. Justification for the exclusion may be on ethical

[74] PDA, s. 1 (4) (b).

[75] Jayashree Watal, 'Intellectual Property and Biotechnology: Trade Interests of Developing Countries', *International Journal of Biotechnology* 2 (2000): 44–55, at 45.

[76] Judy Winegar Goans, *Intellectual Property: Principles and Practice* (Arlington, VA: Nathan Associates, 2014), 86.

[77] Adejoke Oyewunmi, *Nigerian Law of Intellectual Property* (Lagos: University of Lagos Press & Bookshop, 2014), 157.

[78] F. O. B. Babafemi, *Intellectual Property: The Law and Practice of Copyright, Trade Marks, Patents and Industrial Designs in Nigeria* (Ibadan, Nigeria: Justinian Books, 2007), 356.

[79] Joseph Jar Kur, 'Globalization of Intellectual Property Rights and the Regime for the Protection of New Plant Varieties: A Nigerian Perspective', *Journal of Public and Private Law Benue State University, Nigeria* 1, no. 1: 217–31, cited in Mary Imelda Obianuju Nwogu, 'The Role of Nigerian Patents Law in Biotechnology Transfer', *Journal of Law, Policy and Globalization* 31 (2014): 121–25, at 124.

[80] Ibid.

[81] (1980) 447 U.S. 303.

[82] *Ex Parte Hibberd* (1985) 227 USPQ 443; *JEM AG Supply Inc., DBA Farm Advantage Inc. et al. v. Pioneer Hi-bred International Inc.* (2001) 534 US 124.

[83] 65 Law Ed. (2d) 144 1980.

grounds, that allowing patenting of living organisms may promote a materialistic concept of life, raise issues of sanctity of human worth, violate species integrity by encouraging inappropriate human control over animal life, result in cruelty to animals, raise concerns of biosafety, and impact negatively on the environment.[84] Other views are that patenting life forms will constitute interference with the natural world, including issues relating to the devaluation of human life; survival of the family farm; commercialisation of academic research; and agriculture and laboratory animal suffering.[85] Part of the hostile commentary stems from the deontological argument that animal patenting is inherently wrong, because it threatens such crucial moral values as respect for God, species integrity and the value of human life. In contrast, other anti-patenting arguments represent an instrumental view of morality. These arguments emphasise environmental, economic and other harmful consequences that animal patenting might have for society.[86] Animal rights groups saw in it a future full of sad mutant animals twisted into unnatural forms by greedy and inconsiderate genetic engineers.[87] Farm groups considered the prospect of increased control by giant agribusiness corporations, whose demand for royalties on patented animals would surely become yet another threat to the ever-decreasing autonomy of the small farmer.[88] Opposing views opine that the issues at stake are that of animal rights, biosafety and environmental protection, which are not affected by the granting of patents.

There is no gainsaying that biotechnological inventions significantly impact critical aspects of human existence including health, environment, food security and general well-being. The impact of improved plant varieties may improve yield and promote access to food but may also have an adverse effect on the environment especially concerning biodiversity. The use of Genetic Use Restriction Technologies,[89] for instance, may adversely affect farmers who depend on seed from previous yields for new planting seasons.[90] Not only that, but there is also the likelihood of these technologies destroying the natural and traditional seed varieties. The public research system has a critical role to play in ensuring that access to potential benefits of new technologies is guaranteed for poor people and environmental conservation is maintained.[91]

As a member of the WTO, Nigeria has an obligation to protect plant varieties. The provisions for Plant Variety Protection (PVP) are specified in the TRIPS Agreement in Article 27 (3) (b) which states that 'members shall provide for the protection of plant varieties either by patents or by an effective *sui generis* system or by any combination thereof'. This gives the member states the discretion on the type of IPR system they wish to apply. It has been suggested that the *sui generis* system of protection may be best for developing countries as the standard set in the International Conventions for the Protection of New Varieties of Plants (UPOV Convention)

84 See Kevin W. O'Connor, 'Patenting Animals and Other Living Things', *South California Law Review* 65, no. 1 (1991): 597, cited in Oyewunmi, *Nigerian Law of Intellectual Property*, 157.

85 Rebecca Dresser, 'Ethical and Legal Issues in Patenting New Animal Life', *Jurimetrics Journal* 28 (1988): 399–435, at 409.

86 Ibid.

87 Robert P. Merges, 'Intellectual Property in Higher Life Forms: The Patent System and Controversial Technologies', *Maryland Law Review* 47 (1988): 1051–75.

88 Ibid.

89 Often called terminator technology, this refers to genetically modified seeds that can only be used for one planting season. A genetic modification switches on production of a toxin that kills off developing plant embryos. The result is a seed that could be harvested for food but would not produce offspring. The farmers cannot use the seeds from one season in another season.

90 Oyewunmi, *Nigerian Law*, 158.

91 James Abah, M. N. Ishaq and Akaamaa C. Wada, 'The Role of Biotechnology in Ensuring Food Security and Sustainable Agriculture', *African Journal of Biotechnology* 9, no. 52 (2010): 8896–900, at 8898.

seems suitable for them.[92] The convention extends limited protection of plant genera and species, but does not extend protection to end products and the reproduction of plant variety, thereby giving farmers a distinct advantage. It allows developing countries to include exceptions and protection measures for traditional agricultural practices and the traditional knowledge of farmers and local communities.[93]

The benefits of inventive activities to promote increased crop yield, improved varieties and other similar benefits must be weighed against the adverse effects of farmers' traditional practices of saving and replanting seeds. This is especially important in Nigeria as most farmers in the country operate at the subsistence level and farming is the vocation of most rural dwellers. Nigeria is predominantly an agricultural society with approximately 70 per cent of the population engaging in agricultural production at a subsistence level.[94] Thus most of the farmers can hardly afford the expense of purchasing new seeds from private profit-driven biotechnological companies for each planting season.[95] Care needs to be taken to avoid the adverse effect of the genetically modified seeds on the country's agricultural system, with the possible deleterious loss and extinction of the nutrient rich seeds of almost all the crops.

Nigeria recently enacted the Plant Variety Protection Act, which was signed into law on 26 May 2021 with the objective of promoting increased staple crop productivity for smallholder farmers in Nigeria and encourage investment in plant breeding and crop variety development; promote increased mutual accountability in the seed sector; and protect new varieties of plants.[96] Nigeria is signatory to three treaties relevant to plant variety protection, namely TRIPS, the Convention of Biological Diversity (CBD) and the International Treaty on Plant Genetic Resources for Food and Agriculture (ITPGRFA).[97] Nigeria needs to take a cue from India with respect to the protection of plant varieties. India provides for the protection of farmers' varieties, on which the PVPA 2021 is silent.[98]

12.4.1.2 Inventions Contrary to Public Order or Morality

An invention that would be contrary to public order or morality is not patentable.[99] Hence where the publication of an invention will offend the moral sensibilities of reasonably decent members of the society or where the use to which it will be applied is capable of causing public unease because of its immorality or indecency and is therefore contrary to public interest, the invention is not patentable.[100] However, the fact that the exploitation of an invention is prohibited by law does not make it contrary to public order or morality.[101] The PDA however did not define what constitutes public order or morality. Lessons may be learnt from other jurisdictions however in this regard. The provision of the PDA is *in pari materia* with the

92 Folarin Shyllon, *Intellectual Property Law in Nigeria* (Munich: Max Planck Institute for Intellectual Property, 2003), 145.

93 Christoph Antons, '*Sui Generis* Protection for Plant Varieties and Traditional Knowledge in Biodiversity and Agriculture: The International Framework and National Approaches in the Philippines and India', *Indian Journal of Law and Technology* 6 (2010): 89–139, at 89.

94 'Nigeria – Agriculture', *Nations Encyclopedia*, www.nationsencyclopedia.com/economies/Africa/Nigeria-AGRICULTURE.html.

95 Oyewunmi, *Nigerian Law*, 160.

96 The Plant Variety Protection Act (PVPA) 2021, s. 1.

97 Titilayo Adunola Adebola, 'The Regime Complex for Plant Variety Protection: Revisiting TRIPS Implementation in Nigeria' (PhD diss., University of Warwick, 2017), http://wrap.warwick.ac.uk/98751/1/WRAP_Theses_Adebola_2017.pdf.

98 India's Protection of Plant Varieties and Farmers' Rights Act 2001 (PPVFRA), s. 14; Adebola, 'The Regime Complex'.

99 PDA, s. 1 (4) (b).

100 Oyewunmi, *Nigerian Law*, 162.

101 PDA, s. 1 (4) (b).

provision of the European Patent Convention of 1963.[102] The Directive on the Legal Protection of Biotechnological Inventions of the European Parliament (the 'European Directive') declares the following non-patentable, on the grounds that their commercial exploitation would be contrary to public order or morality: human germ line intervention, 'cloning' of humans, commercial use of embryos, and both somatic and germ line genetic intervention in animals that is 'likely to cause suffering without any substantial medical benefit to man or animal'.[103]

Mankind has bred plants and animals for millennia. Breeders have exploited knowledge of dominant and recessive alleles. Moral controversy about genetic engineering stems not from manipulation by breeding, but from recombinant DNA. Some have argued that to engage in germ line intervention, is to 'play God'.[104] Among the first transgenic animals to be produced was the oncomouse. The oncomouse was conceived as a valuable means of furthering cancer research. Harvard College sought patent protection in the United States and several other countries. The case raised general ethical issues regarding transgenic technology in itself and two key issues for the patent system:

1. Should patents be granted at all for animals or animal varieties, particularly for higher-order animals such as mammals, even if they do otherwise meet patentability criteria (novelty, industrial applicability and usefulness, inventive step etc.)?
2. How should moral implications be addressed in relation to specific cases, for example, the question of suffering caused to the transgenic animal?[105]

Different countries resolved the issues differently. In the US, the patent was granted as the claim explicitly excluded humans, apparently reflecting moral and legal concerns about patents on human beings, and about modification of the human genome.[106] The European Patent Office (EPO) applied the patent standards of the European Patent Convention, which contains two key relevant provisions: Article 53 (a) excludes patents for inventions 'the publication or exploitation of which would be contrary to *ordre public* or morality'. Article 53 (b) excludes patents on 'animal varieties or essentially biological processes for the production of … animals'.[107] The EPO decided that the exclusion on patenting animal varieties did not constitute a ban on patenting animals as such. It concluded further that the oncomouse was not an animal variety, so did not fall within that exclusion. In order to address the *ordre public* or morality exception, the EPO developed a utilitarian balancing test. This aimed to assess the potential benefits of a claimed invention against negative aspects, in this case weighing the suffering of the oncomice against the expected medical benefits to humanity. Other considerations could also be taken into account in the balancing test, such as environmental risks or public unease (there was no evidence in European culture for moral disapproval of the use of mice in cancer research, i.e. no moral disapproval of the proposed exploitation of the invention in this case). The EPO concluded that the usefulness of the oncomouse in furthering cancer research satisfied the likelihood of substantial medical benefit and outweighed moral concerns about suffering caused to the animal. The same utilitarian approach to the morality issue was applied by the EPO in the

[102] Louis M. Guenin, 'Patents, Ethics, Human Life Forms', https://guenin.med.harvard.edu/Documents/Ethics%20of%20Patents%20on%20Human%20Life%20Forms.pdf.

[103] Directive 98/44/EC of the European Parliament and of the Council of 6 July 1998 on the Legal Protection of Biotechnological Inventions, Article 6.1.

[104] Ibid.

[105] WIPO, 'Bioethics and Patent Law: The Case of the Oncomouse', *WIPO Magazine*, 1 June 2006, https://rb.gy/ob2apm.

[106] Ibid.

[107] Ibid.

Upjohn case in 1992,[108] but with a different outcome. The patent in question, filed by the Upjohn pharmaceutical company, was on a transgenic mouse into which a gene had been introduced such that the mouse would lose its hair. The objective was to test products to treat human baldness and wool production techniques. The EPO again weighed up benefits (usefulness in research to cure hair loss) and harm (suffered by the mice) but concluded that in this case the latter outweighed the former, such that the exploitation of the invention was contrary to morality and therefore not patentable.[109]

In Canada, the patent examiner initially rejected claims on transgenic animals on the basis that they were not included in the definition of an invention but allowed claims on the process for obtaining the oncomouse. The Supreme Court of Canada ruled in 2002 that higher life forms were not patentable because they were not a 'manufacture or composition of matter within the meaning of invention' of the Patent Act.[110] The Supreme Court interpreted 'manufacture' as a non-living mechanistic product or process. 'Composition of matter' was understood as ingredients or substances that had been combined or mixed together by a person. While microorganisms, or an oncogene-injected egg capable of maturing into an oncomouse, may be a mixture of ingredients and thus patentable under Canadian law, the body of a mouse was not. Moreover, the drafters of the Patent Act (1869) had not had mammals in mind and so the Act did not address higher life forms.[111]

The EPO approach seems to be the best approach for balancing the utilitarian value of the invention to humanity and the harm suffered by the transgenic animal. In addition to the exclusion of inventions from patentability the exploitation of which could be contrary to public order or morality, the Indian Patent Act goes further in excluding inventions the exploitation of which could be prejudicial to human, animal or plant life or health, or to the environment.[112]

The Trademarks Act also prohibits the registration of a deceptive or scandalous mark or one that is contrary to public law and morality.[113] Section 11 provides that it shall not be lawful to register as a trademark or part of a trademark any matter the use of which would, by reason of its being likely to deceive or cause confusion or otherwise, be disentitled to protection in a court of justice or be contrary to law or morality, or any scandalous design.

12.4.2 *Islamic Perspective*

Islamic scriptures (Quran and hadith) emphatically stress ecological considerations and a harmonious relationship with nature.[114] The Quran and hadith are replete with references to nature and environment as powerful signs of God and with ecological exhortations. Islam is a pro-environmental religion that instructs on maintaining a responsible and harmonious relationship between humanity and all living and non-living elements of nature to ensure a sustainable environment. Environmental protection in Islam is based on the concept of stewardship (*khilāfa*), conservation (*ḥifẓ*) and sustainable development (*tanẓīm*). Muslims are entrusted as guardians of the earth, responsible for its preservation.

[108] Cited in ibid.
[109] Ibid.
[110] *Harvard College v. Canada (Commissioner of Patent)* 2002 SCC 76. See also WIPO, 'Bioethics and Patent Law'.
[111] WIPO, 'Bioethics and Patent Law'.
[112] The Indian Patent Act (1970) as amended in 2005, s. 3 (b).
[113] Trademarks Act Cap T13 LFN 2004.
[114] Junaid Qadir and Asad Zaman, 'Sustainable Development Viewed from the Lens of Islam', *International Journal of Pluralism and Economics Education* 10, no. 1 (2019): 46–60, at 51.

> But seek with that (wealth) which Allah has bestowed on you, the home of the hereafter, and forget not your portion of legal enjoyment in this world … and seek not mischief in the land. Verily Allah likes not the mischief makers.[115]

Islam does understand the earth to be made use of by humankind, but it should not be exploited irresponsibly. In the pursuit of livelihood and wealth, human beings must be cautious not to destroy the environment. It is believed that Allah created the whole natural world with perfect wisdom (*ḥikma*) and appropriate environmental balance. The environment and natural ecosystems are considered a fundamental part of faith in Islam. The Quran is replete with verses that discuss nature and instruct on how humanity should handle environmental matters.[116] Islam teaches humanity to use natural resources wisely to maintain the environmental equilibrium set by God. The Quran uses environmental themes in exhorting humankind to be moderate.

> He is the One Who produces gardens – both cultivated and wild, and palm trees, crops of different flavours, olives, and pomegranates – similar in shape, but dissimilar in taste. Eat of the fruit they bear and pay the dues at harvest, but do not waste. Surely, He does not like the wasteful.[117]

Islam in its environmental control teaches that humankind is created by God and shall one day return to Him to give account of his actions. This means that human beings are answerable for all that they do, both the good and the evil. The essence of religious teachings are to maintain unity, balance and sustainability of the ecosystem. However, in the applicative level, the normative teaching has not been implemented properly. There is still an imbalance between theoretical insight and the practical attitude of society. While people have cognitive awareness of the importance of preserving nature, it has not reflected in their practical behaviour.[118] The agenda and activities which lead to the process of preservation and conservation of nature must also contain elements of worship.[119] Thus humans should, in relation to nature, not only use it to achieve certain ends and take benefits but they also have an obligation to maintain and preserve it. Thus it can be stated that nature conservation is a part of religion and becomes the task of humans as caretakers by creating harmonious interaction and togetherness in obedience to God.

12.4.3 *African Traditional Religion and the Environment*

In Africa, Nigeria inclusive, the environment is sacrosanct and treated with great respect, especially in communities where traditional beliefs and practices still prevail.[120] Environmental protection efforts have been made by the people, especially those still governed by customary law. The sacredness of the environment is based on the people's fundamental belief that the spiritual and the secular worlds are intertwined and endowed with divine power

[115] Q 28:77.

[116] For example, Q 2:60, 'And do not commit abuse on the earth, spreading corruption.'

[117] Q 6:142; Fazlun Khalid, 'Islam and the Environment: Ethics and Practice an Assessment', *Religion Compass* 4, no. 7 (2010): 707–17, at 709.

[118] Salamah Noorhidayati, Ahmad Zainal Abidin and Imam Ahmadi, 'Understanding Hadith on Nature Conservation: An Effort to Reinforce Ecological Piety', *ICIGR Conference Proceedings* (2002): 24–35.

[119] Ibid., 29.

[120] James N. Amanze, 'African Approaches to the Protection and Conservation of the Environment: The Role of African Traditional Religions', *Religion and Development* 2, no. 3 (2024): 445–62, 445.

and presence, thereby blurring the line of demarcation between the two worlds.[121] They complement each other in the sense that each derives its meaning, significance and importance from the other. Since the natural world is imbued with the divine, it is considered an extension of the supernatural world. In the absence of written legal frameworks, the environment in Indigenous communities is protected through religious beliefs and practice.

Customary law serves to regulate society in all aspects of life, including the relationship between humans and between humans and the environment. Customary law also serves to regulate the use and management of the environment efficiently for the purpose of preventing environmental damages and maintaining sustainability for the future. The communities that still have strong customary law will tend to preserve the environment and limit usages that cause damage to the environment.

The resource users themselves act as 'managers' and identify as members of a local community rather than as individual scientists or government officials accountable to external authorities. Traditional systems often have a solid moral and ethical framework, with no distinction between nature and culture. In many traditional cultures, nature is considered sacred.[122]

12.5 CONCLUSION

The African traditional belief systems bear some similarities with the Islamic precepts on property ownership and environmental protection and conservation. They both place premiums on communal benefits. Further, there is the belief that human beings are accountable to a Supreme Being for their activities on earth. While the Islamic belief is that the human will give account of his stewardship in the hereafter, the traditional African belief is that a person will reap the fruit of his misdeed immediately. Breaking a taboo entails a punishment in the form of social ostracism, misfortune and even death. If people do not punish the offender, then the invisible world will punish him.

While technology and innovations are important for human development, there is a need to ensure sustainability of the environment by encouraging green technology. While it is also important to incentivise innovation, the current IP regime places as much emphasis on private rights as against public interest, much to the detriment of the environment. There is a need to integrate the traditional knowledge system and environmental practices into the IP and environmental protection systems and the Islamic perspective for sustainability of the environment. Religion can help as the platform to let people key into a more sustainable way of doing business. While there are similarities between Islam and the traditional belief systems on the protection of the environment, the fear of spiritual chastisement tends to make the adherents of a traditional belief system more likely to conform to taboos concerning the environment. Understanding the conservation of the environment as an act of religious worship (*ʿibāda*) is key to embracing sustainable practices and behaviours for the protection of the environment amongst Muslims.

[121] Ibid.

[122] Ezekiel Adesawe, 'Exploring Wilderness in Yorùbá Culture: A Journey of Understanding', *International Journal of Wilderness* 29, no. 2 (2023), https://ijw.org/exploring-wilderness-in-yoruba-culture/.

13

A Critical Appraisal of State-Supported, 'Public' Islamic Environmental Law through the Case Studies of Singapore, Malaysia, and Indonesia

Shazny Ramlan

13.1 INTRODUCTION

The endurance of religious discourse in shaping legal and political discourse in Asia[1] suggests their continued relevance to how their citizens reason with matters of public importance such as environmental protection. In Southeast Asia particularly, Islam, Buddhism,[2] and Catholicism[3] are influential in the public sphere, partly due to their roles in anti-colonial struggle and mass mobilization against postcolonial dictatorial government, as well as their legitimizing of and formal participation in government. Of all these religions, however, only Islamic law exists within the legal systems of many Southeast Asian states. Malaysia, Indonesia, and Brunei are Muslim-majority states where Islamic law is recognized, implemented, and enforced to serve the bulk of its population, whereas Singapore and the Philippines do so for their minority but significant Muslim communities. The degree of Islamic law's implementation in these states also differs depending on their particular historical, political, and social contexts. While Islamic criminal law (*ḥudūd*) is implemented in Malaysia, Brunei, and Indonesia (exclusively in Aceh province), it is not implemented elsewhere. Additionally, the scope of matters governed by 'Islamic law' in most of these states concern personal laws, that is, matrimony, succession, and other 'private law' matters such as endowments (*awqāf*). Enforcement of Islamic law is typically done by Islamic courts established by law and government departments that serve as state religious authorities. Nevertheless, Islamic environmental laws are neither recognized nor enforced by law in lieu of the existence of modern environmental laws and regulations.

[1] See, generally, Jaclyn L. Neo, Arif A. Jamal, and Daniel P. S. Goh (eds), *Regulating Religion in Asia: Norms, Modes, and Challenges* (Cambridge: Cambridge University Press, 2019).

[2] See, e.g., Bardwell L. Smith (ed.), *Religion and Legitimation of Power in Thailand, Laos, and Burma* (Chambersburg, PA: ANIMA Books, 1978); Tomas Larsson, 'Monkish Politics in Southeast Asia: Religious Disenfranchisement in Comparative and Theoretical Perspective', *Modern Asian Studies* 49, no. 1 (2015): 40–82; Matthew J. Walton, *Buddhism, Politics, and Political Thought in Myanmar* (Cambridge: Cambridge University Press, 2017); Eugénie Mérieau, 'Buddhist Constitutionalism in Thailand: When Rājadhammā Supersedes the Constitution', *Asian Journal of Comparative Law* 13, no. 2 (2018): 283–305.

[3] See, e.g., Steven Shirley, *Guided by God: The Legacy of the Catholic Church in Philippine Politics* (Singapore: Marshall Cavendish, 2004); Aloysius Cartagenas, 'Religion and Politics in the Philippines: The Public Role of the Roman Catholic Church in the Democratization of the Filipino Polity', *Political Theology* 11, no. 6 (2010): 846–72.

In this chapter, I analyse the life of Islamic environmental law in Singapore, Malaysia, and Indonesia. 60 per cent of the world's Muslims call Southeast Asia home, and Indonesia is the most populous Muslim-majority country.[4] They share historical and cultural ties, and their Muslims are predominantly Sunnis who follow the Shafiʿi school of law.[5] For the purposes of our discussion, the chapter excludes Brunei Darussalam, which shares these traits, due to its status as an absolute Islamic monarchical state that does not limit the scope of Islamic law in the country in the way the Singapore, Malaysian, and Indonesian governments do. Also, there is an observable trend in these three countries of the use of two non-legal but persuasive instruments – fatwas and mosque sermons – to 'pronounce on' Islamic environmental law, and my main aim is to analyse their utility. However, I also argue that since these instruments are produced with varying degrees and means of state support, their contents, utility, and potential to be more than just pronouncements are limited by the complex entanglements between law, state, and religion underlying that support in the first place.

Before going into the chapter's case studies properly, however, I examine how state support for Islamic environmental law is made possible in modernity in the first place through the law. Such an inquiry is important, as it not only identifies legal avenues for more extensive implementation of Islamic environmental law but also potential conflicts when doing so is seen as contrary to an ideal legal landscape where religion is relegated to and remains within the private sphere. To this end, I examine a phenomenon I call 'public' Islamic environmental law, where constitutional and legal rules validate and enable the application of Islamic law and doctrine in modern environmental governance. I locate public Islamic environmental law within the broader practice of environmental constitutionalism, namely, the constitutional provisioning of environmental protection. I discuss the pros and cons of environmental constitutionalism as a mechanism of environmental governance generally and opine on their implications on Islamic environmental constitutionalism.

13.2 PUBLIC ISLAMIC ENVIRONMENTAL LAW: ENVIRONMENTAL CONSTITUTIONALISM WITH ISLAMIC CHARACTERISTICS

Conventional conceptions of 'public' forms of environmental law are those produced and practised by public institutions. Ranging from environmental legislation and regulations to judicial review of wrongful actions by environmental agencies under administrative law, and the enforcement of littering offences by police officers, public environmental law involves government bodies acting upon sources of law to ensure compliance by citizens. However, it is argued that particular manifestations of Islamic public environmental law exist, even if they are not enforced in the same way as the conventional forms. First, if we look at Islamic constitutions, namely, constitutions where 'supremacy' or 'blasphemy' clauses exist and are worded to 'constrain power holders to … adhere to … [Islamic] law',[6] we can interpret such clauses as implementing Islamic environmental law. Second, even if constitutions do not have these clauses, or clauses that mention religion but do not have a similar constraining effect, there may be other legal and procedural tools to make arguments before judicial bodies on the basis of Islamic environmental law.

[4] 'Islam in Asia: Diversity in Past and Present Exhibition: Muslim Populations', Cornell University Library, 19 May 2022, https://guides.library.cornell.edu/islamasiaexhibit/muslimpopulations.

[5] See, generally, Hussin Mutalib, *Islam in Southeast Asia* (Singapore: ISEAS-Yusof Ishak Institute, 2015).

[6] Keith E. Whittington, 'Constitutionalism', in Gregory A. Caldeira, R. Daniel Kelemen, and Keith E. Whittington (eds), *The Oxford Companion of Law and Politics* (Oxford: Oxford University Press, 2008), 281.

13.2.1 *Environmental Constitutionalism: A Brief Introduction*

Environmental constitutionalism – the adoption of provisions concerning the environment in national constitutions – aims to elevate the importance of environmental protection by according it the highest level of domestic legal protection possible.[7] Today, 148 national constitutions[8] contain environmental provisions, with their adoption premised on a multitude of reasons: legitimacy in the eyes of the international community,[9] civil society demands,[10] and ideological reasons.[11] These provisions take the form of substantive (e.g., right to a healthy environment) and procedural (e.g., right to access to environmental information) rights, environmental duties of the state and citizens, and guiding principles.[12] They need not explicitly concern the environment, but they can be instrumental to environmental protection. These include fundamental rights (e.g., right to life, right to health),[13] and 'structural' provisions 'allocat[ing] . . . environmental regulatory authority across levels of government within particular nations' especially where the constitutions 'divide regulatory authority over certain environmental subject matter between national (federal) and subnational (state/provincial and local) government'.[14]

Judicial enforceability plays a key role in the development of the environmental constitutionalism scholarship. Courts are at the forefront of enforcing the legal protections over the environment. Judicial decisions from environmental litigation have reformatory benefits to signal to other branches of government to endeavour to fill regulatory gaps and of the need for legal and policy reforms.[15] In essence, courts play a major role in advancing environmental rule of law, supporting its core elements: (1) the 'development, enactment, and implementation of clear, strict, enforceable, and effective laws, regulations, and policies'; (2) the 'respect for human rights, including the right to a safe, clean, healthy, and sustainable environment'; and (3) the creation of 'effective rules on equal access to information, public participation in decision-making, and access to justice'.[16] This focus on judicial enforceability also hierarchizes different

[7] Tim Hayward, *Constitutional Environmental Rights* (Oxford: Oxford University Press, 2005), 4; Joshua C. Gellers, 'Explaining the Emergence of Constitutional Environmental Rights: A Global Quantitative Analysis', *Journal of Human Rights and the Environment* 6 (2015): 75–97, at 76.

[8] Number as documented in Roderic O'Gorman, 'Environmental Constitutionalism: A Comparative Study', *Transnational Environmental Law* 6, no. 3 (2017): 435–62.

[9] Heinz Klug, *Constituting Democracy: Law, Globalism and South Africa's Political Reconstruction* (Cambridge: Cambridge University Press, 2000), 48 (on the legitimacy of the post-apartheid ANC government).

[10] Jan Hancock, *Environmental Human Rights: Power, Ethics, and Law* (Oxford: Routledge, 2019), 55–74.

[11] Gellers, 'Explaining the Emergence', 78 (on post-Communist constitutions' adoption of environmental provisions as the embrace of democracy).

[12] David R. Boyd, *The Environmental Rights Revolution: A Global Study of Constitutions, Human Rights, and the Environment* (Vancouver: University of British Columbia Press, 2012), 76.

[13] Inter-American Court of Human Rights, 'On the Environment and Human Rights (State Obligations in Relation to the Environment and the Protection and Guarantee of the Right to Life and Personal Integrity – the Interpretation and Scope of Articles 4.1 and 5.1, in Relation to Articles 1.1 and 2 of the American Convention on Human Rights)', Advisory Opinion OC 23/17, 15 November 2017, para. 63, https://bit.ly/3iVnfd9; Eckard Rehbinder and Demetrio Loperena, 'Legal Protection of Environmental Rights: The Role and Experience of the International Court of Environmental Arbitration and Conciliation', *Environmental Policy & Law* 31 (2001): 282–93, at 283.

[14] Blake Hudson, 'Structural Environmental Constitutionalism', *Widener Law Review* 21 (2015): 201–16, at 202.

[15] Jolene Lin, 'Climate Change Litigation in Asia and the Pacific', in Geert Van Calster, Wim Vandenberghe, and Leonie Reins (eds), *Research Handbook on Climate Change Mitigation Law* (Cheltenham: Edward Elgar, 2015), 578–602, at 580–81; Benjamin Ewing and Douglas Kysar, 'Prods and Pleas: Limited Government in an Era of Unlimited Harm', *Yale Law Journal* 121 (2011): 350–424.

[16] International Union for Conservation of Nature, *World Declaration on the Environmental Rule of Law*, First World Environmental Congress, 26–29 April 2016, www2.ecolex.org/server2neu.php/libcat/docs/LI/MON-091064.pdf.

types of environmental provisions. A clear preference[17] for environmental rights over other types of environmental provisions is present in the scholarship because courts are more likely to enforce environmental rights like other fundamental rights in constitutions.[18] Conversely, it is the general belief that provisions on environmental duties, obligations, and principles exist to guide legislative and executive decision-making, and are not meant to be judicially enforced.[19]

13.2.2 *The Limitations of Environmental Constitutionalism*

Constitutional provisions on the environment can, however, be counterproductive and result in outcomes that harm the environment instead. There are several instances when this has happened.

13.2.2.1 Constitutional Provisions Not Expected to Be Enforced

The first is a reason already mentioned: environmental provisions that are not expected to be enforced. Such constitutional environmental provisions may be included to ground government policies but are not intended to be judicially enforced. In this case, the only way of ensuring government accountability is through administrative review, for which standards of review vary from jurisdiction to jurisdiction. Weis categorizes these into two categories: (1) non-obligatory 'constitutional statements of value' which 'are declaratory in character, meaning that they designate certain values and policies as having fundamental status, but they do not create constitutional obligations with respect to those values or policies';[20] and (2) obligatory (but not judicially enforceable, i.e., 'contrajudicative') 'resource-vesting provisions and directive principles'.[21]

13.2.2.2 Potential and Limitations of Constitutional Interpretation

Second is when the enforcement of environmental rights relies on reading them into other constitutional provisions, such as bill of rights provisions. This is especially the case for former British colonies in Asia, where their Westminster constitutions[22] were drafted with the assistance of British authorities and their 'bill of rights' sections are similarly phrased. Yet, disparities exist across these jurisdictions where judicial interpretation of these provisions are concerned,

[17] See, generally, Ben Boer (ed.), *Environmental Law Dimensions of Human Rights* (Oxford: Oxford University Press, 2015); John H. Knox and Ramin Pejan (eds), *The Human Right to a Healthy Environment* (Cambridge: Cambridge University Press, 2018).

[18] Trevor Daya-Winterbottom, 'The Legitimate Role of Rights-Based Approaches to Environmental Conflict Resolution', in Christina Voigt and Zen Makuch (eds), *Courts and the Environment* (Cheltenham: Edward Elgar, 2018), 59–83; Louis Kotzé, 'Six Constitutional Elements for Implementing Environmental Constitutionalism', in Erin Daly and James R. May (eds), *Implementing Environmental Constitutionalism: Current Global Challenges* (Cambridge: Cambridge University Press, 2018), 13–33.

[19] Lael K. Weis, 'Constitutional Directive Principles', *Oxford Journal of Legal Studies* 37 (2017): 916–45; Lael Weis, 'Environmental Constitutionalism: Aspiration or Transformation?', *International Journal of Constitutional Law* 16 (2018): 836–70, at 836–37, 846–48; Erin Daly, 'Constitutional Protection for Environmental Rights', *International Journal of Human Rights* 17 (2012): 55–76. Daly writes that many constitutional environmental provisions 'are matters of directive principle … designed to galvanize, though not compel, legislative activity to protect the environment' (p. 72).

[20] Weis, 'Environmental Constitutionalism', 843.

[21] Ibid., 844–48.

[22] Andrew Harding, 'The "Westminster Model" Constitution Overseas: Transplantation, Adaptation and Development in Commonwealth States', *Oxford University Commonwealth Law Journal* 4 (2004): 143–66.

especially the right to life. In the case of India, her neighbours in the Indian subcontinent, and Malaysia,[23] environmental rights have been read into the pre-existing right to life in their constitutions. On the flipside, doing this is not the case in Singapore, where judicial interpretation of the right to life is much narrower and the conditions that enable progressive interpretation in her former colonial brethren, such as procedural rules supporting public interest litigation[24] and judicial activism, do not exist.

13.2.2.3 Environmental Constitutionalism in Religious Contexts

Based on the understanding that constitutional provisions in the environmental constitutionalism canon (a) do not have to explicitly concern the environment, (b) can be instrumental in achieving pro-environment objectives, and (c) are (preferably) judicially enforceable, this chapter expands the environmental constitutionalism canon to include the constitutional toolkit of 'constitutional theocracies'.[25] These include religious 'supremacy' or 'blasphemy' clauses that 'constrain power holders to ... adhere to ... religious law'[26] by instituting a state religion and/or subjecting government action and legislation to religious requirements. This chapter also goes further to include other tools of constitutionalism beyond the constitutional text that enables religious values and ideas to ground or motivate environmental litigation, particularly where the public interest is concerned. The chapter refers to this subset of the canon as 'religious environmental constitutionalism'.

Based on previous discussions, however, it is argued that the issues of the developmental state and inter-provision/rights tensions that arise to limit the effectiveness of regular, 'secular', constitutional environmental provisions also impact their religious counterparts when the latter are utilized in a similar fashion. Indeed, as will be shown, these issues catalysed the idea to use religious constitutional clauses as a more morally forceful approach to environmental constitutionalism. 'Ideological' counter arguments, especially when dealing with the human rights of non-Muslims or deviant Muslims' rights in the polity, also complicates inter-provision tensions. This largely stems from two general conventions in the scholarship.

13.2.3 *Recognition of Religious Norms on Environmental Protection through Constitutions*

The constitutional default concerning religion in modern states involves states' regulation of the limits of religious symbolism in the public sphere (e.g., prayer in public spaces, display of religious symbols, religious forms of speech, religion as a criteria for employment)[27] and the protection of individual rights to religious freedom (e.g., the freedom to pray according to one's religious beliefs, the freedom to wear religious paraphernalia, the freedom to speak about one's

[23] While it has been argued that it *can* be implied to also be the case in Malaysia, it is but only one case that has suggested as such in dictum.

[24] Notably, in Singapore, even if the environmental right is judicially recognized and is read into the constitution's right to life and liberty, the strict *locus standi* requirements for litigants to satisfy may prevent the judicial enforcement of the right. Chng suggests an alternative approach to fill this gap is through common law mechanisms in torts and property law. See Kenny Chng, 'Conceptualising a Role for the Common Law in Environmental Protection in Singapore', *Asian Journal of Comparative Law* 16, no. 2 (2021): 218–37.

[25] See Ran Hirschl, *Constitutional Theocracy* (Cambridge, MA: Harvard University Press, 2010).

[26] Whittington, 'Constitutionalism', 281.

[27] Paul Horwitz, *The Agnostic Age: Law, Religion and the Constitution* (Oxford: Oxford University Press, 2011), xv–xvi.

religion, non-discrimination on the basis of religion).[28] Accordingly, religious beliefs concerning the environment and appropriate responses to environmental problems are subject to these legal fictions. However, it has been observed that religion can have a greater constitutional role beyond this archetype when they are constitutionally recognized in some way such that they become 'theocratic' constitutions.[29]

In Muslim-majority jurisdictions in the Middle East, North Africa, and Southeast Asia, the constitutional recognition of Islam brings into effect the inclusion of religious law and doctrines into constitutional and legal discourse.[30] These may come in one or both of these forms: the recognition of Islam as the state religion and the recognition of the sharia as a source of national law. These allow for several postulations: (1) that power of all legislation comes from an 'Islamic' constitution and are legitimized by Islamic doctrine; (2) legislation must be promulgated in accordance with Islamic doctrine; and (3) for government decisions to be regarded 'constitutional', they must be made in accordance with Islamic doctrine. It follows then that environmental constitutional provisions, environmental legislation, and environmental administrative decisions must all be compatible or be made compatible with Islamic law and doctrines. This approach consequently incorporates Islamic law, including its environmental rules, into national legal landscapes.[31]

In Saudi Arabia, for example, the government expressly declares that it is founded on divine law. In its 1992 Basic Law, Islam is proclaimed to be the state religion, and the constitution is the sharia and the Prophetic Sunna.[32] As such, all laws in Saudi Arabia, including its 2001 General Environmental Law, can be presumed to be found on or comply with Islamic norms. Within the Basic Law, Article 32, which imposes on the state an obligation to 'endeavour to preserve, protect and improve the environment and prevent its pollution', can be presumed to espouse Islamic doctrines on environmental protection.[33] Similarly in Iran, its constitution recognizes Islam as the state religion,[34] source of political ideology[35] and principles of governance.[36] Again, within the Iranian constitution, the public obligation under Article 50 to protect the environment and its prohibition of 'all activities, economic or otherwise, which may cause irreversible damage to the environment'[37] can be argued to espouse Islamic doctrines on environmental protection. Furthermore, since Article 4 of the constitution requires that all legislation be promulgated in compliance with an 'Islamic criteria',[38] Iran's 1974 Environmental Protection and Enhancement Act as well as its sectoral environmental legislation are arguably found on and legitimized by Islamic doctrine.[39]

28 Tore Lindholm, W. Cole Durham Jr., and Bahia Tahzib-Lie (eds), *Facilitating Freedom of Religion or Belief: A Deskbook* (Dordrecht: Springer Science+Business Media, 2004), xxxvii–xxxix.
29 Li-ann Thio, *A Treatise on Singapore Constitutional Law* (Singapore: Academy Publishing, 2012), 48.
30 Robert W. Hefner, *Shari'a Politics: Islamic Law and Society in the Modern World* (Bloomington: Indiana University Press, 2011).
31 For a more extensive examination of constitutional provisions on Islam and its normative significance in environmental protection, with a greater number of case studies, see Samira Idllalène, *Rediscovery and Revival in Islamic Environmental Law: Back to the Future of Nature's Trust* (Cambridge: Cambridge University Press, 2021), 20–24, 31–54.
32 1992 Saudi Basic Law, art. 1.
33 Norah b. Hamad, 'Foundations for Sustainable Development: Harmonizing Islam, Nature and Law' (PhD diss., Pace University, 2017), https://bit.ly/38EsUPS.
34 Constitution of the Islamic Republic of Iran, art. 12.
35 Ibid., Preamble.
36 Ibid., art. 2.
37 Ibid., art. 50.
38 Ibid., art. 4.
39 These include the 1995 Air Pollution Act, 2004 Waste Management Act, 1967 Game and Fish Law, 1967 Plant Protection Act and, to a limited extent, the 2004 Fourth Development Plan Act.

In North Africa, the Kingdom of Morocco – a 'sovereign Muslim state'[40] – under its constitution establishes Islam as the state religion in Article 3.[41] The king is also, under the constitution, the Defender of the Islamic Faith and presides over the development and promulgation of Islamic law.[42] All legislation are also only enacted after a vetting process conducted by the Royal Religious Council.[43] As such, it can be argued that the right to a healthy environment under Article 31 has been deemed to be compatible with Islamic doctrine by Morocco's top Islamic jurists, as are its environmental statutes.[44]

Moving on to the Gulf states, Qatar's constitution begins by declaring Islam as its state religion and 'Islamic Law is the main source of its legislations' in Article 1. By implication, then, the government's management of natural resources under Article 29 and duty 'to protect the environment and its natural balance, to achieve comprehensive and sustainable development for all generations' under Article 33 must be performed on the basis of Islamic norms. The same can be implied for its primary environmental statute, the 2002 Environmental Protection Law.

In Southeast Asia, Article 3 of the Bruneian constitution declares Islam as the state religion[45] and the Sultan of Brunei as the religious head.[46] The Bruneian state ideology – *Melayu, Islam, Beraja* (Malay, Islamic, Monarchy) – which was decreed during the proclamation of the country's independence from the UK,[47] mandates among others for key government officials to be Muslim,[48] and all legislation[49] and areas of government policy, from education, economic, and military, to comply with Islamic doctrine (specifically that of the Sunni-Shafi'i school).[50] It can be presumed, thus, that Bruneian environmental laws, regulations, and policies embody Islamic norms, even though environmental rights are not explicitly provided in the constitution.

This list goes on, but a common trait of these jurisdictions is the existence of two constitutional provisions on religion: one establishing Islam as the state religion, and the other making all legislation subject to Islamic doctrine. In this way, not only must the government's decisions be sharia-compliant, but the crafting, debating (as a bill), promulgation, interpretation, and implementation of statutes must honour Islamic beliefs and ethics as constituting the spirit underlying them. Still, it is one thing to draw such a connection between constitutional recognition and how Islamic norms apply to environmental rule of law this way, and another to recognize their application by the authorities, especially the courts. In the following sections,

40 Dahir no 1-11-91 du 27 chaabane 1432 (29 juillet 2011) portant promulgation du texte de la constitution, Preamble: 'Etat musulman soverain'.

41 Ibid., art. 3.

42 Ibid., art. 41.

43 Mohamed Madani, Driss Maghraoui, and Saloua Zerhouni, *The 2011 Moroccan Constitution: A Critical Analysis* (Stockholm: International Institute for Democracy and Electoral Assistance, 2012), 20, https://bit.ly/38Agbhl.

44 For example, Dahir no 1-03-59 portant promulgation de la loi n° 11-03 relative à la protection et à la mise en valeur de l'environnement; Dahir no 1-03-60 du 10 rabii I 1424 (12 mai 2003) portant promulgation de la loi no 12-03 relative aux études d'impact sur l'environnement; Dahir no 1-03-61 portant promulgation de la loi no 13-03 relative à la lutte contre la pollution de l'air.

45 Constitution of Brunei Darussalam, art. 3(1).

46 Ibid., art. 3(2).

47 'Teks Pemashhoran Kemerdekaan Negara Brunei Darussalam Dalam Bahasa Inggeris', in *Koleksi Melayu Islam Beraja* (Bandar Seri Begawan: Jabatan Penerangan, Jabatan Perdana Menteri, 2010), iv.

48 Haji Duraman Tuah. 'Konsep Melayu Islam Beraja Dalam Pentadbiran dan Pengurusan Negara Brunei Darussalam (21 Ogos 1991)', in *Koleksi Melayu Islam Beraja* (Bandar Seri Begawan: Jabatan Penerangan, Jabatan Perdana Menteri, 2010), 36.

49 Constitution of Brunei Darussalam, art. 42(e).

50 Ann Black, 'Ideology and Law: The Impact of the MIB Ideology on Law and Dispute Resolution in the Sultanate of Brunei Darussalam', *Asian Journal of Comparative Law* 3, no. 1 (2008): 1–41, at 4–5.

the chapter explores how such a recognition may manifest in cases where Islam is constitutionally recognized in the aforementioned way.

13.2.4 *Application of Religious Law in Environmental Judicial Review*

13.2.4.1 The Application of the *Ḥisba* Principle in Egypt

Article 2 of the Egyptian Constitution declares 'the principles of Islamic Sharia' as a primary source of Egyptian law.[51] This provision has been interpreted by the Supreme Constitutional Court of Egypt in the famous *Ribā* case[52] as 'impos[ing] on the Legislator, from a political point of view, the duty of purifying the texts of such past legislation and clearing them from any trespass against the said [Islamic] principles'[53] while 'reaching a ruling [i.e., legislation] which does not contradict the principles and general framework of the Sharia in future'.[54] As a result, the Egyptian government is constitutionally bound to consider Islamic principles to form part of its criteria for good governance. One such principle is the *ḥisba* principle that imposes duties on Muslims to 'command good and prevent evil' (*al-amr bi-l-maʿrūf wa-nahī ʿan al-munkar*) by engaging in 'moral criticism' both individually and collectively 'when its practice is manifest'.[55]

Traditionally, the principle forms the basis for state-appointed market inspectors' powers in early Muslim polities to ensure compliance with Islamic commercial regulations by merchants and street vendors[56] as well as the civic duty of citizens to do the same. In modern-day Egypt, the principle manifests in a similar fashion, although the scope has broadened to touch on public law matters. Importantly, it is the basis for the administrative law doctrine of 'the civil calculus' (*al-ḥisābāt al-madaniyya*) imposing upon the state a responsibility to act in the interest and welfare of its citizens in respect to their individual rights;[57] and forms the basis for the right of Muslims to bring lawsuits against alleged violators of statutorily provided 'rights of God'.[58] Consequently, the principle is in effect a double-edged sword because it protects fundamental rights,[59] on the one hand, while also violating them by enabling lawsuits concerning blasphemy, apostasy, and religious deviancy, on the other.[60] Functionally, however, *ḥisba* acts as a principle invokable in public interest litigation,[61] enabling government decisions that result in environmental rights infringement to be challenged under administrative law.

[51] Constitution of the Arab Republic of Egypt, art. 2.

[52] For an English translation of this case, see 'Supreme Constitutional Court (Egypt) – Shari'a and Riba: Decision in Case No 20 of Judicial Year No 1', *Arab Law Quarterly* 1, no. 1 (1985): 100–107. For a commentary on the case, see Saba Habachy, 'Commentary on the Decision of the Supreme Court of Egypt Given on 4 May 1985 Concerning the Legitimacy of Interest and the Constitutionality of Article 226 of the New Egyptian Civil Code of 1948', *Arab Law Quarterly* 1, no. 2 (1986): 239–41.

[53] 'Supreme Constitutional Court (Egypt)', 106.

[54] Ibid., 104.

[55] Knut S. Vikor, *Between God and the Sultan: A History of Islamic Law* (Oxford: Oxford University Press, 2005), 197; Hussein Ali Agrama, *Questioning Secularism: Islam, Sovereignty, and the Rule of Law in Modern Egypt* (Chicago: University of Chicago Press, 2012), 45.

[56] Michael Cook, *Commanding Right and Forbidding Wrong in Islamic Thought* (Cambridge: Cambridge University Press, 2004), 470–79.

[57] Helmy el-Namnam, *al-Ḥisba wa-ḥurriyat al-taʿbīr* (Alexandria: al-Shabaka al-ʿArabiyya al-Maʿlūmāt Ḥuqūq al-Insān, 2012), 184.

[58] Agrama, *Questioning Secularism*, 47–48.

[59] el-Namnam, *al-Ḥisba*, 178.

[60] Mahmoud Salem, 'Blasphemy in New and Old Egypt', Middle East Institute, 12 June 2013, https://bit.ly/3tcV7XF.

[61] el-Namnam, *al-Ḥisba*, 186–87.

In his 2012 book on the use of the principle in Egypt, former Minister of Culture Helmy El-Namnam featured an undated case where lawyer Nabih Taha El-Bahy launched a lawsuit against government officials and institutions[62] and three mining firms[63] for causing air pollution in Egypt. In that case, heard before the Administrative Court of the State Council, Mr El-Bahy argued that the government's failure (through its environmental agencies) to conduct environmental impact assessments before issuing permits to three companies to construct and operate their processing factories adjacent to residential districts violates the expectations arising from the civil calculus. Emphasizing how the air pollution caused by these activities resulted in the suffering of residents living in those districts,[64] Mr El-Bahy argued that the government omissions that led to this violated 'the public right [to a healthy environment] ... of the general public and citizens' and *ḥisba* expectations were not met:

> The Egyptian people put their trust in their choice of leaders for the persons they delegate to preserve all Egyptians, whether concerning health, the economy, or education. And if these people are unable to keep the Egyptian people away from the dangers of chronic diseases by others [i.e., private entities], then their promises bring great sorrow and misery.[65]

Thus, because government officials failed to protect 'the health of citizens when it continued to allow these factories to emit harmful air pollutants',[66] the permits authorizing the construction and operation of the three companies' cement factories are unconstitutional by virtue of Article 2, and the Egyptian government – from the president all the way down the chain of command to the agency granting the permit – should be held accountable, according to Mr El-Bahy.[67] Mr El-Namnam did not explicitly mention if the lawsuit succeeded. However, he affirmatively states that in this case 'we find a great development, which is that the (civil) calculus [i.e., the *ḥisba*] was directed against the President of the Republic as the highest authority in the country, which never happened in the (pre-modern) Islamic era'.[68]

13.2.4.2 Recognition of Religious Reasons for Standing Requirements in Constitutional Review

What if a constitution does not explicitly recognize a state religion, or gives 'supremacy' to the sharia such that Islamic environmental law can be implemented, at least in the normative sense, in modern states? One may suggest that, in the archetypal modern state, one may resort to the right to religious freedom and craft arguments along the lines of religious symbolism and practice. However, religious beliefs can still motivate constitutional arguments without expressly invoking religion in the constitution, and those religious motivations can be 'translated' – in the Habermasian sense – into generally accepted public interest terms. This already grounds much of the environmental advocacy pursued by local and international religious organizations. Still,

62 These are the President of Egypt, the Ministers for Health, Environment, Manpower, and Industry, the Governor of Cairo, the Egyptian Trade Unions President, the Presidential Council, and the National Centre for Human Rights. Ibid., 188.

63 These are Tora Cement Company, Helwan Cement Company, and Asfour Crystal Company based in Cairo. Ibid.

64 Ibid., 189.

65 Ibid., 190.

66 Ibid.

67 Clark B. Lombardi and Connie J. Cannon, 'Transformations in Muslim Views about "Forbidding Wrong": The Rise and Fall of Islamist Litigation in Egypt', in Robert W. Hefner (ed), *Shari'a Law and Modern Muslim Ethics* (Bloomington: Indiana University Press, 2016), 151.

68 el-Namnam, *al-Ḥisba*, 191.

judicial recognition of those motivations to be in line with the public interest provides legitimacy to the environmental cause pursued by religious organizations, and includes religious aspirations for environmental futures into constitutional discourse. The case of religiously motivated environmental constitutional review in Indonesia aptly demonstrates this.

A brief background: the Indonesian constitution declares that the state is 'based on the belief of One Almighty God'[69] but guarantees the freedom of its citizens to embrace and practice any religion,[70] and engage in worship in accordance with their beliefs[71] under Articles 28E and 29, respectively. While the phrase 'belief in One Almighty God' may be interpreted to implicitly recognize monotheistic religions exclusively, the constitution does not expressly recognize one, even though the country is the world's most populous Muslim country. Instead, Islam is statutorily recognized in a select list of theistic religions as state-supported religions.[72] Article 28I(2) thereafter declares that religion cannot be a ground for discrimination.[73] Although religious freedom is 'a human right that cannot be limited under any circumstance',[74] Article 28J(2) imposes on citizens the 'duty to accept the restrictions established by law for the sole purposes of guaranteeing the recognition and respect of the rights and freedoms of others, and of satisfying just demands based upon considerations of morality, religious values, security and public order in a democratic society'.[75]

Although the protection of environmental rights has yet to be argued as an aspect of the broader constitutional right to religious freedom, Indonesian scholars admit that religion plays a normative role in environmental law and policy-making in their country, especially at the local level.[76] One may also argue that the state's 'belief in One Almighty God' sufficiently allows for interpretation that environmental protection in Indonesia shall be guided by a consciousness of the religious values of its people. Islamic non-governmental organizations (NGOs) in Indonesia actively engage in public interest litigation on the basis of the environmental provisions of the Indonesian constitution.[77] Typically, constitutional litigation challenging the constitutionality of environmental and natural resources laws are litigated by private citizens or environmental NGOs such as the Indonesian Forum for the Environment (WALHI) and the Indonesia Centre for Environmental Law (ICEL). However, over the past few years, Islamic NGOs have also appeared as applicants and co-applicants in environmental cases before the Indonesian Constitutional Court. Most prominent of these organizations is Muhammadiyah, one of the oldest and largest Islamic NGOs in the country. While Muhammadiyah has appeared as a co-applicant alongside other Islamic NGOs, it is an organizational objective for them to pursue judicial review as a means of 'constitutional jihad'. In a sense, judicial review constitutes a 'part of their "great legal struggle"' for social justice.[78]

[69] Constitution of the Republic of Indonesia 1945.

[70] Ibid., art. 28E.

[71] Ibid., art. 29.

[72] Presidential Decree No 1/PNPS/1965 on the Prevention of Misuse and/or Insult of Religion (1965 Blasphemy Law), Elucidation, art. 1. See also Melissa Crouch, 'Law and Religion in Indonesia: The Constitutional Court and the Blasphemy Law', *Asian Journal of Comparative Law* 7, no. 1 (2012): 1–46.

[73] Presidential Decree, art. 28I(2).

[74] Ibid., art. 28I(1).

[75] Ibid., art. 28J(2).

[76] A. M. Yunus Wahid, *Pengantar Hukum Lingkungan* (Jakarta: Prenadamedia Group, 2018), 97–106.

[77] Presidential Decree, arts. 28H(1) (the right to a good and healthy environment), 33(3) (state obligation for the natural environment and resources of the country to be used to the greatest benefit to the people), and 33(4) (requirement for the organization of the national economy to be conducted on the basis of, among others, the environment).

[78] Stefanus Hendrianto, *Law and Politics of Constitutional Courts: Indonesia and the Search for Judicial Heroes* (London: Routledge, 2018), 206.

This is largely enabled by a tool of constitutionalism that lies outside the constitutional text – Article 51 of the 2003 Law on the Constitutional Court on standing requirements for judicial review before the Indonesian Constitutional Court. There are two main requirements. First, applicants must fall within at least one of these four categories: (a) individual Indonesian citizens, (b) bodies representing traditional customary (*'ādāt*) communities recognized by law, (c) public and private legal entities, and (d) national agencies. Of these categories, Islamic NGOs classify themselves under the third category and fulfil standing requirements by virtue of being private legal entities.[79] Secondly, they must successfully demonstrate that either a current, possible, or future violation of a constitutional right is or can occur.[80] It is also important to note that even if applicants do not fall within the four categories above or do not definitively demonstrate a present, possible, or future constitutional rights violation, the Constitutional Court can presume the satisfaction of legal standing if the application is made in the public interest.[81]

13.3 'PUBLIC' ISLAMIC ENVIRONMENTAL LAW THROUGH FATWAS AND MOSQUE SERMONS

In modernity, Muslims are left on their own to implement and enforce many religious matters that are not recognized under the law, especially if they are minorities where they live. These include Islamic environmental law. I have posited elsewhere that Muslims can interpret the application of Islamic environmental rules through their constitutions, statutes, and/or legally sanctioned means.[82] Another scholar argues for *awqāf* – as an instrument legally recognized and enforced in most Muslim-majority states – to be used to establish environmental public trusts over land.[83] Alternatively, Muslim communities themselves can engage in 'private environmental governance'[84] where they establish and informally enforce Islamic environmental law at the grassroots level. The Muslim environmentalist movement in Indonesia is an apt example of this kind of environmental 'regulation'.[85] Fatwas and mosque sermons are instruments for such environmental regulation at the communal level; they articulate the Islamic rules governing a Muslim's relationship with the environment in the context of and in response to local circumstances and concerns, and for Muslim communities to enforce upon themselves. However, in the case of many Muslim-majority countries, or those with a significant Muslim population, these instruments are arguably instruments of *public* environmental law because they are made as exercises of political and legal recognition of Islamic law as a part of the national legal system. Before demonstrating this in our three case studies, it is useful to first understand the nature and functions of these instruments as media for pronouncing on Islamic environmental law.

Fatwas are scholarly opinions or advice dispensed by a jurisconsult (i.e., 'mufti') on the Islamic position concerning religious conundrums posed to him by a questioner (*mustaftī*).[86]

79 Law No 24/2003 on the Constitutional Court, art. 51.

80 Ibid., Elucidation, art. 51(1).

81 Constitutional Court Decision No 69/PUU-II/2004 at 66–67; Hendrianto, *Law and Politics*, 140.

82 Shazny Ramlan, 'Implementing Islamic Law to Protect the Environment: Insights from Singapore, Malaysia and Indonesia', *Asia Pacific Journal of Environmental Law* 23 (2020): 202–30.

83 Idllalène, *Rediscovery and Revival*, ch. 5.

84 See Joshua U. Galperin, 'Private, Environmental, Governance', *George Washington Journal of Energy & Environmental Law* 9 (2018): 1–4.

85 Anna M. Gade, *Muslim Environmentalisms: Religious and Social Foundations* (New York: Columbia University Press, 2019), ch. 2.

86 For expositions on the mufti's function in fatwa production, see Wael B. Hallaq, *The Origins and Evolution of Islamic Law* (Cambridge: Cambridge University Press, 2005), 63.

The questioner may be an individual, a court, or even a state organ;[87] and the queries submitted may be conveyed as abstract or hypothetical questions, or a question featuring the factual matrices surrounding a legal conundrum. In response, a fatwa is dispensed by the mufti which addresses the conundrum, although the fatwa must be objective and its contents must be limited to the facts and legal issues the questioner provided.[88] The legal conundrums posed by questioners are generally broad-ranging, from very personal matters (e.g., a family dispute) to contemporary 'big picture' issues such as climate change. In 2018, I submitted a request to Egypt's Dar al-Ifta' for a fatwa addressing two legal conundrums: (1) the duties and obligations of Muslims to the environment, and (2) the limits of a Muslim's compliance with their country's laws.[89] The institute addressed these conundrums with the following fatwa:

> 1. Muslims' duty towards the environment stems from their understanding that man is a vicegerent on earth and God has commanded them to work for development and not destruction. 2. Muslims are commanded in Shari'ah to respect the laws of the countries they live in per the words of God Almighty, 'O you who have believed, obey Allah and obey the Messenger and those in authority among you.' (Surah An-Nisa: 59). This is provided these laws do not contradict the fundamentals of religion. God Almighty knows best.

But the authority for a mufti or a fatwa-issuing body like Dar al-Ifta' to issue fatwas does not simply come from possessing knowledge of the Islamic sciences and the ability to provide answers to the legal conundrums submitted by laypeople such as myself. They must possess recognized qualifications or *ijāza* to issue fatwas. However, it is important to recognize that 'mufti' refers to a position of religious authority by virtue of possessing these qualifications, as well as a government appointment. Since the early days of Islam, Muslim governments have appointed scholars to be muftis in the latter sense, where their fatwas primarily serve to inform, ground, and justify government policies; independent muftis may continue to issue their own fatwas although these are not legally binding unless endorsed by the courts.[90] This state of affairs remains the same today, especially in Singapore, Malaysia, and Indonesia. However, we are only concerned with fatwas issued by government-based or government-endorsed fatwa-issuing bodies.

Unlike fatwas that can only be produced by a select group of learned persons of authority possessing certain qualifications, mosque sermons (*khuṭba*) are delivered by the imam leading congregational prayers in mosques qua *khaṭīb* (sermon-giver) who need not be an Islamic scholar. Sermons may be delivered to congregations impromptu but may also be written beforehand by the mosque's resident Islamic scholars. However, sermons are usually only delivered during congregational prayers on Fridays, the two Eid festivals (Eid al-Fitr and Eid al-Adha), and special sunna prayers organized in response to eclipses or other natural phenomena (e.g., drought). The purpose of mosque sermons is to essentially 'instruct the faithful … in his or her individual duty to God as this is understood in a particular place, at a certain time'.[91] The mosques, Ali Wardak argues, pronounce on the 'rules' of the community in this way; sermons are therefore a medium for mosques to serve its function as 'an important source of the community's morality and moral judgements'.[92]

87 Knut S. Vikør, *Between God and the Sultan: A History of Islamic Law* (Oxford: Oxford University Press, 2005), 141–43.
88 Ibid., 149–150.
89 Ramlan, 'Implementing Islamic Law', 210.
90 Sherman A. Jackson, *Islamic Law and the State: The Constitutional Jurisprudence of Shihāb al-Dīn al-Qarāfī* (Leiden: Brill, 1996), 145–46.
91 M. B. Hooker, *Indonesian Syariah: Defining a National School of Islamic Law* (Singapore: ISEAS, 2008), 129.
92 Ali Wardak, 'The Mosque and Social Control in Edinburgh's Muslim Community', *Culture & Religion* 3 (2002), 201–19, 214–15.

The issues covered by mosque sermons depends on what the imam (or the mosque leadership) deems current, relevant, and necessary, and may range from 'very personal [issues] to the very social – from drinking, eating and dressing to the virtues of cleanliness, honesty, modesty and chastity . . . to duties and obligations to parents, kin, neighbors, the needy, and to the state and society.'[93] The nature of sermons as being directed to an audience of mostly lay Muslims accordingly imposes a set of informal rules to their production as a tool of communication. Most important of these rules are that they must be drafted and delivered to be 'interesting and practically oriented lesson[s] on Islamic morality and values',[94] and they must inculcate a sense of togetherness and community in the congregation by using group pronouns such as 'we' and 'our' in statements reinforcing the community's 'shared sets of moral and religious values'.[95] With respect to the authority of sermons, these instruments are of a lesser degree in terms of authority as compared to fatwas. However, it is argued that they are nonetheless sources of religious information, produced weekly, that inform and remind Muslims of their religious obligations. It is this functionality of mosque sermons that make them appropriate vehicles for pronouncing on Islamic environmental law in our case studies.

13.4 MALAYSIA'S NON-BINDING STATE-LEVEL ENVIRONMENTAL FATWAS AND FEDERAL-LEVEL ENVIRONMENTAL MOSQUE SERMONS

Malaysia has a Muslim-majority population[96] and Islam is recognized in its constitution as 'the religion of the Federation'.[97] Its Islamic legal system is separate from Malaysia's national legal system and supported by a separate Islamic legal profession.[98] Its federal system of government also means that Islamic personal laws and criminal statutes are in effect at both federal and state levels, with individual states possessing their own enabling Islamic legislation, state religious departments (*pejabat agama*), and Islamic courts (*mahkamah syariah*). The Department for the Development of Islam in Malaysia (JAKIM)[99] (a subdivision of the Prime Minister's Office)[100] functions as the federal authority on the Islamic religion.

Accordingly, the production of fatwas and mosque sermon production in Malaysia is also subject to federal or state institutional arrangements. At the federal level, fatwas are issued by the National Fatwa Committee (NFC), a council membered by Malaysia's thirteen state muftis and several appointed experts.[101] They issue non-binding fatwas[102] exclusively at the request of the Conference of Rulers – a council membered by Malaysia's nine[103] hereditary Malay-Muslim

[93] Ibid. at 214.
[94] Ibid.
[95] Ibid.
[96] As of 2020, 63.5 per cent of Malaysians are Muslims: Department of Statistics, Malaysia, 'Launching of Report on the Key Findings Population and Housing Census of Malaysia 2020', 14 February 2022, https://tinyurl.com/4bbu69p3.
[97] Federal Constitution of Malaysia, art. 3.
[98] Dian A. H. Shah and Azizuddin Sani, 'Freedom of Religion in Malaysia: A Tangled Web of Legal, Political, and Social Issues', *North Carolina Journal of International Law and Commercial Regulation* 36 (2011): 647–87.
[99] This is the acronym for its name in Malay: 'Jabatan Kemajuan Islam Malaysia'.
[100] G25 Malaysia, 'Administration of Matters Pertaining to Islam', http://bit.ly/3WjUuLg, 128.
[101] 'Jawatankuasa Fatwa Majlis Kebangsaan Bagi Hal Ehwal Ugama Islam Malaysia', Jabatan Kemajuan Islam Malaysia (JAKIM), http://e-smaf.islam.gov.my/e-smaf/fatwa/latar_belakang/penubuhan.
[102] Farhanin A. Asuhaimi, Nur A. Pauzai, Maheran Makhtar, and Khairun-Nisaa Asari, 'The Role and Position of Fatwa in Malaysian Court', *Pertanika Journal of Social Science and the Humanities* 25 (2017): 227–38.
[103] The nine Malaysian states are Johor, Selangor, Terengganu, Pahang, Perlis, Perak, Kelantan, Kedah, and Negeri Sembilan.

kings – which then approves these fatwas.[104] At the state level, state religious departments can issue fatwas at the request of the head of state (either the state's king or chief minister), a citizen, or on their own. In most states, fatwas are issued by a fatwa committee chaired by a state mufti. In some states, the state muftis of the remaining states have power to issue fatwas on their own but must consult their fatwa committees. In the states of Kedah and Pahang, their state muftis can issue fatwas autonomously without prior consultation.[105] While state-level fatwas are non-binding by default, they can be made legally binding by publication in their respective state government's gazette.[106] Similarly, sermon production in Malaysia is managed by JAKIM at the federal level and state religious departments at the state level.

There are no federal-level fatwas issued by the NFC concerning the environment. However, the fatwa committees of the states of Terengganu and Perlis issued the country's first environmental fatwas in November 2015[107] and February 2016,[108] respectively.

The Terengganu 2015 fatwa deals specifically with the poaching of endangered wildlife, declaring the prohibition against hunting wildlife illegally, with hunting them to the point to extinction being contrary to the Muslim obligation 'to protect Allah's creations'.[109] Interestingly, the fatwa is the result of science–faith collaboration. Prior to the fatwa in 2014, local science-based conservation NGO Rimba launched 'a tiger conservation project in Terengganu . . . and initiated partnerships with faith leaders to engage Muslim grassroot communities, in raising their awareness of the need to protect wildlife'. It was Rimba that encouraged the state Islamic department to enact a fatwa to support their efforts to combat wildlife poaching in the state's forest reserves after a fatwa on the issue was published in Indonesia.[110]

The Perlis 2016 fatwa, titled 'Fatwa on the Pollution of the Environment' (*Fatwa Pencemaran Alam Sekitar*), declared:

1. Islam is an eco-centric religion 'that protects the well-being of humans and nature'.
2. The legal principle of *al-amr bi-l-maʿrūf wa-nahī ʿan al-munkar* (enjoining good and preventing evil) in the sharia applies in this respect.
3. Environmental pollution that adversely impact living beings are generally *ḥarām* (prohibited) unless it achieves a greater good (*maṣlaḥa muktabar*) or prevents a clear and present harm (*mafsada*).
4. Muslims must avoid partaking in environmentally adverse, pollutive activities that can destroy life and disrupt ecosystems.

[104] Zaini Nasohah, 'Undang-undang Penguatkuasaan Fatwa di Malaysia', *Islāmiyyāt* 27, no. 1 (2005): 25–43, at 31–32.
[105] Administration of Muslim Law (Federal Territories) Act 1993, ss. 34 and 37(5); Mufti and Fatwa (Kedah) Enactment 2008, s. 8; Administration of Muslim Law (Pahang) Enactment 1991, s. 36.
[106] Ibid. This is provided as a procedure in all state enactments on the administration of Islamic law.
[107] Adrian David, 'Terengganu First to Issue Fatwa against Wildlife Poaching', *New Straits Times*, 30 November 2015, https://bit.ly/401SPGx.
[108] 'Perlis Fatwa Committee Bans Act of Polluting Environment', *Malay Mail*, 1 March 2016, https://bit.ly/4nUjNzE.
[109] 'Malaysian State Issues "Fatwa" against Wildlife Poaching', *Mongabay*, 14 December 2015, https://bit.ly/4qmDv8R; Beh Lih Yi, 'Islamic Clerics Declare Fatwa on Poachers in Indonesia and Malaysia', *The World*, 5 January 2016, https://theworld.org/article/6714327/2016/01/04/malaysia-indonesia-poaching-fatwa.Unfortunately, the Terengganu poaching fatwa is not accessible online.
[110] Jame Schaefer et al., 'The Efficacy of Using SCB Guidelines to Facilitate Conservation Science-Faith Collaboration: Experiences in the Field', *Frontiers in Environmental Science* 8 (2020): 1–21, at 12. My utmost thanks to one of the co-authors, Dr G. Reuben Clements, for sharing the article with me during his guest lecture via Zoom at the National University of Singapore on 31 October 2023.

5. Pro-environment individual and collective efforts are encouraged in Islam and count as acts of piety (*'amal ṣāliḥ*).[111]

Unfortunately, these fatwas are not gazetted and have no binding effect. The reasons for this are unknown but, as discussed elsewhere, enforceability of these fatwas may be problematic.[112] Interestingly, the Terengganu 2015 fatwa was issued in response to the Indonesian Ulama Council (MUI) fatwa on wildlife conservation issued in 2014.[113]

13.5 FATWAS, MOSQUE SERMONS, AND ISLAMIC ENVIRONMENTAL LAW IN ACTION IN INDONESIA

Unlike Singapore and Malaysia, and despite its Muslim-majority population, the Indonesian constitution does not accord a special status to Islam beyond its recognition of belief in 'One and Almighty God' as normatively fundamental.[114] Instead, Islam is recognized as one of Indonesia's six official religions under its infamous 'blasphemy law' alongside Catholicism, Protestant Christianity, Hinduism, Buddhism, and Confucianism.[115] Legislation on Muslim personal law was enacted in its first decades of independence, but these initially concerned family law exclusively. In 1991, by presidential instruction, the Kompilasi Hukum Islam (KHI) was enacted to guide the enforcement of Islamic family, inheritance (*farā'iḍ*), and endowment (*waqf*) laws. The KHI's enactment was complemented by the establishment of Islamic courts under *Law No. 1 of 1989 on Islamic Judicature* that same year.[116] Islamic criminal law (*ḥudūd*) is implemented and enforced exclusively in Indonesia's autonomous province of Aceh.[117] Despite the existence of a Ministry of Religious Affairs, the Indonesian government relies on the MUI for advice and guidance on Islamic affairs, making the MUI the unofficial state authority on Islamic affairs.[118] The MUI was originally established under the auspices of the Indonesian government in 1975 to function as a platform for Indonesian ulema, scholars, and Islamic organizations to contribute to a collective Islamic voice on national-level issues.[119]

Since its founding, the MUI has produced thousands of 'collective fatwas' at the national and provincial level. However, unlike in Singapore and Malaysia, there is neither legal nor institutional basis for the MUI's production of these fatwas. The two oldest and largest Muslim organizations in the country, Nahdlatul Ulama and Muhammadiyah, are members of the MUI, but they also issue fatwas on their own. Nevertheless, government recognition of the MUI's fatwas as the product of national- and provincial-level consensus amongst Indonesian ulema since 1975 lends them legitimacy and authority *sans* law.[120] Indeed, the MUI is a key player in

[111] Norshariani A. Rahman and Muhammad H. Jalil, 'Awareness of the Role of "Religious People" in Environmental Conservation from the Perspective of Islamic Studies Students', *Creative Education* 12 (2021): 1755–72.

[112] See Ramlan, 'Implementing Islamic Law', 226–27.

[113] Beh, 'Islamic Clerics Declare Fatwa'.

[114] Constitution of Indonesia 1945, Preamble and art. 29(1).

[115] Presidential Decree No. 1/PNPS/1965 on the Prevention of Misuse and/or Insult of Religion, Elucidation, art. 1.

[116] Euis Nurlaelawati, *Modernization, Tradition and Identity: The Kompilasi Hukum Islam and Legal Practice in the Indonesian Religious Courts* (Amsterdam: Amsterdam University Press, 2010), 19–20.

[117] Kamaruzzaman Bustamam-Ahmad, *Islamic Law in Southeast Asia: A Study of Its Application in Kelantan and Aceh* (Bangkok: Asian Muslim Action Network, 2009).

[118] Pradana Boy Zulian, *Fatwa in Indonesia: An Analysis of Dominant Legal Ideas and Mode of Thought of Fatwa-Making Agencies and Their Implications in the Post-New Order Period* (Amsterdam: Amsterdam University Press, 2018), 11.

[119] Majelis Ulama Indonesia, 'Sejarah MUI', Majelis Ulama Indonesia Kabupaten Lamandau, www.mui-lamandau.or.id/pg/sejarah-mui/.

[120] Zulian, *Fatwa in Indonesia*, 9–15.

Indonesian democratic politics precisely because of the effect its authority and its use of fatwas have in advocating and mobilizing social change. In the case of mosque sermons, Islamic organizations, from the MUI to the most rural mosque, are free to produce them since there is no central authority in the likes of the MUIS (Islamic Religious Council of Singapore) or JAKIM to be *the* national producer of sermons. As such, sermons may be produced and delivered organically, as previously explained, by imams leading congregational prayers, either impromptu or prepared beforehand. Notably, Indonesia has a vibrant *khuṭba* publishing industry which the MUI does not dominate, and its many Islamic organizations and millions of independent Islamic scholars can publish them unregulated. Nevertheless, the MUI's legitimacy and authority in Indonesia may imply the credibility of their sermons, which are available online and published as sermon compilation books.[121]

13.6 STATE SUPPORT FOR PUBLIC ISLAMIC ENVIRONMENTAL LAW: AN APPROACH TO STATE CO-OPTATION?

Governments in our case studies appear to provide both explicit and implicit support for Islamic environmental law. Explicit support includes providing legal and institutional bases for fatwa and mosque sermon production, and in the case of the MUIS and JAKIM, vests power and authority to provide religious guidance; they also receive funding directly from the government's budget. Implicit support, on the other hand, are by-products of explicit forms of support, the most significant of which is the legitimacy enjoyed by these religious authorities through their association with the government. In the case of the MUIS and JAKIM, being part of the state bureaucracy has this effect; despite being an NGO, the MUI is legitimized by its longstanding role as the Indonesian government's unofficial advisor on Islamic affairs and its environmental pursuits are funded by the government as well as international NGOs such as the World Bank and Conservation International.[122] However, underlying such support are implied terms arising out of the government's view on its relationship with religion and religious actors, and the limits imposed on the latter's participation in the public sphere according to the state's interests. In other words, the state *co-opts* these actors' environmental efforts to fit overarching government priorities.[123] In Asian contexts, this can be understood as being part of states' broader policy to 'regulate' religion by intervening in the affairs of religious actors 'direct[ly] or indirect[ly], through binding law or otherwise'.[124] Accordingly, in the case of Islamic environmental law, these implied terms limit the scope of *what* rulings are pronounced, the subject matters that are deemed important, and whether environmental efforts by bodies like the MUIS, JAKIM, and MUI can go beyond mere pronouncement of Islamic environmental law to implement and enforce their rulings.

[121] Ramlan, 'Implementing Islamic Law for the Environment', 228.

[122] Anna M. Gade, 'Islamic Law and the Environment in Indonesia: Fatwa and Da'wa', *Worldviews: Global Religions, Culture and Ecology* 19, no. 2 (2015): 161–83.

[123] State co-optation of religion can be defined as when governments 'include religious organizations in its ruling coalition, subsidize them, regulate them, and make them "political partners"': Cheng Tun-jen and Deborah A. Brown, 'Introduction: The Roles of Religious Organisations in Asian Democratisation', in Cheng Tun-jen and Deborah A. Brown (eds), *Religious Organisations and Democratisation: Case Studies from Contemporary Asia* (London: Routledge 2015), 3–40, at 14.

[124] Jaclyn L. Neo, 'Conceptualizing the Regulation of Religion', in Jaclyn L. Neo, Arif A. Jamal, and Daniel P. S. Goh (eds), *Regulating Religion in Asia: Norms, Modes and Challenges* (Cambridge: Cambridge University Press, 2019), 38–58, at 39.

In the case of Singapore, the MUIS being 'bureaucratically embedded in the state'[125] legally and institutionally implies their de facto alignment with government's policies. An examination of MUIS environmental sermons confirms this assumption; the timing in which environmental sermons are produced and delivered almost always coincides with major updates to national environmental and natural resources policy. Indeed, water resources and concerns about its scarcity is a core governmental priority since independence in 1965,[126] and Singapore relies heavily on water imports from Malaysia while progressively building infrastructure for water self-sufficiency.[127] In recent years, however, Malaysia's water reserves have been affected by climate-related factors (e.g., global temperature rises, increased frequency and lengthening of drought, reduced rainfall), leading to a rise in water prices in response to falls in water supply. Two environmental sermons containing water conservation messages, 'Doing Justice towards Allah's Blessings' (March 2016) and 'Balance in God's Creation' (March 2017), were produced and delivered to address the government's announcements of water price increases for 2017 and 2018, respectively.[128] Beyond water resources, the Singapore government declared 2018 and 2019 to be the 'Year of Climate Action'[129] and the 'Year Towards Zero Waste', respectively.[130] The government's announcement of the 'Singapore Green Plan 2030' in late October 2021, a 'whole-of-nation movement to advance Singapore's national agenda on sustainable development'[131] was also received by the MUIS with the production of the sermon titled 'Protecting the Environment' the week after the announcement.[132] More recently, another water conservation sermon was produced in March 2022 in celebration of 'Singapore World Water Day' that 'aims to raise awareness on the importance of keeping water clean and being prudent when using it'.[133]

The same can be said of Malaysia's JAKIM vis-à-vis Islamic environmental law and how its being a government department shapes its pursuit. First, as aforementioned, state-level fatwas can be made legally binding and enforced under Malaysia's Islamic legal system if desired but doing so may be problematic. To elaborate: an environmental harm caused by a Muslim in Terengganu and Perlis may trigger provisions in *both* 'secular' environmental laws (*Environmental Quality Act* 1997 if to an environmental medium, *Wildlife Conservation Act 2010* if to protected animals) *and* 'Islamic' environmental laws (i.e., their state's environmental fatwas), resulting in a case of double jeopardy. This is because enforcement of fatwas, especially the environmental fatwas, is *ex post* in response to violations to the rulings in these fatwas. While

[125] Afif Pasuni, 'Negotiating Statist Islam: *Fatwa* and State Policy in Singapore', *Journal of Current Southeast Asian Affairs* 37, no. 1 (2018): 57–88.

[126] Carl Grundy-Warr and Victor R. Savage, 'Singapore: Sustaining a Global City-State and the Challenges of Environmental Governance in the Twenty-First Century', in Philip Hirsch (ed.), *Routledge Handbook of the Environment in Southeast Asia* (London: Routledge, 2017), 448–69, at 450.

[127] Ibid., 451–54, 461.

[128] Public Utilities Board, 'Water Prices', www.pub.gov.sg/watersupply/waterprice. These prices have since been updated and the original site moved. See also Chew Hui Min, 'Singapore Budget 2017: Water Prices to Increase by 30% from July 1 in Two Phases', The Straits Times, 20 February 2017, http://bit.ly/3L3C4Mk; Andrea Soh, 'Singapore to Raise Water Price by 30% over Two Years', *The Business Times*, 21 February 2017, http://bit.ly/3J91lnU.

[129] Cynthia Choo, 'S'pore Declares 2018 as "Year of Climate Action"', *Today*, 17 November 2017, www.todayonline.com/singapore/spore-declares-2018-year-climate-action.

[130] Ministry of Environment and Water Resources, '2019 Is Singapore's Year towards Zero Waste', press release, 12 January 2019, www.nas.gov.sg/archivesonline/data/pdfdoc/MSE_20191125001.pdf.

[131] Singapore Government, 'SG Green Plan', 11 October 2021, www.greenplan.gov.sg/.

[132] Office of the Mufti, 'Preserving the Environment', MUIS, 5 November 2021, http://bit.ly/3Jf9zuG.

[133] Office of the Mufti, 'Avoiding Wastage Is a Sign of Gratitude to Allah', MUIS, 25 March 2022, http://bit.ly/4ozY4x4.

there are no accessible records of judicial proceedings for fatwa violations in Malaysia,[134] it is disproportionate to prosecute an alleged environmental offender under two different legal systems. Nevertheless, in the case of the Terengganu fatwa, it has been made clear that enforcement of the fatwa is not an active objective, and that the fatwa was the result of Rimba's encouragement for one to support its own efforts to combat wildlife poaching in the state. The Sultan (as head of the Islamic religion of the state)[135] and the state's religious department undertook advocacy roles against wildlife poaching to support the fatwa's compliance, in addition to local clerics being trained on integrating conservation messages in their *da 'wa* (community) work, however, it is not clear if the state sought to co-opt Rimba's work since they form part of Rimba's engagement project with them.[136]

Second, JAKIM's environmental sermons – as in the case of the MUIS – are produced to address the national environmental policies and concerns. JAKIM's first (publicly accessible) environmental sermon in August 2016 sought to garner public cooperation with the government's waste management policy infrastructure. Its sermon in October 2016 spoke of the people's role in natural resource management to prevent environmental disasters such as forest fires, landslides, and the pollution of rivers. Interestingly, this sermon was issued in conjunction with 'National Environment Day' in Malaysia, encouraging the local Muslim community to 'work together and collaborate in efforts to bring prosperity to the earth [and] take what is provided by the earth sustainably and without wastage so that they can be enjoyed by future generations'.[137] In JAKIM's environmental sermons in October 2022, coverage of environmental obligations shifted to emphasize those imposed on political leaders, utilizing Islam's requirement for good governance in that area of policy.[138]

Beyond sermons, National Environment Day seems to also be an avenue for JAKIM to go beyond pronouncing on Islamic environmental law to acting upon it. On 19 October 2019, 'in collaboration with the Selangor Islamic Religious Department and several other agencies', JAKIM organized the 'Clean & Green: Rahmah for All' event[139] to celebrate National Environment Day. The event was held at Pulau Ketam – a Selangor island whose inhabitants are predominantly non-Muslim and Chinese – to 'instill a culture of tolerance and mutual love in communities regardless of race and religion'.[140] The event comprised of a 'clean and green' component, which involved a mass cleaning of the village's common areas and clearing the island of litter,[141] and a '*rahmah* [mercy] for all' component where participants visited and socialized with villagers at their homes, and gifted food items and necessities to them. This event is interesting for several reasons. It firstly highlights the socio-ecological aspect of Islamic

[134] The author's inquiry into this matter reveals that no quantitative research had been done to ascertain why this is the case.
[135] For a video of the Terengganu Sultan's public service announcement regarding the fatwa, see Facebook, 'Harimau Selamanya', www.facebook.com/harimaubuatselamanya/.
[136] Schaefer et al., 'The Efficacy of Using SCB Guidleines', 12–15.
[137] Jabatan Kemajuan Islam Malaysia, 'Tanggungjawab Bersama Melestarikan Alam Sekitar [Collective Responsibility in Preserving the Environment]', JAKIM, 20 October 2016, http://bit.ly/48HlYly.
[138] Jabatan Kemajuan Islam Malaysia, 'Teladan Sepanjang Zaman [An Age-Old Lesson]', JAKIM, 7 October 2022, http://bit.ly/3LkLFOU; Jabatan Kemajuan Islam Malaysia, 'Amanah dan Tanggungjawab [Trust and Responsibility]', JAKIM, 21 October 2022, http://bit.ly/3LkOmAo.
[139] Jabatan Kemajuan Islam Malaysia, 'Kenyataan Media JAKIM Berkenaan Program "Clean & Green: Rahmah for All" [JAKIM Media Release on "Clean & Green: Rahmah for All" Programme]', JAKIM, 29 November 2019, http://bit.ly/4qklqIv.
[140] Ibid.
[141] Ibid.

environmental law, in which the environmental duties of Muslims arise from their relationships with all of God's creation, which includes fellow human beings irrespective of ethnicity and creed. It is unclear if this was intended to be affected by JAKIM, but what is certain is that Islamic environmental law in this case was utilized for a secondary objective: to encourage the preservation of social harmony in Malaysia's ethnically and religiously diverse society.

With respect to Indonesia's MUI, on the other hand, state co-optation is a complex reality. During the authoritarian regime of President Suharto, the MUI was largely a part of the regime's apparatus of legitimacy. This was an era of explicit co-optation when the MUI would issue fatwas in support of President Suharto's policies. However, it is important to note that the MUI is a composite body of hundreds of Islamic organizations and, individually, they are largely autonomous, operationally and ideologically. Indeed, the most prominent ones, such as Nadhlatul Ulama and Muhammadiyah (and their predecessors), were founded and membered by Muslim political leaders who fought for Indonesian independence from the Netherlands, and this remains the case today. When the Suharto regime was toppled in 1998 due to mass unhappiness with its handling of the global recession, these organizations sided with the people and partook in the democratization process thereafter. Subsequently, Islamic political parties founded and supported by these organizations were elected to the legislative and executive branches of government. As such, can we say that co-optation ended with the Suharto regime – or did co-optation remain, but with religious actors being in a position to dictate the terms of engagement to make their relationship with government more of a collaborative endeavour?

Unlike in the case of Singapore or Malaysia, it is difficult to point out a relationship of co-optation between the government and religious organizations like the MUI due to the blurring of a clear distinction between the people of both sides. For example, Indonesia's former Vice President, Kyai Haji Ma'ruf Amin, was the chairman of the MUI and 'Supreme Leader' of the NU prior to his election to the position in 2019. Recent controversial reform to its criminal code to, among others, outlaw pre- and extra-marital sex, also suggest a shift in the Indonesian government's ideological compass towards appeasing religious conservatives.[142] Thus, we cannot definitively conclude on the nature of state–religion relations in Indonesia and whether their working together to tackle policy issues is 'collaboration' or 'co-optation'. Nevertheless, it can be observed that the government recognizes the authority that religious organizations have in fostering compliance in environmental law and policy. This is evinced by how the MUI's 2018 fatwa was issued in response to a request by the then-environment minister, to buttress the ministry's own policies on forest and peatland burning with religious-moral justification. Therefore, a preliminary conclusion we can reach is the adoption of a socio-ecological approach taken by the Indonesian government in this respect – recognizing the role of social actors in successfully implementing environmental policies.

13.7 CONCLUSION

Should we care if Islamic environmental law is enabled by state co-optation? On the one hand, Islamic environmental law can be seen as a fundamental pillar of implementing environmental

[142] Arlina Arshad, 'Indonesian Parliament Approves Legislation to Outlaw Sex Outside Marriage', The Straits Times, 6 December 2022, http://bit.ly/4hFoJ9v.

law that not only decolonizes environmental law[143] but also honours the international obligations of states to create, implement, and enforce environmental rule of law, even if their national circumstances dictate their pace of properly doing so.[144] It also acknowledges the existence of private environmental governance (PEG) as an alternative but concurrent system that exists within society in the non-state to fill the regulatory gaps arising from imperfect policy implementation and legal enforcement.[145] For these, we should laud governments that are willing to include Islamic environmental law as a source of environmental norms in their governance framework. On the other hand, the history of co-optation in our case studies suggests that state support may not always be entirely pursued in recognition of these benefits. The analyses in Section 13.6 sought to flesh out the possibility of non-environmental reasons, justifications, and intentions underlying state support, and to question whether these governments support religious actors implementing Islamic environmental law to gain political points and/or to control how these operate within the general environmental governance framework. The authoritarian pasts and presents of our case studies allow us to be sceptical about this possibility, and be sceptical about the *real* intentions of these governments. Regardless, at least from the perspective of environmental rule of law, such support by governments are steps in the right direction towards achieving our shared environmental objectives.

143 See Usha Natarajan, 'Third World Approaches to International Law (TWAIL) and the Environment', in Andreas Philippopoulos-Mihalopoulos and Victoria Brooks (eds), *Research Methods in Environmental Law* (Cheltenham: Edward Elgar 2017); Michell Lim (ed.), *Charting Environmental Law Futures in the Anthropocene* (Singapore: Springer, 2019), 207–36; Usha Natarajan and Julia Dehm, 'Where Is the Environment? Locating Nature in International Law', *Third World Approaches to International Law Review*, 30 August 2019, https://twailr.com/where-is-the-environment-locating-nature-in-international-law/.

144 Per the principle of common but differentiated responsibilities (CBDR): Ellen Hey, 'The Principle of Common but Differentiated Responsibilities', *United Nations Office of Legal Affairs*, 13 July 2010, https://legal.un.org/avl/ls/Hey_EL.html.

145 See Michael P. Vandenbergh, 'Private Environmental Governance', *Cornell Law Review* 99 (2013): 129–99; Galperin, 'Private, Environmental, Governance', 1; Albert C. Lin, 'Pope Francis' Encyclical on the Environment as Private Environmental Governance', *George Washington Journal of Energy and Environmental Law* 9 (2018): 33–56 (example of faith-driven, as opposed to profit-driven, PEG).

14

Redefining an Islamic 'Good Life'

Environmental Maqāṣid al-Sharīʿa *and* Ijtihād *for the Planet in the Anthropocene*

Wardah Alkatiri

14.1 INTRODUCTION

This chapter embodies a transdisciplinary effort to bridge the gaps between science, environmental humanities, and Islamic environmental law.[1] The entire discussion addresses both the objective reality of the earth as the source of human sustenance, and the objective and subjective aspects of what has been perceived as a human 'good life'. Eventually, I call for exploring the utility of *maqāṣid*[2] and reopening the gates of *ijtihād*[3] to redress the golden balance that has been obliterated between human and nature since industrialization took place in the Islamic world's history.

Following Jenkins' (2005:338–41) useful classification of two different stances towards utilizing Islam for environmental ethics into (i) traditionalist – expressed by Seyyed Hossein Nasr[4] – and (ii) reformist – expressed by Richard Foltz[5] – my position defends some variation on one of these stances. She identified – and therefore, scrutinized – the very idea of progress and the development ideology pointed out to be the main culprits of the crises today (Alkatiri 2021a, 2021b, 2022, 2023, 2024a). By Jenkins' further classification of Islam and ecology scholarship into (i) cosmology – in which one seeks to recruit Islamic resources for reconstructing worldviews – and (ii) jurisprudence – in which the attempt was made to find the mechanism for producing sharia law – I have taken both approaches. Namely, 'cosmology', in Alkatiri (2021a) and a forthcoming paper;[6] and 'jurisprudence' in this present chapter, where she seeks to offer

[1] This chapter is a compilation of my earlier works (Alkatiri 2023, 2024a, 2024b).

[2] *Maqāṣid* is about the purpose of Islamic law. Shaykh Muḥammad al-Ṭāhir b. ʿĀshūr, a great Islamic scholar, defined the *maqāṣid* of Islamic law as the objectives or purposes behind Islamic rulings. He explained the knowledge of *maqāṣid al-sharīʿa* is important for mujtahids (jurists) to not only understand or interpret the texts of sharia, but also to derive solutions to contemporary problems faced by Muslims.

[3] *Ijtihād* is literally the intellectual effort of trained Islamic scholars to arrive at legal rulings not covered in the sacred sources.

[4] Nasr 1998:119.

[5] Foltz takes the view that appealing to a bygone golden age or to the roots of revelation sets ethicists to contentious interpretive work. For him, what we need from religions is to acknowledge, among all possible interpretations available to us, the 'eco-friendly' and 'non-hierarchical ones' (2003:250).

[6] Entitled, 'Ecological and Islamic: Corresponding Critiques of Mainstream Education System – Reconstructing a New Learning Paradigm in the Anthropocene'.

an intelligible appropriation of Islamic resources for environmental ethics and environmental laws.

14.1.1 Fact 1: Living in a Great Upheaval

Times have changed. The prospect of global civilization is now undermined by an unprecedented ecological crisis.[7] The fact is now overwhelming that humankind cannot continue on the path on which it is now heading into the future.[8] This not only asks us to question the very idea of progress and modernism adopted all over the world but it also problematizes the 'development' ideology and the 'perpetual growth' paradigm that became the standard narrative in political and ideological terms.[9] Under this circumstance, this chapter appraises the potential of Islamic law (sharia) to regulate not only the issues of crime and punishment but more crucially in the far-reaching ecologically informed economic system, and being the caretaker of environmental legislation.

The starting premise of this chapter is that the root causes of sustainability problems as scientifically understood are (i) the nature of consumption, (ii) the nature of economy, and (iii) the cultural definition of a 'good life'. Confronted with the reality that many devout Muslims, the Muslim leaders and ulema in the modern world, are in fact entirely indifferent on environmental problems, a flattery that Islam is a 'green religion', which might necessarily make its adherents pay attention to the environment, is in my view disingenuous. Accordingly, she disagrees with facile arguments of some ulema who claim that the quality of one's faith can be measured by the extent of a person's sensitivity and concern for environmental sustainability (Yafie 2006).[10] This chapter contends that awareness is the very first step to any change, and therefore, cultivating the ecological sustainability literacy is badly needed to understand the inescapable laws of Conservation of Mass and Thermodynamics that limit the growth pursued by the 'development' ideology. In such a way, the ulema and Muslim leaders will be sufficiently informed to devise the environmental sharia that correctly situates human society within the context of the earth's limited natural energy flows and resource stocks and, at the same time, comply with the will of God. Given these physical constraints of the planet, the current dominant ethical framework and the endless rat race of modern life have placed us in a riverbed of self-destruction. Technological fixes can temporarily improve conditions, but they cannot move us out of this riverbed of unsustainability. Future paths would have to follow a different riverbed, and this is where Muslims need to redefine a genuinely Islamic development model and its parameters.

Unlike the dominant Eurocentric development paradigm, an Islamic development paradigm should not aim at making it possible for humans to forget God and their own inner reality and being stifled by the prison of their own creation. An Islamic development paradigm needs to have its own criteria for a happiness index that does not envisage life as a big marketplace in which humans are free to roam around and choose objects at will. Even though it is somewhat too late, this chapter urges Muslim-majority countries and sharia-based states to redefine the utilization of natural resources and the objectives of their 'development' projects as per the traditional classifications of *maqāṣid al-sharīʿa* (al-Shāṭibī 2006) into (i) necessities (*ḍarūriyyāt*),

[7] Al-Mizan: A Covenant for the Earth 2022:7.

[8] Ibid., 8.

[9] Ibid.

[10] Ali Yafie is a jurist in Indonesia who affirms that the quality of one's faith can be measured, including by the level of a person's sensitivity and concern for environmental sustainability (Yafie 2006).

(ii) needs (*ḥājiyyāt*), and (iii) luxuries (*taḥsīniyyāt*) in light of Islamic values. This chapter explicates a strong probability that the world has reached a turning point and the road ahead will be mostly downhill. The 'Limits to Growth' analysis (Meadows, Meadows, and Randers 2004)[11] was the linchpin of the argument and laid down the rationales for the need of *ijtihād* for the planet on three fundamental issues in the Muslim world. They are: rethinking (i) the hegemony of development and economic growth paradigm, (ii) the sovereignty of nation states and their competing interests, and paying attention to (iii) the birth control issue vis-à-vis overpopulation.

14.1.2 *Fact 2: Living in Societies with a Paucity of Ecological Literacy*

For a start, I argue how the idea that there are human responsibilities to the natural world has never been made pronounced to the followers of Islam at the ethical, institutional, and material dimensions of the religion.[12] In 'The Loss of Tawhidi Worldview' (Alkatiri 2021a), I spell out historical and sociological factors involved in the gradual erosion of Islam's holistic approach to existence, including the sense of sacred reverence. Certainly, innumerable intellectual attempts on ethics have been advanced in the Muslim world on gender equality, religious pluralism, democracy, and human rights, but not the least of which is addressed to environmental ethics. This chapter draws attention to the central question of ethics on 'how should we live our lives' in a world facing the most serious ecological crisis.

Through the lens of environmental humanities and sociology, I identified what I termed as 'the double-ignorance complacency' being the greatest challenge to be confronted in the Global South generally. There are, on the one hand, a lack of scientific milieu which would be conducive to the scientific understanding of ecological sustainability, and on the other hand, the 'captive mind'[13] among the educated classes and the elites in general. Collectively, these have given rise to two social groups who are largely convivial with one another: one is the progressivists, characterized by unreflective acceptance of liberalism that came in a package deal with right-wing ideology and neoliberal economics, and the other is those who are easily flattered by nativism, including the rhetoric of 'local wisdom'. Local wisdom refers to the notion that traditional or Indigenous knowledge and native science are capable of resolving environmental ills.

Among those in the former group is the progressive liberal-leaning Muslims who eventually came to the service of corporatist development and oligarchy in the Global South (Alkatiri 2022, 2023, 2024a). Elsewhere, despite the rhetoric of local wisdom 'kearifan lokal' promoted since the 1990s in Indonesia's context, the natural environment of Indonesia continued to degrade at an alarming rate and the promise of 'kearifan lokal' remains elusive (Alkatiri 2024b). Meanwhile, it is just as important to recognize the complacency that stemmed from religious fatalism, including the influence of millenarian thought with its apocalyptic expectations of the 'end times' found among the conservative religious Muslims (Alkatiri 2024a).

The chapter has been organized in the following way. By dint of scientific laws, Section 14.2 demonstrates that our planet has boundaries and crossing them puts human life at risk. The

[11] 'Limits to Growth' is not a speculative theory. It follows mathematical logic and conforms to the scientific fact that the earth is a closed system.

[12] Reference is made to the seven dimensions of religion developed by the Scottish scholar of religion Ninian Smart (1998) as a framework for exploring and understanding religion. They are (1) ritual, (2) experiential, (3) mythological, (4) doctrinal, (5) ethical, (6) institutional, (7) material.

[13] Those who adopted development theory uncritically in a wholesale manner (Alatas 1972).

elucidation of a 'closed system' and the concept of 'footprint' will debunk the familiar rhetoric among the libertarians against the calls for degrowth and to put a brake on our economic development. Section 14.3 discusses what science informs us about the current state of the earth – that we are living in a new epoch of our own making, the Anthropocene,[14] and the uncomfortable reality of life on earth in this new phase of planetary history. Section 14.4 articulates the high probability that the world has reached a turning point and the road ahead is likely declining. Together, Sections 14.2, 14.3, and 14.4 develop an understanding of the enormous ethical dilemma imposed by the biophysical constraints of the earth when the world needs to reduce greenhouse gas emissions and protect the remaining forests and wilderness whilst the 'developing countries' are becoming wealthier, thus needing more natural resource stocks and disposing more industrial pollution and emitting more greenhouse gases. Section 14.5 discusses the ethical issues around the notion of a 'good life'. An interesting and important historic twist of events is presented. It has been widely accepted that 'material culture' and its associated economic system originated in Western culture. Surprisingly enough, this fact was now reversed – a recent survey reveals people in developing countries are the world's most materialistic nations, with the Chinese, Indian, Turkish, and South Korean among the likeliest to measure success by material belongings.

14.2 THE EARTH HAS ITS LIMITS TO SERVE THE HUMAN BEING

More than seven billion people currently live on earth. The UN projects that the global population will rise to 9.8 billion people by 2050. Everyone wants to live a long, healthy, happy, and prosperous life. However, is it possible for everyone to live a good life within our planet's limits? This section aims to answer the question with scientific appraisals.

14.2.1 *Footprint: The Hard Truth about Humans' Dependency on Nature*

Most people do not realize that everything they consume, from food to cloth, to every single item they use every day – bags, shoes, telephone, TV, books, cars, cosmetics, medicine, furniture, toys – is made of something which comes from the ground, which we call a 'natural resource'. The 'footprint' analysis estimates that it takes at least 4–6 hectares of productive land to provide water, energy, settlement area, and food for one person living in a rich world city (Wackernagel, Mathis, and Rees 1996). A more recent study in Australia even shows a figure of 8 hectares (WWF 2009 in Trainer 2011:72). If the world's population of 7.9 billion people were to live the American or European urban lifestyles as we have begun to see in big cities in the Global South, we would need 32–62 billion hectares of productive land. That means we need five to ten planets, because it is about five to ten times the size of productive land available on the entire earth.

Ecological footprint measures how fast we consume resources and generate waste compared to how fast nature can absorb our waste and generate resources.

Carbon footprint is the amount of carbon dioxide (CO_2) emissions associated with all the activities of a person or other entity (e.g., building, corporation, country). It includes direct emissions, such as those that result from fossil fuel combustion in manufacturing, heating, and transportation, as well as emissions resulting from activities to produce the electricity associated

[14] Anthropocene is an entirely new phase of planetary history in which human beings have become the driving force, and the human impact on earth has been profoundly noticed.

with goods and services consumed. In addition, the carbon footprint concept also often includes the emissions of other greenhouse gases, such as methane, nitrous oxide, or chlorofluorocarbons (CFCs).

Material footprint is defined in Čuček, Klemeš, and Kravanja (2015) as a global allocation of used raw material extraction to the final demand of an economy.

14.2.2 *A Closed System Has Limits*

Other than scientists, most people have no knowledge about the inescapable fact that the earth – our life-support system – is a *closed system* by the fact that only energy from sunlight enters the earth and *no* matter enters or leaves, except for the rare meteorite. Further, the best way of understanding the ecological limits of the earth is to understand the way matter and energy flow through the natural world.

Two scientific laws that follow describe the limits of what the earth can do. Here it is important to note the difference between scientific laws and scientific facts. Scientific laws are the descriptions of naturally occurring phenomena in the world, whereas scientific facts are simple, one-off observations that have been shown to be true. Scientific laws are generalized observations about a relationship between two or more things in the natural world based on a variety of facts and empirical evidence, often framed as a mathematical statement (Bradford and Hamer 2022).

a. **Conservation of Mass Law** states, for any system closed to all transfers of matter and energy (like the earth), the mass of the system must remain constant over time as the system's mass cannot change, so the quantity can neither be added nor removed. In other words, matter can be neither created nor destroyed. This law describes how humans can never really 'throw something away'. When wastes are discarded, they do not just disappear. They may change location or change into some other form, but they still exist and are likely to have some impact on the environment.

   The Conservation of Mass Law also describes the hard truth about natural resources. There are two kinds of natural resources: renewable and non-renewable. Every non-renewable natural resource (e.g., fossil fuels, metals, minerals, including uranium in nuclear energy) has a beginning, middle, and end of production. These non-renewable resources are formed over long geological periods. Their rate of formation is extremely slow, so they cannot be replenished once they become depleted. Oil (petroleum), natural gas, coal, oil shale, tar sand, and coal bed methane (CBM) are all fossil fuels. It takes from three to six million years to naturally form fossil fuel from the decomposition of dead organisms. That is why they are generally considered non-renewable. With our modern, industrial, affluent, consumer lifestyle, we use fossil fuels in a way that is depleting the available resources much faster than the new ones are being made. Global oil production is now approaching or has already passed an all-time peak and can potentially end our industrial civilization.

b. **Thermodynamic laws.**[15] The first law of thermodynamics says that energy can be changed from one form to another, but it can be neither created nor destroyed. Energy can occur in a variety of forms such as thermal (heat), electrical, magnetic, nuclear, kinetic, or chemical. Most energy changes on the earth can be traced back to a single common source: the sun.

[15] 'Law of Thermodynamics', Encyclopedia.com, www.encyclopedia.com/places/africa/comoro-islands-political-geography/laws-thermodynamics.

> The second law is more profound. It says that the entropy (state of disorder) of a closed system can only increase. Any system and its surroundings tend naturally to have an increasing entropy. Things tend to spontaneously "fall apart" and become less organized. The second law of thermodynamics provides a foundational lens through which to view the challenges inherent in human activity and its interaction with the natural world.

To be clear, the logical conclusion is that the earth is finite, non-growing, closed, and constrained by the laws of thermodynamics. These facts are plain and uncontestable. Any subsystem, such as the economy, physical development, and population must at some point cease growing and adapt itself to a dynamic equilibrium in a way that minimizes the speed of the inexorable deterioration processes. It is important to reiterate here that economics, by all means, is a component of and is dependent upon the natural world. Therefore, economics could never be independent of ecology. Given that the earth is a closed system, the endless economic growth pursued in a finite planet is simply unthinkable. It can therefore be said that the endless growth paradigm in a finite planet is akin to suicide.[16] In light of this, the familiar rhetoric against the 'eco-alarmist' call to put a brake on economic development, in what is commonly referred to as the degrowth movement, has no leg to stand on:

> This is all old news and just another example of muddle-headed doom mongering. People have been saying this for centuries and yet civilisation has never run out of anything. Why should today be any different? If you don't believe me look at historical precedent. Malthus was wrong and his mistakes still prevent most of us (I really mean most of **you**) from thinking clearly. (Tantram 2013)

In a 'closed system' like the earth, the statement 'we haven't run out of anything so we will never run out of anything' does not make any sense. Just because it hasn't happened yet, it doesn't mean it will not.

14.2.3 *The 'Good Life' within Environmental Limits: A Knotty Problem*

The question then is: is it possible for everyone to enjoy a decent life without damaging the planet? Fanning et al. (2022) address these issues by quantifying the link between eleven indicators (relative to the requirements for a good life) and seven environmental pressures (relative to environmental limits) for over 150 countries. Using the doughnut 'safe and just space' framework they show that no country was able to provide these for the citizens while using natural resources at levels that would be sustainable if every other country in the world did the same. Nowhere in the world even comes close. In other words, rich nations live as they do now because they have been taking and using up most of the natural resources and preventing most of the world's people from having anything like a fair share.

Even though the thresholds that Fanning et al. (2022) chose to represent a 'good life' were far from extravagant, the study provided evidence that the universal achievement of these goals could push humanity past multiple environmental limits.

14.3 WHAT SCIENCE TELLS US ABOUT THE CURRENT STATE OF THE PLANET

Section 14.2 shows that the level of consumption, resource use, and ecological impacts of consumer society in varied countries are far too high to be sustained for long or if extended to all

[16] For further deliberation on the contradiction between the limitless pursuit of economic growth and ecological sustainability read, for example, Trainer (2011, 2021), Rees (1992, 2000), and Daly (1996).

people. As a result, this epoch is characterized by climate disruption, biodiversity loss, and pollution escalation along with natural resource crises. The behaviour of consumer society has drastically interfered with the ecological equilibrium, ruining the balance of the earth's interconnected and unified planetary systems, or the *mīzān* in the language of the Quran.

14.3.1 *Climate Change*

For too long, since the first World Conference on the Human Environment in Stockholm in 1972, climate scientists and human ecologists have warned about the impending crisis. The pursuit of endless economic growth is chewing through our living planet, producing poverty, and threatening our existence. In the hope that people might do something about it before it is too late, climate scientists assert that we would not know exactly how the crisis will unfold until it becomes too late to stop. As a matter of fact, climate change is nothing new in the history of the earth's evolution. In the past, the change was caused by variations in solar energy, volcanic eruptions, in the tilt or orbit of the earth around the sun, changing oceanic circulation, and melting permafrost releasing large quantities of methane gas. As modern civilization evolved and the demand for energy increased, it remained renewable for thousands of years with windmills, waterwheels, gravity-fed hydro power, and the use of animal and human power until coal was discovered and, eventually, petroleum and natural gas. From that point on, these fossil fuels were used on a massive scale to fuel the Industrial Revolution. It is important to bear in mind that only as recently as 250 years ago these fossil fuels began to make possible a huge increase in the amount of cheap and productive energy available to humans. Since then, our energy-hungry consumer civilization has been damaging the earth's ecosystems in two ways. Firstly, by gouging and pumping the fossil fuels, coal, oil, and gas, out of the bowels of the earth where they were locked in by geological processes over millions of years, and secondly, by releasing carbon dioxide (CO_2), methane, and other greenhouse gasses into the atmosphere, mainly by burning these fuels. Only recently did we recognize that excess atmospheric CO_2 trapped heat, causing global climate change. Although this gas makes up only less than half of one per cent of the earth's atmosphere, it is crucial to life on earth. By regulating its flow between the terrestrial, oceanic, and atmospheric domains, the carbon cycle maintains the earth's climatic equilibrium.

Climate scientists admonish that the global emissions must be cut by half by 2030 if we stand a chance of averting the worst impacts of warming. We must avoid 1.5°C in global heating beyond pre-industrial times, a critical target of the Paris climate agreement. The urgency to curtail emissions by half by 2030 implies radical changes in all spheres of life. The costs of inaction would be far greater than the costs of taking immediate action. Yet, governments around the world are failing to make necessary changes and engage their citizens in the role they can play to avert the most disastrous consequences of climate change. Hardly any country in the Global North – the cradle of modern civilization – have laid the concrete groundwork for the economic, cultural, and political shifts that will be necessary to deal with the crisis seriously. Only peripheral progress has been made at reducing carbon emissions but, overall, the world is moving too slowly to avoid 1.5°C. As can be expected, the Global South, including Muslim-majority countries with a long list of more pressing everyday life problems, are way behind the necessary tasks. Collectively, most people turn their face away from environmental emergencies; no one likes to think seriously or confront the possibility that they and their loved ones may one day see a world collapsing. In the following sections, it will be demonstrated that the root of this problem is locked deep within the conceptual bedrock of modern economics and dysfunctional cosmology that bring forth the hegemonic world culture we all now live by.

It is a plain fact that economists have occupied much of the climate change policy debates, and for reasons that can be understood, economists will not lend themselves to empowering fundamental changes that would negate their own core principles of mass production, consumer culture, and ideologies of capitalism. Worst of all, every government takes their cue primarily from the economists. This chapter underscores what has been argued by many (e.g., Wackernagel, Mathis, and Rees 1996; Trainer 2011) that our fierce obsessions with economic growth and affluence is suicidal.

14.3.2 *Pollution Escalation*

In any discussion with economists or businesspeople regarding the relationship between economic activities and environmental degradation, Kuznets curve theory serves as an expedient way to shut down a much-needed conversation and avoid the truth amid any hopes of progress on halting deforestation, land conversion, plastic pollution in developing countries, and, lately, solving climate change before it is too late. The joy of the Kuznets curve theory is that the environment is really nothing to worry about. It will solve itself if we just carry on pursuing economic growth. This inverted U graphical representation suggests a hypothesis by Simon Kuznets that in the early stages of industrialization, pollution and environmental damage will rise sharply. As GDP increases, it will eventually peak and begin to fall, as governments begin to legislate for pollution controls and as the economy moves towards services rather than industry.

The theory is certainly appealing, and it would be convenient if it worked. The evidence in the real world is different. If anything, the curve proved right only in the case of air quality, and studies show that water quality also improves, though not on every indicator. On other environmental indicators, studies found no evidence of a peak and decline: deforestation continued, biodiversity loss was not reversed, municipal waste carries on increasing with income and, most importantly of all, carbon emissions did not peak and decline either. In ecological footprint terms, the wealthiest countries clearly consume more of the world's resources and services than poorer countries. In the context of the Global South, major drawbacks of the Kuznets curve theory need highlighting.

14.3.3 *Biodiversity Loss*

Biodiversity – short for biological diversity – means the diversity of life in all its forms: the diversity of species, of genetic variations within one species, and of ecosystems. Biodiversity supports human well-being either directly through enhanced ecosystem functions and services, or indirectly by increasing the resilience of such functions in the face of environmental change. As has been elaborated in Section 14.2.1, the earth supplies services and goods, and the former is often more valuable than the latter. These services include the fundamental role of photosynthesis, nutrient cycles, and the hydrological cycle; the intricate relationship between plant and animal kingdom; and the sensitive role of climate. Current evidence suggests that the more biodiverse a system, the greater stability and resilience the system has. By maximizing key components of biodiversity, we maximize an ecosystem's long-term value.

The reason why this epoch is called the Anthropocene is because the hallmark of this time is a massive transformation of ecosystems for human use. Surely, this process leads to the loss of wilderness and

> multiple impacts on ecosystems from biotic homogenization ... to the rapid erosion of species richness in the most highly transformed areas of Earth. ... At global scales, evidence is mounting that humans are precipitating Earth's sixth mass extinction ... and the collapse of its life support systems. (Seddon et al. 2016)

Meeting the ever-increasing needs of the earth's human population without excessively reducing biodiversity is obviously one of the greatest challenges facing humanity at this point in history. The IPBES Global Assessment Report on Biodiversity and Ecosystem Services announces that biodiversity is declining faster than at any time in human history; the average abundance of native species in most major land-based habitats has fallen by at least twenty per cent since 1900 (Igini 2022), and the World Conservation Body, IUCN, declared that 12,259 species are threatened with extinction (European Commission 2004). Certainly, the 12,259 threatened species are only the tip of the iceberg because nobody knows exactly how many species there are on earth, let alone how they are doing.

14.4 WE HAVE REACHED A TURNING POINT

Many scientists believe that we have passed the tipping point of environmental sustainability already. Among the most recent proclamations of this type are Paul Ehrlich (in Carrington 2018), Spratt and Dunlop (2018), climate scientists (in Corn 2019), and the modelling of Mark Titchener (2022). While the logic of 'Limits to Growth' and 'peak oil' has been around within scientific communities for some time, there is a conventional wisdom that scientists must not frighten the public but rather must focus their attention on technical solutions. For this reason, this discussion has not been made public until quite recently. In titling his book 'Peak Everything', Richard Heinberg (2010) was suggesting that humanity has achieved an unsustainable pinnacle of population size and consumption rates, and that the road ahead will be mostly downhill, at least for the next few decades, until humanity has learned to live within earth's resource limits. He argued that the industrial expansion of the past century or two was made possible only by our use of the concentrated energies of cheap fossil fuels. As a consequence, when oil, coal, and natural gas cease to be cheap and abundant, or when its use has to be regulated to curtail carbon emissions, economic growth will phase into contraction. Heinberg further noted that the shift from growth to contraction will impact every aspect of human existence, at both the macro and micro levels, threatening even our personal psychological coping mechanisms. In 2017, Heinberg penned a note, 'The End of Growth, Seven Years Later', highlighting the latest turn of events that confirm the 'Limits to Growth' warnings that there are clear signs that economic growth is becoming more difficult to achieve worldwide, and that the global economy is approaching inevitable growth limits as the larger ecological systems of which it is a part become depleted, degraded, and destabilized. Heinberg is certainly not alone in such a grim prediction. In a similar vein, political scientist William Ophuls (1992) asserts, 'liberal democracy as we know it ... is doomed by ecological scarcity' and 'such central tenets as individualism may no longer be viable' (3). While offering support for their claims, this chapter aims to propound a cyclical view of time which stands in contradistinction to the outlook of human history as a straight line of movement that underpins the utopianism of modernization (Alkatiri 2021a).

14.5 REDEFINING THE CULTURAL DEFINITION OF A 'GOOD LIFE': AN IMPERATIVE

We don't have a right to ask whether we are going to succeed or not. The only question we have a right to ask is '*what is the right thing to do?*'.

—Wendell Berry (Simplicity Institute 2023)

In view of all that has been presented, it should now be clear that the earth has limited natural resource stocks and energy flows and, accordingly, the endless expansion of economy is illogical at best and suicidal at worst. It thus follows that there is a contradiction between the pursuit of indefinite economic growth and ecological sustainability. As a corollary, it will not be possible for developing countries – including the Islamic world – to follow the levels of consumption, resource use, and ecological impact of the rich countries. The discussion in Section 14.2.2 explicates that the rich countries have been living in ways that are impossible for all to share. In light of this, a 'good life' for all within planetary boundaries has indeed become a problem of ethics. Alan Holland (2010) puts succinctly that it is a matter of 'how simultaneously to procure justice and to safeguard the environment in a world of rapid technological change, riven by inequalities of wealth and power, and driven by the quest for economic growth'. To address the ethical issues raised by environmental limits, we need to rethink our governing notions of a 'good life'. This section explores the cultural dimension of a 'good life'.

14.5.1 *The Nouveau Riche Jumped on the Bandwagon*

A number of studies reveal an interesting fact that at this point in history the Asian and developing nations in general have become extremely materialist in the sense that they are (i) measuring their success by the things the own, or (ii) feeling under a lot of pressure to be successful and make money (Ferdman 2013).[17] Chinese respondents topped the list, coming in more than double the global average in measuring success by their possessions, with Indian and Turkish respondents coming next. Given that the Muslim-majority countries equally fall into the category of developing or under-developed countries, this chapter underscores a key finding in Ferdman's (2013) study, that there is a positive correlation between the stage of a country's development and its tendency to equate money with success.

In the world's largest Muslim nation, Indonesia, for instance, despite the presence of what has been widely held as the world's largest Islamic organizations, namely, the traditionalist Nahdlatul Ulama and modernist Muhammadiyah, and despite the significant cultural power that both possess, both unfailingly condone the development ideology and the state was left to continue pursuing the old obsession of getting rich and powerful at the expense of the integrity of the ecosystem (Alkatiri 2021b). This fact emerges as a striking contrast to the Buddhist country, Bhutan, discussed in the next section. My doctoral research (Alkatiri 2015) reveals two unrecognized implications of Indonesia's economic development on environmental issues. The first is the dramatic increase of consumerism and the prevalant problem of waste in the population at large, and the second is moral confusion. The following illustrates the problem.

In the early twenty-first century, the province of West Java, where the Jakarta-Bandung urban belt resides, had a population of around fifty million. This province generates nearly 50,000 tons of solid waste per day. Only 50 to 60 per cent is collected and the rest is dumped in canals, vacant lots, or burned. Meanwhile, with regard to moral confusion, the growing consumer culture and the emergence of a new middle class have corroded the mentality of the villagers and Indigenous communities, who supposedly live in harmony with nature. The idea that cash and the economy are everything was driven into people's minds, hence, the widespread corruption continues to soar (Gallup 2011; Jakarta Post 2023) and money politics constitutes and sustains patronage (Aspinall 2010; Blunt, Turner, and Lindroth 2012; Muhtadi 2019). Along

[17] Other studies include Beng-Huat 2000; Podoshen, Li, and Zhang 2011; Richins and Dawson 1992; Ferdman 2013.

with the blatant economic inequality, this world's largest Muslim population is also home to a rapidly growing middle-class and its salient phenomenon of the so-called 'Crazy Rich' Indonesians (BBC News 2018). Environmental campaigns by non-governmental organizations (NGOs) that romanticize the image of local communities as the guardian of the rainforests were, thus, perceived as confusing and unrealistic given the changing realities in people's everyday lives. Having been forced to take on the path of modernization, the villagers and Indigenous communities especially were getting confused by the idea that their ancestors' way of life was, in fact, more correct than the modern way (Nguitragool 2012).

Indeed, we live in an era where the balance of economic power is shifting from the Global North to South. China and India are heading to surpass the US and European economies. Compounded by their large populations, rapid economic growth in many Asian countries makes it the most significant consumer market in the world (Asian Equity 2023). As an apprehension of the growth of consumerism, many warn of the unintended consequences of unchecked consumerism in developing countries and its impact on sustainability. Inasmuch as the world is likely to have reached an ecological turning point, radically different ways of carrying out fundamental processes have to be found. This chapter looks at the potential of the Islamic law. Islamic law scholar Hashim Kamali (2011) was of the opinion that the *maqāṣid* method has received renewed attention in recent decades, due to its focus on real life issues of vital concern to people's welfare. According to Kamali (2011), the *maqāṣid*-based approach to sharia had been historically marginalized so much that many reputable texts of *uṣūl al-fiqh* (principles of jurisprudence) did not even assign a section or chapter to the study of the *maqāṣid*. It was not until al-Shāṭibī (d. 1388) that the *maqāṣid* were treated as a credible theme, and an instrument also of flexibility within the corpus juris of the sharia. In his view, the present-day resurgence of interest of the *maqāṣid* has been focused on its relevance to constitutional law, criminal law, family law, and more specific issues such as Islamic finance, genetic engineering, and others.

By his observation, Kamali (2011) notes that the Muslim world is currently witnessing a growing support for accountability, good governance, democracy, and human rights, and the *maqāṣid* were seen to be 'offering a preferable approach to that of the *uṣūl* methodologies to meet the demand of healthy adjustment within the fabric of the sharia' (al-Shāṭibī 2006:246). Herein, this chapter lays hope on the *maqāṣid* approach to reformulate the objectives of the Islamic world's development and redefine the utilization of natural resources, by following the traditional classifications of *maqāṣid al-sharīʿa* in al-Shāṭibī (2006) into (i) necessities (*ḍarūriyyāt*), (ii) needs (*ḥājiyyāt*), and (iii) luxuries (*taḥsīniyyāt*) in light of Islamic values.

14.5.2 *Contemplating the 'Good Life'. Some Conceptual Frameworks*

'How should we live our lives?' – that is the central question of ethics. Interestingly, despite the generality of the formulation in the question, this question has usually been construed narrowly as the question of how individual *humans* should *relate to one another* (Holland 2010). According to Holland, the idea that there are human responsibilities towards the natural world is somewhat new, at least in Western culture, and has only recently begun to surface in mainstream ethical theory. Addressed in the introduction of this chapter, a similar tendency among the devout Muslim societies whereby, in response to the Global Counterterrorism Forum project, Islam was promoted to be only identical with morality, or *akhlāq*, and the *akhlāq* in question refers solely to human interaction with one another (e.g., Nahdlatul Ulama 2012, 2021). Much worse are the liberal Muslims who would make even

Wendell Berry[18] a 'Salafi-Wahhabi' for being not liberal enough in his view of human freedom (see Berry's epigraph under Section 14.5).

As a matter of fact, no matter what the Quran says, Muslims live under the hegemony of the Enlightenment and, hence, the dominant global culture originated in the West. The idea of 'progress', on which the growth ideology was based, constitutes not only the core of the Enlightenment but also a basic element of two ideologies widely adopted in the Muslim world, liberalism and socialism. Given that 'the era of abundance' has passed,[19] both in terms of the abundance of land and natural resources – such as fossil fuels, minerals, clean water, fresh air, and fertile soil – and thus we could not expect to always rely on the abundance of products of technologies that appeared to be always available, our current materialistic and hedonistic lifestyles will not be sustainable in the near future. As a result, we must urgently reconsider our core assumptions about what constitutes a happy and meaningful life. We need to make haste to revise our fundamental assumptions of what constitutes a good and worthwhile life. In 'Capitalising on Religious Lifeworlds' (Alkatiri 2024a), such thoughts have prompted academic debates that renewed the interest in classic philosophical and utopian questions about a 'good life': 'how will we all live comfortably and well within the limited ecological boundaries of the earth?'; 'what is a good life?'; 'how can we live responsibly?'. The article (Alkatiri 2024a) exhibits (i) the counterculture and citizen-led initiatives that stand in contradistinction to the prevailing popular culture and the dominant political-economic paradigms, (ii) the proliferation of intellectual and popular movements that seek to convince the expanding segment of the general public that it is worthwhile to reject the modern, Western, materialistic conception of living happily and well, and to opt for a joyful and creative 'art of living' in which less materialistic pleasure, ecologically responsible behaviour, and consuming differently are dominant. These include ecological citizenship, solidarity economics, eco-minimalism, ecological consumerism, mindfulness, and subjective well-being. This latest development has renewed interest in the classic philosophical questions of happiness, pleasure, well-being, life satisfaction, meaningful life, and, finally, good life. Along this line, an advocate of simple living, Lester Milbrath (1993), provides several suggestions for modes of living that provide quality but do not burden or injure ecosystems. His central idea is summarized as follows:

> The good life as practiced in modern society not only is unsustainable but also is frequently not really good. Quality in living is necessarily subjective, it cannot be defined in physical terms, and can be found in many manifestations. The search for quality is conducted within ourselves and not in a shopping mall . . . The condition of life systems on our planet demand that we cultivate simple lifestyles that are inwardly rich. (Milbrath 1993:261)

Indeed, a good life is an intricate and complex idea, difficult to measure; what makes one person 'happy' might not be the same for another, and there are many factors that determine happiness for each particular person. In the main, there are two conceptions of the 'good life', namely, hedonistic, in which the good life consists of sensual pleasures, and eudaimonic, in which happiness or contentment is achieved through self-actualization and having meaningful purpose in one's life. In other words, a good life from a eudaimonic perspective is best characterized in terms of a worthwhile or meaningful life. Epicurus and Jeremy Bentham are regarded as two founding fathers of hedonist philosophy, whereas Plato, Aristotle, and the Stoics are among the defenders of eudaimonic happiness. Herein, it is relevant to introduce the preference satisfaction theory, also known as the desire theory, according to which a person's good life consists in the

[18] Wendell Berry is an American novelist, poet, and environmental activist. Berry is a prominent defender of agrarian values and supporter of the local economy.

[19] See, for instance, Willsher (2022).

satisfaction of his preferences or, as some would say, his desires. Modern mainstream neoclassical economics assumes a preference satisfaction theory of well-being (Holland 2010). In view of the gargantuan challenges facing us in this epoch as we are entering the end of abundance, we need to move away from the focus on a preference satisfaction towards the notions of a worthwhile or meaningful life. Nonetheless, there is some truth in the hedonist's perspective of happiness that needs consideration as far as it is concerned with a human's basic needs. Pleasure, as the central criterion of hedonism, is not necessarily purely physical in its origins. Practically all hedonists recognize the existence of pleasures derived from non-physical origins such as fame and reputation, friendship and sympathy, and knowledge and art (Britannica n.d.). In light of the latter, a nascent concept of 'sustainable hedonism' (de Geus 1999:93) was proposed as a pleasure independent of the seductions of the world of goods and consumer society, and hence, will not cause any serious environmental pollution or nature degradation. For example, the intense feeling of happiness when looking at a beautiful tree, a bird circling in the sky, or a butterfly in our garden. This kind of hedonism also aims for pleasure for our senses and does so with respect and awe for our natural environment.

Lastly, just as important is the concept of Gross National Happiness (GNH) contemplated by the King of Bhutan, Jigme Singye Wangchuck, in 1972. Emanating from Buddhist spirituality, GNH was proposed as being more important than the economic concept of GDP (Gross National Product). 'Happiness in the king's opinion differs markedly from the common use of that word in common parlance to denote an ephemeral, passing mood due to some temporary external condition like praise or blame, gain or loss' (Barlow 2012). The GNH concept evolved into a socioeconomic development model and received contributions from several Western and Eastern scholars, economists, and politicians. Thirty years later, in July 2011, the United Nations passed Resolution 65/309 that was adopted unanimously by the General Assembly, placing 'happiness' on the global development agenda.

14.6 CONCLUSION

This chapter demonstrates that the relationship between resource consumption and quality of life is a highly pressing issue. It provides evidence that affluence enjoyed in developed countries is built on a global economic system that is, at its core, plainly unjust. The system has enabled the richer countries to control and take far more than their fair share of the world's resources, often by coercive diplomacy with the Structural Adjustment Program (SAP) for justification, aid, trade power, and even military forces whenever necessary, while depriving the poorest countries of the resources needed to live even a minimally decent existence. With these in mind, the richest nations must give up the pursuit of continued growth.

The world has reached a turning point, and the era of abundance is over. To address the ethical issues raised by environmental limits, the Muslims too need to rethink our governing notions of a 'good life'. The developing countries certainly have a right to increase their standards of living to some dignified level, but both the developed and developing countries, the Global North and South, need to have some limiting principles to enable our societies to legitimately say 'enough'.

This chapter hinted at another task to be undertaken in the Islamic world. Redefining the Islamic 'good life' requires educational reforms, by shifting from the anthropocentric worldview in which humans are separate from and superior to the rest of life on earth, towards a unitive (*tawḥīdī*) worldview, in which we appreciate our place as a member in the web of life and being responsible as a *khalīfat Allāh* (viceregent of Allah) to the Owner of the universe.

REFERENCES

Alatas, Syed Hussein. (1972). 'The Captive Mind in Development Studies', *International Social Science Journal*, 34(4).

Alkatiri, W. (2015). 'Muhammad's Nation is Called: The Potential for Endogenous Relocalisation in Muslim Communities in Indonesia'. PhD thesis, University of Canterbury. http://dx.doi.org/10.26021/3870.

(2021a). 'The Loss of Tawhidi Worldview in Islamic World: Another Ecological Consequence of Modernization'. *Comparative Islamic Studies*, 14(1–2): 53–120. https://doi.org/10.1558/cis.20053.

(2021b). 'Re-Imagining Simple Living and Uncertainty. Transitioning to Carbon-Neutral Economy in Developing Countries'. *International Journal of the Asian Philosophical Association*, 14: 43–55. www.asianpa.net/assets/upload/discussions/oVwyPTRputqs1FFQ.pdf.

(2022). 'How about a Green Caliphate? Global Islamic Environmental Governance for Devout Muslim Communities'. *American Journal of Islam and Society*, 39(3–4): 6–56. https://doi.org/10.35632/ajis.v39i3-4.3100.

(2023). 'Undoing Economic Progress, Unraveling Nation-States: Think about the Unthinkable in the Anthropocene'. *Idea Ledger*. https://idealedger.org/research/67.

(2024a). 'Eco-Alarmist Perspective on the Islamic World'. *The International Journal of Islam*, 1(4): 1–25.

(2024b). 'Anti-Fish Campaign: Food Safety and Ethical Issues of Eating Fish from Indonesia', in A. M. Loconto and D. H. Constance (eds), *Agrifood Transitions in the Anthropocene: Challenges, Contested Knowledge, and the Need for Change*. London: Sage, 119–52.

Al-Mizan (2024). www.almizan.earth/islamic-covenant.

Asian Equity (2023). 'Consumption in Asia from a New Perspective: Focusing on Domestic Brands amid a Big Shift in Asia's Consumption Trend'. *Nikko Asset Management*, April 10. www.trustnet.com/news/13373438/fund/sectors.

Aspinall, E. (2010). 'Assessing Democracy Assistance: Indonesia'. *FRIDE Project Report*. www.files.ethz.ch/isn/130783/IP_WMD_Indonesia_ENG_jul10.pdf.

Awanis, S., B. B. Schlegelmilch, and C. C. Cui (2017). 'Asia's materialists: Reconciling collectivism and materialism'. *Journal of International Business Studies* 48: 964–91.

Barlow, Z. (2012). 'The Ecological Worldview: Hearing the Cries of the World'. *Center for Ecoliteracy*. www.ecoliteracy.org/article/ecological-worldview-hearing-cries-world.

BBC News (2018). 'How a Country Suddenly Went "Crazy Rich"'. *BBC*, 16 December. www.bbc.com/news/stories-46529582.

Blunt, P., M. Turner, and L. Lindroth (2012). 'Patronage's Progress in Post-Soeharto Indonesia'. *Public Administration and Development*, 32(1): 64–81.

Bradford, A., and A. Hamer (2022). 'What is a Law in Science?' *Livescience*, 17 January. www.livescience.com/21457-what-is-a-law-in-science-definition-of-scientific-law.html.

Britannica (n.d.). 'Hedonism'. www.britannica.com/topic/hedonism.

Carrington, D. (2018). 'Paul Ehrlich: "Collapse of Civilisation is a Near Certainty Within Decades."' *The Guardian*, 22 March 2018. https://bit.ly/3LEUN1j.

Chua, B.-H. (ed.) (2000). *Consumption in Asia: Lifestyle and Identities*. London: Routledge.

Corn, D. (2019). 'It's the End of the World as They Know It: The Distinct Burden of Being a Climate Scientist'. *Mother Jones*, 8 July. www.motherjones.com/environment/2019/07/weight-of-the-world-climate-change-scientist-grief/.

Čuček, L., J. J. Klemeš, and Z. Kravanja (2015). 'Overview of Environmental Footprints', in J. J. Klemeš (ed.), *Assessing and Measuring Environmental Impact and Sustainability*. Oxford: Butterworth-Heinemann, 131–93.

Daly, H. (1996). *Beyond Growth: The Economics of Sustainable Development*. Boston, MA: Beacon Press.

European Commission (2004). 'Biodiversity Loss: Facts and Figures'. 9 February. https://ec.europa.eu/commission/presscorner/detail/en/MEMO_04_27.

Fanning, A. L., D. W. O'Neill, J. Hickel, and N. Roux (2022). 'The Social Shortfall and Ecological Overshoot of Nations'. *Nature Sustainability*, 5: 26–36.

Ferdman, R. A. (2013). 'Are Chinese People the World's Most Materialistic?'. *The Atlantic*, 16 December. www.theatlantic.com/china/archive/2013/12/are-chinese-people-the-worlds-most-materialistic/282398/.

Gallup (2011). 'Corruption Continues to Plague Indonesia'. https://news.gallup.com/poll/157073/corruption-continues-plague-indonesia.aspx.

de Geus, M. (1999). *Ecological Utopias: Envisioning the Sustainable Society*. Utrecht: International Books.

Heinberg, R. (2010). *Peak Everything: Waking Up to the Century of Decline*. Canada: New Society Publishers.

(2017). 'The End of Growth: Seven Years Later'. *MuseLetter* 311. https://richardheinberg.com/museletter-311-end-growth-seven-years-later.

Holland, A. (2010). 'We Must Give Up Environmental Ethics?', in H. A. M. J. ten Have (ed.), *Environmental Ethics and International Policy*. Paris: UNESCO, 117–44.

Igini, M. (2022). '6 Biodiversity Loss Statistics That Will Blow Your Mind'. *Earth*, 23 August. https://earth.org/biodiversity-loss-statistics/.

Jakarta Post (2023). 'Analysis: Indonesia Today More Corrupt than When Jokowi Took Charge'. www.thejakartapost.com/opinion/2023/02/20/analysis-indonesia-today-more-corrupt-then-when-jokowi-took-charge.html.

Jenkins, W. (2005). 'Islamic Law and Environmental Ethics: How Jurisprudence (*usul al-fiqh*) Mobilizes Practical Reform'. *Worldviews*, 9(3): 338–64.

Kamali, M. H. (2011). 'Maqāsid Al-Shari'ah and Ijtihad as Instruments of Civilisational Renewal: A Methodological Perspective'. *ICR Journal*, 2(2): 245–71.

Meadows, D. H., D. L. Meadows, and J. Randers (1972). *The Limits to Growth*. New York: Universe Books.

Milbrath, L. W. (1993). 'Redefining the Good Life in Sustainable Society'. *Environmental Values*, 2: 261–69.

Muhtadi, B. (2019). *Kuasa Uang: Politik Uang dalam Pemilu Pasca Order Baru*. Jakarta: Gramedia.

Nahdlatul Ulama (2012). 'Inti Agama adalah Akhlak'. *NU Online*, 15 November. www.nu.or.id/nasional/inti-agama-adalah-akhlak-obXZh.

(2021). 'Makna "Rahmat" dalam Rahmatan lil 'Alamin'. *NU Online*, 17 November. https://islam.nu.or.id/syariah/makna-rahmat-dalam-rahmatan-lil-alamin-QVV5U.

Nasr, S. H. (1998). 'Sacred Science and the Environmental Crisis', in H. Abdel Haleem (ed.), *Islam and the Environment*. London: Ta-Ha Publishers, 118–37.

(2001). *Islamic Life and Thought*. Chicago: ABC International.

Nguitragool, P. (2012). 'Environmental Governance in Democratic and Decentralised Indonesia: Between State, Family and Conservation'. *European Journal of East Asian Studies*, 11(1): 45–69.

Ophuls, W. (1992). *Ecology and the Politics of Scarcity Revisited: The Unravelling of the American Dream*. New York: W. H. Freeman and Company.

Podoshen, J. S., L. Li, and J. Zhang (2011). 'Materialism and Conspicuous Consumption in China: A Cross-Cultural Examination'. *International Journal of Consumer Studies* 35(1): 17–25.

Rees, W. E. (1992). 'Ecological Footprint and Appropriated Carrying Capacity: What Urban Economics Leaves Out'. *Environment and Urbanization*, 4(2): 121–30.

(2000). 'Ecological Footprints and the Pathology of Consumption', in R. F. Woollard and A. S. Ostry (eds.), *Fatal Consumption: Rethinking Sustainable Development*. Vancover: UBC Press, 21–51.

Reuter, T. (2010). 'Anthropological Theory and the Alleviation of Anthropogenic Climate Change: Understanding the Cultural Causes of Systemic Change Resistance'. *World Anthropology Network*, 5: 7–32.

Richins, M. L., and S. Dawson (1992). 'A Consumer Values Orientation for Materialism and Its Measurement: Scale Development and Validation'. *Journal of Consumer Research* 19(3): 303–16.

Seddon, N., et al. (2016). 'Biodiversity in the Anthropocene: Prospects and Policy'. *Proceedings of the Royal Society B*, 283: 20162094. https://doi.org/10.1098/rspb.2016.2094.

al-Shāṭibī (2006). *al-Muwāfaqāt fī uṣūl al-sharī'a*. Vol. 2. Cairo: Dār al-Ḥadīth.

Simplicity Institute (2023). http://simplicityinstitute.org.

Smart, N. (1998). *The World's Religions*. Cambridge: Cambridge University Press.

Soper, K. (2007) 'Re-thinking the Good Life: The Citizenship Dimension of Consumer Disaffection with Consumerism'. *Journal of Consumer Culture* 7(2): 205–29.

Spratt, D., and I. Dunlop (2018). *What Lies Beneath: The Understatement of Existential Climate Risk*. Melbourne: Breakthrough – National Centre for Climate Restoration. https://bit.ly/48hKcSB.

Tantram, J. (2013). 'The Limits to Existence: Aligning Economics and Thermodynamics'. *Terrafiniti*. www.terrafiniti.com/aligning-economics-and-thermodynamics/.

Titchener, M. (2022). 'A Simple Climate Model of Earth's Surface Temperature Response to GHG Emissions'. *Engineers for Social Responsibility (ESR)*, 4 April, https://bit.ly/40evhxu.

Trainer, T. (2011). 'The Radical Implications of a Zero Growth Economy'. *Real-World Economics Review*, 57: 71–82, www.paecon.net/PAEReview/issue57/Trainer57.pdf.

(2021). 'Degrowth: How Much Is Needed?'. *Biophysical Economics and Resource Quality*, 6(2): 1–8.

Wackernagel, M., and W. E. Rees (1996). *Our Ecological Footprint: Reducing Human Impact on the Earth*. Gabriola Island, BC: New Society.

Willsher, K. (2022). 'Macron Warns of "End of Abundance" as France Faces Difficult Winter'. *The Guardian*, 22 August. www.theguardian.com/world/2022/aug/24/macron-warns-of-end-of-abundance-as-france-faces-difficult-winter.

Yafie, A. (2006). 'Merintis fiqh lingkungan hidup'. Jakarta: Yayasan Amanah.

15

Islamic Legal Perspectives on Genetically Modified Food (GMF)

Anke Iman Bouzenita

15.1 INTRODUCTION

The term GMF stands for genetically modified food, namely, food products of animal or plant origin with an "engineered" genetic blueprint. The possibilities of recombined DNA in the realm of food and pharmaceutical production are vast and have only begun to be explored. What has already been genetically modified and devised and what can be devised in the future raise a number of questions and concerns. From the Islamic legal (*fiqhī*) perspective, the legally responsible person (*mukallaf*) is asked to follow Islamic legal rules with every action he/she takes. This applies to the research, production, and consumption of genetically modified food as well as to any other human activity. This chapter attempts to assess the reality of GM food and examine the Islamic legal reasoning and concepts that may be applied to this problem.[1]

15.2 THE TECHNIQUES INVOLVED

The insertion of new characteristics into an organism takes place by altering its DNA. The technique involved is referred to as recombinant DNA. This technology consists of combining DNA molecules from different sources into one molecule to create a new set of genes. This DNA is then transferred into an organism, giving it modified or novel genes.[2] Recombinant DNA techniques may involve bacteria or viruses as vectors to carry the recombinant DNA.[3]

15.3 THE REALITY OF GM FOOD

Genetically modified food has already become an aspect of our daily lives as consumers. In most parts of the world, people are – usually without knowing – already consuming GM food.

Genetically modified organisms (GMOs) for human consumption have been vehemently rejected in a number of European countries. Consumer protests have brought about an initial

[1] It does not analyze the usage of GMOs for medical and therapeutic application, as this needs to be investigated independently giving due appreciation to Islamic concepts applicable in medical treatments and their individual permissibility.

[2] "Genetically Modified Organism," *Wikipedia*, https://en.wikipedia.org/wiki/Genetically_modified_organism.

[3] Sharon Walker, *Biotechnology Demystified* (New York: McGraw Hill, 2007), 119f.

ban on GM in some countries (like Austria), although we can perceive that the initially quite restrictive policy is currently being alleviated. Other major industrial countries, like the United States or China, are in general more GMO industry friendly in their legal and economic policies.

Currently, a number of transgenic plants and livestock for human consumption, and highly processed food making use of GM products, are already on the market; others are still in their trial stage. Transgenic plants for human consumption incorporate potatoes, tomatoes, corn, soy, and others, while medical applications, for example, the production of transgenic animals that produce medicine-enriched milk or eggs, are still under development. Transgenic plants that are engineered to produce medication destined for human consumption include tobacco leaves designed by CropTech Corporation, corn producing human monoclonal antibodies against rheumatoid arthritis (Biolex Therapeutics), and trypsin for the biomedical research market (ProdiGene). A number of other trials for medical purposes can be added.[4] Transgenic bananas containing inactivated viruses that cause cholera, hepatitis B, and diarrhea are currently under evaluation. The consumption of these bananas would immunize the consumer against these illnesses.[5] Pathogen resistance aims at engineering resistance to viruses. A transgenic variety of papaya, UH Rainbow, which is now produced in Hawaii, has been engineered to be resistant to the papaya ringspot virus.[6] In the field of agricultural production, GM plants and, to a lesser extent, GM livestock are already a reality. Globally 50 percent of all soybeans are transgenic. In the US, 90 percent of the soybeans and 75 percent of the corn are genetically transformed.[7] The traits engineered into the crops incorporate qualitative and quantitative changes[8] and can be summarized under resistance against insects, pathogens, and herbicide tolerance[9] as well as faster growth. In the realm of livestock, transgenic salmon with a faster and higher growth rate, as developed by Aqua Bounty Technology, has been much criticized due to its ability to decimate the natural fish population by outcrossing. A number of companies are currently developing transgenic faster-growing animals like sheep, pigs, and turkey.[10]

15.4 CONTEMPORARY *IFTĀʾ* AND THE *MAQĀṢID* SCHEME

Contrary to the unanimous prohibition of human cloning, most *fiqh* scholars do not advocate a ban on cloning and the use of genetic engineering in the realm of animals and plants. In this field, it is the increase of agro-economic production and "improvement of the kind," exactly the same argument put forward against human cloning, which is praised as the benefit of genetic engineering.

The Islamic Fiqh Academy in Jeddah pronounced the following statement in 1997: "It is legally permissible (in Islam) to make use of the techniques of cloning and genetic engineering in the fields of bacteria and other microbiological organisms as well as animals and plants, in the framework of the Islamic legal (*sharʿī*) rules, in what realizes benefits and turns away harm."[11]

4 Ibid., 173.
5 Ibid.
6 Ibid., 190.
7 Ibid., 188.
8 Mohammad Tarique al-Rahman, Abdullah al-Ma'mun, and Abu Saim Md. Shahabuddin, "Genetic Modification of Natural Products for Human Consumption: Islamic Perspective," *Proceedings of the International Conference on Biotechnology Engineering: ICBioE '07* (Kuala Lumpur: IIUM Printing, 2007), 144.
9 Walker, *Biotechnology*, 188.
10 Ibid., 198.
11 The announcement's full text is reproduced in Ḥusayn Faḍl Allāh et al., *al-Istinsākh: jadal al-ʿilm wa-l-dīn wa-l-akhlāq* (Damascus: Dār al-Fikr, 1997), 232ff. See also *Resolutions and Recommendations of the Council of the Islamic Fiqh Academy 1985–2000* (Jeddah: Islamic Fiqh Academy, 2000), https://zulkiflihasan.wordpress.com/wp-content/uploads/2009/12/majma-fiqh.pdf, 12.

Since the first steps in genetic engineering have been undertaken, a number of reputable scholars have pronounced their *ijtihād* on related questions. The Syrian scholar Wahba al-Zuḥaylī clearly advocates the benefits this kind of cloning promises mankind, from increasing the productivity of plants to making use of animals for pharmacological aims, and so on. Reproducing animal or plant cell material in the lab and changing the qualities of genes or removing genetic defects are permissible as this constitutes a benefit for mankind or removes harm from them, given that research abstains from playing with creation and avoids things that are of no benefit.[12]

Naṣr Farīd Wāṣil, former chief mufti of Egypt, expounds on the permissiveness of anything leading to the benefit of mankind that does not involve experiments on the human being, such as healing incurable diseases, increasing water supply, and fighting poverty. Such measures are demanded by Islamic law (*maṭlūb shar'an*).[13] More often than not, the question of biotechnology in food and elsewhere is answered on the basis of a scheme of benefit and harm, *maṣlaḥa* and *maḍarra*.[14] It is quite striking that the *fiqhī* discourse on GMF remains in the generality of this paradigm without going into the details of *shar'ī* benefits and harms, assessing their authenticity and conditions with regard to GMOs and weighing them. As a matter of fact, a scrutiny of some cases reveals that the paradigm of benefit and harm runs danger of being superseded by a rather materialistic value system. Whatever is considered a "benefit" within a system based on profit maximization is not necessarily "beneficial" in the sense of *maqāṣid al-sharī'a*. Negative side effects like free and uncontrolled mutations of plants, possible effects on human health, or the equilibrium of creation are hardly discussed as impeding harms in this field. Another striking characteristic in the scholarly discussion to date is that there is hardly any consideration of the probability factor which is inherent to experimental sciences. What *might* accrue in terms of benefit is often treated as a real or existent benefit, whereas the impeding dangers remain unconsidered.

It has to be observed that *iftā'* in the field of genetic engineering generally and GM food particularly hardly evaluates holistic considerations. There are a number of reasons for this phenomenon, of which we ought to be aware. One of these concerns is the procedure of *iftā'* itself. *Iftā'* generally relates to an individual case and is an isolated legal statement on this case. Furthermore, it is very often enacted as a reaction to cases arising from a non-Islamic background and, in the absence of Islamic governance, mistaken for policymaking. It may well be that the mufti looks at a particular GM potato and, after investigation, does not find any evidence to declare its consumption as haram. However, he ought to be aware of the economic and political rationale of the existence of this GM product in his hand *and* the implications of his fatwa. If he simply declares the end product as halal, he automatically gives the green light for import, trade, production, and research. These diverse fields may be subject to different considerations, though. In other words, before declaring it as halal, we should ask: Why should anybody genetically modify this potato? What is the rationale behind this? What are the procedures involved? What consequences does this food have on the environment, human

[12] Faḍl Allāh et al. *al-Istinsākh*, 124f.

[13] Ḥusām al-Dīn Shihāda et al., *al-Istinsākh bayn al-'ilm wa-l-falsafa wa-l-dīn* (Damascus: Markaz al-'Ilm wa-l-Dirāsa wa-l-Nashr, 1998), 126f.

[14] The theory of *maqāṣid*, or the higher objectives of Islamic law, has been formulated by outstanding scholars like Imam al-Shāṭibī in his *Muwāfaqāt*. In a nutshell, it postulates that Islamic law has been revealed to acquire benefits in this world and the afterlife, and to ward off harm from humankind. The main objectives as authenticated by Islamic law are described as "the religion of Islam" and "the Islamic way of life itself" (religion, life, intellect, offspring, and property). Contemporary references to the higher objectives, however, often remain vague and decontextualized.

health, and the local and global economy? After considering all these factors, even the consumption of this potato itself may deserve a second and third thought. A reduction of Islamic *fiqhī* deliberations on GMOs to ad hoc fatwa under separation from the larger context may indeed be harmful. Another reason concerns the contemporary bodies involved in *iftā'*. Generally, we can observe that the body involved lacks the necessary scientific expertise. With knowledge becoming more and more specialized, there is a need to exchange expertise between scholars of the different branches of the sciences, as has repeatedly been demanded.[15]

15.5 THE NECESSITY OF DERIVING THE ISLAMIC LEGAL RULE IN A HOLISTIC CONTEXT

As has been explained above, there is a need to holistically understand the issues related to biotechnology in order to be able to derive the Islamic legal rule. A vital requirement for this is to understand the paradigm of Islam and science as well as the contemporarily predominant secular model of science. This is vital because we need to understand that new developments like biotechnology have emerged from and are developed within a non-Islamic model. Without being aware of the differences between the different models, we run danger of applying Islamic principles in isolation of their sources, rationale, and objectives. The rationale of the existence of biotechnology in food and its objectives need to be evaluated as well as the relationship between Islam and science and its contemporary actualization. Therefore, this chapter deliberates Islamic legal perspectives on GM food while incorporating these holistic aspects.

The main feature of the prevalent secular (capitalist) model is the separation of life from any relation to the hereafter. Capitalist concepts of life stand for an overemphasis on materialism turning into both hedonism and exploitation. Happiness is defined as the accumulation of ever-increasing material assets and satisfaction of artificially created needs. Globalization has finalized the proliferation of a politico-economic model which had already started in the wake of colonization. The *Islamic* model of science, in contrast to this, may be described as *science as developed within the framework of an implemented Islamic reference system*.[16] It is not necessarily a scientific model derived from the texts of revelation, but rather a model that develops within the framework of the rules and guidelines stated in these texts and that does not stand in contradiction to their implications. Specific contributions can be made by Muslims working in this framework and observing the commands of their way of life (*dīn*) as well as by non-Muslims. Research findings or means not in contradiction to this framework can be incorporated. Research questions and the application of research results are in line with the macro framework and conditions as specified by Islamic law.

15.6 GM FOOD AND THE RATIONALE FOR ITS EXISTENCE

With all the variety of provisions (*rizq*), and the manifold kinds of permissible food, vegetables and fruits, meat, cereals, dairy products that Allah has provided, why should there be attempts at "genetically modifying" what is already available in abundance? The involved industries claim that improving the quality and quantity of food suits the demands of an ever-growing world population. Vitamin A-enriched rice to fight consequences of malnutrition for the children of

[15] Shaikh Mohd Saifuddeen b. Shaikh Mohd Salleh, "Ulama Must Understand Biotechnology," *New Straits Times*, September 13, 2003.
[16] References to the Islamic model of science are based on the author's suggestion.

the Third World, faster growing fish or chicken, and pesticide-immune maize plants to feed the growing world population are all part of this aspired agenda. Or are they? A number of critical scientists disbelieve these aspirations.[17]

Upon scrutiny, we will observe that most of the engineered characteristics, such as faster growth, herbicide tolerance, insect and pathogen resistance, and longer shelf life, are either expressions of trying to overcome the side effects of aggressive and highly exploitative monoculture farming methods as used in or promoted by the industrialized nations, or that they are otherwise embedded in a system of profit maximization.

Herbicide tolerance, for instance, is engineered because the usage of herbicides is vital to increase the output of crops in monoculture farming. Herbicide tolerant crops can stand huge amounts of herbicides that would kill any "traditional" crop. This kind of profit maximizing engineering does not account for the implications of an over usage of herbicides to the environment. Effects on the ground water, the consumer who involuntarily takes in even more amounts of chemicals with his regular diet, and the emergence of superweeds by outcrossing (i.e., the transference of genetic modifications to wild plants or other crops) are not accounted for. Always bearing in mind that the monopoly of these transgenic herbicide resistant plant seeds will belong to the same monopolist who provides the matching herbicides: The circle of dependence is closed.

In other words, GM here stands for the attempt to amend the mistakes of an aggressive non-sustainable agricultural system with an even bigger mistake, one whose effects on the natural order of creation cannot be overestimated.

Monocultures are prone to be a favorite feeding and breeding place for highly specialized insects, which then turn into a pest. Insect resistance is engineered into agricultural plants with genes from other species which produce biotoxins. These biotoxins then are present in the plant tissue. Larvae feeding on the plant die at an early stage of development. Among the negative effects of this "pest protection" is that insects develop resistance over time. The total amount of insecticide released into the environment is not reduced and useful insects are also among the victims. It is also to be expected that, if this characteristic is outcrossed, the overall plant–insect equilibrium will be affected.[18] It ought to be added here that crop heterogeneity and alternative agricultural methods may offer the natural alternative for pest control.[19]

Another genetic modification which speaks of changing creation in favor of a particular economic system is to prolong the shelf life of certain crops, such as tomatoes.[20] To emphasize again, these modifications are being undertaken to suit the demands of profit maximization within a capitalist economy. They do not feed the poor or enhance the quality of life.

In the end, GM in agriculture offers expensive non-sustainable solutions to problems caused by a non-sustainable agricultural system and is very swift at offering the same kind of

[17] Charles Benbrook, "Who Controls and Who Will Benefit from Plant Genomics?," *The 2000 Genome Seminar: Genomic Revolution in the Fields*, AAAS Annual Meeting, Washington, DC, February 19, 2000, http://bit.ly/431CCsm; Douglas Boucher, *The Paradox of Plenty: Hunger in a Bountiful World* (Oakland, CA: Food First, 1999); Francis Moore Lappe, Joseph Collins, Peter Rosset, and Luis Esparza, *World Hunger: Twelve Myths* (New York: Grove Press, 1998), 224.

[18] Ricarda A. Steinbrecher, "Ecological Consequences of Genetic Engineering," in Brian Tokar (ed.), *Redesigning Life? The Worldwide Challenge to Genetic Engineering* (London: Zed Books, 2001), 83f.

[19] As stated regarding a field trial in China, Yunnan province, in Youyong Zhu et al., "Genetic Diversity and Disease Control in Rice," *Nature* 406 (2000): 718–22.

[20] GM tomatoes have been developed by the Californian company Calgene under the name of Flavr Savr. The product was introduced to the market in 1994 but taken off the market later. "Genetically Modified Food," *Wikipedia*, https://en.wikipedia.org/wiki/Genetically_modified_food.

problem-creating "solutions" to the problems caused by the initial ones; in other words, the system serves itself. A molecular biologist who left her position with DuPont writes: "Agricultural biotechnology is producing commodities whose sole purpose is to profit the industry that makes them."[21]

15.7 ISLAMIC LEGAL (*FIQHĪ*) DELIBERATIONS ON CONSUMPTION, RESEARCH, AND PRODUCTION OF GMOS FOR HUMAN CONSUMPTION

It was mentioned in the beginning that we should look into the permissibility of GM food from the angle of research, production, and consumption. The reason for this division lies in the fact that, though the consumption of some GM foods, like tomatoes that incorporate fish DNA, may lack evidence to justify their prohibition, this does not necessarily mean that the research and production of these foods should be undertaken by Muslims. Current *iftāʾ* unfortunately focuses on the consumption without deliberation on research and production, while it is conceivable that the verdict on consumption will be extended to the other fields.

From the perspective of a Muslim consumer, the kind of genetic manipulation would be subject to scrutiny in the first place. Given the specified Islamic dietary rules, the first question to be asked generally would be whether any non-halal substance is involved "in the making." On this basis, the author of this chapter will look into the *consumption* of GM food first.

15.7.1 *The Legal Rule on Food*

The original rule on all substances, including food, is their permissibility (i.e., being halal) and purity (*ṭahāra*) unless there is evidence in the Quran and Sunna prohibiting them. The legal maxim "The origin of things is their permissibility as long as there is no evidence prohibiting them" is an expression of this guideline, which the majority of scholars are agreed upon.[22] This general guideline goes back to a number of verses in the Quran: "He is the One who created for you whatever is on the earth" (Q 2:29); "Did you not see that Allah made subservient to you whatever is in the heavens and the earth?" (Q 31:20). Therefore, originally, all substances (including foodstuffs) are permissible unless explicitly prohibited. The number of prohibited food items under Islamic law is comparatively few and includes pork, spilt blood, meat not slaughtered according to Islamic ritual (*al-mayta*), as well as impure animals such as mice, animals and birds of prey, and domesticated donkeys. Originally, any food that was publicly available in Islamic countries was considered to be halal, always presupposing that slaughtering, production, and processing followed Islamic rules. However, with the large amount of food and processed ingredients being imported from non-Islamic countries, and the laxity or negligence in controlling these products, the question needs to be raised whether this original general permissibility still applies.

15.7.2 *GM Food Not Incorporating Non-Halal Substances*

Can we suppose that this general permissibility applies to genetically modified food? GM food may combine DNA of different lawful or unlawful organisms. It seems that most of the fatwa

[21] Sonja E. Schmitz, "Cloning Profits: The Revolution in Agricultural Biotechnology," in Tokar, *Redesigning Life?*, 46.

[22] See Nazīh Ḥammād, *al-Mawādd al-muḥarrama wa-l-najisa fī al-ghidhāʾ wa-l-dawāʾ bayn al-naẓariyya wa-l-taṭbīq* (Beirut: Dār al-Qalam, 2004), 13ff. See also Jalāl al-Dīn ʿAbd al-Raḥmān al-Suyūṭī, *al-Ashbāh wa-l-naẓāʾir fī qawāʿid wa-furūʿ fiqh al-Shāfiʿiyya* (Beirut: Dār al-Salām, 2004), 1:66ff.

councils worldwide have pronounced GM food to be permissible for Muslim consumers, provided that no unlawful substances, for instance of porcine origin, have been used.

The major halal-certifying institutions have followed the approach that the consumption of GM food is permissible. The Islamic Jurisprudence Council (IJC) pronounced this view, and main certifiers like the Islamic Food and Nutrition Council of America (IFANCA), the main North American halal certifying body, follow the same approach.[23] In Indonesia, the Indonesian Ulema Council declared the consumption of GM food permissible "as long as it comes from plants."[24] Concerns have been raised against GM food incorporating genetic material of non-halal origin.

15.7.2.1 Benefits and Harms: Expectable Effects on the Consumer

It has been mentioned that, although scholars of *fiqh* do refer to the *maqāṣid* scheme of benefits and harms, there are certain flaws in the application of the procedure in as far as (a) most of the possible harms remain unmentioned, and (b) economic benefits (of a restricted group) may be mistaken for authentic *shar'ī* ones.

As our immediate question here is possible health effects on the consumer, it may be most appropriate to start with the legal maxim "Harm should not persist." The maxim has its roots in the hadith of the Prophet Muhammad, "There shall be no harm, nor reciprocating harm." According to al-Suyūṭī, one of the subordinate guidelines to this maxim is: "Warding off harms has priority over attracting benefits. . . . If benefit and harm are opposing each other, warding off the harm is mostly preferred, as the preoccupation of the Lawgiver with things He has forbidden is stronger than His preoccupancy with what He has ordered."[25]

On this basis, we should take the benefits and harms of GMOs for human consumption into closer consideration. It ought to be stated here that considered benefits, or *maṣāliḥ*, have to be established as *shar'ī* benefits, meaning they are authentic in that the texts testify to them, and through this testimony in accordance with the higher purposes and limits set by the Lawgiver, Allah. Al-Ghazālī (d. 505 AH/1111 AD) emphasizes the difference between the benefits as intended by the Lawgiver – which need to be observed – and benefits as defined by humans.[26] As the preceding sections have shown, the real purposes and rationale behind GMOs are not necessarily valid *shar'ī* benefits. Further scrutiny may show that there are texts establishing the *maṣlaḥa* involved as nullified (*mulghāt*).[27]

If we were to classify the *maṣlaḥa* involved in this case as one that does not have an origin in the texts, neither to the positive nor to the negative (unrestricted benefit/*maṣlaḥa mursala*) and wanted to follow al-Ghazālī's demands for the acceptance of such,[28] we would arrive at the following conclusions: (1) The benefit involved does not qualify as necessity in the sense that GMF does not cover any of the established objectives of sharia (*dīn*, life, intellect, offspring, property) on an essential level. (2) It is not definitive in that the realization of the "benefit"

[23] It is worth annotating here that certification by IFANCA is recognized and accepted by the Majlis Ulama Indonesia (MUI), the Majlis Ugama Islam Singapura (MUIS), the Muslim World League, Saudi Arabia, and the government of Malaysia. K. Hazzah, "Are GMOs Halal?," *AgBioWorld*, August 4, 2000, www.agbioworld.org/biotech-info/religion/halal.html.

[24] "Muslim Council Approves GM Food," *The Jakarta Post*, July 8, 2003, www.agbioworld.org/biotech-info/religion/muslim-council.html.

[25] al-Suyūṭī, *al-Ashbāh*, 1:215.

[26] Abū Ḥāmid al-Ghazālī, *al-Mustaṣfā min 'ilm al-uṣūl* (Egypt: Dār Qādir, 1904), 1:286f.

[27] Ibid., 284ff.

[28] Ibid., 296.

involved is anything but certain. (3) It is not universal in that GM food has not proven to be a cure for world hunger and a benefit for mankind as propagated, but rather an economic asset for a limited number of multinational companies. With patenting and copyright being active, it has already proven to be an additional means to curb rather than enhance development for those who need it most, the developing countries.

What may be stated about actual, impeding, and possible harms? It is often argued – mainly by advocates of GM food – that there is no substantial evidence to state that GM food is dangerous for human consumption. As a matter of fact, such evidence demands independent long-term research into the respective effects. Negative health effects caused by the consumption of GM food may only materialize after decades. The question, however, remains as to whether these effects will then be led back to their origin, with the growing complexity and interdependence of the mechanisms involved.

Side effects on the consumer have either not been sufficiently researched, or the research has been carried out by the very companies that advocate its usage. Independent research hardly exists, as critics mainly in NGO (nongovernmental organization) platforms frequently comment.[29] Some negative side effects, however, are distinguishable, whereas others will probably only materialize after years of consumption. In addition, research on side effects will naturally focus on what is already known. We should not forget that, as GM food is a new phenomenon, science may not know which side effects to search for in the first place, so that some phenomena appearing after decades may not be linked back to GM food at all.

Is it justifiable to expose millions of consumers to a gigantic field trial with nutrition whose negative effects and possible harms on health, the environment, and ecosystems are unknown?

A number of countries have not legalized GMOs for human consumption but allow it as animal feed. With the human being standing at the top of the food chain, possible negative side effects may be retarded or delayed but not prevented. In this respect, we may think of the critical effect of animal feed in the dissemination of Creutzfeldt-Jakob disease, or "mad-cow disease."[30]

As to the consumption of GM food not incorporating any non-halal substances, it may be considered permissible on a superficial level. The consumer who knowingly consumes this kind of food does thereby not acquire a sin. However, in view of impeding health dangers, a conscious consumption of GMOs ought to be avoided, and relevant authorities should undertake what is in their means to protect consumers from the expectable and unexpected side effects.

What may be stated at this point is that a lot of insecurity is involved in GMOs for human consumption. In the absence of hard data as to its health innocuousness it ought to be treated as doubtful and be avoided in individual consumption – just like any other harmful food.

The case may be different if the food in question has been proven to be so harmful that the consumer knowingly and intentionally exposes his life and health to major types of harm. In this case, a straightforward prohibition would be in place.

The import of GMOs of this kind into the Islamic world ought to be restricted as much as possible. In case of import, the relevant authorities should take all the necessary measurements to impose labelling and leave the last choice to the informed consumer.

Again, the initial question should be that of the rationale of the existence of GM food. Is there an authentic need to produce this kind of food? Or is it rather the material interests of a number of producers that stand at the beginning of the idea?

29 See Tokar, *Redesigning Life?*

30 The *fiqhī* implications of consuming animal products feeding on impure food stuffs are treated under the principle of *jallāla* (Section 15.7.2.5).

15.7.2.2 GMOs Incorporating Non-Halal Substances

In an Islamic context, impermissible organisms and substances such as pork, or dog, mice, birds and animals of prey, or even animal droppings or other waste products would not be made use of for the production of food from the outset. At this point, the different models and approaches of science and their being embedded in a particular way of life come to bear.

However, the question remains as to whether a Muslim may consume GM food produced by others containing genetic material of these impermissible origins; part of our reality being that a great number of processed foods, fruits and vegetables, milk, and meat products on the markets of the Islamic world are produced in and imported from non-Islamic countries.

15.7.2.3 The Principle of *Istiḥāla* and Its Applicability to GMOs Incorporating Non-Halal Substances

The meaning of *istiḥāla*, or transformation, of a substance according to the scholars of *fiqh* is "the change of the substance or transformation of its reality into a different reality."[31]

According to a more modern specialist definition, *istiḥāla* is "the change of a substance into another, different substance, with different physical and chemical characteristics, as a result of chemical changes in the elementary structure of the substance."[32]

Istiḥāla or the (chemical) transformation of a substance has more particularly been described by legal scholars with regard to wine (*khamr*) turning into vinegar. According to the majority view, alcohol is considered to be impure (*najis*). The majority view also states that it may become pure by *istiḥāla*, the chemical transformation into vinegar. Decisive for the permissibility of vinegar is that, first, Prophetic hadith testify to it, and second, the rationale for prohibiting alcohol, its intoxicating quality, is not to be found in vinegar. As articulated in the *uṣūl al-fiqh* maxim "*al-ḥukm yadūru maʿa ʿillatihi wujūdan wa ʿadaman*" ("the legal rule turns with its rationale in presence and absence"), the ruling depends on its effective cause. Thus, when wine transforms into vinegar, the intoxicating property – the *ʿillah* of prohibition – ceases to exist, and vinegar becomes permissible.[33]

However, a prohibition would become effective if the transformation takes place with external influence, for instance by inserting bread, salt, or other substances into the wine, or by moving it from the sun into the shadow, or vice versa. The majority of scholars are agreed that artificial induction of the transformation process does not render the resulting vinegar pure. Another reason for the prohibition of inducing the transformation process is that it would involve material benefits from an unlawful substance, alcohol.

15.7.2.4 The Principle of *Istihlāk* (Extreme Dilution) and Its Applicability to GMOs

There is a strong relationship between the principles of *istihlāk* and *istiḥāla*, in as far as the dissolved substance may also be said to have transformed in terms of developing into a different substance with different characteristics.

[31] Muḥammad Amīn Ibn ʿĀbidīn, *Ḥāshiyat Radd al-muḥtār ʿalā al-durr al-mukhtār: sharḥ tanwīr al-abṣār* (Beirut: Dār al-Kutub al-ʿIlmiyya, 1994), 1:520.

[32] Muḥammad Maḥmūd al-Ḥawarī, "al-Ṭaʿām wa-l-sharāb bayn al-ḥalāl wa-l-ḥarām," paper presented at the Eighth Medical Fiqh Conference of the Islamic Organisation of Medical Sciences, Kuwait, 1995, 19, quoted in ʿAbd al-Ghafūr b. Bashīr Azyuf, "Naẓarāt fī mustajidāt al-ghadhāʾ wa-l-dawāʾ, dirāsa taḥlīliyya naqdiyya" (master's thesis, International Islamic University Malaysia, 2004), 35.

[33] Abū Isḥāq al-Shāṭibī, *al-Muwāfaqāt fī uṣūl al-sharīʿah*, (Cairo: Dār al-Kutub al-ʿIlmiyya, 1997), 2:302–305.

The term *istihlāk* comprises two meanings: first, the usage or consumption of property; and second, mixing a substance with another one in a way that makes its inherent characteristics vanish. They may be said to be "consumed" by the properties and characteristics of the other substance.[34]

The implication of this *fiqhī* principle is the following: If a substance which is forbidden (*muḥarram*) for consumption, or impure (*najis*) in small quantities, is mixed with a pure and permissible substance, with the result that the mixture does not show any properties of the impure substance in taste, color, or smell, the mixing has taken away the characteristics of impurity and impermissibility. In other words, as the substance does not show any properties that would lead to its prohibition, it becomes permissible to use or to consume.[35]

This *fiqhī* principle is based on the following hadith: "Ibn ʿUmar said: I heard the Prophet, when he was asked about any water source which is being frequented by animals of prey and other animals, say: 'If water reaches [the amount of] two jars (*qulla*), it does not carry any impure substance.'"[36] According to Ibn Taymiyya (d. 729 AH/1328 AD), the large quantity here can be taken as an indicator that the reason for establishing the rule of prohibition is that the impurity generally is apparent. If it is consumed (by mixing), it is not apparent anymore. Therefore, the substance is not prohibited.[37] We may conclude that if an impure substance is – rather accidentally – mixed with a pure substance, it does not render the result impure, provided that a total reversion has taken place. The same would apply for small amounts of alcohol being mixed into a liquid, the end result not showing the characteristic of intoxication.[38]

It seems to me that the scholars' intention in these fatwas was to safeguard people's property from destruction. The examples given seem to relate to the accidental and unintentional mixing of lawful with unlawful substances; the scholars usually refer to donkeys, pigs,[39] or dogs[40] falling into salt (mills), ashes of waste attached to bread,[41] mice falling into grease,[42] and other very practical real life incidents of their times.

15.7.2.5 The Principle of *Jallāla* and Its Applicability to GMOs

Scholars of *fiqh* have discussed the principle of *jallāla* and its permissibility, the term *jallāla* describing an animal that feeds on unlawful substances (*jalla*).[43] Are its meat and products, such as eggs and milk, permissible for consumption?

The scholars' views on when exactly an animal comes under the *ḥukm* (ruling) of *jallāla* differ. For the Maliki school, the animal comes under the rule by consuming any amount of *jalla*. For the Shafiʿi school, it qualifies as *jallāla* if the smell of impure food is to be found in its sweat or otherwise. The actual amount of *jalla* taken in is not relevant. The third view states that

34 See Ḥammād, *al-Mawādd al-muḥarrama*, 26.
35 Ibid.
36 Narrated by Abū Dāwūd, al-Tirmidhī, al-Nasāʾī, and Ibn Mājah. See ibid., 27.
37 Quoted in ibid.
38 ʿAbdullāh b. Muḥammad b. Aḥmad al-Ṭarīqī, *al-Iḍṭirār ilā al-aṭʿima wa-l-adwiyya al-muḥarrama* (Riyadh: Maktabat al-Maʿārif, 1992), 227.
39 Ibn ʿĀbidīn, *Radd al-muḥtār*, 1:534.
40 ʿAlāʾ al-Dīn Masʿūd al-Kāsānī, *Kitāb badāʾiʿ al-ṣanāʾiʿ fī tartīb al-sharāʾiʿ* (Beirut: Dār Iḥyāʾ al-Turāth al-ʿArabī, 2000), 1:243.
41 Ibn ʿĀbidīn, *Radd al-muḥtār*, 1:534.
42 al-Kāsānī, *Kitāb badāʾiʿ al-ṣanāʾiʿ*, 1:207, 225.
43 Walīd Khālid al-Rabīʿ, *Aḥkām al-aṭʿima fī al-fiqh al-Islāmī: dirāsa muqārana* (Amman: Dār al-Nafāʾis li-l-Nashr wa-l-Tawzīʿ, 2008), 57.

the animal comes under this rule when most of its fodder consists of *jalla*; in this case, its meat changes and the consumption is disliked (*makrūh*).[44]

As for the consumption of *jallāla*, Mālik b. Anas (d. 179 AH/795 AD) and al-Ḥasan al-Baṣrī (d. 110 AH/737 AD) declare it permissible as the animal does not become impure by consuming impure food. This view is based on the analogy to the consumer of wine whose body does not become impure, and the non-Muslim who consumes prohibited food and is not considered to be impure in himself.[45]

The second view, advocated mainly by the Hanafis and parts of the Shafiʿi school, is that the consumption is discouraged. The third view, propounded by al-Shāfiʿī (d. 204 AH/820 AD), Aḥmad (d. 241 AH/855 AD) (in one transmitted view), and al-Thawrī (d. 161 AH/778 AD), states that the meat of this animal may only be consumed after a period of confinement – which may last as long as the smell is present, or for a period of three days (which was the practice of Ibn ʿUmar) for birds and other animals alike; or a confinement according to the species – three days for birds, seven for sheep, and forty for camels and cows (according to Aḥmad), or, according to the Hanafi school, forty for the camel, twenty for the cow, ten for the sheep, and three days for the chicken.[46] Again, as some contemporary voices may refer (or already have alluded to)[47] this principle, we ought to look at its transferability to GMOs.

First and foremost, feeding on impure food stuff in no way compares to changing the genetic blueprint. The impure food would remain in the consuming animal's system for a certain period of time but then disappears as well as any trace of it in smell, taste, or otherwise. There is no exchange or mutation in the genetic blueprint of either the impure food or the animal that feeds on it. As a precautionary measure, some scholars have, as we have seen, asked for a particular period of time to consume the products of this organism, to safeguard that any non-halal substance has completely vanished from the system. To apply *jallāla* to making use of non-halal organisms in the production of GMOs is indeed an improper analogy.

15.7.2.6 "If Halal and Haram Are Mixed, the Haram Predominates"

The scholars of *fiqh* have formulated other principles that may be of relevance to our case. Among them is the principle "When halal and haram are mixed, the haram is predominant."[48]

Al-Suyūṭī (d. 911 AH/1505 AD) mentions as examples for this, "When the properly slaughtered meat is mixed with not properly slaughtered meat, or cow milk is mixed with donkey milk, or water with urine, none of this is consumed; not even by *ijtihād*, as long as [the substances] are not kept in different containers, because of their being mixed with haram."[49]

This principle seems to be more relevant in its application to GM food as we may not be able to define the apparent characteristics of GMOs and evaluate possible changes and their results.

If we evaluate the case of GMOs incorporating substances from non-halal organisms on the basis of this principle, that is, if we look at it from the perspective of the mixture of two different substances, one being lawful and the other one unlawful, we would give the GMO the rule of

44 Ibid.

45 Ibid.

46 Ibid., 57ff.

47 Abu Bakr Abdul Majeed, "Genethics: Integrating Ethical Reasoning and Scientific Findings," in Abu Bakr Abdul Majeed (ed.), *Bioethics: Ethics in the Biotechnology Century* (Kuala Lumpur: Institute of Islamic Understanding Malaysia, 2002), 78.

48 al-Suyūṭī, *al-Ashbāh*, 1:252.

49 Ibid., 254.

being unlawful (haram). This position has been taken by the Malaysian National Fatwa Council for Islamic Affairs. It concluded in a special meeting on July 12, 1999, that "products, foods and drinks processed by involving swine DNA is against Islamic law and considered *Haram*."[50]

Accordingly, the consumption of the end product would fall under the same rule as the consumption of pork itself. Although the usage of pork and its derivatives will definitely be the most common case of non-halal substances and the one this chapter expounds on most, the list does not end here. I suggest that whatever organism comes under the rule of haram in Islam would fall under the prohibition of usage in combination with other, halal organisms. The end product would be permissible only in a case of utter necessity, namely the permissibility to consume otherwise prohibited food in a case of starvation. This exception does not apply in the *manufacturing* of food.

15.7.2.7 Evaluating from the Outward Appearance

Another approach would be to merely look at the outward appearance of the GMO. If it looks like a tomato, it would be given the rule of one, even if it contains porcine DNA. The GMO looking like a chicken, or having majority chicken characteristics, but having porcine DNA in its genetic blueprint, would be treated as a chicken, and therefore considered to be halal for consumption. *Fiqh* scholars have discussed the status of animals and plants with mixed characteristics, namely characteristics of lawful and unlawful organisms with different results. Al-Suyūṭī gives this example under his discussion of the legal principle "The original status of things is their permissibility, until an evidence proves their prohibition." What comes under this maxim is the animal whose status is unclear; there are two views to it, the more correct one being its permissibility.

As in the cases discussed above, there are a number of incongruities which may stand against the simple transfer or analogy to GMOs. From the outset, we know that genetic material of unlawful organisms has been *deliberately* inserted. In this case, the evidence of prohibition is already there – given that the knowledge about this manipulation is transparent and accessible. The above-mentioned examples of evaluation may come into consideration for the consumer who intends to buy a chicken and is unaware or not able to assess non-halal genetic components – given that genetic manipulation is not labelled. It does not cater as a guideline to work out an original rule on the procedure, production, and the status of the GMO.

15.7.2.8 The Principle of *Ḍarūra* and Its Applicability on GMOs in Consumption and Production

Ḍarūra may be defined in *sharʿī* terms as the state in which something prohibited is acquired, in case the legally responsible person (*mukallaf*) fears that he will otherwise die or that a substantial harm will meet him, his body, property, or honor.[51] The principle of *ḍarūra* has been derived from a number of texts, among them the following Quranic verse: "And who has been forced [by necessity] without wanting it or transgressing, there is no sin on him" (Q 2:173).[52]

The basic idea of *ḍarūra* is that the Lawgiver, Allah, considered it as an exceptional state which takes away the original legal rule of prohibition. However, the state of *ḍarūra* needs to meet two conditions: First, all the available legal ways of overcoming the state of necessity have

50 Abdul Majeed, "Genethics," 78.
51 Ḥammād, *al-Mawādd al-muḥarrama*, 35.
52 See also Q 5:3.

been exhausted and undertaking the prohibited action is the only way left. Should there be any other alternatives, the case and thereby the rule of *ḍarūra* does not apply. Second, *ḍarūra* is to be measured according to the minimal limit necessary to ward it off. The person does not indulge in making use of it, but rather consumes or uses only as much as is needed to cover the immediate emergency.[53] In the framework of the contemporary discussion on food shortage and increasing prices, voices may be raised to apply the rule of necessity or "necessity renders the prohibited lawful" to the consumption and production of GM food.

The idea of food shortage, in the first place, is rather based on a misconception of current global economics in the food sector. The reality is that food is available in adequate quantities, but that is not accessible to growing numbers of people, due to market manipulation, over exporting, and high prices; in other words, man-made factors.[54]

Are GM technologies an answer to this problem? Due to the research and development costs, GM technologies in the production of food make the end product more expensive and thereby even less affordable. They do not cater for an increase in availability at all. As they are subject to the same economic rules, it is to be expected that a larger share of GM food on the market would lead to an aggravation of the current problem of accessibility of food.

In addition, it ought to be noted that the patenting of GMOs for consumption will lead to an even more dominant monopolization of the food market with dire consequences for producers and consumers alike, mainly in countries of the developing world.

The applicability of the principle of *ḍarūra* to GM food is therefore more than limited; it actually applies only in the case of immediate starvation with the existence of GMOs which are prohibited in nature – and only in as far as it covers the immediate need.

The production and research on GM food incorporating non-halal substances is not covered by this principle. All the same, *ḍarūra* would not cater as an argument for the production of GMOs incorporating only halal substances – there is no case for *ḍarūra* in advance planning.

15.8 CONCLUSION: THE TRANSFERABILITY OF THE ABOVE LEGAL MECHANISMS AND PRINCIPLES TO GMOS FOR HUMAN CONSUMPTION

In assessing the transferability of the above discussed principles and guidelines to the GMO status under Islamic law, the rationale of using non-halal substances should be considered in the first place. From an Islamic point of view, the usage of these substances for any product, be it destined for consumption or usage, is not acceptable. The usage of an unlawful substance, or accruing material benefits from it, is not a lawful endeavor under *fiqh*.

I suggest that enzymes, proteins, and other genetic or biochemical material should be considered as part of the *ʿayn*, namely the substance or organism they pertain to and have been taken from, even if they are to a large extent identical with matching materials from other organisms.[55] As such, they would take the rule (*ḥukm*) of the organism they are taken from.

As we have seen, the principles of *istiḥāla, istihlāk*, and *jallāla* are not transferable to the GMO case.

Both *istihlāk* and *istiḥāla* rely on the change or transformation of the substance due to the loss of its characteristics. If the characteristics of the forbidden substance, or rather the characteristics

[53] Ḥammād, *al-Mawādd al-muḥarrama*, 35f.; al-Suyūṭī, *al-Ashbāh*, 1:212.

[54] Mohammad Tariqur Rahman and Abu S. M. Shihabuddin, "Waste Not Want Not," *Islamic Horizons*, March 2009, 28–31.

[55] As a matter of fact, a protein or enzyme is still distinguishable as being of bovine or porcine origin.

which are responsible for prohibiting this substance, are not identifiable in the end product anymore, the latter would take the rule of permissibility.

Both principles rely on the distinctiveness of apparent attributes (*ṣifāt ẓāhira*), which are identifiable as constituting the impurity of a substance. If the rationale and its apparent characteristics underlying the prohibition of a substance are not known, that is, it cannot be established through the known methodology the mujtahid (jurist) usually refers to, these principles may not be applicable at all. But even in case the rationale is known, the limitation to genetic information is not – or not yet – possible.

The insertion of genetic material of an organism into another organism means to bring about a genetic combination with no precedent in biological history and one that would not have occurred naturally. It is not comparable to a simple mixture of two different substances. Even if the quantitative role of an enzyme seems negligible, its qualitative function surely is not.

Also, the intentional induction of the mixture would defy the usage of both principles, *istihlāk* as well as *istiḥāla*, to legitimize the end product.

The principle of *jallāla* seems not to be transferable for the reasons stated above. The same applies to *ḍarūra*, with the knowledge that the consumption of a GMO, should it come under the rule of prohibition, would only be permissible under *ḍarūra* in cases of starvation.

Again, judging from the outward appearance of a GMO – in case it is a developed animal or plant – may be an option on a consumer level, and it may serve as a guideline for a consumer who does not know and cannot verify whether this GMO incorporates non-halal DNA. In this case, the consumer can indeed only judge from the outward appearance. However, if the details of the incorporation of non-halal organisms are provided, the author of this chapter comes to the conclusion that judging from the outward appearance is not an option.

Of the principles discussed above, it seems to me that the only one applicable is the guideline that if halal and haram are mixed, the haram overweighs. On this basis, any organism destined for consumption that incorporates haram substances in its DNA as result of genetic manipulation should take the ruling of being haram.

The chapter has shown that the current *iftā'* procedure often acts out of the Islamic context. *Fiqhī* deliberations on GM food need to take into account the rationale of its existence as well as the societal and scientific model under which it was developed. The contemporary reference to *maqāṣid* often seems to mistake non-*shar'ī* benefits for authentic benefits (*maṣāliḥ*).

Even though there may not be clear-cut evidence for the prohibition of GM food not incorporating non-halal substances, the possible negative side effects on the consumer as well as the proven effects on the ecosystems render it more than doubtful. The case of GMOs combining non-halal substances, however, seems to be clear. *Istiḥāla, istihlāk, jallāla,* and other related legal instruments cannot be transferred to this case to legitimize an end product deliberately inducing genetic material from non-halal sources.

In conclusion, substances taken from prohibited organisms are to be given the same rule as the organism they have been taken from, even on a microbiological level. A mixture of halal and non-halal substances would take the rule of being non-halal.

As to the production and research with GMOs for consumption combining only halal substances, the author's recommendation is that Muslims should seriously reevaluate their participation in the field as it would come under the meaning of changing Allah's creation in unlawful ways. The consumption of such products, even if evidences may not be sufficient to declare it as prohibited for the moment, should be avoided as far as possible – for Muslim and non-Muslim consumers alike – due to inherent and impeding harms.

16

Sheikh Asim Farooq v. Federation of Pakistan

A Case Study

Jawad Hassan

16.1 EDITORS' NOTE

The legal battle of *Sheikh Asim Farooq v. Federation of Pakistan* emerges against a backdrop of profound ecological crisis that has been decades in the making. Pakistan's environmental trajectory tells a story of rapid degradation, systemic neglect, and urgent need for transformative intervention. The nation's forest cover – a critical indicator of ecological health – has plummeted to a mere 1.9 percent of its national territory, positioning Pakistan among the most critically deforested countries in Asia. This is not merely a statistic but a dire warning of impending environmental catastrophe. The roots of this ecological decline are deeply intertwined with complex socioeconomic and historical factors. Colonial-era land management practices, postindependence developmental models, and rapid urbanization have consistently prioritized economic expansion over environmental preservation. Each hectare of forest lost represents more than just trees, it signifies the erosion of biodiversity, disruption of ecological balance, and fundamental threats to human and environmental security.

The consequences of deforestation extend far beyond immediate landscape changes. Reduced forest cover has precipitated a cascade of environmental challenges: increased soil erosion, diminished water retention, compromised air quality, and heightened climate vulnerability. Forests are not merely passive landscapes but active ecological systems that regulate climate, support biodiversity, and provide critical ecosystem services. Their systematic removal threatens not just local ecosystems but contributes to broader regional and global environmental instability. The legal strategy employed in *Sheikh Asim Farooq v. Federation of Pakistan* represented a groundbreaking approach to environmental jurisprudence. By strategically invoking Articles 9, 14, 26, and 38(b) of Pakistan's Constitution, the petitioners constructed a sophisticated argument that repositioned environmental protection as a fundamental constitutional right. Article 9's guarantee of life and liberty was reinterpreted beyond its traditional understanding. No longer was life viewed as mere physical existence but as a holistic concept intrinsically dependent on environmental quality. The right to a clean and safe environment was positioned as a prerequisite for meaningful human life, challenging narrow interpretations of constitutional protections. Similarly, Article 14's protection of human dignity was expanded to encompass freedom from environmental harm. Pollution, ecological degradation, and environmental neglect were framed as direct assaults on human dignity, a profound reimagining of constitutional rights that connected individual well-being with ecological conditions. Articles 26 and 38(b) further broadened the constitutional framework. Equal access to public spaces was reinterpreted to include green spaces, parks, and forests as critical social infrastructure. The state's obligation to ensure well-being was linked directly to ecological sustainability, creating a comprehensive approach to environmental governance.

The court's approach drew from a rich array of legal doctrines that elevated environmental jurisprudence beyond traditional boundaries. The public trust doctrine emerged as a particularly powerful conceptual framework, positioning natural resources as communal assets held in trust by the state for current and future generations. The precautionary principle was strategically deployed to shift the burden of proof to potential environmental disruptors. This approach acknowledges that environmental risks need not be conclusively proven to warrant protective action. It represents a proactive rather than reactive approach to environmental management, recognizing the potentially irreversible nature of ecological damage. Intergenerational equity became a critical philosophical and legal lens. This principle challenges presentist economic models by insisting that current developmental decisions must consider their long-term ecological and social consequences. It roots environmental protection in a broader understanding of human survival and social responsibility.

Perhaps the most innovative aspect of the judgment was the court's deployment of continuing mandamus, a revolutionary judicial approach that transformed the judiciary's role from passive arbiter to active environmental steward. Unlike traditional adjudication that produces a single, finite ruling, this mechanism allowed ongoing judicial oversight and dynamic environmental governance. Over more than a year of hearings, the court maintained active engagement with the case. Government departments were repeatedly summoned, compliance was continuously assessed, and new directives were issued as needed. This approach created a mechanism of persistent accountability, bridging the often-significant gap between legal declaration and administrative action.

The court's directives went beyond traditional legal remedies, embracing technological solutions for environmental monitoring. Geographic information system (GIS)-based tree tracking, digital mapping, and mandatory reporting mechanisms were introduced. Each tree was to be tagged and assigned a unique identification number, creating unprecedented transparency and accountability in environmental management. Municipalities, educational institutions, and housing societies were required to integrate tree plantation into their core infrastructure and planning. This approach embedded ecological awareness into institutional cultures, transforming environmental protection from an external requirement to an intrinsic organizational value.

While not explicitly cited in the judgment, the court's approach resonated deeply with Islamic environmental principles. Concepts like *khilāfa* (stewardship), *amāna* (trust), and *lā ḍarar* (prohibition of harm) provided a theological and philosophical foundation that aligned seamlessly with modern environmental jurisprudence. The Quranic understanding of humans as trustees of the earth, rather than absolute owners, offers a profound ecological ethic. This perspective challenges anthropocentric developmental models, positioning environmental protection as a sacred responsibility rather than an optional consideration.

16.1.1 *Challenges and Limitations*

The implementation of the court's judgment was not without significant challenges. Bureaucratic inertia, fragmented governance, insufficient inter-agency coordination, and political resistance created substantial obstacles. Many local authorities lacked the technical expertise and financial resources to execute large-scale reforestation or effective monitoring. However, the court's insistence on transparency, periodic compliance hearings, and clear reporting requirements ensured that these barriers did not completely derail the process. Stakeholder consultations and a commitment to ongoing oversight created mechanisms for persistent progress. The *Sheikh Asim Farooq* case is part of a broader global trend of judicial intervention in environmental protection. Similar approaches have emerged in various jurisdictions: India's river personhood declarations, Colombia's rights of nature jurisprudence, and Kenya's judicial interventions in ecological preservation. These cases collectively represent a profound shift in legal thinking, recognizing that traditional regulatory frameworks are insufficient to address complex ecological challenges. Courts are increasingly seen as critical institutions for environmental protection, especially in contexts where legislative and executive branches are constrained by short-term political pressures.

16.1.2 *Civil Society and Participatory Governance*

Civil society played a crucial role in the case's success. A network of lawyers, environmental organizations, urban planners, and community groups built public support through strategic media engagement, policy briefs, and community mobilization. The court's receptivity to this participatory approach created a unique space for democratic environmental governance. *Sheikh Asim Farooq v. Federation of Pakistan* transcends its immediate legal context. It represents a model of transformative judicial activism that reimagines constitutional rights, proposes a blueprint for ecological citizenship, and calls for systemic, rights-based environmental protection. The case demonstrates that legal systems can be powerful catalysts for environmental and social transformation. It reframes environmental harm as a fundamental rights issue, suggesting that nature's protection is not a matter of charity but a constitutional and moral imperative. As global ecological challenges intensify, such innovative legal approaches offer hope. They remind us that law is not merely a set of rules but a dynamic instrument for societal evolution and planetary survival. In an era of unprecedented environmental uncertainty, judicial creativity becomes not just admirable, but essential.

JUDGMENT SHEET

IN THE LAHORE HIGH COURT, LAHORE JUDICIAL DEPARTMENT

Writ Petition No.192069 of 2018

Sheikh Asim Farooq **V/S** *Federation of Pakistan etc*

JUDGMENT

JAWAD HASSAN, J. Through the instant petition under Article 199 of the Constitution of the Islamic Republic of Pakistan, 1973 (the "***Constitution***"), the Petitioner has sought directions to the Respondents to, inter alia:

(a) *appraise as to how the National Climate Change Policy, 2012, the National Forest Policy, 2015 and the Forest Policy Statement, 1999 have been implemented to increase the forest cover in Pakistan and Punjab;*

(b) *implement the Forest Act, 1927 (the "**Forest Act**") and the Punjab Plantation and Maintenance of Trees Act, 1974 (the "**Trees Act**") by planting trees;*
(c) *provide reasons for drastic reduction in forest cover in Pakistan particularly in Punjab,*
(d) *increase the forest cover to reach the minimum satisfactory standards of 20-25% necessary for a balanced economy;*
(e) *present a time-line map for the said purposes, and*
(f) *initiate appropriate proceedings against the delinquent officers who have failed to discharge their duties.*

...

PETITIONERS' ARGUMENTS

4. The learned counsel for the Petitioner submits that the Petitioner is a practicing advocate and filing this constitutional petition seeking, inter alia, a writ of mandamus to the Respondents for the implementation of the law and the above mentioned policies, and for enforcement and protection of his fundamental rights guaranteed under Article 9 (right of life liberty), Article 14 (right of dignity), Article 26 (right of access to public places of entertainment) and Article 38(b) (provision of available leisure places) of the Constitution. He submits that Government should implement the Forest Act, the Trees Act, the National Climate Change Policy, 2012, the National Forest Policy, 2015, the Forest Policy Statement, 1999, and the Punjab Forestry Sector (Forests, Watershed, Rangelands and Wildlife) Policy, 1999 because forest area in Pakistan is decreasing rapidly over a year with massive percentage and now as per report, is only 1.9%. He states that trees in forests and other natural resources are covered under the Doctrine of Public Trust and the Government ought to protect them for the enjoyment of the general public rather than to permit their use for private ownership or commercial purposes. He adds that the government's inaction is clearly seen by not protecting the existing forests and trees with massive cutting and also their lack of commitment in planting trees despite of mandatory requirement of Section 3 of the Trees Act. The learned counsel for the Petitioners in their respective petitions also submitted their written arguments and reiterated the contents of the petitions.

...

III. CURRENT SITUATION OF TREES AND FOREST

17. The Petitioners have attached several articles and reports showing several threats to forests, trees and environment in Punjab and Pakistan. It is unfortunate, catastrophic and shocking that the forests of the country are now almost extinct or at decreasing rate. The deforestation is leading to increase in the spread of life threatening diseases. Reports from Yale School of Forestry & Environmental Studies at Yale University and School of Public Health: Center of Health and the Global Environment at Harvard University affirm the fact that deforestation is linked with rise of deadly diseases.

18. It may be noted that the National Environment Information Management System (NEIS), a project of United Nations Development Programme (UNDP), had published a Research Report in 2010 detailing the environment and biodiversity and ecological zones in Pakistan from forests to mountains and threatened flora and fauna and threatened species of animals. The report suggests that deforestation rate in Pakistan is estimated at 0.2% to 0.5% annually, which is the highest in the world and accounts for 4-6% decline in its wood biomass per annum. The total natural forest cover has reduced from 3.59 million hectares to 3.32 million hectares at an average rate of 27,000 hectares annually. The natural resource is decreasing at

such an alarming speed that all the forest area will be consumed within the next few years. Some of the extracts from the Research Report are as follows:

1. **Pakistan is a Forest Poor Country:** Only 4.72 million hectares or 5.36% of its land mass is covered with forests. Table 1.7 of the Report suggests that there is declining forestation trend during the years 2000-2009.
2. **Environmental Benefits of Trees:** The value of intangible benefits is eight times greater than the tangible value of products and services of forestry sector. Many other— intangible — benefits are derived from forest including oxygen production, watershed value, scenic benefits, ecosystem synergism and flow, and a variety of other values essential for human health and quality of life. Forests also provide a number of crucial ecosystem services, for example, their role in sequestering carbon from the atmosphere, protecting upstream watersheds, conserving biodiversity and gene-pools for future generations and in providing landscape beauty.
3. **Biodiversity Conservation:** 60-90% of all terrestrial species are found in forests having widespread economic and medicinal uses still unknown to mankind.
4. **Forests and Carbon Sequestration:** Forests are both a source of carbon dioxide (CO_2) when they are destroyed or degraded and a sink when conserved, managed or planted sustainably. Forest vegetation and soils hold 40% of carbon stored in terrestrial ecosystems.
5. **Forests and Water Quality:** As population grows, the demand for clean drinking water becomes more acute. Besides this, need of water for agriculture, sanitation purpose, cooking needs and other uses is imperative. In Pakistan, 2 decades ago, no one had ever thought of purchasing water, but now people do purchase it, just because of depletion of forests in watersheds. Forest and plant cover are necessary to slow runoff and filter rainwater. When trees are in place, rainwater, which naturally flows downhill to the nearest stream, is slowed. Once slowed, rainwater seeps down to refill underground storage tanks or aquifers. In addition, water may be absorbed by the roots of trees and transpired by leaves so that it can cycle back for use again as rainwater. Forests prevent non-saline drinking-quality water from running off too quickly to mix with the salt water of oceans. Once salty, water takes much longer to re- enter the fresh water portion of the hydrological cycle, where it is most useful to humans.
6. **Forests and Soil Quality:** The roots of trees hold soil in place.
   Fertile soil that is needed to grow crops would otherwise be washed away in rainstorms, decreasing the amount of soil available for agriculture. Rich soil transfers nutrients to food, which contributes to human health.
7. **Biodiversity Conservation:** The forests are one of the largest repositories of biodiversity in the world. By some estimates they contain 60-90% of all terrestrial species found on the planet. Some of these could have widespread economic or medicinal uses that are still unknown to us. The conservation of these valuable genetic resources for future options that are yet undiscovered is thus a valuable service that forests provide.

...

VII. APPLICABLE LAWS ON TREES AND FORESTS

24. Under the Constitution, the subject of Forestry falls in the provincial domain of the provincial governments. The functions of the Federal Government pertaining to Forestry as per Federal Legislative List (Part-II) are limited to national planning and economic coordination, inter-provincial matters and coordination and matters incidental or ancillary thereof. The Article 151 of the Constitution and Federal Legislative List (Part-I) entitles the

Federal Government to regulate import and export of wood and forest products, inter-provincial trade and commerce, and trade and commerce with foreign countries. Constitutionally, implementation of international conventions and agreements related to forests is the sole mandate of the Federal Government.

...

29. The Precautionary Principle finds mention in the Stockholm Declaration 1972 and is enunciated in Principle 15 of the Rio Declaration 1992:

"In order to protect the environment, the precautionary approach shall be widely applied by States according to their capabilities. Where there are threats of serious or irreversible damage, lack of full scientific certainty shall not be used as a reason for postponing cost effective measures to prevent environmental degradation."

This international environmental law, namely, Precautionary Principle has been incorporated into our law through the Shehla Zia judgment and is now a settled part of our domestic jurisprudence.

...

31. The Public Trust Doctrine has been part of the international environmental law since the Stockholm Declaration, 1972 and has entered our law through the Cutting of Trees for Canal Widening Project Lahore case reported at 2011 SCMR 1743; PLD 2018 Lahore 364 – Asghar Leghari Case; 2017 PLD 545 Lahore – Lung Fung Chinese Restaurant Vs. Punjab Food Authority; 2015 SCMR 1520 – Lahore Bachao Tehrik Vs. Dr. Iqbal Muhammad Chauhan; 2015 PLD 522 Lahore – Imrana Tiwana Vs. Province of Punjab; 2015 PLD 112 Lahore – Young Doctors Association Vs. Government of Pakistan; 2011 SCMR 1743 – Cutting of Trees for Canal Widening Project Lahore; 2007 CLC 1358 Lahore – Muhammad Tariq Abbasi Vs. Defence Housing Authority.

B. **The Forest Act, 1927**

32. The Provincial Forest Act, 1927 consolidates the law relating to forests, the transit of forest-produce and the duty leviable on timber and other forest-produce etc in Punjab. Section 2 (c) defines the—forest as — *a reserved forest, protected forest, unclassed forest and village forest and includes wasteland or rangeland*. It may be noted that in the above definition, following four (4) types of forests have been described:

(a). *Sections 3 and 4 empower the Punjab Government to constitute any government forest-land or waste-land a "reserved forest" by issuing notification in the official Gazette.*

(b). *Under Section 29, the Provincial Government may, by notification in the official Gazette, extend the applicability of provisions to any government forest-land or waste-land which is not included in a reserved forest, which is called a "protected forest". Section 32 empowers the Provincial Government to make rules for protected forests.*

(c). *The Provincial Government may also declare a wasteland, not being a reserved forest or protected forest, as "unclassed forest"; and may also direct that all or any provisions of the Forest Act relating to a reserved forest or protected forest, shall apply to an unclassed forest; and may make rules for management of an unclassed forest (Section 28-A).*

(d). *Section 28 empowers the Provincial Government to assign to any village-community the rights of Government over reserved forest, which are then called "village forests". It further empowers the Provincial Government to make rules for management of a village- forest; and to prescribe conditions under which the village community may use the forest produce other than timber and pasture and duties of the village community for the protection and improvement of the forest (Section 28). It may be noted that the provisions relating to the reserved forests are also applicable to the village forests.*

33. Interestingly, the Punjab Government cannot: (a) declare or notify a reserved forest or any part of the reserved forest as being —no longer reserved forest — without the approval of the Provincial Cabinet, (b) allow change in land use of a reserved forest, except for the purposes of right of way, building of roads and development of a forest park, and (c) allow construction of concrete building or permanent structure in the reserved forest (Section 27).

34. On the other hand, the Forest Act also authorizes the Provincial Government to (a) declare any trees or class of trees in a protected forest to be reserved; (b) declare, subject to conditions, that any portion of such forest specified in the notification shall be closed for such term, not exceeding thirty years, and (c) prohibit the quarrying of stone, or the burning of lime or charcoal, or the collection or subjection to any manufacturing process, or removal of any forest-produce in any such forest, and the breaking up or clearing for cultivation, for building, for herding cattle or for any other purpose, of any land in any such forest (Section 30).

35. The Provincial Government also has power to declare forest no longer protected subject to certain restrictions (Section 34-A); to protect forests for special purposes (Section 35); to assume management of forests in case of neglect of, or willful disobedience to, any regulation or prohibition under Section 35, or if the purposes of any work to be constructed (Section 36); for expropriation of forests in certain cases (Section 37); for protection of forests at request of owners (Section 38); to impose duty on timber and other forest-produce (Section 39); to make rules to regulate transit of forest- produce (Section 41); and to movements of timber across Customs frontiers (Section 41-A).

36. Section 78-A empowers the Provincial Government to establish a forest company to oversee the implementation of public private partnership on the assigned forest land or wasteland to a forest company. Further, the Board of Directors of a forest company may be constituted with equal representation from public and private sectors to manage its functioning. The forest company is required to invite applications of eligible persons through a public notice, published in at least two national daily newspapers, for public private partnership for the development of forest on the forest land or wasteland (Section 78-B). Similarly, the Provincial Government is also authorized, itself or through a forest company, to invite proposals for the development of a forest land or wasteland, and to enter into public private partnership for the development, preservation and conservation of a forest land or wasteland, for increase in the productivity of the forest (Section 80-A).

C. The Punjab Plantation and Maintenance of Trees Act, 1974 (the "Trees Act")

37. The Trees Act has been enacted in the public interest to provide for plantation of more trees and maintenance of the same in Punjab. Section 2(c) of the Trees Act, defines "land" as the "land which is not occupied as the site of any building in a town or *village and is occupied or has been let for agricultural purposes or for purposes subservient to agriculture or for pasture, and includes the sites of buildings and other structures on such land*". Section 2(d) defines the "occupier" as "*a person in actual physical possession of the land and shall also include an owner*".

38. Section 3 requires the occupier to plant three (3) trees per acre by the occupier in the prescribed manner, and maintain the same. Section 4 imposes the penalty, in case of contravention of Section 3, of rupee one per tree, after giving an opportunity of hearing to the person concerned. Section 5 empowers the Punjab Government to make rules to carry out the purposes of the Trees Act, to provide for, among others, (a) the manner in which

trees may be planted and maintained; (b) kind of trees to be planted in different areas and the period within which the trees are to be planted; and (c) the procedure for maintaining the record of trees.

...I. **Punjab Village Forest Rules, 2013**

45. Under Rules 3 and 4, a Village Forest Committee is formed which shall suitably demarcate the boundaries of Village Forest. Under Rule 4(b), no person shall collect, cut or remove wood or other forest produce from the Village Forest. Rule 4 (2) prohibits to collect, cut or remove wood or other forest produce from the Village Forest. Rule 5 prohibits a person to cut, injure, and remove any tree grown in a Village Forest.

J. **The National Climate Change Policy, 2012**

46. The National Climate Change Policy provides a framework for addressing the issues that Pakistan faces or will face in future due to the changing climate. The policy provides a comprehensive framework for the development of Action Plans for national efforts on adaptation and mitigation. Clause 3 provides the important climate change threats to Pakistan, which include "further decrease in the already scanty forest cover, from too rapid change in climatic conditions to allow natural migration of adversely affected plant species". This Policy has also constituted the National Climate Change Policy Implementation Committee, with the Minister of Climate Change at the Federal Level as its Chairperson; and the Provincial Climate Change Policy Implementation Committee, with the Provincial Minister for Environment as its Chairperson.

47. Before going any further, it is essential to describe the climate change effect on the Forestry, as described in the National Climate Change Policy:

4.4. Forestry

Climate change is likely to have multi-faceted adverse effects on the ecosystem as a whole, particularly on the already vulnerable forestry sector in Pakistan. The most likely impacts of climate change will be decreased productivity, changes in species composition, reduced forest area, unfavorable conditions for biodiversity, higher flood risks and the like, as portrayed in the Planning Commission Task Force on Climate Change (TFCC) Report. Adaptation in the forestry sector entails the need to restore and enhance Pakistan's forests under sustainable forest management, with particular focus on how these are affected by climate change. This will not only benefit state forests but forest dependent communities and society as a whole.

This policy suggests the Policy Measures relating to the Forestry, which includes (a) the Awareness Raising, (b) Research on adaptation of forests, biodiversity and forest management systems to climate change, (c) Reforms in Governance, (d) Enhancing Adaptive Capacity, (e) Forest Management with afforestation and reforestation programs with plantation suited to the effects of climate change, (f) Arresting Soil Erosion, and (g) Reducing Forest Fires, Disease Outbreaks and Other Damage.

48. Similarly, this Policy requires the Government to take the following policy measures to conserve, restore and protect the biological diversity of Pakistan: ***(a)*** encourage empirical research on flora and fauna in the context of their responses to current and historical climatic changes; ***(b)*** set National Biodiversity Indicators and provide the requisite financial resources for implementation of the Biodiversity Action Plan (BAP); ***(c)*** establish gene banks, seed banks, zoos and botanical gardens to conserve the biological diversity of valuable

species; *(d)* Integrate conservation and protection of biological diversity into various disciplines such as forestry and marine and pastures; (e) encourage involvement of local communities in conservation and sustainable use of biodiversity; *(f)* take necessary measures to establish nature reserves in areas that are rich in biodiversity to preserve their existence; *(g)* establish protected areas in all vulnerable ecosystems, particularly in coastal and marine areas; *(h)* ensure that 'ecosystem based adaptation' is part of an overall climate change adaptation strategy at all levels (national to local); and *(i)* assist genetically impoverished species or those that have important ecosystem functions by providing natural migration corridors as well as assisted migration.

49. Similarly, in Clause 4.6.5, this Policy prescribes the importance of wetlands and requires the Government to ensure control of siltation of wetlands by reducing deforestation and felling of timber in catchment areas. Further, in Clause 5.7, this Policy requires the Government of Pakistan, in collaboration with national entities and support from multilateral agencies, to take the following policy measures in the forestry sector to sequester atmospheric carbon, thereby mitigating climate change: *(a)* set annual afforestation and reforestation targets to increase the country's forest cover; *(b)* strictly prohibit illegal forest cutting and conversion of forest land to non- forest uses; *(c)* enact and enforce laws and regulations required for addressing illegal trade in timber and de-forestation; *(d)* use the vast mass of cultivable wasteland as a carbon sink and to build up organic soil matter; *(e)* provide incentives and alternative fuel and livelihood options to forest dependent communities to prevent deforestation; *(f)* promote farm forestry practices by planting multipurpose fast-growing species to meet the needs for timber, fuel wood and fodder for livestock; *(g)* encourage and support forestry personnel in carbon forestry project development; *(h)* establish linkages with regulated and voluntary carbon markets to promote and encourage forestry mitigation projects in Pakistan; *(i)* secure financial assistance from the World Bank's Forest Carbon Partnership Facility (FCPF) and UN-REDD (Reducing Emissions from Deforestation and Forest Degradation) program as well as from other international sources to formulate a national program for avoiding deforestation and promoting forest restoration; *(j)* prepare the framework for a national REDD strategy on priority basis and ensure its implementation in accordance with international conventions/ processes; *(k)* develop the legal and institutional framework for improved forest management, investment clearly specifying rights to REDD+ credits; and *(l)* restore and establish the blue carbon sequestration capacity of mangroves, sea-grasses and tidal marshes.

50. In relation to the Awareness Raising in Clause 7(c), the Government of Pakistan, in collaboration with the relevant entities, is required to ensure advocacy and mass awareness regarding the importance of water and energy conservation, the impact of climate change on various sectors including forest ecosystems, biodiversity and so on, using mass media, public-private partnerships, students and community mobilization; and incorporate these issues into the formal education systems at all levels.

K. The National Forest Policy, 2015

51. Keeping in view certain facts, this Policy has following three (3) pronged approaches: *(a)* conserving the existing forests by curbing deforestation and promoting conservation, *(b)* bringing more trees in and outside forests by mass afforestation, involving all sections of the society, particularly on communal lands, shamlats and guzara forests, and *(c)* meet International Obligations and Opportunities through scientific planning, legal reforms and capacity building.

52. These approaches are required to be met through the strategic actions, including *(a)* Expand Forest Cover; *(b)* Mass afforestation Programme; *(c)* Integrating Forests with Economic Sectors; *(d)* Ecological Corridors; *(e)* Curb Deforestation and Promote Conservation; *(f)* Regulating Inter-Provincial Timber Movement, Commerce &Trade; *(g)* Reducing Emissions from Deforestation & Forest Degradation under the UNFCCC Agreements on Reducing Emissions from Deforestation and Forest Degradation (REDD+); *(h)* Forest Ownership and Rights; *(i)* Promote Integrated Approach of Forests, Wildlife and Biodiversity Management; *(j)* International Obligations and Opportunities under the three Rio Conventions viz: the United Nations Framework Convention on Climate Change UNFCCC, United Nations Convention to Combat Desertification UNCCD, and the Convention on Biological Diversity CBD; *(k)* Scientific Planning, Policy & Legal Reforms; *(l)* National Institution for Research, Education, Training and Monitoring;

. . .M. **Policy on Controlling Smog, 2017**

54. Paragraph 7 of the Policy EPA has to closely work with Board of Revenue to identify an air mark state land in the vicinity of large cities/town for tree plantation. Furthermore, EPA has to work with forest department to identify suitable tree species and maintain wood lands on indicated pieces of land. Under Paragraph 10, Environmental Protection Department is obligated to conceive and implement projects for greening of industrial existing units. Paragraph 11 of the Policy states that the Provincial Environmental Committee (PEC) shall oversee the implementation of this policy while coordination shall be the responsibility of Environmental Protection Department.

N. **Punjab Environment Policy, 2015**

55. Paragraph 3 of the Policy sets out the goal of the Policy to protect, conserve and restore Punjab Environment to improve quality of life of citizens. Paragraph 4 of the Policy sets out its objectives which, inter alia, includes protection, conservation and improvement of environment, prevention and control of pollution, development and management of environmental resources. Paragraph No. 7.2 recognizes that the desertification is a type of land degradation whereby lands are becoming arid losing water, vegetation and wild life. The Policy states that action is required to formulate and implement a policy for restoring the desertification at provincial and district level. Paragraph 7.9 of this Policy prescribes following actions, amongst others, to ensure sustainable management of natural forest of Punjab and increase tree cover for safeguarding the economic growth, environment, bio-diversity and food security in Punjab province: *(a)* Formulate and implement the Punjab Forest Policy to enhance forest cover up to 25% of the area of the Province to take corrective action to stop deforestation parade; *(b)* Formulate regulatory to prevent forest cutting; and *(c)* Carry out intensive institutional and legal reforms to promote good forest governance.

56. Paragraph 7.10 of the Policy sets out certain actions for conservation and sustainable views of bio-diversity and protected areas: *(a)* To create new national parks and protected areas; (*b*) Develop a comprehensive Provincial Wet Land Policy; (c) Develop Policy for conservation and cultivation of medicinal/economic plants; *(d)* Towns of low park/green belt should be converted into any other activity area; *(e)* Parks and green belt and urban areas should be improved to enhance bio-diversity.

57. Paragraph 7.12 requires that in order to address challenges pose by climate changes and to protect the ozone layer, the Government should identify areas affected by climate change and its impact on water resources, forests and agricultures. Paragraph 8.5 states that promotion of environmental education is vital to sensitize the public at large for prevention

of pollution and preservation of the environment. It proposes the following actions: *(a)* Incorporate subjection of Environment Size in all classes from primary to higher education; *(b)* Induction of —Environment Teacher at school and college levels; *(c)* All public sector universities should launch Ph.D. and M.Phill programs in subject of environment; *(d)* Introduction of short course/diplomas in public and private universities in subject of environment; *(e)* Educational Institutions should provide barriers on road sides through tree plantations; *(f)* Establishment of —Environment Clubs in all educational institutes.

58. Paragraph 11 states that "Provincial Environment Policy Implementation Committee" would be established at the provincial level for effective coordination of this policy. Provincial District and Tehsil Governments would also constitute "Policy Implementation Committee" to ensure implementation of the Policy

O. The Punjab Forest Policy, (Draft) 2018

59. Secretary Forestry, Wildlife and Fisheries Department state that pursuant to orders of this Court dated 31.01.2019, they convened a meeting and prepared draft of Punjab Forest Policy, 2018 (the "Draft Policy").
60. Deputy Director, Ministry of Climate Change states that Draft Policy has been approved by the FW& FD will be approved by the Cabinet in its next meeting.
61. Additional Secretary, Forestry, Wildlife and Fisheries Department stated that they have prepared draft Policy pursuant to orders of this Court after conducting various meetings with all relevant stakeholders and prepared a summary for Chief Minister on 06.05.2019 to allow the draft policy to be placed before Standing Committee of Cabinet on Legislative Business for its approval. He further states that due to massive tree plantation campaign and efforts of Urban Unit, Forest Department has received the demand for tree plantation from various divisions across Punjab in which 5.3 million plants were sold. He points out that on the eve of Forest Day, they have planted more than 7,75,836 trees throughout Punjab
62. Mr. Shahid Rashid Awan, Additional Secretary, Forestry, Wildlife and Fisheries Department appeared and stated that the Draft Policy has been finalized pursuant to orders of this Court after conducting various meetings and consultative sessions on 14.02.2019, 06.03.2019, 15.03.2019 and 25.03.2019 and receiving comments from all stakeholders, government departments, authorities, civil societies as well as the counsel for the Petitioners. He stated that Forest Department has prepared a summary for Chief Minister on 25.04.2019 to allow the draft policy to be placed before Standing Committee of Cabinet on Legislative Business for its approval.
63. Capt.(R) Muhammad Asif, Secretary and Mr. Shahid Rashid Awan, Additional Secretary of Forestry, Wildlife and Fisheries Department stated that pursuant to this Court's order, they have prepared Draft Policy with consultation of Parks and Horticulture Department (PHA), Local Government and Community Development Department, Cooperative Department as well as Urban Unit of P&D Department but Environmental Protection Department could not join the meeting. The Secretary Environmental Protection Department was directed to join the matter for finalization of the Draft Policy.

P. The Punjab Urban and Peri-Urban Forest Policy, (Draft) 2019

64. In Pursuance of order of this Court dated 11.02.2019, Khalid Sherdil, CEO, Urban Unit, P&D and Shahid Rashid Awan, Additional Secretary (Technical) FW&F Department, appeared and stated that on 14.02.2019 they convene a meeting on the draft of "***the Punjab Urban and Peri-Urban Forest Policy, (Draft) 2019***" (the "Draft Policy") which was attended by various Government Departments. They said that they are also in contact with

the other stakeholders and relevant Departments before finalizing the said Draft Policy. In this regard they produced before the Court a booklet containing detailed revised Draft Policy and stated that they will circulate the same amongst the concerned Departments before finalizing the Draft Policy consisting of land/soil for the plantation of the trees, species of the trees, time of the plantation, stock of the trees, responsible executing Departments/ Agencies/Persons.

65. Mr. Khalid Sherdil, CEO, Urban Unit, P&D was directed to convene a meeting on 14.02.2019 and all the concerned departments as well as the Petitioner and other applicants were directed to join the meeting for finalization of draft policy.

66. Pursuant to orders dated 31.01.2019, 11.02.2019 and 19.02.2019, Khalid Sherdil, CEO, Urban Unit, P&D appeared and stated that after revising the Draft Policy, they have prepared a comprehensive document after meetings with stakeholders on 20.02.2019 and 25.02.2019. He further stated that they have taken comments from all stakeholders and circulated comprehensive policy to thirty-six (36) departments in order to obtain their comments and inputs for the Draft Policy and in this respect they have also scheduled a meeting of Stakeholders Consultative Sessions on 05.03.2019 to have discussion and receive input from the government and other stakeholders. He further informed the Court that they are also seeking information from all the stakeholders regarding the area designated for forests, location of area, number of trees to be planted, types of trees, responsible officers and date of plantation.

67. Khalid Sherdil, CEO, Urban Unit, P&D appeared and filed progress report dated 06.05.2019 on Punjab Urban &Peri-Urban Forest Policy. He states that pursuant to orders of this Court, the Urban Unit alongwith Forest Department and other departments of government of Punjab has prepared revised draft and presented the same to various stakeholders.

Khalid Sherdil further states that as per directions of this Court, the Urban Unit started Urban Tree Plantation Campaign, 2019 with industries, housing societies and has identified 270 societies in Lahore which are mentioned in Annex-I of the report alongwith list of industries (Annex-H of the report). He next states that under GIS Mapping, most of the areas are not made part or cover the trees however, the Urban Unit is constantly in touch with Director General, LDA, Director General, PHA and Registrar of the Societies to take action therefore Director General, LDA, Director General, PHA and Registrar of the Societies were directed to appear in person, in order to conclude this case by giving certain directions under writ of mandamus under the respective laws. He points out that in order to implement the policy, Urban Unit needs certain budget from the Planning and Development Department for which they have written letter to the Secretary, therefore, Secretary P&D was directed to appear in person in order to conclude the case. He further points out that Urban Unit has identified 650 industries but they have not planted trees which is in violation of their own undertaking given to Environmental Protection Department when NOC was issued to them under Initial Environmental Examination and Environmental Impact Assessment Regulations, 2000 read with Section 12 of the Punjab Environmental Protection Act, 1997 therefore, the Secretary Environmental Protection Deptt was also directed to appear in person along with permission/NOC granted to industries under the Regulations.

. . .VIII. **URBAN FORESTRY:**

69. Lahore is facing dangerous air pollution, resulting in deaths to citizens. High air pollution and smog are admitted in the Policy, at page 15, wherein it is admitted that afforestation is highly required to combat air pollution, mitigate carbon and improve precipitation. The city

is choking and the need for more than 10 million people is urban forestry based on international best practices, urban forestation which makes the cities in Punjab healthier not for beautification.

70. At the moment, there is no Urban Trees Plantation Policy regarding plantation of trees at urban areas because the Policies only refer forest land and other urban, private and agricultural land are not covered under the issue in hand. Nevertheless, under the Punjab Development of Cities Act, 1976 as well as Lahore Development Authority Act, 1975 and other laws regarding development of societies, there is no clear cut provision for plantation of trees as already held by this Court in *"ANJUM IRFAN versus LAHORE DEVELOPMENT AUTHORITY through Director-General and others"* **(P L D 2002 Lahore 555).**

...XI. **DIRECTIONS:**

83. In view of the above, this Court allows this writ of *mandamus* under Article 199(1(a)(i) of the Constitution and direct the Government Departments performing their functions within jurisdiction of this Court in connection with the affairs of Federation and Province of Punjab and other local authorities under the respective laws, mentioned in this judgment to do anything, they are required by law to do **IN ORDER TO SAFELY MANAGE, CONSERVE, SUSTAIN, MAINTAIN, PROTECT AND GROW FORESTS AND PLANT TREES IN URBAN CITIES** which are as follows:

(1) All the applicable laws and the relevant directions and judgments of the Hon'ble Supreme Court and High Court mentioned herein above, shall be implemented in letter and spirit in order to plant, protect and preserve the forest.

(2) All the Respondents shall take steps to protect, manage and conserve the forests and trees in the Urban Areas, in fact make manifest and obvious efforts, to enlarge the forests and trees in Pakistan and the Punjab.

(3) The requirement for planting three (3) trees per acre by the occupier of a land (Section 3 of the Trees Act) and the penalty of one (1) rupee per tree (Section 4 of the Trees Act) may be revised.

(4) Every responsible Ministry, Division, Department and Authority etc. shall publish the yearly report in which it shall highlight the expansion of the forest area, tree plantation campaign in the Urban Areas and also the action taken by them in compliance of the said laws.

(5) The competent authority is directed to impose the penalty against the relevant officers for omission of their duties, if any, under the respective laws as well as the disciplinary laws and also against the public for cutting the trees.

(6) The Secretary Cooperative and Registrar Cooperative shall issue directions to the housing societies and authorities for ***(i)*** planting at least two (2) trees in the green belt in front of each house mentioning in their allotment letters and bye-laws of the society ***(ii)*** impose heavy penalties and punishments for cutting the same at least Rs.25,000/- per tree and to ***(iii)*** monitor the trees through respective officers of the society/authority. The treatment and maintenance of the trees will be the sole responsibility of the society/authority concerned.

(7) The Punjab Government is also directed to revise and amend such laws where clear direction and command is not entrusted to any authority as under the Punjab Rules of Business, the Secretary Forest, the Secretary Cooperative and the Local Government etc. have clear mandate to make laws and policies, under Schedule-II of the Punjab Government Rules of Business.

(8) It was noted during the hearing that due to the efforts of the Government and other Departments, this year massive tree plantation took place. The same or more effort must be

done and monitored by the relevant authorities each year through proper book logging and designated officers of the area to count, monitor, manage trees every week and submit report and status of the same to the Head of the society/authority for publishing in their annual report. The relevant authority should also number the trees to keep the track of each tree in urban areas (streets, road, parks, market and green belts).

(9) The Department shall, through the media and other means, inform the public and create awareness, including lodging a complaint for any violation of the law for cutting of the trees to the concerned person who maintains data and manages trees and they will take strict action through respective laws. Every area shall have a person to file complaint depending on the jurisdiction of the area and duties of the officers. The Urban Plantation Policy shall be consulted by all the departments.

(10) The Local Government, PHA, DHA, LDA and all others authorities/societies, Secretary Forest and other relevant authorities are directed to define a mechanism for urban forestation by learning from Urban Plantation Policy.

(11) A specific officer may be appointed in a designated area to deal with the issues related to the trees and forest, as the case maybe. If any citizen in their societies or locality feel the need of plantation of trees, such relevant officer may address grievance of the citizen by planting the requisite number of trees by the required authority otherwise they will contact PHA which shall have designated officers for doing such alongwith Forest Department. These trees then shall be again monitored and managed by the said authority.

(12) All the authorities, including DHA, LDA, MDA, FDA and other relevant authorities, are directed to make and adopt comprehensive policies with respect to plantation of trees in urban areas with experience of Urban Plantation Policy and make their own policy under respective laws and immediately start planting of trees with the request to PHA and other departments and maintain the same by imposing fine and penalty to the officers of the area or any citizen.

(13) The school, colleges, higher education institutes, hospitals, parking sites etc. are specifically directed to make policy for planting the trees in open spaces and waiting areas/car parks.

(14) The Government of the Punjab through its respective departments shall make laws in imposing penalty and heavy fine for cutting, removing and damaging any tree with permission of the concerned authority including EPA, PHA and consider all mitigating measures at the time of public hearing of any project such as Initial Environmental Examination (IEE) and Environmental Impact Assessment (EIA).

84. Before parting with this judgment, I appreciate the efforts of all Government Departments whose representatives appeared before this Court from time to time and complied with orders under doctrine of *continuous mandamus* and prepared first ever Urban Trees Plantation Policy for plantation of trees in urban areas including roads, streets, markets, parks and car parks etc. I would also appreciate the efforts of Law Officers, learned counsels, social activists, who played important role for protecting future of citizens of Pakistan regarding massive forest cover and implementation of Urban Trees Plantation Policy throughout the Province of Punjab to have healthy life free from pollution as provided under Article 9 of the Constitution which was introduced by the Hon'ble Supreme Court of Pakistan in "*MS. SHEHLA ZIA AND OTHERS Versus WAPDA*" **(PLD 1994 SC 693)**.

(JAWAD HASSAN) JUDGE

Announced in open Court on the 30th day of August 2019.

17

The Making and Message of Al-Mizan: A Covenant for the Earth

İbrahim Özdemir[*]

17.1 INTRODUCTION

What we have witnessed in recent years alone may be enough to convince any climate change denier, as scorching heat domes smother parts of the US and Canada with record temperatures and blistering heat waves sweep across Pakistan. Torrential rain has caused devastating floods in China, India, Germany, Belgium, Pakistan, Bangladesh, Libya, and Austria. While fires raged in Australia and Siberia, Madagascar was experiencing the world's first famine caused solely by the climate crisis.

Climate change, as observed in the earth's evolutionary history, has roots in various factors such as fluctuations in solar energy, volcanic eruptions, alterations in the earth's tilt or orbit around the sun, shifts in oceanic circulation, and the release of substantial methane gas resulting from permafrost melting. As human civilizations progressed, there was a concomitant rise in energy demand, initially met by renewable sources such as windmills, waterwheels, gravity-fed hydropower, and the utilization of animal and human labor to fulfill various needs for heat, light, and work. This reliance on renewable energy persisted for millennia until approximately 250 years ago, when coal emerged as a primary fuel source during the Industrial Revolution. The widespread use of coal marked a transformative shift in the energy landscape.

In light of this historical evolution, it is noteworthy that a majority of environmental philosophers critique the mechanistic, dualistic, and "techno-industrial" Western worldview as a fundamental contributor to contemporary environmental challenges (Merchant, 1989, p. 84; Warren, 2000, pp. 269–78). Within a postcolonial context, it is imperative to comprehend this worldview as rooted in a logic of power and domination. This logic, which has historically legitimized the exploitation of nature, women, and diverse nations and races, becomes a focal point for critical analysis in understanding the multifaceted challenges posed by the contemporary environmental crisis.

The manifestations of the most pressing contemporary environmental problems – collectively called the "environmental crisis" (e.g., industrial pollution, resource depletion, biodiversity loss,

[*] A preliminary iteration of this manuscript was previously published by *The Minaret of Islam* (No 2, 2022). After a thorough review and extensive revisions, I refined the content. In accordance with academic conventions, I would like to thank *The Minaret of Islam* for their permission for the republication of the revised manuscript at this venue.

climate change, and overpopulation) – are well documented (Hitzhusen & Tucker, 2013, p. 368). Given the urgent need to promote a flourishing, sustainable future, the world's religious communities have much to offer because their religious worldviews and ethical practices greatly influence the attitudes and beliefs that shape most people's concept of nature. The moral imperatives and value systems of religions can mobilize people's sensibilities toward the goals of earth stewardship, here defined as shaping the trajectories of social-ecological change to enhance ecosystem resilience and human well-being (Hitzhusen & Tucker, 2013, p. 368).

This global challenge is one of the significant problems and deserves a global response. As argued in *Al-Mizan*, "the gravity of the looming environmental crisis threatens to eclipse all other crises in human history. Its effects make no distinction between race, religion, culture, or the lines we draw on maps. It should remind us that we are irrevocably connected with the Lord of all in the natural world" (*Al-Mizan*, 2023, p. 45). Therefore, *Al-Mizan* is a humble and sincere attempt, inspired by the Quranic values to understand this and all relevant verses' ontological, psychological, and metaphysical implications: *"To God belong all things in the heavens and on the Earth. And God has ever encompassed all things"* (Q 4:126).

Zamakhsharī (1075–1144), who stands as a prominent figure in twelfth-century Quranic studies and grammar, having crafted the most significant Quran commentary subsequent to al-Ṭabarī's seminal work, is a good example. His interpretation of *"God has not created the heavens and the earth, and all that is between them without [an inner] truth and a term set [by Him]"* (Q 30:8) serves as an illustrative instance of the profound impact the Quran has exerted on shaping the Muslim perspective of the universe throughout various epochs. Zamakhsharī's exposition of the verse underscores the Quran's enduring influence on the Muslim worldview. The verse in question posits that creation is underpinned by truth and is destined for a predetermined temporal span. Zamakhsharī elucidates that the universe's creation is not arbitrary or devoid of purpose, devoid of genuine intent, or profound wisdom. Neither is it fashioned without a clear purpose nor fabricated in perpetuity. Instead, the universe is meticulously brought into existence with inherent truth, wisdom, and a specified duration for its unfolding (Jackson, 2006).

In this scholarly pursuit we focus on developing *Al-Mizan*, an initiative to present an Islamic perspective on environmental matters. The overarching objective is to fortify local, regional, and international efforts in combating climate change and other existential threats to the planet. This endeavor represents a global initiative seeking the active involvement of Islamic scholars and institutions in its formulation and endorsement. *Al-Mizan* is conceived as a reaffirmation of Quranic principles guiding the preservation of nature, strategically articulated to address contemporary and prospective challenges.

At its core, *Al-Mizan* delves into the ethical underpinnings shaping the societal fabric of human existence, exploring the translation of Quranic values into contemporary practices that resonate with the natural world's rhythm. Within the Quranic worldview, nature is not perceived as an inert, purposeless, or meaningless entity; instead, it is posited as a creation sustained and functioning according to a plan (*taqdīr*) reflective of the creative will, knowledge, and power of God (Q 87:2–3). This perspective endows nature with intrinsic value, deeming it "morally considerable" within the Muslim ethos as it has been created with balance, beauty, order, purpose, and meaning. Consequently, *Al-Mizan* is a comprehensive articulation of Quranic principles, fostering an ethical framework that aligns with the dynamic interplay between human society and the natural environment.

Al-Mizan posits that nature possesses inherent moral significance, advocating for a compassionate interconnectedness with humanity, the natural milieu, and sentient creatures. These guiding principles emanate from the principles instituted by the Prophet Muhammad, evolving into a spectrum of regulations and institutions embodying a holistic approach to life. Rooted in Quranic teachings, these principles can be distilled into three overarching categories: the promotion of public welfare, the prohibition of wrongful actions, and the practice of moderation in all endeavors. "*Let there be a community among you that calls for what is good, urges what is right, and forbids what is wrong; they are the ones who have success*" (Q 3:104).

17.2 THE ISLAMIC WORLDVIEW AND AL-MIZAN

The Quran does not use the concept of *tabīʿa* (nature) as it does not imply a creator. When we look at the origins of nature and natural, we can see the complexity of these words and why even believers are mistakenly using them. Their origin is in the Latin word *natura* (birth) and *nasci* (born), deriving from the Greek word *physica* (physics) (Wolff, 2011). Therefore, the concept of nature is a problematic word loaded with history and multiple meanings. Wolff reminds us that "the word is common in daily language; there are many different perspectives about what the word encompasses" (2011).

Therefore, it is essential in this context to notice that the Quran uses the concepts of *kawn*, *kāʾināt*, and *ʿālam* instead of nature (*tabīʿa*). *Kawn* is an adjective derived from the verbal noun *kawn*, cosmos, and creation. It can also refer to the individual creature. The consonantal root is *k-w-n*, whose meanings include "to be," "to create," and "to bring into existence." God's command "Be!" (*kun*) is the occasion for all existence (Akkach, 2005, p. 97; Badawi & Abdel Haleem, 2008).

Therefore, based on the concept of tawhid, *Al-Mizan* affirms God's oneness, which is the bedrock of the Islamic ethos and is the basis of Islamic faith, metaphysics, ethics, law, and spirituality. N. Haq articulates this as follows:

> When one examines these levels in the totality of the Qur'ān, they turn out to interdigitate: on the one hand, the Qur'ānic notion of the natural world and the natural environment is semantically and logically bound up with the very concept of God; on the other hand, this notion is linked with the general principle of the very creation of humanity. The three levels of Qur'ānic discourse, therefore, do not manifest any independent conceptual self-sufficiency of, or a conceptual discontinuity between, the three realms of the divine, of nature, and of humanity. Indeed, this linkage is of fundamental importance to our concerns, for in our reconstruction of the cosmology of the Qur'ān, we can see that the historical-naturalistic is linked to the transcendental-eternal, and this means that there is no ontological separation between the divine and natural environments. At the human psychological level, all this generates a particular attitude to the world as a whole. (Haq, 2001, p. 146)

The Quran opens with the praise of God as "*Lord of the worlds*" (*Rabb al-ʿālamīn*) (Q 1:1). Each of our daily prescribed prayers (salah) begins with these words. The word *Rabb* denotes, on the one hand, the Lord and Master whom we serve and, on the other, the Sustainer who brings each being into existence, then provides for it, who nurtures, develops, and guides it until its destiny is fulfilled. Our ethical obligations focus when we translate *Rabb al-ʿālamīn* accordingly as "*Lord of all beings.*" It is underlined in an early revelation that "EXTOL the limitless glory of thy Sustainer's name: [the glory of] the All-Highest, who creates [everything], and thereupon forms it in accordance with what it is meant to be, and who determines the nature [of all that exists], and thereupon guides it [toward its fulfillment]" (Q 87:1–3). Asad's comment on this verse is very relevant to our purpose here: "He [God] endows it with inner coherence and with qualities consistent with the functions which it is meant to perform, and thus adapts it a priori to the exigencies of its existence" (Asad, 2008, p. 87:1). This due measure (*qadr*) to things, and the balance (*mīzān*) in the cosmos and humanity, makes it clear that humans must first study, understand, and appreciate this divine pattern and then learn not to disturb, corrupt, or violate this *qadr* and *mīzān*.

Haq underlines that "the fulfillment of this commitment is the fundamental moral imperative of humanity" (Haq, 2001, p. 147). Moreover, God is the Creator and Sustainer of the universe and of man, particularly the Giver of guidance for man and He who judges man individually and collectively and metes out merciful justice to him. This "merciful justice" represents orderly creativity, sustenance, guidance, justice, and mercy, fully interpenetrated in the Quranic concept of God as an organic unity (Rahman, 2009, p. 1).

To understand and appreciate how the Quranic values transformed and shaped the minds and hearts of the early Muslim community regarding the natural world, it is crucial to understand pre-Islamic Arabs' perception of nature, as they regarded nature as lifeless, meaningless, and purposeless. This ontological dimension of nature resulted in not feeling any moral compassion and responsibility toward nature and animals. From the beginning, the Quran clarifies that ontologically, in the universe, *"everything has been created with a specific order, duty, meaning, and purpose"* (Q 38:27, 3:190–91, 21:16–17, 23:115).

Accordingly, the natural world did not come into being by accident because of the process of blind and random evolution or chaotic configurations without meaning or purpose: "Who creates [everything], and thereupon forms it in accordance with what it is meant to be, and who determines the nature [of all that exists], and thereupon guides it [toward its fulfillment], Who brings forth green pasture" (Asad, 2008, 87:2–4). It was designed to function with order, balance, and meaning, which imposes a moral responsibility on our shoulders. There was always a theoretical/ontological and practical/moral dimension of Quranic teaching. Therefore, ontologically, "having a firm and well-knit structure with no gaps, no ruptures, and no dislocations," nature has been regarded as "one of the grand handiworks of the Almighty" (Rahman, 2009, p. 2). Like a mirror, the natural world reflects its Creator's power, beauty, wisdom, and mercy.

The Quran further teaches Muslims that the cosmic order was set in place by God, with all life forms having a divinely appointed role in submission to His will (Q 55:1–9). This has resulted in the concept of *mīzān* (divinely ordained balance) in the universe, with all things having their place. God causes the rivers and streams to flow on the earth, upholds the skies, causes the rain to fall, and places the boundary between night and day. In short, the universe, with all its richness and vitality, is the work and art of God, and "there is not a single thing but extols His limitless glory and praise" (Q 22:18, 17:44). The Quran also teaches the practical and moral dimension that humans were given the responsibility to act as stewards and custodians of creation. So, it is a moral imperative for Muslims to live in harmony and "balance" with the creation and God, who is all-encompassing.

Moreover, the Quran also presents God as *"all-powerful, purposeful, and merciful"* (Rahman, 2009, p. 8). This all-powerful God, through His merciful creativity, "measures out" everything, bestowing upon everything the range of its potentialities, its laws of behavior, in sum, its character. Thus, "this measuring, on the one hand, ensures the orderliness of nature and on the other expresses the most fundamental, unbridgeable difference between the nature of God and the nature of man" (Rahman, 2009, p.8). "God, not anyone else, has created the laws by which nature works. This does not mean that man cannot discover those laws and apply them for man's good, for this is what a farmer or a scientist does" (Rahman, 2009, p. 8).

17.3 MĪZĀN AS A COSMIC PRINCIPLE

The etymology of the term *mīzān* is traceable to the linguistic root *w-z-n*, which denotes equality in weight, signifying the equivalence of one entity to another akin object (Ibn Manẓūr, 1956, vol. 13, p. 446). In its primary signification and associated connotations and implications, *mīzān* encompasses the notions of balance, coherence, and equilibrium within a given context or undertaking. Within the context of environmental consciousness, this concept entails ascribing due value to the elements in our surroundings and cultivating a balanced approach characterized by measured and harmonious interactions. This involves fostering relationships marked by moderation, equity, and equilibrium, starkly contrasting various forms of extremism, imbalance, and excess.

Ishak Ozgel in his study on the *mīzān* in the Quranic context provides instances of words stemming from the root *w-z-n* as discernible in twenty-three occurrences within the Quranic text, assuming various grammatical forms. The utilization of this root encompasses its role as a verb in three instances, as a participle (*maṣdar*) in three occurrences, and as the noun "*mawzūn*" in a singular example. Furthermore, the term *mīzān* is deployed in nine instances, with its plural form "*mawāzin*" surfacing in seven cases (Özdemir, 2023, p. 61). Predominantly, the most frequent application is observed in the form of "*mīzān*" and its plural counterpart, "*mawāzin*," with the former being referenced in nine instances.

Within the Quranic context, *mīzān* finds mention in diverse thematic contexts. Notably, in five instances, its invocation underscores the imperative of justice in human relations. Additionally, in two occurrences, the revelation of *mīzān* is explicitly linked to divine revelation. One instance attributes the creation of the universe to the principle of *mīzān*, while another underscores the admonition against distorting this equilibrium. The Quranic usage of *mīzān* accentuates several pivotal points:

- The bestowal of the balance by God through the Book.
- The creation of the universe in accordance with a balanced paradigm.
- Divine injunctions to measure and weigh using a balanced approach.
- The proclamation that all deeds will undergo a balanced assessment in the Hereafter. (Özdemir, 2023, p. 61)

The Quranic utilization of the concept of *mīzān* imposes upon humanity the imperative of embodying equilibrium in their relations with God, fellow beings, and the surrounding environment. When examined through the lens of environmental awareness, the recurrence of *mīzān* in these three domains within the Quran assumes significance, carrying profound implications. The expansive scope of the environmental concept encompasses physical, biological, sociological, and spiritual dimensions, encapsulating the totality of relationships within which human existence unfolds, exerting influence and being influenced.

In this context, preserving natural equilibrium necessitates a conscientious approach whereby individuals tread lightly upon the earth to mitigate entropy within the bounds permitted by physical laws. This entails judicious management of resources to prevent the depletion of the natural environment by economic activities. The Islamic principle of *mīzān* serves as a guiding framework, facilitating the development of an ecosystem accounting system aligned with the intricate ecological processes of the planet. Such a system can, in turn, inform the economy through the establishment of a comprehensive biospheric pricing mechanism. Integrating *mīzān* principles into ecosystem accounting aligns with ecological realities and provides a holistic framework for guiding economic practices in harmony with the biosphere (Qadir & Zaman, 2019).

In the verses of *mīzān* (Q 42:17, 57:25, 55:7–8, 15:19) at least a dual function is evident. The verses provide informative content, articulate underlying purposes, and instigate heightened awareness. As Nursi argues,

> If observed carefully, it will be seen that a perfect and intentional order embraces the whole universe. Traces of choice and flashes of purpose are to be seen in every aspect. What strikes the eyes through the testimony of their fruits is that in everything is a light of intention; in every function, a flash of will; in every motion, a gleam of choice; in every composite whole, a blaze of wisdom. (Nursi, 1996, p. 538)

Concurrently, they summon humanity to acknowledge its ethical obligations through imperative directives and proscriptions governing behavior toward humans and the natural world. At the cognitive stratum, emphasis is placed on establishing equilibrium within the cosmos. Subsequently, human beings are enjoined to reflect upon their duties to maintain equilibrium in their physical surroundings and interpersonal relationships. The cautionary assertion underscores the potential disruption of ecological balance by human transgression of limits (*ṭughyān*) driven by unchecked desires. In response, individuals are instructed to uphold this equilibrium within human relations. Ultimately, the directive is issued to refrain from instigating profound losses, both ecologically and interpersonally, thus underscoring the imperative of avoiding actions that may lead to substantial imbalance and detriment.

In another early chapter, the Quran describes the creation in its perfect balance and with its overreaching moral implications:

> The Firmament has He raised high, and He has set up *the balance* [of Justice] so that you may not transgress [due] *balance*. So, establish *weight with justice* and fall not short in *the balance*. (Q 55:7–9)

The key term here is balance (*al-mīzān*), repeated four times. To quote Yusuf Ali's comments on these verses will suffice for our purpose here as he articulates both ontological and practical dimesons of the text:

> The "balance of justice" in this verse is connected with "the balance" in the following two verses, that men may act justly to each other and observe due balance in all their actions, following the golden mean and not transgressing owing bounds. However, the balance is also connected figuratively with the heavens above in three symbols: (1) Justice is a heavenly virtue; (2) the heavens themselves are sustained by mathematical balance; and (3) the constellation Libra (the balance) is entered by the Sun at the middle of the zodiacal year. For the second part, he argues that A man should be honest and straight in every daily matter, such as weighting out things he is selling, and he should be straight, just, and honest in all the highest dealing, not only with other people but with himself and in his obedience to God's Law. (Ali, 2004)

It is evident from the above discussion that justice and balance are universal laws (of God) and that (as a result) humans should conduct a just and balanced life. When we reflect on the moral implications of these verses, we will see that they alone would be enough for developing an environmental ethic and sustainability from the Quran itself. First, justice and balance are universal. Second, this universal balance is created and sustained by God. Third, humans must attempt to comprehend this universal balance and follow it in social life and overall environmental interaction. Any sincere follower of the Quran must conclude from all these – be he/she a philosopher, a scientist, an economist, an engineer, a technocrat, a statesman, or an ordinary human being – that he/she must respect, care, and preserve this balance in their relations with nature and society. Time and time again, the Quran's insistence on the absolute and infinite character of God on the one hand and the finitude of everything other than God is very significant in current discussions about sustainable economics and development. Therefore, any new economic and developmental theory that claims to be Islamic should presuppose this conceptual framework as a core axiom (Foltz et al., 2003; Mergaliyev et al., 2021; Asutay, 2013).

In conclusion, this verse draws attention to the fact that everything in the universe, from the big to the small, has a cosmic balance and equilibrium most suitable for humanity's benefit. In addition, it is stated that if a man does not maintain and distort this state of affairs, corruption will arise on land and sea due to his thoughtlessness and not considering the balance as a cosmic principle created and sustained by God (Q. 30:41).

17.4 BACKGROUND OF *AL-MIZAN*: A COVENANT FOR THE EARTH

Given what is happening globally, we see ever-increasing religious engagement with environmental issues and climate change. We are witnessing growing collaboration between religious organizations, scientific research forums, civil society groups, and international organizations. In this context, The Faith for Earth Initiative was established by the United Nations Environment Programme (UNEP) in 2017 and tasked with strategically engaging and partnering with faith-based organizations to collectively contribute toward achieving the Sustainable Development Goals (SDGs) and Agenda 2030. The strategic framework was predicated upon three overarching and interconnected objectives, which seek to mobilize faith-based actors and resources toward implementing innovative methodologies conducive to harmonious coexistence with the natural environment. These objectives are (1) Strengthen Partnership with Faith-Based Organizations' Leadership for Policy Impact; (2) Green Faith-Based Organizations' Investments, Operations, and Assets; and (3) Establish an Accessible Knowledge-Based Support System using faith scripts and scientific evidence (UNEP, n.d.).

In this spirit, the Faith for Earth Initiative was key in organizing Muslim environmentalists to produce a document later called *Al-Mizan: A Covenant for the Earth*. The name is inspired by the Quranic use of the term *mīzān*, as mentioned above. As a first step, at the 8th Islamic Conference of Environment Ministers (ICEM) held in Rabat in October 2019, the strategy of "enhancing the role of cultural and religious factors in protecting the environment and achieving sustainable development in the Islamic World" was approved. This indicated Islam's religious and civilizational duty to contribute toward addressing topical issues in the management of the earth and the environmental crises we face today. Then, the cooperative work on this project was launched in 2020 with a group of scholars and those interested in Islam and the environment from different countries and disciplines. Most of them had previously contributed to drafting the Islamic Declaration on Climate Change (2015).

After this development, a prevailing sentiment emerged, underscoring the imperative for the expeditious establishment of a global platform that integrates environmental concerns with Islamic teachings while concurrently fostering the incubation of Islamic perspectives on nature. Such an initiative is deemed urgent to illustrate Islam's potential as a catalytic agent for sustainable development and conscientious environmental stewardship. Furthermore, it would accentuate the influential role of culture and religion in instigating the necessary behavioral transformations, complementing the concurrent application of scientific, technical, and policy-oriented solutions to address ecological crises. To this end, the Islamic World Educational, Scientific, and Cultural Organization, the Islamic Foundation for Ecology and Environmental Sciences, Uskudar University, Istanbul, the Qur'anic Botanic Garden, the College of Islamic Studies at Hamad Bin Khalifa University in Qatar, and the UNEP Faith for Earth Initiative came together to discuss the founding of an Islamic covenant designed to showcase Islam's teachings on the environment and help the world's 1.8 billion Muslims to embrace sustainability as part of their everyday lives.

Therefore, *Al-Mizan* attempts to articulate an Islamic environmental understanding of nature that is open to all horizons of human life and open to other religions. It is infused with a desire to affirm our interconnectedness and inseparability from nature. The first draft was shared with over 300 Islamic institutions and eminent environmentalists worldwide for feedback and consultation. The last draft was submitted to Al-Azhar University in Cairo and the Muslim Council of Elders for their feedback and approval. The latter is an independent international organization and was established in 2014 in Qatar to promote peace in Muslim communities. The council unites Muslim scholars, experts, and dignitaries known for their wisdom, sense of justice, independence, and moderateness. After careful study and discussion, both institutes approved the text with their feedback. *Al-Mizan's* core team tried their best to evaluate all feedback and benefit from them. We hope it will represent an institutional Muslim covenant prepared by diverse Islamic scholars that address the global Islamic community and humanity, like the Pope's Encyclical *Laudato Si'* (Francis, 2015).

17.5 THE CORE TEAM

The core team, overseen by the UNEP Faith for Earth Initiative, comprises representatives from esteemed institutions, including the Islamic World Educational, Scientific and Cultural Organization, Morocco; the Islamic Foundation for Ecology and Environmental Sciences, UK; Uskudar University, Istanbul, Türkiye; the Qur'anic Botanic Garden; and the College of Islamic Studies at Hamad Bin Khalifa University in Qatar. Tasked with delivering administrative support and overseeing the institutional facets of *Al-Mizan*, the core team is constituted of the following individuals:

- **Dr. Iyad Abumoghli**, Director of UNEP Faith for Earth Initiative.
- **Dr. Ibrahim Ozdemir**, Professor of Philosophy, the Founding Director of Uskudar University Forum on Environmental Ethics, Uskudar University, Istanbul, Türkiye.
- **Fazlun Khalid**, Founding Director of the Islamic Foundation for Ecology and Environmental Sciences (IFEES), UK.
- **Othman Llewellyn**, senior expert, the National Commission for Wildlife Conservation and Development, Saudi Arabia.
- **Dr. Abdelmajid Tribak**, Head of Environment at ISESCO and winner of the Mohamed VI Prize for Islamic Thought and Studies, Morocco.
- **Aishah Ali Abdallah**, EmbraceTheEarth, an ecological leadership program in Saudi Arabia.
- **Dr. Fatima Saleh Al-Khulaifi**, the Qur'anic Botanic Garden, Qatar.
- **Dr. Evren Tok**, the College of Islamic Studies, Hamad Bin Khalifa University, Qatar.
- **Kamran Shezad**, Director of the Islamic Foundation for Ecology and Environmental Sciences (IFEES/EcoIslam).

17.6 THE MESSAGE OF AL-MIZAN

The ethos underpinning the covenant is rooted in the tenet of tawhid, signifying the unequivocal affirmation of the oneness of God. As mentioned earlier, tawhid is the foundational pillar of the Islamic worldview and constitutes the cornerstone of Islamic ethical principles. Consequently, *Al-Mizan* commences by comprehensively depicting and evaluating the contemporary global milieu, encouraging readers to contemplate. The narrative encompasses humanity's legacy, particularly emphasizing the ramifications of pervasive climate change. Despite the diverse array of challenges articulated, the imperative stance adopted by Muslim environmentalists is one of unwavering "active hope," signifying a collective optimism in finding viable solutions and surmounting the present crisis. To underscore the ontological underpinnings and the essence of *Al-Mizan*, the introductory paragraph is aptly encapsulated by the following excerpt:

> We begin with praise and gratitude to God, the Lord of all beings, to the number of stars in the sky, the drops of rain, the waves of the waters, the leaves of the trees, the grains of sand, and all the atoms throughout the Heavens and the Earth.
>
> The Earth on which we live – within the unutterably vast and glorious cosmos – reflects the all-transcendent glory of God, the All-Sustaining Lord of the worlds of being, beyond our grasp. Its community of life, of which we are a part, is exquisite beyond all telling, evanescent, and more precious than mortal beings can comprehend, for it reflects the grace and mercy of the Lord of all.
>
> Each thing God has created is a sign of His power, wisdom, and grace, and we seek insight, understanding, and guidance from these signs. He has unfolded all things in equilibrium with each other, in need of one another, and all give aid to one another. Nothing is created wantonly or in vain.
>
> All are created in Truth and for Right, and each has rights on us: that we care for it in reverential awe for its Lord, in compassion unwithheld, and in utmost beauty and good.
>
> To serve the Lord of all by working for utmost good is the most profound purpose of our lives, for God "*...created death and life to try you, which of you work most good...*" (67:2).
>
> (*Al-Mizan*, 2023, p. 1)

Based on this ontological foundation, it is articulated that with a reflection on our planet and the cosmos, Muslims may better appreciate how the Islamic worldview instructs them to relate to the earth we live on and realize that it is a multifaceted relationship of moral responsibility. The main chapters of *Al-Mizan* are as follows:

1. **An Appraisal of the State of the Earth:** The Human Legacy – What our Hands have Wrought, Global Climate Change, The Loss of Biological Diversity, Political Economy.
2. **Signs in the Cosmos and the Earth:** Cosmic Equilibrium, Khilāfah fī'l-Ard – Responsibility on the Earth.
3. **The Ecological Ethos and Ethics of Islam:** The Ethics of Tawhid, Reverential Care, Show Compassion toward those on Earth, The Signs of the All-Merciful, Spiritual Practices, A Beautiful Exemplar – A Mercy to All Beings.
4. **Equity, Fairness, and Justice in Sharing the Sources of Life:** Prosperity in Perspective, Development and Lifestyle, The Sources of Life, Our World in Debt – Between Exploitation and Contribution, Between Frugality and Wasteful Excess.
5. **Principles and Practices for Tending the Earth:** The Aims of the *Sharīʿah*, Benefits and Detriments, Rights and Wrongs, Harvesting our Food – *Halāl* and *Tayyib*, Protecting the Sources of Life, Ethical *Sharīʿah*-based Policies, Securing Right, Averting Wrong, Annex: A Way Forward, and A Prayer.

Therefore, *Al-Mizan* can be considered a wake-up call for Muslims, who now comprise a fifth of the population of humankind on earth. It reminds Muslims that the distinctive aspects of their faith suggest that they should contribute more to environmental awareness, protection, and sustainability of the cosmic order created and sustained by God. The core messages are summarized as follows:

- The cosmology of our faith is rooted in the recognition that all things in the heavens and the earth support one another to the glory of the Lord of all, who holds human beings responsible for working good on the earth and keeping far from wreaking devastation in it.
- The ethos and ethics of our faith, as exemplified in the life of the Prophet, are steeped in revering the Lord of all creation in our treatment of every creature and devotion to the Lord of all by working utmost good and beauty in all we do and responding to the grace of the All-Merciful that encompasses all things through compassion that sets no limits.
- The Islamic value system is based on the principles of compassion and mercy. The first pioneer of compassion in Islam certainly is the Prophet Muhammad himself, whom the Quran presents as "*a mercy for all creatures*" (*raḥma li-l-ʿālamīn*) (Q 21:107). As the Messenger of God, he presented his followers with outstanding examples of how compassion can be a source of moral responsibility toward all creatures in the concept's original meaning. Most importantly, he presented a new worldview based on compassion and mercy; as God says in the Quran, "*Your Lord had inscribed for Himself [the rule of] Mercy*" (Q 6:54). As a reflection of divine mercy, the Prophet insisted on animals' protection and kind treatment. It showed that Muslims should act kindly toward all living beings through their deeds and sayings. When mentioning neighbors' rights, he formulated it with a sense of compassion, saying, "*he is not a believer whose stomach is filled while his neighbor goes hungry*" (Bukhari). Here, the Prophet implies that it is part of being a true believer to feel the suffering and pity of hungry fellows and even extend the boundary of compassion to include all creatures: "*The Most Merciful One is merciful towards those who are merciful. Act kindly to those on the earth so that those in the heavens [the angels] will be merciful to you*" (Özdemir, 2022).
- The economic values of our faith are embodied in frugal moderation while taking joy in the sources of life for humankind and other living beings, respecting their inherent limits by forsaking wasteful excess for just, equitable sharing of their fruits, and forsaking exploitation of the earth and its inhabitants for charity and cultivation.
- The law of our faith and the policies and practices derived from it aim to secure the rights and the welfare of all things, to secure good and avert harm, and to realize the human responsibility of *khilāfa* (stewardship) on the earth.

In consideration of the preceding, it makes the following pledges:

- To urge educators to experience the joy of learning about natural creation in the wild viscerally and then to arrange visceral contact with wild nature to compel participants to understand, respect, and care for it (see para. 3.11).
- To urge all our fellow Muslims, particularly those who teach the young, to study the example of the Prophet Muhammad deeply, upon him be peace and the blessing of God, concerning tending the earth and its communities of life and strive to realize his example in their lives (see para. 3.23).
- To urge Muslim jurists, economists, and ecologists to work with their countries' administrations and local communities to prescribe measures that do not compromise the ability of future generations to meet their own needs and that do not threaten the integrity of nature or the survival of other species (see para. 4.7).

- To remind leaders and decision-makers that it is essential that people of all social and ethnic groups, traditional societies, and Indigenous people be consulted without discrimination and that the weakest be held as strongest until their rights are fully secured, and the strongest held as weakest until they comply fully with the law (see para. 4.26).
- To call upon conservation agencies, nongovernmental organizations, conservation advocates, faith-based groups, and local communities in the Islamic countries to recognize the value of *ḥimā*s and analogous traditional protected areas and other effectively managed conserved areas, such as *agdāl*, *ḥawṭa*s, and the like, and to empower the traditional managers in whom lies the cumulative inherited cultural knowledge that is embodied in these practices to continue managing them (see para. 5.20).
- To urge conservation agencies, nongovernmental organizations, conservation advocates, faith-based groups, and local communities in all countries to set up effectively and equitably managed protected areas and other effective area-based conservation measures, whatever they may call them, that embody the ethical principles of the *ḥimā*, which conserve areas of particular importance for biodiversity and ecosystem services, are ecologically representative and well connected, and are integrated into the broader landscapes and seascapes (see para. 5.20).
- To urge Islamic communities globally to set about reviving the *waqf* (charitable endowments) system that has led the way in establishing exemplary conservation practices in the past (see para. 5.24).
- To urge all governments and jurists in Islamic countries to issue an unequivocal condemnation of scorched-earth tactics and the use of nuclear and other weapons of mass destruction, to strive to ensure that their governments abjure them, and to work together with other countries for their elimination (see para. 5.26).
- To urge policymakers, planners, and designers in Islamic countries and worldwide to endorse the vision that humans should plan and design harmoniously with the natural world, the universal *mīzān* created and sustained by God (see para. 5.28).

17.7 CONCLUSION

Within the contemporary landscape, the imperatives presented by climate change underscore the need for innovative narratives and metaphors that elucidate the cosmos and our situational dynamics within it. This approach facilitates responses to climate challenges marked by creativity and discernment. The Quran, grounded in its early verses, consistently underscores the concept of *mīzān*, inviting its readers to engage in contemplation and exploration of the celestial and terrestrial realms. These encompass a diverse array of observable environmental elements, ranging from clouds, seas, grapes, and dates to olives, flies, the moon, the sun, fish, camels, bees, mountains, rain, and wind, thus encapsulating a comprehensive spectrum of natural phenomena.

The Quran emphasizes that every facet of creation is a miraculous sign (*āya*) of God, extending an invitation to humanity for contemplation. Significantly, the Quran explicitly includes nonhuman animals among God's miraculous signs, both as part of a general category and as a specific species. This perspective underscores the interconnectedness of the natural world and positions all elements of creation as divine manifestations, fostering a deeper understanding of the environment and its intrinsic significance within the larger cosmic framework (Q 2:164, 7:73, 16:79).

On the other hand, as all things have been created with balance, purpose, and measure (Q 54:49) thoughtless consumption, wastefulness, and extravagance are ethically wrong and prohibited. Wastefulness is not only the careless consumption of natural resources but also is to be disrespectful toward God, the Creator, and the Owner of all the bounties. For this reason, eating and drinking licit food is lawful in Islam, but wastefulness is forbidden: "*Eat and drink, but do not waste. Surely, He does not like the wasteful*" (Q 7:31).

Therefore, the message of *Al-Mizan* involves a meticulous exposition, elaboration, and defense of the Quranic worldview, undertaken with a discerning and critical mindset. The foundational argument posits that the universe should be comprehended as an ongoing process of creative emergence orchestrated by God. A central tenet posits the unity and coherence of nature as an integrated structure devoid of gaps, ruptures, or dislocations. Governed by inherent laws ingrained by God, nature operates autonomously but not autocratically, lacking inherent justification for its existence or the capacity to self-explain (Rahman, 2009, p. 2).

Al-Mizan, therefore, serves as a summons to the Muslim community to reassess its economic, legal, political, and ethical frameworks, which have predominantly originated from Western influences in contemporary times. This encompasses examining not only natural and social sciences but also the institutions underpinning this paradigm of thought. It initiates a critical inquiry into fundamental aspects of human existence, encompassing inquiries into the essence and purpose of the universe, human beings, knowledge and value, meaning and rationality, and the overarching significance of life itself. *Al-Mizan* provides the underpinnings for an environmentally sustainable alternative culture, positioned as a counterforce to supplant the prevailing culture rooted in a Western materialist and consumption-oriented worldview. This prevailing worldview serves as the foundation for the existing economic, social, and political world order, against which *Al-Mizan* advocates for a transformative alternative.

It reminds us that addressing the exigencies of the environmental crisis mandates a comprehensive reevaluation of our self-perception and our role within the world through the lens of the Quranic worldview. *Al-Mizan* contends that genuine solutions to formidable and impending challenges necessitate a departure from delegating the responsibility solely to a "political world" that, as asserted, has been predominated by individuals – politicians, corporate leaders, bureaucrats, media figures, military authorities, and intelligence magnates – devoid of foundational values, ideals, and principles, where the pursuit of power has devolved into a mere short time vested interest (Gare, 1996, p. 2). Therefore, *Al-Mizan* advocates for an ethos of authentic democratic participation and moral responsibility in shaping resolutions to pressing issues.

Al-Mizan hopes to serve as a poignant reminder, beckoning not only to the Muslim community but also to Muslim scientists, scholars, philosophers, policymakers, industrialists, and farmers alike. It enjoins them to explore the universe and self, invoking an ecological interpretation of the Quran that positions them as integral facets of a singular narrative – interwoven and mutually reliant. In recognition of the divine orchestration characterized by *Al-Mizan*, signifying balance, measure, and purpose in creation and sustenance, individuals across these diverse domains are urged to cultivate lives and construct economic and financial systems marked by sustainability. Such systems are envisioned to be rooted in principles of justice, equality, and a profound regard for the well-being of both humanity and the natural world.

REFERENCES

Akkach, S. (2005). *Cosmology and Architecture in Premodern Islam: An Architectural Reading of Mystical Ideas*. Albany: SUNY Press.

Ali, A. Y. (2004). *The Holy Qur'an: Text, Translation and Commentary*. India: Goodword Books.

Asad, M. (2008). *The Message of the Qur'an*. London: The Book Foundation.

Asutay, M. (2013). "Islamic Moral Economy as the Foundation of Islamic Finance." In V. Cattelan (ed.), *Islamic Finance in Europe*, Cheltenham: Edward Elgar Publishing, pp. 55–68.
Badawi, E., and Abdel Haleem, M. (2008). *Arabic–English Dictionary of Qur'anic Usage*. Leiden: Brill.
Foltz, R. C., Denny, F. M., and Baharuddin, A. (eds.) (2003). *Islam and Ecology: A Bestowed Trust*. Cambridge, MA: Harvard University Press.
Francis, Pope (2015). *Laudato Si': On Care for Our Common Home*. Vatican City: Vatican Press.
Gare, A. (1996). *Nihilism Inc.: Environmental Destruction and the Metaphysics of Sustainability*. Como, NSW: Eco-Logical Press.
Haq, S. N. (2001). "Islam and Ecology: Toward Retrieval and Reconstruction." *Daedalus*, 130(4), 141–77.
Hitzhusen, G. E., and Tucker, M. E. (2013). "The Potential of Religion for Earth System Governance." *Ecology and Society*, 18(1), 368–76.
Ibn Manẓūr, M. (1956). *Lisān al-ʿArab*. Beirut: Dār Ṣādir.
Islamic Declaration on Climate Change (2015). Islamic Relief Worldwide and Islamic Foundation for Ecology and Environmental Sciences, Istanbul. https://unfccc.int/news/islamic-declaration-on-climate-change.
Jackson, R. (2006). "Mahmud Ibn Umar Al-Zamakhsharī (1075–1144)." In *Fifty Key Figures in Islam*. London: Routledge, 91–96.
Merchant, C. (1989). *The Death of Nature: Women, Ecology, and the Scientific Revolution*. San Francisco: Harper & Row.
Mergaliyev, A., Asutay, M., Avdukic, A., and Karbhari, Y. (2021). "Higher Ethical Objective (Maqasid al-Shari'ah) Augmented Framework for Islamic Banks: Assessing Ethical Performance and Exploring Its Determinants." *Journal of Business Ethics*, 170(4), 797–834.
Al-Mizan (2023). "Al-Mizan: A Covenant for the Earth." United Nations Environment Programme (UNEP) Faith for Earth Initiative. www.unep.org/al-mizan-covenant-earth.
Nursi, S. (1996). *The Words*. Istanbul: Sozler Publications.
Özdemir, İ. (2022). *Care for Creation: An Islamic Perspective*. London: Viverealtrimenti.
(2023). *Mîzân: Dünya ile Bir Sözleşme*. Istanbul: Üsküdar Üniversitesi Yayınları.
Qadir, J., and Zaman, A. (2019). "Sustainable Development Viewed from the Lens of Islam." *International Journal of Pluralism and Economics Education*, 10(1), 46–60.
Rahman, F. (2009). *Major Themes of the Qur'an*. Chicago: University of Chicago Press.
UNEP (n.d.). "Faith for Earth Initiative." United Nations Environment Programme, Nairobi. www.unep.org/about/who-we-are/faith-earth-initiative.
Warren, K. J. (2000). *Ecofeminist Philosophy: A Western Perspective on What It Is and Why It Matters*. Lanham, MD: Rowman & Littlefield.

18

Towards Environmental Sustainability

A Reflection on Islamic Epistemologies and Models for Sustainable Development

Nematollah Azizi

18.1 INTRODUCTION

The natural resources and environment serve as the cornerstone of national wealth in every country, crucial for achieving development objectives. Yet, environmental crises are escalating rapidly, signalling the deterioration of these invaluable resources (Steffen et al., 2018; Bigdeli and Maleki, 2022; Sawari and Biranvand, 2022; Azizi, 2024). Without intervention, their condition is bound to deteriorate further under current exploitation methods. Consequently, the challenges of environmental degradation and climate change have become paramount worldwide concerns (Lampert, 2019). Many societies are now transitioning towards sustainable environmental management and production practices after years of overuse (Bringezu and Bleischwitz, 2009). The current situation reflects an unprecedented strain on the delicate balance between humanity and nature, exacerbated by rapid technological advancements and lagging efforts to mitigate adverse economic, cultural, and moral impacts. Environmental irregularities have sparked profound concerns among environmentalists, thinkers, and social reformers (Baba Oghli, 2013). In response, sociologists have increasingly scrutinized human environmental behaviors, recognizing their significant impact on environmental issues and threats, which are influenced by various factors (Shafai Moghadam and Niazi, 2019).

Therefore, it is widely acknowledged that human activities significantly contribute to exacerbating environmental problems and climate change. While some issues stem from ignorance or lack of awareness, many result from complex economic, political, and social dynamics (Wang et al., 2020). Irresponsible behavior like deforestation, fossil fuel use, and industrial pollution are major contributors to global warming, leading to severe weather events and environmental consequences (Swim et al., 2011; Ahmadi, 2019). On the other hand, unbalanced economic and industrial growth has caused further harm, with greenhouse gas emissions and environmental damage increasing rapidly. Many societies have collapsed due to an inability to adapt to these unsustainable practices (Diamond, 2005). Recognizing this, the United Nations formulated seventeen Sustainable Development Goals (SDGs) in the 2030 Agenda for Sustainable Development to address these challenges (UNDP, 2015). Urgent action, therefore, is needed from policymakers, practitioners, and all societal institutions to revise development policies and strategies for environmental sustainability calling for fundamental changes in legal approaches, production procedures, and active engagement from social, cultural, scientific, and educational institutions to offer creative solutions to this crisis (Basheer et al., 2022).

18.2 THE CONCEPT OF SUSTAINABLE DEVELOPMENT

Sustainable development has emerged as a pivotal concept amidst the complex challenges of balancing economic, social, and environmental factors (Shi et al., 2019). Initially rooted in concerns over rapid industrialization and resource depletion, the term gained prominence with the publication of the Brundtland Report in 1987, which defined it as development meeting present needs without compromising future generations (WCED, 1987). This laid the groundwork for a three-dimensional approach – economic, social, and environmental – underscored at the 1992 UN Conference on Environment and Development in Rio de Janeiro. The subsequent adoption of Agenda 21 and the Millennium Development Goals marked significant global commitments to sustainable development, culminating in the 2015 SDGs (UNDP, 2015).

Sustainable development serves as a crucial framework for promoting economic stability and social equity while safeguarding the environment. By encouraging practices that prioritize resource conservation and resilience, it mitigates the risks of economic collapse associated with unsustainable exploitation. Moreover, sustainable development endeavors to combat poverty by fostering inclusive economic growth and enhancing access to essential services like healthcare and education. By addressing inequalities in resource distribution and opportunities, it builds stronger and more cohesive societies. Sustainable development also facilitates access to clean water, nutritious food, and healthcare, thereby reducing health risks linked to environmental degradation. Furthermore, it drives innovation and the adoption of cleaner technologies, stimulating economic growth and job creation in emerging sectors. Businesses embracing sustainable practices earn trust and loyalty from consumers, enhancing their long-term success. Aligning with ethical and moral principles, sustainable development promotes responsible behavior towards the environment, society, and future generations. By prioritizing long-term planning and considering the needs of future generations, it safeguards against shortsighted decision-making that could compromise future well-being. Overall, sustainable development offers a comprehensive approach to addressing environmental, social, and economic challenges, striving to create a more equitable, resilient, and prosperous world for present and future generations. The reappropriation of sustainable development involves stripping away its institutional and conceptual framework and redefining it through a paradigmatic lens. This new perspective has highlighted diverse critical drivers. Diemer (2019) outlines six key drivers that characterize the new perspective on sustainable development:

(a) Addressing Social and Controversial Issues: Sustainable development encompasses challenges such as climate change, biodiversity loss, and resource depletion, embracing risk and uncertainty in conventional knowledge.
(b) Transdisciplinarity and Complexity: Embracing complexity, sustainable development necessitates a transdisciplinary approach, drawing from scholars like Edgar Morin.
(c) Methodology of System Thinking: Sustainable development adopts a system thinking methodology, recognizing the interconnectedness of various systems.
(d) Integration of Multiple Dimensions: Considering environmental, social, economic, cultural, and governance dimensions, sustainable development requires balancing and trade-offs.

(e) Redefinition of Spatial and Temporal Scales: Long-term thinking fosters solidarity between generations and acknowledges irreversibility in decision-making.
(f) Values and Principles for Behavioral Change: Grounded in values such as sustainability and equity, sustainable development promotes behavioral change towards responsible practices.

Today, sustainable development is recognized as a holistic concept that integrates economic, social, and environmental dimensions, acknowledging their interconnectedness. As the concept evolves, there is a growing emphasis on inclusive and adaptive approaches, incorporating local and Indigenous knowledge alongside religious, social, and cultural values to tackle contemporary challenges effectively (Sultana and Muhammad, 2018). Integrating Islamic epistemological models into global efforts for environmental sustainability offers a promising avenue for comprehensive and intelligent management of environmental policies and actions. Drawing on principles of stewardship, justice, and balance from Islamic teachings, this integration can provide valuable insights and strategies for addressing environmental issues. Furthermore, incorporating Islamic perspectives fosters a deeper understanding of humanity's role as stewards of the earth and promotes harmonious coexistence with nature. This inclusive approach respects diverse cultural and religious viewpoints on environmental stewardship, fostering cooperation and mutual respect towards sustainability goals. Ultimately, integrating Islamic epistemological models enriches discussions on environmental sustainability and enhances the likelihood of achieving positive global change.

18.3 ISLAMIC THOUGHTS ON SUSTAINABLE DEVELOPMENT

It is widely accepted by the majority of Muslim scholars that in Islam, the basic goal of development is to create an environment that enables people to enjoy spiritual, moral, and socio-economic well-being in this world and success in the hereafter (they refer to this conception of well-being as *falāḥ*). The distinct view of Islamic teachings on development is based on the innate human dignity that God has granted to all mankind. In this respect, the Quran unambiguously declares:

> We have bestowed dignity on the progeny of Adam ... and conferred on them special favours, above a great part of Our creation.
>
> (Q 17:70)

The Islamic conception of development is based on the fact that God Almighty created the universe and appointed man as successor on the earth to carry out the task of rebuilding according to Islamic law. The first verse of the opening chapter of the Quran states, "Praise be to Allah, the Cherisher and Sustainer of the Worlds." Yusuf Ali states that "the Arabic term Rabb usually translated as Lord also has the meaning of cherishing, sustaining and bringing to maturity. Allah cares for all the Worlds He has created" (Ali, 2014, p. 14). Therefore, the Islamic worldview emphasizes the unity of God across all major monotheistic religions, with Islam seen as the final revelation in a continuum of past religions. Central to this worldview is the concept of tawhid, or the oneness of God, which governs the universe in a balanced and harmonious manner. Therefore, humanity, as God's stewards (*khalīfa*), is tasked with maintaining this balance and harmony in the natural order (*fiṭra*), guided by the Quran and the teachings of the Prophet Muhammad. These sources provide moral guidance and legal rulings, emphasizing consciousness, accountability in the afterlife, and compassion towards all living beings (Hasan,

2006; Al-Jayyousi, 2016; Khan and Haneef, 2022). In the economic sphere, Islam promotes the protection of public goods and prohibits usury (*ribā*), instead advocating for zero-interest and risk-sharing in Islamic banking. Alms (zakat) and trust funds (*waqf*) serve as mechanisms for fostering social equity and supporting those in need (Hasan, 2006; Fazreena and Zuhdi, 2015; Al-Jayyousi, 2016). Islamic law evaluates matters in light of their objectives (*maqāṣid*), which include religion, life, posterity, reason, and property rights. These principles guide sustainable development efforts, aiming to establish a balance between environmental, economic, and social dimensions while upholding moral values and ethics (Chapra, 1993). Ultimately, sustainable development from an Islamic perspective seeks to enable individuals to lead healthy and responsible lives with moderation, ensuring the well-being of present and future generations in harmony with the natural world (Chapra, 1993; Fazreena and Zuhdi, 2015; Al-Jayyousi, 2016).

Islam provides a comprehensive framework for understanding humanity's relationship with the environment, emphasizing stewardship and responsibility (Al-Jayyousi et al., 2022), with the Quran and hadith offering guidance on environmental matters and addressing environmental issues and the Prophet Muhammad's life serving as a model for justice and equity (Hasan, 2006). According to the Islamic perspective, the earth is a gift from God to humanity, but this gift comes with responsibilities. The Quran teaches that nature reflects divine wisdom and provides signs for those who reflect (Khalid, 2002). For instance, the Quran highlights the significance of water, animals, plants, and natural processes, emphasizing the interconnectedness of all living beings (Q 16:65–69). The Prophet Muhammad urged his followers to treat the environment with care, advising against harming women, children, the elderly, animals, crops, or trees. This recognition of the intrinsic value of nature underscores the inseparable connection between humans and their surroundings. The Quran offers profound guidance regarding our role as caretakers of the earth and the imperative of safeguarding the environment. It highlights God's creation in perfect balance and proportion (Q 54:49), emphasizing the beauty and harmony of His creation. Moreover, it underscores human responsibility on earth (Q 2:30), urging respect for all creation (Q 6:38), preservation of the environment and nature (Q 21:32), and the avoidance of corruption (Q 2:60). These verses emphasize the importance of environmental stewardship and ethical conduct in maintaining the earth's natural balance and beauty.

Therefore, as Khan and Haneef (2022) have highlighted, on the one hand, Islam places a strong emphasis on human capital development, which aligns with SDGs 3 and 4, focusing on health and education, respectively. This emphasis serves as a catalyst for economic growth (SDG-8). Additionally, Islamic principles such as zakat and *waqf* offer effective social financial tools to address various SDGs, including poverty alleviation (SDG-1), hunger eradication (SDG-2), gender equality (SDG-5), and reducing inequality (SDG-10). On the other hand, Islamic finance provides long-term financing solutions like *ṣukūk*, which can be instrumental in building sustainable infrastructure (SDG-9) and developing sustainable cities (SDG-11). Furthermore, Islamic principles derived from the Holy Quran can positively contribute to several SDGs. For instance, the principle of *waṣatiyya* (moderation) can promote sustainable consumption and production (SDG-12), while the concept of *khilāfa* (vicegerency on earth) can guide the responsible utilization of water and sanitation (SDG-6) and energy (SDG-7).

Furthermore, other principles such as *maṣlaḥa* (public interest) can inform the sustainable management of natural resources, while *salām* (peace) and *al-ʿadl wa-l-iḥsān* (justice and benevolence) support efforts towards achieving SDG-16 (peace, justice, and strong institutions). Finally, the principle of *taʿāwanū ʿalā al-birr* (cooperation in goodness) encourages partnerships and collaboration, contributing to the realization of SDG-17 (partnerships for the goals).

In light of these brilliant teachings and principles, the community could protect and preserve the environment for future generations, aligning with the principles of sustainability and responsible stewardship wisely and effectively.

18.4 TIMELESSNESS OF THE ISLAMIC PARADIGM

Muslims believe that the core principles and values of Islam are timeless and applicable to all people and ages. This belief is rooted in the idea that the Quran, as the holy book of Islam, is a message for all of humanity, not bound by a specific historical or cultural context. Some scholars argue too that there is a need for continuous reinterpretation of Islamic principles to address modern challenges. This is particularly relevant in a rapidly changing world where new ethical, social, and technological issues emerge. Based on this, Islamic jurisprudence, or *fiqh*, allows *ijtihād* for the interpretation and adaptation of Islamic teachings to address new challenges and changing circumstances. *Ijtihād*, which refers to independent reasoning and interpretation, is a fundamental concept in Islamic legal tradition. The process of *ijtihād* can lead to the development of new models and approaches within the framework of Islamic ethics. For example, scholars may explore how Islamic principles can guide issues related to economics, governance, human rights, and environmental sustainability in the twenty-first century. It is important to note that within the Islamic tradition there are diverse interpretations and schools of thought. Different scholars and communities may have varying perspectives on how *ijtihād* should be conducted and what the outcomes should be. However, the idea of *ijtihād* and the reinterpretation of Islamic teachings for contemporary contexts is a subject of ongoing discussion and debate among Muslim scholars and communities. Indeed, it reflects the dynamism and adaptability of Islamic jurisprudence to address the challenges and complexities of the modern world while staying true to the core values of Islam.

The basic pillars of the idea of sustainable development are the unity of destiny and the common future, and this concept is clearly seen in the hadith of the Prophet:

> The example of the person abiding by Allah's order and restrictions in comparison to those who violate them is like the example of those persons who drew lots for their seats in a boat. Some of them got seats in the upper part, and the others in the lower. When the latter needed water, they had to go up to bring water (and that troubled the others), so they said, "Let us make a hole in our share of the ship (and get water) saving those who are above us from troubling them." So, if the people in the upper part left the others to do what they had suggested, all the people of the ship would be destroyed, but if they prevented them, both parties would be safe.[1]

This hadith indicates the importance of the unity of destiny and the common future in the context of Islamic values and sustainable development and also sheds light on the concept of cooperation and joint participation to preserve the public interest and stand against pollution and environmental problems. It contains many examples and lessons, including:

1. The Unity of Fate: This hadith shows the importance of understanding that we all share in sufferings and benefits. If harm is done to one person, it will affect everyone. This has been reflected in the poem of the famous Iranian poet Saadi Shirazi, who says:

[1] al-Bukhārī, *Ṣaḥīḥ*, the Book of Company, chapter 6, hadith 1.

Human beings are members of a whole
In creation of one essence and soul
If one member is afflicted with pain
Other members uneasy will remain
If you have no sympathy for human pain
The name of human you cannot retain

This is evident in the context of sustainable development where we must consider the effects of our actions on the environment and society in general.

2. Cooperation and Solidarity: This hadith also encourages cooperation and solidarity between individuals and communities to face shared challenges. We must work together to preserve the environment and a better future for everyone.
3. Shared Responsibility: This hadith mentions that the people who lived in the lower part of the ship lived in the knowledge that they would not be righteous if they did not act. This indicates that everyone must do their duty and contribute to the protection of the environment and public interests. In the Quran, too, humanity's concern for preserving the environment is a moral responsibility.

In the context of sustainable development and environmental protection, we can conclude that joint action and unity in efforts are vital to face environmental challenges and maintain a sustainable future for future generations.

The most important thing that distinguishes the Islamic approach to preserving the environment is highlighting the values of rationalization in consumption through moderation in all human actions. God Almighty said: "And We made you a moderate nation" (Q 2:143). Therefore, extravagance in anything and by any means is forbidden in Islam, as God Almighty said: "And eat and drink, and do not be extravagant. Indeed, God does not like the extravagant" (Q 7:31). He also said: "Eat from its fruit when it bears fruit and pay its due on the day of its harvest, and do not be extravagant. Indeed, He does not like the extravagant" (Q 6: 141). From an economic point of view, Islam has called for moderation even in spending. God Almighty said: "And those who, when they spend, are neither extravagant nor stingy, and there is stability in between" (Q 25:67).

Therefore, from an Islamic view, sustainable development is striving diligently to do the work to reach the state of satisfaction that achieves happiness according to universal laws established by God Almighty; it is a balanced and comprehensive development in which one side does not dominate another. It is economic, social, humanitarian, environmental, technical, and administrative development, and it is material, spiritual, and participatory development (Gadri, 2023). In this process, no one is excluded, and no one is deprived of its positive impacts. It preserves the environment from pollution, tampering, and waste, and is development that gives the present generations their rights without undermining the rights of future generations. To this end, it is emphasized that the best possible means must be applied, and the principles of justice must be adopted. It also seeks to continuously advance individuals, qualifying and preparing them to conduct the desired development process to achieve well-being for them in their life, and to bring them the honor that God has bestowed upon them in this life and avoiding what God Almighty has forbidden.

There may not be a significant distinction between the concept of sustainable development according to the Islamic perspective and its contemporary counterpart familiar through international institutions. However, certain unique aspects of Islamic development differentiate it from the contemporary understanding:

(a) Islamic development is seen as a form of worship to God, yielding rewards in both worldly life and the hereafter.
(b) It encompasses both material and spiritual dimensions.
(c) Islamic development is governed by a disciplined legal authority, primarily the Quran and Sunna, which provide directives and guidelines to regulate and rationalize the process.
(d) It is inclusive and nondiscriminatory, transcending gender, color, belief, or race.
(e) Islamic development is not merely an option but a religious obligation, binding on both individuals and nations.

18.5 STEWARDSHIP AND TRUST

Two critical principles regarding man's position in the universe, stewardship and trust, are important concepts in the context of environmental ethics and sustainability (Arafa, 2014). In Islamic theology, the concept of stewardship (*khilāfa*) means that humans are considered stewards or caretakers of the earth, responsible for its well-being and the well-being of all creatures (Redwan, 2018). This concept is rooted in the Quran, where it is mentioned that humans are God's vicegerents (*khalīfa*) on earth. The concept of stewardship implies the responsible management and utilization of resources. Therefore, as pointed out by Sayem (2023, p. 273) the Quran portrays human identity in a twofold manner: as the vicegerent of God on earth and as the servant of God. This dual identity entails both honor and responsibility. On the one hand, humans are designated as vicegerent or representative of God (*khalīfa*), which emphasizes their exceptional dignity. On the other hand, this dignity is accompanied by great responsibility, emphasized by the terms *ʿabd Allāh* (servant of God) and *amāna* (trust). Thus, human life is characterized by responsibility, humility, service, and stewardship over God's creation. This implies that humans are entrusted with the task of caring for the earth and its inhabitants on behalf of God. Therefore, as stewards, humans have the responsibility to manage and utilize the earth's resources wisely and sustainably.

Muslims are encouraged to use natural resources wisely and avoid wastefulness. With the task of stewardship, God both honors and tests man. If man is allowed to make use of nature on the one hand, then, on the other hand, he is responsible for the balanced and sustainable use of it. For nothing is in man's possession; rather, he rules over the entrusted property that God has placed at his disposal.

> Verily we offered the entrusted property (*amāna*) to the Heavens and the Earth and the Mountains; but they refused to undertake it, being afraid thereof: but man undertook it; he was indeed unjust and foolish. (Q 33:72)

> Thus, We have made you trustees (*khulafāʾ*) on the earth after them, to see how you would act. (Q 10:14)

From a Quranic perspective, humans are considered trustees (*khalīfa*) of the earth's resources. This principle underscores the ethical obligation of ensuring that natural resources are used sustainably, with a focus on long-term conservation. The principle of *amāna* entails that the earth has been entrusted to man and it must be cared for and protected accordingly. As such, he has the task of cultivating the earth sustainably and maintaining ecological balance.

> Children of Adam, dress well whenever you are at worship, and eat and drink [as We have permitted] but do not be extravagant (*mīzān*): God does not like extravagant people. (Q 7:31)

The principle of trust emphasizes that natural resources are entrusted to humans for their use, but this use should be in line with ethical and sustainable principles. It underscores the importance of considering the needs of future generations (sustainability) and ensuring that resources are not depleted nor degraded to the detriment of future inhabitants of the earth. These principles align with broader environmental ethics and the concept of sustainable development, emphasizing the ethical responsibility to care of the earth and its resources. They call for a balanced approach to resource use, one that meets the needs of the present without compromising the ability of future generations to meet their needs. In practice, this entails sustainable resource management, conservation efforts, responsible consumption, and ethical decision-making in matters related to the environment. These principles also reflect the idea that environmental conservation is not just an ecological or scientific concern but also a moral and ethical imperative deeply rooted in religious and philosophical beliefs. They provide a strong ethical foundation for addressing environmental challenges and fostering a harmonious relationship between humans and the natural world. The idea that God is the sole proprietor of the earth reinforces the notion that humans do not have absolute ownership over the planet and its resources. Instead, they are entrusted with the earth's resources and are expected to use them in accordance with God's guidance, which includes principles of justice, equity, and sustainability. Therefore, while humans are beneficiaries of the earth's resources, it is essential to emphasize that this benefit should not entail the reckless exploitation of nature. Consequently, exploitation that leads to environmental degradation and harm to other creatures. Additionally, Islamic environmental safety is based upon the principle of "use" without "abuse." Environmental protection under the Islamic legal scheme does not differ from any modern environmental legal system.

Accordingly, the goal of the Islamic development process is to achieve man's material and moral happiness in a way that is consistent with the sharia's intention of establishing his caliphate on earth. Therefore, the human being is the focus of Islamic development and central to this process, making it a prime area for comprehensive development of human capabilities and skills, both material and moral. The centrality of the human being as the focus of Islamic development and its goal gives priority to education, so that it prioritizes educational development before other areas of development.

18.6 MODERATION AND JUSTICE IN ISLAM

Moderation and justice in Islam, often referred to as *al-wasaṭiyya*, is a fundamental concept that encourages and promotes balance, equity, and a middle way in all aspects of life. It plays a significant role in contributing to sustainable development within Islamic societies. This concept constitutes an important ethical and behavioral framework in Islam and is considered key to maintaining balance and stability in Muslim societies and promoting understanding and cooperation between different cultures and societies. This approach is considered an integral part of the teachings of the Islamic religion and is believed to contribute to achieving justice, peace, and stability in societies. In connection with the importance of adopting a moderate approach in the personal and social life of the believers, the Quran reminds us:

> O people of faith, be firm and steadfast for God and bear witness to justice, truth and righteousness, and of course you should not be enmity of a group to go out of the way of justice, do justice, which is closer to piety [than any action]. And fear God, surely God is aware of everything you do.
>
> (Q 5:8)

This distinctive approach emphasizes balance, justice, compassion and tolerance, and moderation in religious behavior. From this perspective, first, Muslims have been reminded that they must avoid indulging in excessive extremism and reduce extremism in all matters. Second, they must be fair in their dealings with others and respect the rights of individuals and communities. Third, they must treat others with kindness and understanding and be prepared to tolerate differing opinions and beliefs. Fourth, they must properly understand the teachings of Islam and avoid neglecting worship or indulging in religious extremism. For this, it is important that an Islamic educational system institutionalizes and promotes the principles of justice and fairness in the social, cultural, and economic matters of individuals and communities, and emphasizes that an appropriate and moderate way must be sought to deal with issues and make decisions.

Additionally, an individual's cognition, experience, and attitude about the environment will inevitably affect the way they interact with the natural environment (Mishal et al., 2017). The correlation between human overindulgence and environmental contamination is a well-established concern in the field of environmental science (Ma et al., 2021). Addressing this issue involves recognizing the ecological limits of our planet, promoting sustainable practices, and fostering a culture of moderation and responsibility in our interactions with the environment. This approach is essential for safeguarding the well-being of both current and future generations and protecting the planet's ecosystems. However, most studies conducted on the environmental crisis have confirmed the close relationship between human extravagance in dealing with the environment and environmental destruction in all its forms (Chu and Karr, 2017; Garcia et al., 2021; Bsoul et al., 2022). Extravagance has led to diverse environmental catastrophic crises whose impacts are not limited to humans alone but extends to whole ecosystems, endangering life on the planet. There is no doubt that the best way to save humanity or the environment from the effects of extravagance and depletion of natural resources in vain or without concern for dangers is to return to the approach of moderation.

However, the call for moderation and justice does not imply passivity in the face of environmental challenges. Rather, it obliges humanity to actively engage in the stewardship and reconstruction of the earth, fulfilling the trust of succession (*khilāfa*) entrusted to them by God. They must deal with natural systems and the environment in a way that enables him to develop their life without excessive use of natural resources or by oppressing the rights of others. For this, many Islamic traditions call for environmental protection and attention to public hygiene through the establishment of precise controls and clear standards.

18.7 ISLAMIC ETHICAL ENVIRONMENTAL PRINCIPLES

Islamic ethical environmental principles provide guidance for individuals, communities, and societies to interact with the natural world in a manner that is respectful, sustainable, and just. These principles operate at various levels, including the macro (societal and policy level), meso (community and organizational level), and micro (individual and personal level). Therefore, by integrating these Islamic ethical environmental principles at the macro, meso, and micro levels, individuals, communities, and societies can contribute to the protection, preservation, and sustainable management of the environment in accordance with Islamic teachings and values.

At the macro level, Islam emphasizes the concept of stewardship (*khilāfa*), where humans are regarded as custodians or trustees of the earth. This principle calls for the development of policies and governance structures that prioritize environmental conservation, sustainable development, and the equitable distribution of resources. In addition to this, Islamic ethics underscore the importance of justice (*'adl*) in all aspects of human conduct, including environmental management, which requires policies and initiatives that promote environmental justice, ensure fair access to natural resources, and address environmental inequalities and disparities. Furthermore, sustainability is a central theme in Islamic teachings, emphasizing the need to use natural resources responsibly (*taqwā*) and ensure their preservation for future generations. This, in turn, guides the development of policies and strategies for sustainable development, resource management, and environmental conservation.

At the meso level, Islam encourages consultation and collaboration within communities (shura) to address shared challenges and make collective decisions. Shura (community engagement) promotes community-based initiatives, partnerships, and grassroots movements for environmental protection, conservation, and sustainable development. Islamic ethics emphasize the importance of social responsibility (*takāful*) and solidarity towards others, including future generations and nonhuman beings. This principle encourages organizations, institutions, and businesses to integrate environmental considerations into their operations, supply chains, and corporate social responsibility initiatives. More importantly, Islam emphasizes the importance of seeking knowledge (*taʿlīm*) and promoting awareness about environmental issues and ethical responsibilities, which calls for educational programs, outreach campaigns, and community-based initiatives to raise awareness about environmental conservation, sustainable lifestyles, and Islamic environmental ethics.

At the micro level, Islam places a strong emphasis on personal piety and righteousness (*taqwā*) in all aspects of life, including interactions with the environment. These principles guide individuals to adopt environmentally conscious behavior, such as conserving water and energy, reducing waste, and practicing moderation in consumption. Furthermore, in the form of environmental ethics (*amāna*), Islam teaches that humans are entrusted with the earth and its resources and will be held accountable for their stewardship, which instills a sense of moral responsibility and environmental consciousness in individuals, motivating them to care for the environment and minimize their ecological footprint in daily life. Additionally, Islamic teachings encourage ethical consumption practices (halal and *ṭayyib*) that prioritize the well-being of humans, animals, and the environment. At this level, these principles guide individuals to make informed choices about their consumption habits, opting for sustainable, organic, and ethically produced goods.

By presenting the Islamic conceptual model for environmental sustainability (Figure 18.1), I have sought to elucidate Islamic ethical environmental principles across three action levels: macro, meso, and micro. At the macro level, stewardship (*khilāfa*) underscores two pivotal principles: Responsible management and care of the earth, and custodianship over natural resources. Moving to the meso level, conservation (*ḥifẓ al-bīʾa*) embodies three key principles: the protection of biodiversity, preservation of ecosystems, and the sustainable use of resources. Lastly, at the micro level, moderation (*ʿiffa*) highlights three critical principles: avoidance of waste and extravagance, balance in consumption habits, and respect for the rights of future generations.

These ethical principles not only foster eco-harmonization and solidarity but also guide all main dimensions of sustainable development in a wise and satisfactory manner. By effectively directing the sustainable development process, these principles contribute to the realization and accomplishment of the Sustainable Development Goals (SDGs) effectively and successfully.

As shown in the Islamic conceptual model, Islamic development models rooted in faith-based principles have emerged as alternative paradigms. But, as Al-Jayyousi (2017) has asserted, their realization remains a subject of ongoing experimentation, primarily due to the inherent challenge of striking a balance between tradition and modernity. Despite this, the works of many

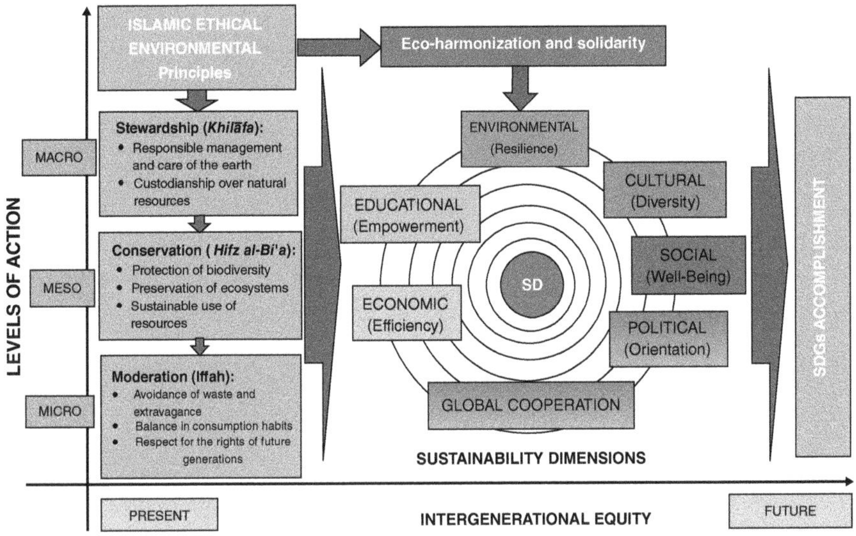

FIGURE 18.1 Islamic conceptual model on enviromental sustainability

Muslim scholars, such as Hasan (2006), Marsuki, (2009), Astrom (2011), Abdulrahman (2011), and Al-Jayyousi (2012) have been promoting the spiritual dimensions of sustainable development, especially according to the following key principles:

1. Acknowledging the spiritual dimension within the Sustainable Development Goals (SDGs) framework implies a holistic approach to human well-being. While the SDGs primarily address material needs such as poverty alleviation, education, and healthcare, integrating spirituality recognizes that individuals have deeper existential needs beyond material comforts.
2. Spiritual development can contribute to inner fulfillment and happiness, which are essential components of overall well-being. While economic prosperity and social progress are vital, they may not guarantee happiness if individuals lack a sense of purpose, meaning, or connection to something greater than themselves.
3. Spirituality often encompasses values and ethics that guide human behavior towards compassion, empathy, justice, and environmental stewardship. Integrating spiritual principles into sustainable development efforts can foster a culture of responsibility towards one another and the planet, promoting long-term harmony and balance.
4. Many spiritual traditions emphasize the importance of community and social cohesion. Strengthening social ties and fostering a sense of belonging can enhance resilience and solidarity within communities, contributing to more sustainable development outcomes.
5. Spirituality often includes a reverence for nature and a recognition of humanity's interconnectedness with the environment. Integrating spiritual perspectives into environmental conservation efforts can inspire greater respect for the natural world and promote sustainable practices that preserve ecosystems for future generations.
6. Practices such as meditation, mindfulness, and contemplation are integral to many spiritual traditions. These practices can enhance mental health, resilience, and overall well-being, complementing efforts to address psychological stress and promote mental wellness within sustainable development agendas.

7. Recognizing and respecting diverse spiritual beliefs and cultural traditions is essential for sustainable development that is inclusive and equitable. Upholding cultural heritage and spiritual practices within communities contributes to social cohesion and enriches the collective tapestry of human experience.

Indeed, incorporating the spiritual aspect into the SDGs framework thus enriches development efforts by addressing not only material needs but also the deeper dimensions of human existence, fostering a more holistic and sustainable approach to improving quality of life for all. In this regard, scholars such as Nasr (1997) argue that the Quranic understanding of human ethical responsibility, encapsulated in concepts like *khilāfa*, *ʿabd*, and *amāna*, can contribute to environmental sustainability. Therefore, by emphasizing humans' moral responsibility as stewards of God's creation, the Quranic perspective suggests a way to promote environmental sustainability while honoring human dignity and divine purpose.

1. Islamic teachings provide logical and practical support for environmental sustainability.
2. Incorporating Islamic guidelines, such as the concepts of *khilāfa* and *amāna*, can help reverse current environmental degradation.
3. Quranic terms like *ʿadl, iḥsān, isrāf, tabdhīr, fasād*, and *ākhira* offer guidance on how to treat the environment and why it is essential to care for it.
4. The Quran emphasizes the importance of maintaining ecological equilibrium in human activities.
5. By integrating ethically oriented sustainability strategies inspired by Quranic principles, humans can enhance their stewardship of the environment and promote its well-being.

18.8 CONCLUSION

The convergence of values and ethics from diverse cultural and religious backgrounds can contribute to a more inclusive and comprehensive approach to sustainable development, recognizing the interconnectedness of human well-being and the health of the planet. Regarding this, it is argued that there is a great potential in the Islamic environmental traditions focusing on justice, degrowth, and harmony between human and nature, to provide a unique model for a transition to sustainable development. This assertion reflects a perspective that has gained traction in the field of environmental ethics and sustainability (Al-Jayyousi, 2012). Therefore, it is worthy to highlight that the concept of development in Islam is an integral part of the Islamic faith, based on the values of Islam inspired by the Quran and Sunna, and it is an obligation imposed by Islam on individuals and groups.

This chapter explored the Islamic perspective on stewardship, trust, moderation, and justice in the context of environmental ethics and sustainability. It delves into the Quranic teachings and Islamic ethical principles that emphasize humans' roles as stewards of the earth and the importance of responsible management and utilization of resources. Additionally, it highlights the significance of moderation, justice, and ethical conduct in addressing environmental challenges and fostering sustainable development.

The chapter sought to effectively integrate Quranic verses and scholarly insights to illustrate how Islamic teachings provide a comprehensive framework for environmental stewardship and sustainability. By emphasizing the ethical responsibilities embedded in Islamic principles, such as stewardship (*khilāfa*), trust (*amāna*), moderation (*al-wasaṭiyya*), and justice (*ʿadl*), it underscored the importance of harmonious coexistence between humans and the natural world. Furthermore, the chapter elucidated how these principles operate at different levels – macro, meso, and micro – to guide individuals, communities, and societies towards sustainable practices and ethical conduct. It emphasizes the interconnectedness between spiritual well-being, environmental stewardship, and sustainable development, highlighting the holistic approach advocated by Islamic teachings.

The incorporation of the Islamic conceptual model for environmental sustainability provided a comprehensive framework for understanding and implementing Islamic ethical principles in environmental conservation and sustainable development efforts. By integrating spiritual dimensions into the Sustainable Development Goals (SDGs) framework, the chapter underscored the importance of addressing not only material needs but also the deeper dimensions of human existence. Overall, this chapter articulated the Islamic perspective on environmental ethics and sustainability, offering valuable insights into how Islamic principles can guide individuals and societies towards a more balanced and responsible relationship with the environment.

REFERENCES

Abdulrachman, S. M. (2011). "Integrating Spiritual Dimension in Sustainable Development Strategy: An Islamic Perspective." *OIDA International Journal of Sustainable Development*, 2, 51–64.

Ahmadi, A. (2019). "Analysis of the Effects of Environmental Hazards on the Stability of the Security of Border of Rural Areas (Case Study: Villages of Sarovabad, Kurdistan, and Middle of South Khorasan)." *Geography and Regional Urban Planning*, 9, 161–88.

Ali, A. Y. (2014). *The Meaning of the Glorious Qur'ān: Text & Commentary*. Lahore: Shaikh Muhammad Ashraf.

Arafa, M. A. (2014). "Islamic Policy of Environmental Conservation: 1,500 Years Old – Yet Thoroughly Modern." *European Journal of Law Reform*, 16, 465–504.

Astrom, Z. H. O. (2011). "Paradigm Shift for Sustainable Development: The Contribution of Islamic Economics." *Journal of Economic and Social Studies*, 1, 73–82.

Azizi, N. (2024). "Higher Education for Sustainable Development: What Can Be Learnt from Islamic Academic Tradition." In H. Schuetze, M. Osborne, R. Zhang, and A. Y. Adamu (eds.), *Higher Education and Its Contribution to the SDGs*. Manchester: Manchester University Press.

Baba Oghli, M. (2013). "An Overview of the Environmental Crisis in Iran Centered around Air Pollution and Destruction of Water Resources." *Economic Journal – Monthly Review of Economic Issues and Policies*, 13, 59–72.

Basheer, M., Nechifor, V., and Calzadilla, A. (2022). "Balancing National Economic Policy Outcomes for Sustainable Development." *Nature Communications*, 13, 5041.

Bigdeli, V., and Maleki, S. (2022). "Evaluation of the Effects of Human Hazards on the Instability of Natural Resources and the Rural Environment in the Central Part of Alborz, Qazvin Province." *Sustainable Agricultural Science Research*, 2, 1–14.

Bringezu, S., and Bleischwitz, R. (2009). *Sustainable Resource Management: Global Trends, Visions and Policies*. New York: Routledge.

Bsoul, L., Omer, A., Kucukalic, L., and Archbold, R. H. (2022). "Islam's Perspective on Environmental Sustainability: A Conceptual Analysis." *Social Sciences*, 11, 228.

Chapra, M. U. (1993). *Islam and Economic Development*. Islamabad: Islamic Research Institute.

Chu, E. W., and Karr, J. R. (2017). "Environmental Impact: Concept, Consequences, Measurement." *Reference Module in Life Sciences*, B978-0-12-809633-8.02380-3.

Diamond, J. (2005). *Collapse: How Complex Societies Choose to Fail or Survive*. New York: Penguin.

Diemer, A. (2019). "Six Key Drivers for Sustainable Development." *International Journal of Environmental Sciences and Natural Resources*, 18, 1–29.

Fazreena, N., and Zuhdi, M. (2015). "Sustainability and Role of Theology: Islamic Perspectives." *Al-Qimah Al-Mudhafah: Journal of Management Science*, 1, 1–10.

Gadri, I. (2023). "The Role of Islamic Legislation in Achieving Sustainable Development." *International Humanitarian and Natural Sciences Journal*, 4, 7.

Garcia, A. C., Ambrose, A., Hawkins, A., and Parkes, S. (2021). "High Consumption: An Unsustainable Habit That Needs More Attention." *Energy Research & Social Science*, 80, 228.

Hasan, Z. (2006). "Sustainable Development from an Islamic Perspective: Meaning, Implications, and Policy Concerns." *Journal of King Abdulaziz University Islamic Economics*, 19, 3–18.

Al-Jayyousi, O. R. (2012). *Islam and Sustainable Development: New Worldviews*. London: Routledge.

(2016). *Islam and Sustainable Development: New Worldviews*. London: Routledge.

(2017). *Integral Innovation: New Worldviews*. London: Routledge.

Al-Jayyousi, O., Tok, E., Saniff, S. M., Wan Hasan, W. N., Janahi, N. A., and Yesuf, A. J. (2022). "Re-Thinking Sustainable Development within Islamic Worldviews: A Systematic Literature Review." *Sustainability*, 14, 7300.

Khalid, F. (2022). "Islam and the Environment." In P. Timmerman (ed.), *Social and Economic Dimensions of Global Environmental Change*, vol. 5. Chichester: Wiley, 332–9.

Khan, F., and Haneef, M. A. (2022). "Religious Responses to Sustainable Development Goals: An Islamic Perspective." *Journal of Islamic Monetary Economics and Finance*, 8, 161–80.

Lampert, A. (2019). "Over-Exploitation of Natural Resources Is Followed by Inevitable Declines in Economic Growth and Discount Rate." *Nature Communication*, 10, 1419.

Ma, H., Chen, W., Ma, H., and Yang, H. (2021). "Influence of Publicity and Education and Environmental Values on the Green Consumption Behaviour of Urban Residents in Tibet." *International Journal of Environmental Research and Public Health*, 18, 10808.

Marsuki, M. Z. (2009). "Religious Agendas towards Sustainable Development: An Islamic Perspective." *Malaysian Journal of Science and Technology Studies*, 7, 22–38.

Mishal, A., Dubey, R., Gupta, O. K., and Luo, Z. (2017). "Dynamics of Environmental Consciousness and Green Purchase Behaviour: An Empirical Study." *International Journal of Climate Change Strategy Management*, 9, 682–706.

Nasr, S. H. (1997). "Islam and Environmental Crisis." In A. R. Agwan (ed.), *Islam and the Environment*. New Delhi: Institute of Objective Studies, 31–51.

Redwan, A. (2018). "When the Earth Speaks Against Us: Environmental Ethics in Islam." *Yaqeen Institute for Islamic Research*, 20 September. https://yaqeeninstitute.org/read/paper/when-the-earth-speaks-against-us-environmental-ethics-in-islam.

Sawari, M., and Biranvand, N. (2022). "Challenges of Applying Environmentally Sustainable Operations among Wheat Farmers in Khorram Abad City." *Water and Sustainable Development*, 8, 87–98.

Sayem, Md. A. (2023). "Islam and Environmental Ethics: A Qur'anic Approach." In S. S. Kwan and W. Chow (eds.), *Asian Spiritualities and Social Transformation*. Hong Kong: Springer, 263–76.

Shafai Moghadam, E., and Niazi, M. (2019). "Meta-Analysis of Studies on the Relationship between Environmental Awareness and Environmental Behavior in Iran." *Scientific Quarterly of Environment and Transsectoral Development*, 67, 51–64.

Shi, L., Han, L., Yang, F., and Gao, L. (2019). "The Evolution of Sustainable Development Theory: Types, Goals, and Research Prospects." *Sustainability*, 11, 7158.

Steffen, W., et al. (2018). "Trajectories of the Earth System in the Anthropocene." *Proceedings of the National Academy of Sciences*, 115, 8252–59.

Sultana, R., and Muhammad, N. (2018). "Role of Indigenous Knowledge in Sustainable Development." *International Journal of Development Research*, 8, 18902–06.

Swim, J. K., Clayton, S., and Howard, G. S. (2011). "Human Behavioral Contributions to Climate Change: Psychological and Contextual Drivers." *American Psychologist*, 66, 251–64.

United Nations Development Programme (UNDP). (2018). *Human Development Indices and Indicators Statistical Update*. New York: UNDP.

United Nations Sustainable Development. "Agenda 21." Proceedings of the United Nations Conference on Environment & Development, Rio de Janeiro, Brazil, June 3–14, 1992.

Wang, C., Cardon, P. W., Liu, J., and Madni, G. R. (2020). "Social and Economic Factors Responsible for Environmental Performance: A Global Analysis." PLoS ONE, 15, e0237597.

World Commission on Environment and Development (WCED). (1987). *Our Common Future*. Oxford: Oxford University Press.

19

Arabic Treatises on Environmental Pollution up to the End of the Thirteenth Century

Lutfallah Gari

19.1 INTRODUCTION

Physicians have studied the causes and treatment of widespread illnesses, or crowd diseases, both endemics and epidemics, as part of medicine. A handful of books in this field were translated into Arabic during the "translation period" of Arab/Islamic intellectual history (eighth to ninth centuries AD). Among these were the works of Hippocrates and Galen. Two of Hippocrates' works, *Airs, Waters, and Places* and *Epidemics*, were among the most influential later used by Arab physicians.

This chapter is a sort of a handlist, limited in scope to a brief review of Arabic works that studied environmental pollution as a cause of various illnesses, endemic and epidemic. It reviews only the treatises written solely on this subject, unless the issue was treated in depth within some compendiums. In addition to the contents, I mention any original and important ideas in the treatise. Other researchers have treated this subject briefly, and their works are cited in the references. But several of the treatises listed in this chapter were not known when those works were published, and this led to some erroneous assumptions, which are corrected below.

This chapter deals only with the genre of treatises mentioned above. The subject of protection of public health against the effects of pollution was also treated in other nonmedical books. Among these are the "market and industry inspection manuals" (*ḥisba* books) and the books of "jurisprudence of civil works," which are regulations for civil works and buildings (*aḥkām al-bunyān*).

Table 19.1 gives the titles and bibliographical data of the treatises under review. It also shows the year when the author died, according to both the hijri (Arabic lunar) year (AH) and the Gregorian year (AD). The period covered in the chapter is up to the end of the seventh century AH/thirteenth century AD. This is because the Black Death took place in the fourteenth century AD and encouraged several authors of that time to write about epidemics and plagues. These later works have been studied before.[1]

[1] M. W. Dols, *The Black Death in the Middle East* (Princeton, NJ: Princeton University Press, 1977).

19.2 AL-KINDĪ (NINTH CENTURY)

Until the 1970s it was generally assumed that the latter medieval physicians who wrote on plague did not cite the works of al-Kindī.[2] This is no longer true because al-Tamīmī, whose book was discovered later, cites the treatise on *Incenses Purging the Atmosphere against Epidemics* on seven pages. He says:[3]

> These are recipes of incenses which I extracted from a treatise by Ya'qūb b. Isḥāq al-Kindī to Aḥmad b. al-Mu'taṣim [the Abbasid prince] on making incenses which purge air spoilage.

> وهذه صفات دخن استخرجتها من رسالة ليعقوب بن إسحاق الكندي إلى أحمد بن المعتصم في أعمال الأبخرة المصلحة لفساد الهواء

From these extracts, it appears that the sources used by al-Kindī were firstly books of the Sabian or Mandaean sect – descended from the Babylonian star-worshippers – and secondly, Indian books. Hence, the treatise of al-Kindī is about incenses that combat air pollution according to the available knowledge from his sources and experience.

19.3 QUSṬĀ B. LŪQĀ (NINTH AND TENTH CENTURIES)

Qusṭā wrote and translated many books. His works on environmental issues are given in Table 19.1. One of these is a small treatise *On Contagion*. He defines contagion as a transmission from an ill body to a healthy one. He then describes the means of contagion and gives examples of transferrable diseases. He assigns two causes to widespread illnesses: firstly, the surrounding air, and secondly, contagion/infection.[4] He relates contagion to environmental pollution by saying:[5]

> Surrounding air differs greatly according to different effects on it. These are either from the earth or from the sky. Factors relating to the earth include [i] vapors ascending from forests and swamps; [ii] other ground humidities, such as the smoke ascending from mountains and furnaces; [iii] corpses and other dry bodies which emit smoke when they are burned; and [iv] other decayed things which emit bad fumes and stinky odours when heated by the sun and nature. Heavenly factors include extreme heat in summer and extreme cold in winter. These factors cause the common illnesses that overwhelm most people. The most obvious cause is air spoilage which results from these factors.

> يعرض فيه من هذه الأحداث تعم أكثرهم، يكون أظهر حدوثها عن فساد الهواء بماالهواء المحيط يختلف اختلافا كبيرا، على قدر اختلاف التأثرات التي تحدث فيه: إما من الأسباب الأرضية كالبخارات التي ترتفع من السباخ والغياض وسائر الرطوبات الأرضية كالأدخنة التي ترتفع من الجبال والأتاتين وغيرها من الأجرام اليابسة التي إذا عملت فيها النار انقادت منها دخانا، وكجثث القتلى وغيرها من الأشياء العفنة التي إذا فعلت فيها الحرارة الشمسية والطبيعية أحدثت منها بخارات رديئة وروائح منتنة. وإما من أسباب سمائية، كالحر المفرط في الصيف والبرد المفرط في الشتاء، كان كثيرا ما يعرض للناس أمراض مشتركة

His *Medical Regime for the Pilgrims to Mecca* is a traveler's health guide especially written for a pilgrim to Mecca. The following "chapters" of the treatise are related to environmental pollution and how to cope with various natural resources. Each "chapter" is one page long on average.

- Chapter 4: On the diseases that arise from the blowing of the different kinds of winds.

[2] Ibid., 29n.
[3] Y. Sh'ār (ed.), *Māddat al-baqā' li-l-Tamīmī al-Maqdisī* (Cairo: The Institute of Arabic Manuscripts, 1999), 177–83.
[4] G. Bos (ed.), *Qusṭā Ibn Lūqā's Medical Regime for the Pilgrims to Mecca* (Leiden: Brill, 1992), 5.
[5] H. Fahndrich (ed.), *Abhandlung über die Ansteckung von Qusta Ibn Luqa* (Stuttgart: Franz Steiner Verlag Wiesbaden, 1987), 22–24.

- Chapter 6: On rheum, defluctions, and cough that are caused by changes of weather, and their treatment.
- Chapter 7: On eye diseases that are caused by change of weather, by dust, or winds, and their treatment.
- Chapter 8: On the examination of different waters in order to find out which is the best.
- Chapter 9: On the improvement of contaminated water.
- Chapter 10: On lack of water and ingenuity in finding means of quenching one's thirst.
- Chapter 12: On the treatment of stings and bites of all kinds of vermin.[6]

Qusṭā was a translator who lived during the aforementioned "translation period." The influence of Galen's ideas can be traced in his works.[7] A treatise entitled *On Epidemics and Their Causes* was ascribed to Qusṭā,[8] but a study of its content, made by the author of this chapter, showed that it is the work of Abū Sahl al-Masīḥī, which will be reviewed below.

19.4 AL-RĀZĪ (RHAZES) (NINTH AND TENTH CENTURIES)

Here, we meet another prolific author, especially in medicine. His extant works in the subject of our study are given in Table 19.1. In his work *On Types of Water*, the subject is treated from the medical, geological, and physical points of view. He cites Hippocrates, Dioscorides, Rufus, Galen, Alexander of Tralles, Ibn Māsawayh, ʿAlī b. Rabban al-Ṭabarī, and Ḥunayn.[9]

In his *Epistle on Chronic Coryza at the Bloom of the Roses*, he describes the effect of pollen dust on the respiratory system.[10]

Al-Rāzī is well known as the most free-thinking of the major philosophers of Islam. His medical works are typically free of dogmatism, following the Hippocratic reliance on clinical observations. His criticism of Galen had the potential, in time, to bring down the whole theory of humors and the scheme of the four elements on which ancient medicine was grounded.[11] Among his ideas appearing for the first time in a book is the positioning of dwelling units uphill and upwind from infected areas.[12]

19.5 IBN AL-JAZZĀR (TENTH CENTURY)

Ibn al-Jazzār did not travel outside the region of Ifriqiya (today's Tunisia), yet he was the author of a book on epidemics in Egypt (Table 19.1). This made him the subject of bitter criticism by the Egyptian physician ʿAlī b. Riḍwān, whose book is reviewed below. Ibn al-Jazzār's work is not extant, except for small extracts by al-Tamīmī and Ibn Riḍwān. Al-Tamīmī quotes the compositions of three syrups that were composed by Ibn al-Jazzār. These syrups were made as health protectors when crowd diseases attack the community. Ibn Riḍwān acuses Ibn al-Jazzār of being

6 Bos, *Qusṭā's Medical Regime*, 21–23.

7 Dols, *The Black Death*, 87.

8 Ibid., 29; F. Sezgin, *Geschichte des Arabischen Schrifttums: Medicine* (Leiden: Brill, 1970), 3:271, 327. Sezgin noted that the treatise cannot be Qusṭā's because it was written upon the request of Khwarazm-Shah (the King of Khwarazm) Ma'mūn, who died in AH 407/AD 1016, while Qusṭā died around AH 300/AD 912.

9 Ibid., 290.

10 F. Hau, "Summary of Rāzī's Epistle on Chronic Coryza at the Bloom of the Roses," *Journal for the History of Arabic Science* 1, no. 1 (1977): 123.

11 L. E. Goodman, "al-Razi," in *Encyclopaedia of Islam* (2nd ed.) (Leiden: Brill, 1995), 8:474.

12 H. al-Bakri (ed.), *al-Manṣūrī fī al-ṭibb li-l-Rāzī* (Kuwait: Institute of Arab Manuscripts, 1987), 225.

weak in Greek philosophy, besides writing about an environment that he did not see. He quotes the erroneous statements of Ibn al-Jazzār and then comments on them one by one.

Nevertheless, Ibn al-Jazzār deserves credit for being the first author in the genre of medical geography books, which study the environmental conditions of a specific town. This genre includes the works of ʿAlī b. Riḍwān, Ibn Jumayʿ, Yaʿqūb al-Isrāʾīlī, and ʿAbd al-Laṭīf al-Baghdādī (Table 19.1). Some researchers have claimed that Ibn Buṭlān (d. AH 458/AD 1066) gave a brief description of Baghdad.[13] However, this "description" is very brief and does not give any valuable information.[14]

19.6 AL-TAMĪMĪ (TENTH CENTURY)

Compared to other treatises, al-Tamīmī's book is voluminous (Table 19.1). Its contents are broadly classified as follows:

1. Views of Hippocrates, Aristotle, and Ahrun on the subject. The author devotes special sections to each of these scholars. He also quotes other non-Arab scientists throughout the book.
2. Description of polluted air types in the Islamic states and their relationship to weather and geographical conditions.
3. Diseases resulting from air pollution and their infectious nature.
4. Hygienic procedures for protection against contagion when epidemics occur.
5. Types of incense that treat/combat air pollution. Many of these were developed by the author himself.
6. Treatment of stagnant water, which produces various types of pollution.
7. Drugs that strengthen the immune system. Here he cites Indian sources, among others.
8. Usage of perfumes, music, and psychotherapy to strengthen the body against infection.
9. Descriptions of smallpox and measles, together with their remedies.
10. Drugs for healing those who caught airborne diseases. Many of these were prepared by al-Tamīmī himself.[15]

This work of al-Tamīmī was listed as lost until the late 1970s,[16] or even the 1980s.[17] Because it was only discovered recently, a number of important ideas in it have been ascribed to later authors. Examples are (i) preventive measures that include sour juices and pickles, ascribed to Tashkupruzade (d. AH 968/AD 1561)[18] and (ii) methods for improving air quality and increasing body resistance to diseases, ascribed to Ibn Khātima (d. ca. AH 775/AD 1373).[19] These subjects were discussed in detail by al-Tamīmī.

19.7 ABŪ SAHL AL-MASĪḤĪ (TENTH AND ELEVENTH CENTURIES)

If al-Tamīmī's work is important in its pioneering details, al-Masīḥī is outstanding in being organized and clear. In nineteen manuscript pages, he presents an "engineered report,"

[13] M. W. Dols and A. S. Gamal, *Medieval Islamic Medicine: Ibn Ridwan's Treatise "On the Prevention of Bodily Ills in Egypt"* (Berkeley: University of California Press, 1984), 53.
[14] J. Schacht and M. Meyerhof (ed. and trans.), *The Medico-Philosophical Controversy between Ibn Butlan of Baghdad and Ibn Ridwan of Cairo* (Cairo: The Egyptian University, 1937), 89.
[15] Shʿār, *Māddat al-baqāʾ*.
[16] Dols, *The Black Death*, 29.
[17] S. K. Hamameh, *Background of History of Arabic Medicine* (Amman: Yarmouk University, 1986), 280.
[18] Dols, *The Black Death*, 99, 333.
[19] Ibid., 99, 100.

classifying crowd diseases in terms of their causes and specifying a certain remedy for each type of disease.

Al-Tamīmī, in comparison, lists many recipes without specifying when and why they are used. Therefore, al-Masīḥī's work is a key to many other works like that of al-Tamīmī.

The treatise is divided into four sections, each one called a *jumla* (group), as follows: (1) the necessity of air to life; (2) changes in air contents and the effects of these changes on health; (3) the ways by which epidemics harm the body; (4) prevention and treatment according to the type of epidemic.

In the second section, or *jumla*, we see a clear distinction between endemic illnesses (*al-amrāḍ al-bilādiyya*), epidemics (*al-wabāʾ*), and calamities (*al-mawtān*). In this section the author also gives three causes of epidemics: (i) excessive humidity and warmth in the air compared to usual conditions at that time of the year; (ii) excessive dryness in the air; (iii) air being changed into an abnormal condition, or when abnormal detrimental fumes are mixed with it. This last condition, particularly, causes calamity.

In section four the epidemics are classified according to the causes given in section two, and al-Masīḥī then specifies the remedies for each type.[20]

19.8 IBN SĪNĀ (AVICENNA) (TENTH AND ELEVENTH CENTURIES)

Ibn Sīnā's *Qānūn* is very important on this subject. Chapters in it were devoted to (i) mold; (ii) types of water, their quality, and treatment; (iii) illnesses caused by impurity in water; (iv) air spoilage and its effect; (v) designing houses and selecting their location according to health considerations; (vi) food quality and its effects; and (vii) animals transmitting pollution or observed at the time of plague. He mentions as a sign of an approaching plague that rats and subterranean animals flee to the surface of the earth, behave as if they are intoxicated, and die. This important phenomenon was mentioned by Ibn Sīnā for the first time.[21] Some of these ideas are treated in depth in another work of Ibn Sīnā entitled *Repelling General Harm from the Human Body* (see Table 19.1). It discusses types of harmful air: hot, cold, coal smoke, perfumes, northerly wind, southerly wind, moving from one air to another, epidemics caused by air putrescence, and stagnant and moving air. It also describes waterborne harms and treatment by different types of water: forest water, sulphur water, alum water, sulfate water, arsenic water, verdigris water, ammonia water, copper water, tar water, saline water, bitter water, sour water, beer, strong black liquor, light transparent liquor, and stored liquor.[22]

19.9 ʿALĪ B. RIḌWĀN (ELEVENTH CENTURY)

As mentioned in Section 19.5, Ibn Riḍwān wrote his work to rebut Ibn al-Jazzār. According to Ibn Riḍwān, Ibn al-Jazzār was not only a foreigner to Egypt, he also lacked knowledge of Greek medical theory. Ibn Riḍwān was a strong exponent of the thought of Hippocrates and Galen.[23] His treatise covers the following issues: (1) the specific causes of pollution in Egypt (more exactly Metropolitan Cairo); (2) the temperament of Egypt; (3) the necessity to adapt to the local

[20] A. S. al-Masīḥī, "Fī taḥqīq amr al-wabāʾ wa-1-iḥtirāz minhu idhā waqaʿa," ed. L. Qārī, *Journal for the History of Arabic Science* 13 (2005): 5–55.
[21] Dols, *The Black Death*, 89.
[22] M. Z. al-Bābā (ed.), *Min muʾallafāt Ibn Sīnā al-ṭibbiyya: Kitāb dafʿ al-maḍārr al- kulliyya ʿan al-abdān al-insāniyya* (Aleppo: Aleppo University Institute for the History of Arabic Science, 1984).
[23] Dols and Gamal, *Ibn Ridwan's Treatise*, 19, 65.

environment; (4) disturbances and corruption of air there; (5) the causes of epidemics; (6) a geographical comparison of various parts of Metropolitan Cairo; (7) a geographical comparison of Metropolitan Cairo and rural areas; (8) the methods of improving the quality of air, water, and food in Egypt; (9) appropriate medical remedies for ill bodies; (10) the advantages of living in Metropolitan Cairo; (11) an emphasis on a proper regime and prophylaxis rather than remedial treatment.[24]

19.10 IBN JUMAYʿ (TWELFTH CENTURY)

Here, we meet another study of the specific environment of a city. Ibn Jumayʿ wrote about Alexandria, where he examines the various parts of the city, conducts field reviews of drinking water sources and how they are polluted, and studies types of food and drink. After demonstrating the city's shortcomings, he gives appropriate advice to eliminate pollution and avoid illnesses. He also gives special advice to the physicians who work in the city.[25]

Ibn Jumayʿ was influenced by Ibn Riḍwān, not only in the overall subject but also in repeating some of his predecessor's ideas. For example, Ibn Riḍwān mentioned that "Burga rams are imported to Egypt. Their transportation creates aridity in their bodies, dryness, and humors that are unlike the temperament of the Egyptians. For this reason, most of the rams get sick when they enter Egypt. After settling down in Egypt for a suitable length of time, their temperament changes and agrees with that of the Egyptians."[26] Ibn Jumayʿ repeats the same points about Burga rams, but without giving any credit to Ibn Riḍwān.[27]

19.11 YAʿQŪB AL-ISRĀʾĪLĪ (AL-ASʿAD AL-MAḤALLĪ) (TWELFTH CENTURY)

Yaʿqūb states in the introduction that when he visited Damascus in AH 598/AD 1202, he was asked several questions. His treatise on *The Temperament of Damascus* is composed of the answers to those questions, one of which was about the temperament of Damascus, its location, and differences from Egypt. It is composed of four "articles" (*maqālāt*) over thrity-one pages (see Table 19.1). Only the first article (of ten pages) is devoted to the question of Damascus and Egypt, although the whole treatise is named after that article. That article is divided into three sections: (i) presenting the seven climates and proving that the equator is not a temperate zone; (ii) Egypt's temperament; and (iii) the temperament of Damascus.[28] In his opinion Egypt is healthier than Damascus because of the differences in weather and terrain. He therefore gives several pieces of advice regarding suitable diet in Damascus to avoid the common illnesses there.[29]

19.12 ʿABD AL-LAṬĪF AL-BAGHDĀDĪ (TWELFTH AND THIRTEENTH CENTURIES)

ʿAbd al-Laṭīf was a Baghdadi physician who was in Cairo when a great famine and spread of illness occurred in AH 597–98/AD 1201–2. In his book we have a graphic and detailed

[24] Ibid., 69–72.

[25] M. ʿAsīrī and S. al-Bishrī (eds.), *Ṭabʿ al-Iskandariyya li-Ibn Jumayʿ* (Mecca: Umm al-Qura University, 1997).

[26] Dols and Gamal, *Ibn Ridwan's Treatise*, 90–91.

[27] ʿAsīrī and al-Bishrī, *Ṭabʿ al-Iskandariyya*, 69, 70.

[28] R. Şeşen et al. (eds.), *Catalogue of Islamic Medical Manuscripts in the Libraries of Turkey* (Istanbul: Research Centre for Islamic History, Art and Culture, 1984), 390; Y. al-Isrāʾīlī, "Mizāj Dimashq wa-waḍʿihā wa-tafāwutihā min Miṣr," ed. Lutfallah Gari, *ʿĀlam al-Makhṭūṭāt wa-l-Nawādir* 8, no. 2 (2004): 428–57.

[29] al-Isrāʾīlī, *Mizāj Dimashq*, 428–57.

eyewitness account of this occurrence as well as other chapters dealing with ancient monuments of Egypt at that time, plants, animals, exotic foods, buildings (including public baths), and ships. It also contains a progressive study of the River Nile and its floods, so vital to the life and economy of Egypt at that time. This is a famous and important work, which has been studied by several researchers. It contains valuable information concerning environmental pollution. Examples are:

1. The effect of weather conditions and the rise of the Nile river on the health of people. Here he follows Ibn Riḍwān in saying that the people of Upper Egypt are healthier than those of Lower Egypt.[30]
2. The social effects and the behavior of people at times of crisis. Some researchers thought that he was talking about an epidemic,[31] while actually he was describing a calamity that resulted from drought and famine.[32]
3. The proper design of houses and city planning. He observed the use of wind catchers – the towers containing ventilation shafts in houses. The Egyptians had firm sewage channels and their streets, markets, and houses were wide and comfortable.[33]
4. The bath houses were designed with proper ventilation, ample lighting, and elevated vaults.[34]

19.13 IBN AL-QUFF (THIRTEENTH CENTURY)

Ibn al-Quff's work (Table 19.1) belongs to the literary genre of preventive medicine, as did Ibn Sīnā's work. Other works of this genre showed less concern about environmental issues.[35] Ibn al-Quff's book is considered outstanding among all the others, being the most comprehensive, finest, and most original. It was not surpassed until the time of the European Renaissance in its precision, scope, contents, and objectivity.[36] Among the subjects of the book are (1) water quality and treatment; (2) causes of epidemics; and (3) diet and health protection of people according to the terrain and weather in their areas.[37]

19.14 IBN AL-NAFĪS (THIRTEENTH CENTURY)

Ibn al-Nafīs wrote a voluminous commentary on Hippocrates' *Epidemics I* and *III*. But this commentary does not add much new to the field. In his introduction, Ibn al-Nafīs mentions that his task is limited to explaining the statements of "the leader Hippocrates" (*al-Imām Abuqrāṭ* in his Arabic wording) and justifying his claims. He decided to avoid any side issues and arguments against the opponents of Hippocrates, because these controversies were mentioned in other works written by the commentator.[38]

30 Dols and Gamal, *Ibn Ridwan's Treatise*, 92, 93; K. Hafuz Zand, J. A. Videan, and I. E. Videan (trans.), *The Eastern Key: Kitāb al-Ifādah wa'l-I'tibār of 'Abdallatif al-Baghdādi* (London: George Allen & Unwin, 1965), 27.

31 Zand et al., *The Eastern Key*, 7; Dols, *The Black Death*, 33.

32 Ibn Ḥajar al-'Asqalānī, *Badhl al-mā'ūn fī faḍl al-ṭā'ūn*, ed. A. I. A. al-Kātib (Riyadh: Dār al-'Āṣima, 1999), 368; al-Nuwayrī, *Nihāyat al-arab fī funūn al-adab* (Cairo: General Egyptian Book Organization, 1992), 29:12.

33 Zand et al., *The Eastern Key*, 179.

34 Ibid., 183.

35 S. K. Hamarneh (ed.), *Ibn al-Quff al-Karaki's Book on Preventive Medicine and the Prevention of Health* (Amman: University of Jordan, 1989), 12–13.

36 Ibid.

37 Ibid., 176, 180–92, 216, 217.

38 Ibn al-Nafīs, Sharḥ Kitāb Apidhimiyā (Cairo: National Egyptian Library MS 583, Ṭibb-Tal'at), folios 1a, 1b.

TABLE 19.1 *List of Arabic treatises dealing with environmental pollution up to the end of the thirteenth century AD*

No.	English title	Arabic title	Author	Condition (manuscript or printed)	Folios or pages
1	*Causes of Heavenly Fatal Toxicants, Named Epidemics*	رسالة في إيضاح العلة في السمائم القاتلة السمائية، وهو على القول المطلق الوباء	al-Kindī (d. ca. AH 200/AD 873)	Not extant[a]	
2	*Drugs Curing Detrimental Odours*	رسالة في الأدوية المشفية من الروائح المؤذية	=	Not extant[b]	
3	*Incenses Purging the Atmosphere against Epidemics*	رسالة في الأبخرة المصلحة للجو من الأوباء	=	Not extant, but al-Tamīmī (see below) cites it[c]	7 printed pages are extant
4	*On Contagion*	كتاب في الإعداء	Qusṭā b. Lūqā (d. ca. AH 300/AD 912)	Printed in Stuttgart, 1987	9 printed pages
5	*Medical Regime for the Pilgrims*	رسالة في تدبير سفر الحج	=	Printed in Leiden, 1992	34 printed pages
6	*Epistle on Chronic Coryza at the Bloom of Roses*	مقالة في العلة التي من أجلها يعرض الزكام لأبي زيد البلخي في فصل الربيع عند شمه الورد	al-Rāzī (Rhazes) (d. AH 313/AD 925)	Printed in Aleppo, 1977[d]	3 printed pages
7	*The Reason That Simūm [Hot Wind] Kills Most Animals*	السبب في قتل ريح السموم أكثر الحيوان	=	Manuscript in Tehran[e]	fols. 90a–91a (3 ms. pages)
8	*On Types of Waters*	رسالة في المياه	=	Manuscript in Tehran[f]	fols. 224b–242a (36 ms. pages)
9	*On Epidemics*	الرسالة الوبائية	=	Manuscript in Istanbul[g]	fols. 493b–502a (18 ms. pages)
10	*Causes Generating Epidemics in Egypt: Methods of Prevention and Treatment*	نعت الأسباب المولدة للوباء في مصر وطريق الحيلة في ذلك وعلاج ما يتخوف منه	Ibn al-Jazzār (d. AH 369/AD 980)	Not extant, but small extracts are given by al-Tamīmī and ʿAlī b. Riḍwān	Small extracts
11	*Surviving Material about Treating Air Spoilage and Avoiding Epidemics*	مادة البقاء بإصلاح فساد الهواء والتحرز من ضرر الوباء	al-Tamīmī (d. ca. AH 390/AD 1000)	Printed in Cairo, 1999	700 printed pages

TABLE 19.1 (*cont.*)

No.	English title	Arabic title	Author	Condition (manuscript or printed)	Folios or pages
12	*Investigation on the Nature of Epidemics, Their Prevention, and Cure*	رسالة في تحقيق أمر الوباء والاحتراز منه وإصلاحه إذا وقع	Abū Sahl al-Masīḥī (d. AH 401/ AD 1010)	Edited by the current author	49 printed pages
13	*Repelling General Harm from the Human Body*	دفع المضار الكلية عن الأبدان الإنسانية	Ibn Sīnā (Avicenna) (d. AH 428/ AD 1037)	Printed in Aleppo, 1984	63 printed pages
14	*On the Prevention of Bodily Ills in Egypt*	دفع مضار الأبدان بأرض مصر	ʿAlī b. Riḍwān (d. AH 460/ AD 1068)	Printed in 3 different editions: Berkeley, Baghdad, and Cairo	63 printed pages (US edition)
15	*The Nature of Alexandria*	طبع الإسكندرية	Ibn Jumayʿ (d. AH 594/ AD 1198)	Printed in Mecca, 1997	74 printed pages
16	*The Temperament of Damascus: Its Location and Difference from Egypt*	مزاج دمشق ووضعها وتفاوتها من مصر	Yaʿqūb al-Isrāʾīlī (d. ca. AH 600/AD 1204)	Edited by the current author	11 printed pages
17	*Instruction and Admonition on the Things Seen and Events Observed in the Land of Egypt*	الإفادة والاعتبار في الأمور المشاهدة والحوادث المعاينة بأرض مصر	ʿAbd al-Laṭīf al-Baghdādī (d. AH 629/ AD 1231)	Printed in several editions, e.g., Paris, 1810; London, 1964; Damascus, 1982; Baghdad, 1987	96 printed pages
18	*Prevention of Health and Avoiding Ills*	جامع الغرض في حفظ الصحة ودفع المرض	Ibn al-Quff (d. AH 685/ AD 1286)	Printed in Amman, 1989	363 printed pages
19	*Commentary on Epidemics*	شرح كتاب أبيذيميا	Ibn al-Nafīs (d. AH 687/ AD 1288)	Manuscript in Istanbul and Cairo	Cairo copy is in 193 folios (386 pages)

[a] E. Savage-Smith, S. Swain, and G. J. van Gelder (eds.), *A Literary History of Medicine: The ʿUyūn al-anbāʾ fī ṭabaqāt al-aṭibbāʾ of Ibn Abī Uṣaybiʿah* (Leiden: Brill, 2020), 3-1:578, no. 155.
[b] Ibid., 577, no. 132.
[c] Shʿār, *Māddat al-baqāʾ*, 177–83.
[d] Hau, "Rāzī's Epistle," 123.
[e] Sezgin, *Geschichte des Arabischen Schrifttums*, 3:289.
[f] Ibid., 290.
[g] Şeşen et al., *Islamic Medical Manuscripts*, 115.

The latter authors who cited Ibn al-Nafīs were not influenced by this commentary. They referred to another book of his, namely the *Summary of Qānūn* (*Mujāz al-Qānūn*), which has a commentary on the important plague description of Ibn Sīnā.[39]

39 Dols, *The Black Death*, 29, 88, 89.

19.15 CLASSIFICATION OF THE TREATISES

Table 19.1 lists twenty books related to the field of environmental pollution. Most of them have been mentioned in this chapter – a few are not extant. The topics covered in these books are:

- Pollution and contagion (1, 4, and 9 in the table)
- Medical geography and the environmental conditions of specific cities: Alexandria, Cairo, and Damascus (10, 14, 15, 16, 17)
- Remedies, treatments, and combating illness (2, 3, 11,12)
- Prevention of air and water pollution (8, 13, 18)
- Clinical observations (19)
- Conservation of health for travelers (5)
- Effects of weather (6, 7, 20)

Some of the authors made genuine contributions to the field. I have mentioned, for example, those who studied specific localities. Others did no more than relying on the Greek theory of humors and miasma. Ibn al-Nafīs, for example, known in the history of medicine for the discovery of the lesser blood circulation, wrote two lengthy commentaries on Hippocrates, but upon reviewing the extant one of those commentaries I do not find anything new. The common factor linking all the authors is that they were all concerned with environmental pollution and how to protect human health from its effects.

20

Islamic Environmental Law Revisited as an Academic Discipline

Empowering Community-Led Compliance in Muslim Countries

Ridoan Karim

20.1 INTRODUCTION

In recent decades, there has been a notable increase in environmental legislation. However, these laws have not been effectively implemented and enforced, leading to inadequate outcomes in addressing environmental issues.[1] The United Nations' Intergovernmental Panel on Climate Change (IPCC) has echoed these concerns in its 2018 special report on climate change, highlighting the ongoing failure of nations to uphold environmental laws.[2] This persistent inability to meet climate change targets puts the world at great risk, approaching a critical point from which recovery may be unattainable.

Generally, the establishment of environmental rule of law goes beyond the mere functioning of governmental institutions. Hence, ensuring compliance is a far from straightforward task. While the entities governed by the law, including state agencies, individuals, and corporations, are obligated to adhere to the established legal framework, the decision to do so or not is fundamentally rooted in moral considerations.[3] This complexity arises from the fact that human behaviour and decision-making are influenced by a multitude of non-legal factors, making the issue of compliance a formidable challenge. Therefore, in order to foster compliance with environmental regulations, there is a need for embracing alternative normative sources alongside top-down, state-enforced approaches. It particularly highlights the value of well-established sources like religion, which primarily operate at the social level and originate from the bottom up.

Moral rules, whether enforced as social norms or institutionally enforced as religio-legal norms, have the potential to influence environmental regulations and foster compliance at the social level. Islamic environmental law, also known as environmental *fiqh*, bring these moral rules into the legal and social framework and may assist Muslim countries in striving for environmental justice. Islamic teachings place a strong emphasis on the concept of *khilāfa*, which pertains to stewardship and underscores the responsibility of humans to act as caretakers of the earth. Islamic teachings discourage extravagance, waste, and excessive consumption of

[1] Jan G. Laitos and Lauren Joseph Wolongevicz, 'Why Environmental Laws Fail' (2014) 39(1) *William & Mary Environmental Law and Policy Review*, 1–51.

[2] International Panel on Climate Change (IPCC), Special Report: Global Warming of 1.5°C, www.ipcc.ch/sr15/.

[3] See Brian Bix, *Jurisprudence: Theory and Context* (London: Sweet & Maxwell, 2012), pp. 181–90.

resources. Furthermore, Islamic environmental law acknowledges the intrinsic value of biodiversity and emphasizes the importance of preserving ecosystems and protecting animal welfare. Moreover, Islamic environmental law urges Muslims to proactively address climate change by reducing greenhouse gas emissions, promoting renewable energy sources, and adopting sustainable agricultural practices.

By incorporating these principles as religious and legal norms, Muslim countries can promote sustainable practices, ensure the fair distribution of resources, and encourage community participation in decision-making processes. Since many Muslim-majority countries have implemented legislation and established institutions to govern Muslims' affairs on a national level through the sharia, Islamic environmental governance structures have the potential to benefit marginalized communities and vulnerable groups by ensuring their inclusion in environmental decision-making. This fosters environmental justice and promotes the fair distribution of environmental benefits. Empowering local communities to take responsibility for their environmental obligations through such structures can lead to bottom-up compliance, resulting in greater sustainability and environmental well-being.

The concept of 'Islamic environmental law' is widely recognized among Muslims.[4] However, from the perspective of environmental law scholars, it might be considered premature to engage in discussions specifically about Islamic environmental law. Technically speaking, there is no established field or area of study dedicated to Islamic environmental law.[5] Nonetheless, certain aspects of the sharia can potentially be utilized for environmental preservation purposes. Islamic environmental ethics have been explored in various essays written by Muslim legal environmental scholars.[6] However, the majority of these studies primarily focus on highlighting the ecological significance found in religious texts.[7] As a result, it can be argued that Islamic environmental law remains a distinct and evolving component within the legal system. The evolving nature of Islamic law suggests that studying Islamic environmental law as an academic discipline is warranted. There are several compelling reasons supporting this argument. Firstly, it offers an opportunity to explore the intersection between religious teachings and environmental principles within Muslim-majority countries and communities. Secondly, studying Islamic environmental law as an academic discipline or as a subdiscipline of environmental law and environmental justice enables us to tackle the distinctive obstacles encountered by marginalized communities and vulnerable groups in these countries. It facilitates a deeper examination of how Islamic principles can be employed to ensure the equitable distribution of environmental benefits. Such understanding can contribute to the development of inclusive governance structures and decision-making processes that actively involve all stakeholders, especially those who have traditionally been marginalized. Furthermore, investigating Islamic environmental law within the framework of environmental justice adds value to the broader discourse on sustainability and ecosystem preservation.

To emphasize the benefits, this chapter aims to thoroughly examine Islamic environmental law as an academic discipline, highlighting its unique perspective and values that contribute to its practical implementation in Muslim countries. Additionally, it suggests that studying Islamic environmental law in academic discourse can serve as a catalyst for scholars and practitioners to

[4] Samira Idllalene, *Rediscovery and Revival in Islamic Environmental Law: Back to the Future of Nature's Trust* (Cambridge: Cambridge University Press, 2021), pp. 31–53.
[5] Ibid.
[6] Ibid.
[7] Ibid.

delve into the exploration of how Islamic principles can be translated into concrete actions and policies that foster sustainability and environmental well-being.

20.2 CONVENTIONAL ENVIRONMENTAL LAW VERSUS ISLAMIC ENVIRONMENTAL LAW

In recent decades, there has been a noticeable rise in collective global endeavours to protect and preserve the natural surroundings.[8] Prominent examples of these efforts include the Stockholm Declaration on the Human Environment in 1972, the Montreal Protocol of 1987, which prohibited the use of chlorofluorocarbons (CFCs), the Kyoto Protocol of 1997 aiming to reduce greenhouse gas emissions and combat climate change, and the subsequent Paris Agreement. These agreements exemplify the growing trend towards environmental preservation. Moreover, given the imminent danger posed by human-induced climate change and the potentially disastrous consequences that lie ahead for humanity in the twenty-first century and beyond, the importance of international collaboration in safeguarding and regulating the environment becomes even more evident. Despite the ongoing endeavours of international organizations to establish worldwide benchmarks for environmental preservation and the reduction of greenhouse gas emissions, several problems persist.[9]

As per a report by the United Nations (UN), there exists a recurring challenge within international environmental laws.[10] This challenge is a widespread issue encountered in various other international legal systems, wherein enforcement methods are found to be insufficient. While this revelation undoubtedly raises concerns about the future of our planet, it may not come as a surprise to those familiar with the progression and application of international law. Throughout the twentieth century, international organizations and agreements have faced an ongoing challenge due to the inadequate presence of enforcement mechanisms, which persists and hinders the successful implementation of effective global policies by the international community in the twenty-first century.

Consequently, international environmental agreements, such as the Paris Agreement, often include voluntary provisions, rendering the UN unable to enforce compliance among individual signatories.[11] Furthermore, governments of signatory states may demonstrate hesitancy in strictly adhering to the obligations set forth in the Paris Agreement, given the absence of a guarantee for universal adherence by all signatories. Alongside this uncertainty, governments may encounter financial limitations when implementing stringent environmental regulations, as they could potentially incur substantial costs.

However, it is crucial to acknowledge that the enforcement of environmental laws is not exclusively a concern at the international level. National environmental law, which governs environmental protection within a country's borders, also encounters substantial challenges when it comes to enforcement.[12] In fact, national environmental law grapples with similar issues, such as the lack of effective enforcement mechanisms. This predicament can be

[8] Tseming Yang and Robert V. Percival, 'The Emergence of Global Environmental Law' (2009) 36 *Ecology Law Quarterly*, 615–64, at 627.

[9] See Matúš Štulajter, 'Problem of Enforcement of an International Law: Analysis of Law Enforcement Mechanisms of the United Nations and the World Trade Organization' (2017) 33(2) *Journal of Modern Science*, 325–35.

[10] United Nations Environmental Programme (UNEP), *Environmental Rule of Law: First Global Report* (Nairobi: UNEP, 2019), https://bit.ly/4003MSK.

[11] Annalisa Savaresi, 'The Paris Agreement: A New Beginning?' (2016) 34(1) *Journal of Energy & Natural Resources Law*, 16–26.

[12] Laitos and Wolongevicz, 'Why Environmental Laws Fail'.

attributed to various factors, including limited resources, institutional weaknesses, corruption, and conflicting priorities.[13]

For nearly two centuries, regulations designed to oversee resource utilization and environmental protection have been based on flawed perceptions about the fundamental nature of the environment, humanity, and their intricate relationship.[14] For instance, a significant proportion of regulations pertaining to the environment and natural resources are built upon the underlying belief that humans should receive primary benefits, prioritizing human interests above those of nature and the planet that sustains both humanity and the natural ecosystem.[15] These anthropocentric rules are rooted in notions of human superiority and exceptionalism, aiming primarily to advance human benefits and well-being.[16]

Islamic environmental law differs from the anthropocentric approach by recognizing the interconnectedness and interdependence of humans, nature, and the planet. It emphasizes the concept of stewardship (*khilāfa*), trust (*amāna*), and responsibility towards the environment as a trust from God rather than prioritizing human interests above all else. In Islamic environmental law, the well-being of humans is indeed important but is balanced with the well-being of all creation. Islamic teachings encourage the protection and conservation of the natural environment, including the preservation of biodiversity, sustainable resource management, and the prevention of pollution and harm to ecosystems. It also emphasizes the concept of *ḥisba*, which refers to the duty of Muslims to enjoin what is good and prevent what is harmful. This includes promoting environmental sustainability, social justice, and ethical conduct towards the environment. Muslims are encouraged to be mindful of their actions and strive for harmony between human activities and the natural world, which is known as 'creating the balance', or *mīzān* in Arabic.

Furthermore, it is worth noting that until relatively recently, there was a prevailing belief in the near-boundless nature of earth's resources. It was only when resources started dwindling or becoming entirely depleted that humans began to contemplate the existence of finite planetary boundaries that impose restrictions on resource consumption. As a consequence of these erroneous perspectives, numerous regulations aimed at regulating human behaviour and mitigating disruptions to earth's systems and resources. However, Islamic principles, from the very beginning, encourage the sustainable use of natural resources and prohibit wastefulness and overexploitation. They condemn extravagance (*isrāf*) or waste (*tabdhīr*) and corruption of the earth (*fasād fī al-arḍ*), which prohibit excessive consumption and actions that harm the environment.

Another factor contributing to the lack of success in conventional environmental law stems from the tendency of environmental and natural resource laws to be rooted in two impractical models.[17] The first model assumes a certain understanding of how nature functions. Traditionally, it has been believed that nature attains stability when undisturbed by human intervention, implying that it is self-regulating.[18] However, the reality is that nature operates as a 'complex adaptive system' that thrives on constant non-linear change rather than stability. It is

[13] See Irene Villanueva Nemesio, 'Strengthening Environmental Rule of Law: Enforcement, Combatting Corruption, and Encouraging Citizen Suits' (2014) 27 *Georgetown Environmental Law Review*, 321–42.

[14] Laitos and Wolongevicz, 'Why Environmental Laws Fail'.

[15] See William Leiss, 'Modern Science, Enlightenment, and the Domination of Nature: No Exit?' (2007) 2(2) *Fast Capitalism*, 49–58, https://fastcapitalism.uta.edu/2_2/leiss.html.

[16] See 'Environmental Ethics', Stanford Encyclopedia of Philosophy, http://plato.stanford.edu/entries/ethics-environmental/#IntChaEnvEth.

[17] See Johan Rockström et al., 'A Safe Operating Space for Humanity' (2009) 461 *Nature*, 472–75.

[18] Ibid.

essential to recognize that humans are not external observers but rather inherent and interconnected parts of this system.[19] Therefore, we cannot simply 'leave nature alone'. This is why the concept of stewardship in Islamic environmental law is so important. It implies that humans have a duty to actively care for and manage the earth's resources while being mindful of the long-term consequences of their actions. This includes conserving ecosystems, protecting biodiversity, and ensuring equitable access to resources for both present and future generations.

The second unrealistic model of conventional environmental law is based on flawed notions of human behaviour. One enduring and cherished belief, particularly among economists, is that humans are rational beings solely driven by self-interest and the pursuit of personal welfare maximization.[20] However, human behaviour often deviates from this rational actor model, as individuals frequently exhibit altruistic tendencies or make choices influenced by emotional and cognitive biases rather than strict welfare maximization. Islamic environmental law addresses the flawed notion of human behaviour by recognizing the multi-dimensional nature of human beings and their motivations. It acknowledges that humans are not solely driven by self-interest and the pursuit of personal welfare maximization. Instead, Islamic teachings recognize the existence of altruistic tendencies and the influence of emotional and cognitive biases in human decision-making. Islamic environmental law emphasizes the importance of ethical conduct and moral responsibility in the relationship between humans and the environment. It encourages individuals to consider the broader implications of their actions on both human welfare and the well-being of the natural world. This recognition of the moral and ethical dimensions of human behaviour helps to counterbalance the narrow focus on self-interest often prevalent in conventional environmental law. The concept of *iḥsān* plays a significant role. *Iḥsān* refers to acts of kindness, excellence, and doing what is right. It encourages individuals to go beyond their self-interest and to act in a way that benefits not only themselves but also their communities and the environment.

Many of the flawed assumptions and inaccurate models of conventional environmental laws have played a role in shaping the 'Four Troubled Eras' of environmental and natural resource laws.[21] In Era I, known as the 'Use' era, resources were perceived as inexhaustible and pollution-resistant, with a predominant emphasis on immediate human benefit within the legal framework.[22] Era II, the 'Conservation' era, marked a shift towards recognizing the importance of resource preservation for future generations.[23] However, the prevailing belief that natural resources are meant solely for human use remained dominant, even as laws aimed to manage and conserve resources for future human needs. Subsequently, with a growing awareness of planetary boundaries, legal policies transitioned from resource management to preservation (Era III) and then environmental protection (Era IV).[24] In Era III the focus was on preserving specific lands and species, such as wilderness areas, parks, and endangered wildlife that were facing depletion.[25] Era IV laws were designed to safeguard environmental goods, including air and water, which were increasingly subject to pollution.[26] Nevertheless, during both Eras III and IV, laws still maintained an anthropocentric perspective and continued to perceive humans as

[19] Simon Levin et al., 'Social-Ecological Systems as Complex Adaptive Systems: Modeling and Policy Implications' (2013) 18(2) *Environment and Development Economics*, 111–32.
[20] See Daniel Kahneman, *Thinking, Fast and Slow* (New York: Farrar, Straus and Giroux, 2011).
[21] Laitos and Wolongevicz, 'Why Environmental Laws Fail'.
[22] Ibid.
[23] Ibid.
[24] Ibid.
[25] Ibid.
[26] Ibid.

separate from nature.[27] This is where the fundamental fallacies underlying traditional legal responses to natural resources and environmental goods lie.

Islamic environmental law offers an alternative framework that challenges these flawed assumptions. It recognizes the intrinsic value of the natural environment and the interconnectedness between humans and the earth. It incorporates ethical principles such as justice, equity, and compassion. Islamic environmental law also encourages responsible behaviour, sustainable practices, and the consideration of broader implications for both human welfare and the well-being of the natural world. Therefore, the evolving nature of Islamic environmental law necessitates its study as an academic discipline that intertwines with environmental justice and conventional environmental laws. In the next section, the aim is to present compelling reasons that support this argument and explore how Islamic environmental law, within the framework of environmental justice and conventional environmental law, contributes value to the broader discourse on sustainability and ecosystem preservation.

20.3 ISLAMIC ENVIRONMENTAL LAW: AN ACADEMIC DISCIPLINE

To effectively decrease greenhouse gas emissions, it is crucial for major fossil fuel producers to separate their economies from the key factors that contribute to the ongoing rise in global temperatures. Among these contributors are nations like Saudi Arabia, Qatar, and the United Arab Emirates (UAE), which incorporate Islamic principles into their legal systems and societal fabric. Although other Muslim-majority countries such as Indonesia, Malaysia, Bangladesh, India, and Pakistan do not enforce Islamic law formally, a substantial portion of their population embraces fatwas and other Islamic legal sources as moral compasses. Therefore, it is imperative to explore the potential incentives embedded within Islamic law that foster active participation in the shift towards environmentally sustainable practices. This exploration entails investigating the extent to which Islamic law can be utilized as a mechanism to integrate principles of energy and environmental justice into the legal framework of a wider Islamic community.

The Islamic Declaration on Climate Change holds a significant position in the contemporary discourse of Islam and its stance on climate change.[28] This influential declaration was unveiled through a collaborative effort by the Organisation of Islamic Cooperation, Islamic Educational, Scientific and Cultural Organization (ISESCO), and the International Islamic Fiqh Academy during a joint symposium. By highlighting the moral obligations entrusted to Muslims, it underscores the urgent need to mitigate the impacts of climate change. To exemplify the call for sustainable living among Muslims, the declaration specifically references the practices of the Prophet (hadith), including the establishment of protected conservation areas (*ḥimā*), advocating a modest lifestyle, and promoting asset recycling through repair or charitable giving. Furthermore, the declaration draws strength from Quranic verse 30:41, providing additional support for its argument:

> Corruption has spread on land and sea as a result of what people's hands have done, so that Allah may cause them to taste the consequences of some of their deeds and perhaps they might return to the Right Path.

The declaration offers captivating perspectives on the topic of environmental justice. Notably, it advocates for affluent nations to redirect their focus from unethical exploitation of the

[27] Ibid.

[28] The Islamic Declaration on Global Climate Change was launched in Istanbul during a two-day event called the International Islamic Climate Change Symposium, held on 17–18 August 2015.

environment towards its preservation, simultaneously aiming to uplift the living conditions of impoverished populations worldwide. Additionally, the declaration emphasizes the collective responsibility of individuals across nations to prioritize adaptation efforts and provide substantial support to the most vulnerable countries with limited capacity for adaptation. This approach holds wealthier nations and high carbon emitters accountable for addressing climate injustice while promoting a universal obligation to adapt in a manner that safeguards the interests of minority groups. Moreover, the declaration holds significant value in delving into the potential spiritual consequences for those who disregard the imperative of climate action.

However, it is crucial to acknowledge the limitations of the declaration. While it receives support from legal organizations such as the Fiqh Academy, it does not possess the status of a fatwa specifically addressing environmental justice. The moral authority of the Quran and Sunna cannot be invoked solely by presenting a multitude of relevant quotations, as demonstrated in the declaration. To achieve a consensus on environmental justice, it is probable that jurists would need to rely on *ijtihād*, which entails the application of independent juristic reasoning. Nevertheless, many scholars and practitioners tend to compare Islamic environmental law with conventional environmental law,[29] rather than recognizing that the principles and perspectives within Islamic environmental law have a unique potential to contribute to the broader field of environmental justice. Although the connection between Islamic environmental law and environmental justice may not be explicitly explored by some scholars, it does not diminish the relevance and applicability of Islamic principles in addressing environmental justice concerns. One reason for the prevailing focus on comparing Islamic environmental law with conventional environmental law is the desire to bridge the gap between Islamic teachings and modern legal frameworks. This approach aims to demonstrate the compatibility and applicability of Islamic principles within the existing legal systems, fostering integration and acceptance. However, it is crucial to expand the discourse beyond this comparative approach and explore the intrinsic connections between Islamic environmental law and environmental justice.

Islamic environmental law emphasizes the interconnectedness of human beings with nature, the responsibility of stewardship, and the need for social and environmental justice.[30] These principles align with the core tenets of environmental justice, such as the fair distribution of environmental benefits and burdens, public participation, and addressing historical injustices.[31] Moreover, incorporating Islamic environmental law within the framework of environmental justice can foster a more inclusive and comprehensive approach to environmental governance. By recognizing the unique contributions of Islamic principles we can enrich the discourse with alternative perspectives and solutions that may be particularly relevant to Muslim-majority regions or communities. This inclusive approach promotes cultural diversity and acknowledges the potential of different religious and ethical systems to contribute to environmental justice.

[29] See Shazny Ramlan, 'Implementing Islamic Law to Protect the Environment: Insights from Singapore, Malaysia, and Indonesia' (2020) 23(2) *Asia Pacific Journal of Environmental Law*, 202–30; Damilola S. Olawuyi, 'Introduction to Environment and Environmental Law', in *Environmental Law in Arab States* (Oxford: Oxford University Press, 2022), pp. 3–32.

[30] Labeeb Bsoul et al., 'Islam's Perspective on Environmental Sustainability: A Conceptual Analysis' (2022) 11(6) *Social Sciences*, 228.

[31] Yoshira O. Van Horne et al., 'An Applied Environmental Justice Framework for Exposure Science' (2023) 33(1) *Journal of Exposure Science & Environmental Epidemiology*, 1–11.

The principles of Islamic environmental laws, such as tawhid,[32] *khalīfa*,[33] *amāna*,[34] and *mīzān*[35] are more connected to the core principles of environmental justice, such as equity,[36] participation,[37] precaution,[38] and accountability.[39] Islamic environmental laws and environmental justice principles share common values such as equity, fairness, and the recognition of the interdependence of humans and nature. Both perspectives emphasize the importance of inclusive decision-making processes that involve all stakeholders, particularly marginalized communities. Islamic environmental laws, when combined with environmental justice principles, can help address historical and ongoing environmental injustices by ensuring equitable access to environmental resources and reducing disproportionate burdens. Environmental justice seeks to rectify historical injustices by ensuring that vulnerable communities are not disproportionately affected by environmental hazards as a part of distributive justice.[40] Islamic environmental law echoes this principle by emphasizing the fair distribution of natural resources and the need to prevent environmental harm. Islamic principles such as *ḥisba* (accountability) and *iḥsān* (acting with excellence and justice) can contribute to addressing environmental disparities and promoting social equity.

Moreover, environmental justice emphasizes the importance of inclusive decision-making processes that involve affected communities as a part of procedural justice.[41] Islamic environmental law emphasizes consultation, consensus-building, and public participation, as demonstrated by the Islamic concept of shura (consultation). Incorporating Islamic principles into environmental justice frameworks can enhance public engagement and ensure that marginalized communities have a voice in environmental decision-making. Environmental justice also recognizes the need for redress and compensation for communities that have historically suffered environmental harm as a form of corrective justice.[42] Islamic law provides a framework for restorative justice through concepts such as *diya* (compensation) and *qiṣāṣ* (retaliation). These principles can be applied to environmental contexts, fostering accountability and promoting reparative measures for communities affected by environmental degradation.

Hence, Islamic environmental law should be regarded as an academic discipline that incorporates the principles of both conventional environmental law and environmental justice. Indeed, Islamic environmental law endeavours to address conventional environmental law by incorporating the principles of environmental justice into the theoretical discourse on

[32] The concept of tawhid, or the oneness of God, forms the foundation of Islamic environmental ethics. It recognizes the interconnectedness of all living beings and highlights the need for harmony and balance in the natural world.

[33] Humans are regarded as *khalīfa*, or trustees, on earth and are responsible for protecting and preserving the environment for future generations.

[34] The principle of *amāna* refers to the trust that humans have been given by God to safeguard the earth and its resources.

[35] The concept of *mīzān* highlights the importance of maintaining a balance and avoiding excess or waste.

[36] Environmental justice demands equal access to environmental resources, services, and decision-making processes for all individuals and communities.

[37] Meaningful public participation is crucial for inclusive and just environmental decision-making.

[38] Environmental justice emphasizes the precautionary principle, which encourages preventative action to protect human health and the environment in the face of uncertain risks.

[39] Environmental justice requires accountability and responsibility from both governmental and private entities for their actions and their impact on communities.

[40] See Mary Menton et al., 'Environmental Justice and the SDGs: From Synergies to Gaps and Contradictions' (2020) 15 *Sustainability Science*, 1621–36.

[41] Derek Bell and Jayne Carrick, 'Procedural Environmental Justice', in Ryan Holifield et al. (eds), *The Routledge Handbook of Environmental Justice* (Abingdon: Routledge, 2017), pp. 101–12.

[42] See Matthew D. Adler, 'Corrective Justice and Liability for Global Warming' (2007) 155(6) *University of Pennsylvania Law Review*, 1859–67.

contemporary environmental principles. However, Islamic environmental law cannot be understood without referring to Islamic environmental ethics. It is important to note that Islamic environmental law and Islamic environmental ethics are related concepts but they are not synonymous. While Islamic environmental ethics provides the moral and ethical guidance, Islamic environmental law translates those ethical principles into legal obligations and regulations. Islamic environmental law is a practical application of Islamic environmental ethics within a legal framework. By incorporating the principles of Islamic environmental ethics into the broader framework of environmental justice, we can address social and environmental disparities, ensure equitable access to a clean and healthy environment, and foster sustainable practices.

The contributions of Islamic environmental law, grounded in principles of distributive justice, procedural justice, and corrective justice, offer valuable insights and approaches to the global discourse on environmental protection and sustainability. By embracing diverse perspectives and incorporating Islamic environmental ethics into environmental justice frameworks, we can work towards a more inclusive, equitable, and sustainable future for all. By positioning Islamic environmental law as an academic discipline that compares and contrasts the conventional knowledge of environmental law and environmental justice, scholars can contribute to the development of a more inclusive and multidimensional understanding of climate justice.

Now that we understand that Islamic environmental law is an integral part of environmental justice rather than only conventional environmental law, will non-Muslim countries, in addition to Muslim countries, incorporate it into their curricula? While Islamic environmental law may have initially been viewed as a domain specific to Muslim-majority countries,[43] its relevance and contributions extend beyond religious boundaries. The inclusion of Islamic environmental law in non-Muslim countries' curricula would undoubtedly offer several benefits. First and foremost, it would foster a more comprehensive and inclusive understanding of environmental law and justice. By acknowledging the unique principles and perspectives within Islamic environmental law, educational institutions can enrich their students' understanding of environmental governance and the diverse approaches to sustainability and relate it to theology. Introducing Islamic environmental law into the curricula of non-Muslim countries would also promote cultural diversity and cross-cultural dialogue. It would offer an opportunity for students to explore different ethical frameworks and legal traditions, fostering an appreciation for the values and contributions of various cultures. This intercultural exchange can lead to greater empathy, understanding, and collaboration in addressing global environmental challenges.

Nevertheless, the incorporation of Islamic environmental law into non-Muslim countries' curricula should be approached with sensitivity and respect for diverse perspectives. It is essential to provide balanced and comprehensive education that encompasses various religious and ethical frameworks, ensuring that students gain a well-rounded understanding of environmental governance.

20.4 ISLAMIC ENVIRONMENTAL LAW FOR MUSLIM COUNTRIES

Islamic environmental law emerged in the sphere of environmental ethics alongside other religious traditions during the late 1970s, 1980s, and 1990s.[44] It represents a contemporary response from Islamic scholars to the global call for addressing environmental challenges.

[43] Idllalene, *Rediscovery and Revival*, 31–53.
[44] See Erhun Kula, 'Islam and Environmental Conservation' (2001) 28(1) *Environmental Conservation*, 1–9.

Notably, the World Wildlife Fund for Nature (WWF) organized meetings in 1986 and 1995, bringing together religious leaders from Buddhism, Christianity, Hinduism, Judaism, and Islam.[45] The purpose of these gatherings was to engage in discussions on the role of religion in safeguarding the natural world and exploring its potential contributions to this significant undertaking.[46]

From that period onwards, Islamic religious leaders and scholars have undertaken commendable initiatives to create 'international instruments' that express the official position of the worldwide Muslim community on vital environmental issues. Notable illustrations of these endeavours include the Islamic Declaration on Sustainable Development and the Islamic Declaration on Global Climate Change. Within Islamic law, environmental preservation has consistently held great importance, evident in the numerous Quranic verses directly addressing environmental concerns and the extensive history of implementing protective measures rooted in Islamic theology.[47] The Quran, the holy scripture of Islam, and the Sunna, encompassing the teachings, actions, and judgements of the Prophet Muhammad as documented in the hadith, serve as the principal sources of Islamic jurisprudence. Islamic jurisprudence has undergone transformations over time to address contemporary legal, political, and practical challenges that may not have been explicitly addressed in the primary texts. In order to facilitate scholarly interpretation, a comprehensive framework known as *ijtihād*[48] has been developed by Islamic scholars. In Islam, the study of theology and the legal sciences are intricately intertwined, forming an inseparable union.

The beauty of Islamic theology lies in its profound understanding of the interconnectedness between law and theology within the context of environmental responsibilities. Rooted in the concepts of cosmic symbiosis and human stewardship, Islam emphasizes the recognition of God as the Creator and the inherent natural order of the universe. This natural order, governed by a delicate equilibrium, highlights the intricate harmony and purposeful existence of all things. As humans possess reason and freedom of choice, Islam seeks to awaken individuals to align with their innate primordial essence and restore harmony with the natural world.

In today's Muslim world, Islamic environmental law is being widely embraced and implemented in various forms, all while upholding the universal core principles on which it is founded. The constitutional frameworks of the majority of contemporary Muslim-majority nations have shifted from theocratic systems to more liberal and democratic structures. Concurrently, Islamic law has undergone a significant transformation, moving away from its predominantly jurist-centric approach to incorporating European-style legal frameworks and legislation. Consequently, the application of Islamic law within Muslim states has become more limited in scope, primarily focusing on personal legal matters like marriage, divorce, or inheritance.

Even within democratic constitutional frameworks, Muslim governments have the capacity to integrate Islamic law, including Islamic environmental law, into their national legal systems.

[45] 'World Wildlife Fund Begins a "New Alliance"', *The New York Times*, 30 September 1986, www.nytimes.com/1986/09/30/world/world-wildlife-fund-begins-a-new-alliance.html.

[46] Ibid.

[47] Willis Jenkins, 'Islamic Law and Environmental Ethics: How Jurisprudence (Usul Al-Fiqh) Mobilizes Practical Reform' (2005) 9(3) *Worldviews: Global Religions, Culture, and Ecology*, 338–64.

[48] *Ijtihād* is a concept within Islamic law (sharia) that refers to the process of independent reasoning and interpretation of the legal sources by qualified scholars. It is the effort made by Islamic jurists to derive legal rulings (fatwas) on new or emerging issues based on the foundational sources of Islamic law, namely the Quran, hadith (sayings and actions of the Prophet Muhammad), the consensus of scholars (*ijmā'*), and analogical reasoning (*qiyās*).

This phenomenon is evident in countries such as Saudi Arabia, Egypt, and Pakistan.[49] In Saudi Arabia, where Islam holds the status of the official religion and the constitution is rooted in sharia and the Prophetic Sunna, the government explicitly upholds its adherence to divine law. Consequently, it can be inferred that all regulations within Saudi Arabia, including the Environmental Act No. 193, promulgated by Royal Decree No. M/34 of 2001, are either based on or aligned with Islamic law.[50] Article 32 of the Constitution of the Kingdom of Saudi Arabia, which mandates the state's obligation to preserve, protect, and enhance the environment,[51] aligns with the responsibilities of *khilāfa*.

In both Egypt and Pakistan, the incorporation of Islamic law into their democratic constitutional frameworks enables the application of Islamic principles in public interest cases presented before national courts. The Constitution of the Arab Republic of Egypt, specifically in Article 2, acknowledges Islamic sharia as the primary legal source.[52] Islamic law in Egypt extended to environmental issues as well, showcasing the broad range of applications of Islamic law in modern legal contexts.[53] On the other hand, in Pakistan, where Islam is the official religion and plays a foundational role in governance, the Supreme Court has acknowledged the harmonious coexistence of Islamic values, including justice, equality, and democracy, with fundamental secular rights.[54] Furthermore, Article 184A of the Constitution of the Islamic Republic of Pakistan was incorporated, taking inspiration from Islamic values, to institute the mechanism of public interest litigation (PIL).[55] Although there have been no distinct PIL cases exclusively focused on environmental rights grounded in Islamic principles, various PIL cases addressing environmental issues in Pakistan, including *Shehla Zia and Others v. WAPDA*[56] and the *Human Rights Case*[57] on environmental pollution in Balochistan, serve as illustrations of the tangible realization of the Islamic entitlement to seek justice and uphold related rights.

Additionally, the integration of Islamic law, including Islamic environmental law, into the national legal systems of Muslim-majority regions outside the Middle East is a significant and evolving phenomenon.[58] The Islamic faith in Southeast Asia encompasses unique attributes resulting from the amalgamation of Indigenous cultural customs with Islamic doctrines and sharia tenets.[59] Noteworthy is the shared civilizational, cultural, and religious heritage among

49 Damilola S. Olawuyi, 'Sources of Environmental Law in Arab States', in *Environmental Law in Arab States* (Oxford: Oxford University Press, 2022), pp. 33–54.

50 Ibid.

51 Ibid.

52 See Tamir Moustafa, 'The Islamist Trend in Egyptian Law' (2010) 3(3) *Politics and Religion*, 610–30; Clark B. Lombardi, *State Law as Islamic Law in Modern Egypt: The Incorporation of the Sharī'a* (Leiden: Brill, 2006), pp. 123–40; Clark B. Lombardi, 'Constitutional Provisions Making Sharia "A" or "The" Chief Source of Legislation: Where Did They Come From? What Do They Mean? Do They Matter?' (2013) 28(3) *American University International Law Review*, 733–74.

53 Clark B. Lombardi and Connie J. Cannon, 'Transformations in Muslim Views about "Forbidding Wrong": The Rise and Fall of Islamist Litigation in Egypt', in Robert W. Hefner (ed.), *Shari'a Law and Modern Muslim Ethics* (Bloomington, IN: Indiana University Press, 2016), pp. 145–49.

54 *Benazir Bhutto v. The Federation of Pakistan* (1988) PLD SC 416 (Supreme Court of Pakistan). See Muhammad Afzal Zullah, 'Human Rights in Pakistan' (1992) 18(4) *Commonwealth Law Bulletin*, 1343, 1346.

55 *Chaudhry Akbar Ali v. Secretary, Minister of Defence, Rawalpindi* (1991) SCMR 2114 (Supreme Court of Pakistan) 2116. For a brief summary of PIL in South Asia, see Ridwanul Hoque, *Judicial Activism in Bangladesh: A Golden Mean Approach* (Newcastle upon Tyne: Cambridge Scholars Publishing, 2011), pp. 90–91.

56 PLD 1994 SC 693 (Supreme Court of Pakistan).

57 PLD 1994 SC 102 (Supreme Court of Pakistan).

58 Shazny Ramlan, 'Religious Law for the Environment: Comparative Islamic Environmental Law in Singapore, Malaysia, and Indonesia' (2019), NUS Centre for Asian Legal Studies Working Paper 19/03.

59 Ibid.

nations such as Malaysia, Indonesia, and Singapore, situated within the Malay Archipelago or Nusantara, which showcases parallel manifestations of these distinctive characteristics.[60]

By tapping into the academic discourse on Islamic law and the environment, and channelling the knowledge into policy, local communities in Muslim countries can be empowered to take responsibility for their environmental obligations. In addition to the general principles and ethical teachings of Islamic law, the issuance of fatwas (religious rulings) plays a significant role in shaping Islamic environmental law. Evidently, in 2011, the Ulama Council of Indonesia (MUI) issued a fatwa declaring destructive mining operations as forbidden (haram) in Islamic law.[61] The fatwa emphasized that mining companies should not harm ecosystems, destroy biodiversity, or cause poverty in local communities.[62] It recommended that the government be more selective in permitting and enforce existing laws with significant penalties for polluters.[63] In 2014, the MUI also issued a fatwa prohibiting activities that threaten endangered species with extinction. The fatwa referenced Quranic passages and hadith, emphasizing the responsibility of believers to care for creatures on earth.[64] The fatwa urged the government to take stronger measures to protect endangered species, businesses to restore damaged ecosystems, religious leaders to promote environmental understanding, and all Muslims to actively participate in conservation efforts.[65] Additionally, in 2016, the MUI issued an environmental fatwa banning slash and burn farming, considering it as religiously forbidden (haram).[66]

While these fatwas do not hold legal authority in Indonesia, they have received support from the secular government. The moral condemnation provided by the fatwas, in addition to legal punishments, aims to deter arsonists and raise awareness about environmental issues. The influence of these fatwas has extended beyond Indonesia, with other Islamic leaders in countries like Bangladesh, Malaysia, Nigeria, and Pakistan considering similar fatwas on environmental matters.[67] In addition to fatwas, mosques, community centres, and educational institutions can also play a pivotal role in disseminating knowledge and fostering environmental consciousness based on Islamic teachings. Imams and religious leaders can incorporate environmental ethics into sermons and religious education, emphasizing the importance of environmental stewardship within an Islamic framework.

One of the significant advantages of utilizing Islamic law for environmental empowerment is its potential to foster bottom-up compliance. Islamic law encourages people and communities to take ownership of their acts by placing a strong focus on individual accountability. Communities may also contribute collectively to sustainable practices by encouraging individuals to incorporate environmental concepts into their everyday lives. This bottom-up compliance also creates a sense of ownership, which leads to long-lasting behavioural changes. Hence, local knowledge and practices may develop that can eventually be leveraged to develop context-specific solutions, enhancing the effectiveness and relevance of environmental initiatives. This bottom-up

60 Ibid.

61 'MUI Issues Fatwa against Rogue Mining Companies', Pusat Pengajian Islam, Universitas Nasional (Jakarta), http://ppi.unas.ac.id/mui-issues-fatwa-against-rogue-mining-companies/.

62 Ibid.

63 Ibid. See also 'Environmental Fatwas of Indonesia', Harvard Divinity School, https://bit.ly/43TUfup.

64 Protection of Endangered Species to Maintain the Balanced Ecosystems, Fatwa no. 04/2014, Ulama Council of Indonesia, http://ppi.unas.ac.id/wp-content/uploads/2014/10/Fatwa_MUI-libre.pdf.

65 Ibid.

66 'Environmental Fatwas of Indonesia'.

67 Sarah Hiddleston, 'Can "Green Fatwas" Combat Climate Change?', *Nature Middle East*, 22 November 2016, www.natureasia.com/en/nmiddleeast/article/10.1038/nmiddleeast.2016.208.

compliance also strengthens community cohesion, as environmental goals are pursued collectively, building a sense of shared purpose and unity.

20.5 CONCLUSION

Islamic environmental law transcends mere legal considerations and encompasses a socio-legal phenomenon rooted in environmental justice objectives, necessitating comprehensive exploration from an academic standpoint. Its potential influence on comparative environmental law, overarching frameworks in environmental legislation, and the intricate interplay between law, religion, and justice should not be overlooked. This chapter serves as a catalyst, igniting inspiration and motivation for further research and advancements in the field of Islamic environmental law, particularly from the perspective of justice. By leveraging the academic discourse on Islamic law and the environment and translating knowledge into effective policies, local communities in Muslim countries can be empowered to embrace their environmental responsibilities with a sense of ownership and commitment.

21

Animal Ethics in Islam

Sarra Tlili

[The Mussulmans] are tender almost to infirmity to the brute creation. (Anonymous 1809, p. 3)

The Mussulman preserves the lives of the lower animals solicitously. Though he considers the dog impure, and never makes a friend of him, he thinks it sinful to kill him, and allows the neighbourhood and even the streets of his towns to be infested by packs of masterless brutes, which you would get rid of in London in one day. The beggar does not venture to destroy his vermin: he puts them tenderly on the ground, to be swept up into the clothes of the next passer-by. There are hospitals in Cairo for superannuated cats, where they are fed at the public expense. (Bacon and Whately 1860, p. 144)

I think that Cartesianism belongs, beneath its mechanicist indifference, to the Judeo-Christiano-Islamic tradition of a war against the animal. (Derrida 2008, p. 101)

Perhaps no animal has a harder time in the Islamic world than the dog.

(Capper 2016, p. 78)

21.1 INTRODUCTION

The roughly two centuries that separate the first two statements from the last two have led to a remarkable change in the presentation of Islam's position on animals in Western texts. In early modern literature, the "Mussulman" or "Mahometan" could be barbarian and deceitful or chivalrous and magnanimous, yet in both cases, his charity to the "brute creation" was affirmed. As early as the seventeenth century, Francis Bacon gave the example of the Turks, whom he depicted as "a cruel people, who nevertheless are kind to beasts, and give alms, to dogs and birds" to corroborate the view that inclination to goodness was deeply imprinted in "man," though – as his example presumably showed – it could be misplaced (Bacon 2010). Indeed, Muslims' compassion could be a sign of the nobility of their character or of the debility of their minds, or could simply be explained away as unrepresentative of their true nature, but in all cases it was seldom questioned.

More recent literature reflects a complex but overall less positive image. Although Jacques Derrida's (2008) claim that Islam is at war against the animal is not shared by more informed critics, it is still representative of a tendency among many ethicists to dismiss the tradition as anti-animal by mere association with its older monotheistic siblings. This position is generally inferred from the fact that, like Judaism and Christianity, Islam authorizes the instrumental use of animals and killing for food. From such well-established themes these ethicists cursorily reach unfounded ones, including the odd idea that Islam gives humans dominion over nonhuman animals or even that it is at war with animals, as Derrida claims.

More informed assessments are more favorable; nonetheless, the growing consensus appears to be that although Islam fares better than some other faith traditions, it still falls short of attending adequately to the needs of nonhuman creatures. Richard Foltz writes, "The Islamic tradition does indeed offer much that can lend itself to respect for species other than our own, but it also contains much that is problematic from an animal rights activist point of view. Even much of what could resemble animal rights within the tradition is unheeded by most Muslims or unknown to them" (Foltz 2006, p. xii).

Kristen Stilt states that the "rules of Islamic law on animal welfare, established in the seventh century, do more to protect animals than the laws of any country today" (Stilt 2008, pp. 8–9), yet she also cites the example of Egypt, a majority-Muslim country that fares very poorly in world surveys of animal welfare, "receiving an 'F' on an 'A' to 'G' grading scale in 2014 from the organization World Animal Protection" (Stilt 2017, p. 5). Modern assessments thus reflect the view that at the normative level Islam is not as animal-friendly as was previously assumed, whereas at the empirical level Muslims' treatment of nonhuman animals has deteriorated.

Meanwhile, many Muslims continue to insist not only that their tradition is highly attentive to the wellbeing of nonhuman creatures but even that it offers one of the best moral hopes in this regard. Such discussions, however, fall short of building a solid enough case in defense of this claim. For example, Mawil Izzi Dien lists many protections that the tradition extends to nonhuman animals, including the fact that owners are required to continue to spend time, money, and effort on their aged and diseased animals even if they no longer expect to benefit from them to illustrate the level of care that Islam accords to nonhuman creatures, but he glosses over the question of killing for food (Izzi Dien 2000, p. 45). Failure to adequately address such a crucial point undermines his case.

Although the reasons behind these conflicting perspectives are too complex to be fully addressed here, a few can be highlighted. First, recent discussions indicate that Muslims' attitudes toward nonhuman animals have deteriorated. Contradictory assessments seem thus to reflect at least in part changes at the empirical level. Second, the prism through which the tradition is evaluated is no longer the same. Whereas in missionary and travel literature the average observer was a layperson with, at best, no more than a casual commitment to nonhuman animals' well-being, in recent scholarship the tradition is increasingly evaluated from the standpoint of animal rights advocacy. More importantly, cultural, ideological, and political sensitivities play a major part in shaping this debate. On the traditional Muslim side, several works take the form of apologies seeking to resist perceived or real Western attempts at cultural and moral hegemony. On the Western side, many Muslim and non-Muslim authors subject the tradition to a narrow, West-centric version of animal advocacy while often failing to apply the same critical scrutiny to the animal rights discourse.

The aim of this chapter is to assess the current debate on animal ethics in Islam and consider the extent to which it has helped the modern reader understand this tradition's position on this subject. I will first discuss a group of texts that share the preoccupation of demonstrating the superiority of the tradition, thus exhibiting a clearly apologetic tone, then I will turn to the debate on animal ethics in Western academia. By raising challenging questions, the latter holds the promise of delving deeper into the subject, but at its current stage much of it is still affected by serious problems. In conclusion I will explain why the subject of animal ethics in Islam deserves careful study. This chapter approaches animal ethics in Islam through a critical examination of both apologetic and academic discourses, focusing on how methodological assumptions shape contemporary interpretations of the tradition.

21.2 APOLOGETIC LITERATURE

A substantial portion of modern writing on animals in Islam takes the form of apologetic literature, which warrants examination because of its influence on both internal Muslim discourse and external scholarly assessments. Several works dealing with the so-called subject of animal rights in Islam share the preoccupation of demonstrating the tradition's superiority in this area. To achieve this goal, one of the oft-repeated arguments consists of the reminder that "Islam" predates the "West" by many centuries in extending "rights" to animals. This argument is often intended to silence critics by reminding them that whereas the West has "just discovered" that animals are worthy of moral consideration, Islam can boast of having included them in its moral compass since its inception. In these discussions, however, Islam is typically reduced to its scriptural teachings, especially reports describing Muhammad's compassionate treatment of nonhuman animals and enjoining Muslims to do the same. The questions of whether, to what extent, and in what ways these teachings have shaped the intellectual and empirical dimensions of the tradition generally fail to receive adequate attention. Discussions about animal rights often focus narrowly on scriptural teachings, neglecting how these ideals have actually shaped Muslim thought and practice. Many writings in this area are more concerned with defending Islamic tradition against Western criticisms than with analyzing or addressing animal welfare issues within Muslim societies themselves.

Although the cultural anxieties underpinning this type of discourse deserve to be acknowledged and addressed, these works' contribution to the field of animal ethics is less than satisfactory. This approach not only fails to attend carefully to questions arising from genuine concern for nonhuman animals but generally also posits an essentialized understanding of Islam, the animal, and of cultural differences. This is not to suggest that these authors do not have a point. In fact, ample evidence shows that overall premodern Islamic tradition takes the interests of nonhuman animals very seriously and that it has developed a sensible animal ethics model; however, this does not mean that the tradition is entirely innocent of problematic views and practices nor that all its positions are intuitively graspable. Concerns surrounding the issue of killing for food are particularly legitimate and deserve to be addressed.

Moreover, Islamic tradition is too complex to be reduced to its scriptural teachings. Of course, these teachings have played an important role in shaping Muslims' attitudes toward other creatures, but they have never been the only determining factor. The very claim that Islam extends "rights" to nonhuman animals is problematic, not only due to its anachronistic nature[1] but also because it seems inconsistent with the principle of monotheism due to the sense of entitlement that seems inherent in the concept of rights. Even the notion of the animal is not as simple as it may appear. Are human beings part of the animal world? Does our conception of the animal typically extend to insects? Answers to these and related questions are not without important ethical implications.

More problematically, the apologetic approach may be a contributor to negative attitudes toward nonhuman animals. Failure to engage critically with the emerging set of problems characterizing humans' impact on nonhuman life in the modern age, including in the Muslim

[1] The notion of rights, as William Edmundson notes, "first became unmistakably prominent during the period of modern intellectual history known as the Enlightenment, which ... had its beginnings in the early seventeenth century and ran to the end of the eighteenth" (Edmundson 2012, p. 13).

world, is likely to produce a false sense of reassurance, thus arguably facilitating the perpetuation of negative practices and attitudes toward nonhuman animals. This approach can even be theologically problematic. If "Islam" truly takes the lives and well-being of nonhuman animals seriously, as this literature consistently emphasizes, then the sense of appeasement derived from these apologies seems to run counter to this attitude.

This said, the cultural and political anxieties underlying the apologetic discourse should not be dismissed as irrelevant to this discussion. Like gender issues, animal advocacy has too often been used to racialize and dehumanize others and to exercise moral imperialism. Glen Elder, Jennifer Wolch, and Jody Emel have shown how "in the contemporary United States, racialization of others is fostered by postcolonial interpretations of the human–animal boundary or divide" (Elder et al. 1998, p. 80). A use of animals that falls outside the norm of what a dominant culture deems acceptable (such as killing a dog for food as opposed to killing her for biomedical research in the modern West, for example) can be interpreted as an act of cruelty and treated as a symbol of savagery, thus potentially becoming legally and socially costly to the person or group who enacts it.

Like other groups who have been subjected to Western imperialism, Muslims have enough good reasons to be wary of Western animal advocacy. From colonial times to the present, this principle has often been used as a pretext for the infliction of acts of physical and social violence against them. Animal advocacy in colonial Egypt, for example, was a cause defended by the highest British official in the country, Lord Cromer, "who clearly believed in the inferiority of non-European humans" (Baring 1908, p. 586). Such paradox can perhaps explain why, as Alan Mikhail (2014) observes, "many British anti-cruelty advocates in colonial Egypt expressed their animal welfare politics through violence toward human animals" (p. 179). More recently, many animal rights campaigns in Europe have been denounced as smear campaigns against Jews and Muslims (Bergeaud-Blackler 2016). To some Muslims these campaigns may seem particularly ironical as animal advocacy in the West is not without Islamic roots. Jeremy Bentham, the eighteenth-/nineteenth-century British philosopher whose oft-cited footnote condemning animal cruelty (Bentham 1879) is credited by many as one of the first triggers of animal advocacy in the West, is a case in point. "The very first sentence of that footnote" writes James Carson, "shows that a seminal text in Western philosophical discourse on animal rights draws on non-Western sources (Hinduism and Islam)" (Carson 2013, p. 171).

Apologetic literature on animal ethics is thus not without value. It is a useful source for the study of the intersection between animal ethics, on the one hand, and cultural and colonial tensions, on the other. Besides, it gives access to a wealth of primary material, mostly from the hadith, but also from other sources, including the Quran and legal texts. Moreover, despite its apologetic tone, it is not devoid of interesting analytical insights. Some works also occasionally sermonize their Muslim readers by stressing the importance of treating other animals well and reminding them of the afterlife consequences of such treatment, therefore seeking to create a concrete positive impact on the lives of other animals. However, the critical merit of these works is rather limited and, even more problematically, they generally fail to address emerging problems, such as factory farming and animal transportation. If apologetic writings tend to emphasize moral defense, Western academic treatments approach the tradition from a more critical distance, raising different but equally consequential interpretive challenges.

21.3 WESTERN ACADEMIA

The Western academic landscape is more complex. Thus far, the field has contributed excellent studies and raised important questions, but much of it still suffers from serious drawbacks. On the positive side, Western academics approach the tradition more critically and revisit foundational texts and doctrines from new angles. This approach has invigorated the debate and promises deeper analyses. On the downside, much of the literature suffers from methodological flaws and factual inaccuracies. Perhaps because much of the debate is undertaken by non-Islamicists who, due to language and training limitations, have no direct access to primary sources and only a cursory appreciation of the tradition's intellectual history; misreadings, oversimplifications, and forthright misinformation prevail in much of the literature. Moreover, while showing much critical insight toward Islamic tradition, the debate often fails to approach animal ethics theories with similar critical rigor. These limitations often lead to ambivalent positions and one-sided readings whereby the complexity of ethical dilemmas and pressures of lived reality fail to be given adequate attention.

21.3.1 *Critical Approach*

G. H. Bousquet's article comparing attitudes toward nonhuman animals in the three monotheisms is probably the first to offer an academic treatment of animal ethics in Islam (Bousquet 1958). The article's explicit comparative frame is helpful in identifying Islam's distinctive features and situating its views of animals in a wider context. Bousquet observes, for example, that unlike Indian traditions, the three monotheisms share an anthropocentric premise consisting of the belief that animals are created for the sake of humans. Regardless of this observation's accuracy, the comparative approach can reveal previously unnoticed features and allows one to see things in more perspective.

From Bousquet's comparison, Islam emerges as the most attuned of the three monotheisms to the well-being of nonhuman animals. The author offers an interesting metaphor to the effect that when the Judaic seed of compassion was thrown on Christian soil it could not grow any roots, but when the same seed fell on Islamic soil it found a fertile ground that allowed it to thrive. Interestingly, Bousquet's analytical approach does more to illustrate this positive side than the apologetic discourse for, unlike the latter, this author looks beyond doctrinal and legal stipulations and considers how concern for animals permeates daily life, shapes personal piety, and represents a social ideal to which everyone is encouraged to aspire.

Some of Bousquet's ideas did not stand the test of scrutiny. More recent research has demonstrated that Indian traditions are as guilty of anthropocentrism as their monotheistic counterparts (Nelson 1998; Waldau 2002) and that the anthropocentric character of the three monotheisms is mitigated by a theocentric dimension linked to the spiritual abilities that all three traditions ascribe to nonhuman animals (Bauckham 2002; Tlili 2017b). Nonetheless, the author not only offers useful analyses, but he also calls attention to themes that deserve further inquiry. He observes, for example, that seemingly similar practices can be underlain by widely divergent motivations. For instance, in both Egypt and France one finds institutions that seem to denote respect for – or even liberality toward – dogs. In the former case this consists of endowments benefiting these animals whereas in the latter it consists of cemeteries where the wealthy bury them. Bousquet argues that despite their seeming similarity the sentiments underlying these practices have nothing in common.

It took the field a few decades since Bousquet's work to witness the appearance of new contributions. Of these, James Wescoat's article "The 'Right of Thirst' for Animals in Islamic Law: A Comparative Approach" (Wescoat 1995) not only sheds light on a little-studied point (*ḥaqq al-shirb*, i.e., the right of access to water, otherwise known as "the right of thirst") but, unlike Bousquet's article, it pays closer attention to the topic's empirical dimension. In Wescoat's analysis, the Islamic legal system once again emerges as very attentive to the well-being of nonhuman animals – far more so than contemporary western legal systems – but the author also notes the disconnect between the normative and the empirical dimensions. Under colonial, political, and economic pressures, traditional legal stipulations have lost much of their weight, leading to lack of observance of many religious doctrines and legal stipulations. Although Wescoat recognizes that neither Western nor Muslim countries are likely to formally adopt Islamic rulings about animals, he argues that these rulings can still be relevant not only to Muslims but also to Westerners. In the former case teachings about animals can continue to shape individuals' behavior, whereas in the latter it can become a resource for reformers who seek to rework existing laws or frame new ones. Basheer Ahmad Masri's Animal Welfare in Islam (Masri 2007) and even more so Richard Foltz's Animals in Islamic Tradition and Muslim Cultures (Foltz 2006) incorporate animal rights theory and challenge anthropocentrism. However, Foltz is critiqued for sometimes oversimplifying Islamic texts and underestimating the ethical complexities of vegetarianism and veganism. Even plant-based diets have hidden moral costs, and animal rights philosophies often extend moral consideration mainly to animals similar to humans. Alan Mikhail's *The Animal in Ottoman Egypt* (Mikhail 2014) demonstrates how social, political, and technological changes shaped human–animal relations, emphasizing the importance of lived realities over abstract ideals. The field increasingly values nuanced, context-sensitive analysis and cautions against sweeping generalizations when addressing animal ethics in Muslim societies.

21.3.2 *Misinformation, Misinterpretation, and Oversimplification*

The following case studies are presented not as isolated scholarly errors but as illustrative of recurring patterns of misinterpretation within the literature. The need to include sections on Islam in multivolume works at a time when the field of animal ethics was in its infancy seems to have led some editors to seek the help of non-specialists, something that resulted in less than satisfactory contributions. A short article in the first edition of the *Encyclopedia of Animal Rights and Animal Welfare* illustrates this problem. The author, no less an authority than Paul Waldau, who has developed some of the most nuanced conceptual tools for the study of animal ethics in religion, emphasizes Islam's anthropocentric character, which he presents as barely mitigated by a dimension of responsibility toward nonhuman animals. The same article, however, reveals the author's unfamiliarity even with basic aspects of Islamic tradition, let alone the Quran and the other texts that he discusses. For example, Waldau places the sacrificial holiday (*ʿīd al-aḍḥā*), which occurs on the tenth day of the last (twelfth) month of the Islamic calendar (Dhu'l-Hijja), at the end of the month of Ramadan, the ninth month of the Islamic calendar when Muslims fast from dawn to sunset. Among the unfortunate results of this misinformed approach is the casual affirmation that the Quran contains negative views of other animals (Waldau 1998). Indeed, the closer one studies this scripture the more such affirmation proves questionable (Tlili 2010, 2012). Of course, the Quran, like any other text, lends itself to multiple interpretations; however, a careful reading using Waldau's very conceptual tools yields a surprisingly nonanthropocentric outlook. Another unfortunate outcome is the presentation of marginal opinions as if they were central to the tradition's worldview while failing to point to legal, theological, and other scholarly debates, which are more serious in character and have played a more important role in shaping Muslims' attitudes toward nonhuman creatures. Obviously, this uninformed and selective approach serves to perpetuate stereotypes more than provide useful information about the tradition.

Although the field has since grown considerably, the problem of misinformation persists. In a more recent piece – nearly two decades following the publication of Waldau's article – Daniel Capper (2016) offers a more rounded and detailed reading of the tradition which, nonetheless, includes serious inaccuracies. One of the points Capper seeks to make is that, although in Islam nonhuman animals are believed to have souls, the tradition ascribes them a lower type of soul, what he refers to as "*nafs* [*sic*] *al-ammara*, a base soul that pursues needs, wants, and survival." In contrast, he argues, humans have a higher type of soul, even though the mainstream Islamic tradition actually recognizes nonhuman animals as having a higher soul (*rūḥ*) and moral accountability in the afterlife, granting them complexity and protecting them from being judged by human moral standards, marking an essential departure from prevalent anthropocentric attitudes and protecting nonhuman animals from practices similar to the animal trials conducted in medieval Europe (Evans 1906; Oldridge 2005, chap. 3).

Although most Muslims accept that nonhuman animals will be resurrected and judged in the hereafter, the potential impact of this theme on nonhuman animals' status did not receive adequate attention. Muslims generally do not question the principle of nonhuman animals' afterlife because both the Quran and – even more explicitly – the Prophetic tradition (hadith) establish this principle. Remarkably, when the same scriptural sources are examined carefully one discovers that even the difference between human and nonhuman's final destinies is not founded on anthropocentric premises. This difference is generally linked to a Quranic verse stating, "We have offered the Trust (*amāna*) to the heavens, the earth, and the mountains, but they shied away from it and declined to assume it; however, the human being assumed it. He was utterly unjust, utterly haughty" (Q 33:72). The intensity of humans' afterlife destiny is thus linked to a choice in which they and other creatures were involved at a primordial time. When the *amāna* (trust) was offered to various creatures, the human being was the only creature that rushed to accept it. One also should not forget that this unwise move elicited divine criticism. The *amāna*, as Quran exegetes explain, consists of the bargain to be tested in this life in return for either eternal (or long-term) reward or punishment in the hereafter. The different treatment reserved for humans is therefore the result of a risky choice that they alone seem to have made. It should be reminded also that, because of this choice, not only heaven but also the hellfire is populated mainly by humans. Thus, had Capper studied the "soul" and "afterlife" motifs more carefully he would not have exempted the tradition from critical assessment, but he would have offered a more accurate diagnosis.

Misinformation and misreadings are even more salient in Katherine Perlo's *Kinship and Killing* (Perlo 2009). The author takes up the daunting task of proposing an explanation for what she perceives as mixed legacies toward nonhuman animals in four world traditions (Judaism, Christianity, Islam, and Buddhism) and to refute the claim that "a given author's faith is overwhelmingly or essentially pro-animal" (Perlo 2009, p. 1). Perlo seems to reject, or at least de-emphasize, the sacred nature of religion, arguing that human attitudes are the immediate source of religious doctrines, which are then projected on divine or otherwise sacred beings or sources. She attributes the presence of both pro- and anti-animal teachings in these traditions to the fact that humans have mixed feelings toward other creatures, something that results in what she describes as doctrines of "aggression," "evasion," and "defense." Doctrines of "aggression," she explains, are ones that seek to justify the oppression of animals "in terms of their naturalness, inevitability, or inherent morality" (Perlo 2009, p. 6), whereas the doctrine of "evasion" "diverts attention from exploitative practices by introducing precepts of kindness within the power structure or emphasizing its benevolent aspect" (Perlo 2009, p. 7). Finally, the doctrine of "defense," she writes, seeks to protect people from "actual revenge or attack, symbolic revenge in the form of illness or other manifestations of a bad conscience, or one's own pain caused by identification with that of another" (Perlo 2009, p. 8).

Commenting on this approach, Geoffrey Barstow (2017) writes, "Unfortunately, Perlo is hampered by her attempt to identify strategies that cut across all world religions. In her attempt for breadth, she can sometimes miss important aspects of individual traditions (particularly non-Western traditions such as Buddhism)" (p. 12). This comment applies equally to her treatment of Islamic tradition. The section on Islam reveals not only the author's less than adequate familiarity with the tradition but also a surprising failure to cite even English sources accurately. For example,

Perlo takes Basheer Ahmad Masri's "conceptual" vegetarianism to mean that he has become an actual vegetarian (Perlo 2009, p. 95). Indeed, although Masri says that he "has become a vegetarian by conviction," he also adds that his "metabolism got so used to meat that a complete change over to a vegetarian diet has now become very difficult" (Masri 2007, p. 57). Thus, in his own words Masri affirms that, in practice, a vegetarian diet is beyond his ability. Perlo also misnames the medieval author (ʿIzz al-Dīn) b. ʿAbd al-Salām (d. 660/1262) as "Al-Salam" (Perlo 2009, p. 97). Her referencing of hadith reports is unintelligible. Apparently under the impression that specific numbers have been assigned to given reports across hadith works, she gives the numbers of "books" and "chapters" within hadith compilations but fails to provide the title of the actual compilations and the names of their compilers. Someone with no prior knowledge of her cited material will not be able to locate her hadith citations (Perlo 2009, p. 102).

These oversights are symptomatic of deeper problems consisting of the misrepresentation and misreading of core themes. For example, Perlo raises the possibility that the Prophet Muhammad was largely a vegetarian without mentioning her sources or explaining how she has reached this conclusion. She then proceeds to discount Muhammad's alleged vegetarianism as a sign of asceticism rather than compassion toward nonhuman animals. Like many other Arabs, she maintains Muhammad was attracted to Syrian Christianity with its mystical-ascetic bent. These Arabs, she writes, "emulated the Syrian Christian monks by swearing off meat and drink and becoming wandering ascetics, or *hanifs*" (Perlo 2009, p. 97). This view not only misrepresents Muhammad's biography and teachings – for contrary to Perlo's claim, the Prophet is reported to have explicitly shunned asceticism (Muslim 1991, vol. 2, p. 1020)[2] and to have slaughtered his own animals and consumed meat (Muslim 1991, vol. 3, p. 1563) – but it also glosses over the meaning of the word *ḥanīf* and takes no note of the rich debates around it both in traditional and modern sources.

Aside from failing to spell out why mentioning it in the first verse (or, for that matter, even in the title) would be a sign of importance, Perlo, again, misrepresents the Quran and its adjacent exegetical literature. Whereas Sura al-Fīl (Q 105) speaks neither favorably nor unfavorably about the elephant, Muslim exegetes point out that, though one or more elephants were part of what Perlo describes as a "sacrilegious power," the eponymous elephant resisted his human masters and refused to attack the Kaaba and was accordingly spared the severe punishment that the "birds sent by Allah" inflicted on the army.[3] Some accounts mention that another (or other) elephant(s) did the opposite and, like the human culprits, was/were punished (Tlili 2012, pp. 104–5). If one is to take these exegetical accounts as consonant with the Quranic narrative, the elephant after whom the sura is titled stands out for doing the right thing and accordingly reaps the benefits. From these exegetical commentaries, elephants also come across as capable of making moral choices and of assuming the ensuing consequences, which implies that they are treated as responsible beings. Furthermore, these commentaries indicate that species membership has no bearings on one's status and divine treatment. Both principles are determined by the level of one's consciousness of God and obedience to him.

Obedience to God, however, is not necessarily a virtue in Perlo's view. Rather, she finds the principle of divine voluntarism a sign of authoritarianism and argues that this doctrine "has been

[2] The hadith scholar Muslim b. al-Ḥajjāj reports on the authority of Anas who said, "One Companion of the Prophet, peace and blessings be upon him, . . . said, 'I will not get married'; another said, 'I will not eat meat'; and a third said, 'I will not lie down on a comfortable bed [meaning, I'll stay up in prayer at night].' [When he heard this] the Prophet praised God then said, 'Why do some people speak like this when I myself observe prayer then sleep, observe fasting on certain days and eat regularly on others, and marry women? Whoever shuns my way has no relation to me.'"

[3] Referring to the army of Abraha, who ruled Yemen in the name of the Ethiopian king, the Negus, and whose army according to Islamic sources attacked Mecca a few decades prior to the advent of Islam.

used to suppress instincts of sympathy" (Perlo 2009, p. 96). Such reductionism is in fact the most problematic aspect in Perlo's approach. Although her thesis that religious doctrines are projected on, rather than derived from, scriptural and other religious sources is not without merit, her casual dismissal of centuries-long efforts to grapple with difficult ethical dilemmas as no more than self-serving strategies can hardly count as serious scholarship. Perlo reduces Ashʿarī theology to one decontextualized citation highlighting God's freedom to do what he wants with his creation, as if this stance was reached arbitrarily or this single citation can do justice to the full complexity of Ashʿarī thought (Perlo 2009, p. 96). The polysemous nature of the theme of Abraham's sacrifice of his son is reduced to no more than "a symbol of divine authority outweighing natural sentiment in the human context" (Perlo 2009, p. 95). It should also be noted that, while proposing these provocative readings, Perlo offers little analysis to defend or corroborate them. This is a missed opportunity, for had she combined her critical approach with adequate study of primary and secondary sources she could have contributed useful insights.

Because many claims about Islamic views on animals rest on specific Qurʾanic terms, careful philological analysis is necessary to assess the validity of these interpretive moves. The growing acceptance of this supposed dominion notwithstanding, there is clear disagreement on its scriptural foundation. Lisa Kemmerer (2006) situates it in the Quranic notion of "*tamkīn*"[4] (p. 347) whereas Patricia Crone (2004) links it to the notions of "*tafḍīl*"[5] and "*taskhīr*"[6] (p. 354). Capper (2016), on the other hand, links it to the notions of *amāna*[7] and *istikhlāf*[8] and finds some support for it in the Quranic statement that God created the human being in the "fairest stature." Of course, the main reason behind this disagreement is that no verse in the Quran gives humans dominion over other creatures. This leads these and other scholars to attach the biblical notion (Genesis 1:26) to a variety of Quranic themes that highlight God's favors toward humankind. Ultimately, thus, this is guilt by association. The Quran is automatically assumed to mimic the Bible and is criticized for ideas it does not even express. A more careful approach, even if premised on the assumption that the Quran subscribes to the principle of human exceptionalism, should have sought to understand and evaluate this scripture's own version of this principle instead of conflating its position with that of another scripture. Such approach shows lack of interest in evaluating the Islamic scripture according to its own terms.

Returning to some of these notions,[9] close analysis shows not only that none of them corresponds to the biblical idea of dominion but also that none of them can be used unproblematically to defend the principle of human privilege. The verbal form *makkana*, from which the notion of *tamkīn* is derived, means primarily "to settle," "to secure," and "to establish." The lexicographer Edward Lane (1968) translates "*makkanahu*" as "he gave him a place, he assigned him a place, and settled, or established him" (vol. 8, p. 3022). Arthur Arberry (1955) translates the verse adduced by Kemmerer as: "We have established you [i.e., humankind, *makkanākum*] in the earth and there appointed for you livelihood; little thanks you show" (p. 171). Muhammad Asad (2003) translates the same verse as "Indeed, O men [*sic*], We have given you a [bountiful] place on earth, and appointed thereon means of livelihood for you: [yet] how seldom are you grateful!" (p. 232). The medieval exegete al-Ṭabarī (d. 310/923) paraphrases the pertinent sentence in this verse saying, "We [God] have paved and smoothed for you,

[4] This notion is mentioned in Q 7:10, among other verses.
[5] This notion occurs in Q 17:70.
[6] Crone refers to Q 45:13, but the notion occurs in numerous other verses.
[7] This notion occurs in Q 33:72.
[8] This notion occurs in Q 2:30 and 95:4.
[9] For the notions of *taskhīr*, *tafḍīl*, and *istikhlāf* and for more on *amāna* and the "fairest stature" depiction, see Tlili 2012.

humankind, the earth and made it a place where you can settle, an expanse adapted to your movements, and a comfortable place where you can rest."

This is not to deny that an element of authority is detectable from later interpretations. Al-Zajjāj (d. 311/923), for example, defines the word *tamkīn* as "putting [someone] in possession and giving them power (*al-tamlīk wa-l-qudra*)" (al-Zajjāj 1988, vol. 2, p. 320). Thus, in this exegete's understanding God has given humans ownership in the land and has endowed them with power, but neither the Quranic verse nor al-Zajjāj say that this is power or authority *over other creatures*. What al-Zajjāj means is probably that God has provided humans with opportunities, skills, and abilities (*qudra*) that are perceived as necessary for their survival. This is a far cry from prevalent interpretations of the biblical notion of dominion.

But even if absent from al-Zajjāj's interpretation, the idea of "authority over other creatures" emerges in more recent works. The Tunisian exegete al-Ṭāhir b. ʿĀshūr (d. 1973) comments on verse 10 of Sura al-Aʿrāf saying, "We have given you power over the matters of the earth *and enabled you to handle its creatures* (*khawwalnākum al-taṣarrufa fī makhlūqātihā*) thanks to the faculty of reason that God has instilled in humankind" (Ibn ʿĀshūr 1984, p. 33, emphasis added). Similarly, the Arabic dictionary *al-Muʿjam al-wasīṭ* defines the verb *makkana* as "*jaʿala lahu sulṭānan*," a definition that seems to convey the idea of authority over others, as in non-Quranic Arabic the word *sulṭān* means authority that is linked to ruling and kingship (Ḍayf 2003, p. 881). Moreover, even if *The Study Quran* (Nasr et al. 2015) renders the idea of *tamkīn* as "to establish on earth," the translators suggest as another possible interpretation that God has given or *delegated* to humankind certain powers in the world, an idea that is reminiscent of the notion of dominion (detectable from the notion of delegation).[10]

Of course, these interpretations should be studied not for what they have to say about the Quran but rather about the interpreters' worldviews. This brief survey seems to point to a growing trend of anthropocentrism in Islamic thought, whereby humans and their role on earth become more central with time. In fact, studies of other Quranic terms, such as *jahl* ("ignorance"), *khalīfa* ("vicegerent"), and *rūḥ* ("soul"), have already introduced this thesis. These works not only show that the meaning of certain words has evolved over time, but they also explore the significance of such change (Steppat 1989; Izutsu 2002; Tlili 2017a).

Be that as it may, the Quranic verse itself continues by explaining that God has "appointed livelihood" for humankind on earth. The verse thus seems merely to seek to remind humans that their ability to be functional and earn a living on earth is a grace from God. Remarkably, as well, the verse proceeds to point out that humans rarely give thanks. Far from highlighting humans' special status, the verse seems rather to highlight their inherent vulnerability and utter dependence on God, on the one hand, and their failure to show gratitude for God's grace toward them, on the other. The ability to turn such criticism into something that bespeaks human privilege, whether attempted by Muslims or non-Muslims, seems remarkable.

Equating the notion of *amāna* with dominion is another awkward attempt to find a Quranic equivalent for the biblical notion. The word neither carries a connotation of authority nor, to my knowledge, has it ever been rendered as dominion prior to Capper's translation. As noted earlier, *amāna* simply means "trust." Although the verse does not specify the nature of this trust, a survey of exegetical literature shows that this notion has more often been understood as a burden than as a

10 Interestingly, the translators adduce the medieval exegetical work *Tafsīr al-Jalālayn* in support of this interpretation (Nasr et al. 2015), but this is a rather implausible interpretation of this *tafsīr*, which does not even comment on the meaning of *makkana* in this verse. The translators may have inferred this from al-Ṣuyūṭī's and al-Maḥallī's commentaries on the notion of *tamkīn* elsewhere in the Quran, but even this does not make their interpretation more plausible. Space limitations preclude a fuller treatment of this point in this chapter, but it is my hope to return to this point in a future project.

privilege: It is about the bargain of either believing in God and being righteous or failure thereof in return for eternal/long-term reward or punishment. Muslims who saw in the verse an element of human privilege had to grapple with the verse's negative comment that the human being proved to be "utterly unjust" and "utterly haughty" (*ẓalūm* and *jahūl*) for entering this momentous bargain. It should also be noted that although the verse highlights something that may be unique to humans – the fact that out of many creatures they alone jumped on *amāna* – the offer to carry this burden was given to other creatures before humans jumped on it. Thus, humans are not that exceptional.

Similarly, the "fairest proportion" depiction can be treated as a sign of human exceptionalism only when taken out of context. The full passage where this phrase occurs says, "We have created the human being in the fairest proportion, *then reduced him to the lowest of the low*, save those who have believed and do righteous deeds, they shall have unlimited reward" (Q 95:4–6, emphasis added). Clearly, then, whatever status can be inferred from the fourth verse in this passage is affected by the fifth one. Moreover, the comparison in this verse does not necessarily involve humans and other creatures. Many exegetes understand it in the sense that out of innumerable potential shapes in which God could have created the human being he chose for them the best possible one (Tlili 2014, p. 64). Seeing in the "fairest proportion" depiction a sign of human exceptionalism and then treating this interpretation as a foundation for the principle of dominion can thus be achieved only through decontextualized and selective reading strategies. This, of course, is not to maintain that Islamic sources did not adduce these and other Quranic themes to corroborate anthropocentric claims, for they have. However, to equate the Quran with its interpretations and, even more problematically, to selectively treat the most anthropocentric interpretations as representative of this scripture's worldview, while failing to even allude to readings that convey different perspectives even when the latter are more widely accepted, betrays a preconceived insistence to treat the Quran as an anthropocentric text without much regard to what it actually says.

21.4 CONCLUSION

Taken together, these debates reveal how shifts in interpretive frameworks, rather than doctrinal absence, have shaped modern assessments of animal ethics in Islam. Though inexhaustive, I hope that the foregoing has illustrated some of the strengths and weaknesses of the current debate on animal ethics in Islam. At some level, this chapter may simply be a reminder of the value of scholarly rigor and of the need to consider how cultural and ideological biases can affect the quality of one's research. In its defensive attitude, the apologetic discourse has generally taken little notice of and barely benefited from the invaluable conceptual tools that have grown out of the current debate on animal ethics in Western scholarship. This results in two major problems. First, because the apologetic discourse is mostly descriptive, it fails to discern the principles and ideals that underlie religious teachings on animals and to articulate an animal ethic that is intelligible across cultural boundaries. Second, the defensive attitude precludes the possibility of taking serious notice of the tradition's own shortcomings.

The animal advocacy discourse is similarly hampered by cultural and ideological biases. This is not to suggest that advocacy is inherently problematic. Nor is apologetic discourse for that matter. Indeed, both apology and advocacy are in some sense inevitable and desirable as they endow discourse with meaning. Rather, this is a problem because at its current stage much of the advocacy discourse does not adhere to the standards of scholarly rigor. This is clear not only in the methodological problems and factual inaccuracies highlighted earlier but also in the unexamined colonial undertone of certain positions. One, for example, wonders what kind of criteria are adopted in assigning Egypt an "F" grade for its treatment of nonhuman animals. To what extent are such criteria shaped by Western worldviews, and what qualifies an organization that is inevitably shaped by one set of cultural ideals to serve in this universal capacity?

This chapter, however, hopes to be more than just such a reminder. Indeed, the foregoing discussion points to a consensus among informed observers that Islamic tradition has thought very deeply about the subject of animal ethics even if many remain dissatisfied with some of its positions. Muslims' attitudes toward animals have deteriorated in modern times, and even the premodern tradition is guilty of many imperfections but, overall, premodern Muslim scholars gave the subject utmost attention and developed a well-thought-out ethic. Even if many may continue to reject some of the tradition's positions, I believe that this ethic deserves serious attention and that it has much to contribute to the current debate. This is the case especially now with the so-called political turn, which focuses on animals' positive rights as opposed to the conventional rightist position, which is mainly preoccupied with animals' negative rights (right to be free from harm). As some work has already started to show, premodern Islamic law developed a highly sophisticated and carefully thought-out model of such positive "rights," or rather, protections (Tlili 2015). Modern ethicists could benefit from the Shafiʿi and Hanbali ethics models, as jurists from these two schools prioritize the interests of nonhuman animals nearly across the board (the notable exception pertains to the permissibility of killing for food but, again, such permissibility should be studied within a larger frame that thinks more deeply about the institution of domestication and related issues). Careful study of these models can thus be a great resource in modern debates.

The mechanisms and strategies used to inspire reverence for life and motivate compassion toward other creatures among Muslims – the type into which the early modern testimonies cited at the beginning of this chapter provide a glimpse – may even be worthier of study. Ample evidence indicates that up until a couple of centuries or even decades ago this ethic was still vibrant in Muslim lands (in some circles it continues to be so). Although many of the teachings that nurtured this ethic are time- and culture-contingent, understanding them can still be useful, not only in formulating a coherent animal ethic but also an effective one.

REFERENCES

Anonymous. 1809. *Monthly Review* 59: 1–7.

Arberry, Arthur. 1955. *The Koran Interpreted: A Translation*. London: George Allen & Unwin.

Asad, Muhammad. 2003. *The Message of the Qur'an*. Bristol: The Book Foundation.

Bacon, Francis. 2010. Of Goodness and Goodness of Nature. www.westegg.com/bacon/goodness.html.

Bacon, Francis, and Richard Whately. 1860. *Bacon's Essays: With Annotations*. London: John W. Parker and Son.

Baring, E. 1908. *Modern Egypt*. London: Macmillan.

Barstow, Geoffrey. 2017. *Food of Sinful Demons: Meat, Vegetarianism, and the Limits of Buddhism in Tibet*. New York: Columbia University Press.

Bauckham, Richard. 2002. Joining Creation's Praise of God. *Ecotheology* 7: 45–59.

Bentham, Jeremy. 1879. *The Principles of Morals and Legislation*. London: Oxford University Press.

Bergeaud-Blackler, Florence. 2016. Animal Rights Movements and Ritual Slaughtering: Autopsy of a Moribund Campaign. In *Islam and Public Controversy in Europe*. Edited by Nilüfer Göle. New York: Routledge, pp. 187–200.

Bousquet, Georges Henri. 1958. Des Animaux et de leur traitement selon le Judaïsme, le Christianisme et l'Islam. *Studia Islamica* 9: 31–48.

Capper, Daniel. 2016. *Learning Love from a Tiger: Religious Experiences of Nature*. Oakland: University of California Press.

Carson, James P. 2013. "One of Folly's Puppies": Austen and Animal Studies. In *Global Jane Austen: Pleasure, Passion, and Possessiveness in the Jane Austen Community*. Edited by Laurence Raw and Robert G. Dryden. New York: Palgrave Macmillan, pp. 165–88.

Crone, Patricia. 2004. *Medieval Islamic Political Thought*. Edinburgh: Edinburgh University Press.

Ḍayf, Shawqī, ed. 2003. *al-Muʿjam al-wasīṭ*. 4th ed. Cairo: Maktabat al-Shurūq al-Dawliyya.

Derrida, Jacques. 2008. *The Animal That Therefore I Am*. Edited by Marie-Louise Mallet. Translated by David Wills. New York: Fordham University Press.

Edmundson, William A. 2012. *An Introduction to Rights*. New York: Cambridge University Press.

Elder, Glen, Jennifer Wolch, and Jody Emel. 1998. Le Pratique Sauvage: Race, Place, and the Human–Animal Divide. In *Animal Geographies: Place, Politics, and Identity in the Nature-Culture Borderlands*. Edited by Jennifer Wolch and Jody Emel. London: Verso, pp. 72–90.

Foltz, Richard. 2006. *Animals in Islamic Tradition and Muslim Cultures*. Oxford: Oneworld.

Ibn ʿĀshūr, al-Ṭāhir. 1984. *al-Taḥrīr wa-l-tanwīr*. Tunis: al-Dār al-Tūnusiyya li-l-Nashr.

Izutsu, Toshihiko. 2002. *Ethico-Religious Concepts in the Qurʾān*. Montreal: McGill.

Izzi Dien, Mawil. 2000. *The Environmental Dimensions of Islam*. Cambridge: The Lutterworth Press.

Kemmerer, Lisa. 2006. *In Search of Consistency: Ethics and Animals*. Leiden: Brill.

Lane, Edward. 1968. *An Arabic–English Lexicon*. Beirut: Librairie du Liban.

Masri, al-Hafiz Basheer Ahmad. 2007. *Animal Welfare in Islam*. Leicestershire: The Islamic Foundation.

Mikhail, Alan. 2014. *The Animal in Ottoman Egypt*. New York: Oxford University Press.

Muslim b. al-Ḥajjāj. 1991. *Ṣaḥīḥ Muslim*. Beirut: Dār al-Kutub al-ʿIlmiyya.

Nasr, Seyyed Hossein, Caner K. Dagli, Maria Massi Dakake, Joseph E. B. Lumbard, and Mohammed Rustom, eds. 2015. *The Study Quran: A New Interpretation and Commentary*. New York: HarperOne.

Nelson, Lance E. 1998. *Purifying the Earthly Body of God: Religion and Ecology in Hindu India*. Albany: SUNY Press.

Perlo, Katherine Wills. 2009. *Kinship and Killing: The Animal in World Religions*. New York: Columbia University Press.

Steppat, Fritz. 1989. God's Deputy: Materials on Islam's Image of Man. *Arabica* 36: 163–72.

Stilt, Kristen. 2008. *Animal Welfare in Islamic Law*. Cairo: Animal People.

2017. Constitutional Innovation and Animal Protection in Egypt. *Law and Social Inquiry* 42: 1364–90.

al-Ṭabarī, Ibn Jarīr. 2008. *Jāmiʿ al-bayān ʿan taʾwīl āy al-Qurʾān*. Cairo: Dār al-Jawzī.

Tlili, Sarra. 2010. The Meaning of the Qur'anic Word "*Dābba*": "Animals" or "Nonhuman Animals"? *Journal of Qur'anic Studies* 12: 167–87.

2012. *Animals in the Qur'an*. New York: Cambridge University Press.

2014. All Animals Are Equal, or Are They? The Ikhwān al-Ṣafāʾ's Animal Epistle and Its Unhappy End. *Journal of Qur'anic Studies* 16: 42–88.

2015. Animal Would Follow Shāfiʿism: Legitimate and Illegitimate Violence to Animals in Medieval Islamic Thought. In *Violence in Islamic Thought from the Qurʾān to the Mongols*. Edited by Robert Gleave and István T. Kristó-Nagy. Edinburgh: Edinburgh University Press, pp. 225–44.

2017a. From Breath to Soul: The Quranic Word *Rūḥ* and Its (Mis)interpretations. In *Arabic Humanities, Islamic Thought: Essays in Honor of Everett K. Rowson*. Edited by Joseph Lowry and Shawkat Toorawa. Leiden: Brill, pp. 1–21.

2017b. I Invoke God, Therefore I Am: Creation's Spirituality and Its Ecologic Impact in Islamic Texts. In *A Global History of Literature and the Environment*. Cambridge: Cambridge University Press, pp. 107–22.

Waldau, Paul. 1998. Islam. In *Encyclopedia of Animal Rights and Animal Welfare*. Edited by Marc Bekoff. Westport: Greenwood Press, pp. 291–92.

2002. *The Specter of Speciesism: Buddhist and Christian Views of Animals*. Oxford: Oxford University Press.

Wescoat, James, Jr. 1995. The "Right of Thirst" for Animals in Islamic Law: A Comparative Approach. *Environment and Planning D: Society and Space* 13: 637–54.

al-Zajjāj, Abū Isḥāq Ibrāhīm. 1988. *Maʿānī al-Qurʾān wa-iʿrābuhu*. Beirut: ʿĀlam al-Kitāb.

22

Islamic Finance and Environmental Law

Dalal Aassouli and Damilola S. Olawuyi

22.1 INTRODUCTION

This chapter examines the potential contributions of Islamic finance as an important faith-based approach for financing environmental policies and programs in Islamic countries. It examines the preconditions for designing and implementing Islamic green finance, and current barriers to its application in Islamic countries.

Islamic countries face pressing environmental threats that require a paradigm shift in how economic systems operate, including the management of environmental resources. Consequently, many Muslim-majority countries, including Malaysia, Indonesia, Morocco, Jordan, Pakistan, and the United Arab Emirates (UAE), as well as multilateral institutions working within Muslim-majority countries, have recently undertaken or financed projects to combat climate change, expand renewable energy generation, develop sustainable transportation, and enhance policies around environmental sustainability.[1] In this regard, initiatives that aim to promote the transition to a green economy have emerged in many of these countries.[2] Nongovernmental organizations (NGOs) and international institutions such as the United Nations (UN) and multilateral development banks (MDBs) took the lead in promoting this "greening" movement in an attempt to create more awareness and mobilize more financing globally for green projects. The year 2015, particularly, was critical for the international development community as it set three major agreements for the coming decade: the Sustainable Development Goals (SDGs), their effective financing, and climate change.[3] The

[1] B. Goud and T. Al-Mubarak, *Environmental Impact in Islamic Finance* (London: RFI Foundation, 2018).

[2] The United Nations Environment Programme defines a green economy as low-carbon, resource efficient, and socially inclusive: https://bit.ly/3JqIcoX. See, for example, Indonesia's Green Bond and Green Sukuk Framework and Malaysia's SRI Sukuk Framework.

[3] The 2015 United Nations Climate Change Conference (COP21) was held in Paris, France, during which parties to the United Nations Framework Convention on Climate Change (UNFCCC) reached an agreement (the Paris Agreement) to undertake ambitious efforts to combat climate change (see https://unfccc.int/process-and-meetings/the-paris-agreement/what-is-the-paris-agreement). As of September 2017, out of 196 signatories of the Paris Agreement, 166 have ratified it. Among the OIC countries, forty-three members have ratified it, whereas thirteen members have the status of signatory (see SESRIC, "OIC Environment Report 2017," www.sesric.org/files/article/586.pdf). The same year saw the organization of the Third International Conference on Financing for Development in Addis Ababa, Ethiopia. The Addis Agenda provides a new global framework for financing sustainable development (see https://bit.ly/43X5CBV).

purpose is to tackle the dual challenge of overcoming poverty and protecting the planet, with the ultimate goal of improving people's quality of life and well-being. Development finance institutions also recognized the need for a paradigm shift on how development should be financed in order to unlock the resources needed to achieve the SDGs and climate mitigation, especially as the financing resources needed are expected to surpass current development financial flows. According to estimates by the International Renewable Energy Agency (IRENA), additional investments of about US$15 trillion is required for the period 2019–50 for climate change mitigation and adaptation projects across the world.[4] With other reports and studies also indicating that Islamic countries will need sustained funding of between US$700 billion and US$1 trillion every year to achieve the SDGs,[5] there is a clear need for alternative and additional sources of financing to support low-carbon and sustainable infrastructure development projects in Islamic countries.[6] Public funds alone will fall short in reaching these investment needs. Consequently, more than half of the additional finance that will be needed for sustainable infrastructure over the next fifteen years must come from alternative sources, such as private investment, as well as from development agencies and multilateral, regional, and national development banks.[7]

Islamic finance has emerged as one of the most promising alternative mechanisms through which additional capital can be mobilized to advance environmental development programs and projects in Islamic countries across the world.[8] Islamic finance promotes the financing of investment activities and projects in accordance with the tenets and procedures of sharia law. One distinguishing feature of Islamic finance, as compared to conventional financing methods, is that parties agree to abide by Quranic injunctions and Prophetic practice in structuring the transaction. For example, the Quran and hadith prohibit the levying of interest (*ribā*). Therefore, in selecting Islamic financing, parties choose to exclude *ribā*.[9] Furthermore, Islamic finance instruments are free from excessive risk, uncertainties, or ambiguities (*gharar*), speculation, or gambling (*maysir*), as well as transactions that are prohibited or forbidden in Islamic faith (haram). In addition to ensuring that financial transactions are underpinned by genuine economic activities, parties engaged in Islamic finance arrangements agree to share profits and losses in accordance with pre-determined and mutually agreed ratios, without any

[4] International Renewable Energy Agency (IRENA), *Global Energy Transformation: A Roadmap to 2050* (Abu Dhabi: IRENA, 2019).

[5] Islamic Finance Council, "Islamic Finance and the SDGs: Framing the Opportunity," May 2020, https://bit.ly/47MjZtP, pp. 21–22. See also D. Olawuyi, "Advancing Innovations in Renewable Energy Technologies as Alternatives to Fossil Fuel Use in the Middle East: Trends, Limitations, and Ways Forward," in D. Zillman, M. Roggenkamp, L. Paddock, and L. Godden (eds.), *Innovation in Energy Law and Technology: Dynamic Solutions for Energy Transitions* (Oxford: Oxford University Press, 2018), pp. 354–70; J. Meltzer, N. Hultman, and C. Langley, *Low-Carbon Energy Transitions in Qatar and the Gulf Cooperation Council Region* (Washington, DC: The Brookings Institution, 2014), pp. 40–45; I. J. Bachellerie, *Renewable Energy in the GCC Countries: Resources, Potential, and Prospects* (Jeddah: Gulf Research Center, 2012).

[6] D. Olawuyi, "Financing Low-Emission and Climate-Resilient Infrastructure in the Arab Region: Potentials and Limitations of Public-Private Partnership Contracts," in W. L. Filho (ed.), *Climate Change Research at Universities: Addressing the Mitigation and Adaptation Challenges* (New York: Springer, 2017), pp. 533–47.

[7] J. Meltzer, "Financing Sustainable Infrastructure," The Brookings Institution, July 2016, https://bit.ly/49QdvN8, pp. 1–5; IRENA, "Perspectives for the Energy Transition: Investment Needs for a Low-Carbon Energy System," March 2017, https://bit.ly/3LwZDxp.

[8] Islamic Finance Council, "Islamic Finance and the SDGs."

[9] For example, AAOIFI Standard No. 17 on investment *ṣukūk* states that "the prospectus must not include any statement to the effect that the issuer of the certificate accepts the liability to compensate the owner of the certificate up to the nominal value of the certificate in situations other than torts or negligence nor that he guarantees a fixed percentage of profit." AAOIFI, "Shari'ah Standard No. 17: Investment Sukuk," 2015, https://aaoifi.com/ss-17-investment-sukuk/?lang=en, at 5/1/8/7.

party being guaranteed a fixed or risk-free return. Sharia-compliant modes of financing include profit and loss sharing partnerships (*muḍāraba*), profit and loss sharing joint ventures (*mushāraka*), building and construction contracts (*istiṣnāʿ*), forward sale contracts (*salam*), and leasing (*ijarah*), as well as Shari'ah-compliant securities (*sukuk*).[10]

In light of the fact that global Islamic financial services industry assets reached approximately US$3.9 trillion in 2024 and continue to record robust double-digit growth, Islamic finance has significant potential to mobilise the financing required for countries to advance green and sustainability-oriented projects.[11] For example, the use of *ṣukūk* for environmental and SDG-related initiatives (i.e., "green *ṣukūk*") as a potential funding solution has grown over the last years.[12] Generally, a green bond is an investment vehicle that integrates the fiduciary element of fixed-income instruments with an awareness of mitigation and adaptation to the climate, thus providing investors with climate-related investments.[13] For example, the International Capital Market Association (ICMA) defines a green bond as any type of bond instrument whose proceeds will be exclusively applied to finance or refinance, in part or in full, new or existing eligible green projects that advance environmental objectives.[14] In line with these principles, green *ṣukūk* has emerged as a sharia-compliant mode of financing, in full, new or existing environmental and low-carbon development projects and assets. It is based on the increasing recognition of the potential role for religion, or at least philosophical approaches stemming from religion, to address the environmental crisis.[15]

Despite the growing awareness of the potential of Islamic finance as a faith-based approach to financing environmental projects and programs, a number of legal and governance challenges continue to stifle its widespread application across the Islamic world. Since environmental and SDG-linked Islamic finance initiatives are still at the early stages of development across the Islamic world, clear operational guidelines, best practices, and principles for integrating Islamic finance approaches into mainstream environmental laws and planning processes are yet to fully emerge. Similarly, environmental management in Islamic countries is held back by partial coverage of environmental issues in regulations and policies; limited availability of environmental data and their use for priority setting; low quality of environmental assessment systems; weak policy implementation; limited public information; and minimal consideration of environmental issues in sector ministries.[16] Understanding the guiding principles and normative requirements for applying Islamic finance in environmental law and planning can help Islamic countries to plot a path for integrating financial instruments into environmental law

[10] See N. Saleh, "Definition and Formation of Contract under Islamic and Arab Laws," *Arabic Law Quarterly* 5(2) (1990), pp. 101–16.

[11] Islamic Financial Services Industry Stability Report 2025, www.ifsb.org/wp-content/uploads/2025/05/IFSI-Stability-Report-2025.pdf.

[12] For example, in 2018 HSBC Amanah (the Malaysian Islamic banking arm of HSBC Holdings) issued an RM 500 million (US$120.63 million) *ṣukūk* tied to SDG programs. See "HSBC Issues First Islamic Bond Tied to U.N. Development Goals," *Reuters*, October 4, 2018, https://bit.ly/3LC7b1L. See also, Islamic Finance and Sukuk, "Indonesia Raises $3bn in Sovereign Sukuk including $1.25bn Green Sukuk," https://bit.ly/4qSDOZ8.

[13] D. Aassouli, M. Asutay, M. Mohieldin, and T. C. Nwokike, "Green Sukuk, Energy Poverty, and Climate Change: A Roadmap for Sub-Saharan Africa," World Bank Group Policy Research Working Paper No. WPS 8680, 2018, https://bit.ly/4hUJ9LC.

[14] International Capital Markets Association (ICMA), "The Green Bond Principles," June 2018, www.icmagroup.org. See also Article 1 of Qatar's "Rules for the Offering and Listing of Sukuk and Bonds on Financial Markets," Qatar Financial Markets Authority, November 2010, which defines *ṣukūk* as a debt certificate issued according to conditions in compliance with Islamic sharia.

[15] U. F. Moghul and S. Safar-Aly, "Green Sukuk: The Introduction of Islam's Environmental Ethics to Contemporary Islamic Finance," *Georgetown International Environmental Law Review (GIELR)*, 27(1) (2015), pp. 1–60.

[16] See SESRIC, "OIC Environment Report 2019," September 2019, www.sesric.org/publications-detail.php?id=488.

and policymaking. This chapter unpacks the nature, scope, and guiding principles of Islamic green finance as an important faith-based approach for financing environmental policies and programs in Islamic countries.

This chapter proceeds in five sections. After this introductory section, Section 22.2 discusses the drivers of Islamic finance and the implications for environmental law in Islamic countries. Section 22.3 analyzes the legal and institutional barriers to Islamic green finance in Islamic countries. Section 22.4 discusses the need for good governance approaches that mainstream Islamic law tenets and principles into environmental legislation, policies, programs, and funds in order to create the appropriate regulatory environment for Islamic green financing. Section 22.5 is the conclusion.

22.2 DRIVERS OF ISLAMIC FINANCE AND THE IMPLICATIONS FOR ENVIRONMENTAL LAW IN ISLAMIC COUNTRIES

Islam has always had a great influence on the formation of individual Muslim communities and the policymaking of Muslim states, including environmental policy.[17] Concepts such as *iḥyā' al-arḍ al-mawāt* (land revitalization or reclamation), *ḥimā* (reserves), *ḥarīm* (inviolable/protective zones), and *waqf* (charitable endowments) have existed since the time of the Prophet Muhammad.[18] From the sharia sources (Quran and hadith) and many others, Muslim jurists derived principles and laws regarding interactions with natural resources and animal life that today may be described as "sustainable."[19] At present, the role of Islam in environmental protection can be seen in the formation of different Islamic organizations and the emphasis given to Islam as a motive for the protection of the environment.[20]

In fact, the Muslim world has consciously connected moral virtue to financial markets in Islamic banking and finance.[21] Islamic finance's principles offer an alternative for investors seeking a more ethical use of their funds. Since its modern development in the 1970s, the industry developed significantly with an annual two-digit growth and an expansion beyond traditional markets. However, this growth has not benefitted the social and environmental developments. Recent debates suggest that there should be a convergence between Islamic finance and socially responsible investing (SRI) that integrates environmental, social, and governance (ESG) considerations.[22] However, those ethical values are inherent in the Islamic economy, and the current disconnect between theory and practice is due to various factors.

Islam highlights the moral objective of human existence and offers a moral and ethical code of conduct that influences individual behaviors towards humankind and society. Therefore, it impacts every aspect of everyday lives and cannot be disconnected from society. In this model, the Islamic economic system is based on Islamic law (sharia), whereby economic transactions are guided by a set of moral and ethical principles such as justice, solidarity, honesty, fair competition, public interest, transparency, equity, and the prohibition of usury (*ribā*),

[17] M. Y. Izzi Deen, "Islamic Environmental Ethics, Law, and Society," in R. S. Gottlieb (ed.), *This Sacred Earth: Religion, Nature, Environment*, 2nd ed. (New York: Routledge, 2004), pp. 142–50.

[18] M. A. 'Arafa, "Islamic Policy of Environmental Conservation," *European Journal of Law Reform* 16(2) (2014), pp. 465–504.

[19] Moghul and Safar-Aly, "Green Sukuk."

[20] Izzi Deen, "Islamic Environmental Ethics."

[21] Moghul and Safar-Aly, "Green Sukuk."

[22] See A. J. Yesuf and D. Aassouli, "Exploring Synergies and Performance Evaluation between Islamic Funds and Socially Responsible Investment (SRIs) in Light of the Sustainable Development Goals (SDGs)," *Heliyon* 6(8) (2020), e04562.

speculation (*gharar*), and illicit activities (alcohol, weapons, etc.). The system also encourages social responsibility through profit redistribution. The main instruments are almsgiving (zakat), endowment (*waqf*), charity (*ṣadaqa*), and interest-free loans (*qarḍ al-ḥasan*). An Islamic moral economic system should therefore endeavor to support the overall goals of Islamic law (*maqāṣid*), to promote welfare (*maṣlaḥa*), and prevent harm (*mafsada*).[23] These considerations are important for overall human well-being (*falāḥ*).

To understand the Islamic moral economy system, it is important to examine two key concepts: vicegerency (*khilāfa*) and the objectives of Islamic law (*maqāṣid al-sharī'a*). *Khilāfa* or *istikhlāf* in Arabic is the act of custodianship. Vicegerency signifies the position of humans as the dwellers and occupiers of the earth who will build a civilization on earth and inhabit it (*'imār*).[24] The Quran refers to the concept of *khilāfa* on many occasions (Q 2:30, 38:26, 6:165, 7:129). God has assigned to humans the responsibility of building and developing (*'imār* or *'imāra*) the earth for their benefit and the one of future generations. *Khilāfa* is therefore linked to *'imāra* and *'ibāda* (worship) whereby the three acts constitute the purpose of human existence.[25] It is an intergenerational responsibility (*amāna*) that implies engagement, willingness, capacity, and effort. The *amāna* of man as a viceregent is to build up a civilization for the good of all humanity and his environment according to God's will.[26] It also requires good governance in order to manage the earth's resources based on justice and sustainability. This implies that man has only a usufruct right of the environment and the exercise of the usufruct is counterbalanced by accountability.[27] This definition is in line with the concept of sustainable development, which is defined as development that meets the needs of the present without compromising the ability of future generations to also meet their needs.[28]

Islamic law, on the other hand, has many universal guiding principles that pertain to the protection of the environment. These include the inviolability of human life; the protection of animals and plants; saving land, water, and air; and protecting against noise pollution.[29] The concept of environment is used extensively in sharia law, including its application in discussions of the natural environment, the social environment, and the economic environment.[30]

When discussing the concept of *khilāfa* it is also important to consider the concept of *maqāṣid al-sharī'a*. The term *maqṣid* (pl. *maqāṣid*) means objective, principle, intention, end, telos (in Greek), or finality.[31] The science of *maqāṣid al-sharī'a* analyzes the purpose behind the rules and prescriptions of Islamic law. *Maqāṣid* are also the group of divine intentions and moral concepts that Islamic law is based on, such as justice, human dignity, free will, social cooperation, chastity, magnanimity, and facilitation.[32]

Al-Ghazālī, in *al-Mustaṣfā min 'ilm al-uṣūl*, states that "the higher objectives of religion for human beings are five: preserving their faith, their life, their reason, their filiation, and their

[23] M. U. Chapra, *The Islamic Vision of Development in the Light of the Maqasid Al-Shari'ah* (London: The International Institute of Islamic Thought, 2008).
[24] S. Sikandar Shah Haneef, "Principles of Environmental Law in Islam," *Arab Law Quarterly* 17(3) (2002), pp. 241–54.
[25] A. al-Iṣfahānī, *al-Dharī'a ilā makārim al-sharī'a*, ed. A. al-Yazīd al-'Ajamī (Cairo: Dār al-Kutub al-'Ilmiyya, 1987).
[26] Sikandar Shah Haneef, "Principles of Environmental Law."
[27] 'Arafa, "Islamic Policy of Environmental Conservation."
[28] World Commission on Environment and Development (WCED), *Our Common Future* (Oxford: Oxford University Press, 1987).
[29] Sikandar Shah Haneef, "Principles of Environmental Law."
[30] 'Arafa, "Islamic Policy of Environmental Conservation."
[31] M. Ṭ. Ibn 'Āshūr, *Maqāṣid al-sharī'a al-Islāmiyya* (Tunis: Dār al-Salām, 2014).
[32] J. A. Jasser, *Maqāṣid al-Sharī'ah: A Beginner's Guide* (London: The International Institute of Islamic Thought, 2008).

wealth." Anything that aims at preserving these five objectives is a benefit (*maṣlaḥa*) and anything that negatively impacts them is a harm (*mafsada*).[33] Other contemporary scholars have integrated new objectives linked to contemporary global issues such as the environment and human dignity. Among them is ʿAbd al-Majīd al-Najjār, who suggests a classification of *maqāṣid al-sharīʿa* based on four components: the value of human life, the human being, the society, and the material environment.[34] The material environment comprises both wealth and the environment. According to al-Najjār, the preservation of wealth consists in its acquisition and development, preventing its damage, and promoting ownership, whereas the preservation of the environment consists in protecting it against damage, pollution, and excessive use of its natural resources as well as its development.

The analysis of the concepts of *khilāfa* and *maqāṣid* shows the multidimensional ethical and moral considerations that lead to the overall well-being of humans. The Islamic economic system is therefore based on the concepts of *khilāfa* and *maqāṣid al-sharīʿa*, whereby humans are custodians of wealth (*māl*), which includes both material and monetary wealth, and have a fiduciary responsibility that is governed by ethical and moral values (*akhlāq*). This explains the exclusion of certain sectors and transactions, such as usury (*ribā*) and weapons, which are considered to be unethical and against moral values. Linking ethics to religion also implies that humankind is responsible for its own actions and behavior.

From an environmental perspective, Islam expects human beings to conserve the environment.[35] Islamic environmental ethics are based on the concept that all human relationships are established on justice (*ʿadl*) and equity (*iḥsān*).[36]

Thus, sustainability issues including environmental concerns are, by nature, embedded in the "*maqāṣidī*" approach of development, on which the Islamic economy is based, and whereby its objectives and guiding moral and ethical principles aim at improving the living conditions and social well-being of humans and the society. This comprehensive and multidimensional system needs to function in harmony so that it achieves its objective of offering a moral-based value solution for the economic, environmental, and social problems faced by humanity. Therefore, the dichotomy between economic development and social and environmental developments will lead to similar deficiencies faced by the capitalist financial system.

22.3 LEGAL AND INSTITUTIONAL BARRIERS TO ISLAMIC GREEN FINANCE IN ISLAMIC COUNTRIES

Despite the growing awareness on the potential of Islamic green finance as a faith-based approach to financing environmental projects and programs, a number of legal and governance challenges continue to stifle its wide application across the Islamic world. This section develops a profile of the key barriers and limitations to the application of Islamic green finance in environmental governance and planning.

[33] Abū Ḥāmid al-Ghazālī, *al-Mustaṣfā min ʿilm al-uṣūl*, ed. Ḥamza b. Zuhayr Ḥāfiẓ, Medina/Jeddah: [n.p.], 1993, vol. 1, p. 174.

[34] ʿA. al-Najjār, *Khilāfat al-insān bayna al-waḥī wa-l-ʿaql* (London: The International Institute of Islamic Thought, 1981).

[35] Izzi Deen, "Islamic Environmental Ethics."

[36] A. M. al-Damkhi, "Environmental Ethics in Islam: Principles, Violations, and Future Perspectives," *International Journal of Environmental Studies* 65(1) (2008), pp. 11–31.

22.3.1 *Lack of Comprehensive and Standardized Green Islamic Finance Legislation and Policies*

One of the most significant barriers to the wide-scale adoption of Islamic green finance is the absence of clear and standardized legal frameworks and policies that will guide the design, approval, and implementation of environment and SDG-linked projects and initiatives as well as direct financing to climate projects. In 2014, the Securities Commission Malaysia (SC) introduced the Sustainable and Responsible Investment (SRI) Sukuk Framework in order to facilitate the creation of an ecosystem that promotes sustainable and responsible investing for SRI investors and issuers.[37] A few years later, in 2018, the Republic of Indonesia (ROI) developed a Green Bond and Green Sukuk Framework under which it planned to finance or refinance eligible green projects via the issuance of "green bonds" and "green *ṣukūk*."[38] However, several other Islamic countries are yet to formulate the applicable requirements and principles that will guide sustainable and responsible investments and green *ṣukūk* markets.[39] Due to the diverse interpretation of Islamic financial law, coupled with extant legal debates on the sharia compliance of some of the different forms of Islamic finance instruments, the task of standardization and a coherent definition of Islamic financial law, generally, has remained difficult across the Islamic world.[40] Despite standardization efforts by entities such as the Islamic Financial Services Board (IFSB) and the Accounting and Auditing Organization for Islamic Financial Institutions (AAOIFI), interpretational complexities remain in the regulation of Islamic finance transactions, which has limited their wide adoption and enforcement in key sectors such as energy, environment, and infrastructure development.[41] This undertone of conflict and the lack of standardization in Islamic financial law has made the task of outlining the guiding principles for the design, application, and implementation of Islamic green financing a complex endeavor.[42] For example, green financing options are underpinned by strong incentives such as tax holidays, concessional loans, subsidized interest rates, grants for technical assistance, guarantees, and debt-for-nature swap programs, which increase their attractiveness from an investment standpoint.[43] Given the complexities of questions as to the sharia compliance of some of the different forms of such incentive programs in the context of Islamic *ṣukūk* and other Islamic green financing programs, clear legal and policy guidelines that clarify such questions will have to be developed.

[37] See Securities Commission Malaysia, "Sustainable and Responsible Investment Sukuk Framework: An Overview 2019," https://bit.ly/4hV4bK7.

[38] See Ministry of Finance Republic of Indonesia, "Indonesia's Green Bond & Green Sukuk Initiative 2018," https://bit.ly/47B8VRK.

[39] E. Richardson, "The UAE and Responsible Finance: Can Responsible Finance Ṣukūk Help the UAE in Fulfilling Its Sustainability Ambitions?," *Arab Law Quarterly* 34(4) (2020), pp. 313–55, https://doi.org/10.1163/15730255-BJA10013; Qatar Financial Center, "Cross Border Opportunities: Qatar Islamic Financial Hub Report 2019," https://bit.ly/3LumOZi, stating that Qatar is yet to tap into the SRI and green *ṣukūk* markets (p. 34).

[40] See J. Ercanbrack, "The Standardization of Islamic Financial Law: Lawmaking in Modern Financial Markets," *The American Journal of Comparative Law* 67(4) (2019), pp. 825–60; M. F. Khan, "Setting Standards for Shariah Application in the Islamic Financial Industry," *Thunderbird International Business Review* 49(3) (2007), pp. 285–307; A. Shaharuddin, "Defining Harmonisation of Shariah Rulings in Islamic Finance," *Arabic Law Quarterly* 30(3) (2016), pp. 292–304.

[41] Ercanbrack, "Standardization of Islamic Financial Law."

[42] R. Ali and M. Kamal, "Standardising Islamic Financing: Possibility or Pipe Dream?," *Business Law International* 10 (2009), p. 19.

[43] A.-L. Amin, T. Dimsdale, and M. Jaramillo, "Designing Smart Green Finance Incentive Schemes: The Role of the Public Sector and Development Banks," April 2014, www.cbd.int/financial/gcf/giz-smartgreen2014.pdf.

For example, what are the sharia-compliant incentives that Islamic green financing will offer to increase their widespread uptake and attractiveness from the lender's perspective?[44]

Furthermore, as can be learned from countries such as Canada and the United States where green financing options have grown exponentially, green financing programs are often backed by strong cap and trade policies and legislation that place a price on carbon emissions.[45] In such contexts, green financing grows as companies and entities try to meet their carbon offset obligations. Lack of clear and comprehensive climate change laws in several Islamic countries, especially Middle East and North African (MENA) countries, as well as an absence of market-based carbon pricing programs (such as carbon taxation), means that the focus on responsible investment and environmental financing remains generally weak.[46] While climate awareness and action are increasing across the Islamic world, a comprehensive review of global climate change laws reveals that many of the Islamic countries do not have specific legislation on climate change.[47] Enacting climate change and comprehensive environmental laws with robust performance requirements will create the necessary legal obligations and impetus for companies and entities to advance green and low-carbon technologies and climate-smart infrastructure development projects. An increase in the scale of green and environmental projects would significantly increase the demand for green financing, including green *ṣukūk*.

Enacting clear laws and policies on Islamic green financing can also be very helpful in addressing underlying barriers and gaps in wider energy and environmental policies that may deter the successful implementation of Islamic green financing.[48] For example, many rentier states in the MENA region maintain significant fossil fuel subsidies for domestic energy consumption.[49] Apart from contributing to high energy consumption rates and inefficiency, a heavily subsidized energy sector can hinder the market-based functionality and the cost–benefit calculations of lenders and investors when it comes to developing environmentally sustainable renewable energy and climate change projects. This could result in significant policy mismatch and slow development of environmental projects that require financing. Reforming energy subsidies as well as introducing robust renewable energy programs and policies will not only increase the portfolio of projects that require environmental financing, but could also provide a basis for channeling government subsidies into green programs. De-risking Islamic finance will also include streamlining the applicable regulations to make them clearer and less cumbersome

44 For example, in Malaysia, in order to promote greater utilization of green *ṣukūk* and to attract green issuers, several incentives were introduced: (i) tax deduction until year of assessment on issuance costs of SRI *ṣukūk* approved or authorized by the SC; (ii) income tax exemption to the issuers of the Green SRI *ṣukūk* grant for applications received by the SC; (iii) tax incentives for green technology activities in energy, transportation, building, waste management, and supporting services activities; and (iv) financing incentives under the Green Technology Financing Scheme (GTFS) with total fund allocation of RM 5 billion until 2022. See Securities Commission Malaysia, "Sustainable and Responsible Investment."

45 A. Jones, "Principles for Investment Grade Policy and Projects," report produced for the Capital Markets Climate Initiative, May 2012, https://bit.ly/3WK59iD.

46 D. Olawuyi, "Energy Poverty in the Middle East and North African (MENA) Region: Divergent Tales and Future Prospects," in I. Del Guayo, L. Godden, D. N. Zillman, M. F. Montoya, and J. J. Gonzalez (eds.), *Energy Law and Energy Justice* (Oxford: Oxford University Press, 2020), pp. 254–72.

47 Sabin Center for Climate Change, "Climate Change Laws of the World," https://climate-laws.org.

48 See UNDP, "Derisking Renewable Energy Investment: A Framework to Support Policymakers in Selecting Public Instruments to Promote Renewable Energy Investment in Developing Countries," December 1, 2020, www.undp.org/publications/derisking-renewable-energy-investment, which discusses the need to address the underlying barriers that cause risk in climate financing intitatives.

49 See IMF, "Energy Subsidies in the Middle East and North Africa: Lessons for Reform," March 2014, www.imf.org/external/np/fad/subsidies/pdf/menanote.pdf.

for potential investors.[50] Moreover, climate policies enable the directing of finance to green projects. A good example is India, where the Reserve Bank of India has established priority sector lending requirements.[51]

The success of Islamic green financing is highly dependent on having in place strong and comprehensive environmental laws and policies that place an obligation on companies and entities to develop and finance environmental projects and initiatives. Considering the importance of Islamic financing to environmental protection and sustainable infrastructural development, it is important for governments in Islamic countries to provide supportive legal and regulatory frameworks that will accelerate the recognition, financing, and implementation of Islamic green financing. Fast-tracking the adoption of robust environmental standards, climate change legislation, and renewable energy policies could open up green investment, which will not only achieve environmental objectives but could also stimulate social and economic co-benefits and progress.

22.3.2 *Lack of Standardized Contractual Framework*

One of the key causes of risks and disputes in climate financing is the lack of a clear, detailed, contractual framework that allocates risks.[52] Given that the application of Islamic financing for green and SDG-linked projects is still in the early stages of development, clear and detailed information on how risks, returns, and responsibilities will be allocated are yet to comprehensively emerge. This has made it difficult for investors to clearly ascertain the underlying commercial terms, risks, and responsibilities for designing, financing, building, and maintaining infrastructure projects using green *ṣukūk* and other Islamic finance instruments. In countries with mature green financing markets this information is available in model contracts that have been compiled by national authorities, after consultation with private sector stakeholders, to clearly establish the underlying commercial principles that green financing projects should follow.[53] A standard form of green *ṣukūk* agreement, for example, can make it easier for investors to perform long-term risk analyses and assessments while determining investment locations. It also enhances the transparency standardization and certainty of the financing process. For example, financial de-risking on the part of the lender could include having clear operational guidelines and contract templates in place, which would reduce the possibility of conflict or risk at all stages of the project life cycle. Limiting risks on the part of a prudent investor will involve a careful investigation of the scope and nature of projected risks, especially how risks of governmental interference, project confiscation, or nationalization and midterm changes in contractual terms have been allayed in lending instruments.

As Islamic countries increasingly embrace green *ṣukūk* and other green Islamic financing options, it is important for regulators, in conjunction with financial institutions and private sector stakeholders, to evolve clear, credible, and market-tested precedent for the wide range of green Islamic finance instruments. Standardized green finance models developed in other jurisdictions can provide guidance for developing standardized terms and conditions on Islamic green financing. Such templates can be reworked to reflect local market realities and

[50] UNDP, "Derisking Renewable Energy Investment." See also UNDP, "Catalyzing Climate Finance: A Guidebook on Policy and Financing Options to Support Green, Low-Emission and Climate Resilient Development," April 2011.

[51] UNEP Inquiry, "Green Finance For Developing Countries: Needs, Concerns and Innovations," August 2016, https://bit.ly/4p1XtUW.

[52] Richardson, "The UAE and Responsible Finance."

[53] Ibid. See, for example, PLC Finance, "Islamic Finance: Standard Documents," https://bit.ly/43mFdgI.

to ensure consistency with existing legislation and government requirements; for example, local content requirements, sharia-compliant contractual terms, responsible product sourcing, and local employment practices.

22.3.3 *Structural and Institutional Integration Questions*

The effective implementation of green Islamic finance models for environmental programs and infrastructure will require the collaborative participation of a wide range of government institutions, agencies, and departments. For example, given that green lending is linked to environmentally responsible projects, the active participation of the ministry of environment in standard setting and verification will be essential, while financial institutions and regulators will have roles to play in approving such specialized lending options. Similarly, the ministry of the interior is often responsible for granting approval for project execution. Also, the ministry of economy and commerce will need to grant approvals for foreign agencies to carry out investment activities, while other ministries, such as power, energy, and transportation, have prominent roles to play in approving all energy efficiency related projects to be executed under their ministries. In addition, developing a pipeline of sustainable green infrastructure projects at the national levels could facilitate attracting private investment by providing information and the long-term visibility of projects.[54] This wide range of institutional actors underscores the importance of coordination among these ministries. With solid intergovernmental coordination, granting and getting approval for green and SDG-linked projects will be less cumbersome and more straightforward. Such coordination will also simplify the process of passing information between government ministries, thereby removing inefficiencies and bureaucracies.[55] To effectively implement green Islamic financing, the importance of strengthening existing government institutions and establishing direct synergies between all government institutions, both new and old, to fast-track and simplify the implementation of financed projects cannot be overemphasized.

There is also a need to designate a focal entity that will coordinate with other relevant agencies and ministries to reduce the administrative and licensing requirements for green Islamic financing initiatives. For example, an existing financial authority or department can be designated as the one-stop shop to accelerate the process of obtaining relevant approvals and licences for green Islamic financing initiatives. Not only will this simplify the process of dialogue and information exchange amongst key stakeholders and prospective participants, but it could also accelerate the development of best practices and policy instruments amongst financial institutions so as to ensure that requirements and approaches are standardized and complementary.[56]

22.3.4 *Capacity Gaps*

Flowing from the lack of comprehensive legislation and institutions on green Islamic financing across many parts of the Islamic world is that lawyers and non-lawyer experts in financial spheres are yet to evolve sufficient technical capacity and skills that are directly relevant for structuring green Islamic financing contracts and investments. For example, what are the required due

[54] Aassouli et al., "Green Sukuk."
[55] Olawuyi, "Energy Poverty."
[56] Amin et al., "Smart Green Finance."

diligence and contractual negotiation steps for allocating project risks and minimizing disputes between private and public sector participants? Such questions must be sufficiently understood by administrators, policy leaders, project evaluators, investment bankers, auditors, and lawyers involved in formulating Islamic green financing policies and project requirements. Lack of awareness on climate change, green technologies, environmental law principles, SDGs, and other core concepts that underpin green financing by policymakers, project developers, and financiers is a key factor that continues to slow down the uptake and development of Islamic green financing initiatives. For example, in many countries, Islamic banking institutions are largely staffed by bankers with a limited understanding of environmental law concepts and principles, while environmental agencies and institutions that understand green technologies and risks are rarely involved in formulating Islamic financing instruments and policies. Without understanding the principal assumptions and motives of environmental law and green financing, developing risk-free Islamic green financing instruments will be difficult.

The required level of sophistication to successfully navigate the entire project chain of an Islamic green-financed project can be improved in many countries through tailored capacity development programs. To promote Islamic green financing, it is important to strengthen the capacity of Islamic financial institutions in core areas of green technology, SDGs, and environmental law. Financial institutions can also improve their internal capacity by employing environmental lawyers and practitioners who are trained to examine and assess legal risks across the entire value chain of energy and environmental projects and design green financial incentives.

The foregoing gaps and barriers in the design, development, and implementation of Islamic green financing can be addressed holistically by Islamic countries by putting in place adequate law and policy frameworks that provide the required supportive enabling regulatory environment. Section 22.4 discusses required good governance approaches for advancing Islamic green financing at national and local levels.

22.4 ADVANCING ISLAMIC GREEN FINANCING: THE NEED FOR GOOD GOVERNANCE APPROACHES

National authorities in Islamic countries must realize the importance of Islamic green financing as an alternative, and mutually supportive, platform through which the high costs of financing environmental and SDG-linked infrastructure development can be progressively met. Furthermore, with reduced oil income, revenue drop, and increased demand on government budget, countries must look to private sector participation in developing the infrastructure required to achieve sustainable and climate resilient cities.[57] Success lies in the abilities and commitment of governments across the Gulf Cooperation Council (GCC) to address the above-noted limitations and barriers through a good governance approach to Islamic green financing. A good governance approach aims to comprehensively mainstream Islamic law tenets and principles into environmental legislation, policies, programs, and funds, and vice versa, in addition to embedding climate mitigation and adaptation strategies in national budgets. It seeks to address legal and regulatory gaps to green investments, while also creating incentives

[57] Most of the international climate finance discussions emphasize the importance of using various instruments, such as de-risking, to mobilize additional private sector financing. This process is usually defined as blending, whereby public resources are leveraged in order to mobilize additional private investments allowing for a larger investment to take place than if one was to rely on public resources alone (Aassouli et al., "Green Sukuk").

for financial institutions and private sector investors to increase their participation in sharia-compliant financing for energy efficiency and low-carbon projects. For example, as earlier noted, the success of Islamic green financing is highly dependent on having in place strong and comprehensive environmental laws and policies that place an obligation on companies and entities to develop and finance environmental projects and initiatives in the first place. Given the interconnectedness of sectorial laws and policies, the need for coherent and systemic application of Islamic law and environmental law principles cannot be overemphasized. For example, in virtually all Islamic countries, the constitution recognizes Islam as a source of law.[58] This constitutional recognition means that, even when Islamic notions are not clearly integrated into environmental laws, Islamic principles have strong roles to play in the design, implementation, and approval of environmental initiatives and programs. What is required is for countries to clearly practicalize such intersections and linkages by integrating Islamic perspectives and approaches in the design, approval, financing, and implementation of environmental programs and initiatives. Good governance is about systemic integration to ensure greater coherence, accountability, transparency, and coordination by all key actors and sectors.[59] To improve the efforts for the implementation of Islamic green financing models, the following points should be considered.

The starting point is for national authorities in Islamic countries to accelerate the standardization of Islamic financial law through clear legislation that clarifies and addresses legal contentions and ambiguities. Such comprehensive legislation should, amongst other things, establish fiscal and tax incentives for investments in the renewable energy sectors and harmonize the conflicting laws and regimes on Islamic financing. Most importantly, legislation in this area should establish clear energy efficiency, emission reduction, and renewable energy performance standards across key sectors of the economy in order to create incentives for green financing. Furthermore, there is a need for wider reform of energy policies and investment laws that could serve as a disincentive to Islamic green financing. For example, existing energy subsidy systems that do not deter overconsumption will need to be reexamined and reformed in order to create a competitive and attractive Islamic green financing market.[60] Furthermore, stringent local laws on repatriation of earnings, investment taxation, insurance, and dispute resolution may also serve as disincentives for private sector participation and investments in Islamic green financing initiatives. It will therefore be necessary for countries to review and fundamentally reform extant investment laws and institutions that could hinder the robust implementation of Islamic green financing.

Secondly, to promote Islamic green financing it is important to designate a focal institution or administrative unit that will coordinate the design, approval, and implementation of best practices, contract templates, and operational guidelines on the application of Islamic green financing across various sectors. Apart from serving as a one-stop shop that will streamline the approval processes for projects, such an institution would also provide capacity development opportunities for administrators to acquire technical knowledge about the methods, requirements, and challenges of Islamic green financing. By designating and empowering a focal institution on Islamic green financing initiatives, project participants, financial institutions,

58 D. Olawuyi, "Sustainable Development and Water-Energy-Food Nexus: Legal Challenges and Emerging Solutions," *Journal of Environmental Science & Policy* 103(1) (2020), https://doi.org/10.1016/j.envsci.2019.10.009.

59 Ibid.

60 Eliminating these subsidies releases funds for green investment by stimulating demand for renewable energy. An OECD analysis suggests that most countries would realize real income gains of 4 percent by unilaterally eliminating subsidies, in addition to a 10 percent reduction in greenhouse gas emissions by 2050 compared with normal activity (Aassouli et al., "Green Sukuk").

and national authorities across multiple sectors can obtain relevant information and develop an institutional understanding about the process and methodology for de-risking Islamic green financing contracts and projects.

Thirdly, given that Islamic green financing is an emerging development across Islamic countries, regional interaction and knowledge sharing between countries with experience and practice can help promote expertise on how Islamic green financing can accelerate infrastructure development in the region, especially in the context of climate-smart infrastructure. While countries such as Malaysia, Indonesia, and the UAE have some experience with green *ṣukūk*, several other Islamic countries have little to no experience at all. In this regard, Aassouli and colleagues suggest a roadmap that supports policymakers in creating a green *ṣukūk* market in sub-Saharan Africa. The roadmap tackles three key objectives – maintaining financial stability, meeting climate finance needs, and promoting Islamic financing – by leveraging regional financial integration initiatives.[61] It is therefore important to promote the cooperation and knowledge sharing between regional networks and institutions, within and outside of the Islamic regional bodies, on how Islamic green financing models can help facilitate large-scale infrastructure development. Regional centers and platforms that can also enhance the exchange of ideas, best practices, and knowledge on existing financing opportunities, model contracts, and practical steps for de-risking projects. A regional knowledge-sharing platform could help capture the common challenges and approaches in the design and implementation of green *ṣukūk* and other sharia-compliant financing initiatives in Islamic countries.

22.5 CONCLUSION

Islamic financing provides viable opportunities for Islamic countries to attract additional financing, technical expertise, skills, and commitment from the private sector in the development, financing, implementation, and maintenance of large-scale environmental infrastructure projects. Lack of widespread and sustained implementation of green Islamic finance initiatives across the Islamic world is exacerbated by the absence of robust environmental, climate change, and renewable energy obligations and performance standards. These barriers must be addressed if Islamic countries are to leverage the potentials of green *ṣukūk* and other Islamic green financing portfolios to attract additional financing for SDG-linked infrastructure projects and developments.

The adoption of renewable energy laws in Morocco and Jordan, for example, shows that there is a growing interest in, and increased regulatory support for, low-carbon and energy efficacy projects. As more of such laws become more widely adopted across Islamic states, especially in MENA countries where climate change impacts on livelihoods and the achievement of the SDGs are increasingly apparent, the financing gap for climate projects will require the acceleration of resource mobilization initiatives and alternative financing strategies such as green Islamic finance. It is therefore critical for Islamic countries to establish good governance approaches for advancing Islamic green financing at national, regional, and local levels.

SELECT BIBLIOGRAPHY

Aassouli, D. et al. "Green Sukuk, Energy Poverty, and Climate Change: A Roadmap for Sub-Saharan Africa," World Bank Group Policy Research Working Paper No. WPS 8680, 2018, https://bit.ly/4hUJ9LC.

[61] See Aassouli et al., "Green Sukuk."

'Arafa, M. A. "Islamic Policy of Environmental Conservation 2014," *European Journal of Law Reform* 16(2) (2014), pp. 465–504.

Chapra, M. U. *The Islamic Vision of Development in the Light of the Maqasid Al-Shari'ah*, London: The International Institute of Islamic Thought, 2008.

Izzi Deen, M. Y. "Islamic Environmental Ethics, Law, and Society," in R. S. Gottlieb (ed.), *This Sacred Earth: Religion, Nature, Environment*, 2nd ed., New York: Routledge, 2004, pp. 142–50.

Moghul, U. F., and Safar-Aly, S. "Green Sukuk: The Introduction of Islam's Environmental Ethics to Contemporary Islamic Finance," *Georgetown International Environmental Law Review (GIELR)*, 27(1) (2015), pp. 1–60.

Olawuyi, D. "Energy Poverty in the Middle East and North African (MENA) Region: Divergent Tales and Future Prospects," in I. Del Guayo, L. Godden, D. N. Zillman, M. F. Montoya, and J. J. Gonzalez (eds.), *Energy Law and Energy Justice*, Oxford: Oxford University Press, 2020, pp. 254–72.

"Sustainable Development and Water-Energy-Food Nexus: Legal Challenges and Emerging Solutions," *Journal of Environmental Science & Policy* 103(1) (2020), https://doi.org/10.1016/j.envsci.2019.10.009.

Sikandar Shah Haneef, S. "Principles of Environmental Law in Islam," *Arab Law Quarterly* 17(3) (2002), pp. 241–54.

23

Towards an Islamic Energy Ethic and Praxis

Saffet Abid Catovic

This chapter explains some ways in which one of the significant faith communities, the Muslims, now numbering worldwide over 1.8 billion, can recognize and understand their relationship with the earth and its resources according to the sharia (sacred law)[1] as derived from their sacred texts of the Quran[2] and the hadith and Sunna[3] of the Prophet Muhammad, and some ways in which this environmental ethical understanding and associated practices need to be revived practically going forward.

In Islam, the link between doing one's religious duty to Allah (God) through proper service and interaction with one's fellow human beings and other creatures is essential and clearly established. The Quran uses the Arabic terms *ḥabl Allāh* and *ḥabl al-nās*: a rope that connects human beings to Allah along the vertical plane, and a rope that connects human beings to the rest of creation in the horizontal plane. Each rope conditions and is conditioned by the other. This in turn creates mutual rights, duties, and obligations between humankind and Allah (*ḥuqūq Allāh*) and humankind and the rest of creation – "worshippers" (*ḥuqūq al-ʿibād*). This type of link and positive interaction can be described broadly as ethics.

[1] The word sharia literally means "a waterway that leads to a main stream, a drinking place, and a road or the right path." From this meaning, the word sharia was used to refer to a path or a passage that leads to an intended place, or to a certain goal. Although the word sharia and its different derivative forms are mentioned in five places in the Quran, its extensive usage came much later, for the words Islam and *dīn* (religion) were more commonly employed to express the same meaning in the early days of Islam. Sharia (sacred or divine law), conceptually, refers to a set of rules, regulations, teachings, and values governing the lives of Muslims. However, these rules and regulations, contrary to how they are often described by many non-Muslims, cover every aspect of life. Sharia embraces worship, morals, individual attitude, and conduct, as well as the political, social, economic, criminal, and civil spheres.

[2] Muslims hold the Quran as being the uncreated divine word/speech (Logos) whose wording and meaning are both from Allah. It is the first of the two universally accepted primary sources of *hidāya* (guidance) and sharia for Muslims. All English translations of Quranic verses cited throughout are taken from Abdullah Yusuf Ali, *The Holy Quran*, https://quranyusufali.com.

[3] Hadith is the Arabic word for the sacred sayings of the Prophet Muhammad as remembered and recorded by his *ṣaḥāba* (companions), *azwāj* (wives), or *ahl al-bayt* (literally "people of the house" – immediate familial relations). It is also used in connection with the term Sunna (traditions), which includes Prophetic actions and approvals as well as sayings as they pertain to the sacred (bearing in mind that Islam does not maintain the same duality and apparent concrete separation of sacred/profane as found in the modern Western Judeao-Christian context, but rather a more fluid continual spectrum; a more appropriate term might be religious – but this too, like all such terms, is value-laden). It is the second of the two universally accepted primary sources of *hidāya* and sharia for Muslims.

Human beings have been charged with *amāna* (trust) (Q 33:72), that is, the just (*ʿadl*) and effective (*iḥsān*) administration of all that has been placed under our control and use (*taskhīr*) in our multifaceted role as *khalīfa* – stewards, caretakers, or guardians (Q 6:165).

Ethical understandings and insights occur and are communicated within religious traditions. A useful working definition of "religious tradition" is one put forth by Joseph Runzo: "A religion or a religious tradition consists of a complex set of social elements – symbols and ritual, myths and stories, concepts and truth-claims – which a community believes gives ultimate meaning to life by connecting the religious adherent to the transcendent." A religious life thus rests on a specific claim about the nature of reality, about how meaning and value are to be achieved, and about what is the desired end for humankind. To follow a religious life in part is to follow a moral life, which in turn is informed by and informs one's ethical point of view. Ethics, then, is the reasoning about morality, and is situated in the person, community or society, place, and time of its making. Notably, both "ethics" (from the Greek *ethos, ethike*) and "morality" (from the Latin *mos, mores*) mean customs or sacred customs of the people. The challenge of environmental crisis brought on by global warming and climate change caused the construction of environmental ethics and spurred the world's religions to develop their own set of environmental ethics based on their religious values.

Islamic ethics have historically been incorporated within the Islamic science (*ʿilm*) known as *ʿilm al-akhlāq*. Linguistically, the Arabic term *akhlāq* (plural of *khuluq*) means character, nature, and disposition. The word *akhlāq* is closely related and connected to *khāliq* (creator) and *makhlūq* (creation). Therefore, linguistically speaking, *akhlāq* assumes a good, wholesome, sound, and positive relationship between the Creator and creation, and between and among creatures. The term *khuluq* appears in the Quranic verse "And You (Muhammad) are on an exalted standard of character (*khuluq ʿaẓīm*)" (Q 68:4) and was the essence of the Prophet Muhammad's self-described mission when he said, "I have been sent to perfect good character."

Over the centuries, different Muslim scholars from across the theological spectrum have devoted much time, thought, research, and scholarly writings to this matter. A common thread through these diverse views is that the scope of Islamic ethics or *ʿilm al-akhlāq* is wide, comprehensive, and far-reaching because it deals with the relationship between human beings and their Creator, Allah, and human beings and all other creatures. In all these senses the *maqāṣid* (goals) of the sharia (which I will discuss later) give practical form to ethical norms and seek to construct human life on the basis of *ḥisba* (accountability) – *amr bi-l-maʿrūf wa-nahy ʿan al-munkar* (enjoining the right and forbidding the wrong). Maulana Maududi in his *tafsīr* (exegesis) of the Quran has defined *maʿrūf* as historically and universally accepted good that is "known, well-known, generally recognized, beneficence, and approved by Shariah," and *munkar*, which is the opposite of *maʿrūf*, as historically and universally accepted wrong that is "bad, evil, detestable, disagreeable, abominable, disapproved."[4] In general, what is good (*maʿrūf*) and approved are the halal and the lawful according to Islam. What is evil (*munkar*) and disapproved are the haram, the prohibited in Islam. The enactment of the *ḥisba* is a societal or communal obligation (*farḍ al-kifāya*), meaning it rests within the power of the state and legitimate governmental authorities, but should the state fall short in carrying this out with justice and fairness then the responsibility and obligation devolves to the individuals (*farḍ al-ʿayn*), who are the members of that state.

[4] Sayyid Abul Aʿla Mawdudi, *The Islamic Way of Life*, ed. Khurshid Ahmad and Khurram Murad (Leicester: The Islamic Foundation, 2001), p. 8.

The question for the Muslim is not who owns these resources – whether water, the soil, its vegetation, plant and animal life above, or its minerals (including fossil fuel deposits) beneath – for in all these cases it is Allah who owns them (Q 6:73, 10:55).

The scheme of life envisaged by Islam is a complete whole that revolves around the central concept of tawhid (divine unity, oneness). For the believing Muslim, Islam is not a mere appendage to life, it is life itself.[5] The primary basis of an Islamic worldview is the idea of tawhid, or the oneness of Allah. A worldview based on tawhid sees this universe as originating from Allah, returning to Him, and centered about Him. The unity of Allah has several corollaries, including the unity of all religions (not uniformity or unanimity), the unity of humanity with all its diversity (not sameness), and the unity of creation. The universe and all it contains originates from the power of the Word, the active singular Will from which all creation came to exist – "*kun fa-yakūn*" ("be and it is").[6] The fact that all groups[7] of living beings owe their existence directly to Allah and therefore stand on the same footing is beautifully expressed in the verse "There is no beast that walks on the earth and no bird that flies on its two wings which is not Allah's creatures like yourselves. No single thing have We neglected in Our Decree."[8] This verse gives some idea of the sanctity to which all life is held in Islam or what Thomas Berry refers to as the "rights of living species."[9]

In an oft-cited hadith by Muslims involved in the environmental "green" movement, the Prophet Muhammad said: "Indeed, the world is sweet and green, and Allah is making you successors in it to see how you act. So be mindful of this world."[10] This is similar to the Quranic *āya* (verse, but also the term used for "sign" in nature) "It is He who has made you *khalā'if* (guardians/caretakers) of the earth; He has raised you in ranks, some above others, that He may try you in the gifts He has given you; for your Lord is quick in punishment yet He is indeed Oft-Forgiving Most Merciful" (Q 6:165). According to this view, human beings have been charged with the *amāna* (Q 33:72) in our multifaceted role as *khalīfa* (Q 6:165). This trust not only encompasses the web of human relations but extends outward in ever-expanding concentric circles to include all within the natural world. In another hadith, the Prophet observed a timeless truth and worldly reality when he said: "Muslims have common share (*arfāq*) in three [things]: grass [herbage/vegetation for ourselves and the animal world, both domesticated and wild], water, and fire [including power – sourced by fossil fuels and other sources of nonrenewable and renewable energy]."[11] According to Islamic juridical (*fiqhī*) terminology, *arfāq* is that which is held in common or commonage so that all humans (and I would also hold that in many cases nonhumans as well) have an inalienable right to benefit from it and to expect its prudent use and just and equitable distribution. The question for the Muslim is not who owns these resources, for they belong to Allah. Therefore, ownership in Islam is more in keeping with the concept of trusteeship, a type of individual interim ownership. Abdullah Yusuf Ali, a commentator of the

5 An insightful observation about the real-life implications of divine unity for a faithful and practicing Muslim was put forth by Sayyid Qutb when he noted "Islam chooses to unite heaven and earth in one spiritual organism ... For the center of its being and the field of its action is human life in its entirety, spiritual and material, religious and worldly. Muslims must practice their faith in their social, legal and economic relationships. One of the characteristic marks of this faith is the fact that it is essentially a unity. It is at once worship and work, religious law and exhortation." Sayyid Qutb, *Social Justice in Islam* (Oneonta, NY: Islamic Publications International, 1999), pp. 7–8.

6 Q 36:82.

7 The Quran refers to nonhuman communities of creatures as *umam* (nations/societies) like humans (Q 6:38).

8 Q 6:38.

9 Thomas Berry, *The Great Work: Our Way into the Future* (New York: Bell Tower, 1999), p. 82.

10 *Saḥīḥ Muslim*, hadith no. 2742.

11 *Sunan Abī Dāwūd*, hadith no. 3477.

Quran, says of Q 33:72, regarding *amāna*: "There is no trust if the trustee has no power, and the trust implies that the giver of the trust believes and expects that the trustee would use it according to the wish of the creator of the trust, and not otherwise."[12]

Most, if not all, conflicts throughout human history can be directly or indirectly tied to the fair access and/or just control over these finite, life-sustaining resources.

In other words, the guardian of the trust has a high degree of freedom and accompanying responsibility (and accountability) in the use (or misuse) of the given trust. Hence the focus of concern is rather on "who" has the right to determine, and to what extent, access to those nonrenewable resources, their distribution, and consumption. From a *fiqhī* (jurisprudential) perspective within the various *madhāhib* (jurisprudential schools of thought) there are several kinds of this type of individual ad interim ownership that have been discussed by Muslim scholars over the years. In general, most Muslim scholarship has had the tendency to defer most forms of those nonrenewable resources held in common to the state's ownership, who in turn is expected to adminster them in the public interest and for the public common good (*maṣlaḥa mursala*). The historic experience of this type of state-administered and state-run ownership, especially as it pertains to the modern period and to resources like fossil fuels, has been mixed at best.

Our problem as humans is that we are not sharing these common resources equitably, neither horizontally (among the living human and nonhuman beings, and in particular between the geopolitically developed Global North and the underdeveloped Global South), nor vertically (among the living and the yet to be born – intergenerational equity) through implementing ecologically conscientious, environmentally friendly, and sustainable development practices and policies.

In response, global faith communities and their respective religious leadership have declared their intent to battle climate change with the release of statements and declarations that articulate their religious environmental ethics. These include the Papal Encyclical on the Environment and Climate Change, *Laudato Si'*, and similar faith-based declarations made by other faith communities, sects, and denominations. At a historic meeting of over sixty Muslim scholars, academics, and environmental activists from over twenty countries held in Istanbul, Türkiye, an Islamic Declaration on Global Climate Change was adopted.[13] This bold grassroots initiative was driven by various nongovernmental organizations (NGOs) including Greenfaith, Islamic Relief Worldwide, the Islamic Foundation for Ecology and Environmental Sciences, Climate Action Network (CAN) International, and Our Voices. Specifically, the Islamic Declaration on Climate Change affirms the United Nations goal of limiting global warming to "well below 2°C, and pursuing efforts to limit the temperature increase to 1.5°C above pre-industrial levels," consistent with the Paris Agreement adopted at COP21.[14] The declaration calls for the reduction and limitation of anthropogenic fossil-fuel combustion and the resultant CO_2 and other greenhouse gas emissions.[15] The declaration is notably distinctive among statements previously issued by Muslim organizations as well as among declarations from other

[12] Abdullah Yusuf Ali, *The Holy Qur'an: Text, Translation and Commentary* (Beltsville, MD: Amana, 1989), p. 1080.

[13] Islamic Declaration on Global Climate Change, August 17–18, 2015, http://islamicclimatedeclaration.org/islamic-declaration-on-global-climate-change/.

[14] United Nations Framework Convention on Climate Change (UNFCCC). Paris Agreement, art. 2(1)(a), December 12, 2015, UN Doc. FCCC/CP/2015/10/Add.1. "Holding the increase in the global average temperature to well below 2°C above pre-industrial levels and pursuing efforts to limit the temperature increase to 1.5°C."

[15] Islamic Declaration, especially section III, which states the moral duty to reduce anthropogenic emissions from fossil fuels.

faith communities in that it explicitly calls for a rapid phase-out of fossil fuels, a transition to 100 percent renewable energy, and increased financial and technological support from major greenhouse-gas emitters (the geopolitical Global North and China) to vulnerable communities in the Global South.[16] These communities include peoples of color who disproportionately suffer from climate impacts and among whom the majority of the world's Muslims reside.[17] Wealthy and oil-producing nations (of which the USA is now number one) are urged to phase out all greenhouse gas emissions by 2050. All people, leaders, and businesses are invited to commit to 100 percent renewable energy in order to tackle climate change, reduce poverty, and achieve sustainable development. This pattern cannot continue indefinitely and is unsustainable because it is destroying the resources or conditions upon which it depends. Writ small, this call put forth in the declaration is for divestment from fossil fuels assets, stocks, and capital investments.

This concept of not disturbing the earth is in keeping with the Quranic injunction "to walk softly on the earth" (Q 25:63). Scholars of *tafsīr* inform us that this walking softly on the earth is exemplified by the Prophet Muhammad, who was himself the embodiment of the Quran – "a walking Quran." His manner of walking was to place his feet firmly on the ground as if he was always walking downhill and not to penetrate or disrupt it. Hence, a more "green" ecological reading of this verse is to not cause harm to the earth. In modern environmental terminology, it includes reducing our carbon footprint that results from the burning of fossil fuels and is driven by our overconsumption. It is also part of *raḥma* (mercy), and hence the sharia, to adhere to the general principle of not being the cause of harm or hurt to one another. In the words of the Prophet Muhammad: "There should be neither harming nor reciprocating harm."[18] The mechanism of harming or violating the earth is *fasād* (corruption), or as contemporary Muslim scholars like Dr. Yusuf Qaradawi have interpreted the term, "pollution" in the earth, which the Quran holds is the result of what "the hands of man have wrought" (Q 30:41) – anthropogenic. Muslims must strive to follow this Prophetic best example – *uswa ḥasana* – in all aspects of their lives, including our investment decisions.

Broadly speaking, the divestment campaign asks all investors, not just corporate or institutional, NGOs, or organized religious communities and bodies, but also individuals, to consider cleaning up their investment portfolios; but the operative question is, how? The immediate challenge is to convince and persuade these investors to do this. General arguments about saving the earth for future generations, while correct and generally appealing, will not by themselves push many to action in terms of investments. Religious language, however, which is grounded in our particular faith traditions, and which speaks about matters of the soul, life, salvation, and eternal standings (heaven and hell), can be very persuasive in moving the faithful to take action.

I will briefly outline some ways in which Muslim investors, concerned about ethical, halal (religiously permissible and sanctioned) investments, can be reached and persuaded to become part of the movement. These are not the the only means and at this point constitute an outline. I invite anyone who can contribute to this effort in any way to add to the discussion and help

16 Ibid., sections III–IV, calls for "a complete phase-out of fossil fuels" and "a swift transition to 100% renewable energy" and urges "the countries and corporations of the developed world and oil-producing economies" to provide support to vulnerable nations and communities.

17 Asian Pacific region: 61.7 percent; Middle East/North Africa: 19.8 percent; sub-Saharan Africa: 15.5 percent. "The Future of the Global Muslim Population," Pew Research Forum on Religion, www.pewresearch.org/religion/.

18 *Sunan Ibn Mājah*, hadith no. 2340.

make this happen. A hot button these days is the sharia, or Islamic sacred law. I am not going to revisit this broad and multifaceted subject here, but would like to highlight the following facts:

1. Shariah, or Islamic law, influences the legal code in most Muslim countries.
2. According to the Pew Research Center 2013 survey findings, most Muslims (around the world) believe the sharia is the revealed word of Allah rather than a body of law developed by men based on revelation. Many Muslims say the sharia should be the law of the land in their Muslim-majority country; however, the survey reveals divergent opinions about the precise application of "the hows of implementing" Islamic law.[19]

Given this reality, strategically connecting to and including the fossil fuel divestment issue within the sharia is critical. To divest is to uphold and fulfill the purposes and objectives of the sharia, and therefore to ensure that one's Islam is complete and sound, and that to do otherwise is to violate the sharia and compromise one's Islam; conveying this to the faithful is a critical step in this process. Initially this requires a lot of scholarly work within Islamic society. Islam has been characterized by some as the Lutheran priesthood of the believers par excellence, which means there is no denominational executive council or papal authority. It starts with proposing the ideas and sharing them with scholars across the religious spectrum and the geographic Muslim world. This in turn will result in critiques of the ideas and debate, subsequent deliberation, and consensus building. The good news is that the proposals and sharing has begun, and debate is soon to follow.

Then follows the tactical design of new sharia-compliant financial investment instruments (for corporate, NGO, nonprofit, religious, institutional, and individual investors) that allow those who divest to reinvest in halal investments, including those that include renewable and clean energy projects and stocks in their portfolios; as they are already doing by avoiding investing in non-sharia-compliant, so-called sin stocks (alcohol, gambling, etc.).

Here, then, is my initial and humble contribution to this endeavor and undertaking: sharia literally means the trodden path that leads to the water well, the source of life – or the water way (stream) that leads to the river and sea itself, analogous to the Hebrew term halakha (the way to go). A classic and widely referenced definition of the sharia give by Sunni scholar Ibn al-Qayyim al-Jawziyya states, in part:

> The foundation of the sharia is wisdom and the safeguarding of people's interests in this world and the next. In its entirety it is justice, mercy, and wisdom. Every rule that transcends justice to tyranny, mercy to its opposite, the good to the evil, and wisdom to triviality does not belong to the haria. The Sharia is Allah's justice and mercy amongst His people. Life, nutrition, medicine, light, recuperation, and virtue are made possible by it. Every good that exists is derived from it, and every deficiency in being results from its loss and dissipation, for the sharia, which Allah entrusted His prophet to transmit, is the pillar of the world and the key to success and happiness in this world and the next.[20]

By the fourth century after the death of the Prophet, these principles and objectives were formally categorized and organized into an architectural framework by the ulema (scholars) and jurists into the sacred science of *maqāṣid al-sharīʿa* (higher objectives of sacred law). Of particular note is the work of the polymath scholar Abū Ḥāmid al-Ghāzālī, who wrote

[19] See "The World's Muslims: Religion, Politics and Society," Pew Research Center, April 30, 2013, www.pewforum.org/2013/04/30/the-worlds-muslims-religion-politics-society-overview.

[20] Ibn al-Qayyim al-Jawziyya. *Iʿlām al-muwaqqiʿīn ʿan Rabb al-ʿālamīn* (Beirut: Dār al-Kutub al-ʿIlmiyya, n.d.), pp. 11–12.

categorically that the sharia pursued five basic objectives: preservation (*ḥifẓ*) of faith (*dīn*), life (*nafs*), lineage/posterity/family (*nasl*), intellect (*ʿaql*), and wealth/material resources/property (*māl*), and that these were to be protected as absolute priorities. He observed, "Whatever ensures the safeguard of these five principles serves public interest and is desirable, and whatever hurts them is against public interest and its removal is desirable." Al-Ghazālī's five basic categories or essentials (*al-ḍarūra al-khamsa*) remain the same, but the order is changed by some scholars and others have added additional categories to them.

In reference to these categories, it has been observed by Dr. Hashim Kamali and others "that Maqsid Shariah (Higher Objectives of Sacred Law) is still open for further development and enhancement. The nature of this development and enhancement must reflect the priorities of our age and the change of circumstances that we encounter as a result."[21] In fact, this is a must; what is referred to as *tajdīd al-ʿaql wa-l-fahm* (renewal of mind and understanding) is to cope with the challenge of modernization and globalization (and, I would add, climate change). These are the objectives whose fulfillment is essential for the establishment of welfare in this world and in the hereafter, in the sense that if they are ignored then coherence and order (*taqdīr*) cannot be established, the balance (*mīzān*) will be disrupted, and *fasād* (chaos, disorder, and corruption) will be rife in this world.

Our communities, nation, the world environment, and our very future are threatened by rising global temperatures caused by greenhouse gas emissions resulting primarily from the burning of fossil fuels. Projections by the Intergovernmental Panel on Climate Change,[22] whose scientific integrity has been affirmed repeatedly through rigorous peer-reviewed processes, and overwhelming scientific consensus, have concluded unequivocally that the earth's temperature is warming, that the burning of fossil fuels is largely responsible, and that climate change will cause grave humanitarian, ecological, and financial damage on a global scale. In the coming century, this fact will displace and impoverish hundreds of millions of people globally and will increase illness, injury, and death rates due to the spread of infectious diseases, heat waves, and severe weather-related disasters. Climate change also causes grave damage to the ecological systems on which human civilization and all forms of life depend, thus undermining the very goals and objectives of the sharia.

Traditionally, strategies and policies put forth by environmentalists with respect to limiting and controlling greenhouse gas emissions driven by climate change focused on reducing demand and restraining consumption. These included curbing excess and waste and this strategy is very much in keeping with the Quranic injunction as found in verses like "O children of Adam! Wear your beautiful apparel at every time and place of prayer: eat and drink: but waste not by excess, for God loves not those who waste" (Q 7:31). This ethic of conservation and restraint is exemplified by the growing global grassroots Green Ramadan Movement, an example of which is the Islamic Society of North America's (ISNA) multifaceted Our Masjid Is Greening Ramadan campaign. Its "Ramadan: When Less Is More" theme is an example of implementing Prophetic ecological friendly practices at the community level and committing to the "greening" of mosque facilities. This commitment has also been made at the national level by the Morrocan Ministry of Religious Affairs. On the government level, a carbon tax (sometimes referred to as carbon fee and dividend (CF&D) approach and championed by the Citizens Climate Lobby (CCL) among others) would see those who consume more carbon pay more for the products and resources that they use and consume and would lead to more carbon equity.

[21] Muhammad Hashim Kamali, *Maqāṣid al-Sharīʿah: Ijtihād and Civilisational Renewal* (London: IIIT, 2011), p. 43.
[22] Berry, *The Great* Work, p. 111; Intergovernmental Panel on Climate Change, www.ipcc.ch/.

An exploration of new ways and means, especially through the use of modern technologies to capture and sequester carbon from the air, and the strengthening of traditional policies that seek to do this through nature's proven and time-tested way of tree planting and control of deforestation, are excellent ideas and they are making slow but steady progress (more slowly in the US than elsewhere, but that is par for the course). Given sufficient time, and implemented together, they would reduce carbon emissions gradually and in significant ways. Time, however, is precisely what we do not have. In Sura al-ʿAṣr (Q 103) the Quran mentions that time is running out for human beings to believe and do the right thing. A growing number of respected environmental scientists and economists have stated that in order to stem a global warming disaster, we must stop burning fossil fuels and keep at least 50 to 75 percent of fossil fuel reserves in the ground. To do otherwise is to overwhelm the planet's physical systems, heating the earth far past the red lines drawn by scientists.

It is not just the macro effects of greenhouse gas emissions and the resultant global warming that is of concern, but also the immediate health and well-being of the children, our future. But what type of future are we providing for our children and their children, who are our most precious gift from Allah and whose care, existence, and future we have been entrusted with is inextricably linked and connected with all of the noble goals of *maqāṣid al-sharīʿa*. A recent UNICEF study has found that air pollution is a major contributing factor in the deaths of around 600,000 children under five every year, and it threatens the lives and futures of millions more every day. As UNICEF Executive Director Anthony Lake has said, "Pollutants don't only harm children's developing lungs – they can actually cross the blood-brain barrier and permanently damage their developing brains – and, thus, their futures. No society can afford to ignore air pollution."[23] Satellite imagery confirms that around 2 billion children live in areas where outdoor air pollution, caused by factors such as vehicle emissions, heavy use of fossil fuels, dust, and burning of waste, exceeds minimum air quality guidelines set by the World Health Organization. South Asia has the largest number of children living in these areas, at 620 million, with Africa following at 520 million. East Asia and the Pacific has 450 million children living in areas that exceed guideline limits. (All the areas cited in this study are areas of high Muslim population.) The study also examines the heavy toll of indoor pollution, commonly caused by use of fuels such as coal and wood for cooking and heating, which mostly affects children in low-income, rural areas. Together, outdoor and indoor air pollution are directly linked to pneumonia and other respiratory diseases, which account for almost one-in-ten deaths of children under five, making air pollution one of the leading dangers to children's health. "We protect our children when we protect the quality of our air. Both are central to our future."[24] The sharia, Islam, and Allah require no less from us.

In 1963, during his speech at the historic Civil Rights March on Washington, DC, the great American civil rights leader Reverend Dr. Martin Luther King Jr. stated the following regarding the civil rights of African-Americans, which is equally applicable today in the context of the ravages of climate change: "We are now faced with the fact that tomorrow is today. We are confronted with the fierce urgency of now. In this unfolding conundrum of life and history, there 'is' such a thing as being too late. This is no time for apathy or complacency. This is a time for vigorous and positive action."[25]

[23] UNICEF, "Pollution: 300 Million Children Breathing Toxic Air," October 31, 2016, www.unicef.org/press-releases/pollution-300-million-children-breathing-toxic-air-unicef-report UNICEF.

[24] Ibid.

[25] Martin Luther King Jr., "I Have a Dream." Speech delivered at the March on Washington for Jobs and Freedom, Lincoln Memorial, Washington DC, August 28, 1963.

Is it not time for Muslims, believers, our mosques, and our institutions to revive their responsibilities as *khulafāʾ al-arḍ* (caretakers of the earth)? As Allah informs the faithful in the Quran:

> Has not the Time arrived for the Believers that their hearts in all humility should engage in the remembrance of Allah and of the Truth which has been revealed (to them), and that they should not become like those to whom was given Revelation aforetime, but long ages passed over them and their hearts grew hard? For many among them are rebellious transgressors. Know you (all) that Allah gives life to the earth after its death! Already have We shown the Signs plainly to you, that you may learn wisdom. (Q 57:16–17)

24

The Protection of Basic Natural Resources and Man under Islamic Law

A New Tool for Sustainable Development and Greening of the Environment

Mohamed A. 'Arafa

Islamic believers, known as Muslims, prevail in numerous countries in the Middle East. Humankind is observed as having stewardship over, or being a guardian or trustee of, the environment.[1] One of the rudimentary theories in Islamic environmental law is the concept of creation along with *fiṭra* (natural purity – a concept that 'encompasses an altruistic spirit, thoughtfulness in action, and a conservationist bias').[2] Building on the idea that God created the earth, the Quran and the Sunna, along with other sources of this divine law, disclose that God provides for humanity by putting everything in service to humans.[3] This principle demonstrates that man is part of nature, and God expects him to make ethical selections in response to what he encounters on earth.[4]

In this respect, there are four notions that address the principle of sustainable development according to modern positive environmental standards: 'parties need to preserve natural resources for the benefit of future generations'; 'natural resources may only be exploited in a manner that is "sustainable"'; 'the use of natural resources must be "equitable"'; and 'environmental considerations must be integrated into economic and other development plans and programmes, and developmental needs must be taken into account in applying environmental objectives'.[5] Comparing these notions to the Islamic attitude on natural resources and environment, a great resemblance will be acknowledged. The core and purpose of maintainable growth exists in Islam as the term 'sustainable development' has been emphasised in light of sharia values.[6] The Quranic provisions designate that in his role as viceregent, man should not exercise absolute dominion over nature or abuse the environment, but rather should take what he needs abstemiously and moderately in order to serve the Creator while maintaining the natural equilibrium that He ordained.[7]

As a result, the Quran stipulates that God has granted man, in effect, a usufruct and a right of tenancy with a precondition attached – 'he has granted man the right to live on Earth and to use

[1] F. Denny, 'Islam and Ecology: A Bestowed Trust Inviting Balanced Stewardship', *Earth Ethics* 10 (1998): 10.

[2] N. Mohamed, 'Revitalizing an Eco-Justice Ethic of Islam by Way of Environmental Education: Implications for Islamic Education' (PhD diss., Stellenbosch University, 2012), https://core.ac.uk/download/pdf/37348584.pdf.

[3] Ibid., 10.

[4] G. E. Roughton, 'The Ancient and the Modern: Environmental Law and Governance in Islam', *Columbia Journal of Environmental Law* 32 (2007): 107.

[5] G. W. Mugwanya, 'Global Free Trade vis-a-vis Environmental Regulation and Sustainable Development: Reinvigorating Efforts towards a More Integrated Approach', *Journal of Environmental Law & Litigation* 14 (1999): 418.

[6] Roughton, 'The Ancient and the Modern', 107.

[7] Ibid.

to the extent that he carries out God's will and preserves what God has granted him'.[8] In the same vein, Roughton notes that Fazlun M. Khalid refers to man's rights on earth as usufructuary – God is the only proprietor of the earth and everything in it, while man may use it for its utility only.[9] Other environmental intellectuals have added that, in light of sharia prohibitions against environmental waste and mismanagement, man's usufructuary privileges come with a supplementary obligation to preserve and develop the earth for the benefit of upcoming generations.[10] Sustainable development is deep seated in Islamic norms as the Quran inspires man to rationally approach the environment.[11] The equilibrium (balance) conception also supports the idea that man should act with control and reasonableness towards nature and the natural surroundings.[12]

In addition to giving everything on earth a divine purpose, under the Islamic environmental model, God has formed and created a stable and measured environment for His creations that is sensibly calculated so that they may effectuate His devotions.[13] Thus, it is mandatory that man conserve the proportions and stability of the environment that God created rather than disrupting or distracting this equilibrium.[14] Therefore, it is recommended that man's regular relationship to the rest of God's creation should be one of 'ecological utilization', whereby he lives according to God's will while protecting natural resources and averting degradation of the natural world created by God.[15] The *mīzān/al-tanāsub* norm (due proportion), mentioned in several Quranic verses, guides Muslims' connections with the environment, and designates that man must use the environment cautiously and only in ways that serve the balance.[16] This equilibrium is the keystone of sustainable development, and hence the concept of 'balance' or 'equilibrium' in Islamic international environmental law is comparable to the modern notion of sustainable development in the contemporary environmental international statutes and agreements.[17]

The crucial function of all creatures as signs of their Creator establishes the foremost sound legal basis for environmental management. In Islamic law, the requisite of elementary natural

[8] Ibid. See also M. R. al-Ḥalw, *Qānūn ḥimāyat al-bī'a fī ḍaw' al-sharī'a* (Beirut: Dār al-Maṭbū'āt al-Jāmi'iyya, 1999), 55–59.

[9] See, generally, F. M. Khalid, 'Islam and the Environment', in P. Timmerman (ed.), *Encyclopedia of Global Environmental Change* (Chichester: Wiley, 2002), 332–39.

[10] Ibid., 335.

[11] 'A. 'A. Fahmī, *al-Qawā'id al-Rūmāniyya wa-l-fiqhiyya* (Houston: Islamic University of North America (Mishkāh), 2013), www.muslim-library.com/dl/books/English_Legal_Maxims_of_Islamic_Jurisprudence.pdf, 150.

[12] Khalid, 'Islam and the Environment', 7. Regarding the 'balance' principles, Khalid says, 'All creation has an order and a purpose and is in a state of dynamic balance. If the sun, the moon, the stars did not bow themselves, *i.e.*, serve the purpose of their design, it would be impossible for life to function on earth' (ibid.).

[13] The Quran explains that God established the earth in an equilibrium that human beings may not disturb. God says, 'He raised the heaven on high and set the balance of all things, that you might not transgress that balance. Give just weight and full measure' (Q 55:1–18); and 'Sovereign of the heavens and the Earth, who has begotten no children and has no partner in His sovereignty; who has created all things and ordained them in due proportion' (Q 25:2).

[14] See M. R. Hassanien, 'Greening the Middle East: The Regulatory Model of Environmental Protection in the United States–Oman Free Trade Agreement, a Legal Analysis of Chapter 17', *Georgetown International Environmental Law Review* 23 (2011): 478.

[15] Ibid. See also Khalid, 'Islam and the Environment', 6–7: 'One could say with a reasonable degree of certainty that the environmental problems we see today would not have happened in a society ordered in accord with Islamic principles because its world view defined limits to human behavior and contained excess.' See, generally, F. M. Khalid, 'Islamic Pathways to Ecological Sanity: An Evaluation for the New Millennium', *Journal of Industrial Ecology* 3 (2000): 6–7.

[16] Khalid, 'Islam and the Environment', 6–7.

[17] Khalid, 'Islam and the Environment', 6–7. The perception of Islamic justice, which is a comprehensive concept that comprises several sorts of legal adjudication, has been used in a number of cases related to environmental protection in Muslim countries.

resources is based upon texts from the Quran and the Prophet Muhammad's teachings, along with the juristic principles. It should be noted that *fiqh* means the apprehension of sharia principles, in which 'legal theory' of Western legal doctrine is part of Islamic philosophy.[18] *Fiqh* was developed principally as an area of Islam that tried to comprehend sharia without entering into the area of 'jurisprudence', or the philosophy of law in its Western conception.[19] The sharia juristic principles must be inferred within the development of Islamic jurisprudence known as *uṣūl al-fiqh* (principles of jurisprudence).[20] Accordingly, the interpretation and implementation of basic Islamic legal norms, and the nature of this law, have been the focus of numerous debates among Muslim scholars.[21]

On the other hand, *al-wājibāt* (duties) in sharia are of central significance. Marcel Boisard has the following view: 'Islam offers a uniting and cohesive vision of humankind, of society, and of the world.'[22] In this framework, individual duties complement but also limit individual rights.[23] The Islamic stress on duties over rights is so noticeable that one scholar termed Islamic law 'an endless discussion on the duties of a Muslim'.[24] This Islamic conception of social improvement is a mutual effort, whereby 'individuals, communities and indeed the state act as the instruments by which these ideals are translated into practice'.[25] Hence, all human beings – as well as wildlife and livestock – have the right to share in the earth's resources, as man's mishandling of any resources is prohibited and the best use of all natural resources, both living and dead, is *farḍ* (mandatory). Section 24.1 is an analysis of the protection of the basic natural elements within the Islamic justice principles.

24.1 WATER: IMPORTANCE, LEGAL PROTECTION, AND THE CASE FOR CLEAN WATER LAW

Islam considers water as the origin of life, plants, and animals, as all living organisms depend on water for their survival, existence, and for the continuation of their life.[26] Also, water is the

18 It should be noted that Islamic law (sharia) is different from Islamic *fiqh* (jurisprudence). In other words, *fiqh* refers to the understanding of Islamic rules and principles. There are four major Sunni schools of jurisprudential thought (*madhāhib*) in Islam, and these schools have influenced the enlargement of the sharia in addition to the Shia school of Islam. Islamic law is *juristic*, meaning its rubrics have been evolved throughout history by the scholarly writings of Muslim jurists. See, generally, K. M. Khan, 'Juristic Classification of Islamic Law', *Houston Journal of International Law* 6 (1983–84): 23.

19 Ibid.

20 For further elaboration of the secondary sources of Islamic law, see, generally, I. Abdal-Haqq, 'Islamic Law: An Overview of Its Origin and Elements', *Journal of Islamic Law & Culture* 7 (2002): 27, 56 (defining Islamic law, explaining the main elements of sharia along with its various sources, and discussing the methodologies and various schools of Islamic jurisprudence).

21 Ibid. Indeed Islamic law principles are the theme of questioned understandings in Islamic history and in the contemporary world. See, generally, A. F. Ḥusayn, *Uṣūl al-fiqh al-Islāmī* (n.p., 2006).

22 Odeh Al-Jayyousi et al., 'Re-Thinking Sustainable Development within Islamic Worldviews: A Systematic Literature Review', *Sustainability* 14 (2002): 2.

23 Ibid.

24 F. Rahman, *Islam and Modernity: Transformation of an Intellectual Tradition* (Chicago: University of Chicago Press, 1982), 32 (quoting Professor Santillana).

25 A. Nanji, 'The Right to Development: Social and Cultural Rights and Duties to the Community', in *Proceedings of the Seminar on Islamic Perspectives on the Universal Declaration of Human Rights*, UN Doc. HR/IP/SEM/1999/1 (Part II, Section 2), 1999. See also J. Morgan-Foster, 'Third Generation Rights: What Islamic Law Can Teach the International Human Rights Movement', *Yale Human Rights & Development Law Journal* 8 (2005): 73–74 (explaining the importance of duties and strong support for solidarity rights in Islamic law).

26 A. A. Bagader, A. T. El-Sabbagh, M. Al-Glayand, and M. Y. Samarrai, 'Environmental Protection in Islam', *IUCN Environmental Policy & Law Paper*, no. 20 (1994): 6.

habitat of many creatures. Water also has other socio-religious functions, as it helps man remain *ṭāhir* (ritually pure) – to clean his body and clothes from all dirt and impurities so as to meet God clean and pure.[27] Therefore, there is no doubt that preservation of this natural resource is vital for all creatures in the world, and it is thus mandatory in Islamic law. At this point, an Islamic juristic principle governing this protection is 'whatever is indispensable to fulfill the imperative is imperative'.[28]

Accordingly, any act that obstructs or harms the ecological balance and biological and social functions of this resource, either by polluting, poisoning, or exhausting it with materials or substances that would degrade the environment, necessarily leads to the damages or ruin of life itself.[29] A related Islamic juristic norm stipulates, 'what leads to the prohibited is prohibited'.[30] Furthermore, excess use of water is forbidden, even if water is abundant, and water cannot be monopolised in Islamic water law. Hence, upstream farms cannot monopolise water.[31] Should water be insufficient for all farms, older ones have priority over newer ones. The same principle applies to underground water.[32] The Prophet bathed with two litres of water and performed ablutions with half a litre.[33]

The fundamentals of Islamic water law guarantee that water is accessible to all members of the Muslim *umma* (community), as it is considered common public property.[34] This is why in several modern Muslim nations, such as Egypt, statutes consider 'water resources as belonging to the whole society (the state, or the public domain)'.[35] An individual's water right is restricted by

[27] The Quran states in this regard: 'We made from water every living thing' (Q 2:164); 'Verily . . . in the rain that God sends down from heaven, thereby giving life to the earth after its death' (Q 21:30); and 'It is He who has made the sea of service, that you may eat thereof flesh that is fresh and tender' (Q 16:14).

[28] Bagader et al., 'Environmental Protection in Islam', 7.

[29] Bagader et al., 'Environmental Protection in Islam', 7.

[30] The *majalla al-aḥkām al-ʿadliyya* (Majalla) provides that 'people have the right to use water from all sources, including those on private property. Private acquisition or sale of water or water rights is still uncommon in the Islamic world. Although water may be acquired through ownership of land on which it is located, the right of the public to use such water for specific purposes cannot be denied.' It is worth mentioning that the Majalla is the first compilation and codification of Islamic civil and commercial law and was enacted by the Ottoman Empire in 1869 for the use of then recently established civil courts, and was later found in many forms in most Islamic nations. See F. M. Goadby, 'The Moslem Law of Civil Delict as Illustrated by the Mejelle', *Journal of Comparative Legislation & International Law* 21 (1939): 62.

[31] Ibid.

[32] Ibid. See A. Ahmad, 'Islamic Water Law as an Antidote for Marinating Water Quality', *University of Denver Water Law Review* 2 (1999): 169, analysing the traditional law regulating water pollution in Muslim countries, showing the attitude of the law towards the environment generally, and the development of water resources and subsequent allocation of water rights. In this respect, Ahmad argued: 'Water may not be reduced to the domain of private proprietorship. . . . Maintaining the public character of water is the best way to reclaim its quality and enhance optimum utilization of available resources in those societies. The water laws of many developing countries are still based on or influenced by Islamic law. Considering the traditional worldview of Islam on water resources and water quality maintenance, it is a paradox that in Muslim countries water quality continues to deteriorate without any appreciable effort either by the public or the authorities to abate it. Islamic law treats water as distinct from other environmental elements, removes it from the pack of normal legal entitlements, and assumes its constant purity. Available data shows that water quality in Muslim nations is deteriorating due to enormous development challenges and rapid growth. Thus, water quality degradation is an emerging pollution problem in these countries that needs to be arrested quickly' (ibid.).

[33] *Ṣaḥīḥ Muslim* and *Ṣaḥīḥ al-Bukhārī*.

[34] Ibid. See also al-Ḥalw, *Qānūn*, 199, 255–68.

[35] D. A. Caponera, *Principles of Water Law and Administration: National and International* (London: Routledge, 1992), 68. 'In spite of subsequent written water laws introduced by external powers or other governments, the basic principles of Islamic water law are still observed and strictly followed, as local customs and usages, by the population' (ibid.).

its priority and preference of use, and it is not a product for limited proprietorship or exclusive possession, despite personal expenses in its attainment or sanitisation.[36]

In this regard, the Prophet set forth the standard when he stated: 'All members of the community are equal partners in three things: water, fire, and pasture.'[37] By the same token, good management and water maintenance are explicit requirements under sharia rules as there is no reason to engage in water excess, not even for what is considered one of the most imperative pillars of Islam, *wuḍūʾ* (ritual ablution).[38]

As a common natural resource, water in Islamic law falls in the category of *ḥuqūq Allah* (rights of God). These rights are connected directly to God because their enforcement is highly underlined by Him, as these include the public interest concerns as a whole with no particular attachment to any person.[39] These rights cannot be graced, remitted, exonerated, or compromised unless *nadam* (regret or repentance) is fulfilled, and the qadi (judge), the state, or the plaintiff has no discretionary power within their strict implementation, distinguishing them from *ḥuqūq al-ʿibād* (individual rights), which are mostly contractual or tortious.[40] In one practical case, *al-Dahhak v. Muhammad b. Maslama*, the plaintiff (the former) wanted to obtain water by digging a canal, and the only method by which he could reach the water was by excavating through the land of the defendant (the latter); the defendant strongly opposed the idea of digging a canal and laying it through his property. Caliph ʿUmar b. al-Khaṭṭāb decided in favour of the plaintiff, irrespective of the defendant's strong opposition.[41]

Under the notion of mandatory duty in Islamic water law, the public authorities have a greater liability in defending water as a resource than they do in enforcing other laws.[42] This responsibility is settled once the government (state) takes progressive steps to clean and refresh polluted waters or to keep them in their natural situation by regulating polluters' deeds.[43] Islamic norms and values require that water be kept free from contamination so that it may endure to achieve its religious and social functions, as well as serve as an appropriate environment for numerous beings, as polluted water cannot be used for any legitimate purpose such as drinking, swimming, washing, or navigation.[44] Thus, a big resemblance can be observed between Islamic water law and the current positive laws regulating water quality as contract law, property law, environmental law, and tort law.[45] A liability that results from water pollution under Islamic

[36] Ibid., 69. 'No one can refuse surplus water without sinning against Allah and against man. Also animals must not be allowed to die of thirst, and the water which remains after a man has quenched his thirst must be given to them. It would seem that the Prophet Mohammad declared that water should be, together with pasture and fire, the common entitlement of all Muslims, that he prohibited the selling of it, and that he had established a community of water use among men' (ibid.).

[37] Ibid. See, generally, D. A. Caponera, *Water Law in Moslem Countries* (Rome: Food and Agriculture Organization of the United Nations, 1973), 38–39. The Prophet stated: 'No one shall urinate in stagnant water, and avoid the abhorrent act of emptying your bowels near water sources, in the middle of the road, and in the shade' (*Ṣaḥīḥ Muslim*).

[38] The Prophet himself illustrates this issue. The Prophet observed his Companion's extravagance in his use of water and asked, 'What is this wastage, O Saʿd?' Saʿd said, 'Is there wastage even in washing for prayer?' 'Yes, even if you are by a flowing river!' the Prophet replied. Bagader et al., 'Environmental Protection in Islam', 6.

[39] Ahmad, 'Islamic Water Law', 7. 'A. b. M. al-Māwardī, *al-Aḥkām al-ṣultāniyya wa-l-wilāyāt al-dīniyya* (n.p., 1978), 273.

[40] Ahmad, 'Islamic Water Law', 7.

[41] Ibid.

[42] Hassanien, 'Greening the Middle East'.

[43] Ahmad, 'Islamic Water Law', 7.

[44] Ibid.

[45] Ibid. See also O. A. Bakhashab, 'Islamic Law and the Environment: Some Basic Principles', *Arab Law Quarterly* 3 (1988): 287–98, at 287, 293. S. H. Nasr, *Religion and the Order of Nature* (New York: Oxford University Press, 1996), 281.

jurisprudence is *contingent* that one cannot 'own' water and is consequently liable for polluting public property.[46] One's state of mind is immaterial to the liability's inquiry, making intent-based defences inapplicable and ineffective.

24.2 AIR: SIGNIFICANCE AND LEGAL PROTECTION

All creatures on the earth depend on air for breathing, and wind helps plants reproduce and exemplify the perfection and wisdom of God.[47] Conservation of the air is required in Islamic law. The Islamic juristic rule governing the protection of air identifies it as an essential aspect of life: 'whatever is necessary to fulfill the imperative is imperative'.[48] Air pollution is a disruption of the religious and social roles of the air, and any activity to impede these functions represents an attempt to disturb and transgress God's ordering of the universe along with an obstruction of man's role in the development of the world.[49] The legislative Islamic principles regulating the fortification of air are akin to those of water – as rights to the benefits derived from natural resources held in common: abusing rights is forbidden and punished; scarce resource exploitation is controlled; mutual welfare is secured; and benefits are protected and damages have to be either contained or reversed.[50] In other words, sharia evolved within the strategies set by four ideologies agreed upon by Muslim scholars over the centuries: 'the interest of the community (public interest) takes superiority over the individual (private) interests'; 'relieving hardship takes precedence over endorsing benefit'; 'a bigger loss cannot be prescribed to lessen a smaller loss and a bigger benefit takes precedence over a smaller one'; and 'a smaller harm can be arranged to evade a bigger damage and a smaller benefit can be dispensed with in preference to a bigger one'.[51]

24.3 LAND AND SOIL: CONCEPT AND ISLAMIC LEGAL ENVIRONMENTALISM

The Creator has made the land a source of living and sustenance, as human beings were created from water and soil. Land is home to many creatures, soil is used to grow food, and mountains perform a role in stabilising the earth's crust.[52] Islamic law considers the whole earth a place of

46 U. F. Moghul and A. A. Ahmed, 'Contractual Forms in Islamic Financial Law and Islamic Inv. Co. of the Gulf (Bahamas) Ltd. v. Symphony Gems N.V. & Ors.: A First Impression of Islamic Finance', *Fordham International Law Journal* 27 (2003): 150–51 (discussing the viewpoint of Islamic finance and its relation to the environment).

47 Bagader et al., 'Environmental Protection in Islam', 6. See also al-Ḥalw, *Qānūn*, 150.

48 Bagader et al., 'Environmental Protection in Islam', 6. See also W. M. H. El-Malik, *Minerals Investment under the Shari'a Law* (Alphen aan den Rijn: Kluwer Law, 1993), 55.

49 God says, 'Behold! . . . In the change of the winds, and the clouds which they trail between the sky and the Earth, here indeed are signs for people that are wise' (Q 2:164).

50 Khalid, 'Islam and the Environment', 3.

51 Ibid., 4. See F. M. Mangunjaya and J. E. McKay, 'Reviving an Islamic Approach for Environmental Conservation in Indonesia', *Worldviews* 16 (2012): 286–305, explaining an approach to combine Islamic principles of environmental protection with traditional methods of conservation, presenting an Islamic theology of creation care and highlighting some projects in the Muslim world: '(1) to strengthen standing of state law, especially with respect to environmental justice in the sector of mining; (2) provide correct clarification and understanding to all levels of society regarding religious law with respect to issues connected with the natural environment; and, (3) attempt to apply moral and ethical norms and sanctions to those concerned regarding the importance of environmental care in the mining sector'.

52 The Quran states: 'It is He Who has made the Earth manageable for you, so traverse ye through its tracts and enjoy of the sustenance which He furnishes' (Q 67:15); and 'Behold, thy Lord said to the angels: I am about to create man from clay' (Q 38:71).

worship, as the Prophet decreed: 'The whole earth has been made a place of worship for me, pure, and clean.'[53] Accordingly, it is required that humans maintain the soil's productivity and not expose it to erosion by any means (flood, wind, frosting, grazing, mining, etc.), but instead enhance its fertility and efficiency.[54] Legally speaking, and according to the Islamic norm 'what leads to the prohibited is prohibited', destruction, corrosion, and abuse of fertile land are prohibited.[55]

24.4 ANIMALS AND PLANTS: IMPORTANCE AND THE ISLAMIC LEGAL IDEAL

Without doubt, no one may possibly deny the vitality of plants and animals as living resources of massive benefits. Without them, neither man nor other species could endure.[56] Plants and animals produce food from energy for man and all other creatures; provide man with medicine, oil, timber, fuel, leather, medicine; enrich the soil; preserve the water by detaining its run-off; moderate the climate; and produce oxygen.[57] Under sharia law, the Prophet Muhammad ordered Muslims to treat animals well, telling a story about a woman who will go to hell for torturing a cat.[58] In addition, ʿUmar b. al-Khaṭṭāb said, 'If a mule stumbled in Iraq, I will be held responsible before God, for not having paved the road for it.'[59]

Islamic environmentalism prohibits the prolonged slaughtering of animals. The Prophet stated, 'When you slaughter, slaughter with goodness. Let each of you sharpen his blade and let him give ease to the animal he is slaughtering.'[60] Fishing and hunting for food is permitted under Islamic law; however, the Prophet cursed anyone using a creature as a target and the taking of life as a mere sport.[61] Moreover, killing animals with fire is haram (forbidden) and absolutely banned, as the Prophet Muhammad stated that an earlier prophet had ordered the burning of an anthill after an ant stung him. God corrected him: 'Because an ant stung you, you have destroyed a whole nation that worships God.'[62] On the basis of the Sunna, Muslim legal mujtahids/ulema (jurists) have ruled that God's creatures possess *ḥurma* (inviolability), which exists even in wartime, as the Prophet forbade killing any animal such as ants, bees, or captured livestock, as killing them is considered to be an act of corruption in what God proscribed.[63] Also, the Prophet prohibited the baseless cutting of trees and the burning of the enemy's trees.[64] Moreover, animals enjoy a detailed body of legal rights in Islamic law, and their rights are

[53] Bagader et al., 'Environmental Protection in Islam', 8.
[54] Ibid., 9.
[55] Ibid. See also al-Ḥalw, *Qānūn*, 288–302.
[56] al-Ḥalw, *Qānūn*, 112–19.
[57] God considers them as living societies like mankind, and they praise and worship God. In this domain, the Quran reads: 'Then let man look at his food, for that We pour forth water in abundance, and We split the earth in fragments, and produce therein corn, and grapes and nutritious plants, and olives and dates ... for use and convenience to you and your cattle' (Q 80:24); 'See ye the fire which ye kindle? Is it ye who grow the tree which feeds the fire, or do We grow it?' (Q 56:71); 'There is not an animal that lives on the Earth, nor a being that flies on its wings, but forms part of communities like you' (Q 6:38); and 'The seven heavens and the Earth, and all beings therein, declare His glory' (Q 17:44).
[58] God says, 'We have not sent you but a mercy to all beings' (Q 21:107).
[59] al-Ḥalw, *Qānūn*.
[60] See *Sunan* of Abū Dāwūd.
[61] Bagader et al., 'Environmental Protection in Islam', 11.
[62] *Ṣaḥīḥ Muslim* and *Ṣaḥīḥ al-Bukhārī*.
[63] Bagader et al., 'Environmental Protection in Islam', 11.
[64] Ibid.. The Prophet said, 'If any Muslim plants a tree or sows a field, and a human, bird or animal eats from it, it shall be reckoned as charity from him' (*Ṣaḥīḥ Muslim* and *Ṣaḥīḥ al-Bukhārī*).

enforceable by courts and public authorities.[65] According to this logic, one environmental Muslim scholar offered the following argument on the Prophetic traditions:

> The rights of livestock and animals with regard to their treatment by man: These are that he spent on them the provisions that their kinds require, even if they have aged or sickened such that no benefits comes from them; that he not burden them beyond what they can bear; that he not put them together with anything by which they are injured, whether of their own kind or other species, and whether by breaking their bones or butting or wounding; that he slaughter them with kindness if he slaughters them and neither flay their skins nor break their bones until their bodies have become cold and their lives expired; that he not slaughter their young within their sight; that he set them apart individually; that he make comfortable their resting places and watering places; that he puts their males and females together during their mating seasons; that he not discard those which he takes in hunting; and that he neither shoot them with anything that breaks their bones nor bring about their destruction by any means that renders their meat unlawful to eat.[66]

The world we occupy is a sign of God's creation, as is the environment of our innermost selves. They originate from one source and are attached by only one objective, which is to serve the divine will.[67]

24.5 PROTECTION OF MAN FROM HARM UNDER ISLAMIC ENVIRONMENTAL LAW

In Islamic law, protection of man is based upon texts and juristic doctrines developed by Muslim jurists in order to account for modern life through *ijtihād* (individual reasoning).[68] The correlation between man and the universe is well defined and illuminated in the Quranic provisions and the Prophetic traditions as follows:

(a) a relationship of meditation, consideration, and observation of the creation and what it encompasses;
(b) a linkage of justifiable and maintainable utilisation, improvement, and service for man's benefit and for the satisfaction of his interests and welfares; and
(c) a relationship of attention, care, devotion, and nurture for man's good works are not restricted to the benefit of the human species but rather cover the benefit of all creatures.[69]

Damage of all forms is forbidden under Islamic law, and one of the most significant juristic principles is *dar' al-mafāsid awlā min jalb al-maṣāliḥ* (averting harm takes precedence over the

65 Bagader et al., 'Environmental Protection in Islam', 11.
66 See 'I.'A. b. 'Abd al-Salām, *Qawā'id al-aḥkām fī maṣāliḥ al-anām* (Egypt: al-Maktaba al-Ḥusayniyya al-Miṣriyya, 1934), 121, discussing individual rights, and the legal and moral claims of other creatures upon each legally responsible person. He said, 'It is, however, significant that in Islam the concept of rights or legal claims enforceable by law applies to animals as well as human beings' (ibid.).
67 The chief correlation is that between the Creator and the rest of His creation, the Creator Himself determined a subsidiary one – that between man and the other creatures. Khalid, 'Islam and the Environment', 3.
68 For further details on *ijtihād*, see, generally, N. Goolam, 'Ijtihad and Its Significance for Islamic Legal Interpretation', *Michigan Law Review* (2006): 1444–45, explaining the notion of *ijtihād* as a source of law in Islamic law, its definition, theoretical underpinnings, its role in the interpretation of the Islamic provisions, and historical development of the concept throughout the diverse ages of Islam.
69 The Prophet Muhammad said, 'There is a reward in doing well by every living thing' (*Ṣaḥīḥ al-Bukhārī*). See also Fahmī, *al-Qawā'id*.

acquisition of benefits) and *lā ḍarar wa-lā ḍirār* (there shall be no harming others or reciprocating harm).[70] Accordingly, all actions that intend to reach goods and secure benefits by way of fulfilling human needs, developing communications, and providing services of all aspects of life (agriculture, industry, trade, mining, etc.) should be carried out without any injuries, harm, or acts of *fasād* (corruption) or *ifsād* (mischief).[71] Hence, it is essential that safeguards and precautions be taken into consideration within the processes of developing and implementing such performances, as they may not be accompanied by or result in any form of avoidable damage.[72]

24.6 WASTES, EXHAUSTS, DRUGS, AND TOXIC SUBSTANCES: RECYCLING IN ISLAM

All waste and exhaust resulting from man's daily acts, industrial activities, and the use of advanced and modern technologies worldwide should be judiciously reduced for the advancement of environmental protection against devastation or other negative impacts on the natural world.[73] A further central Islamic principle related to the protection of man in this area is the Islamic prohibition regarding insensitive consumption, that is, extravagance and profligacy.[74] Extravagance is not only the inconsiderate consumption of natural resources but also constitutes a sign of disrespect towards the Owner and the Creator of all bounties (God).[75] Islamic law prohibits excessive use of resources and requires that waste be kept to a minimum. As the Quran states, 'Eat and drink, but waste not.'[76]

70 Bagader et al., 'Environmental Protection in Islam'. See also J. al-Ṣuyūṭī and Z. al-ʿĀbidīn b. Nujaym, *al-Ashbāh wa-l-naẓā'ir* (Cairo: Dār al-Ḥadīth, 2013).

71 See K. Hamdy, 'Islamic Perspectives on Natural Resources Management and Sustainability', *IIFET 2000 Proceedings* (2001), 1: 'The complexity of natural resources management has challenged the most willing governments and their most dedicated scientists. . . . Recently more professionals have turned to religious teachings about nature and society, in order to tackle those intangibilities. In this context . . . efforts have been dedicated to the use of Islamic sources of law to inform natural resource management efforts. . . . In Islam, the use of natural resources for consumption and profit lies at the juncture between individual worship (*ʿibadat*), and group transactions (*muʿamalat*). . . . The relationship between human society (*ummah*) and the natural environment is a defining factor of Muslim human ecology.' Also, Hamdy asks, 'Does religion have a place in natural resource governance? And, if it does, do basic religious teachings have what it takes to judiciously inform the arduous task of sustainable balancing of the three constraints of greed [i.e., self-interest], efficiency, and fairness, that shape the decision-making processes of natural resource management?' (ibid.).

72 Ibid. See also M. Abu-Sway, 'Towards an Islamic Jurisprudence of the Environment: Fiqh Al-Biʿah fil-Islam', Belfast Islamic Centre, 2000, https://tinyurl.com/2py63yew.

73 See I. Ozdemir, 'An Islamic Approach to the Environment', *Islam Awareness*, 27 August 2013, www.islamawareness.net/Nature/environment_approach.html. 'The concept of divine unity is the basis and essence of Islam. Divine unity is apparent in the unity of humanity and of nature. God's vicegerents on the Earth, the holders of His trust, are therefore primarily responsible for preserving the unity of creatures, the integral wholeness of the world, the flora and fauna, and wildlife and natural environment. Thus, "unity", "trust", and "responsibility" are the three basic concepts of Islam. These principles are at the same time the chief pillars of the Islamic environmental ethic. They form also the fundamental values taught by the *Qur'an*.'

74 Ibid.

75 Ibid. 'According to Islam, everything in the universe is created by God. It is God Who adorns the skies with the sun, the moon and the stars, and the face of the earth with flowers, trees, gardens, orchards, and the various animal species. It is again God Who causes the rivers and streams to flow on the Earth, Who upholds the skies (without support), causes the rain to fall, and places the boundary between night and day. The universe together with all its richness and vitality is the work and art of God, that is, of the Creator. It is again God Who creates all plants and animals as pairs, in this way causing their procreation.'

76 Q 7:31.

Similarly, Islamic law requires that waste be carefully disposed of, towards which end a juristic rule states: 'Damage shall not be eliminated by means of similar or greater damage.'[77] Any polluting or altering substance (e.g., toxic or chemical materials used in factories, houses, private or public spheres) should be treated at source with the best available treatment measures or reliable effective techniques. Care should be taken in the removal and dumping of any detrimental products to avoid greater environmental damages, including natural and social injuries.[78] Similarly, Islamic environmental principles inspire the recycling and reutilisation of waste. As the Prophet Muhammad stated, 'No one shall urinate in stagnant water, and avoid the abhorrent act of emptying your bowels near water sources, in the middle of the road, and in the shade.'[79] Thus, it is essential that all possible precautions are taken to avoid any harmful damage to the environment and to reduce any deleterious effects. The Islamic principle 'a private injury is accepted to avert a general injury to the public' protects man along with the natural and social environment.[80]

24.7 PESTICIDES AND INSECTICIDES

These same Islamic principles and juristic rules apply equally to pesticides, insecticides, and herbicides, as using such ingredients should not result in any form of corruption or damage to man and the environment.[81] In other words, such substances must not cause any harm to man or other creatures, even if this leads to some losses in agricultural productivity. Thus, control and banning of whatever may cause potential harm to man or the ecosystem is required, even if this control or proscription may affect some personal interests under Islamic law.[82] If the use of pesticides is inevitable, then the concept of *ḍarūra* (necessity) applies.[83] In this way, Islamic law encourages scientific research and the use of the least destructive means, as *al-ḍarūrāt tubīḥ al-maḥẓūrāt* (necessities render prohibited things permissible) – 'every necessity is to be assessed according to its seriousness' and 'what is permitted due to an excuse ceases to be as such with the cessation of that excuse'.[84] It should be underscored that necessity is defined as where a person has to violate the law in spite of himself to prevent an inescapable evil befalling him, even

77 al-Ḥalw, *Qānūn*, 215–24.

78 Ibid., at 226–28. See also, S. Zafar, 'Environmental Sustainability in Islam, Echoing Sustainability in MENA', *ECOMENA*, 8 June 2013, www.ecomena.org/sustainability -islam/. 'Islamic beliefs, traditions and values provide an effective and comprehensive solution to the current environmental challenges faced by the human race. Islam has a rich tradition of highlighting the importance of environmental protection and conservation of natural resources. According to Islamic law, the basic elements of nature – land, water, fire, forest, and light – belong to all living things, not just human beings.'

79 *Ṣaḥīḥ Muslim* and *Ṣaḥīḥ al-Bukhārī*.

80 al-Ḥalw, *Qānūn*, 230. In case any negative injuries occur, we should search for less innocuous substitutions or harmful options.

81 Ibid., 312–15.

82 Ibid., 316–19. See also T. Cisse, 'Islam, the Environment, and the Use of Vetiver Grass', 2008, www.vetiver.org/SEN-cisse2.pdf.

83 Ibid. See also Bagader et al., 'Environmental Protection in Islam'.

84 al-Ḥalw, *Qānūn*, 316–19. In Islamic jurisprudence (*fiqh*), Muslim jurists along with the mufti/sheikh (leader) explained these rules within the following guidelines:

(a) Objection in Islamic *fiqh* is reserved for omitting what is agreed to be a requirement and performing something that is agreed to be unlawful. Objection is not for issues where there is a difference of opinion.

(b) It is recommended to remove oneself from controversial issues.

(c) Whoever is afflicted with something controversial must follow the opinion of those who permit it.

though it is in his power not to transgress the law and allow the evil to befall him or someone else.[85]

It is measured by its extent thereof, and renders prohibited things permissible only to the extent necessary, and this legal regulation is derived from the Quranic verse concerning simplifying and easing sufferings and hardships.[86] In addition, it is important to show consideration at times of hardship.[87]

It is obvious that all the above-mentioned Islamic principles apply equally to radioactive substances, disruptive noise (which everyone has a duty to minimise),[88] and natural catastrophes (floods, storms, volcanic eruptions, earthquakes, epidemics, etc.), as they are a means of testing people's patience and, of course, whenever appropriate, precautions must be taken to mitigate catastrophes and acts of man that may cause disasters on a large scale.[89]

To summarise, Islamic law maintains that 'damage shall be eliminated and removed to the extent that is possible'. However, the preventative means that are taken should not lead to other confrontational influences within the scope of the Islamic principle that 'damage shall not be eliminated by means of similar damage'.

85 Bagader et al., 'Environmental Protection in Islam'.

86 For instance, drinking alcoholic beverages or eating pork or the meat of unslaughtered animals is not permitted except at times of necessity, because these are times when exceptions are permissible. God says, 'He imposed no hardships upon you in religion' (Q 2:286); and 'God does not burden any soul with more than it can bear' (Q 22:78).

87 H. Z. Rahim, 'Ecology in Islam: Protection of the Web of Life a Duty for Muslims', *Washington Report on Middle East Affairs*, 1991, 65, www.wrmea.org/1991-october/ecology-in-islam-protection-of-the-web-of-life-a-duty-for-muslims .html.

88 In this regard, the Quran states: 'And be moderate in thy pace, and lower thy voice; for the worst of sounds without doubt is the braying of the donkey' (Q 31:19).

89 In this respect, God says, 'Mischief has appeared on land and sea because of what the hands of man have earned' (Q 30:41).

25

Faith-Based Approaches to Ecological Harmony and Environmental Protection

Nadia B. Ahmad[*]

25.1 INTRODUCTION

This chapter delves into the origins of faith-based approaches to environmental law. These alternative viewpoints to the environmental law canon offer additional legal mechanisms for environmental protection, including, for instance, climate change adaptation measures.[1] World religions emphasize the duty of the individual to care for the environment instead of a rights-based approach as expressed; for example, in international human rights law in terms of the human right to a healthy environment.[2] The origins of these faith-based traditions can be traced to Judaism, Christianity, Islam, Hinduism, Buddhism, Jainism, Zoroastrianism, Daoism, Shintoism, Sikhism, and others.[3] The scope of religious law is broad, but I focus on the interconnections of faith and ecology in world religions. The emphasis on righteousness lays the foundation for the religious command to protect the environment.[4]

The failure to enforce environmental rights and norms worldwide necessitates finding alternative sources of ecological obligation, such as that which could be derived from religious rules for faith practitioners. "Intergenerational equity is also a chief concern of climate change adaptation efforts and sustainable development. According to much religious teaching, present generations should keep the environment healthy and safe for inheritance by future generations."[5] An appreciation of the nexus between ecology and faith shows that faith traditions provide centuries-old legal customs and norms for environmental ethics and can add to the understanding of the public trust doctrine and impact various international law agreements and modalities.[6] While considering faith-based approaches more generally, this chapter focuses on the protections found in Islamic law in particular, because its framework of environmental ethics

[*] An earlier version of this chapter appeared in *Rutgers Race and the Law Review*.

[1] Nadia Ahmad, *Recognizing the Role of Religion in Environmental Legal Norms*, 32 St. Thomas Law Review 24, 24–25 (2019).

[2] "This duty is rooted in the belief that the Earth in its totality is a creation of the Creator, and that both the individual and the State are enjoined to take responsibility for creation as part of religious duties." Ibid.

[3] Ibid.

[4] "In sacred scriptures, humans have a divine mandate to improve nature and dispose of impurities as they find them. This purification is focused on bringing order and progress to nature without destroying it in the endeavor." Ibid.

[5] Ibid.

[6] Ibid.

allows for resisting the twin assaults to religious freedom and the environment. Identifying faith-based approaches to environmental protection assists in the conservation of religious identity and the protection of the environment.[7] Religious environmental ethics have not been well addressed in the context of international environmental law in its current iteration, and this shortcoming may be contributing to the failure of international environmental law to protect the environment. Faith-based approaches can help formulate an international order that is more ethically driven, more ethically consistent, and less contradictory.[8]

This chapter is structured as follows. First, I highlight the role of sacred thought for creating justifications for environmental ethics. Then, I lay out the general principles of specific religions with respect to the environment and discuss some of the shortcomings of faith-based environmental laws as alternative legal norms. I conclude by looking at how faith-based approaches to environmental law can be reframed as a heterodox formulation of environmental ethics and how to bring these into the fore as legal constructs. The reformulation of environmental ethics through religious principles can work to broaden mechanisms for environmental protection.

25.2 THE RISE OF FAITH-BASED APPROACHES

Religious worldviews are a contributing factor in creating environmental degradation and human misery in its various forms all over the world, whether today or in centuries past. For the same reason, religious worldviews have the powerful potential to help shape sustainable and inclusive worldviews with the aim of environmental protection. Psychologists define religion as "a system of beliefs in a divine or superhuman power, and practices of worship or other rituals directed towards such a power."[9] The importance placed on worship and rituals suggests that community activities connect people together, based on how the term "religion" comes from the Latin *religio*, derived from *ligo*, meaning "to tie or bind."[10] As opposed to "religion," definitions of spirituality tend to place more "emphasis on the individual and on subjective experience," explaining it more broadly as "a transcendent dimension within human experience … discovered in moments in which the individual questions the meaning of personal existence and attempts to place the self within a broader ontological context."[11] While appreciating how religion and spirituality have been used interchangeably in various contexts, this chapter recognizes the distinction between them. Religion offers a systematic means to connect to the world and its problems in ways that other connections may not.

Philosopher Roger Gottlieb explores the current environmental crisis and how religions have entered an "ecological phase."[12] People who are religious have had to become political and environmental activists.[13] However, there are also objections to ecological religion.[14] For instance, one complaint is that democratic societies do not need religion involved in their

[7] Ibid.
[8] Ibid.
[9] Michael Argyle & Benjamin Beit-Hallahmi, The Social Psychology of Religion 1 (Routledge, 1st ed. 2013).
[10] Ibid. (quoting Gerard Saucier & Katarzyna Skrzypińska, *Spiritual but Not Religious? Evidence for Two Independent Dispositions*, J. of Personality 1257, 1259 (Oct. 2006)).
[11] Ibid.
[12] Roger S. Gottlieb, *Introduction: Religion and Ecology: What Is the Connection and Why Does It Matter?, in Oxford Handbook of Religion and Ecology* 4 (Roger S. Gottlieb ed., 2006), https://bit.ly/47WtNS7.
[13] Ibid. at 6.
[14] Ibid.

political life to solve their problems.[15] Religions have served as tools for political intolerance, bigotry, sexism, racism, and homophobia. In fact, religion was used to provide a moral basis for colonization and conquest of the Americas through the notion of Manifest Destiny.[16] Religious arguments were provided in favor of slavery and ethnic cleansing.[17] Nonetheless, environmental movements are "hospitable to religion."[18] This is because they tend to be more open to spirituality than many other political movements.[19] The mission of environmental groups is to protect all life and religion has a similar purpose towards the inclusion and cohesion of life.[20]

Industrialized countries need to account for previous centuries of greenhouse emissions by providing low-cost transfer of skills, technology, and capital to emerging economies so that they can modernize without relying on carbon-based energy.[21] Religion offers a sense of environmental justice, creating a sense of duty to the environment and to others, because religious rhetoric carries a powerful moral authority.[22] The religious duty to protect the environment precedes international environmental law instruments.[23] In the same way that the civil rights movement stood on a religious high ground, the environmental movement can also harness this authority for its purposes.[24] Indeed, in the 1970s, environmentalists claimed ecology more as a religion, arguing that interests the law serves are derived from how the natural world is seen, understood, and used.[25]

Efforts to bring religious insights to international environmental debates are not new. In the past, international religious meetings on the environment, such as the Global Forum of Spiritual and Parliamentary Leaders, have been held in Oxford, Moscow, Rio, and Kyoto.[26] The Tehran Seminar on Environment, Culture, and Religion was held in Iran in 2001 and another meeting on "Environment, Peace and the Dialogue of Civilizations and Cultures" was organized in 2005.[27] Both of these were sponsored by the Iranian government with the support of the United Nations Environment Programme.[28] The International Union for the Conservation of Nature organized the first panel on "Spirituality and Conservation" at the World Conservation Congress in Barcelona in 2009.[29] Religion can assist humanity (as

[15] Ibid. at 7.

[16] Donald M. Scott, The Religious Origins of Manifest Destiny, NAT'L HUMANITIES CTR., http://nationalhumanitiescenter.org/tserve/nineteen/nkeyinfo/mandestiny.htm.

[17] See, generally, Crystal Silpar, *Christian Devils: How the Bible Was Used to Mobilize Oppression of Native Americans*, MEDIUM (Feb. 20, 2018), https://bit.ly/4piGUUY; see also Noel Rae, *How Christian Slaveholders Used the Bible to Justify Slavery*, TIME (Feb. 23, 2018), https://time.com/5171819/christianity-slavery-book-excerpt/.

[18] GOTTLIEB, *supra* note 12, at 11.

[19] Ibid.

[20] Ibid. at 10.

[21] Burns H. Weston, *Climate Change and Intergenerational Justice: Foundational Reflections*, *VT. J. ENVTL. L.* 375, 404 (2008).

[22] Lisa A. Binder, *Religion, Race, and Rights: A Rhetorical Overview of Environmental Justice Disputes*, *WIS. ENVTL. L. J.* 1, 16 (1999).

[23] Edith Brown Weiss, *The Evolution of International Environmental Law*, 54 JAPANESE Y.B. INT'L L. 1, 2 (2011).

[24] Chika Okafor, *Returning to Eden: Toward a Faith-Based Framing of the Environmental Movement*, 26 VILL. ENVTL. L. J. 215, 262 (2015).

[25] Jedediah Purdy, *American Natures: The Shape of Conflict in Environmental Law*, 36 HARV. ENVTL. L. J. 169, 228 (2012).

[26] Mary Evelyn Tucker, *Religion and Ecology*, *in* OXFORD HANDBOOK ON THE SOC. OF RELIGION 823 (Peter B. Clark ed., 2009).

[27] Mary Evelyn Tucker, *World Religions and Ecology for a Flourishing Future*, PATHS TO SUSTAINABILITY 193 (May 8, 2018), https://bit.ly/485OkUA.

[28] Ibid.

[29] Ibid.

guardians/stewards) to advocate and protect the rights for future generations to come.[30] The following sections survey religious doctrine on the environment.

Whether from an anthropocentric or a biocentric perspective, more adequate environmental values need to be formulated and linked to areas of public policy. Scholars of religion, as well as religious leaders and laity, are key players in this articulation process. Such an alliance of scholars, religious leaders, and activists is creating common ground for dialogue and creative partnership in envisioning and implementing long-range, sustainable solutions to some of our most pressing environmental problems. This is critical because the attitudes and values that shape people's concepts of nature come primarily from religious worldviews and ethical practices. Religions have been significant catalysts for humans in coping with change and transcending suffering while at the same time grounding humans in nature's rhythms and earth's abundance. The creative tensions between humans seeking to transcend this world and yearning to be embedded in this world are part of the dynamics of world religions.

25.3 ENVIRONMENTALISM THROUGH FAITH

Each of the religions discussed in this chapter carry a wide set of rules, customs, and laws relating to environmental governance; however, I focus only on specific aspects of each particular religion to demonstrate the creative and normative possibilities of the use of such ideas in heightening environmental protection. As an academic exercise, this discussion is meant to provoke an appreciation for nature through faith and provide the foundational basis for alternative legal norms for environmental protection nationally, subnationally, and internationally through mutual cooperation and action.

25.3.1 *Christianity, Environmental Ethics, and the Public Trust Doctrine*

Ancient traditions have governed natural resource use by humans and their relationship with the environment. Religious scholar Gretel Van Wieren notes that Christian approaches to environmental ethics are not monolithic, fully agreed-upon principles, but recognize that individuals "should be *against* the unjustified destruction of nature and *for* the care of God's Earth."[31] She also explains that Christian environmental ethicists focus on the idea that humans have a capacity to live with mutual respect and understanding with other creatures and creation as a whole.[32] Of the many Christian denominations, Lutheran traditions call on their members to challenge the practices where God's creation is made into commodities in an unjust way, which negatively impacts the poor.[33] Regardless of the religion, the common theme of protecting the environment is pervasive.

Barry Law School's Center for Earth Jurisprudence filed an amicus brief on behalf of the Global Catholic Climate Movement and the Leadership Conference of Women Religious in

[30] Sasha Hollis, *Old Solutions to New Problems: Providing for Intergenerational Equity in National Institutions*, *N.Z. J. Envtl. L.* 25, 60 (2010).

[31] Gretel Van Wieren, Restoring Earth, Restored to Earth: Christianity, Environmental Ethics, and Ecological Restoration 33 (2011) (unpublished PhD dissertation, Yale University).

[32] Ibid.

[33] Gyula Bándi, *Richness of Traditions: Environmental Traditions*, 49 Annales U. Sci. Budapestinensis de Rolando Eotvos Nominatae, 137, 145 (2008).

support of a constitutional climate change lawsuit brought by twenty-one young plaintiffs from across America in 2016.[34] As reported by EcoWatch News:

> Catholic groups filed the brief to make their views known that the youth's legal claims are rooted in U.S. [legal] traditions and parallel Roman Catholic tenets. The Global Catholic Climate Movement is an international network of more than 250 Catholic organizations and individuals, including Pope Francis and Catholic bishops. The Catholic group is raising a strong voice in global climate change discussions, relying on the Pope's encyclical, Laudato Si': On Care for Our Common Home.[35]

A representative of the Global Catholic Climate Movement has said:

> Laudato Si' reminds us that "[i]ntergenerational solidarity is not optional, but rather a basic question of justice, since the world we have received also belongs to those who will follow us." By supporting this initiative, we join our voices with the young plaintiffs who are calling for climate justice and the protection of the atmosphere for generations to come.[36]

Ileana Porras describes the encyclical as offering "a careful analysis of the root causes of environmental degradation, mapping out the complex linkages and tensions between globalization, economic growth, liberalized trade, unsustainable patterns of consumption and production, environmental degradation, involuntary migration, immiseration and growing inequality."[37] Porras postulates:

> The call to ecological conversion draws on the profound spiritual idea of conversion, which at its simplest can be described as a radical re-orientation of perspective that informs our goals and therefore guides our choices and actions. In the religious tradition, a conversion depicts both a turning point and a journey. The turn is both a turning away from and a turning towards. Paradoxically, this shift in perspective is experienced at the same time as a momentous break, away from deeply entrenched habitual patterns of thought and action, and as a minor adjustment, for in the moment of conversion we merely rediscover our original orientation and destination.[38]

Porras argues that Francis provides the groundwork for an integral ecology, which parallels the notion of sustainable development.[39]

The public trust doctrine is a way for citizens to stand as beneficiaries holding clear public property interests in natural resources, rather than as weakened political constituents making increasingly desperate environmental appeals to their public officials.[40] The public trust doctrine relies on the idea that the government holds natural resources in trust for its citizens and carries the fiduciary obligation to protect these resources for present and future generations.[41]

[34] Center for Earth Jurisprudence, *Center for Earth Jurisprudence Authors Amicus Brief in Constitutional Climate Change Lawsuit*, EARTH JURIST (Jan. 21, 2016), https://bit.ly/48hK59E (quoting Our Children's Trust, *Pope Francis Part of Amicus Brief Filed in Support of Teen's Landmark Climate Change Lawsuit*, ECOWATCH (Jan. 20, 2016), https://bit.ly/3XBe2LH).

[35] Ibid.

[36] Pope Francis, Encyclical Letter, *Laudato Si'*: On Care for Our Common Home (June 18, 2015), https://bit.ly/3XvEw11.

[37] Ileana M. Porras, *Laudato Si', Pope Francis' Call to Ecological Conversion: Responding to the Cry of the Earth and the Poor – Towards Integral Ecology*, 109 AJIL UNBOUND 136, 136 (2015).

[38] Ibid. at 137.

[39] Ibid. at 139.

[40] Mary C. Wood, *Atmospheric Trust Litigation across the World*, in FIDUCIARY DUTY AND THE ATMOSPHERIC TRUST 99, 106 (Ken Coghill et al. eds., 2012).

[41] Ibid.

The trust is rooted in the law as a characteristic of sovereignty itself.[42] The public trust is a common law doctrine that conserves navigable waters and tidal lands for public use, and institutes a duty in governments to guard such public use.[43] Christian environmental ethics expand the latitude of legal norms to apply for international environmental law rulemaking.

25.3.2 *Islam and Natural Resource Extraction*

The rules governing Islamic law principles for environmental protection, sustainability, and economic development rest on the juristic principles of Islamic law, known as *uṣūl al-fiqh*. The principles of Islamic law consider the origins of these sources as well as their methodological framework. Islamic law looks at what constitutes the discipline and how it is differentiated from the actual practice.[44] The Quran emphasizes the duty of the individual Muslim to care for the environment instead of a rights-based approach.[45] This duty is rooted in the belief that the earth in its totality is a creation of God, and that both the individual and the state are enjoined to take responsibility for God's creation as part of their religious duties.[46] Muslim thought about nature is shaped by several passages in the Quran, which exalt nature as the work of God:

> So set thou thy face steadily and truly to the Faith: (establish) Allah's handiwork according to the pattern on which He has made mankind: no change (let there be) in the work (wrought) by Allah. That is the standard Religion: but most among mankind understand not.[47]

The Quran also calls on humans to purify nature.[48] The Quran indicates, "Truly he succeeds that purifies it, and he fails that corrupts it!"[49] Under Islamic teachings, humans have a divine mandate to improve nature and dispose of impurities as they find them.[50] This purification is focused on bringing order and progress to nature – but not destroying it in the process.[51] The limits of nature should not be exceeded, as stated in the Quran, "Do no mischief on the earth, after it hath been set in order, but call on Him with fear and longing (in your hearts): for the Mercy of Allah is (always) near to those who do good."[52] God requires humans to observe nature's boundaries and draws near to believers who do good to the earth. The air is part of creation for Muslims. As in many other religions, it is often associated with the wind:

> It is He Who sendeth the winds like heralds of glad tidings, going before His mercy: when they have carried the heavy-laden clouds, We drive them to a land that is dead, make rain to descend

42 Harrison C. Dunning, *The Public Trust: A Fundamental Doctrine of American Property Law*, 19 Envtl. L. 515, 524 (1989); Mary C. Wood, *Advancing the Sovereign Trust of Government to Safeguard the Environment for Present and Future Generations (Parts I and II)*, 39 Envtl. L. 43, 68–69 (2009).

43 *Public Trust Doctrine*, Black's Law Dictionary (10th ed. 2014), defining "public-trust doctrine" as "the principle that navigable waters are preserved for the public use, and that the state is responsible for protecting the public's right to the use."

44 Ziauddin Sardar, *Islamic Science: The Contemporary Debate, in Postcolonial Sci. and Tech. Stud. Reader* 373–74 (Sandra G. Harding ed., 2011).

45 Yaser Khalaileh, *Islamic Principles for the Conservation of the Natural Environment*, 42 *Envtl. L. Rep. News & Analysis* 10280, 10288 (2012).

46 Ibid.

47 Q 30:30.

48 See Q 91:9–10.

49 Ibid.

50 Ali Ahmad, *Islamic Water Law as an Antidote for Maintaining Water Quality*, 2 U. Denv. Water L. Review 169, 179 (1999).

51 M. Rafiq & Mohammed Ajmal, *Islam and the Present Ecological Crisis, in World Religions and the Environment* 123 (O. P. Dwivedi ed., 1989).

52 Q 7:56.

> thereon, and produce every kind of harvest therewith: thus shall We raise up the dead: perchance ye may remember.[53]

The wind is akin to divine messengers and should not be fouled by humans. Air pollution thus represents a violation of God's ordering of nature. "Verily, all things have We created in proportion and measure."[54] There is a balance to nature as God has created it. According to Islam, air is a part of that balance and should be maintained in a pure state. Otherwise, a society may face tangible losses. Nature, including the air and all creatures who draw breath from it, is fair in its original state and should not be defaced by humanity. All elements of nature are to be considered common property of every creature – not just humans.[55] The Quran predicts the air pollution experienced today as a result of smoke, gas, and other emissions.[56] Corruption of the air spreads because of human activity, which damages the environment.[57]

The failure to completely achieve the goal of recognizing and establishing legal environmental rights and norms in Muslim-majority countries in the Middle East supports the idea of finding another source of obligation, such as Islamic rules that bind Islamic states, some of which constitute major sources of environmental pollution. Incidentally, some of the populations in the Arabian Gulf have the highest per capita carbon footprints in the world, including Qatar and the United Arab Emirates, and also have significant influence on oil and gas markets, namely, Saudi Arabia, Qatar, and the United Arab Emirates. They also happen to be strongly influenced by Islam. In Muslim-majority states, these arguments may find more resonance compared with more secular arguments, and thus may be strategically deployed.

25.3.3 *Judaism and Reducing Consumption*

Jewish teaching posits God created the environment and that humans are not allowed to misuse it.[58] As God's agents, humans are allowed to use God's creation with limits (those limits are established by God).[59] For instance, the saving of human lives above all else leaves itself open to the critique of deep ecologists and anthropocentricism. But it also has emancipatory potential in terms of addressing environmental injustice, unequal access to the environment, and unequal impact of environmental damage. The Sabbath, by limiting use of resources, is a way of living a sustainable life.[60] The halakhah, which is the collective body of Jewish religious laws from the written and Oral Torah, disallows wasteful consumption (including of resources).[61] Judaism recommends caution when using modern materials and chemicals and consideration of their impact.[62] In fact, there are many Jewish religious teachings that mandate the proper disposal of waste by industrial production to be kept far away from "human habitation."[63] The principle of

[53] Q 7:57.
[54] Q 54:49.
[55] Al-Hafiz B. A. Masri, *Islam and Ecology*, in ISLAM AND ECOLOGY 6 (Fazlun Khalid & Joanne O'Brien eds., 1992).
[56] Rafiq & Ajmal, *supra* note 51, at 128.
[57] Masri, *supra* note 55, at 9.
[58] Lawrence Troster, *10 Teachings on Judaism and the Environment*, HUFFINGTON POST (June 6, 2011), www.huffpost.com/entry/10-teachings-on-judaism-a_b_844973.
[59] Ibid.
[60] Ibid.
[61] Ibid.
[62] Ibid.
[63] Ibid.

bal tashchit ("do not destroy") prohibits needless destruction, and senseless damage or waste.[64] Judaism encourages preservation of the planet, as it is a loan from God.[65] Jewish sacred texts further the idea of intergenerational equity and support for policies that address climate change and promote conservation. The greatest moral obligation is the principle of *pikuach nefesh* ("to save human lives above all else") and this can be accomplished by education and the prevention of environmental health risks, ultimately by preserving the earth today and for future generations.[66] In Judaism, the scriptures indicate if the Messiah comes while you are planting a tree, you must first finish planting and then you go to the Messiah.[67]

25.3.4 *Hinduism, Buddhism, Jainism, and Cosmic Ecology*

Religious schools originating in India, such as Hinduism, Buddhism, and Jainism, believe in a balanced cosmic ecology that does not separate the human species from the rest of nature.[68] The concept of the sanctity of life is clearly part of Hinduism in the sense that Hindu teachings recognize that "only God has absolute sovereignty over all creatures; thus, human beings have no dominion over their own lives or non-human life."[69] As a result, "humanity cannot act as a viceroy of God over the planet, nor assign degrees of relative worth to other species."[70] This notion of the divine Being as expressed in the Yajurveda states: "The loving sage beholds that Being, hidden in mystery, wherein the universe comes to have one home; Therein unites and therefrom emanates the whole; The Omnipresent One pervades souls and matter like warp and woof in created beings."[71] The sacredness of God's creation means no damage may be inflicted on other species without adequate justification. Therefore, all lives, human and nonhuman, are of equal value and all have the same right to existence.[72]

According to Buddhism, the root causes of climate change can be understood as cravings, delusions, and aversions.[73] Religion can facilitate climate change work by engaging members of faith-based groups, building a community to support sustainability practices, sharing physical resources, offering ethical guidelines, and providing new paradigms of well-being.[74] Wisdom is the Dharma's first principle to mitigate climate change.[75] The second principle is ethical conduct (compassionate concern for all living beings), and the third is mindfulness (enhancing

[64] Religious Action Center of Reform Judaism, *Jewish Views on the Environment*, Reform Judaism, https://reformjudaism.org/jewish-views-environment.
[65] Ibid.
[66] Ibid.
[67] Ibid.
[68] Oren Perez, *Reflections on an Environmental Struggle: P&O, Dahanu and the Regulation of Multinational Enterprises*, 15 Geo. Envtl. L. Rev. 1, 28 (2002); see generally Christopher G. Framarin, Hinduism and Environmental Ethics: Law, Literature, and Philosophy (Routledge, 1st ed. 2014).
[69] Onkar Prasad Dwivedi, *Satyagraha for Conservation: Awakening the Spirit of Hinduism, in This Sacred Earth: Religion, Nature, Environment* 153 (Roger S. Gottlieb ed., 1996).
[70] Ibid.
[71] Yajurveda 32.8.
[72] Ibid.
[73] Statement, International Dharma Teachers, The Earth as Witness: International Dharma Teachers' Statement on Climate Change (Jan. 8, 2014), https://oneearthsangha.org/articles/dharma-teachers-statement-on-climate-change/.
[74] Paul L. Jones, *The Religions of the World Agree: Being Sustainable Is a Moral Imperative; So, How Can We Bring the Ecology of Faith Home?*, Sustainable Benefits (Oct. 3, 2017), https://sustainablebenefits.com/tag/green-products/ (citing Gary Gardner, Inspiring Progress: Religions' Contributions to Sustainable Development (2006)).
[75] International Dharma Teachers, *supra* note 73.

our awareness by noticing when we cause harm to the environment).[76] The *Earth as Witness: International Dharma Teachers' Statement on Climate Change* from 2014 states:

> We must recognize that without swift and dramatic reductions in fossil fuel use and major efforts to increase carbon sequestration, global temperatures will rise close to or beyond [two] degrees C. This increase will lead to injury and death for millions of people worldwide and the extinction of many of the Earth's species.[77]

Buddhism works to overcome the theory–practice divide through the concept of sustainable economies.[78] Mechanisms for bridging this gap include the institutional example and dissemination of the *dhamma* ("teachings") from Buddhist-based organizations, charismatic inspiration and leadership, examples from the laity, as well as educating and communicating with society to highlight the relevance of Buddhist views in mitigating the conflict and adversity of a host of global environmental, cultural, social, and economic problems. These multiplicities of agenda items show how breaking silos of religion can lead to better sustainability outcomes. In Bhutan, Mahayana Buddhism is the state religion, yet in practice the balance between development and conservation is difficult to achieve.[79] Bhutan is concerned about biodiversity protection to preserve endangered species from vanishing from the common heritage list.[80]

In Jainism, a key tenet is that "everything [is] attributed to [the] self and [the] self attributes everything to nature."[81] Its philosophy promotes resolving all types of crises by imparting faith and knowledge.[82] "When man is free from *Karma*, the environment will naturally be restored to its original purity."[83] The theory of Karma is essential in resolving crises, because it deals with cause and effect.[84] "According to this theory, by exploiting natural and human resources, man is causing not only environmental crisis, but also self-inviting an influx of Karma."[85]

25.3.5 *Zoroastrianism*

In Zoroastrianism, *asha* means purity, righteousness, and a good order.[86] Members of the faith are to act as responsible agents of the environment in order to acquire plenty of food, pleasant surroundings, and absence of illnesses.[87] Neglect of the environment is seen as turning away from the pursuit of *asha*, surrendering to evil.[88] Zoroastrians are renowned farmers and gardeners because of their understanding of the relationship between humanity and earth and water.[89] In some Iranian Zoroastrian communities, after the birth of a child and after the death of a loved

[76] Ibid.
[77] Ibid.
[78] Akadémiai Kiadó, *Sustainability and Sufficiency: Economic Development in a Buddhist Perspective*, 29 Society and Economy 155, 177 (2007).
[79] Shera Lhundup, *The Genesis of Environmental Ethics and Sustaining Its Heritage in the Kingdom of Bhutan*, 14 Geo. Int'l Envtl. L. Rev. 693, 694, 698 (2002).
[80] Ibid. at 699.
[81] J. Geetha, Environmental Awareness in Jainism 60 (2003) (unpublished PhD dissertation, University of Mysore), http://hdl.handle.net/10603/90291.
[82] Ibid.
[83] Ibid. at 62.
[84] Ibid.
[85] Ibid.
[86] Shahin Bekhradnia, *Zoroastrianism and the Environment*, in Revelation and the Environment *AD 95–1995* 149 (Sarah Hobson & Jane Lubchenco eds., 1995).
[87] Ibid. at 150.
[88] Ibid.
[89] Ibid.

one, a fruit-bearing tree is planted in their honor.[90] Life could not exist without water. Water is not a lifeless creation but a divine Being worshipped as *Avan Yazad*.[91] Air is a divine Being worshipped as *Mino Ram*.[92] Minerals are considered sacred, and when we deplete the natural resources, our good health is also depleted, because for the earth to maintain a healthy ecology, it also needs its minerals.[93] Zarathushtis are directed not to pollute nature even at death.[94] They do not bury or cremate, instead they use an ecofriendly alternative: the "rays of the Sun to decontaminate and dispose" of the corpse.[95]

25.3.6 *Other Eastern Faith Traditions: Daoism, Shintoism, and Sikhism*

Daoism is centered on nature and the belief that struggling against the natural world is certain to fail.[96] The movement of nature (water, clouds, wind) is a balance of yin and yang forces, and the earth and sky display the movement of qi (energy-substance).[97] It is believed that if qi is disrupted, it can result in disaster.[98] There must be a balance between yin and yang forces, which can be recreated artificially (e.g., the artificial mound balancing the stream running in front of the Forbidden City in Beijing).[99] Deep ecology generally is a philosophy addressing the environmental crisis by combining thoughts of environmental movements and religion.[100] Its platform consists of eight basic principles: (1) human and nonhuman life have intrinsic value; (2) the diversity and richness of life forms contribute to the realization of these values; (3) humans may only reduce this richness and diversity to satisfy vital needs; (4) the flourishing of nonhuman life requires a decrease of the human population; (5) the interference of humans with the nonhuman world is excessive and worsening; (6) policy must be changed; (7) ideological change: appreciating life quality instead of increasingly higher standards of living; (8) by subscribing to these points we have an obligation to attempt the necessary changes.[101]

In Shintoism, the land, its nature, and the creatures in it are children to Kami (deity).[102] Jinja Honcho, the representative body of all Shinto shrines in Japan, urges that we must take responsibility and address environmental issues.[103] Shintoism advises that we "shift our point of view and look at our environment with the spirit of 'reverence and gratitude,'" like how a parent cares for their children.[104] In Sikhism, the *Guru Granth*, which is the Sikh scripture,

[90] Ibid. at 150–51.

[91] Pervin J. Mistry, Zoroastrianism: Its Stewardship for all Creation, the Animate and the Inanimate, The Parliament of World's Religions, Presentation at the Parliament of World's Religions (Dec. 5, 2009), https://bit.ly/3K6zXas.

[92] Ibid.

[93] Ibid.

[94] Ibid.

[95] Ibid.

[96] David Wright, The Environment and the Dao Copyright Society for Anglo-Chinese Understanding (SACU) 2001: China Now 153, 16, www.sacu.org/daoenv.html.

[97] Ibid.

[98] Ibid.

[99] Ibid.

[100] W. Ambrosius, *Deep Ecology: A Debate on the Role of Humans in the Environment* 8 U. Wis. L. J. of Undergraduate Res. 1, 1 (2005), www.uwlax.edu/urc/jur-online/pdf/2005/ambrosius.pdf.

[101] Ibid. at 2.

[102] Jinja Honcho, *Shintoism, in Faith in Conservation: New Approaches to Religions and the Environment* 127 (Martin Palmer & Victoria Finlay eds., 2003).

[103] Ibid. at 129.

[104] Ibid.

asserts that the purpose of humanity is to achieve a harmonious state with the earth and all its creations.[105] There are approximately 25 million Sikhs worldwide.[106]

25.4 RESPONDING TO ENVIRONMENTAL THREATS WITH THE RELIGION

In *God, the Bible and the Environment: An Historical Excursus on the Relationship between Christian Religion and Ecology*, anthropologist Marco Damonte explores several theological works including Pope Francis's *Laudato Si'* and Lynn Townsend White Jr.'s position on Christianity and ecological problems.[107] Damonte's work describes Christianity as the most anthropocentric religion, thus resulting in exploitation of nature.[108] White accuses Christianity of (1) considering humans above all beings, thus creatures are to service mankind; (2) monotheism prevents humans from forming a relationship with nature; (3) the denial of metempsychosis causes a decline in value of the animal world; (4) deserts and wild places are thought to have no intrinsic value due to their biblical depiction; (5) indifference to the material world is due to appreciation of the transcendent world; and (6) "the apocalypse implicit in the final judgment and the relative annihilation are not compatible with an ethic environment."[109] White urges for Christianity to drop its dogmas.[110] "The human task towards nature has to have the qualities of a good administration, not of a dictator, nor a cold person."[111] The links between religious identification and commitment to the environment are crucial because the environmental attitudes will vary among Judeo-Christian denominations.[112] White's criticism could apply equally to Judaism and Islam.

Religion helps people cope with natural disasters because it offers explanations and perceptions, but not humanly caused environmental disasters (e.g., Chernobyl).[113] Environmental legislation faces difficulties, and philosophical controversies exist that prevent ecologists from overcoming such difficulties.[114] Environmental philosopher Mark Sagoff states that "after 60 years of standing on the mountainside beseeching the sky, mathematical theorists should concede that the hope for a theoretical and deductive, as distinct from an empirical and inductive, ecology reflects a religious faith more than a rational expectation."[115] Bioethics and religious scholar Harold Coward studies the impact of religion on the environment by changing

[105] Paula J. Posas, *Roles of Religion and Ethics in Addressing Climate Change*, 7 Ethics in Sci. & Envtl. Pol. 1, 12 (2007), www.gci.org.uk/Documents/E80.pdf.

[106] Steve Almasy, *Who Are Sikhs and What Do They Believe?*, CNN (May 25, 2018), www.cnn.com/2012/08/05/us/religion-what-is-a-sikh/index.html.

[107] Marco Damonte, *God, the Bible and the Environment: An Historical Excursus on the Relationship between Christian Religion and Ecology*, 5 Religion Beyond Anthropocentrism 27, 27 (2017).

[108] Ibid. at 30, 32.

[109] Ibid. at 33.

[110] Ibid. at 37.

[111] Ibid. at 41.

[112] Carl M. Hand & Kent D. Van Liere, *Religion, Mastery-Over-Nature, and Environmental Concern*, 63 Soc. Forces 555, 557 (1984).

[113] Suzanne Keller, *Ecology and Community*, 19 B.C. Envtl. Aff. L. Rev. 623, 623 (1992).

[114] Dustin R. Turin, *Environmental Problems and American Politics: Why Is Protecting the Environment so Difficult?*, 6 Inquiries J. 1, 1 (2014), www.inquiriesjournal.com/articles/943/environmental-problems-and-american-politics-why-is-protecting-the-environment-so-difficult (stating that tackling environmental problems today is more difficult because the nature of the problems have changed from scientific and technocratic in nature to almost exclusively relating to political issues).

[115] Mark Sagoff, *Ethics, Ecology, and the Environment: Integrating Science and Law*, 56 Tenn. L. Rev. 77, 146 n.347 (1988).

patterns of consumption and reproduction (as social force).[116] He argues for a partnership between international law and world religions.[117] Even though the United Nations may be able to convince governments through agreements, these agreements are written in a modern language that appear foreign to many cultures.[118] Thus, if these documents were to be translated into the norms of religions such as Hinduism, Islam, or Buddhism, there will be a better chance that ordinary people would embrace them and change their behavior.[119]

In 2013, researchers studied the relationship between a country's religion and its biodiversity areas.[120] The study showed that Christian countries, particularly Catholic ones, had more areas set aside for nature than other countries.[121] However, another study found that Christian fundamentalists are less willing to spend money on conserving the environment than Catholics.[122] Therefore, this study suggests that behavior towards nature is influenced by the type of Christianity.[123] For instance, another study showed that the Maasai people in Kenya who had converted from their traditional faith to evangelical Christianity did not have a positive attitude towards wildlife; in fact they had a higher intent to kill lions.[124] Conservationists need not ignore religion.[125] The Alliance for Religion and Conservation's (ARC) most successful project was convincing fishermen on an island off the coast of Tanzania to give up dynamite fishing.[126] They did so by showing the local sheikhs passages of the Quran promoting environmental behavior.[127] The sheikhs then shared the information with the fishermen, who were devout Muslims.[128]

25.5 CONCLUSION

Many conflicts couched as religious conflicts are, in fact, natural resource conflicts. To practice religion as a means of peacebuilding, harmony, and reconciliation will work to resolve ongoing conflict. To consider religion as protecting the environment and limiting pollution will work to improve problems of climate change adaptation, pollution, toxicity, chemical spills, wildlife loss, and migration. Religion can serve not only to divide but also unite. The recognition of religious harmony with environmental sustainability is crucial for protecting the planet from greed and avarice. With the rise of petro-capitalism, religion can be used as a wedge for divisive action for enhancing market competition of fossil fuel commodities to increase demand and prices for oil and natural gas. On the other hand, religion can be the Klaxon call to halt construction and infrastructure expansion for the preservation of nature. Legal norms for environmental protection nationally, subnationally, and internationally would be strengthened by the use of faith-based approaches to environmental protection. The process of making and unmaking international law for the environment entails reimagining the role of religion to broaden the legal conversation through the religious audience.

[116] Harold Coward, *Religious Responses to the Population Sustainability Problematic: Implications for Law*, 27 Envtl. L. 1169, 1169 (1997).
[117] Ibid. at 1185.
[118] Ibid. at 1180.
[119] Ibid.
[120] Niki Rust, *Religion Can Make Us More Environmentally Friendly – or Not*, BBC Earth (Feb. 7, 2017), www.bbc.com/earth/story/20170206-religion-can-make-us-more-environmentally-friendly-or-not.
[121] Ibid.
[122] Ibid.
[123] Ibid.
[124] Ibid.
[125] Ibid.
[126] Ibid.
[127] Ibid.
[128] Ibid.

26

Charting the Future of Islamic Environmental Law in an Age of Planetary Crisis

Nadia B. Ahmad, Saba Kareemi, Erum K. Sattar, and Oluwakemi A. Ayanleye

As we stand at the precipice of unprecedented environmental collapse with climate tipping points accelerating, biodiversity loss reaching extinction-level rates, and social-ecological systems under extreme stress, the urgent need for transformative approaches to environmental governance has never been more apparent. This handbook has demonstrated that Islamic environmental law offers not merely an alternative perspective but a necessary and profound reimagining of humanity's relationship with the natural world. The convergence of spiritual obligation, legal innovation, and ecological stewardship presents pathways forward that transcend conventional regulatory approaches and speak directly to the moral dimensions of our planetary crisis.

The chapters in this volume collectively argue that we are witnessing what can only be described as a civilizational inflection point. The scale and velocity of environmental degradation demand responses that match the magnitude of the challenge. Traditional Western legal frameworks, while valuable, have proven insufficient to address systemic ecological breakdown. The anthropocentric assumptions underlying much of contemporary environmental law have failed to generate the transformative change necessary to halt planetary degradation. It is precisely at this juncture that Islamic environmental law emerges as both historically grounded and urgently contemporary. The theological foundation of humans as *khalīfa* (stewards) of creation provides a framework that fundamentally reorients legal thinking from exploitation toward responsibility. This is not merely a philosophical shift but a practical reorientation that demands institutional transformation, legal innovation, and spiritual awakening. The concept of *mīzān* (balance) offers sophisticated tools for understanding and implementing ecological justice that Western environmental law has struggled to achieve through purely secular mechanisms.

26.1 ESTABLISHING ISLAMIC ENVIRONMENTAL LAW AS A SCHOLARLY DISCIPLINE

The institutionalization of Islamic environmental law as a formal academic discipline represents one of the most critical tasks ahead. As Professor Ridoan Karim argued in Chapter 20, this requires systematic curriculum development, methodological sophistication, and sustained scholarly investment. Yet establishing this discipline demands more than academic infrastructure; it requires a fundamental recognition that environmental protection constitutes a core dimension of Islamic jurisprudence, not a peripheral concern. Several concrete steps must be prioritized. First, Islamic universities and law schools must integrate environmental law into core *fiqh* curricula, moving beyond occasional seminar offerings to comprehensive degree programs. This includes developing specialized tracks in Islamic environmental jurisprudence that combine traditional textual analysis with contemporary ecological science. Second, research centers dedicated to Islamic environmental law must be established across Muslim-majority countries, creating networks of scholars who can engage in sustained collaborative research. Third, the development of standardized methodologies for interpreting classical Islamic texts in light of contemporary environmental challenges requires urgent attention. The scholarly infrastructure must also include translation projects that make classical Arabic environmental texts accessible to contemporary researchers, as well as digitization efforts that preserve historical documents while making them available for analysis. Professor Lutfullah Gari's work in Chapter 19, revealing extensive environmental awareness in historical Arabic texts, demonstrates the rich intellectual heritage that remains largely untapped.

One of the most significant contributions of this handbook lies in demonstrating how classical Islamic institutions can be adapted to address contemporary environmental challenges. The transformation of the *ḥimā* system from elite privilege to community-centered conservation, as analyzed by Professor Gari in Chapter 10, provides a model for institutional evolution that maintains spiritual grounding while embracing practical innovation. This bridging requires what we might call "creative fidelity" – remaining true to foundational principles while developing new applications that address unprecedented challenges. The integration of Islamic principles into constitutional environmental rights, as demonstrated in Pakistani jurisprudence, reveals the adaptability of Islamic legal thinking.

However, this bridging must avoid both uncritical traditionalism and wholesale modernization. The tension identified by Professor Mehran Kamrava in Chapter 6 between Islamic environmental ethics and rentier political economies illustrates the complex institutional challenges that must be navigated. Effective bridging requires institutional transformation that aligns political and economic structures with environmental imperatives.

26.2 URGENT RESEARCH PRIORITIES

Several research priorities emerge as critical for advancing Islamic environmental law in response to planetary crisis. First, the development of Islamic climate jurisprudence represents an urgent necessity. This includes not only theoretical frameworks but practical legal instruments that can be implemented through courts, regulatory agencies, and international agreements. The work on climate litigation must be expanded to develop comprehensive legal strategies that can be deployed across Muslim-majority countries. Second, the intersection of Islamic finance and environmental protection, as explored by Professors Dalal Aassouli and Damilola S. Olawuyi in Chapter 22, requires immediate attention. Green *ṣukūk* and other Islamic financial instruments offer powerful tools for mobilizing capital toward environmental protection, but their development requires sophisticated legal frameworks that ensure both sharia compliance and ecological effectiveness. Third, the relationship between Islamic environmental law and emerging technologies demands urgent research. Professor Anke Iman Bouzenita's analysis of genetically modified food in Chapter 15 provides a model for how Islamic jurisprudence can engage with biotechnology, but this work must be expanded to address artificial intelligence, geoengineering, renewable energy systems, and other technologies critical to environmental transition.

Fourth, the development of Islamic frameworks for environmental justice represents a crucial research priority. The work by Professor Nadia B. Ahmad in Chapter 7 on military emissions and ecological justice points toward broader questions about how Islamic principles can address environmental inequality both within and between nations. This includes developing Islamic approaches to climate reparations, environmental racism, and intergenerational justice.

The translation of Islamic environmental principles into effective policy requires institutional innovation that goes beyond traditional legal mechanisms. The Malaysian model analyzed by Shazny Ramlan in Chapter 13, which integrates muftis and sharia councils into environmental governance, provides one approach, but broader institutional experimentation is necessary. This includes the development of Islamic environmental courts with specialized jurisdiction over ecological cases, the creation of sharia-compliant environmental regulatory agencies, and the establishment of Islamic environmental arbitration mechanisms for resolving disputes. Additionally, the integration of Islamic environmental principles into international environmental law requires diplomatic innovation and the development of multilateral agreements that recognize diverse legal traditions. The Al-Mizan declaration examined by Professor İbrahim Özdemir in Chapter 17 demonstrates the potential for Islamic environmental principles to contribute to global environmental diplomacy. However, this requires moving beyond symbolic declarations toward binding international agreements that incorporate Islamic legal principles alongside other religious and secular approaches.

26.3 EDUCATIONAL TRANSFORMATION AND CONSCIOUSNESS CHANGE

Perhaps most importantly, the future of Islamic environmental law requires fundamental educational transformation that cultivates ecological consciousness alongside legal expertise. Professor Nematollah Azizi's call in Chapter 18 for environmental education grounded in Islamic epistemology represents a crucial direction. This educational transformation must occur at multiple levels: from children's Islamic education through to advanced legal training.

The integration of environmental awareness into Islamic religious education represents a particularly urgent priority. Mosques, madrasas, and Islamic schools must become centers for ecological consciousness, where environmental protection is understood as fundamental to Islamic faith and practice. This requires curriculum development, teacher training, and the creation of educational materials that connect Islamic teachings with environmental science. Similarly, the training of Islamic legal scholars must be fundamentally reimagined to include ecological literacy. Future muftis, judges, and legal advisors must understand both classical Islamic texts and contemporary environmental science. This interdisciplinary training represents a significant departure from traditional legal education but is essential for developing Islamic environmental law as a practical discipline.

One of the most distinctive contributions of Islamic environmental law lies in its integration of spiritual and legal dimensions. Professor Wardah Alkatiri's analysis of *ḥayāt ṭayyiba* (a good life) in Chapter 14 and Imam Saffet Catovic's theological argument for fossil fuel divestment in Chapter 23 demonstrate how environmental protection becomes a spiritual practice rather than merely a regulatory obligation. This spiritual dimension offers unique resources for motivating environmental action that secular environmental law struggles to provide. The connection between environmental protection and spiritual development creates powerful incentives for individual and collective behavioral change. However, realizing this potential requires the development of practical spiritual disciplines that connect daily religious practice with environmental action. This includes the development of Islamic environmental understandings, the integration of ecological themes into Friday sermons, the creation of environmental pilgrimages that connect spiritual development with ecological awareness, and the establishment of eco-mosques that model sustainable practices.

The planetary nature of environmental crisis demands that Islamic environmental law develop transnational dimensions that transcend national boundaries. This requires building solidarity between Muslim communities facing different environmental challenges while recognizing shared spiritual and legal foundations. The work on environmental justice in Gaza, Iraq, and Afghanistan presented in Chapter 7 demonstrates how Islamic environmental law can address the environmental dimensions of conflict and occupation. This transnational cooperation must include the development of Islamic environmental networks that connect scholars, activists, and policymakers across Muslim-majority countries. It also requires building bridges with environmental movements in other religious traditions, as suggested by the interfaith approach in Chapter 25. The planetary crisis demands collaborative responses that draw on diverse wisdom traditions while maintaining the integrity of each tradition's distinctive contributions.

26.4 TECHNOLOGY, INNOVATION, AND ISLAMIC ENVIRONMENTAL FUTURES

The future of Islamic environmental law must engage seriously with technological innovation while maintaining spiritual grounding. This includes developing Islamic frameworks for evaluating emerging technologies, creating sharia-compliant approaches to renewable energy development, and establishing Islamic criteria for environmental technology assessment. The development of Islamic environmental technologies represents a particularly important frontier. This includes not only the application of existing technologies within Islamic legal frameworks but the development of new technologies guided by Islamic environmental principles. Solar energy systems designed according to Islamic architectural principles, water management technologies that incorporate classical Islamic water law, and agricultural techniques that combine traditional Islamic farming practices with contemporary ecological science represent examples of this technological integration.

Ultimately, the future of Islamic environmental law points toward what we might call "ecological *khilāfa*," a form of environmental stewardship that integrates spiritual responsibility, legal innovation, and ecological wisdom. This represents more than policy reform or legal development; it constitutes a fundamental reimagining of human civilization according to Islamic principles. Ecological *khilāfa* would organize society around the recognition that humans are trustees of creation with obligations to protect and nurture the natural world. This would transform everything from urban planning and economic systems to educational curricula and spiritual practices. It would create institutions that prioritize ecological health alongside human welfare, recognizing that these are ultimately inseparable.

Such a vision requires courage, creativity, and sustained commitment. It demands moving beyond reactive responses to environmental crisis toward proactive transformation guided by Islamic principles. It requires building alliances between religious and secular environmental movements while maintaining the distinctive contributions of Islamic environmental thought.

The development of Islamic environmental law as a robust discipline requires sophisticated methodological innovations that can bridge classical Islamic jurisprudence with contemporary environmental science. This methodological challenge is particularly acute given the temporal gap between classical legal texts and modern ecological understanding. Future scholarship must develop hermeneutical approaches that can interpret historical sources in light of contemporary environmental knowledge while maintaining fidelity to original meanings and intentions. The development of comparative methodologies represents another crucial frontier. Islamic environmental law must engage systematically with other legal traditions, both religious and secular, to identify areas of convergence and divergence. This comparative work can reveal unique contributions of Islamic approaches while identifying opportunities for legal harmonization and cross-tradition learning. The growing field of comparative environmental law provides models for this kind of interdisciplinary engagement.

Additionally, the development of empirical research methodologies specifically adapted to Islamic environmental law represents an urgent priority. This includes ethnographic studies of how Islamic environmental principles are actually implemented in Muslim communities, quantitative analysis of the environmental effectiveness of Islamic institutions like *waqf* and *ḥimā*, and longitudinal studies tracking the evolution of Islamic environmental consciousness in different cultural contexts.

26.5 ECONOMIC TRANSFORMATION AND ALTERNATIVE DEVELOPMENT MODELS

The chapters in this handbook reveal a fundamental tension between dominant economic models and Islamic environmental principles. Professor Kamrava's analysis of Gulf rentier economies demonstrates how resource extraction creates institutional impediments to environmental protection, while Professor Alkatiri's critique of consumerism challenges growth-oriented development paradigms. The future of Islamic environmental law requires developing alternative economic models that align with both Islamic principles and ecological limits. This economic transformation must begin with a fundamental reconceptualization of wealth, progress, and development. The Islamic concept of *baraka* (blessing) offers resources for understanding prosperity in terms that transcend material accumulation. Similarly, the principle of *wasaṭiyya* (moderation) provides frameworks for economic activity that avoids both poverty and excess. These concepts must be translated into concrete economic policies and institutional arrangements.

The development of Islamic circular economy models represents a particularly promising direction. The prohibition of waste (*isrāf*) in Islamic law aligns closely with circular economy principles that seek to eliminate waste through closed-loop production systems. Islamic finance principles that prohibit speculation (*gharar*) and exploitation (*ribā*) offer foundations for economic systems that prioritize long-term sustainability over short-term profit maximization.

The revival and modernization of traditional Islamic economic institutions offer additional pathways for economic transformation. The *waqf* system, analyzed by Professor Erum K. Sattar in Chapter 9, provides a model for community-controlled resource management that prioritizes long-term sustainability over short-term extraction. Modern adaptations of *waqf* could include environmental conservation trusts, renewable energy cooperatives, and community-supported agriculture initiatives guided by Islamic principles.

The translation of Islamic environmental principles into effective legal mechanisms requires sustained judicial innovation and institutional creativity. The Pakistani constitutional jurisprudence examined by Professors James R. May and Erin Daly in Chapter 5 demonstrates how courts can interpret environmental protection as a fundamental right rooted in Islamic concepts of human dignity. This judicial creativity must be expanded and systematized across Muslim-majority countries. The development of Islamic environmental standing doctrines represents a crucial legal innovation. Traditional Islamic law recognizes the concept of *maṣlaḥa* (public interest) as grounds for legal action, but this must be expanded to include environmental protection and the rights of future generations. The appointment of environmental guardians (*awliyāʾ al-bīʾa*) who can represent ecological interests in legal proceedings offers one model for expanding legal standing beyond immediate human interests.

Islamic environmental law must also develop sophisticated frameworks for environmental liability and compensation. The concept of *diya* (blood money) in Islamic criminal law provides precedents for environmental compensation systems that could address pollution, habitat destruction, and climate damages. However, these frameworks must be adapted to address collective rather than individual harms and to account for intergenerational impacts. The integration of traditional Islamic dispute resolution mechanisms with environmental protection offers additional opportunities for legal innovation. The institution of *taḥkīm* (arbitration) could be adapted to address environmental disputes through panels that include both legal scholars and environmental scientists. Similarly, the principle of *ṣulḥ* (reconciliation) could guide restorative approaches to environmental justice that prioritize healing and restoration over purely punitive measures. Importantly, the development of Islamic environmental criminal law represents an urgent necessity. The Quranic concept of *fasād* (corruption) provides theological foundations for treating severe environmental crimes as offenses against divine order. This could support the development of ecocide legislation that criminalizes systematic environmental destruction while providing Islamic theological justification for such laws.

26.6 INTERNATIONAL LAW AND GLOBAL GOVERNANCE

The planetary scope of environmental crisis requires that Islamic environmental law engage systematically with international environmental law and global governance mechanisms. This engagement must move beyond symbolic participation toward substantive contribution to international legal development. The Al-Mizan declaration examined by Professor Özdemir provides a model for this engagement, but much more comprehensive work is needed. The development of Islamic approaches to international environmental agreements represents a priority. This includes developing Islamic legal frameworks for evaluating and implementing international environmental treaties, creating mechanisms for ensuring that international obligations align with Islamic legal principles, and contributing Islamic perspectives to the ongoing development of international environmental law. The integration of Islamic environmental principles into United Nations frameworks offers particular opportunities for global influence. The UN Sustainable Development Goals (SDGs) provide spaces for Islamic environmental contributions, but this requires systematic engagement by Islamic legal scholars and practitioners. Similarly, the ongoing development of international climate law creates opportunities for Islamic perspectives to influence global climate governance.

The establishment of Islamic environmental courts with international jurisdiction could provide additional mechanisms for global environmental governance. Such courts could adjudicate disputes between Muslim-majority countries involving transboundary environmental issues while developing Islamic environmental jurisprudence through case law. This could contribute to the broader development of international environmental judicial mechanisms. Furthermore, the development of Islamic environmental diplomacy requires sustained attention. This includes training Islamic diplomats in environmental law and policy, creating networks of

Islamic environmental lawyers who can contribute to international negotiations, and developing Islamic positions on key international environmental issues.

The ultimate success of Islamic environmental law depends not only on scholarly development and institutional innovation but on grassroots mobilization and community implementation. The transformation of environmental consciousness at the community level represents perhaps the most critical challenge for Islamic environmental law. This community mobilization must begin with the development of Islamic environmental pedagogy that can reach diverse audiences across different educational levels and cultural contexts. The creation of Islamic environmental curricula for children that integrate Quranic teachings with ecological science represents a fundamental priority. Similarly, adult education programs that help Muslim communities understand the environmental dimensions of their faith could catalyze widespread behavioral change.

The development of community-based Islamic environmental projects offers additional opportunities for grassroots implementation. This includes the establishment of eco-mosques that model sustainable practices, the creation of Islamic permaculture projects that demonstrate ecological farming techniques, and the development of Islamic environmental action groups that can advocate for policy change at local levels. The integration of environmental themes into Islamic ritual and spiritual practice represents another important dimension of community mobilization. The development of environmental prayers, the incorporation of ecological consciousness into pilgrimage experiences, and the creation of Islamic environmental festivals could help embed environmental awareness into the fabric of Muslim religious life.

Additionally, the training of Islamic religious leaders in environmental issues represents a strategic priority for community mobilization. Imams, scholars, and community leaders who understand both Islamic environmental principles and contemporary environmental challenges can serve as powerful advocates for environmental action within Muslim communities. This requires developing training programs, educational materials, and support networks for religious leaders engaging with environmental issues.

26.7 WOMEN'S LEADERSHIP AND GENDER DIMENSIONS

The future of Islamic environmental law must explicitly address gender dimensions and create space for women's leadership in environmental governance. While this handbook includes important contributions from female scholars, the broader development of Islamic environmental law must systematically integrate feminist perspectives and address the particular ways that environmental degradation affects women. Islamic environmental law must recognize that women often bear disproportionate burdens from environmental degradation while simultaneously possessing crucial knowledge about environmental management and conservation. The development of Islamic environmental jurisprudence that recognizes women's environmental knowledge and leadership represents both a justice imperative and a practical necessity for effective environmental governance.

This includes examining how classical Islamic legal concepts like *qiwāma* (responsibility/stewardship) can be interpreted to support women's environmental leadership rather than restrict it. Similarly, the principle of *shūra* (consultation) requires ensuring that women's voices are included in environmental decision-making processes at all levels. The development of Islamic environmental organizations led by women and focused on women's environmental concerns represents another priority. This includes addressing issues like environmental health impacts on maternal and child health, women's roles in sustainable agriculture, and the intersection of environmental justice with gender justice.

26.8 YOUTH ENGAGEMENT AND INTERGENERATIONAL JUSTICE

The concept of intergenerational justice embedded in Islamic environmental law requires particular attention to youth engagement and leadership development. The current environmental crisis will disproportionately affect young people and future generations, making their engagement in Islamic environmental law development both urgent and necessary. This step requires developing Islamic environmental education programs specifically designed for young people that combine Islamic teachings with environmental activism. Young Muslims around the world are already demonstrating leadership in environmental movements, and Islamic environmental law must provide frameworks that support and channel this activism.

The establishment of Islamic environmental youth organizations that can advocate for environmental protection while developing expertise in Islamic environmental law represents a strategic priority. These organizations could serve as training grounds for future Islamic environmental lawyers and as advocates for intergenerational justice within Muslim communities. Additionally, the integration of Islamic environmental law into Islamic higher education requires particular attention to engaging young scholars and students. This includes developing scholarship programs, research opportunities, and career pathways for young people interested in Islamic environmental law. The future of the discipline depends on cultivating a new generation of scholars and practitioners committed to environmental justice and Islamic legal innovation.

26.9 DIGITAL INNOVATION AND KNOWLEDGE DISSEMINATION

The development of Islamic environmental law in the digital age requires leveraging technology for knowledge creation, dissemination, and implementation. The COVID-19 pandemic demonstrated both the possibilities and limitations of digital engagement, creating opportunities for global collaboration while highlighting digital divides that must be addressed. The creation of comprehensive digital archives of Islamic environmental texts represents a fundamental infrastructure need. This includes not only digitizing historical manuscripts but developing searchable databases that allow scholars to identify environmental themes across the vast corpus of Islamic literature. Artificial intelligence and machine learning tools could assist in this textual analysis while requiring careful attention to cultural sensitivity and scholarly accuracy. The development of Islamic environmental law databases that track contemporary legal developments, court decisions, and policy innovations could support both scholarly research and practical implementation. These databases should be accessible to scholars, practitioners, and community members while maintaining appropriate standards for scholarly accuracy and cultural sensitivity.

Digital platforms for Islamic environmental education offer additional opportunities for knowledge dissemination. Online courses, webinar series, and virtual conferences can connect Islamic environmental scholars and practitioners across global networks while making specialized knowledge accessible to broader audiences. However, these digital initiatives must address issues of digital equity and linguistic diversity to ensure broad accessibility. The development of Islamic environmental law apps and digital tools that can help Muslims integrate environmental consciousness into daily religious practice represents another frontier for digital innovation.

These could include carbon footprint calculators based on Islamic ethical principles, prayer apps that incorporate environmental themes, and digital platforms for organizing community environmental action.

26.10 MEASURING IMPACT AND EVALUATING EFFECTIVENESS

As Islamic environmental law develops as a discipline and practice, sophisticated frameworks for measuring impact and evaluating effectiveness become paramount. This requires developing metrics that can assess both the scholarly development of the discipline and its practical effectiveness in promoting environmental protection. Academic metrics must go beyond traditional measures like publication counts and citation indices to include measures of interdisciplinary engagement, policy influence, and community impact. The development of Islamic environmental law as a truly interdisciplinary field requires evaluation frameworks that can assess contributions across different academic domains and practical applications. Practical effectiveness measures must address both environmental outcomes and social justice impacts. This includes developing indicators that can track the environmental performance of institutions guided by Islamic environmental principles, the effectiveness of Islamic environmental policies in achieving conservation goals, and the success of Islamic environmental education in changing behavior and consciousness.

The development of Islamic environmental indicators that align with both Islamic values and environmental science represents a particular challenge. These indicators must be culturally appropriate while maintaining scientific rigor, and they must address both material and spiritual dimensions of environmental well-being. Additionally, longitudinal studies tracking the development of Islamic environmental consciousness and practice within Muslim communities could provide crucial data for evaluating the broader impact of Islamic environmental law development. These studies could track changes in environmental behavior, policy preferences, and spiritual understanding related to environmental issues. We stand at a moment of decision that will determine the future of life on earth. The environmental challenges we face are unprecedented in human history, but so too are the resources available for response. Islamic environmental law offers profound wisdom, practical tools, and spiritual motivation for addressing planetary crisis. However, realizing this potential requires urgent action across multiple fronts: academic, legal, spiritual, economic, and political.

The convergence of multiple crises, climate breakdown, biodiversity collapse, social inequality, and spiritual emptiness, creates both unprecedented challenges and unique opportunities for transformative change. Islamic environmental law emerges from this convergence not as a marginal academic specialty but as a potential catalyst for civilizational transformation guided by divine guidance and human wisdom. The scholars, practitioners, and communities engaged with Islamic environmental law must move beyond academic discourse toward practical implementation. This handbook provides the intellectual foundation, but the real work lies ahead in courtrooms and classrooms, in mosques and policy councils, in communities and international forums. The future of Islamic environmental law depends on our collective willingness to translate spiritual vision into legal reality and legal innovation into environmental transformation.

This translation requires courage to challenge existing power structures that benefit from environmental degradation, creativity to develop new institutions and practices that align with Islamic principles, and commitment to sustained engagement across generations. It requires building alliances with environmental movements worldwide while maintaining the distinctive spiritual and legal contributions of Islamic tradition. The planetary crisis calls us to our highest possibilities as Muslims and as humans. Islamic environmental law offers a path forward that honors both spiritual tradition and ecological necessity. The question that remains is whether we will have the wisdom and courage to walk this path with the urgency that our moment demands.

As this handbook demonstrates, Islamic environmental law is not a historical curiosity but a living tradition with profound contemporary relevance. Its future lies not in museums or libraries but in the active engagement of scholars and practitioners committed to environmental justice and spiritual transformation. The convergence of ecological crisis and spiritual opportunity creates unprecedented possibilities for Islamic environmental law to contribute to planetary healing. The time for incremental change has passed. The scale of environmental crisis requires transformative responses that can only emerge from the deepest sources of human wisdom and moral commitment. Islamic environmental law offers access to such sources, but only if we are willing to engage with both traditional wisdom and contemporary urgency with the full measure of our intellectual, spiritual, and practical capabilities.

The work begins now. The future of Islamic environmental law, and perhaps the future of human civilization, depends on our response to this sacred calling. This is not merely an academic project or a policy initiative but a spiritual imperative that demands nothing less than the transformation of human consciousness and institutions in service of divine creation. The earth itself calls us to this work, and our response will determine whether future generations inherit a world of ecological abundance or ecological collapse. May this handbook serve not as a conclusion but as a beginning; the beginning of a new chapter in Islamic legal development that rises to meet the challenges of our time with wisdom, courage, and unwavering commitment to justice for all creation.

Index

For EU product safety concerns, contact us at Calle de José Abascal, 56–1°,
28003 Madrid, Spain or eugpsr@cambridge.org.

www.ingramcontent.com/pod-product-compliance
Ingram Content Group UK Ltd.
Pitfield, Milton Keynes, MK11 3LW, UK
UKHW050955290926
15470UKWH00006B/1827
* 9 7 8 1 0 0 9 3 3 2 0 8 8 *